Washington

Washington

Denise Fainberg

SECOND EDITION

The Countryman Press ✳ Woodstock, Vermont

Interior photographs by the author unless otherwise specified.

Explorer's Guide Washington
978-0-88150-974-8

Maps by Erin Greb Cartography, © The Countryman Press
Text and cover design by Bodenweber Design
Composition by PerfecType, Nashville, TN

Published by The Countryman Press, P.O. Box 748, Woodstock, VT 05091

Distributed by W. W. Norton & Company, Inc., 500 Fifth Avenue, New York, NY 10110

Printed in the United States of America

10 9 8 7 6 5 4 3 2 1

EXPLORE WITH US!

Welcome to *Washington: An Explorer's Guide*. This updated edition in the Explorer's Guide series will help you discover not only the Evergreen State's better-known attractions but also its back roads and hidden corners. With the state's 71,303 square miles of forest, ice, and rock, including four major volcanoes, a wild ocean coast and an inland sea, orchards, sagebrush desert, ghost towns and high-tech pioneers, not to mention a world-class city in a jewel-like setting, you have a lot of exploring to do. All listings here have been included on the basis of interest and merit; no payment is accepted for inclusion.

WHAT'S WHERE

This alphabetical section includes important information for quick reference and particular highlights.

LODGING

Innkeepers are not charged for inclusion in this guide. I have tried to include accommodations in a variety of price ranges for travelers ranging from families to retirees to outdoorspeople, from the budget-conscious to the leisure-oriented. Listings, in alphabetical order, concentrate on bed & breakfasts and independently owned, historic, or unique hotels, as well as lodges, inns, cabins, and some independently owned, friendly motels. Chains and franchises are included only where there are no, or few, other choices. Prices quoted are generally for doubles unless otherwise indicated, in a range from the smallest room in low season to the largest in high season. Prices listed, current for 2011, are subject to change. Room tax is not included; room tax ranges from 7.2 percent to 8.9 percent, and some localities also have city or county taxes.

RESTAURANTS

In most sections, please note a distinction between *Dining Out* and *Eating Out*. By their nature, restaurants included in the *Eating Out* group are generally less expensive and less formal. Both groups' listings are in alphabetical order.

KEY TO SYMBOLS

- ✎ The crayon appears next to lodgings, restaurants, and attractions that accept or are geared to children. Many bed & breakfasts have age restrictions; when in doubt, ask.
- ♿ The wheelchair symbol appears next to lodgings and restaurants that are partially or fully wheelchair-accessible.
- 🐾 The paw appears next to accommodations that accept pets, always with prior approval and usually for a fee. Consult with the innkeeper.
- 🎖 The blue ribbon appears next to lodgings or restaurants that offer particularly good quality for the price.

We would appreciate any comments or corrections. Please address correspondence to Explorer's Guide Editor, The Countryman Press, P.O. Box 748, Woodstock, VT 05091, or e-mail countrymanpress@wwnorton.com.

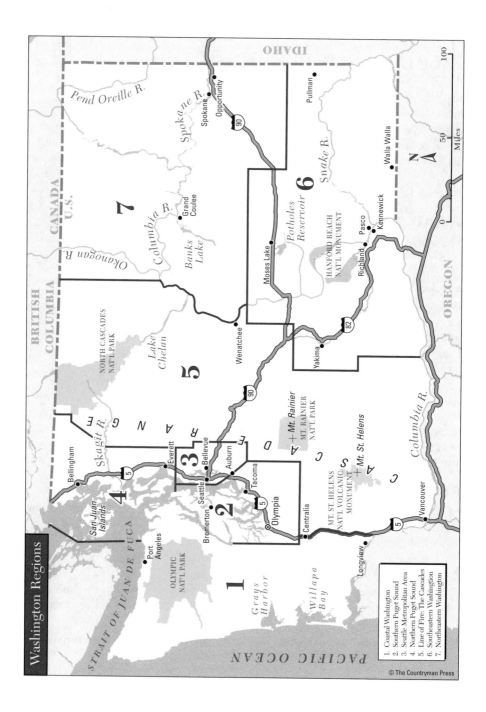

Washington Regions

IDAHO

Pend Oreille R.

Spokane R.

Spokane • • Opportunity

[90]

Pullman •

Snake R.

Walla Walla •

N

0   50   100
Miles

Columbia R.

Grand Coulee •

Banks Lake

Potholes Reservoir

6

HANFORD REACH NAT'L MONUMENT

Richland •
Pasco •
Kennewick •

7

Okanogan R.

BRITISH COLUMBIA

CANADA
U.S.

NORTH CASCADES NAT'L PARK

Lake Chelan

5

Moses Lake •

Wenatchee •

[90]

OREGON

Mt. Rainier
MT. RAINIER NAT'L PARK

Yakima •

[82]

Columbia R.

Skagit R.

R A N G E

Bellingham •

[5]

Everett •

Bellevue •

3

Seattle •
Bremerton •
Auburn •

C A S C A D E

Mt. St. Helens

Tacoma •

4

San Juan Islands

2

Olympia ⊙

[5]

Port Angeles •

OLYMPIC NAT'L PARK

STRAIT OF JUAN DE FUCA

Centralia •

MT. ST. HELENS NAT'L VOLCANIC MONUMENT

Vancouver •

[5]

Longview •

1

Grays Harbor

Willapa Bay

PACIFIC OCEAN

1. Coastal Washington
2. Southern Puget Sound
3. Seattle Metropolitan Area
4. Northern Puget Sound
5. Line of Fire: The Cascades
6. Southeastern Washington
7. Northeastern Washington

© The Countryman Press

CONTENTS

MAPS

ACKNOWLEDGMENTS

I t's impossible to recognize individually all the people who help on a project of this size. Nonetheless, I'd like to thank all those who gave me guidance, showed me around, and otherwise helped me get acquainted with their areas, particularly: Dana Haynes, of the Spokane Regional Convention and Visitors Bureau; Katie Heaverlo, of the Yakima Valley Visitors and Convention Bureau; Nancy Trucano, of the Cascade Loop Association; Jessica Robinson, of the Leavenworth Chamber of Commerce; Kauilani Robinson, of Seattle's Convention and Visitors Bureau; and all the innumerable docents, guides, forest rangers, hosts, question-answerers, and others without whom I would have had much less to say! Thanks also to the production team at Countryman Press; to all my family and friends for putting up with months of abstraction; and, last but not least, my son and daughter-in-law, Harell and Tiffany Firestone, who shared some of their favorite Seattle places with me.

INTRODUCTION

The Evergreen State should really be called the Water State. Yes, there are plenty of evergreens here—hundreds of thousands of acres of some of the world's tallest forests—but how would those forests exist without the famous Northwest rain and coastal fogs? The city of Seattle gleefully points out that its annual rainfall, about 37 inches, is actually less than New York's. Which is true but disingenuous. In Seattle it's seasonally concentrated, which means this: The area gets a fairly sparkling July and August, with rain—at 90 percent of New York's precipitation—distributed liberally the rest of the year. In the winter of 2006, the city approached its all-time record of 33 straight days of rain with more actual volume than during its previous 33-day record. But it's true the summers are glorious.

Besides these waters from above, there are the waters here below. The Pacific and the vast inland waterways of the Strait of Juan de Fuca, Puget Sound, and the Georgia Strait teem with marine life and offer a multitude of protected harbors and shipping ports—one reason why so much more Northwest wealth collected around Puget Sound than, say, in Spokane or Walla Walla. Those towns had their magnates, and many others in the most unlikely places felt poised to become the next Boston or Chicago just as soon as the railroad terminus came. But the termini naturally went to places like Tacoma and Seattle, where deep-draft boats could moor safely, which eventually led to cities and technological developments and Boeing and Microsoft.

Then there are the rivers, spawned by springs, snowmelt, and glaciers. Mount Rainier and the North Cascades are the most glaciated areas in the United States outside of Alaska. Even the state's arid interior, which gets just 8–15 inches of rain a year and is far from green, ever, is bisected by the great Columbia looping across the state from north to south, then east to west. Columbia Basin salmon runs allowed Native cultures to flourish for millennia in an otherwise harsh environment. The great dam projects beginning in the 1930s spelled the decline of that era. The tamed rivers, though, brought electricity, industry, and greatly expanded agriculture to these remote regions—heavens, now they even have *vineyards*.

Most of the population, however, still lives west of the Cascades, and western Washingtonians sometimes say, half-jokingly, that their cultural climate too is a by-product of the rain: When even these outdoor-loving citizens are confined indoors much of the time, what is there to do but be creative? This reasoning is used to explain Seattle's sometimes quirky cultural scene—after all, it was the birthplace of grunge. At the very least, it may explain Starbucks.

Parts of Washington, such as Long Beach, Mount Rainier, even the remote San Juan Islands and remoter town of Stehekin, began attracting leisure travelers as early as the 1890s with fine hotels and special boat and train transport— surprisingly, since Washington became a state only in 1889. The state boomed during 1887–1891, as the railroads followed the discovery of minerals, unbelievable fisheries, and mechanized lumbering. Not a few citizens did remarkably or at least respectably well and could afford vacations. Other areas of the state, such as the North Cascades, the far northeastern corner, and the desert south, had to wait for today's highways before receiving many visitors. There are still plenty of places where, even in summer, you'll have lots of room to yourself.

This book is arranged by regions, from generally west to east and south to north. Each of the seven regions is broken down into subregions, and within these chapters, subjects are arranged by area of interest rather than by town. For instance, within the Southeastern Washington region, the Yakima Valley chapter lists museums in the whole valley, from Naches to Prosser, then farmers' markets, historic sites, and so forth, rather than providing a town-by-town breakdown. This will enable you to find the activity you're interested in within each chapter.

A counsel of prudence: Beyond Puget Sound and the I-5 corridor, Washington has lots of wide-open space. Temperature extremes east of the Cascades are common year-round. Make sure you know where the next gas station is. Carry water, especially in summer, for you and your car. In winter, carry tire chains and blankets. The maps in this book will get you started, but a detailed road map is another good bit of gear for your explorations of the Evergreen State.

WHAT'S WHERE IN WASHINGTON

AGRICULTURE People have been farming in Washington since the Hudson's Bay Company appropriated huge tracts and cleared them for crops to support its own needs. Generally, farming came after forestry—the giant trees were felled, then the soil plowed, as settlers and Oregon Trail emigrants trickled in. It was only after the Puget Sound area had "filled up" that a backwash of homesteaders discovered the fertility of the land east of the Cascades. Once irrigated, the eastern river valleys became the fruit bowl of the nation. Washington is still the largest apple producer in the nation and the second-largest wine-grape producer, with apricots, peaches, cherries, and berries also very plentiful. And the state ranks fourth in wheat production, mainly in the Palouse country of the southeast.

AIR SERVICE Seattle-Tacoma International Airport (SEA), located (where else?) between Seattle and Tacoma, is the state's major airport. Sea-Tac (not to be confused with the town of SeaTac) is served by most major and quite a few minor airlines. Smaller commercial airports around the state include Bellingham (BLI), Pasco (PSC), Pullman (PUW), Spokane (GEG), Walla Walla (ALW), Wen-atchee (EAT), and Yakima (YKM). Horizon Air and United Express serve most of these.

AMTRAK (800-USA-RAIL; www .amtrak.com) has three routes through Washington: Amtrak Cascades, from Eugene, Oregon, to Vancouver, British Columbia; the Coast Starlight, from Seattle to Los Angeles; and the Empire Builder, from Seattle to Chicago via Washington's remarkable Stevens Pass and Spokane, with a spur from Spokane to Portland along the scenic Columbia Gorge.

ANTIQUES Washington is not a very old state, yet antiques are a virtual industry in some towns, particularly Centralia and Snohomish. A partial listing of dealers may be found online (www.antiquesnavigator.com).

AREA CODES Washington residents east of the Cascades are known as "five-oh-niners," since that entire half of the state is covered by area code 509. The west side is more complicated: Seattle, its environs, and, perversely, Bainbridge Island are 206; the Everett, Redmond, and Bellevue areas are 425; the Tacoma region, including the southern Kitsap Peninsula, is 253; and the northern Kitsap area, along with most of western Washington whether north or south of the Seattle-Tacoma corridor, is 360.

BEACHES Washington has two kinds of saltwater beaches: those on the long, straight Pacific coast, which are mostly sandy except near the northern end, where they get rocky, and which total about 157 miles; and those of the intricate inland waterways of Puget Sound, the Strait of Juan de Fuca, and the multitude of islands amid it all. These latter beaches are largely rocky and rich in tidal pools. Unfortunately, public access to the saltwater shores is limited. In the Puget Sound area, about 79 percent of beaches are privately held, so even though beaches are technically public property below the high-tide mark, you can't necessarily get there. The Pacific coast is somewhat better off since 65 miles belong to Olympic National Park and much of the Long Beach Peninsula is public. (Strangely, though, vehicles are allowed to drive on many public beaches, which by law are still considered part of the state highway system, and drivers are required only to observe the rules of the road and a speed limit of 25 miles per hour. So watch out.)

BICYCLING This book includes only a fraction of the bike trails in Washington, where road and mountain biking are practically art forms and many towns make efforts to include cycling in their transportation plans. A mine of information and help is available from the Washington Bicycle Alliance (206-224-9252; bicyclealliance.org), 311 Third Avenue South, Seattle 98104.

BIRDING With its diversity of habitats, Washington also has a diversity of birds—the state checklist now includes 475 species—and of course the state is on the Pacific Flyway. Audubon Washington and the Washington Department of Fish and Wildlife are collaborating on the **Great Washington Birding Trail,** a collection of birding itineraries around the state. So far, birding maps of the Cascade Loop, Coulee Corridor, and Southwest Loop are available through Audubon Washington (206-652-2444; www.wa.audubon.org), 5902 Lake Washington Boulevard South, Seattle 98118.

BOATING Both sailboats and motorboats crisscross Washington's nearly 5,000 square miles of water. Vessels with a motor exceeding 10 horsepower or used in federal waters must be licensed through the state Department of Licensing unless they're already licensed in another state. There are many marinas in the coastal zones and some along the Columbia River; I list only a few, but you can find a directory of public moorage slips online (www.washingtonports.org).

BUREAU OF LAND MANAGEMENT The BLM manages only about 400,000 acres in Washington (as opposed to 15 million in Oregon). Its land covers mostly dry eastern acreage, where it tries to fulfill several sometimes contradictory roles as custodian of mineral resources, archaeological sites, range-land, fisheries, water, and recreation. Its Washington offices are at 1103 North Fancher Road, Spokane 99212 (509-536-1200), and 915 North Walla Walla Road, Wenatchee 98801 (509-665-2100). Contact these for a list of recreational sites on BLM land, or check online (www.blm.gov). Uses generally include hiking, camping, fishing, and wildlife viewing.

BUS SERVICE Greyhound (800-231-2222; www.greyhound.com) still offers long-haul service between some Washington cities. Some regions have fairly good public systems; for information, check the Getting Around section in relevant chapters.

CANOEING AND KAYAKING In these activity sections in each chapter, I recommend waters where motor use is restricted, or at least minimized, though some spots are popular for both types of recreation. For more destinations and information, check online (www.kayakonline.com).

CITIES There are 281 incorporated towns in Washington. Seattle is the behemoth, with some 612,000 inhabitants (though 1.5 million in the metropolitan area). Tacoma and Spokane vie for second place, with 204,200 and 206,900, respectively. Then comes Vancouver, Washington, with 155,000, while the capital city, Olympia, comes way down the list with about 46,000. The smallest is Krupp (in the Mid-Columbia Basin north of Moses Lake), with a population of 60 in 2010.

CLAMMING AND CRABBING Gathering clams and other shellfish requires a license from the Washington Department of Fish and Wildlife (360-902-2464) and is limited to certain seasons just as hunting and fishing are.

Licenses may be bought online (wdfw .wa.gov) or at many sporting-goods stores. Also check the shellfish hotline (800-866-5431) for closures due to red tide or other toxins.

CLIMATE Washington's image as a state of constant rainfall is only about half true. Almost exactly half true, in fact. While its western zone, from the ocean to the Cascade crest, does receive rather astonishing precipitation, the area between the Cascades and the Idaho border—about half the state—is largely desert (technically called "shrub-steppe"). This is because the mountains wring out so much moisture from incoming Pacific weather systems that there's little left for the east side. (Occasionally there are secessionist murmurs from the eastern halves of Washington and Oregon, but that's another story.) Even on the west side, though, there is wide variation, from the 140-inch annual rainfall in the Hoh rain forest to the 18 annual inches falling on parts of Whidbey Island and the San Juan Islands, which lie in the rain shadow of the Olympic Mountains.

COLUMBIA RIVER The great "river of the West" is *the* defining natural feature of the state, though Oregon and Canada both share it. Originating in the Canadian Rockies, it divides Washington neatly in two on its 1,200-mile way to the sea, generating gargantuan numbers of kilowatts as it falls over 11 dams and greening parts of the interior plateau. Before the era of electricity, it powered several inland Indian cultures with its prodigious salmon runs. For a rather large geographic feature, it escaped discovery for years as explorers tacked up and down the Pacific coast, passing it in the fog or tricked by the offshore breakers crashing on the bar at its mouth. In 1792 the American

strangely dressed androids marching into the water or see their breathing tubes bobbing about. Locations and qualified diving outfitters that will train you and take you underwater are listed in the relevant chapters.

EMERGENCIES Each chapter lists hospitals or urgent-care clinics in the Medical Emergency section. In case of need, call one of these, or dial 9-1-1.

EVENTS The events selected for inclusion in this book in the Special Events sections are those that reflect the local traditions, culture, or economy, whether those of the majority, Native American, or immigrant communities.

captain Robert Gray crossed the bar, discovered the estuary, and named the river after his ship, the *Columbia Rediviva*. A few days later, he ran into British captain George Vancouver up the coast and casually mentioned his discovery. Vancouver, who had missed it, hastened south, entered the river, and claimed the territory for England, setting the stage for decades of contention between the two nations. It was hoped, forlornly, that the Columbia might be the Northwest Passage, an imagined waterway that would link the Great Lakes with the Pacific. The journey of Lewis and Clark proved that the Columbia wasn't the hoped-for waterway, but it did become the final highway for generations of Oregon Trail emigrants.

FARMERS' MARKETS Nearly every Washington village and town has its farmers' market selling succulent produce from neighboring fields. Shopping at these is often a convivial affair as well as a utilitarian trip. The Washington State Farmers' Markets Association (www.wafarmersmarkets.com) maintains a list of farmers' markets throughout the state.

FERRIES Washington State Ferries (206-464-6400 or 888-808-7977; www .wsdot.wa.gov/ferries) is a division of the Washington State Department of Transportation, 2901 Third Avenue, Suite 500, Seattle 98121. The ferries provide service across and around Puget Sound, to the San Juan Islands, and to Vancouver Island, British Columbia. They are almost as important to the Washingtonian image as they are to transportation—and they're a lot of fun to ride.

COUNTIES Washington is divided into 39 counties, from Adams to Yakima. The most populous is King County, with about 1.9 million people; the least is Garfield in the southeastern corner of the state, with a mere 2,100 souls.

DIVING Washington has an interesting submerged life, and at many dive spots along its shorelines you'll find

FISHING Washington offers surf, river, and lake fishing for species including trout, salmon, sturgeon, and halibut. Most fishing requires a license from the state Department of Fish and Wildlife (360-902-2464; wdfw.wa.gov) and can be purchased online and at many sporting-goods stores. Be sure to check about seasons and limits, too.

GARDENS In parts of the state, especially the Kitsap and Olympic peninsulas and the islands, gardening reaches near-manic proportions, like the plants themselves. Selected nurseries and outstanding public gardens are listed for these areas. Some localities offer garden tours, which are listed by the local chambers of commerce.

GEOGRAPHY Those who make decisions about such things have divided the state into six geographic regions, which, coincidentally, nearly parallel the sections of this book: the thickly forested **Olympic Mountains and Coast Range** along the ocean; the **Puget Sound Lowlands,** between the Cascades and the Olympics, comprising Washington's great population centers and its inland sea; the **Cascade Range,** running from Mount Adams in the south to Mount Baker in the north, bisecting the state; the **Columbia Plateau** covering most of southern and central Washington, rocky and arid but for the loess-covered Palouse Hills; and a segment of the **Rocky Moun-**

tains covering the northeastern corner of the state.

GEOLOGY The beauty of the western states is that they wear their geology on their sleeves. *A Roadside Geology of Washington,* by Robert Alt and Donald Hyndman (Mountain Press Publishing), is a handy guide to the formations you'll see around the state. In it you'll read about the former coastline, somewhere around Idaho, and how the state built itself up through accretion as the movement of tectonic plates brought several landmasses to our shores. You'll learn, too, about the layers of lava that built the Columbia Plateau before floods churned it into the Channeled Scablands and the relatively recent births of Washington's proud volcanoes. How's that for a summary of several geologic eons? You really have to see it to believe it.

GOLF COURSES This volume lists some of the golf courses that can now be found in virtually all parts of the state (well, maybe not the Channeled Scablands). For additional listings, check online (www.golfwashington.com or www.worldgolf.com).

GUIDES AND OUTFITTERS A list of outfitters experienced in various recreational excursions such as fishing, horse or llama trekking, rafting, and hunting can be obtained from the Washington Outfitters and Guides Association (509-997-1080; www .woga.org), Box 1125, Twisp 98856.

HIGHWAYS The state's main arteries are **I-5,** running north from Portland, Oregon (and California), to Vancouver, British Columbia, by way of Washington's metropolis, Seattle, and **I-90,** which runs east from Seattle to Spokane and points east. Other west-east routes include **US 2,** which starts in Everett and heads to Spokane before crossing into Idaho; **US 12,** which starts in Aberdeen and heads to Walla Walla; and brave **WA 20,** which crosses Washington's entire northern tier, from Port Townsend to Newport, and gets hardly any credit for it. **US 97** crosses the Columbia near The Dalles, Oregon, and runs north up the state's midsection to Oroville and then Canada. **US 101** circles the Olympic Peninsula, more or less paralleling the coastline: along Hood Canal from Olympia to Port Townsend, then along the Strait of Juan de Fuca to Forks, then along the Pacific coast to Aberdeen.

HIKING In the Hiking sections of this book, I include hikes of varying lengths and for a variety of ability levels, including some wheelchair-accessible trails, representative of each particular area's scenery and natural history. Naturally, these hikes represent only a fragment of the trails available in Washington. Many detailed guidebooks to Washington's trails are on the market, such as *100 Classic Hikes in Washington,* by Ira Spring and Harvey Manning (Mountaineers Books); *Foghorn Outdoors Guide to Washing-* *ton Hiking,* by Scott Leonard (Avalon); and *Accessible Trails in Washington's Backcountry: A Guide to 85 Easy Outings,* by Washington Trails Association and Dan Nelson (Mountaineers Books).

HISTORICAL MARKERS The state Department of Transportation has put up 52 roadside interpretive markers at various places around the state, mostly on scenic byways, from which you can learn some little-known facts of Washington history (see below). A list can be printed out from the WSDOT website (www.wsdot.wa.gov).

HISTORY The human history of Washington state began before anyone knew about it, some 10,000 years ago—or is it 13,000?—when people came across the Bering Strait or maybe along the coast. The discovery of Kennewick Man has thrown previous neat theories into confusion. The area's written history, at least, may be said to begin in the 1770s when the Spanish and British began to explore their competitive options along the Pacific coast, all the while with discovery of a Northwest Passage in the back of their minds. Captain James Cook proceeded all the way to Alaska without finding it.

Kettle Falls, and American Protestants farther south. It's not clear why Marcus and Narcissa Whitman, after trekking all the way from the East Coast to Fort Vancouver, where they bought supplies and rested, trekked back to the Walla Walla Valley (the Spaldings, with whom they had traveled, went even farther east, into what's now Idaho) to build their mission compound. But they did; more missionaries were sent out, supposedly in response to Indian requests; the missionary settlements encouraged fortune seekers from back east; and when the massacre occurred at the **Whitman mission** in 1847, a consequence of a measles epidemic and Mr. Whitman's abrasive personality, U.S. troops were sent in to protect a growing settler population.

By this time, the British had agreed to remove themselves to north of the 49th parallel; the "Oregon Territory," filling up with Oregon Trail emigrants, had become unambiguously American. By 1853, the northern part of the territory was no longer Oregon but Washington Territory; the treaties of 1855 "settled" the Indians on reservations, though unrest flared for a couple of decades; and in 1889 Washington became a state.

Having ridden into the Union on the crest of America's Gilded Age, Washingtonians are nothing if not enterprising. You can read the story of ambitious expansion in the **Jefferson County Courthouse** in Port Townsend and the ornate department stores and banks of downtown **Ellensburg** and **Walla Walla;** you can see the shadows in the reservation museums, the graves of **Chief Seattle** and **Chief Joseph,** even in the deeds and speeches of Isaac Stevens, the first territorial governor, recorded in displays at the **state capitol** in Olympia. And you can see the new skyscrapers of

Bruno de Heceta, following the yarns of the Greek Juan de Fuca, found his way to the strait that now bears his name, bringing in Spanish place names. As luck would have it, in 1792 Captains Robert Gray and George Vancouver got to the Columbia River's estuary at nearly the same time (see *Columbia River,* above) and established conflicting claims to the banks of the mighty river.

For decades, there was an uneasy cohabitation of British and Americans in this wild territory. In a letter dated July 4, 1803, President Thomas Jefferson commissioned the Corps of Discovery; within a few years, American furrier John Jacob Astor built his trading post at the mouth of the Columbia, modestly naming the town-to-be after himself. British fur companies moved with no less celerity to take advantage of the resources. Soon Hudson's Bay Company forts were scattered over the Northwest, from **Spokane** and **Colville** to **Nisqually** and **Vancouver, Washington**—you can still visit most of them—while American trappers moved about south of the Columbia.

Next, missionaries arrived: French Jesuits on the northern reaches of the Columbia, where you can see the oldest extant church in Washington at

Seattle, a skyline radically remade in the past 30 years. Although Washington has suffered in the current recession, like everywhere else, it always seems quick to pick up the pieces.

HOT SPRINGS Due to the geothermal activity of its mountains, Washington has a number of natural hot springs, some remote and some easily accessible, some developed as resorts and some not. Throughout the book, I note those that are (more or less) easy to reach. *Touring Washington and Oregon Hot Springs,* by Jeff Birkby (Falcon/Globe Pequot), is a useful guide if you are a hot-springs buff.

INDIAN RESERVATIONS Washington is home to 29 federally recognized tribes, though some of these are actually groups of tribes, or members of tribes, that were thrown together on reservations in the late 1800s—the Colville Confederated Tribes, for instance, are made up of 12 bands, including a band of Nez Perce, while the Yakama Nation is composed of members of 14 different bands and tribes. These tribes have 29 reservations, of which the largest are the Colville and Yakama reservations. Several reservations—among them the **Yakama, Colville, Makah, Squaxin, Suquamish,** and **Jamestown S'Klallam**—welcome visitors through museums (noted in the relevant chapters' Museums listings), casinos, or, increasingly, art galleries, as young tribal artists receive recognition and encouragement.

There are also a number of tribes without federal recognition, often because they did not sign on to the 1855 "agreements" ceding their lands to the United States. These include the **Wanapum,** near Priest Rapids Dam; the **Chinook** of southwestern Washington; the **Duwamish** of Puget Sound (Chief Seattle's mother's tribe); and several others. Without federal recognition, these tribes don't have reservations. Most federally recognized tribes have their own websites; links and a map of reservations are available online (www.goia.wa.gov).

LEWIS AND CLARK "Lewis and Clark schlepped here" advertises one hostelry on the Long Beach Peninsula. Did they ever. After a horrendous autumn trek through the Bitterroots (the snow was already deep), they entered what is now Washington at the convergence of the Clearwater and Snake rivers on October 10, 1805. Their progress is noted with memorial plaques along the Snake and Columbia rivers, where they made their way downstream, trading with various tribes and noting the changing landscape. The explorers remarked on widespread eye infections among the Plateau Indians, complained about dried salmon, appreciated *wapato,* a potato-like root, and ended up eating dogs and their own horses (one wonders what Clark's dog, Seaman, thought about that). The Corps of Discovery reached Long Beach, at last, in mid-November, just in time to spend a miserable, wet winter on the Oregon side of the Columbia. Although the bicentennial celebrations were less exuberant than expected, the memory of the Corps of Discovery is very much alive on both sides of the river—the romance of a small band charting unknown territory is part of the American mythos. Most of us, after all, have followed in their footsteps.

LIBRARIES Almost every town in Washington has a public library, and in most of them you can catch up on your e-mail. The library system got a big boost in the late 1800s and early 1900s when Andrew Carnegie funded

MILEAGE Mileages indicated in this guide are approximate. Keep a map handy and ask for directions if necessary—this is a generally friendly state.

MUSEUMS The Museums listings in each chapter cover every sort of collection in the state, from the grand art collections (such as those at the Seattle Art Museum and Tacoma's Museum of Glass) to the memorabilia repositories of tiny rural communities. Sometimes these smaller museums have prized items, such as Native American baskets, an 1870 wedding dress, or a cookstove you may remember from your childhood (the past, as William Faulkner said, isn't dead; it isn't even past). Several Indian reservations have museums of tribal history and culture; notable among these are the Makah Cultural and Research Center in Neah Bay and the Yakama Nation Museum in Toppenish. Then there are science museums and those devoted to specific interests such as antique radios or telephones—in short, the possibilities are limited only by your stamina.

libraries all over the country. A remarkable number of Washington's libraries came about this way, and many of them are still libraries, though some have been converted to other uses.

MAPS You can order highway maps from the state Department of Transportation's website (www.wsdot.wa .gov/publications/highwaymap/order). Maps are also distributed at many highway rest areas.

MUSIC FESTIVALS Various kinds of music festivals take place annually around the state; I list them under Special Events in relevant chapters. Some are the Centrum Festival of American Fiddle Tunes in Port Townsend, the Orcas Chamber Music Festival on Orcas Island, Port Townsend's Centrum Summer Chamber Music Festival, and Richland's Tumbleweed Folk Music Festival.

MUST-SEE SIGHTS Okay, this is it: You absolutely have to see Mount Rainier; Olympic National Park; the Columbia River *somewhere* along its length, preferably the Columbia River Gorge; Seattle, of course (if you have to choose one site, make it Pike Place

Market); the San Juan Islands; Cape Disappointment at the mouth of the Columbia River; and what's left of Mount St. Helens after its 1980 eruption. You really should drive the North Cascades Scenic Highway (WA 20), ride on a Washington State Ferry, and go whale-watching, too. This is my personal, subjective list, which coincides more or less with the "Top 10" list compiled online (www.travel-in-wa .com)—which adds Lake Chelan, Grand Coulee Dam, and Snoqualmie Falls, all of which are pretty spectacular, too. You don't have to see the Space Needle except from the outside.

NATIONAL FORESTS Washington is home to the Colville, Okanogan-Wenatchee, Mount Baker–Snoqualmie, Gifford Pinchot, and Olympic national forests, and it shares the Umatilla National Forest with Oregon. These amount to about 8.5 million acres, a considerable area in which to recreate, whether you choose an organized campground or picnic area or delve deep into the wilderness areas (see below) and Mount St. Helens National Volcanic Monument, also administered by the U.S. Forest Service. Campgrounds in national forests are often, but not always, free; check with the

relevant office. Parking in national forests usually requires a Northwest Forest Pass ($5 per day or $30 per year; available at Forest Service offices and some local businesses).

NATIONAL PARKS Washington has three national parks: Mount Rainier, Olympic, and North Cascades. These pristine tracts are among the jewels of the national park system. North Cascades is the newest and most remote and has few tourist amenities. Venerable Mount Rainier gets heavy traffic but is a must-see; go off-season or get off the main roads. Olympic, though highly popular, is fairly uncrowded even in summer. The National Park Service also administers several national recreation areas and a few national historic sites and parks. All these are treated in part 1, Coastal Washington; part 5, Line of Fire: The Cascades; and part 7, Northeastern Washington. Check the Guidance section of the relevant chapters for contact information.

NEWSPAPERS Washington's two primary papers are the *Seattle Post-Intelligencer* (now online only) and the *Seattle Times*. Smaller but still proud dailies include the *Spokane Spokesman-Review,* the *Tacoma News Tribune,* the *Tri-Cities Herald,* the *Olympian,* and the *Yakima Herald Republic.*

PACIFIC CREST TRAIL The Appalachian Trail turned out to be such a good idea that western states wanted a long-distance trail, too. The Pacific Crest Trail (PCT) runs from Mexico to Canada through California, Oregon, and Washington. For information on hiking on, protecting, finding shelter along, or anything else on this premier 2,650-mile national scenic trail, contact the Pacific Crest Trail

can be found on a map on the WSDOT website (www.wsdot.wa.gov).

RESTAURANTS Food in Washington runs the gamut from steak and potatoes to various types of haute cuisine (Japanese, French, Italian, "fusion"), and eateries can be holes-in-the-wall or high-class and high-priced. I include a bit of everything, concentrating on what's good and affordable (there's plenty) while allowing for the special-occasion places, too. If the state can be said to have a regional cuisine, it's Northwest—that means good, fresh seafood; plenty of local fruits and vegetables; and often range-fed meats. Sometimes these ingredients are prepared in combinations you don't often see elsewhere, such as salmon in blackberry sauce. Even if it's surprising, it's memorable when well done.

ROAD REPORTS For information on road conditions, construction projects, snow, and other kinds of traveling inconveniences, check online (www.ws dot.wa.gov/traffic) or call 5-1-1 or 800-695-ROAD.

RV PARKS Few parks for recreational vehicles are listed in this guide, unless they have unusual locations or a

Association (916-285-1846; www.pcta .org), 1331 Garden Highway, Sacramento, CA 95833.

RECOMMENDED READING Some worthy titles include *The River of the West,* by Robert Clark (Picador); *Snow Falling on Cedars* and *East of the Mountains,* by David Guterson (Harcourt); *A Roadside Geology of Washington,* by David Alt and Donald Hyndman (Falcon/Globe Pequot); *A Traveler's History of Washington,* by Bill Gulick (Caxton Press); *The Egg and I,* by Betty MacDonald (Harper Paperbacks); and *Mount Rainier: A Visitor's Companion* and *The Olympic Peninsula: A Visitor's Companion,* by George Wuerthner (Stackpole Books).

REST AREAS The state Department of Transportation operates 46 safety rest areas, 28 of them on the interstate system. Most have handicapped-accessible restrooms, pay phones, pet walking areas, picnic tables, and traveler information; many even offer free coffee. You may spend up to eight hours in any rest area. Their locations

pleasant family atmosphere. However, if an RV is your mode of travel, you can find detailed listings of many RV parks online (www.rvpark.com).

SCENIC BYWAYS Washington has 61 routes in its scenic byways system, offering tours of the state's varied terrain; check www.wsdot.wa.gov for listings. Washington also has six nationally designated scenic drives, which means they pass through scenery that is outstanding even by national standards. Most of these are mentioned under Scenic Drives throughout the text. I also include a few routes that have no official status but are pretty and/or interesting.

STATE FORESTS National forests account for most of the public forestland in the state, but the Washington State Department of Natural Resources (360-902-1100) manages quite a number of state forests. These tend to be lands that have been logged once or twice and are in various stages of regrowth; some are listed in this book. They are often open to recreation such as hiking, mountain biking, all-terrain-vehicle use, and primitive camping, though because they are "working" forests, you may share them with logging trucks and equipment.

STATE PARKS The Washington State Parks and Recreation Commission (360-902-8844; www.parks.wa .gov), 1111 Israel Road SW, Olympia 98504, administers 120 state parks and recreation areas, with more coming down the pipeline. These are usually lovely natural areas offering picnicking, hiking, boating, or other activities; some have visitors centers or interpretive programs. There is a $10 parking fee for day use ($30 for an annual pass); camping and boat launching (other than kayaks or canoes) also involve a fee. You can reserve a camp-

site at some parks (888-226-7688), but some don't take reservations.

STATE TRIVIA Washington's state bird is the **American goldfinch.** The state tree is the **western hemlock;** the state flower is the **coast rhododendron.** The state song is "Washington, My Home," but the state folk song is Woody Guthrie's "Roll On, Columbia, Roll On," commissioned by the Bonneville Power Administration. Guthrie ended up writing 26 songs to accompany the BPA's promotional movie on the newly completed Bonneville and Grand Coulee dams. The state fish is the **steelhead trout;** the state gem is **petrified wood.** Unsurprisingly, the state dance is the **square dance;** the state fruit is the **apple.** The state fossil is the **Columbian mammoth,** of which examples have been found on the Olympic Peninsula. The state marine mammal is, of course, the **orca.** Washington even has a state grass: **bluebunch wheatgrass,** a dryland bunchgrass. The state's nickname is the **Evergreen State,** though that has never made official. And its unofficial territorial motto is **ALKI,** an Indian word meaning "someday." This comes from the 1850s settlement on Elliott Bay, which was hopefully named New York. It failed to thrive, though, so people dubbed it "New York Alki." After a short time, the settlers moved to a more favorable location across the bay, which became Seattle. The site of the original settlement is now called Alki Point.

STATISTICS Washington's current population is about 6.5 million (as compared to 357,232 in 1890, the year after statehood was granted), of whom about 600,000 live in Seattle—though nearly 1.800 million live in King County, where Seattle is located. Washington is the 18th-largest state, with a total area of 71,303 square miles, of which 66,544 is actual landmass; the rest is water. The state's highest point is the summit of Mount Rainier, at 14,410 feet (some say 14,411, but who's counting?), and its lowest point is sea level—found in many places around the state. Bordered by Canada, Idaho, Oregon, and the Pacific Ocean, Washington's geographic center is 10 miles westsouthwest of Wenatchee. The state's northernmost point is the 49th parallel; its southernmost point lies near Washougal along the Columbia River; the easternmost spot is a piece of desert along the Snake River at the Idaho-Oregon border; and the westernmost point is Cape Flattery, which is also the northwesternmost point of the continental United States.

TAXES State sales tax is 6.5 percent, which is levied on most goods and services except food (prepared food, however, is taxed); counties and cities also levy sales tax, so in places like Seattle, you may pay close to 10 percent on purchases (waivers exist for some sales to nonresidents). The tax on lodging includes sales tax plus various local and regional taxes and may amount to 7.2–10.2 percent. There is, however, no state personal income tax.

TRAVEL INFORMATION Washington State Tourism (800-544-1800; www.experiencewa.com) will happily send you a package to help you start planning your travels here. Its website has been recently revamped; don't even try to navigate it with an operating system older than Windows 2000. Each region also has its visitors bureau or chamber of commerce, listed under Guidance in each chapter, and these also will be glad to give or send you information.

UNIVERSITIES Washington has six public universities: the University of Washington in Seattle, with branches in Bothell and Tacoma; Washington State University in Pullman, Spokane, Tri-Cities, and Vancouver; Central Washington University in Ellensburg; Eastern Washington University in Cheney; Evergreen State College in Olympia; and Western Washington University in Bellingham. Private four-year colleges include Walla Walla and Whitman colleges in Walla Walla, Gonzaga and Whitworth in Spokane, and Pacific Lutheran University and the University of Puget Sound in Tacoma. Antioch University, based in Ohio, also has a branch in Seattle.

WEATHER Forecasts appear on the state Department of Transportation website (www.wsdot.wa.gov). You can also check with the National Weather Service (206-526-6087 or 509-224-5992; www.nws.noaa.gov). Generally speaking, the east side of the state is either cold and dry or hot and dry, while the west side is cool and damp or warm and damp. The highest temperature recorded in Washington was 118 degrees Fahrenheit in 1961, at Ice Harbor Dam near Pasco; the lowest

was a disastrous −48 degrees in 1968, at Mazama and Winthrop.

WHALE-WATCHING With gray whales passing by on their regular Mexico-to-Alaska migrations, plus resident and transient orca pods, minkes, and occasional humpbacks, there's hardly an excuse for *not* seeing a whale if you're anywhere near Puget Sound or the Pacific coast. Whale-watching boats based in the San Juan Islands, Edmonds, Port Townsend, and Whidbey Island offer you every opportunity, though they're a bit hard on your pocketbook (averaging $50 for a half-day tour). Orcas often come right up to the western shore of San Juan Island in summer.

WILD AND SCENIC RIVERS Though Washington's wildest river, the Columbia, has been trammeled, portions of the Klickitat, White Salmon, and Skagit rivers are designated "Wild and Scenic," popular for rafting, fishing, or just enjoying a clean, natural stream.

WILDERNESS AREAS Almost every chapter in this book describes some wilderness area or other. Wilderness areas, which do not have amenities other than trails, are great areas to visit, but remember that their purpose is to be a place where humans make no lasting mark. Pack your litter out, bury your waste, camp lightly—and take water, extra food, warm clothing, a knife, a flashlight, a map, and a light or whistle for signaling. You're on your own out here. They're administered by the national forests (see above).

WILDLIFE With its variety of habitats and many wild areas, Washington supports a great variety of creatures, from the whales of Puget Sound to the golden-mantled ground squirrels that

want to share your picnic. Reportedly, grizzlies occasionally wander in from the north or east; wolves, absent for decades, are trickling back (and are not infrequently, but still illegally, shot). There are bobcats, cougars, and black bears about, but you're more likely to see elk, deer, coyotes, and maybe moose in the Rocky Mountain foothills; very likely you'll spot ravens, eagles, and ospreys. Be aware of rattlesnakes in the drier regions. And—I shouldn't have to say this—please don't feed the wildlife.

WILDLIFE AREAS Washington has 23 national wildlife refuges, both large and small, ranging from marine islands to deserts. Many are quite accessible from main roads, such as Nisqually, Ridgefield, Dungeness, and Grays Harbor. Others are farther from civilization but still on proper roads and rather spectacular—Conboy, Turnbull, and Little Pend Oreille, to name a few. Some are islands you can approach by boat but must avoid landing on, such as Protection Island and some of the smaller San Juans; these islands protect quantities of nesting seabirds. For details, contact the U.S. Fish and Wildlife Service (360-753-9440 or 800-344-WILD; www.fws.gov). State wildlife areas range from the Skagit River Estuary to Grouse Flats, near the Idaho border; for information check with the Washington Department of Fish and Wildlife (360-902-2200; wdfw.wa.gov), 600 Capitol Way North, Olympia 98501.

WINE Washington lies between 45°30′ and 49° north latitude, which, as its wine industry never tires of pointing out, is roughly that of France's wine areas. (Roughly indeed—and it must be pointed out that their climates are quite different: Washington's industry is heavily irrigation depend-

ent.) From a few experimental vineyards in the Columbia Valley in the 1970s, wine grapes have become the state's fourth-largest fruit crop. Today the Columbia Valley alone would keep a taster busy for several days. The principal growing areas are the Yakima and Walla Walla valleys, with vineyard after vineyard along the winding roads. The Tri-Cities are close behind despite their extreme aridity, and the vines are creeping ever northward up the Columbia Valley as far as Wenatchee and even Chelan, with a few appearing as far off as Spokane and Puget Sound. Wines produced run from your every-day chardonnay to some quite impressive (and pricey) merlots, pinot noirs, and dessert wines. For information and suggested itineraries, consult the Washington Wine Center (206-667-9463; www.washingtonwine.org), 1201 Western Avenue, Seattle 98101.

WINTER SPORTS As a mountainous northern state, Washington presents many opportunities for snow sports such as skiing, snowshoeing, and otherwise enjoying winter. These, whether ski resorts or trail networks, are generally listed under Winter Sports in the relevant chapters.

Coastal Washington

INTRODUCTION

*Great joy in camp we are in View of the Ocian, this great Pacific
Ocean which we been So long anxious to See. and the roreing
or noise made by the waves brakeing on the rockey Shores
(as I Suppose) may be heard distinctly.*

— *Captain William Clark, November 7, 1805*

Actually, they weren't there yet. The Corps of Discovery, under Captains Lewis
and Clark, were still on the lower Columbia River, near what is now Altoona in
Wahkiakum County. The ocean was more than 20 miles distant, and it would take
them more than a week to get there, pinned down as they were in "dismal nitches"
along the riverbanks in the miserable November storms.

But they may be forgiven the premature announcement. The Columbia estuary
is so broad—a good 5 miles at that point, and widening—and turbulent even in
good weather that Clark quite reasonably thought the expanse that was opening
before them was the sea and the "roreing" of its waves just that. Soon enough, he
was forced to recognize that this river could have ocean-sized waves, and his journal records his admiration for the Indians who crossed over in their canoes while
the Corps was immobilized, wet, and cold.

The lower Columbia is moody at the best of times, and from the safety of a
snug inn, its storms are romantic. Summer is calmer; often mists hang over the
water, permitting glimpses of pine-clad mountains on one or the other bank, much
as in a Japanese painting, and the occasional still, sunny day invites paddling
around the sloughs. But always there is humidity, and vegetation is rampant. The
river's huge volume and the nearby Pacific see to that.

The Indians of the lower river and coast had early if sporadic contact with
Europeans. Since the 1600s, Spanish, English, and Russian ships had plied the
coast, exploring, occasionally killing, and often trading. Lewis and Clark remarked
on Indians who spoke some English and more who possessed goods such as iron
kettles or European clothes. Contact meant the tribes were also swept by disease,
so that by the time the Corps of Discovery arrived, the population may already
have been diminished. But Clark does note several populous villages, and the company camped near one (now called Chinook) for a fortnight while scouting what is
now the Long Beach Peninsula and trying to decide what to do next.

As everyone now knows, the decision was taken not by the captains but by a vote of every member of the party, including Sacagawea (or Sacajawea) and Clark's slave, York. It was to go over to Oregon, where they spent a perfectly lousy (in both senses) winter and moved temporarily beyond the scope of this book. We will meet them later on their return to Washington's shores.

Settlement came slowly to the rugged river mouth, but it did come. By the late 1800s, small active communities bustled along the banks, all built up hurriedly around canneries or lumber mills and all facing the water; there were no roads, and the river was the highway. When roads did come, in the 1930s, the river traffic dried up, and many towns along its banks shrank or vanished. Today you can see pilings where factories or whole villages once were built over the water. Nature reclaims them now.

North of the river lie the Willapa Hills, an even more thinly populated area of heavily exploited forest bordered by I-5, from Longview and Kelso north to Chehalis, to the east and Willapa Bay and Grays Harbor to the west. Formerly busy ports, wholly dependent on lumber or fish, most of the few towns along these shores—from Ilwaco to Westport—are struggling with these industries' decline.

Still farther north, a straight, wild coast stretches some hundred miles from Grays Harbor to Cape Flattery. Most of this coastline is roadless, a haunt of seals and whales, solitary hikers on Olympic National Park's wilderness beaches, and a number of coastal tribes. The lower portion, from Ocean Shores to Moclips, has long been a destination of beachwalkers and wave watchers.

Behind the coast rise the formidable Olympic Mountains. Even today, few roads enter but do not cross the range. There was no record of anyone's success-fully crossing them even by foot until a five-man expedition led by James Christie did it as a newspaper stunt in 1889. It took five months, and they almost didn't make it. Today, protected by numerous wilderness areas surrounding Olympic National Park, the rugged peaks and valleys are explored by hikers, climbers, and skiers.

To the north and east on the Olympic Peninsula are the small towns along the Strait of Juan de Fuca, Puget Sound, and Hood Canal that grew up either on dreams of empire or on the grit of labor and trade. From Neah Bay to Port Angeles, towns along the strait offer spectacular views of a wild shoreline and Vancouver Island looming in the distance. Historic Port Townsend sits at the gateway to Puget Sound; Quilcene south to Shelton lie along the west shore of Hood Canal.

With the Olympic Mountains and rugged Pacific coast in such proximity, the scenery in this region is endless—and so are the recreational opportunities. Olympic National Park is one of the jewels in the national park system's crown, and it's so vast a place, you can easily find solitude even in midsummer. Not long ago, the Olympic Peninsula was a hardscrabble place to live, and parts of it still are. But efforts to diversify the local economy and encourage tourism are flourish-ing; you'll now find lavender farms, wineries, arts and music festivals from Port Angeles to Port Townsend, as well as—and this hasn't changed—seafood stands everywhere. If you've never tried wild Pacific salmon, you'll get your chance here in Coastal Washington.

LOWER COLUMBIA RIVER AND WILLAPA BAY

I f you like ambling along unfrequented back roads, the lower Columbia is your kind of place. Even the main artery, WA 4 from I-5 to US 101, isn't very busy, and the small side roads through sleepy farmland are even less so. Here or there, you'll find a roadside plaque noting where Lewis and Clark camped, a small park or a wildlife refuge, or a little town with a cozy café overlooking the river. Villagers from Cathlamet to Chinook, towns that are largely overlooked by tourists, tend to live ordinary lives in an extraordinary setting, gaining a living from farms or what's left of the river traffic.

All this bucolic country culminates in wild, rocky Cape Disappointment, where the river meets the Pacific and where the Corps of Discovery did finally meet the ocean. In fact, Captain Clark took an excursion up what is now the Long Beach Peninsula, remarking on a large beached sturgeon and carving his initials in a tree. The tree is long gone, but you can follow his route along the Discovery Trail from Ilwaco to Long Beach. You can also see the first completed installment of the Confluence Project, a series of four works by architect Maya Lin celebrating the river and Lewis and Clark's journey along it.

Long Beach itself has been a resort for more than a century, which has resulted in a salty mix of proud Victorian houses and tourist kitsch. Nevertheless, it's a remarkable natural feature—a 30-mile-long sandbar cast up by the river's prodigious output—and the farther north you go, the prettier it gets. With the Pacific on one side and Willapa Bay on the other, it's also a prime spot for oysters and migratory birds as you wander through the villages of Ocean Park, Oysterville, and Nahcotta.

Across the bay from the northern tip of the peninsula is a quiet stretch of coastline on WA 105, from the tiny hamlets of Tokeland and Grayland to Westport. Inland, the US 101 towns of Raymond and South Bend, which see few visitors, are linked to I-5 at Chehalis by lonely WA 6, on the northern side of the Willapa Hills.

GUIDANCE Cowlitz County (360-577-3137; www.co.cowlitz.wa.us), 1900 Seventh Avenue, Longview 98632.

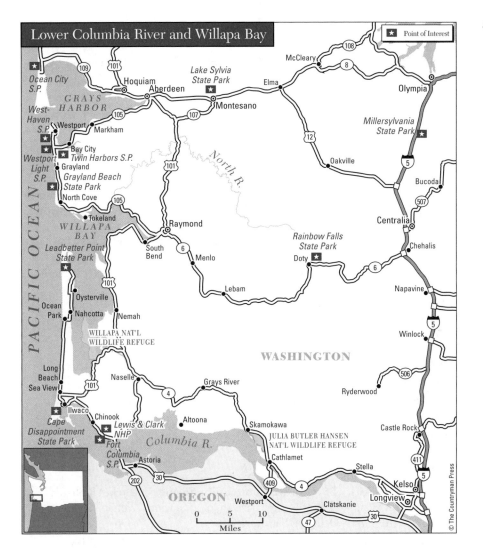

Lower Columbia River and Willapa Bay

★ Point of Interest

© The Countryman Press

Cranberry Coast Chamber of Commerce (360-267-2003 or 800-473-6018; www.cranberrycoastcoc.com), Box 305, Grayland 98547.

Grays Harbor Chamber of Commerce (800-321-1924; www.graysharbor.org), 506 Duffy Street, Aberdeen 98520.

Long Beach Peninsula Visitors Bureau (360-642-2400 or 800-451-2542; www.funbeach.com), corner of US 101 and WA 103, Box 562, Seaview 98644.

Mount St. Helens Cowlitz County Tourism Bureau (360-577-3137; www.visitmtsthelens.com), 105 Minor Road, Kelso 98626.

Vancouver USA Regional Tourism Office (360-750-1553 or 877-600-0800; www.visitvancouverusa.com), 101 East Eighth Street, Vancouver 98660; **Visitor**

Information Center (877-224-4214), 1501 East Evergreen Boulevard, Vancouver 98661.

Wahkiakum County Chamber of Commerce and Visitor Information Center (360-795-9996; www.wahkiakumchamber.com), 102 Main Street, Cathlamet 98612.

Westport-Grayland Chamber of Commerce (800-345-6223; www.westport -graylandchamber.org), 2985 South Montesano Street, Westport 98595.

Willapa Harbor Chamber of Commerce (360-942-5419; www.visit.willapa harbor.org), 405 Commercial Street, Raymond 98577.

GETTING THERE Exit **I-5** onto **WA 4** at Longview or Kelso and follow it west in a leisurely fashion along the bottomlands and river towns to **US 101** at Willapa Bay. Or exit I-5 onto **WA 6** at Chehalis and follow it west to US 101 at Raymond. From Raymond, **WA 105** loops along Willapa Bay, the Pacific coast, and Grays Harbor back to US 101. US 101 goes south from Grays Harbor at Cosmopolis to the coastline at Ilwaco. From Ilwaco, **WA 103** extends north up the Long Beach Peninsula.

GETTING AROUND **Pacific Transit** (360-875-9418 or 360-642-9418; www .pacifictransit.org) provides bus service around Pacific County from Aberdeen to Astoria, Oregon.

MEDICAL EMERGENCY **Ocean Beach Hospital** (360-642-3181; www.ocean beachhospital.net), 174 First Avenue North, Ilwaco.

St. John Medical Center (360-414-2000), 1615 Delaware, Longview.

Willapa Harbor Hospital (360-875-4503; www.willapaharborhospital), 800 Alder Street, South Bend.

✷ To See

FARMERS' MARKETS **Cowlitz Community Farmers' Market** (360-785-3883), Cowlitz County Event Center parking lot at Seventh Avenue, Longview. Open 9–2 Tues. May–Oct.; 9–2 Sat. Apr.–Oct.

Ilwaco Saturday Market (360-244-1117), Waterfront Way at Port of Ilwaco. Open 10–4 Sat. May–Sept.

Public Market on the Willapa (360-942-2123), Fourth and Heath Streets, Raymond. This covered market is open 10–4 Fri. and Sat. late Jan.–mid-Dec.

Two Islands Farm Market (360-849-4145), Stockhouse's Farm, 59 West Birnie Slough Road, on Puget Island opposite Cathlamet (take the ferry). Open 3–6:30 Fri. May–Oct.

FARMS AND GARDENS **Little Island Farm** (360-849-4492), 316 East Little Island Road, Cathlamet. Call for hours. Situated on Puget Island in the Columbia River, the farm raises goats, turkeys, chickens, and eggs, as well as flowers and a wide variety of fruits and vegetables. Order meat in advance or come by for produce and eggs.

Stockhouse's Farm (360-849-4145; www.stockhousesfarm.com), 62 West Birnie Slough Road, Cathlamet. Call for hours. Also on agricultural Puget Island, Stockhouse's offers all kinds of vegetables and flowers, a pumpkin patch, and chicken and duck eggs. They also have a **guest cottage** ($100; $500 per week) among the gardens.

FOR FAMILIES ♂ **Kite shops,** Pacific Highway, Long Beach. There are two reasons why one major and two minor kite festivals happen in Long Beach: the constant breezes and the long, flat beach. Visit a kite shop and go fly a kite. For instance:

Above It All Kites (360-642-3541; www.aboveitallkites.com), 312 Pacific Boulevard South, Long Beach.

Stormin' Norman's (360-642-2929), 205 Pacific Avenue South, Long Beach.

♂ **Marsh's Free Museum** (360-642-2188; www.marshsfreemuseum.com), 409 South Pacific Avenue, Long Beach. Open 9–6 daily in winter; 9–8 daily in summer. Free. This is basically a large souvenir shop with some really bizarre stuff, such as Jake the Alligator Man, a two-headed calf, a shrunken head, and more innocuous but curious items, including a collection of antique music machines. It's like a carnival sideshow frozen in time. Small children may enjoy this and a lot of other beach kitsch found around town.

HISTORIC HOMES **Colbert House** (360-642-3078), corner of Spruce and Quaker streets, Ilwaco. Open Memorial Day–Labor Day for self-guided tours. The Colberts were a fishing family who built this house in 1872 in what was once Chinookville, a town slightly upriver of here that no longer exists. In 1883 the house was moved downriver and enlarged; now it's restored and refurbished as a comfortable turn-of-the-20th-century home.

Ocean Park homes. A tour of this little town reveals several sober New England–style homes and the **Wreckage,** a log cabin built of salvaged piling poles. A self-guided tour is available from the Long Beach Peninsula Visitors Bureau (see *Guidance*).

Seaview homes. This town, platted in 1881, soon became a fashionable resort whose first vacationers arrived by stagecoach. Many settled in, at least part-time, and built elegant homes. Today the town is like Long Beach's older, steadier aunt. A self-guided tour of many Victorian homes is available from the Long Beach Peninsula Visitors Bureau (see *Guidance*). Among them are the homes of two senators.

Senator Tom Bloomer's mansion, 1004 41st Place, Seaview. Built in 1890, it has marble from quarries he owned in Alaska.

Sou'wester Lodge, 3728 J Street, Seaview. This was built in 1892 as the summer home of Senator Henry W. Corbett of Oregon.

See also Fort Columbia under *Historic Sites,* as well as *Lodging*.

HISTORIC SITES **Grays River Covered Bridge,** on WA 4 just east of the town of Grays River. This is the last covered bridge in use in Washington. Dating from 1905, it sits among bucolic farmland and hosts a festival in August (see *Special Events*).

Lewis and Clark mentioned several sites in their journals that are recognizable today or are marked by plaques. Here they're listed from east to west.

County Line Park, off WA 4 at Rosburg, at the end of the road. At the Cowlitz-Wahkiakum county line, a plaque records where the Corps of Discovery spent the night of November 6, 1805. The following night's camp is as yet unmarked, though it's the one where Clark made the entry noted at the beginning of this section.

Megler Rest Area, on WA 401 just east of Astoria Bridge. This is the site of a marker for the "dismal nitches" where the Lewis and Clark party was miserably confined by storms.

Station Camp State Park, on US 101, 2 miles southeast of Chinook. This 1-acre park is near the approximate location of the Corps's last campsite of their westward journey. Here they finally saw the Pacific and, most regrettably, shot a California condor.

Fort Columbia (see below) and **Cape Disappointment state parks.** Captain Clark and a party of 11 made a three-day trip up what's now the Long Beach Peninsula, crossing this area and Cape Disappointment.

The Discovery Trail, 8 paved miles from Ilwaco to Long Beach. This hiker-biker path retraces William Clark's route as he scouted up the beach. Several bronze sculptures commemorate findings from his notes: the discovery of a huge sturgeon, a whale's skeleton, and a tree in which he carved his initials (which has never been found).

Fort Columbia State Park (360-902-8844), US 101, Chinook. Open 6:30 AM–9:30 PM in summer; 8–5 in winter. Built on a high knoll, this fort is one of several batteries established in the late 1800s to protect the Columbia estuary; others are Fort Stevens on the Oregon side and Fort Canby at Cape Disappointment. Fort Columbia was staffed from 1896 to 1947, through the Spanish-American War, World War I, and World War II, after which it was turned over to the state. Today the 593-acre park invites a stroll along the row of handsome officers' houses dating from the early 1900s and around somber gun emplacements; if you're lucky, a bald eagle may soar overhead. The park includes a 25-table picnic area, an **interpretive center** featuring fort history (open 11–4 Sun.–Thurs. and 11–5 Fri.–Sat. in summer; 11–4 Fri.–Mon. in Sept.), and the **Commander's House Museum** (open 11–4 daily). Two period houses are available for **vacation rentals** (888-226-7688): the Steward's house, which sleeps 4, and Scarborough House, sleeping 12.

Naselle Pioneer Lutheran Church, on US 101 at milepost 7. Also more than a hundred years old and as austere as St. Mary's Catholic Church (see below), this church still has an active congregation.

Oysterville, on WA 103 near the north end of Long Beach Peninsula. This hamlet's historic homes and church look like a bit of New England removed to the wild West Coast. In fact, many of its early settlers and oyster entrepreneurs hailed from the Northeast. This village on the quiet bay side of the peninsula was once the seat of Pacific County, till gallants from South Bend seized the court documents by night in 1893 and spirited them home across Willapa Bay, where they reside to this day. Perhaps more important, Oysterville was the capital of the West Coast oyster industry for several decades. Flyers for a **self-guided walking tour** of the sober clapboard homes are available at the church, which also offers concerts in summer.

Pacific County Courthouse, corner of Cowlitz and Vine streets, South Bend. Open 8–4:30 weekdays. Here you can visit the current home of the county court files that were removed from Oysterville (see above). This grand 1910 building, a tribute to the area's golden age, stands at the crest of a hill overlooking Willapa Bay, flanked by the Victorian homes of lumber (and oyster) barons. A Tiffany dome 35 feet in diameter caps the atrium, faux marble columns run around the gallery, and dark wood trim and a mosaic floor lend yet more gravitas. It's still the county courthouse, with departments and offices radiating from the atrium.

St. Mary's Catholic Church, on US 101 near milepost 2, in the ghost town of **McGowan.** Built in 1904, this church's compact sanctuary of weathered shingles faces the Columbia River like the pioneer church it is. It still doesn't have utilities, and kerosene lamps are used for the occasional services.

Willie Kiel's Grave, on WA 6 about 2 miles southeast of Raymond. In 1855 the family of Dr. William Kiel set out on the Oregon Trail, bound for Willapa Bay. His 19-year-old son, Willie, was to head the wagon train; however, he died of malaria just before departure. The grief-stricken father put his son's body in a lead-lined coffin filled with whiskey and placed it in a wagon at the head of the train. Willie was finally buried the day after Christmas near the head of the bay, where a monument indicates his grave. The family moved on to Oregon about a year later.

MUSEUMS Cranberry Museum and Demonstration Farm (360-642-5553; www.cranberrymuseum.com), 2907 Pioneer Road, Long Beach. Museum open 10–5 daily Apr.–Dec. 15; farm open 8 AM–dusk daily. Cranberry cultivation began here when a visitor from Massachusetts observed native berries growing in the wetlands and said, "Aha." Cranberries are now cultivated in propitious spots along the Washington and Oregon coasts, though the industry has had its ups and downs since the 1870s; the Ocean Spray company has a facility in nearby South Bend. The museum exhibits cranberry-farming tools and the growing cycle; the farm is open for self-guided walking tours.

Columbia Pacific Heritage Museum (360-642-3446; www.columbiapacific heritagemuseum.org), 115 SE Lake Street, Ilwaco. Open 10–4 Tues.–Sat., 12–4 Sun. $5 adults, $4 seniors over 55, $2.50 children 12–18; free every Thurs. This museum focuses on the exploration and settlement of the lower Columbia River, including exhibits on the local Chinook culture and, naturally, a nod to Lewis and Clark. One room is, curiously, devoted to Gerard d'Aboville, who made landfall at Ilwaco after crossing the Pacific in a kayak in 1990. Out in back are a depot and train car from the old Ilwaco Railroad and Navigation Company, which used to carry mail, passengers, and especially oysters between Nahcotta, on the Long Beach Peninsula, and Ilwaco, where they were loaded on steamers for the California market (1889–1930). Since the steamer schedule depended on the tide, the train schedule followed suit and was popularly called the "Clamshell Railroad." The upstairs gallery has an intriguing collection of dollhouses.

Lewis and Clark Interpretive Center (360-642-3029), Ilwaco. Open 10–5 daily. $5 adults, $2.50 children 7–17. Lighthouse tours $2.50 adults, children under 17 free. This newly renovated center sits, appropriately, on a high hill overlooking the vast mouth of the Columbia River. The views extending across to Oregon and far out to sea are in themselves fitting testimony to the magnitude of the Corps of Discovery's 1804–1806 journey, commissioned by President Jefferson to find a water route to the Pacific and to report on all points in between. The interpretive center commemorates the remarkable expedition in a series of murals lining a descending ramp, a collection of tools and artifacts used on the journey, details of their scientific discoveries, and exhibits on the precontact Native cultures of the area. For lighthouse enthusiasts, a bonus is the "lighthouse room," with a large Fresnel lens on display. You can also tour the **North Head Lighthouse.**

Westport Maritime Museum (360-268-0078; www.maritimemuseum-ghlight house.org), 2201 Westhaven Drive, Westport. Open 10–4 daily in summer; 12–4 Thurs.–Mon. in fall and spring; 12–4 Sat.–Sun. and holidays in Jan.–Feb. $5 adults, $2 children 5–15. Lighthouse tours 10–4 daily in summer; $5. Housed in a 1939 Nantucket-style former Coast Guard station right on Westport's waterfront, this museum explains not only the life of the station but also early life on Willapa Bay ("early" meaning about 1900). Nearby, take a look at **Grays Harbor Lighthouse,** the tallest in Washington.

Northwest Carriage Museum (360-942-4150; www.nwcarriagemuseum.org), 314 Alder Street, Raymond. Open 10–4 Wed.–Sat. year-round; 12–4 Sun.–Tues. Apr.–Sept. $3 adults, $1 children 6–18, $7 families. Horse-and-buggy enthusiasts can enjoy 21 antique carriages, including a landau that appeared in *Gone with the Wind*.

Pacific County Historical Society and Museum (360-875-5224; www.pacific cohistory.org), 1008 West Robert Bush Drive (US 101), South Bend. Open 11–4 daily. Free. This museum has a rather dense collection of local memorabilia— photos, furniture, oyster- and cranberry-harvesting equipment, and more.

River Life Interpretive Center (360-795-3007; foska@pacifier.com), Redmen Hall, 1394 West WA 4, Skamokawa. Open 1–4 Thurs.–Sun. Suggested donation $2 adults, $1 children. This 1894 schoolhouse is now home to a museum of Skamokawa's history. Like many Columbia River towns, Skamokawa is much reduced. It used to be a rail terminus, shipping out lumber and fish from the can-nery. Photos show how the early houses were built on pilings, whole streets and neighborhoods of them; roads didn't come in till later. The second floor is an art gallery; from there you can climb the tower, ring the school bell, and enjoy a nice river view. (The Red Men were a fraternal organization active in the 19th and early 20th centuries. They bought the schoolhouse in 1926.)

Wahkiakum Historical Museum (360-795-3954), 65 River Street, Cathlamet. Open 1–4 Fri.–Sun. May–Oct. Suggested donation $3 adults, $1.50 seniors. This little house displays a way of life that existed here not long ago, with a wooden Columbia River boat out back and old-fashioned fishing and farming tools, cook-ware, toys, and other small-town treasures indoors.

Willapa Bay Interpretive Center (360-665-4547), 273rd Place, Nahcotta. Open 10–3 Fri.–Sun. Memorial Day–Labor Day. Free. San Francisco had an insatiable demand for oysters in the heady gold rush days, and many of those oysters came from Willapa Bay. Small, sweet, and in seemingly endless supply, the Pacific oyster was shipped out in such quantity, down the Clamshell Railroad and out by ship from Ilwaco, that it soon became commercially extinct. But Willapa's oyster indus-try goes on, now producing introduced Japanese species. At this reproduction oys-ter station halfway up the Long Beach Peninsula, you can learn about the industry that built the peninsula. The oyster beds lining much of the shore are jealously guarded, so you might take advantage of public access here.

✍ **World Kite Museum and Hall of Fame** (360-642-4020; www.worldkite museum.com), 303 Sid Snyder Drive, Long Beach. Open 11–5 daily May–Sept.;

11–5 Fri.–Tues. Oct.–May. $5 adults, $4 seniors, $3 children. The only museum in the United States dedicated completely to kites, this facility quadrupled in size in 2006 with expanded exhibits on the history of kites, military uses of kites, kite photography (including an aerial view of San Francisco after the 1906 earthquake)—in short, everything for the kite lover. Hands-on workshops are offered, too.

NATURAL WONDERS Long Beach, about 30 miles from the Columbia to the tip of the peninsula. This beach is claimed to be the longest continuous sand beach in the United States. The spit was formed by sediment washed down the Columbia River and pushed north by the prevailing coastal currents. Dependent on the vagaries of wind and water, its actual shoreline is fluid, though less so since the jetties at the river's mouth were built. The beach along which Captain Clark walked in 1805 was about a mile east of the present beach. About 1–2 miles wide, with some forest down its spine, the peninsula runs due north from the mouth of the Columbia, with the Pacific battering its west side and quieter Willapa Bay to the east.

Virtually the entire ocean side of the peninsula consists of broad, flat, sandy beach that is open for walking, kite flying, picnicking, and more. *Exhilarating* is the word that comes to mind. For a leisurely stroll, the Long Beach Boardwalk runs above the beach for half a mile, offering expansive ocean views and interpretive displays.

No swimming is allowed; ubiquitous signs warn of treacherous currents, and the surf is always heavy. Since the maximum water temperature is about 55 degrees Fahrenheit, you wouldn't want to swim anyway. For better or worse, the beach is also open to vehicles, which must observe a speed limit of 25 miles per hour and all rules of the road.

SCENIC DRIVES Wahkiakum Ferry (360-795-3301), ferry landing on WA 409 on Puget Island (via short bridge from Cathlamet). $5 per car, $3 per motorcycle, $2 per bike, $1 per pedestrian. A ferry ride isn't exactly a drive, but this is the oldest one still operating on the lower Columbia River. Carrying half a dozen cars, it runs hourly through the summer from Puget Island to Westport, Oregon, offering vistas of the broad river and steep green slopes on each side.

WA 4, 77 paved miles from Longview to Long Beach. This quiet highway winds along the banks and bottomlands of the moody lower Columbia through small towns and fertile farmland. Several sites where Lewis and Clark stopped are marked with historic plaques (see *Historic Sites*), and you'll pass two wildlife refuges (see *Wilder Places*), Fort Columbia State Park (see *Historic Sites*), and breathtaking Cape Disappointment. But the main attraction is the pastoral environment. Uncrowded and not at all touristy till you get to Long Beach, it's almost a step back to an earlier era.

✷ To Do

BICYCLING Apollo Activities (360-642-4260), 106 Sid Snyder Drive, Long Beach. Bikes can be rented here.

Discovery Trail, 8 paved and gravel miles from Ilwaco to Long Beach. This trail winds through the dunes near several towns.

Long Beach Peninsula, WA 103. Back roads are straight and level.

Puget Island, via WA 409 and short bridge from Cathlamet. The rural island has gentle rides through farmland. The country roads of Pacific and Wahkiakum counties also lend themselves to road bikes.

Willapa River Trail, 5.5 paved miles between Raymond and South Bend. This trail follows the Willapa River.

CAMPING Cape Disappointment State Park (888-226-7688), on WA 100 at Cape Disappointment. Open year-round; reservations recommended, especially in summer. One hundred thirty-seven standard sites, 60 full-hook-up sites, 18 sites with water and electricity, and 5 primitive sites. Also yurts and rustic cabins. ADA restrooms and showers.

Grayland Beach State Park (888-226-7688), on WA 105, 5 miles south of Westport. Open year-round. Fifty-eight full-hook-up sites, 42 sites with water and electricity, 4 primitive sites, and 16 yurts. A 0.25-mile interpretive trail leads from the campground to 1.5 miles of spectacular beach.

Long Island (360-484-3482), in Willapa National Wildlife Refuge in Willapa Bay, accessible only by boat. No reservations. Twenty-four primitive campsites.

Rainbow Falls State Park, on WA 6, 35 miles east of Raymond. No reservations. Forty-five tent sites, 8 utility sites, and 3 hiker-biker sites.

Skamokawa Vista Park (360-795-8605), 13 Vista Park Road, Skamokawa; located below Redmen Hall (see *To See—Museums*) and across the creek. A full-service park with tent and RV sites and five yurts.

Twin Harbors State Park (888-226-7688), on WA 105, 3 miles south of Westport. This beach park has 250 tent sites, 49 rather crowded utility sites, and 2 yurts.

CANOEING AND KAYAKING Lower Columbia River Water Trail (www .columbiawatertrail.org), 146 miles from Bonneville Dam to the Pacific. This water trail is for nonmotorized craft.

Willapa Bay Trail (www.wwta.org/trails), around entire perimeter of the bay. Also for nonmotorized craft.

Secondwind Sports (360-642-4052; www.secondwindsports.net), on WA 104, Long Beach. The intrepid may wish to try sea kayaking, an exhilarating sport but one requiring stamina, strength, the proper equipment, and training. This outfitter will take you out, give you lessons, or just rent you a boat.

Columbia River Kayaking (360-795-8300; www.skamokawakayak.com), 1391 WA 4, Skamokawa. They offer rentals, lessons, and tours among the sloughs, islands, and open waters of the lower Columbia River.

GOLF Peninsula Golf Course (360-642-2828), 9604 Pacific Highway, Long Beach. Nine holes.

Surfside Golf (360-665-4148), 31508 J Place, Ocean Park. Nine holes.

Willapa Harbor Golf Course and RV Park (360-942-2392; www.willapagolf andrv.com), 2424 Fowler Street, Raymond. Nine holes.

HIKING Cape Disappointment State Park, on WA 100 at Cape Disappointment. Seven miles of hilly hiking trails lead to two lighthouses and magnificent views of the mouth of the Columbia River.

The Discovery Trail, 8 paved and gravel miles from Ilwaco to north Long Beach. It commemorates Captain William Clark's investigation of the peninsula.

Leadbetter Point State Park, on WA 103, 18 miles north of Long Beach, just short of the peninsula's tip. Seven miles of trails meander through woods, dunes, beach grass, and sand. Undeveloped except for a parking area and restrooms. Few tourists wander this far, so this is a good place for a quiet forest or beach walk— except in winter, when it generally floods. Part of the beach may be closed Mar.–Sept. to protect nesting snowy plovers.

Willapa River Trail, 5.5 miles between Raymond and South Bend. This paved riverfront trail is open to hikers and bikers (see *Bicycling*).

✳ Wilder Places

PARKS Cape Disappointment State Park (360-642-3078), on WA 100, 2 miles south of Ilwaco. Open 6:30 AM–10 PM in summer; 6:30–4 in winter. It's not hard to recapture the elation of Lewis and Clark's team upon viewing the Pacific when you stand on the rocky headland of Cape Disappointment and behold the mighty Columbia flowing into the sea many feet below, the Pacific stretching out to all eternity. With 1,880 acres and 27 miles of rocky shoreline, this is one of the most visited parks in the system, with old-growth forest, beach, lakes, tidal pools, and plentiful wildlife. The newest attraction is the first installation of the **Confluence Project,** a series created by Maya Lin at key confluences along the river system that aim to integrate landscape, history, and culture. There's historical interest in the **Lewis and Clark Interpretive Center** (see *To See—Museums*); **Cape Disappointment Lighthouse,** one of the oldest on the West Coast (1856), and **North Head Lighthouse;** and the largest **Coast Guard search-and-rescue station** in the Northwest. The Columbia River bar is one of the most dangerous river bars in the world, called the graveyard of the Pacific because of the hundreds of wrecks that have taken place here (some of which are still visible on both the Oregon and Washington sides). For an unusual place to stay, you might try one of the lighthouse keepers' **cottages** (see *Lodging*).

Day-use activities include picnicking, surfing, fishing, and beachcombing on Half Moon Bay.

Westport Light State Park, on Ocean Avenue about 1 mile west of Westport. Day use only. Open 6 AM–10 PM in summer; 8–6 in winter. This 212-acre park next to Grays Harbor Lighthouse at Westport is the trailhead for a 1.3-mile ADA path leading to **Westhaven State Park,** on Jetty Road near the marina in Westport. This small park just south of the jetty is popular with surfers but shrinking due to erosion—it's down to 60 acres, from 79. The path, winding among the dunes, offers several benches and a glimpse of birdlife among the back-dune shrubbery.

See also *To Do—Camping*.

WILDLIFE REFUGES Julia Butler Hansen Columbian White-Tailed Deer National Wildlife Refuge (360-795-3915), 46 Steamboat Slough Road, Cathlamet. Open daily dawn to dusk; headquarters open 7:30–4 Mon.–Fri. The Columbian white-tailed deer is an endangered subspecies of the white-tailed deer commonly found in the eastern United States. This refuge was set aside in 1972 to provide enough habitat to increase its numbers, so you'll find a combination of woodland, wetland, and even hayfields along the Columbia River floodplain. River otters and a few Roosevelt elk also live on the refuge. A road allows you to drive through slowly and observe the wildlife.

Lewis and Clark National Wildlife Refuge (360-795-3915), 46 Steamboat Slough Road, Cathlamet. Accessible only by boat, this is a refuge principally for migratory waterfowl that consists of 8,313 acres of islands and sandbars adjacent to the Julia Butler Hansen National Wildlife Refuge (see above). The islands are artificial, a by-product of shipping-channel dredging.

Willapa National Wildlife Refuge Headquarters (360-484-3482), 3888 US 101, Ilwaco. Established in 1937, this four-unit system protected the bay at a time when many estuaries were being radically altered by draining, dredging, and pollution. At headquarters, a short woodland trail celebrates the restoration of a small salmon stream with a series of sculptures. The refuge's varied habitats—tidal flats, dunes, and old-growth forest—create great wildlife viewing, except in fall when the refuge is open to hunting. The most popular units are **Long Island,** with boat access only, and **Leadbetter Point,** an old-growth forest threaded with trails at the tip of the Long Beach Peninsula (see *To Do—Hiking*). Leadbetter Point harbors wintering flocks of waterfowl and protected snowy plover nests on the beach in summer. Unusually, the refuge allows camping, on Long Island only (see *To Do—Camping*).

✳ Lodging

BED & BREAKFASTS

Ilwaco

China Beach Retreat (360-642-2442; www.chinabeachretreat.com), 222 Robert Gray Drive. A sister house of the Shelburne Inn (see *Seaview*), it's called China Beach because of the Chinese cannery workers who lived in barracks on this cove. Off the road and looking out over a marsh, the retreat's three luxurious rooms are removed, as intended, from distractions beyond the occasional bear or eagle. A full breakfast is included. $179–289.

Inn at Harbour Village (360-642-0087 or 888-642-0087; www.innat harbourvillage.com), 120 Williams Avenue NE. This gray-shingled house was once a church—and still has a 1928 chapel for weddings! Set on a hill in downtown Ilwaco, it's a bit away from the beach attractions but close to Ilwaco's renovated port and just 2 miles from Cape Disappointment. The nine rooms are comfortably old-

fashioned, and the parlor has a fireplace. A continental breakfast is included. No pets. $115–185.

Ocean Park

✍ ✿ **Charles Nelson Guesthouse Bed and Breakfast** (360-665-3016 or 888-862-9756; www.charlesnelson bandb.com), 26205 Sandridge Road. This solid two-story house was a Sears and Roebuck kit bought in the 1920s. Now nicely renovated, it's in a restful setting on the quiet part of the peninsula, with three bedrooms and several common areas, including a parlor, sunroom, and gardens. A full breakfast is included. Child- and pet-friendly. $170–190; special winter rates available.

Seaview

The Shelburne Inn (360-642-2442 or 800-INN-1896; www.theshelburneinn .com), 4415 Pacific Highway. Built in 1896, this inn has been sheltering vacationers since the peninsula became a resort for Portland businessmen and their families. Owners David Campiche and Laurie Anderson bought the place in 1977 and have lovingly made it one of the premier inns of the region. The rambling green Victorian sits modestly on its corner lot, but inside, the warm fir paneling, Oriental rugs, and spectacular antique furnishings offer fin de siècle luxury. However, the mattresses are state-of-the-art pillow tops, and all 15 rooms have private baths. A family-style breakfast is included. The on-premises **Shelburne Restaurant and Pub** has won awards for fine dining (see *Where to Eat*). Supervised children welcome. No pets. $139–199; packages available.

South Bend

Russell House Bed and Breakfast (360-875-6487 or 888-484-6907; www.russellhousebb.com), 902 East Water Street. This imposing turreted home on a hill was built in 1891 by John Russell as an anniversary present for his wife (well, it was their silver wedding anniversary). Seven guest rooms from snug to spacious are decorated in full-blown Victorian style, brass bedsteads, draperies, and all; most have bay or garden views and private baths. A full breakfast is included. $60–145.

COTTAGES AND CABINS

Long Beach

Boardwalk Cottages (360-642-2305 or 800-569-3804; www.boardwalk cottages.com), 800 Ocean Boulevard South. Ten cottages near the board-walk, from studio-sized to two bed-rooms, have kitchens, gas fireplaces, and decks. No pets. $89–145.

Ocean Park

Shakti Cove Cottages (360-665-4000; www.shakticove.com), 25301 Park Avenue. Ten shingled cabins stand around a glade and a small pond a short walk from the beach. Shakti is a quiet getaway friendly to gays of both sexes

(one cabin has quite a number of female fertility statuettes). Pets with responsible owners are welcome. $80–110.

INNS AND HOTELS

Nahcotta

Moby Dick Hotel, Restaurant and Oyster Farm (360-665-4543; www.mobydickhotel.com), 25814 Sandridge Road. Far from the madding crowds, Moby Dick sits near the north end of the peninsula, where you can slow down and hear the wind blow—and not much else. The hotel came about in 1929; in 1931 the Clamshell Railroad stopped running (demand for oysters must have crashed with the stock market), and the hotel fell on hard times. Refurbished and reopened in 1990, the hotel now boasts a style that might best be called "neo-deco"—eclectic but homey in a 1930s sort of way, with stuffed armchairs, Asian touches, and period art. Phones and TVs are eschewed. Tranquil grounds slope down to the bay through flower and organic vegetable gardens, past an outdoor sauna and a yurt. It's just different enough. Some of the 10 rooms have shared baths. Homegrown oysters have—temporarily, it is hoped—disappeared from the full-breakfast menu due to concerns about pesticides in Willapa Bay. Children welcome. Pets welcome for a fee. $90–150.

Skamokawa

The Inn at Lucky Mud (800-806-7131; www.luckymud.com), 44 Old Chestnut Drive. The name comes from Kurt Vonnegut's *Cat's Cradle*, which is the sort of inspiration you might expect from a guy named Sunrise—though I suspect the coastal winters may play a part, too. Notwithstanding, the relaxed, elegant, and immaculate house is wonderful to come back to after you've been wandering trails around the 40-acre property. Tucked back in the woods along the lower Columbia, it's a fine place to get away from it all. Jessica and Sunrise Fletcher will cook you a full breakfast, and dinner too if you like. Oh, and there's an 18-hole disc golf course. No pets. $110–120.

Tokeland

🐾 **Tokeland Hotel** (360-267-7006; www.tokelandhotel.com), 100 Hotel Road. On a lonely little peninsula jutting into the north end of Willapa Bay stands the Tokeland Hotel. The spot doesn't exactly look like Grand Central Station, but in the mid-1800s anyone going from Portland to Seattle—there was considerable traffic because of the oyster trade and an evolving government—went by stage and boat, and the Tokeland Peninsula was a land-water connection that many visited. Later, tourism took hold, and the lodgelike hotel officially became a hostelry in 1898. But owners William and Lizzie Kindred had already been housing and feeding travelers for years, as her homesteading parents had done before her. Of course, they had to enlarge their home a bit. Today it has two gabled ends connected by a long main section, much like the national park lodge at Mount Rainier, and the atmosphere of a remote Victorian beach hotel. The floors creak, and the rooms share bathrooms, but the airy rooms with their brass or carved wooden bedsteads are refreshing, and you've got some real atmosphere here. The on-site dining room (open 8–8) offers country-style home cooking for breakfast, lunch, and dinner, which is a good thing as it's quite a way to another restaurant. $48.50–65.

MOTELS

Long Beach

🐾 🏠 **Arcadia Court Hotel** (877-642-2613; www.arcadiacourthotel.com),

405 Ocean Beach Boulevard North. "Lewis and Clark schlepped here." At that point, they doubtless would have appreciated this small, old-fashioned beach motel. Simple queen and king rooms and one- and two-bedroom suites come with complimentary use of a beach wagon; suites have kitchens. $45–169.

Seaview

🐾 🏠 **Seaview Motel and Cottages** (360-642-8008), 3728 Pacific Highway. Larry and Amy Cook run these homey lodgings. Rooms are small but spotless and cheery, with sparing but tasteful decoration. Children and pets welcome. $50–129.

COTTAGES

Long Beach

Akari Bungalows (360-642-5267; www.akaribungalows.com), 203 Bolstad Avenue. These cottages—1930s on the outside, rock fireplaces and pillow-top mattresses on the inside—range from studio-sized to two bedrooms, with kitchen or kitchenette. $85–175.

✳ Where to Eat

DINING OUT

Ilwaco

Pelicano Restaurant (360-642-4034; pelicanorestaurant.com), 177 Howerton Way SE, Port of Ilwaco. Open from 5 PM Wed.–Sun. The menu changes with the season but always features fresh Pacific seafood as well as "landlubber food," often with an Asian touch. And the view over the harbor is fine.

Seaview

The Depot (360-642-7880; www .depotrestaurantdining.com), 1208 38th Place. Open from 5 PM Wed.–Mon. It actually is a 1905 depot of the Clamshell Railroad, aka the Ilwaco Railroad and Navigation Company, which carried people and oysters between Nahcotta and Ilwaco for several decades. Chef Michael Lalewicz refined his seafood-cooking skills in tidewater Maryland and was formerly at the Shoalwater Inn restaurant at the Shelburne Inn (see below). The casual, fine-dining experience he's created here offers seafood, game, and vegetarian choices, with steak Americano, too.

The 42nd Street Café (360-642-2323; www.42ndstcafe.com), 4201 Pacific Way. Open 8–2 and 4:30 to closing. The menu is eclectic (mousseline of portobello mushrooms, anyone?), and chef Cheri Walker plays the harp on Sunday nights—you know you're onto something slightly different. Organic beef and a variety of clams, shrimp, oysters, and more, often prepared with a Cajun twist, make this one of the most popular eateries on the peninsula. *Wine Press Northwest* gave the café a "Best Washington Wine List" designation—the list is extensive and almost entirely Northwest.

The Shelburne Restaurant and Pub (360-642-4150; www.theshelburne restaurant.com), 4415 Pacific Way. Open 8–3 and 5–8:30 daily; dinner reservations recommended. Formerly the Shoalwater Inn, the Shelburne Inn's in-house restaurant (see *Lodging*) continues a fine-dining tradition that has attracted patrons from far-flung Portland and Seattle for more than a century. Seafood, as local as possible, takes pride of place on the menu, but landlubbers will appreciate choice duck, lamb, and other seasonal offerings, all prepared with an expert hand. The pub offers more casual fare, sometimes with live music.

EATING OUT

Long Beach
Long Beach Thai Cuisine (360-642-2557), 1003 Pacific Highway. Opened in spring 2005 by an enthusiastic young couple, the restaurant looks like humble, hopeful Thai restaurants everywhere, but some of the best Thai food anywhere is served here. Favorite dishes are juxtaposed with startling new ones such as mango and fruit curries—surprising and delicious. The chef obviously has a delicate yet bold touch, and her husband serves with gusto. This is one of the best deals around.

Lost Roo (360-642-4329; www.lost roo.com), 1700 South Pacific Highway. Open for lunch and dinner Wed.–Mon. No, the owners are not Aussies, but they met backpacking in Brisbane. This does not seem to have affected the menu (despite the Roo Burger)—even the fish-and-chips is served tempura-style. Mostly it's hearty Northwest fare, with good Northwest beer and wine to boot.

Ocean Park
The Berry Patch (360-665-5551), 1513 Bay Avenue. This friendly café in peaceful Ocean Park serves homemade ice cream and all-you-can-eat fish-and-chips.

Skamokawa
Duck Inn (360-795-3655), 1377 WA 4. Open 8 AM–9 PM daily. When I asked where I could eat sturgeon, this is where I was pointed. A down-home type of place with moody views of the Columbia River, the Duck Inn naturally takes advantage of the river's bounty. Straightforwardly prepared native fish dishes are the draw, but traditional steak, chicken, and pork dinners share the menu.

✳ Selective Shopping

FOOD Brady's Oysters (360-268-0077 or 800-572-3252), 3714 East Oyster Place, Westport. Visit or order—oysters all ways, plus crab, clams, fish, and so forth.

Nelson Crab, Inc. (800-262-0069; www.nelsoncrab.com), WA 105, Tokeland. The Nelson family founded one of the earliest West Coast crab canneries in 1934 and have been at it for three generations. Shop online or on the Tokeland spit; you'll find not only crab, and not only canned.

SPECIAL SHOPS The Port of Ilwaco (360-642-3143; www.portof ilwaco.com), 165 Howerton Avenue, Ilwaco. As well as a marina and port, there's a small but hopeful shopping center here. Besides your usual boat-yard stores, you'll find art galleries and nautical gifts at **Nautical Brass** (360-642-5092).

✳ Special Events

August: **Covered Bridge Celebration** (360-795-0419), Grays River Covered Bridge, Grays River. A race, scenic trolley rides, music, farmers' market, Model T races, and more celebrate the bridge.

Washington International Kite Festival (360-244-0669; www.kitefestival .com), Long Beach. A week of kite competition and celebration is held during the last week of August.

October: **Cranberrian Fair** (360-642-3446), Ilwaco Heritage Museum, Ilwaco. Celebrate the cranberry with food, crafts, music, and dancing. $5, with shuttle buses to the cranberry and kite museums (see *To See—Museums*).

WESTERN OLYMPIC PENINSULA

Sticking up like a hitchhiker's thumb, the Olympic Peninsula looks like a geographic afterthought. And in a way, it is: The mountains' sharp edges show them to be young, as mountains go. Settlement, too, came fairly late here. Towns on the peninsula's fringe, important for trade and defense, grew up in the 1860s, but the interior was too impenetrable and the Pacific coastline too dangerous for would-be settlers to make much of a dent. The result is a sprinkling of small towns around the edges, a national park in the middle, and national forest and wilderness areas in between: one of the wildest, least penetrated areas you might find south of the 49th parallel.

This chapter covers the peninsular lowlands on the west side of the Olympic Mountains, but "lowlands" is a relative term: The lands from the water's edge extend into the Olympic foothills toward the national park. They include the Olympic National Forest and wilderness areas surrounding the park.

Visitors to the Western Olympic Peninsula often pass through Aberdeen and Hoquiam without stopping, perhaps staying at Ocean Shores or another of the small towns south of the large Quinault Indian Reservation. For a short way, US 101 hugs the coastline north of Kalaloch, inviting a beach walk, before the road swings inland again. At the town of Forks, WA 110 heads west to La Push on the tiny Quileute Indian Reservation; US 101 continues north through Beaver and Sappho, where it turns east. From Sappho, WA 113 leads to WA 112, which heads west through Clallam Bay and Sekiu to Neah Bay; this road hugging the Strait of Juan de Fuca is among the most spectacular in the world. The Makah Reservation on Cape Flattery at Neah Bay has a wonderful cultural museum, besides being at the northwesternmost point of the continental United States. You'll feel like you're at the end of the earth.

GUIDANCE Clallam Bay–Sekiu Chamber of Commerce (877-694-9433; www.clallambay.com), Box 355, Clallam Bay 98326. Open daily May–Sept.

Forks Recreation and Information Center (360-374-2531 or 800-443-6757; www.forkswa.com), 1411 South Forks Avenue, Forks 98331. Open 10–4 Mon.–Fri., 10–5 Sat., 11–4 Sun.

Grays Harbor Chamber of Commerce (800-321-1924; www.graysharbor.org), 506 Duffy Street, Aberdeen 98520.

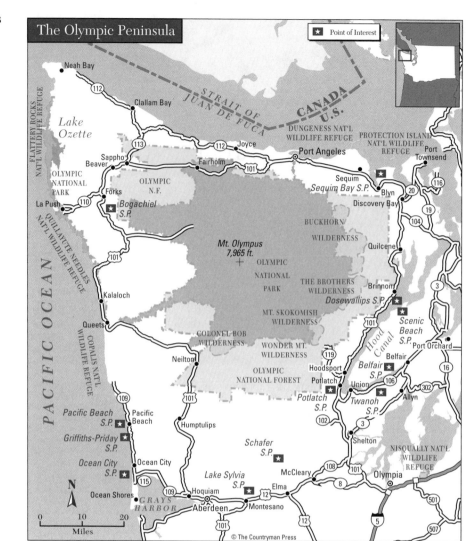

The Olympic Peninsula

★ Point of Interest

Neah Bay

112

Clallam Bay

FLATTERY ROCKS NAT'L WILDLIFE REFUGE

STRAIT OF JUAN DE FUCA

CANADA U.S.

DUNGENESS NAT'L WILDLIFE REFUGE

PROTECTION ISLAND NAT'L WILDLIFE REFUGE

Port Townsend

116

Lake Ozette

113

112 Joyce

Port Angeles

Sappho

Beaver

Fairholm

101

Sequim

Sequim Bay S.P. ★

Blyn 20

19

OLYMPIC NATIONAL PARK

OLYMPIC N.F.

Forks

Discovery Bay

104

La Push 110

Bogachiel S.P. ★

BUCKHORN WILDERNESS

Quilcene

QUILLAYUTE NEEDLES NAT'L WILDLIFE REFUGE

Mt. Olympus 7,965 ft.

OLYMPIC

OLYMPIC NATIONAL PARK

THE BROTHERS WILDERNESS

Brinnon

3

101

Dosewallips S.P. ★

PACIFIC OCEAN

Kalaloch

MT. SKOKOMISH WILDERNESS

Scenic Beach S.P. ★

Port Orchard

Queets

COLONEL BOB WILDERNESS

WONDER MT. WILDERNESS

119

Belfair

COPALIS NAT'L WILDLIFE REFUGE

Neilton

OLYMPIC NATIONAL FOREST

Hoodsport

Belfair S.P.

16

Potlatch

106

302

109

101

Potlatch S.P. ★

Union ★

Twanoh S.P.

Allyn

Pacific Beach S.P. ★

Pacific Beach

Humptulips

102

3

Shelton

NISQUALLY NAT'L WILDLIFE REFUGE

Griffiths-Priday S.P.

Schafer S.P. ★

Ocean City S.P. ★

Ocean City

McCleary

108

101

Olympia

N

115

Lake Sylvia S.P. ★

Elma

8

501

Ocean Shores

109

Hoquiam

12

GRAYS HARBOR

Aberdeen

Montesano

12

0   10   20
Miles

101

12

5

507

© The Countryman Press

Ocean Shores Chamber of Commerce (360-289-2451), 873 Point Brown Avenue NW, Ocean Shores 98569.

Olympic National Forest Headquarters (360-956-2402), 1835 Black Lake Boulevard SW, Olympia 98512.

GETTING THERE From **I-5** in Olympia, take **WA 8 and US 12** west to Aberdeen and Hoquiam. From there, **WA 109** continues west and north through Ocean Shores to Moclips; **US 101** heads north through Forks to Sappho. Or, from Seattle, take the ferry to Bainbridge Island and follow **WA 305 and 3** north to the Hood Canal Bridge, which takes you to the northeastern peninsula via **WA 104,** then US 101 west to Sappho. From Sappho, take **WA 113** north, then **WA 112** west to Clallam Bay and Neah Bay.

www.clallamtransit.com), 830 Lauridsen Boulevard, Port Angeles. There's cheap
bus service between Sequim, Port Angeles, Forks, and La Push and links with Jefferson Transit (see the Eastern Olympic Peninsula chapter).

MEDICAL EMERGENCY **Forks Community Hospital** (360-374-6271), 530
Bogachiel Way, Forks.

✳ To See

FARMERS' MARKETS **Forks Open Aire Market** (360-374-6789), US 101,
next to the **Timber Museum,** Forks. Open 10–3 Sat. mid-May–mid-Oct.

Gray's Harbor Street Fair (360-532-8443), Broadway between Heron and
Wishkah streets, Aberdeen. Open 11–4 Sun. early June–Aug.

HISTORIC HOMES **Hoquiam Castle** (360-533-2005; www.hoquiamcastle.com),
515 Chenault Avenue, Hoquiam. Tours 1–4 Wed.–Sat. $4. Robert Lytle completed
this opulent home in 1901; its turreted, 10,000-square-foot majesty almost
demands a moat. Remarkably, the house stayed in the family until 1950, when it
was auctioned off and abandoned. Restoration began in 1968, and in 1999 the
house opened as a bed & breakfast (see *Lodging*). With remarkable antiques
throughout, such as a nickel-plated stove, a hand-carved oak dining room set, and
crystal chandeliers, the castle is a sort of memory palace of the frontier barons.
The Lytle House next door was built from 1897 to 1900 in the Queen Anne style.

MUSEUMS **Aberdeen Museum of History** (360-533-1976; www.aberdeen
-museum.org), 111 East Third Street, Aberdeen. Open 10–5 Tues.–Sat., 12–4 Sun.
Mar.–Oct.; 10–5 Tues.–Sat. Nov.–Feb. Suggested donation $2 adults, $1 seniors
and students, $5 families. The life and times of Grays Harbor is brought to life in
this unexpectedly spacious museum. Vintage equipment fills mockups of an early-
20th-century fire station, logging camp, and schoolhouse—some of the early fire
trucks are remarkable. Scenes from Aberdeen's early decades make up an intriguing slide show.

Forks Timber Museum (360-374-9663), on US 101, Box 873, Forks 98331. Open
seasonally. Donation requested. In the middle of the rain forest, Forks has long
lived on timber. The museum holds logging equipment and memorabilia, including
a fire lookout tower.

Makah Cultural and Research Center (360-645-2711; www.makah.com
/museum), Box 160, Neah Bay 98357. Open 10–5 daily except Thanksgiving,
Christmas, and New Year's Day; may also close in extreme weather. $5 adults, $4
seniors and students, children under five free. The Makah Reservation occupies
Cape Flattery at the very farthest tip of the Olympic Peninsula. This is the tribe
that's been getting varied press about its resumption of whaling. In this fascinating
museum, you can see both whaling and sealing canoes and a host of artifacts from
a village buried by a mudslide five hundred years ago at Ozette, about 15 miles
south of here. The amazingly preserved and beautifully displayed items include
baskets and woven blankets. Did you know a special breed of dog was kept to provide wool and only died out a century or so ago?

✍ **Polson Museum** (360-533-5862), 1611 Riverside Avenue, Hoquiam. Open 11–4 Wed.–Sat., 12–4 Sun. Apr.–Dec.; 12–4 Sat.–Sun. Dec.–Mar. $4 adults, $2 students, $1 children under 12, $10 families. Formerly the 26-room home of the Polson family, it was donated to the city in 1976 and now interprets the history of Hoquiam through Polson family artifacts, photos, and themed rooms—logging, sports, children, and so forth.

SCENIC DRIVES **The Pacific Coast Scenic Byway,** about 280 paved miles from Aberdeen north, east, then south to Olympia. US 101 follows a neat arc around the peninsula and the edge of Olympic National Park. It's all scenic, really. When you have a mountain range ringed with evergreen forests and rugged coasts, what's not scenic? From Aberdeen the route north is inland from the coast to glacial Lake Quinault, where the highway jogs west to the Pacific. Along this stretch of misty coast fringed with Sitka spruce, the shore is part of the national park. The route heads inland again, where the park is edged by clear-cuts of unfortunate number and size, especially as the route heads north through Forks, the population and tourism center of the Western Olympic Peninsula. At Sappho, US 101 heads east into the park at Lake Crescent and continues on its loop back to Olympia (see the Eastern Olympic Peninsula chapter).

WA 112, about 70 paved miles from Port Angeles west to Cape Flattery. For spectacular views of the Strait of Juan de Fuca and Vancouver Island, follow this winding highway out along the ragged coast, past infrequent villages, to the northwesternmost point of the continental United States—Cape Flattery, on the Makah Reservation. You'll have to walk the last 0.75 mile, on forest duff and boardwalk, to the headland. Tatoosh Island, the straits, and the Pacific offer an unsurpassable view of wild beauty. You may have puffins and eagles for company. A $7 permit is required for nonresident vehicles visiting the reservation for recreational purposes; this can be bought at the Makah museum, the Makah Tribal Center, the Makah Marina, or Washburns' General Store—all are easy to find in tiny Neah Bay.

THE OLYMPIC RAIN FOREST CAN BE ADMIRED FROM THE PACIFIC COAST SCENIC BYWAY.

place—not surprisingly, as the gray, misty climate seems perfect for vampires. The
Forks Chamber of Commerce website (www.forkswa.com) has a slide show of Twilight sites you may want to take in.

✳ To Do

BICYCLING Queets River Road, about 12 paved miles; from US 101, 8 miles
east of Queets, turn north. This is a near-wilderness ride.

Undie Road, 5 paved miles; from US 101, 5 miles south of Forks, turn left. A
quiet ride is the 5 miles to the Bogachiel trailhead (the Bogachiel Trail itself is not
for bikes).

US 101. Road biking is feasible along the highway, but the shoulder is often narrow, and you share the road with RVs.

Mountain Biking

Lake Sylvia State Park, 2.5 miles of mountain biking trails; off US 12, 1 mile
north of Montesano.

Mount Muller Trail, 13-mile loop; from US 101 north of Lake Crescent, start at
Klahowya Campground.

West Fork Humptulips Trail, 9.5 rugged miles from Pete's Creek trailhead to
FR 2204. For late-summer rides only, due to high water after spring runoff.

Rentals

Rainforest Paddlers (866-457-8398), 4883 Upper Hoh Road, Forks. This outfitter also rents mountain bikes on the peninsula's west side.

CAMPING Bogachiel State Park (360-374-6356), on US 101, 6 miles south of
Forks. No reservations. Thirty tent sites, six sites with hook-ups. Shower and ADA
restroom.

Cottonwood Campground (360-374-6131), on Hoh River, 16 miles south of
Forks, 2.5 miles west of US 101 on Oil City Road. This Department of Natural
Resources campground has seven sites, restrooms, and river access.

Hoh Oxbow Campground (360-374-6131), on US 101 south of Hoh Rainforest
Road. This Department of Natural Resources campground has seven wooded
campsites and restrooms.

Lake Sylvia State Park (888-226-7688), off US 12 east of Grays Harbor and 1
mile north of Montesano. Thirty-five tent sites and two primitive hiker-biker sites.

Ocean City State Park (888-226-7688), on WA 115, 1 mile north of Ocean
Shores. One hundred forty-nine tent sites and 29 RV sites. ADA restrooms and
showers.

Olympic National Forest campgrounds are mostly vehicle-accessible; no reservations: **Campbell Tree Grove,** 21 sites and 10 walk-in sites, no water; **Coho,** 46
sites and 10 walk-in sites; **Falls Creek,** 21 sites and 10 walk-in sites; **Gatton
Creek,** 15 tent-only sites, no water; **Klahanie,** 20 sites, no water; **Klahowya,** 55
sites; **Willaby,** 31 sites, no water.

Pacific Beach State Park (reservations 888-226-7688), off WA 109, 15 miles north of Ocean Shores. Open year-round. Twenty-two standard sites and 42 RV sites (electricity only).

Schafer State Park (360-482-3852), 12 miles north of US 12 at Elma on East Satsop Road. Campground closed Oct.–Apr. Forty-one regular tent sites, two primitive tent sites, six RV sites, and one ADA site. Restrooms and shower; no reservations.

CANOEING AND KAYAKING Rainforest Paddlers (866-457-8398), 4883 Upper Hoh Road, Forks. They offer trips and rentals along the rain-forest rivers and estuaries, as well as kayak trips down the Quillayute River to the Pacific.

HIKING Big Tree Grove, 0.5–4 miles; from ranger station or Willaby Campground just off South Shore Road. A system of easy loop trails range through old-growth forest along the south shore of Lake Quinault.

Olympic National Forest. Some hiking trails, mostly rugged, run through the three national forest units adjoining the national park on the west side. The southernmost unit runs from the Quinault Reservation east to Lake Cushman; the middle unit is between the Quinault and Queets rivers; and the northernmost unit runs north from the Calawah River past US 101. Contact **Pacific (South) Ranger District** (360-374-6522), 437 Tillicum Lane, Forks 98331; or **Pacific (North) Ranger District** (360-288-2525), Box 9, Quinault 98575. See also *Wilder Places— Wilderness Areas.*

Pioneer's Path Nature Trail, 0.6 mile, wheelchair-accessible, at Klahowya Campground, on US 101, 9 miles west of Lake Crescent. Signs describe pioneer life along the Sol Duc River.

✳ Wilder Places

PARKS Bogachiel State Park (360-374-6356), on US 101, 6 miles south of Forks. Open year-round. On the edge of the Hoh Rain Forest, this state park's 123 acres along the Bogachiel River are heavily wooded. If you can't go to the Amazon, come here; it's closer and cooler.

Griffiths-Priday State Park (360-289-3553), off WA 109, 21 miles north of Hoquiam. Day use only; open year-round. Between the Copalis River and the ocean, this lonely stretch of dunes and beach includes Copalis Spit, a wildlife refuge.

Lake Sylvia State Park (888-226-7688), off US 12 east of Grays Harbor and 1 mile north of Montesano. Open year-round. Nearly 3 miles of lakeshore.

Ocean City State Park, on WA 115, 1 mile north of Ocean Shores. Open year-round. This rather exposed 170-acre beach park gets a lot of wind and rain, not to mention riptides and currents. However, it's a good spot to see migratory birds and wildflowers in season.

Pacific Beach State Park (360-276-4297), off WA 109, 15 miles north of Ocean Shores. Open year-round. This small park has half a mile of windy shoreline and heavy surf. Otters are sometimes visible.

Schafer State Park (360-482-3852), off US 12 at Elma and 12 miles north on East Satsop Road. Day use only; open year-round. Deep in the forest between Puget Sound and the Pacific, Schafer sits on the Satsop River, where fishermen come to seek steelhead and salmon. Fishing and camping are the primary activities (see *To Do—Camping*).

WILDERNESS AREAS Colonel Bob Wilderness, 11,961 acres; 68 miles southeast of Forks, reached via South Shore Quinault Lake Road. Steep and rugged, like all the terrain in the Olympics, Colonel Bob Wilderness lies on the southwestern slopes of the range and gets 150 inches of rainfall a year. Forests and undergrowth are lush, though there are no lakes or major watercourses here, strangely. There are 12 miles of rugged trails. If you venture in, be aware of the probability of rain and consequent hypothermia.

WILDLIFE REFUGES Grays Harbor National Wildlife Refuge (360-753-9467), western edge of Hoquiam, next to Bowerman Field Airport. Open dawn to dusk daily. Designated in 1990, this refuge with acres of mudflats is a haven for hundreds of thousands of shorebirds flying north in spring; smaller numbers stop in fall. A 1-mile path leads to the tip of Bowerman Spit for viewing.

Olympic Coast National Marine Sanctuary, including Flattery Rocks National Wildlife Refuge, Quillayute Needles National Wildlife Refuge, and Copalis National Wildlife Refuge (360-457-6622; www.olympiccoast.noaa.gov), 115 Railroad Avenue, Suite 301, Port Angeles 98362. From the middle of the Strait of Juan de Fuca down to the Quinault Reservation, this huge marine sanctuary protects 135 miles of coast below the low-tide line and 20–40 miles out to sea. These cold Pacific waters are some of the most prolific anywhere, harboring deep-sea corals; shoals of herring, salmon, and halibut; the rare but recovering sea otter; whales; and vast numbers of seabirds. With the underwater zone protected by the sanctuary and the exposed islands and rocks by the three national wildlife refuges (which are off-limits), 3,310 square miles of marine habitat are managed for conservation. Visitors generally experience the sanctuary from the beach; educational programs are available through Olympic National Park and the Olympic Institute (see the Olympic National Park chapter) and the **Makah Cultural and Research Center** (360-645-2711), Box 160, Neah Bay 98357.

✳ Lodging

BED & BREAKFASTS

Forks

🐾 **Miller Tree Inn Bed and Breakfast** (360-374-6806 or 800-943-6563; www.millertreeinn.com), Box 1565, Forks 98331. This big old farmhouse just outside Forks has the feeling of an old shoe, from the comfy sofa and easy chairs in the living room to the books and board games for a rainy day—and the boot dryers are a nice touch. Seven guest rooms range from cozy queen-bedded rooms to suites sleeping three or four. Sit out on the porch or under the huge trees after exploring the rain forest—or, hey, just sit on the porch anytime. Children over seven welcome; children seven and under may stay with parents in the Orchard Suite, a one-bedroom apartment, where pets are also welcome. $115–205.

River Inn (360-374-6526), 2596 Bogachiel Way. Two and a half miles west of Forks, the River Inn sits in a bucolic setting under tall Sitka spruces on the banks of the Bogachiel River. You might see elk in the evening. The inn caters mostly to fishermen, with winter packages that include fishing guides and accommodations. Open Oct.–Apr. Children over 14 only. $200.

Hoquiam

Hoquiam Castle (360-533-2005; www.hoquiamcastle.com), 515 Chenault Avenue. In 1999 this opulent house opened as a bed & breakfast, and since 2004, owner Donna Grow has operated it with her daughters Kathy and Pat. Four guest rooms, all with private bath and two with four-poster beds, pamper with every conceivable turn-of-the-20th-century luxury, with remarkable antiques throughout. Among other events, the castle specializes in murder mysteries, for which it is the perfect setting. Children over 12 are welcome; pets are not. $145–195; $125–175 off-season.

COTTAGES AND CABINS

Clallam Bay

Chito Beach Resort (360-963-2581; www.chitobeach.com), 7639 WA 112. This is where you want to go when you die—except you don't have to wait until then for a visit. Far out on the northern reaches of the peninsula, halfway between Clallam Bay and Neah Bay, right on the rocky shoreline, you can sit and watch the whales, otters, or seals go by. Ecotourists, say the owners, are their biggest customer base. That said, it's a pretty romantic spot as well—you can walk for miles on the beach or hole up in your tile-floored, artfully decorated cabin. Three cabins have full kitchens, private entrances and decks, and views, while the big house has two bedrooms and a woodstove. Families are welcome in the house, children over six in the cab-

ins. Cabins $$120–150; house $160–215.

The Lost Resort (360-963-2899; www.lostresort.net), 20860 Hoko-Ozette Road. Three one-room log cabins are on remote Lake Ozette; also 30 primitive campsites with showers and bathrooms nearby, plus a general store and deli. Campsites $15 (no reservations); cabins $65 with electricity and linens provided.

HOSTELS

Forks

Rain Forest Hostel (360-374-2270), on US 101 between mileposts 169 and 170 (between Forks and Ruby Beach), 169312 US 101. Accessible by bus, with some changes, from Seattle or Tacoma, this is a budget spot for backpackers, families, or backpacking families exploring the Western Olympic Peninsula. Shuttle service is available to Olympic trailheads. There are 26 beds Mar.–Oct. and 14 beds Nov.–Feb. Dorm bed $10 adults, $5 children; private room $18 per couple; family rooms charged per person.

MOTELS

Beaver

☗ **Hungry Bear Café, Motel and RV Park** (360-327-3225; www.hungrybearcafemotel.com), on US 101 at milepost 206. They say it's centrally located—well, it *is* roughly halfway between Lake Crescent and Forks, in the middle of a working forest. The motel has 10 rustic, wood-paneled rooms (one with kitchenette). Pets subject to approval. The camping area (open year-round) has 12 sites with full hook-ups and room for tents; on-site bathrooms. Good thing the café is on the premises, with all-day breakfast, sandwiches, burgers, steaks, and seafood. Rooms $55–95.

✴ Where to Eat

EATING OUT

Forks

Hard Rain Café and Mercantile (360-374-9288; www.hardraincafe .com), 5763 Upper Hoh Road. Open 97. Near the Hoh Rain Forest, this café offers hearty breakfasts before your active day and Oly Burgers (and more) afterward. There is also a campground for tents or RVs and a simple cabin; inquire for rates.

Pacific Pizza (360-374-2626), 870 South Forks Avenue. Open for lunch and dinner daily. Hungry hikers find hearty pizzas, pasta dishes, and panini in central Forks.

Taquería Santa Ana (360-374-3339), 80 Calawah Way. Open 11–9 daily. This hole-in-the-wall is possibly your best deal in Forks—cheap, hearty, homestyle Mexican food. Cash only.

Neah Bay

The Warmhouse Restaurant (360-645-2077), 1471 Bayview Avenue. Open for breakfast, lunch, and dinner Mon.–Sat. Whether you've come to watch birds, see the Makah museum, or buy some smoked salmon, don't miss this spot overlooking the Makah Marina for fresh seafood, burgers, pasta, or steaks. The decor is spare natural wood with Native decorative touches, such as the mat-patterned ceiling.

Ocean Shores

Mike's Seafood Restaurant and Fish Market (360-289-0532; www .oceanshoresseafood.com), 830 Point Brown Avenue NE. Open 11–10 Mon.–Sat., 12–8 Sun. Completely without pretension, Mike's is the place either to buy seafood as fresh as you can get it or simply to eat it. Grab a table (it can get crowded), then check the menu for specialties such as the smoked salmon sampler or old reliables such as halibut or oysters.

Quinault

🍴 **Salmon House Restaurant** (360-288-2535; www.rainforestresort.com), on US 101 at Rainforest Resort Village, 1 mile east of Lake Quinault Lodge. Open 4–9 daily year-round, plus 8–noon daily in summer. Here you'll find a variety of salmon dishes made with salmon supplied by the nearby Quinault tribe, as well as other seafood and steaks. A children's menu is available.

✴ Special Events

April: **Grays Harbor Shorebird Festival** (800-303-8498), Hoquiam. Also takes place in Grays Harbor National Wildlife Refuge.

August: **Makah Days** (800-443-6757), Makah Reservation. Three days of festivities include canoe races, traditional games, singing and dancing, a salmon bake, and fireworks.

EASTERN OLYMPIC PENINSULA

The eastern Olympic Peninsula runs from Shelton, at the southwestern end of the Kitsap Peninsula, along the western shore of Hood Canal through the small towns of Hoodsport, Brinnon, and Quilcene; up to Port Townsend on the Quimper Peninsula at the mouth of Puget Sound; and west to Port Angeles on the Strait of Juan de Fuca and WA 112 as far as Joyce. Visitors tend to focus on historic Port Townsend, with its grand Victorian homes and even grander city hall (the city's movers and shakers once thought it would be the terminus for a continental railroad—a wild improbability if you look at a map). The only Victorian seaport still registered on the West Coast and very proud of its maritime heritage, the place was a busy marine hub as early as the 1860s. Today the town's lively arts community supports independent bookstores, galleries, and cultural events.

A more recent tourist discovery is Sequim (pronounced "skwim"), a 35-mile drive west of Port Townsend. Sequim sits in an odd rain shadow north and east of the Olympic Mountains that shelters lavender farms and even wineries. Port Angeles, with fantastic shoreline views, is the gateway to Olympic National Park and also to Victoria, British Columbia, with ferry service to Vancouver Island across the Strait of Juan de Fuca.

In addition to these towns, this chapter covers the eastern peninsular lowlands from the shoreline back into the Olympic Mountain foothills, including the eastern units of Olympic National Forest and their wilderness areas surrounding the park. Like the park itself, the confluence of Puget Sound and the Strait of Juan de Fuca is a crossroads for spectacular wildlife—in this case orcas, seals, eagles, and many seabirds.

GUIDANCE North Olympic Peninsula Visitor and Convention Bureau (800-942-4042; www.olympicpeninsula.org), 338 West First Street, Suite 104, Port Angeles 98362.

Olympic National Forest Headquarters (360-956-2402), 1835 Black Lake Boulevard SW, Olympia 98512.

Port Angeles Chamber of Commerce and Visitors' Center (360-452-2363; www.portangeles.org), 121 East Railroad Avenue, Port Angeles 98362.

Port Townsend Visitor Information Center (888-ENJOYPT; www.ptguide .com), 440 12th Street, Port Townsend 98368.

GETTING THERE From I-5 in Olympia, take **US 101** north through Shelton, Quilcene, Sequim, and Port Angeles and beyond to Lake Crescent. From Port Angeles, **WA 112** heads west through Joyce toward Clallam Bay.

Or, from Seattle, take the ferry to Bainbridge Island and follow **WA 305 and 3** north to the Hood Canal Bridge, which takes you to the peninsula via **WA 104** to US 101 just north of Quilcene.

From Discovery Bay, **WA 20** heads north to Port Townsend; other highways on the Quimper Peninsula visit Port Ludlow, Chimacum, Port Hadlock, and Indian and Marrowstone islands.

Ferries also dock directly at Port Townsend, from Whidbey Island (see part 4, Northern Puget Sound), and at Port Angeles, from Victoria, British Columbia.

From Seattle-Tacoma International Airport, **Olympic Bus Lines** (800-457-4492) runs to Port Angeles and Sequim.

GETTING AROUND Clallam County Transit (360-452-4511 or 800-858-3747; www.clallamtransit.com) and **Jefferson Transit** (360-385-4777 or 800-371-0497; www.jeffersontransit.com) provide bus service around the northern rim of the peninsula, from Puget Sound to La Push.

MEDICAL EMERGENCY Jefferson Healthcare (360-385-2200), 834 Sheridan Avenue, Port Townsend.

Olympic Medical Center (360-417-7000), 939 Caroline Street, Port Angeles.

✳ To See

FARMERS' MARKETS Nash's Organic Produce (360-683-4642; www.nashs produce.com), 1865 East Anderson Road, Sequim. Open 9–5 Tues.–Sun. Nash Huber grows a wide variety of organic produce on his Dungeness Valley farm and sells it in the farm store.

Port Angeles Farmers Market (360-460-0361; portangelesfarmersmarket.com), 125 East Front Street, Port Angeles. Open 10–2 Wed. and Sat. year-round.

Port Townsend Farmers Market (360-379-9098; ptfarmersmarket.org), 620 Tyler Street, Port Townsend. Open 3–6 Wed. June–Sept.

Sequim Open Aire Market (360-460-2668; sequimmarket.com), Sequim. Two locations: corner of Sequim and Washington streets, open 3–6 Wed. June–Jan.; Cedar Street, open 9–3 Sat. June–Jan.

✿ **Sunny Farms Country Store** (360-683-8003), 261461 US 101 West, Sequim. Open 8–8 daily. A comprehensive farm and produce store under one roof, this is your place to find local fruits and vegetables, and lots of them, plus a butcher shop, feeds, gardening supplies, and a café—in short, a proper country store.

FARMS AND GARDENS Since the decline of dairy farming in the Dungeness Valley, this dry, warm area around Sequim has turned to **lavender farming.** Most of the farms participate in the annual Lavender Festival in July (see *Special Events*). Some farms that allow visitors to wander the fragrant fields, learn about the varieties of lavender, and purchase some of their products include the following:

Cedarbrook Lavender and Herb Farm (800-470-8423; www.cedarbrook lavender.com), 1345 South Sequim Avenue, Sequim. Open 10–5 Mon.–Sat.

The Cutting Garden (360-670-8671; www.cuttinggarden.com), 303 Dahlia Llama Lane, Sequim. Open 10–6 daily, including weekends if no events are scheduled (check website). Admire the spacious gardens with a great variety of flowers and/or buy plants.

Lost Mountain Lavender (360-681-2782 or 888-507-7481; www.lostmountain lavender.com), 1541 Taylor Cutoff Road, Sequim. Open by appointment. With 120 varieties on just 3 acres, this farm lets you pick a bundle or just have a picnic.

Olympic Lavender Farm (360-683-4475; www.olympiclavender.com), 1432 Marine Drive, Sequim. Open during harvest season; call for hours. Here you can pick your own, see the lavender still where essential oils are extracted, and buy plants and products.

HISTORIC HOMES Port Townsend, founded in 1851, is replete with the homes of successful merchants, sea captains, and other Victorian worthies. **Tours of Port Townsend homes** occur in March and September; 90-minute guided tours of the **historic "uptown" and "downtown"** are offered summer weekends by the **Jefferson County Historical Society** (360-385-1003; $10). Some highlights include the following:

John Quincy Adams House, corner of F and Tyler streets, Port Townsend. This turreted Victorian was built in 1887 by Albert C. Adams, a descendant of the Massachusetts Adamses (the ancestors were revolutionaries; the descendant was a real estate speculator). It's now privately owned, so unless it's included in a tour, only the exterior can be admired.

Lucinda Hastings Spec House, 505 Cass Street, Port Townsend. Lucinda is supposed to have been the first white woman to come to Port Townsend, in 1852. She had this house built in 1890, in the last hurrah before the bust of 1892. Six other identical houses in town are still standing, also built by the Hastings family as investments. This one has been extensively remodeled but has some original fir flooring. It's privately owned, so unless it's included in a tour, only the exterior can be viewed.

Rothschild House, corner of Taylor and Franklin streets, Port Townsend. Open 11–4 daily May–Sept. $4 adults, $1 children under 12. D. C. H. Rothschild was a far-flung member of the Rothschild family who apparently came west to seek his fortune. This implies that he didn't start out with one. He did have stores, though, in Bellingham and California, and established one in busy Port Townsend in 1858. Ten years later, he had done well enough to build this house, where he and his wife raised five children. Much more sober than many of the Victorian homes gracing Port Townsend, it could be almost any modest American farmhouse. Its sobriety concealed a comfortable four-bedroom home with a parlor, dining room, kitchen, and bath. Quite well preserved, it still has wallpaper dating from 1885 and many original furnishings, including a mahogany piano. Now a state park, the house is open for visits. The gardens have been restored with heirloom peonies and lilacs.

HISTORIC SITES Bell Tower, Jefferson Street, Port Townsend. This tower was put up in 1890, and for more than 50 years it was the city's fire alarm. It's quiet now, but the little 0.1-acre park site has fine views of downtown Port Townsend and the bay.

Fort Flagler State Park (360-385-3701), on the northern tip of Marrowstone Island. Fort Flagler and Fort Worden (see below) are two of a battery of forts that were placed around Puget Sound in the late 19th century; most are now state parks. At Fort Flagler, a **military museum** occupies one of the former barracks; open 11–4 daily June–Sept., 11–4 Fri.–Sun. May, 11–4 Sat.–Sun. Oct.–Apr. Guided tours of the other buildings are available by arrangement. The park, which lies opposite Fort Worden and Fort Casey on Whidbey Island (forming a defensive triangle at the mouth of Puget Sound), has almost 4 miles of shoreline, the Marrowstone Lighthouse, and a campground. To get there, see *Scenic Drives.*

Fort Worden State Park (360-344-4400), 200 Battery Way, Port Townsend. This military base operated from 1897 to 1953. You may have seen it in the movie *An Officer and a Gentleman,* much of which was filmed here. Its many historic buildings include the **Commanding Officer's House,** restored and furnished in late Victorian style; a former barracks that is now a youth hostel; **Point Wilson Lighthouse;** and the curious **Alexander's Castle** overlooking the sound, built by a Scottish immigrant for his wife. Also in the park is the **Coast Artillery Museum;** open 11–4 daily Memorial Day weekend–Labor Day. The **Port Townsend Marine Science Center and Natural History Museum** (see *Museums*) and **Centrum Performing Arts Center** (see *Entertainment*) are also located here. Miles of trails, boat moorage, and a campground provide recreation.

Jefferson County Courthouse (360-385-9100), 1820 Jefferson Street, Port Townsend. Open 8:30-4:30, Mon.-Fri. The huge brick edifice on the hill, with its numerous points and turrets and 124-foot-tall clock tower, seems out of proportion for a town of eight thousand people. Ah, but in those days—it was completed in 1892—Port Townsend still had ambitions of becoming the primary port on Puget Sound. This hope, based on the parallel expectation of a railroad terminus, had buoyed it through the 1880s, when many of the town's imposing homes were built (see *Historic Homes*). The railroad went elsewhere, and the financial collapse of 1892 all but quashed that idea. But the proud courthouse remains, governing the county with a dignity befitting its aspirations.

MUSEUMS ♂ **Arthur D. Feiro Marine Life Center** (360-417-6254; feiro marinelifecenter.org), Port Angeles City Pier, Railroad and Lincoln streets, Port Angeles. Open 10–5 Tues.–Sun. Memorial Day weekend–Labor Day, 12–4 Sat.–Sun. the rest of the year. $4 adults, $3 children 4–17. Here are "touch tanks" for hands-on creature contact, as well as hands-off displays of the strange and varied denizens of the Olympic deep: starfish, giant octopuses, sea anemones.

Jefferson County Historical Museum (360-385-1003; www.jchsmuseum.org), 540 Water Street, Port Townsend. Open 11–4 daily. $4 adults, $1 children 3–12. This museum offers an overview of the county's story, from the original inhabitants through Captain George Vancouver's explorations to maritime history and Chinese immigration.

♂ **Port Townsend Marine Science Center and Natural History Museum** (360-385-5582; www.ptmsc.org), in Fort Worden State Park, 532 Battery Way, Port Townsend. Open 11–5 Wed.–Mon. mid-June–Labor Day; 12–4 Fri.–Sun. the rest of the year. $5 adults, $3 children. Standing on pilings, appropriately, this center offers an introduction to Puget Sound's natural history, showing off native marine plants and animals through various replicated habitats. On land, exhibits include marine geology, fossils, interpretive programs, and field trips to Protection Island.

Squaxin Island Tribe Museum and Research Center (360-432-3851 or 360-432-3839; www.squaxinislandmuseum.org), 3851 Old Olympic Highway, Shelton. Open 9–5 Wed.–Sat., 1–5 Sun. $5 adults, $4 seniors, $2 children 5–12. The Squaxin tribe calls itself the People of the Water, and the exhibits in this large, modern facility draw out the relationship between nature and culture as applied to the tribe's traditional and modern life. Of particular interest are unique five-hundred-year-old artifacts from a village unearthed nearby.

NATURAL WONDERS Dungeness Spit, 3 miles north of US 101 on Kitchen-Dick Road, midway between Port Angeles and Sequim. Seen from the bluffs above, the yellow sickle of this spit seems thrown onto the blue seascape to reap—what? Jutting 5.5 miles into the Strait of Juan de Fuca, it is said to be the longest natural sand spit in the world. The entire spit is part of the 631-acre **Dungeness National Wildlife Refuge** (360-457-8451), administered by the U.S. Fish and Wildlife Service. Its leeward (east) side is a haven to many migratory birds and home to an isolated population of tufted puffins as well as young salmon and steelhead; to the windward side you may see whales, seals, or sea lions. The leeward side is closed to protect breeding birds, but a trail leads along the western, windward side all the way to the **Dungeness Lighthouse;** tours of the lighthouse are offered daily. Check tide tables before walking on the spit: It is low and narrow. There is a $3 parking fee.

SCENIC DRIVES Pacific Coast Scenic Byway, about 280 paved miles from Olympia north to Port Townsend, east to Port Angeles, and south to Aberdeen. US 101 follows a neat arc around the peninsula, skirting first the placid inlets of Puget Sound to Shelton and the shore of Hood Canal, then turning east past Discovery Bay and Sequim across the sunny plains to Port Angeles, where it makes a slight course correction to pass lovely Lake Crescent within the northern edge of Olympic National Park.

Quimper Peninsula back roads, about 23 paved miles from Discovery Bay to Fort Flagler State Park. This peaceful meander leaves US 101 at Discovery Bay and follows WA 20 north along blue water and across the Quimper Peninsula, which juts off its mother peninsula like a fractal to delimit Puget Sound from the Strait of Juan de Fuca. After 8 miles, take WA 19 southeast 3 miles to WA 116 east through Port Hadlock and across a small bridge to Marrowstone Island. WA 116 continues north the length of the island along postcard-perfect inlets to arrive at Fort Flagler State Park (see *Historic Sites*), about 10 miles from WA 119.

✳ To Do

BICYCLING Back roads around Sequim and Port Angeles are amenable to leisurely cycling, being gently rolling with views of lavender farms, pastures, and the Strait of Juan de Fuca.

Fort Worden State Park (see *Historic Sites*) rents bikes: $15 for the first hour, $10 for each subsequent hour.

Olympic Discovery Trail, 40 paved miles from Blyn to Port Angeles. This hiking trail is open to cyclists as well and will eventually stretch 120 miles from Port Townsend to La Push on the Pacific.

Olympic National Forest trails. Some are open to mountain bikes; check with the **Hood Canal Ranger District** (360-765-2200), Box 280, Quilcene 98376.

PT Cyclery (360-385-6470), 252 Tyler Street, Port Townsend. This shop has bike rentals, sales, and maps.

BIRDING **Port Townsend Marine Science Center cruises** (360-385-5582), from Point Hudson Marina (see *Boating*), Port Townsend, to Protection Island. Visit the nesting site of 70 percent of the seabirds in Puget Sound.

BOATING **City Pier** (Port of Port Angeles, 360-417-4550), 338 West First Street, Port Angeles. This marina offers transient moorage in summer.

John Wayne Marina (360-417-3440), Sequim Bay, Sequim. This is a full-service marina on nearby Sequim Bay. John Wayne used to bring his yacht here before it was a marina, hence the name.

Point Hudson Marina (800-228-2803), 320 Jefferson Street, Port Townsend. In the historic district at the site of a former Coast Guard station, this marina is here to welcome your boat.

Port Angeles Boat Haven (360-457-4505 or 800-228-2803), Ediz Hook, Port Angeles. This marina operates year-round.

Port Townsend Boat Haven (800-228-2803), 1 mile west of Hudson Marina, Port Townsend. Larger than its sister marina, this is also open year-round.

Sound Experience (360-379-0438), 2900 Washington Street, Port Townsend. Daysails or multiday sails and educational programs are offered on the schooner *Adventuress.*

Wooden Boat Foundation (360-385-3628; www.woodenboat.org), at Point Hudson Marina, 320 Jefferson Street, Port Townsend. Open 9–5 Mon.–Fri., 10–4 Sat. Free. There's nothing as splendid as messing around in a boat—especially a wooden boat. It's only natural that one of the nation's three remaining Victorian seaports should have an organization entirely devoted to spreading enthusiasm for boats, both as part of its cultural heritage and just because, well, it's fun. The foundation down on the harbor offers classes for children and adults in sailing, boatbuilding, racing, and just about everything maritime. If you didn't bring your own boat, you can rent a wherry here or borrow a longboat 5–6:30 PM Fri. The foundation also sponsors the annual Wooden Boat Festival (see *Special Events*). The **Chandlery** offers boat-related items and gifts, from books to bells.

CAMPING **Lake Cushman Resort** (360-877-9630; lakecushman.com), 7211 North Lake Cushman Road, Hoodsport. Open Apr.–Oct. Fifty-two standard sites ($15–60), 20 sites with hook-ups ($20–32), and 11 cabins ($65–135).

Chimacum County Park (360-385-9160), Rhody Drive, Chimacum; on WA 19, 10 miles south of Port Townsend. Eight campsites. Restrooms.

Dosewallips State Park (888-226-7688), on US 101 at Brinnon. Seventy tent sites, 55 utility sites, 3 platform tents, and 3 cabins. ADA restrooms and showers.

THE PORT TOWNSEND WATERFRONT

Dungeness Recreation Area (360-683-5847), a county park at the entrance to Dungeness National Wildlife Refuge. Open Feb.–Sept. Sixty-four sites with no electricity or water to individual sites. Half the sites are reservable.

Fort Flagler State Park (888-226-7688), on WA 116, 8 miles northeast of Port Hadlock (see *To See—Scenic Drives*). Fifty-nine tent sites, 58 utility sites, 2 primitive sites, and 1 Cascadia Marine Trail site. ADA restrooms.

Fort Worden State Park (360-344-4400), 200 Battery Way, Port Townsend. Eighty sites in a historic fort with beaches, views, a marine science center, and the Centrum Performing Arts Center (see *To See—Historic Sites*).

Lake Leland County Park (360-385-9129), off US 101, 7 miles north of Quilcene. Twenty-two primitive sites with outhouses and a boat launch. No water or garbage collection.

Old Fort Townsend State Park (360-385-3595), 0.5 mile off WA 20, 2 miles south of Port Townsend. Campground closed late Oct.–early Apr. No reservations. Forty standard sites and three primitive sites.

Olympic National Forest campgrounds are mostly vehicle-accessible; no reservations: **Big Creek,** 23 units (tent or small trailer sites), water and toilets; **Brown Creek,** 20 units; **Collins,** 16 units, no water; **Dungeness Forks,** 10 tent sites and drinking water; **Falls View,** 30 units, no water; **Hamma Hamma,** 15 units, no water; **Lena Creek,** 13 units, water and toilet; **Seal Rock,** 41 tent sites.

Pleasant Harbor State Park (360-753-5771), on US 101, 2 miles south of Brinnon. This satellite park of Dosewallips State Park has marine moorage only.

Potlatch State Park (888-226-7688), on US 101, 3 miles south of Hoodsport. Open year-round. Thirty-six standard tent sites, 35 utility sites, and 2 primitive sites.

Salt Creek Recreation Area (360-928-3441), off WA 112, 12 miles west of Port Angeles, on Camp Hayden Road. No reservations. This county park is also a marine sanctuary with 92 campsites, 3 ADA restrooms, trails, and beach access.

Sequim Bay State Park (888-226-7688), on US 101, 3 miles southeast of Sequim. Forty-nine standard tent sites, 15 RV sites, and 3 primitive sites. Restrooms and showers (some ADA), water, beach access, and clamming.

See also *Wilder Places—Parks.*

CANOEING AND KAYAKING **Dungeness Spit,** north of Sequim. To the east of Port Angeles, the lee side of the spit is quieter than Ediz Hook.

Ediz Hook and the Port Angeles waterfront. Kayakers plying the waters between the hook and the harbor get an up-close look at the huge Rayonier plant and the cargo ships loading and unloading.

Olympic Raft and Kayak (888-452-1443; www.raftandkayak.com), 123 Lake Aldwell Road, Port Angeles. They will rent you kayaks or canoes for flatwater paddling or take you out sea kayaking along Dungeness Spit.

Point Hudson Marina, Port Townsend (see *Boating*). Sea kayaking is big in the coastal communities. If you have your own sea kayak, you can launch from the beach or dock at Port Townsend's marina.

PT Outdoors (360-379-3608; www.ptoutdoors.com), 1017-B Water Street, Port Townsend. They offer sea kayaking instruction, tours, and rentals.

GOLF **Discovery Bay Golf Club** (360-385-0704; www.discoverybaygolfclub.com), 7401 Cape George Road, Port Townsend. Eighteen holes.

Dungeness Golf Course (360-683-6344; www.dungenessgolf.com), 1965 Woodcock Road, Sequim. Eighteen holes.

Port Ludlow Golf Course (888-793-1195), 751 Highland Drive, Port Ludlow. Twenty-seven holes.

Port Townsend Golf Course (360-385-4547; www.porttownsendgolf.com), 1948 Blaine Street, Port Townsend. Nine holes.

HIKING Port Townsend has a network of **city walking and biking paths;** ask for a map of the trails at **City Hall** (360-379-5047), 250 Manson Street, Port Townsend.

Dungeness Forks Forest Service campground, off US 101, 4.5 miles south of Sequim, on Palo Alto Road. There are trails, camping, and drinking water.

Fort Worden State Park (360-344-4400), 200 Battery Way, Port Townsend. You may like to stroll the beach at this fort that marks the entrance to Puget Sound (see *To See—Historic Sites*). You may see whales, eagles, shipping, Coast Guard patrols, or the occasional Trident submarine surfacing on its way to or from the submarine base at Bangor, across the sound.

Lena Lake Trail, 3 miles from the end of FR 25 to the Lena Lake Campground; trailhead 8 miles from US 101. This trail makes a gentle ascent to the lake and 29 primitive campsites.

Native American Nature Trail, at Seal Rock Forest Service campground, on US 101, 10 miles south of Quilcene. The trail is paved and wheelchair-accessible.

Olympic Discovery Trail (www.olympicdiscoverytrail.com), 40 miles from Bryn to downtown Port Angeles (see *Bicycling*). This path winds past meadows, woods, and people's backyards till it comes to the Port Angeles waterfront, then takes a 4-mile spur out Ediz Hook. Several access points allow for shorter trips.

See also *Wilder Places*.

WHALE-WATCHING **Puget Sound Express** (360-385-5288), 431 Water Street, Port Townsend. Whale-watching cruises are offered in season, $64–94.

✴ Wilder Places

PARKS **Chetzemoka Park,** Jackson and Blaine streets, Port Townsend. More than 5 acres on a slope overlooking Admiralty Inlet, Chetzemoka is a jewel of a city park dating from 1904, with flower and water gardens, a playground, a bandstand, and access to the beach below. The name honors a prominent local Indian who was friendly with early settlers.

Dosewallips State Park (360-796-4415), on US 101 at Brinnon. Open year-round. With a mile of shoreline along Hood Canal and another mile along the Dosewallips River, this park provides both fresh- and saltwater recreation—boating, diving, shellfish harvesting, even swimming—and plentiful wildlife.

Fort Flagler State Park (360-385-1259), on WA 116, 8 miles northeast of Port Hadlock (see *To See—Scenic Drives*). Camping, crabbing, trails, and a historic area are located on beautiful Marrowstone Island.

Fort Worden State Park (360-344-4400), 200 Battery Way, Port Townsend. The historic fort has beaches, views, a marine science center, and the Centrum Performing Arts Center (see *To See—Historic Sites*).

Old Fort Townsend State Park (360-344-4400), 0.5 mile off WA 20, 2 miles south of Port Townsend. Open year-round. Tall firs part to reveal the Cascades across Admiralty Inlet. "Old Fort Townsend" was developed as a fort in 1856 to protect settlers and had a turbulent life—shut down for being unfit in 1859, rebuilt in 1874, burned down in 1895. Given this record, the U.S. Army used the place for defusing enemy munitions during World War II. Its military history at an end, it now offers rest and recreation among the firs, with camping, interpretive trails, boating, and diving.

Potlatch State Park (360-877-5361), on US 101, 3 miles south of Hoodsport. Open year-round. This 57-acre park on Hood Canal is popular for shellfish harvesting, boating, and camping.

Seal Rock Forest Service campground, on US 101, 2 miles north of Brinnon. With beach access, it's popular for clamming and oystering; there's an ADA beach-viewing area, too.

Sequim Bay State Park (360-683-4235), on US 101, 3 miles southeast of Sequim. Open year-round. The calm waters of Sequim Bay, being protected by long sandbars, were missed by the first three expeditions to come by. Like Sequim itself, the park is in a deep rain shadow and receives only 17 inches of rain a year—this only 40 air miles from the Hoh Rain Forest. Nonetheless, it's sometimes possible to snowshoe here in winter. The nearly 1 mile of shoreline offers camping, shellfish gathering, boating (with 424 feet of summer moorage), wildlife watching, and swimming—for the hardy.

Olympic National Park is nearly surrounded by Olympic National Forest, which contains four large wilderness areas on the east side of the peninsula:

The Brothers Wilderness, 16,682 acres; reached via Hamma Hamma Road or Duckabush Road, about 10 miles west of Brinnon. This wilderness is thickly forested but also very steep, hot in summer, and wet otherwise. The Brothers, a 6,866-foot peak, is a climber's goal; four hiking trails of various degrees of difficulty penetrate the interior.

Buckhorn Wilderness, 44,258 acres; via FR 2750, about 12 miles south of Sequim. Very steep slopes keep this wilderness wild (except for a 216-acre mining claim). Several rugged to moderate trails lead to mountain tarns and meadows. Most trails are open to pack animals.

Mount Skokomish Wilderness, 10,815 acres; via WA 119, about 11 miles west of Hoodsport. This wilderness area has four rocky peaks over 6,000 feet, including 6,404-foot Mount Skokomish, with old-growth Douglas fir on the lower slopes. Some 10 miles of very steep trails lead to Mildred Lakes and Mount Rose.

Wonder Mountain Wilderness, 2,049 acres; via FR 2055, about 20 miles north-west of US 101 between Potlatch and Shelton. Closed Oct.–May. This small wilderness has no trails, so you have to travel cross-country through deep forest and high pinnacles. You won't find many people here. Map and compass skills are essential.

WILDLIFE REFUGES **Dungeness National Wildlife Refuge** (360-457-8451), 3 miles north of US 101 on Kitchen-Dick Road, midway between Port Angeles and Sequim. Open dawn to dusk daily. $3 per family. Five-and-a-half-mile-long Dungeness Spit sticks out into the Strait of Juan de Fuca like a fishhook. Two smaller spits on the leeward side nearly enclose Dungeness Harbor, whose tidal ponds and flats house many birds in late summer and fall, especially brants; you can also see puffins, harlequin ducks, and peregrine falcons. You can walk out to the **lighthouse** at the end of the spit, although certain areas are closed to protect wildlife.

Dungeness River Audubon Center (360-681-4076; www.dungenessrivercenter .org), 2151 West Hendrickson Road, Sequim. Open 10–4 Tues.–Sat., 12–4 Sun. Located in **Railroad Bridge Park** on the tumbling Dungeness River, this educational center is a joint venture of the local Audubon Society and the Jamestown S'Klallam tribe, whose ancestral lands these are. The center offers exhibits on the watershed and its flora and fauna, plus trails and bird walks.

Olympic Coast National Marine Sanctuary (360-457-6622; www.olympic coast.noaa.gov), 115 Railroad Avenue, Suite 301, Port Angeles. From the middle of the Strait of Juan de Fuca down to the Quinault Reservation, the marine sanctuary protects 135 miles of coast below the low-tide line and 20–40 miles out to sea. These cold waters are some of the most prolific anywhere, harboring deep-sea corals; shoals of herring, salmon, and halibut; the rare but recovering sea otter; whales; and vast numbers of seabirds. Including the underwater zone protected by the sanctuary, 3,310 square miles of marine habitat are managed for conservation. Visitors generally experience the sanctuary from the beach; educational programs are available through Olympic National Park, the Olympic Institute, and the Makah tribe (see the Western Olympic Peninsula chapter).

Protection Island National Wildlife Refuge (360-457-8451), Discovery Bay, between Sequim and Port Townsend. This 364-acre island is closed to protect seals and nesting seabirds, but motorboat tours are available through **Puget Sound Express** (360-385-5288) and kayak tours through **PT Outdoors** (360-379-3608 or 888-754-8598). Vessels must stay 200 yards offshore. See also *To Do—Birding*.

✍ **Salt Creek Recreation Area** (360-928-3441), 3506 Camp Hayden Road, Port Angeles; off WA 112, 12 miles west of Port Angeles. This county park has 196 acres of bluffs, forests, tidal pools, and beach. Also on-site are playgrounds and the remains of Fort Hayden, a World War II military installation. The tidal pools are part of the Olympic Coast National Marine Sanctuary (see above), where you can investigate but not interfere with the peculiar life forms of the intertidal zone.

✳ Lodging

BED & BREAKFASTS

Chimacum

Solstice Farm (360-732-0174; www.solsticefarmstay.com), 6503 Beaver Valley Road. Linda Davis and Jeff Rueff started taking guests on their farm in 2010. Help with the chickens, garden, and sheep if you want, or just relax after a farm breakfast. Two rooms in the new farmhouse have private baths. Children under 13 free. No pets or credit cards. $105.

Port Angeles

Angeles Inn Bed and Breakfast (360-417-0260 or 888-552-4263; www.angelesinn.com), 1203 East Seventh Street. Situated on a quiet side street in town, this large contemporary house has four guest rooms (two with shared bath), a living room, and a reading room. Rates include full breakfast. Children over five welcome. No pets. $85–145.

Domaine Madeleine (888-811-8376; domainemadeleine.com), 146 Wildflower Lane. For an isolated romantic getaway, maybe even a honeymoon—definitely a special occasion—Domaine Madeleine is situated in splendid isolation on the shores of the Strait of Juan de Fuca, surrounded by 5 acres of gardens. Three rooms and two cottages are beautifully appointed. Rates do not include breakfast. Rooms $160–310; cottages $145–265.

✍ **Elwha Inn** (360-457-6540; www.elwharanch.com), 905 Herrick Road. Out of town on the way to Lake Crescent, this 95-acre horse ranch is in the beautiful Elwha River valley. Two suites (one with two bedrooms) and a cabin all have decks looking out on the national park and come with down comforters, living rooms (the cabin has a full kitchen), and VCRs. Breakfast is included but optional (reduced rates without). Children welcome. Rooms $120–165; cabins $140–160.

Five Sea Suns Bed and Breakfast (800-708-0777; www.seasuns.com), 1006 South Lincoln Street. Five guest rooms in this 1926 neoclassical home are themed to the seasons (including Indian summer); some have private balconies and nice Olympic views. Rates include breakfast. Children over 12 welcome. No pets. $115–175.

Inn at Rooster Hill (877-221-0837; www.innatroosterhill.com), 112 Reservoir Road. A house set on a hill with seven bedrooms welcomes couples, families, singles, and groups, with an optional murder mystery on the side. Children over 10 welcome. $99–189.

Port Townsend

Blue Gull Inn (888-700-0205; www.bluegullinn.com), 1310 Clay Street. Built in up-and-coming Port Townsend in 1868 as a family home, this house has six guest rooms with private baths and Wi-Fi. $105–140.

Commander's Beach House (360-385-1778 or 888-385-1778; www.commandersbeachhouse.com), 400 Hudson Street. Built for Coast Guard officers, this imposing Colonial-style house is right on the beach, with views of the sound and Mount Baker. Four tidy, cozy rooms are your haven here. $120–145.

Holly Hill House (360-385-5619 or 800-435-1454; www.hollyhillhouse.com), 611 Polk Street. This dignified 1872 house is surrounded with owner Nina Dortch's bright gardens, including dozens of rosebushes and an upside-down Camperdown elm (apparently, if you plant one upside down, its exposed roots will grow branches). The place has been lovingly maintained and lived in, so that its lovely design is both impressive and welcoming. Four snug guest rooms and a large suite come with full breakfast. Children over 12 welcome. No pets. $99–190.

Old Consulate Inn (360-385-6753 or 800-300-6753; www.oldconsulateinn.com), 313 Walker Street. This imposing mansion was in fact a German consulate from 1908 to 1911, when Port Townsend was still an important international port. With its tower, several gables, and curved, columned porch gazing over the city, the inn certainly screams importance. The inside matches, with a formal parlor, two fireplaces, a piano, a library, a billiard room, and appropriate antique furniture. Eight guest rooms include a honeymoon suite in the tower. Rates include full breakfast, afternoon tea, and evening drinks and dessert. Children over 12 only. No pets. $99–210.

Ravenscroft Inn (360-385-2784 or 800-782-2691; www.ravenscroftinn.com), 533 Quincy Street. Ravenscroft

offers eight quietly pampering guest rooms of varying sizes in a Nantucket-style house—two stories with balconies looking out to sea. Unlike many of Port Townsend's lodgings, its decor is comfortably modern, and it's billed as a romantic retreat with amenities such as fireplaces and verandas. Rates include full breakfast. No children or pets. $150–210.

Sequim

Dungeness Barn House (360-582-1663; www.dungenessbarnhouse.com), 42 Marine Drive. This house was originally a dairy barn when it was built in 1924. Gradually it was converted to a home and now offers guests two suites and lush gardens, all overlooking the strait. $99–175; 10 percent discount for military and teachers.

FOREST SERVICE CABINS

Olympic National Forest (360-765-2200; www.recreation.gov). They sleep four to six people. Reservations required.

Hamma Hamma Cabin, on US 101, 14 miles north of Hoodsport, then 6 miles west on Hamma Hamma River Road. It has two bedrooms, a kitchen, and a bathroom, but you must bring your own drinking water. Sleeps six. $50.

Interrorem Cabin, on US 101, 20 miles north of Hoodsport, then 4 miles west on Duckabush Road. This log square has one bedroom, a kitchen, and a living room with a futon. There's no water or electricity, but propane is furnished. Sleeps four. $50.

Louella Cabin, on US 101 south of Sequim State Park; call for directions. This cabin has two bedrooms, a living room, and a kitchen. There's propane and electricity but no running water. Sleeps six. $60.

GUESTHOUSES

Port Townsend

Takaki House (360-385-9748; www .mtakaki.com), 1617 Washington Street. Not a guesthouse exactly, nor a B&B, these two guest rooms share a roof with Margaret Takaki's art gallery. If you enjoy understated elegance, harbor views, and all the comforts of home, including a kitchen and Wi-Fi, this is the place to spend a weekend or more. Don't miss Ms. Takaki's sculpture and ceramics. From $100.

HOSTELS

Port Townsend

Olympic Hostel (360-385-0655 or 800-909-4776; www.olympichostel .org), in Fort Worden State Park, 272 Battery Way. Located in an old barracks, the Hostelling International hostel is a clean and friendly crossroads for travelers from around the world. A total of 30 beds in men's and women's dorms plus several private rooms. There's also a spacious kitchen, a common room with a piano, and free parking. Dorm bed $28 nonmembers, $15 children under 18; private room $66.

HOTELS

Port Townsend

Ann Starrett Mansion (800-321-0644; www.starrettmansion.com), 744 Cleary Street. This very exuberant 1889 Queen Anne Victorian house was built for Ann Starrett by her husband, George, who had her portrait painted into the solar calendar lining the top chamber of the 70-foot-tall tower. A spiral staircase without visible means of support runs from the ground floor right up the tower, where a ruby oculus is illuminated at the summer solstice. The whole is unique even among Port Townsend's collection of Victoriana, and of course it's furnished with opulent Victorian taste, from rugs to fireplaces to furniture. There are six guest rooms in the house, from the Nanny's Room (it really was) to the Master Suite, and three rooms in the Carriage House; the **Wisteria Cottage,** 1005 Quincy Street, contains the Garden Suite and Honeymoon Suite, both of which welcome children, curiously. Guest rooms $129–225; carriage house $115–185; cottage $139–210.

Belmont Hotel (360-385-3007; www.thebelmontpt.com), 925 Water Street. One of Port Townsend's several surviving Victorian hotels, the Belmont is one of the oldest, dating from 1885. It wasn't as genteel then as it is today, however, but a tavern and restaurant, with offices above. Now the offices are respectable Victorian-style rooms, with private baths no less, and the **restaurant** is of course nonsmoking. $79–129.

Manresa Castle (360-385-5750 or 800-732-1281; www.manresacastle .com), Seventh and Sheridan streets. Charles Eisenbeis was an immigrant from Prussia who owned or partly owned many businesses in town, such as a brick factory, a bakery, a lumber mill, a bank, and more. It was almost natural, then, that he was elected Port Townsend's first mayor, in 1878. It's not known whether that was the proximate cause of his building this 30-room home with towers and mansard windows, but that's what he did, completing it in 1892. It was immediately dubbed "Eisenbeis Castle." Perhaps it reminded him of Prussia.

The name "Manresa" came from the Jesuits who bought the place in 1927. When they left in 1968, there was really nothing to do but turn it into a hotel. The rooms now have all modern conveniences and elegant Victorian-style decor. The **Castle Key Restaurant** is in the original dining room. $109–229.

Palace Hotel (800-962-0741; www
.palacehotelpt.com), 1004 Water
Street. This dignified brick building
with arched windows and 14-foot ceilings was erected by Captain Tibbals, a
seafarer from the age of 10. The ground
floor was, naturally, a saloon, while the
upstairs rooms were rented out. The
15 rooms today are fancifully named
after the prostitutes who reputedly
worked here from 1925 to 1933. However, major renovations—uncovering a
1921 mural, putting in stained-glass
windows and skylights, and using late-
Victorian furniture (some original)—
have turned the hotel into a period
piece providing all the modern comforts for today's tourists. All the rooms
have private baths, and some have
kitchenettes. $59–229.

& **The Swan Hotel** (360-385-6122 or
800-824-4738; www.theswanhotel
.com), 216 Monroe Street. More modern in decor than the Victorian hotels
in town, the Swan still looks like a sea
captain's house, with its square shape
and widow's walk overlooking the Point
Hudson Marina. Two of the eight
rooms are wheelchair-accessible, and
all are comfortably appointed, with
access to the wraparound decks. Four
cottages offer even more privacy.
$90–185.

MOTELS

Port Townsend

Tides Inn (360-385-0595 or 800-822-
8696; www.tides-inn.com), 1807 Water
Street. It calls itself a waterfront motel,
but it's been designed to blend in with
the local late-Victorian architecture,
with bow windows, cedar paneling, and
balconies. Like Fort Worden State
Park, it was featured in the film *An
Officer and a Gentleman*. A newer
wing is less traditional. Rates include
breakfast. No pets. $60–239.

Sequim

 Sequim Bay Lodge (800-622-
0691; www.sequimbaylodge.com),
268522 US 101. Double and king
rooms, fireplaced suites, and hot-tub
suites are choices in this lodge-style
motel overlooking Sequim Bay. Pets
allowed in some units. $79–175.

RESORTS

Port Angeles

Log Cabin Resort (360-928-3325;
www.logcabinresort.net), 3183 East
Beach Road. This low-key family resort
on the unfrequented north shore of
Lake Crescent sits among tall old
cedars and Douglas firs. The original
log hotel, built in 1895 by a customs
officer from Port Townsend, burned
down in 1932. The current resort came
about in the early 1950s, but the rustic
wooden buildings have a timeless feel.
Accommodations include lodge rooms
and a range of rustic cabins, from log
"sleeping" cabins without plumbing to
kitchenette units. A general store, café,
and restaurant serve basic needs. You
can also rent a canoe, kayak, or row-
boat here or arrange a rafting trip with
nearby Olympic Raft and Kayak (see
To Do—Canoeing and Kayaking).
Cabins $94–161; lodge rooms $121.

✳ Where to Eat
DINING OUT

Port Angeles

C'est Si Bon (360-452-8888; www
.cestsibon-frenchcuisine.com), 23
Cedar Park Road. Open 5–11 Tues.–
Sun. The price tag makes this definitely a destination for a special night
out, and so does the decor—something
like a crystal palace—but you're not
likely to find French recipes like these
elsewhere on the Olympic Peninsula.
Offerings range from stuffed quail to
magret de canard to coquilles Saint-

Jacques. The wines come from Washington, California, Australia, and, of course, France.

Port Townsend
Silverwater Café (360-385-6448; info@silverwatercafe.com; www.silver watercafe.com), 237 Taylor Street. Open for dinner daily, for lunch Mon.–Sat., and for Sunday brunch (10:30–2:30). Alison and David Hero firmly believe in the joys of fresh, local foods. So, apparently, do their friendly and energetic staff. Creative uses of the best the Northwest has to offer include dishes such as lavender pepper ahi, troll-caught salmon in white wine sauce, and steaks exclusively from Oregon beef. If you're a vegetarian, you might like the wild mushroom, rice, and leek cakes with Dijon sauce. Add a respectable wine list, scrumptious desserts made by David, 11 coffee choices, or proper leaf tea, and you get a perfectly satisfying dining experience.

EATING OUT
Port Angeles
Michael's Seafood and Steak House (360-417-6929; www.michaelsdining .com), 117-B East First Street. Open for dinner daily. In the basement below the Country Aire health food store, Michael's is a casual bistro whose menu is based on Mediterranean recipes and Northwest ingredients: You can get paella, ravioli, or clam chowder. Michael buys as much as possible from local, organic farms, and he has a full bar, too.

Port Townsend
Khu Larb Thai (360-385-5023; www .khularbthai.com), 225 Adams Street. Open 11–9 Sun.–Thurs., 11–10 Fri.–Sat. If you tire of Port Townsend's abundant Northwest cuisine, Khu Larb Thai provides something completely different. Well, not completely: Mussels in curry sauce represent a happy

marriage, and halibut with lemongrass sauce is a neat twist. A full palette of Thai spices accent the many soups, meats, and poultry dishes. Khu Larb is a welcome stop for vegetarians, too, with delicious spicy tofu, ginger tofu, and other nonmeat selections.

Lanza's Ristorante (360-379-1900), 1020 Lawrence Street. Open for dinner Tues.–Sat. Lanza's pasta was voted the best in the county eight years in a row. A lively place, it serves pizza, pasta, seafood, and Italian specialties in a casual setting, with a children's menu and music on the weekend.

The Otter Crossing Café (360-379-0592), Point Hudson Marina. Open for breakfast, lunch, and dinner Mon. and Wed.–Sat., 9–3 Sun. This place has a terrific view of Puget Sound and specialties such as smoked salmon hash, fried oysters, and lingonberry crêpes.

✱ Entertainment
THEATER Centrum Performing Arts Center (360-385-3102; www .centrum.org), in Fort Worden State Park, 272 Battery Way, Port Townsend. Centrum is a venue for performing arts of all kinds (including poetry readings; it's the home of Copper Canyon Press), as well as workshops and creative retreats.

Rose Theater (360-385-1089; www .rosetheater.com), 235 Taylor Street, Port Townsend. Today an art-film theater, the Rose opened in 1907 as a local playhouse, vaudeville theater, and, yes, movie house.

✱ Selective Shopping
ART Ancestral Spirits Gallery (360-385-0078), 701 Water Street, Port Townsend. Featuring contemporary Native American art.

Forest Gems (360-379-1713), 807 Washington Street, Port Townsend.

Work by Harvey Windle, who sculpts West Coast wood.

Gallery 9 (360-379-8881), 1012 Water Street, Port Townsend. Showcases work by more than 30 local artists.

BOOKS William James Bookseller (360-385-7313), 829 Water Street, Port Townsend. Carries all those books you've been looking for.

✳ Special Events

May: **Rhododendron Festival** (360-379-4855; www.rhodyfestival.org), Port Townsend. A bike tour, parade, and Rhody Run fill out a week of flower-filled events.

June: **Centrum Summer Chamber Music Festival** (360-385-3102; www.centrum.org), Fort Worden State Park, Port Townsend.

June–September: **Olympic Music Festival** (360-732-4800; www.olympicmusicfestival.org), Quilcene. Enjoy music on a century-old dairy farm.

July: **Centrum Festival of American Fiddle Tunes** (360-385-3102; www.centrum.org), Fort Worden State Park, Port Townsend.

Jazz Port Townsend (360-385-3102; www.centrum.org), Fort Worden State Park, Port Townsend.

Sequim Lavender Festival (877-681-3035; www.lavenderfestival.com), Sequim. There's a street fair in downtown Sequim and tours of surrounding farms.

September: **Wooden Boat Festival** (360-385-3628; www.woodenboat.org), Port Townsend. Workshops, tours, activities, and lots of wooden boats.

OLYMPIC NATIONAL PARK

So dense and rugged is the Olympic interior that it was only successfully traversed in 1889, on an expedition hastily mounted by James Christie and the *Seattle Press*. Strangely, the five-member party chose to cross in winter, hauling a boat with all their provisions up the Elwha River. (What is it about northwesterners?) By stages, they were obliged to give up on the boat and most of their equipment. After five months, during which they lost their remaining gear and nearly starved, they emerged at the mouth of the Quinault River.

This north-south crossing inspired further explorations—albeit in summer. As early as 1890, some of those who had beheld the mountains' grandeur were calling for the creation of an Olympic National Park. Following a long tug-of-war prefiguring many later environmental battles, the park was created by a stroke of Franklin D. Roosevelt's pen in 1938. It's said that the boundary between the park and adjacent national forestland is visible from space.

Today the park comprises 922,651 acres, including a narrow, nearly roadless strip of forested coastline. Those seemingly impenetrable mountains are not actually that high: Mount Olympus tops out at 7,980 feet. It's the dense vegetation and the radial drainage, creating innumerable folds, that make them so hard to get through—and so scenic. To stand anywhere in the high country is to confront massed jagged peaks surrounded by tall forests. Scraped from the seafloor, bent and uplifted by ungentle tectonic forces, and finally sculpted by glaciers, the Olympic formations are far less regular than their volcanic neighbors to the east. From alpine meadows to the temperate rain forest of the western slopes, the Olympics are, for want of a better word, stupendous.

Paved roads enter the park at several points, but they don't get very far. The interior remains roadless, but a network of hiking trails enables you to see much of the wilderness as it was in 1890—or 1790, for that matter. A 60-mile, nearly roadless coastal stretch that was added later is another equally wild world. Many visitors to Olympic National Park make a foray into the Hoh Rain Forest, but with the park's nearly 1 million acres to explore, plus hot springs to soak in after an active day, there's so much more to see.

GUIDANCE Hoh Rain Forest Visitor Center (360-374-6925), 18113 Upper Hoh Road, Forks 98331; off US 101 about 20 miles southeast of Forks. Open daily in summer (hours vary); 10–4 Fri.–Sun. in spring, fall, and winter.

Hurricane Ridge Visitor Center, end of Hurricane Ridge Road, about 17 miles south of Port Angeles. Open daily in summer (hours vary); 10–4 daily in spring, fall, and winter if the road is open.

Olympic National Park Visitor Center (360-565-3130; www.nps.gov/olym), 3002 Mount Angeles Road, Port Angeles 98362. Open daily; hours vary seasonally.

South Shore Quinault Ranger Station, South Shore Quinault Road next to Quinault Lodge (see *Lodging*).

Wilderness Information Center (360-565-3100), 1 mile off US 101, behind Olympic National Park Visitor Center (see above), Port Angeles. Open 8–4:30 Sun.–Thurs., 7:30–5:30 Fri.–Sat. May 1–June 22; 7:30–6 Sun.–Thurs., 7:30–7 Fri.–Sat. June 23–Sept. 4. Wilderness permits, trail reports, backcountry trip planning, and the like.

GETTING THERE There are many access points. Entry fee is $15 per vehicle for a week or by America the Beautiful Pass or Olympic National Park Annual Pass.

North: Mount Angeles Road, from **US 101** in Port Angeles, leads to Hurricane Ridge; Elwha River Road, from US 101 west of Port Angeles, leads to several trailheads; US 101 follows the south shore of Lake Crescent; Sol Duc Road, from US 101 just west of Lake Crescent, leads to the hot springs.

West: Upper Hoh Road, from US 101 south of Forks, leads to the Hoh Rain Forest; Queets Road, from US 101 just east of Queets, leads up the isolated Queets River; North Shore and South Shore roads, from US 101 near Amanda Park, follow along the shore of Quinault Lake.

East: WA 119, from US 101 at Hoodsport, leads to Lake Cushman; other roads from US 101 lead into foothills but not the park itself—FR 25 (up the Hamma Hamma River), Duckabush Road, and Dosewallips Road, among others.

MEDICAL EMERGENCY Dial 9-1-1 (though cell phone access in the park is minimal). Emergency rooms are located in Forks, Port Angeles, and Port Townsend (see Western Olympic Peninsula and Eastern Olympic Peninsula chapters).

✳ To See

CHAMPION TREES Twelve feet of rain per year naturally brings about some champion trees—that is, the largest living specimens of their species. These are some of the more accessible ones in or near the national park:

Alaska cedar, 124 feet tall. Drive along Lake Quinault on North Shore Road, stopping at the Skyline Ridge trailhead, about 0.5 mile before the road ends. It's about a 5-mile hike to the tree; you have to be motivated.

Douglas fir, a co-champion, 212 feet tall and 44 feet in diameter. Drive some 13 miles on the Queets Road to its end, then walk up the Queets River Trail 2.4 miles. Turn left at the sign and continue 0.2 mile.

Sitka spruce, 191 feet tall. Drive along Lake Quinault on South Shore Road about 2.5 miles from US 101. The tree is in Olympic National Forest just past the Quinault Ranger Station.

Western red cedar, 159 feet tall with a whopping 63.5-foot circumference. Drive along Lake Quinault on North Shore Road about 1 mile from US 101. This fantastically gnarled tree, practically a forest in itself, is thought to be 1,200 years old. This one is a must-see.

FOR FAMILIES Olympic National Park Visitor Center (360-565-3130), 3002 Mount Angeles Road, Port Angeles. Open daily; hours vary seasonally. Free. The center provides a good introduction to the natural history of the Olympics, with pressed plants, animal tracks, a kids' discovery room, and more. On the grounds you'll find an 1887 trapper's cabin and a Native seal-hunting canoe.

NATURAL WONDERS Deer Park, via Deer Park Road, south of US 101 from east of Port Angeles. Closed fall–spring. A long gravel road leads to an elevation similar to that of Hurricane Ridge; Deer Park has spectacular scenery, too, and fewer people. Eagles are often seen soaring over the deep valleys below. A couple of trailheads and a small campground afford entry to the wilderness for the intrepid.

Hoh Rain Forest, via Upper Hoh Road, east of US 101, 90 miles west and south of Port Angeles. A small visitors center and interpretive trails explain the nature of the forest occupying the Hoh River valley, which is part of the **temperate rain forest** covering most of the park's west side. Near-constant precipitation from the cold northern Pacific amounts to a good 12 feet of rain a year, creating a cool, densely green jungle of giant hemlocks, Sitka spruces, and Douglas firs, with moss growing on trees, trees growing on trees, huge ferns, and other oversized ground covers.

Hurricane Ridge, via Mount Angeles Road, south of US 101 at Port Angeles. Open daily mid-May–mid-autumn; Sat.–Sun. in winter, weather permitting. There's a small visitors center with a café and gift shop, and several walking trails begin here. This is probably the park's most popular destination because of the views. The narrow, hairpin-bend road from Port Angeles up to the mile-high ridge is quite a trip in itself. When you get to the top, you have the entire Olympic range spread out before you to the south, one jagged peak in front of another. Looking the other way, to the north, you can see the ragged coast and Vancouver Island across the blue Strait of Juan de Fuca. Go in the late morning or afternoon to avoid fog. Quite nearby, you might see mountain goats, introduced and apparently not native.

Lake Crescent, on US 101, 20 miles west of Port Angeles. This glacier-carved lake is nearly 10 miles long and 660 feet deep. Enclosed by high, forested hills, its dark waters exert a certain fascination; there are even rumors of a water monster. Many faithful vacationers return year after year to stay at Lake Crescent Resort (see *Lodging*) or the Log Cabin Resort (see Eastern Olympic Peninsula chapter). You never do see many people actually *in* the water, but then you wouldn't expect to, with maximum lake temperatures of about 60 degrees Fahrenheit.

Olympic coast, 65 miles from Quinault Reservation to Makah Reservation. The southern section, from Kalaloch to the Hoh River, is right on US 101. Beaches along this stretch are easily accessible, including **Kalaloch Beach,** near Kalaloch Resort (see *Lodging*), and **Ruby Beach.** The rest of the park's coast is more isolated. **Rialto Beach** and **First Beach** are near La Push, on either side of the Quillayute River; **Second Beach** and **Third Beach** are accessible only by trail. All of these are reached via WA 110 west of US 101 at Forks. (Access to Second Beach is occasionally blocked due to disputes between the Park Service and the Quileute tribe, whose tiny reservation adjoins the park at La Push.) You might have to climb over mats of huge driftwood trees that wash down the rivers and up

VIEW OF HURRICANE RIDGE, PART OF OLYMPIC NATIONAL PARK'S STUPENDOUS MOUNTAINOUS INTERIOR.

the beaches, and you'll have to walk anywhere from 0.25 mile to 2 miles just to get there, but the expanses of empty beach and ocean are truly stupendous. Tidal pools, sea stacks, whales, and sea lions overwhelm the eye. The wilderness beach can be hiked south from Third Beach to the Hoh River and north from Rialto Beach to Point of the Arches, which is reached via a trail from Lake Ozette (see *To Do—Hiking*). If you walk the isolated wilderness beach, be aware of the tides, which can cut you off between trails over the headlands.

✳ To Do

BICYCLING Spruce Railroad Trail, 4 unpaved miles on the north shore of Lake Crescent. Biking is not permitted on national park trails except this one. This was the track of a railway built to ship Sitka spruce out to use for building planes during World War I. The track was completed in 1918 and never used.

CAMPING Fifteen **developed campgrounds** in the park offer drinking water (at least in summer), ADA restrooms unless otherwise noted, but no showers. No reservations are taken except for Kalaloch (www.recreation.gov): **Altaire,** on Elwha River Road, 30 sites; **Deer Park** (see *To See—Natural Wonders*), 14 tent sites, no water, no ADA restrooms, open summer only; **Dosewallips,** via Dosewal- lips Road (5.5-mile walk-in due to road washout at time of this writing), 30 tent sites, no water, no ADA restrooms, open summer only; **Elwha,** on Elwha River Road, 40 sites; **Fairholm,** on the west shore of Lake Crescent, 88 sites, open sum- mer only; **Graves Creek,** at the end of South Shore Road on Quinault River, 30 sites, no ADA restrooms; **Heart o' the Hills,** on Mount Angeles Road near the main visitors center, 105 sites, no water in winter; **Hoh,** on Upper Hoh Road at Hoh Rain Forest Visitor Center, 88 sites; **Kalaloch,** on US 101 at the south end of wilder- ness beach, 170 sites; **Mora,** on WA 110 west of US 101 at Forks, north side of Quil- layute River, 94 sites; **North Fork,** at the end of North Shore Road on North Fork Quinault River, 7 sites, no water, no ADA restrooms, no trailers; **Ozette,** at the end of Hoko-Ozette Road off WA 112 west of Clallam Bay, at the north end of Ozette

Lake, 15 sites; **Queets,** at the end of Queets Road (not safe for trailers or RVs), 20 tent sites, no water; **Sol Duc,** at the end of Soleduck River Road, off US 101 west of Lake Crescent, near hot springs, 82 sites, open summer only; **Staircase,** at the end of Lake Cushman Road, off US 101 at Hoodsport, 56 sites.

Additionally, nearly 100 **backcountry sites** offer primitive camping via hiking trails and require wilderness permits. For information, contact **Wilderness Center Information Center** (360-565-3100) in Port Angeles. See also *Hiking*.

CANOEING, KAYAKING, AND RAFTING The **Hoh, Sol Duc,** and **Elwha rivers** offer class II–III kayaking and river rafting.

Olympic Raft and Kayak (888-452-1443; www.raftandkayak.com), 123 Lake Aldwell Road, Port Angeles. They rent kayaks or canoes for flatwater paddling.

Rainforest Paddlers (866-457-8398; www.rainforestpaddlers.com). They also rent kayaks or canoes for flatwater paddling.

FOR FAMILIES Olympic Park Institute (360-928-3720), 111 Barnes Point Road, Port Angeles. Located on Lake Crescent near the Lake Crescent Resort (see *Lodging*), the institute offers field courses and educational adventures for teenagers and adults. Lodging and meals in the rain forest are provided.

HIKING Both the coastal and interior parts of the park have exquisite hiking trails for all ability levels. It's always wise to visit the nearest ranger station (see *Guidance*) before starting out to check for road washouts or trail closures. Some classic hikes include the following:

Coastal strip: From **Lake Ozette,** two boardwalks go to the Pacific: the **Cape Alava Trail,** 3.3 miles, and the **Sand Point Trail,** 3 miles. For a 9-mile loop, connect these two trails with a 3-mile stretch on the beach. From **Rialto Beach,** walk north along the remote shoreline to Hole in the Wall or farther. Watch the tides along these beach walks.

Deer Park: From US 101, 5 miles east of Port Angeles, turn south on Deer Park Road and drive about 16 miles (the first 8 miles are paved) up to the Deer Park Ranger Station. Several trails start here. The **Obstruction Point–Deer Park Trail,** 7.4 miles, changes only 600 feet in elevation through alpine meadows and mountain forests but is strenuous nonetheless. The short initial stretch is level and gives great views, including possible golden eagles.

Hurricane Ridge: From US 101 in Port Angeles, take Mount Angeles Road 18 miles up to the Hurricane Ridge lodge and visitors center, from which several trails radiate. The **Hurricane Hill Trail,** 1.5 miles, perhaps the most used (for good reason), winds up to a knob with views of razorback Olympic ridges in one direction and the Strait of Juan de Fuca in the other. (Of course, it might all just as easily be wrapped in fog; afternoons are clearer.) Look for grouse, too. The first 0.5 mile is paved and wheelchair-accessible but has steep drop-offs. If you have the time and energy, the trail connects with several others for a more energetic hike. A challenge is the **Hurricane Hill–Elwha Trail,** 5.8 miles, which descends 5,200 feet from Hurricane Ridge to the Elwha River.

Lake Crescent: Several steep trails can be accessed from the resort on US 101. The **Barnes Creek Trail,** 3.3 miles, rises 1,400 feet; it's strenuous, but you'll walk through lovely old-growth forest. **Mount Storm King Trail,** 1.7 miles, climbs 2,000 feet to a ridge with lake views. An easier stroll is the **Marymere Falls Trail,** 1 mile, through the same forest (the first 0.75 mile is wheelchair-accessible) to the 90-foot falls.

Olympic Hot Springs: From US 101 west of Port Angeles, turn left on Elwha River Road and continue to the Boulder Creek trailhead. Take a relaxing walk (2.5 miles) to the ruins of a 1930s resort and soak in the backcountry springs (clothing optional).

Sol Duc Hot Springs: From US 101 west of Lake Crescent, take Sol Duc River Road to its end at the hot springs. A network of trails near the springs can take you deep into the mountains. At the end of the road, the **Sol Duc Falls Trail,** 0.8 mile, leads through a forest to the falls. The **Sol Duc River Trail,** 7.2 miles, follows the river back into the hills, joining other backcountry trails.

West-side rain forest: From the **Hoh Rain Forest Visitor Center,** via Upper Hoh Road from US 101 about 20 miles southeast of Forks, two **short loops** (0.75 mile and 1.25 miles) guide visitors from around the world through a sample of this temperate rain forest of giant Sitka spruces and big-leaf maples. A third trail (0.25 mile) is wheelchair-accessible. If you are particularly energetic, the **Hoh River Trail,** 17 miles, carries on to Glacier Meadow. The lesser-known **Bogachiel Trail,** 25 miles, traverses similar habitat along the wild Bogachiel River to the north of the Hoh.

HOT SPRINGS Olympic Hot Springs, via Elwha River Road from US 101 west of Port Angeles to the Boulder Creek trailhead. These springs near the Elwha River are decidedly informal. There was a resort here once, but it fell into ruin and is now frequented at all times of year by those willing to hike 2.5 miles on the old road. However, some of the pools reportedly fail water-quality tests. There's a walk-in campground across the creek from the springs.

Sol Duc Hot Springs, via Sol Duc River Road about 10 miles from US 101, 28 miles west of Port Angeles. Open Mar.–Oct. $10.75 adults, $8 seniors and children. When a settler was led to these steaming springs by Indians, he had the brilliant idea of charging others for the same pleasure. You can still enjoy the springs for a fee, and even enjoy dinner and an overnight stay at the Sol Duc Hot Springs Resort (see *Lodging*) or the **Sol Duc Campground** (360-327-3398).

WINTER SPORTS Hurricane Ridge: In winter, the hiking trails here become cross-country ski trails; there's also a downhill ski area (tow rope) and room for snowshoeing. **Hurricane Ridge Visitor Center** (360-565-3130) is open Sat.–Sun. and holidays Dec.–Mar. Rentals are available at the center, which also offers guided snowshoe walks.

✸ Lodging

RESORTS

Amanda Park
Lake Quinault Resort (360-288-2362; www.lakequinault.com), 314 North Shore Road. On the meditative north shore of Lake Quinault, this quiet 1940s resort in the rain forest has nine units sleeping 2–10. Lawns slope down to the lake, where you can paddle a kayak or canoe. Not far away is the 1,200-year-old champion western red cedar (see *To See—Champion Trees*). $ 128–199.

Forks

🐾 ☙ **Kalaloch Resort** (360-962-2271; www.olympicnationalparks.com), 157151 US 101. The first buildings here were constructed quixotically of driftwood, before there was a road. Cabins followed in the 1930s, when US 101 was built, and today's Main Lodge sits on a bluff overlooking the lonely Pacific coast. You can choose between rooms in the rustic lodge, cabins with kitchens and fireplaces, and motel units. The **Kalaloch Lodge Restaurant** serves seafood, breakfasts, and simple lunches, with a children's menu available. It's your only food option except for the small grocery store. Pets allowed in cabins. $139–325.

Port Angeles

Lake Crescent Resort (360-928-3211; www.lakecrescentlodge.com), 413 Lake Crescent Road. One of the grand old national park lodges, with its shining wood lobby and great stone fireplace, this one was privately built in 1916 for a burgeoning tourist trade on the then remote lakeshore. Over the years, additional buildings and several cottages have been added to the grounds, so it has become quite a complex. Historic lodge rooms share bathrooms; newer rooms have private baths. The cottages have one or two bedrooms, and some have fireplaces. Cottage season is May–mid-Oct., though some are open Sat.–Sun. in winter. The **dining room** overlooking the lake is open daily in season (dinner reservations required). Lodge rooms $105–169 (some with shared bath); cottages $108–465.

☙ **Sol Duc Hot Springs Resort** (360-327-3398; www.visitsolduc.com), Box 1269, Port Angeles 98362. To get here you drive 11 miles through deep forest down Sol Duc River Road, accompanied by the babbling Sol Duc River. At the road's end are the hot springs. The pool is surrounded by 32 cabins, 6 of which have kitchens; each has its own bathroom and sleeps four. Rates include pool access. **The Springs Restaurant** offers casual, tasty Northwest cuisine for breakfast and dinner; open early May–mid-Oct. Some units allow pets. $163–362.

Quinault

Lake Quinault Lodge (360-288-2900; www.visitlakequinault.com), Box 7, Quinault 98575. On the National Register of Historic Places, this 1926 lodge offers traditional amenities such as billiards, horseshoes, and badminton, plus some the founders might not have though of: high-speed Internet access, for example. An 1880s log hotel was replaced with this grand two-floor structure, all beams and dark wood and stuffed furniture—in short, all the qualities of a fine wilderness lodge. Lodge rooms have period-style furniture; a newer building has 36 more-modern rooms; the 1923 Boathouse Annex has 8 rooms and a veranda. Room rates include the use of two walking sticks. Rent a canoe or a bike to explore the lake and environs. The **Roosevelt Dining Room** is named for Franklin D. Roosevelt, whose 1937 visit resulted in the establishment of Olympic National Park the following year. Dinners feature Pacific seafood, steaks, and prime rib, but it's open for breakfast and lunch, too. Pets allowed in Boathouse Annex. $104–329.

✳ Where to Eat

EATING OUT Just about the only dining options in the park itself are at the various **lodges** (see *Lodging*).

Southern Puget Sound

OLYMPIA AREA

TACOMA AREA

KITSAP PENINSULA AND
BAINBRIDGE ISLAND

INTRODUCTION

When your children's children think themselves alone in the
field, the store, the shop, upon the highway, or in the silence of
the pathless woods, they will not be alone. In all the earth there
is no place dedicated to solitude. At night when the streets of
your cities and villages are silent and you think them deserted,
they will throng with the returning hosts that once filled them
and still love this beautiful land.

—Chief Seattle, 1854

It's a fine speech, and if Chief Seattle (or Sealth, in the Salish pronunciation) didn't exactly say those words, he certainly ought to have. It's not clear whether he did. A leader of the Suquamish people inhabiting much of the western Puget Sound area, Sealth made an impassioned speech at the treaty talks of 1854 (which were less talks, actually, than exercises in Governor Isaac Stevens's frankly expressed goal of dispossessing the Indians) near what is now Seattle. The chief spoke in his native Lushootseed, a Salish language. Possibly this was put into the Chinook jargon by an Indian interpreter for the benefit of other tribes represented, but the speech did not appear in English or in print until 1887. That year, one Henry Smith printed a "transcript" in the *Seattle Sunday Star*. Smith had indeed been present at the 1854 meeting and supposedly taken notes, but he had only a rudimentary knowledge of Chinook, and scholars have expressed doubt as to whether he would have understood enough of the speech to render a credible translation 33 years later. Phrases that occur in some versions, such as "sable braves" or "glad-hearted maidens," seem fairly unlikely to have come from the lips of an actual Indian leader. Smith probably grasped the gist as best he could and made up for his deficiencies with a healthy dose of Victorian poesy.

Chief Sealth tried to do his best in a bad time. He was born before the first white incursions into his country and died nearly a stranger in his own land. He tried to navigate his people through the swift and irreversible seizure of their lands by a policy of accommodation, and along the way, he became a Catholic and a friend of Seattle businessman "Doc" Maynard. The best anyone could have done in the face of the march of empire wouldn't have been good enough, and as happened with other tribes, those of the southern sound were confined to small reservations that were promptly rendered smaller by treaty breaches. (Rumors are that Chief Sealth was not well pleased when the city was named in his honor, as it meant his name would henceforth be loosely bandied about, and he demanded financial compensation.)

Sealth's world has changed more than he could have imagined, from the state capitol's golden cupola at Olympia to the massive container ports of Tacoma and Seattle, to the Bremerton shipyards and the now diminishing lumber mills. Puget Sound is still an inland sea, though. The tribes necessarily lived with, from, and by the water. Not only is the territory a patchwork of solid and liquid, but it can rain so long and so hard, especially in winter, that you wonder if sky and sea have changed places. Water was and to a large extent still is the highway, from the canoe days to the "mosquito fleet" to the Washington State Ferries. Water defines even the Seattle-Tacoma metropolitan area, with its wharves, fishing boats, and water-front parks. The low, green Kitsap Peninsula to the west, much indented by bays and inlets and attached to the mainland by only a slender neck of land, is home to a renascent Native canoe-building and canoe-paddling tradition. Often overlooked as a backwater, so to speak, on the way to the Olympic Peninsula, the Kitsap is a world unto itself, becoming recognized as a quick getaway for caffeine-jittery Seat-tleites. In fact, some have reversed the process: Bainbridge Island, connected by bridge to the Kitsap Peninsula where Chief Sealth is buried, is now a bedroom community whose residents commute to the city by ferry.

OLYMPIA AREA

T he race is not always to the swift. Olympia beat out Seattle and several other Washington cities in 1889 to become the state capital at a time when it was little more than a burg at the edge of a swamp. (In fairness, one has to add that, at the time, few cities in the state were terribly impressive.) Even today Olympia is probably the most modest city of the Puget Sound agglomeration, with only about 45,000 inhabitants to Greater Seattle's nearly 4 million or Tacoma's 200,000. Instead of housing the Washington State History Museum, Olympia has only a branch of it. But the city does have the state capitol, and though the area's accommodations base is rather small, it has a selection of pleasant restaurants—the way to a legislator's heart must lie through his or her stomach. The presence of Evergreen State College leavens the mix with alternative films, music, and the occasional demonstration.

Olympia is a good walking city, whose compact downtown area has cozy cafés and tea shops to duck into if it rains, which is more than likely. If you get tired of walking, go for a paddle on Budd Inlet or drive to nearby Priest Point Park or Tolmie State Park. Oh, and it's in an earthquake zone; ask someone to show you where the capitol dome columns are out of alignment, a vestige of the damaging 2001 Nisqually quake.

GUIDANCE Lacey Chamber of Commerce (360-491-4141; www.laceychamber .com), 8300 Quinault Drive NE, Lacey 98503.

Olympia-Lacey-Tumwater Visitor and Convention Bureau (360-704-7544 or 877-704-7500; www.visitolympia.com), 103 Sid Snyder Avenue, Olympia 98501.

State Capitol Visitor Center (360-902-8881; www.ga.wa.gov/visitor), 416 Sid Snyder Avenue, Olympia 98504.

Tumwater Area Chamber of Commerce (360-357-5153; office@tumwater chamber.com; www.tumwaterchamber.com), 5304 Littlerock Road SW, Tumwater 98512.

GETTING THERE Olympia, Lacey, and Tumwater can be reached by car from the south or northeast on **I-5.** Yelm and Tenino are south of Olympia on **WA 507; WA 510** connects Yelm to Lacey.

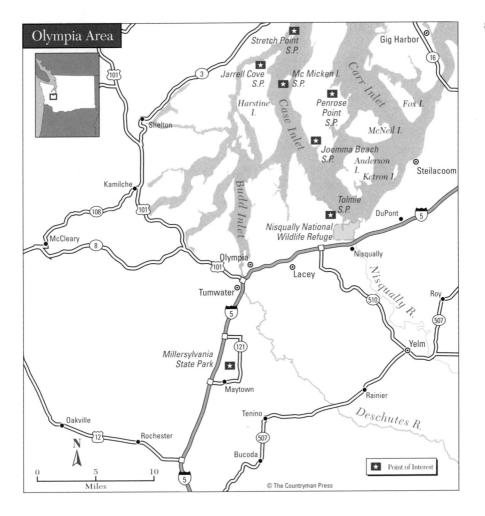

Olympia Area

Point of Interest

© The Countryman Press

Seattle-Tacoma International Airport is 46 miles northeast of Olympia via I-5. From Sea-Tac Airport, **Black Hills Transportation** (360-786-0636) serves Lacey and Tumwater.

AMTRAK (800-USA-RAIL; www.amtrak.com) has two train routes—AMTRAK Cascades and Coast Starlight—that stop in nearby Lacey at 6600 Yelm Highway SE.

Greyhound (360-357-5541 or 800-231-2222; www.greyhound.com) stops in Olympia at 107 Seventh Avenue SE on its Portland-Seattle run.

GETTING AROUND **Intercity Transit** (360-786-1881 or 800-287-6348; www .intercitytransit.com) provides bus service in the southern Puget Sound area with connections to Seattle and Aberdeen. All buses have external bike racks. The local office of **Olympia Transit Center** is at 222 State Avenue; open 6:30 AM–7 PM Mon.–Fri., 9–5:30 Sat.–Sun.

MEDICAL EMERGENCY Capital Medical Center (360-956-2574; www.capital medical.com), 3900 Capital Mall Drive SW, Olympia.

Pacific Walk-In Clinic (360-455-1350), 3928 Pacific Avenue SE, Lacey. Provides urgent and minor trauma care 9–7 Mon.–Fri., 9–5 Sat.–Sun.

Providence St. Peter Hospital (360-491-9480; www.providence.org/swsa), 413 Lilly Road NE, Olympia.

✳ To See

CULTURAL SITES Monarch Contemporary Art Center and Sculpture Park (360-264-2408; www.monarchsculpturepark.com), 8431 Waldrick Road SE, Tenino. Grounds open dawn to dusk year-round; indoor gallery open by appointment June 7–Oct. 5.

FARMERS' MARKETS ✍ Olympia Farmers Market (360-352-9096; www .olympiafarmersmarket.com), 700 Capitol Way North. Open 10–3 Thurs.–Sun. Apr.–Oct.; 10–3 Sat.–Sun. Nov.–Dec. This market has provided a colorful outlet for local farmers since 1975. Bins of rosy apples, green peppers, juicy peaches, and more beckon, while meat, fish, bakery, cheese, and other stalls make this a market such as you might find in any European town. Plus—buy a meal at any of the permanent café booths and enjoy your curry, taco, seafood dish, or lasagna at a picnic table while you watch other shoppers.

FOR FAMILIES ✍ Rie Munoz Gallery (Eastside Gala-Rie; 360-325-8135, 360-943-3354, or 800-448-9975; www.gala-rie.com), 2384 Crestline Boulevard, Olympia. Open 11–5:30 Wed.–Fri., 11–4 Sat. Children and adults love Rie Munoz's portraits of life in Alaska.

THE OLYMPIA FARMERS MARKET

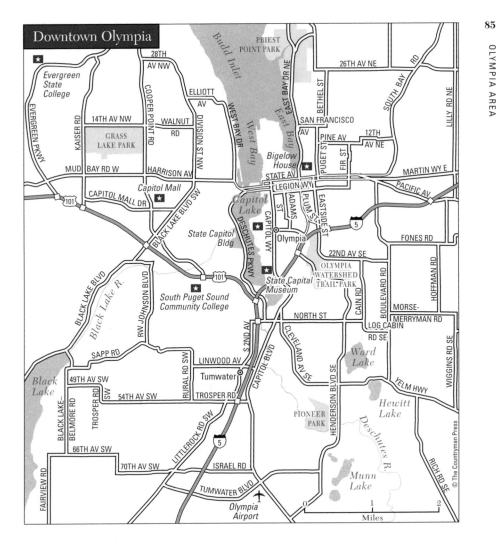

Downtown Olympia

GARDENS Yashiro Japanese Garden (360-753-8380), 1010 Plum Street SE, Olympia. Open dawn to dusk. Free; parking at city offices next door. Named for Olympia's sister city in Japan, this garden is a half-block refuge wedged between I-5 and bustling Plum Street—"walls" of pine and cedar provide a remarkable sound barrier. Paths meander through blended native and Japanese plantings, punctuated here and there by stone lanterns.

HISTORIC HOMES Bigelow House Museum (360-753-1215; bigelowhouse museum@yahoo.com; www.bigelowhouse.org), 918 Glass Avenue NE, Olympia. Open 1–4 Sat.–Sun. in summer; by special arrangement in off-season. $5 adults, $3 seniors and students, $1 children under 12; includes guided one-hour tour. When the young lawyer Daniel Bigelow came west on the Oregon Trail in 1851, he didn't know he'd become a grand old man of the Washington legislature. He and fellow emigrant Ann Elizabeth, a schoolteacher, married in 1854 and by 1860 had built their house in the Carpenter Gothic style popular at the time. In it they raised eight children. It remained in the family with its accumulated furnishings, memorabilia, and other appurtenances for 140 years and today is open briefly for tours.

The Byrd House, 1106 Olympia Avenue NE, Olympia. Not open to the public. Built in 1891 with a two-story porch, cornices, railings, and more by Mary Ellen Byrd near the homes of her mother and sisters (a couple of which still stand), this privately owned house displays the cautiously exuberant style permitted by the growth of local sawmills. Compare it to the Steele House (see below).

Crosby House Museum (360-943-9884), in Tumwater Historical Park (see *Wilder Places—Parks*), 703 Deschutes Way North, Tumwater. Open 1–4 Fri. and Sun. Apr.–Oct. Free. The Crosby House was built about 1860 by Nathaniel and Cordelia Jane Crosby, who would become grandparents of the better-known Bing. Nearly lost to highway construction, the house is now on the National Register of Historic Places as part of the Tumwater Historical District.

The Hale House, 902 Tullis Street NE, Olympia. Not open to the public. This is really a cottage, a sort of miniaturized Queen Anne Victorian with abundant gables and decorative work. Built in 1882, it was the home of Captain Calvin Hale and his wife, Pamela; she became the county superintendent of schools.

Henderson House Museum (360-754-4217), in Tumwater Historical Park (see *Wilder Places—Parks*), 602 Deschutes Way, Tumwater. Open 1–4 Thurs. and Fri. Free. The Hendersons were only the next-to-last residents of Henderson House, occupying it from 1939 to 1974. The pared-down, Queen Anne–style structure was built in 1905 for William Naumann of the Olympia brewery. This house was nearly lost to highway construction but is now on the National Register of Historic Places as part of the Tumwater Historical District.

The Patnude House, 1239 SE Eighth Avenue, Olympia. Not open to the public. Charles Patnude, who had a brickyard, built his house in 1893 on a foundation of his own bricks. Not a purist, he mixed Carpenter Gothic, Italianate, and Queen Anne elements for a rather cheerful-looking residence that today is privately owned.

South Capitol Historic Neighborhood. As the capitol complex grew up in the early 1900s, its environs became a desirable residential area. Today four hundred historic buildings, still mostly homes, display the gamut of early-20th-century popular architectural styles. In fall, sugar maples blaze along Maple Park Drive. **Walking tour** brochures of the district, covering both sides of Capitol Way between 15th and 26th avenues SE, Olympia, are available at the State Capitol Visitor Center (see *Guidance*).

The Steele House, 1010 Franklin Street SE, Olympia. Not open to the public. This house was built by army surgeon Alden Steele when he retired in 1870. A rather typical house of the period, it is constructed of vertical planks running from the foundation to the roof; whether this style was gleaned from Indian plank houses or is a result of convergent development of building styles is unclear. Its boxy shape is relieved only by a porch and small bay window.

Tumwater Ready Cut Homes, 1500 block of SW Columbia Street, Olympia. In 1922, Tumwater Lumber Mills began to market this early form of the kit house. More than five hundred were put up around Olympia in the 1920s and 1930s. A row of five, built as demonstration models, can be seen here, from the outside only.

The White House, 1431 11th Avenue NE, Olympia. Now the Swantown Inn (see *Lodging*). With a three-story tower and many decorative flourishes, this is a monument to the optimism of the early statehood period and its builders, William and Amanda White. When first built in 1893, it stood above Swantown Slough, which was later filled in for residential expansion.

HISTORIC SITES End of the Oregon Trail, corner of Legion Way and Capitol Way, Olympia. A monument marks the end of the Oregon Trail here. There's another End of the Oregon Trail in Oregon City, Oregon, but it was all Oregon Territory until 1853, and some emigrants ignored the fertile Willamette Valley, instead bearing north. Among these were black settlers discouraged by discriminatory landholding laws Oregon had enacted in its pre–Civil War bid for statehood. These pioneers became Washingtonians.

Old Capitol Building (360-725-6000; www.k12.wa.us), 600 South Washington Street, Olympia. Open 8–5 Mon.–Fri. It's now the state school superintendent's office, but from 1901 to 1928 the Chuckanut Sandstone building was the state capitol. Brochures for self-guided tours are available at the State Capitol Visitor Center (see *Guidance*).

State Capitol Campus (360-902-8880; www.ga.wa.gov/visitor), along Capitol Way between Maple Park Drive, 11th Avenue, Jefferson Street, and Capitol Lake, Olympia. Washington Territory was run first from an attic, then a clapboard house, and then respectable sandstone offices. But statehood encouraged a leap (bitterly resisted by some) to larger, more grandiose quarters, and in 1910 ground was broken for the neoclassical complex overlooking Capitol Lake. Fifty acres of grounds designed by the Olmsted brothers of New York include a **conservatory, sunken gardens,** and several **war memorials.** A **story pole** created by the Snohomish chief William Shelton in the 1930s has unfortunately been removed due to decay. A field of five thousand bronze wheat stalks, part of the **World War II Memorial,** resounds in the wind like church bells. The **State Capitol Visitor Center** (360-902-8881), 416 Sid Snyder Avenue, Olympia, has brochures and information on these and the following sites:

The Governor's Mansion (360-902-8880). Tours Wed. Free; reservations required. This 1908 Georgian-style building predates the capitol complex. It was intended to be temporary but soldiers magnificently on.

Legislative Building (the one with the dome). Tours hourly 10–4 Mon.–Fri., 10–3 Sat.–Sun. Free. You can also tour on your own with a self-guiding brochure.

The Temple of Justice, just north of the Legislative Building (see above). Open 8–5 Mon.–Fri. Besides housing the state supreme court, this building offers a series of placards detailing the colorful history of justice in Washington, from territorial times on.

MUSEUMS *The Hands-On Children's Museum* (360-956-0818; www.hocm .org), 106 11th Avenue SW, Olympia. Open 10–5 Mon.–Sat., 12–5 Sun. $7.95 over age 2, $6.95 seniors and grandparents, $5.95 toddlers 10–23 months. free 5–9 first Fri. each month. Especially popular on rainy days, the Children's Museum makes a nice break for kids, whatever the weather. Dozens of interactive exhibits let children design a waterfront, load cargo, build, experiment with marine currents, create works of art, explore the crawl-through stomach, and more. Friendly staff help maintain a happy, orderly environment.

Lacey Museum (360-491-0857), 829½ Lacey Street SE, Lacey. Open 11–3 Thurs.–Fri., 9–5 Sat. Free. In what used to be Lacey's city hall, this museum traces the town's history from the Oregon Trail to the present through photos, furnishings, and tools.

Olympic Flight Museum (360-705-3925; www.olympicflightmuseum.com), 7637-A Old Highway 99 SE, Olympia. Open 11–5 daily in summer; 11–5 Tues.–Sun. Oct.–Dec.; 11–5 Wed.–Sun. Jan.–Apr.; closed Thanksgiving and Christmas. $7 adults, $5 children 7–12. Children can play in some of the vintage military aircraft, mostly dating from World War II. The museum also has a large collection of model planes.

Washington State Capital Museum (360-753-2580; www.wshs.org/wscm), 221 21st Avenue NW, Olympia. Open 10–4 Sat. or by appointment. $2 adults, $1.75 seniors, $1 children 6–18, $5 families. The stately 1923 Mission Revival home of banker Clarence Lord is now a branch of the Washington State History Museum in Tacoma. Ground-floor exhibits detail Olympia's settlement and rise to state capital, while the second floor is dedicated to changing art exhibits focused on the Pacific Northwest. The lush grounds include an ethnobotanical garden displaying plants traditionally used by Northwest tribes.

SCENIC DRIVES North Olympia shoreline loop, about 25 paved miles. A leisurely drive north along East Bay Road takes you past marinas to Priest Point Park; continue north on Boston Harbor Road to the end of the peninsula protecting Budd Inlet. Follow Libby Road, Woodard Bay Road, Shincke Road, South Bay Road, and Johnson Point Road to follow the shoreline along Henderson Inlet. Take 63rd Avenue NE east to Tolmie State Park, then head south on Marvin Road and west on South Bay Road to return via a pleasant rural loop route.

WALKING TOURS Tenino Sandstone (360-264-2368), Tenino. Sandstone from deposits in the Tenino area was considered particularly suitable for building from the late 1800s to the 1930s. Today the town swimming pool is located in the old sandstone quarry. A walking tour (call for a brochure) passes 15 Tenino sandstone buildings in the small town of the same name, most about a hundred years old.

✴ To Do

BICYCLING Capital Bicycling Club (360-956-3321; www.capitalbicycleclub .org), Box 642, Olympia 98507, publishes a guide to cycling in the area.

Capitol State Forest (360-577-2025 or 360-902-1600; www.dnr.wa.gov; www .capitolforest.com), 160 miles of trails plus fire roads. Of several access points, the easiest is on Waddell Creek Road; from I-5 take exit 95, about 15 miles southwest of Olympia. The forest's 90,000-plus acres of woods offer routes for mountain bikers of all skill levels. Most of these are shared with hikers, horses, or even motorcycles (see *Hiking* and *Wilder Places—Nature Preserves*). Logging also may be under way; check ahead to ensure a quiet camping experience. In winter the forest can be quite wet.

Chehalis Western Trail and **Yelm-Tenino Trail,** mostly paved but away from roads, are open to cyclists as well as foot traffic (see *Hiking*).

Thurston County's scenic country roads (see Capital Bicycling Club above) are also popular with road bikers. The nice thing about these rural routes is that there are frequent settlements where you can stop for calorie replacement:

Boston Harbor–Fish Trap Loop, 22 miles. Cycle past marinas, small hamlets, and (thoughtfully) the San Francisco Bakery.

Johnson Creek Loop, 40 miles. Ride from Millersylvania State Park through bucolic southern Thurston County, past Skookumchuck Lake and Alice's Restaurant and Winery.

Yelm and Fort Lewis Military Reservation loop, 32 miles. Take in old-growth fir stands, preserved prairies, and awe-inspiring views of Mount Rainier (note the small signs designating volcano evacuation routes).

CAMPING Capitol State Forest (360-577-2025 or 360-902-1600; www.dnr .wa.gov; www.capitolforest.com) has several access points—easiest is on Waddell Creek Road; from I-5 take exit 95, about 15 miles southwest of Olympia. Most of the seven low-tech tent campgrounds (90 campsites total) have restrooms and drinking water but no showers or electric hook-ups: **Fall Creek,** 8 sites; **Margaret McKenny,** 25 sites; **Middle Waddell,** 24 sites, no drinking water; **Mima Falls,** 5 sites; **North Creek,** 5 sites; **Porter Creek,** 16 sites; **Sherman Valley,** 7 sites.

Millersylvania State Park (360-753-1519; reservations 888-226-7688; www.parks .wa.gov), 12245 Tilley Road South, 10 miles south of Olympia. One hundred twenty tent sites and 48 RV sites, with many amenities, including a playground.

CANOEING AND KAYAKING Cascadia Marine Trail, 140 miles from Olympia to the Canadian border (where it becomes the British Columbia Marine Trail). **Washington Water Trails Association** (206-545-9161; www.wwta.org) has charts and information. The trail starts at Percival Landing in Olympia on Budd Inlet and extends north up Puget Sound. Devoted paddlers get a duck's-eye view of the island-splashed inland sea, plus possibly seals, sea lions, and orcas. Water-trail campsites—for nonmotorized boaters only—are available at many state parks and other facilities along the way; some may require reservations. Neophytes can just paddle around Budd Inlet.

GOLF Capitol City Golf Course (360-491-5111), 5225 Yelm Highway SE, Olympia. Eighteen holes. Reputed to be the best course in wet weather.

Delphi Golf Course (360-357-6437), 6340 Neylon Drive SW, Olympia. Nine holes.

The Golf Club at Hawk's Prairie (800-558-3348), 8383 Vicwood Lane, Lacey. Eighteen holes.

Tumwater Municipal Golf Course (360-943-9500; www.ci.tumwater.wa.us), 4611 Tumwater Valley Drive, Tumwater. Eighteen holes.

HIKING Capitol State Forest (360-577-2025 or 360-902-1600; www.dnr.wa.gov; www.capitolforest.com), more than 160 miles of trails, plus gravel roads. Of several access points, the easiest is on Waddell Creek Road; from I-5 take exit 95, about 15 miles southwest of Olympia. About half the paths (80 miles) are for nonmotorized use; open to horses and cyclists, too, with 6 miles for hikers only; in summer many trails are even shared with ATVs and motorcycles. Unfortunately, dumping and random target shooting have become problems in the forest. Some short hikers-only trails include these: **Cedar Creek Trail,** 2.8 miles; **McLane Creek,** 1.5 miles; **Mima Mounds,** 3.3 miles; **North Creek to Sherman Valley,** 1.6 miles.

Chehalis Western Trail, 30 miles, from Woodard Bay south to Yelm-Tenino Trail (see below). **Thurston County Parks** (360-786-5595; www.thurston-parks.org) has converted this disused railroad right-of-way to a foot and bicycle trail that meanders through quiet parks, farmland, forest, and wetlands.

Mima Mounds Preserve (360-902-1434), 2.5 miles of easy trails, 12 miles south of Olympia; from I-5 take exit 95 west through Littlerock, turn right on Waddell Creek Road, and continue 1 mile. Some are paved, winding among the mysterious mounds (see *Wilder Places—Nature Preserves*).

Nisqually National Wildlife Refuge (360-753-9467), 5.5 miles of trails; 100 Brown Farm Road, 8 miles east of Olympia; from I-5 take exit 114 and follow the signs (see *Wilder Places—Wildlife Refuges*). $3/car. A track and shorter spurs—some wheelchair-accessible—circle the refuge with views of tidal flats, wetlands, and Puget Sound.

Priest Point Park, (360-753-8380), 2600 East Bay Drive NE, Olympia. north of Olympia. Has several miles of woodland and beach trails.

Tolmie State Park (360-456-6464; www.parks.wa.gov); from I-5 take exit 111 and head north, following the signs, for about 5 miles. This park has 3 miles of wood-land and beach trails.

Yelm-Tenino Trail, 14.5 miles. **Thurston County Parks** (360-786-5595; www .thurston-parks.org) has converted this disused railroad right-of-way to a foot and bicycle trail that parallels WA 507 through the hamlet of Rainier.

See also *Wilder Places—Parks*.

UNIQUE ADVENTURES ✐ **Wolf Haven International** (800-448-9653; www .wolfhaven.org), 3111 Offut Lake Road, Tenino. Open 10–4 Mon., Wed., and Sat., 12–4 Sun. Apr.–Sept.; 10–4 Sat., 12–4 Sun. Oct.–Jan. and Mar.; closed Feb. Admission with tour only; $9 adults; $8 seniors, active military, and students; $7 children 3–12. If your kids, or you, hear the call of the wild, take an hour-long tour of this 80-acre sanctuary in rural Thurston County. Wolf Haven cares for wolves that have been too habituated to humans to be rehabilitated to the wild— "pets" whose owners couldn't cope, zoos that had no room, and a handful of wolf-dog hybrids. It is also one of three sites that works with the U.S. Fish and Wildlife Service to prepare Mexican gray wolves for release into the wild. An enthusiastic guide will introduce you to the dozen or so wolves "on tour," explaining their biol-ogy, behavior, and needs. All wolves are in large circular enclosures, mostly in (sterilized) pairs. Summer and fall bring special educational programs for children and adults.

✳ Wilder Places

NATURE PRESERVES Capitol State Forest (360-577-2025 or 360-902-1600; www.dnr.wa.gov; www.capitolforest.com); of several access points, the easiest is on Waddell Creek Road; from I-5 take exit 95, about 15 miles southwest of Olympia. Hikers, cyclists, hunters, and off-road-vehicle enthusiasts share this 91,650-acre forest with commercial logging operations. The state seems to satisfy most of the people most of the time by allocating 87 miles of trails for motorized and 80 for nonmotorized use (see *To Do—Bicycling*), with 6 miles for hikers only (see *To Do—Hiking*); most motor trails close in winter. The 420 miles of roads and 7 campgrounds with a total of 90 campsites (see *To Do—Camping*) make it a popular outdoor getaway for nearby urbanites.

Mima Mounds Natural Area Preserve (360-902-1600), 12 miles south of Olympia; from I-5 take exit 95 west through Littlerock, turn right on Waddell Creek Road, and continue 1 mile. Acres of upturned bowls 6 feet high and up to 30 feet across, covered with grasses and wildflowers—that's what the Mima Mounds look like. Theories of their origin run from patterns of frost heaving at the end of the last Ice Age to the work of busy gophers (which, however, are no longer in evidence). At this Department of Natural Resources site, 2 miles of trails and a viewing platform grace the 450-acre fragment of what was once thousands of acres of mounded prairie.

PARKS Heritage Park (360-753-8380), 330 Fifth Avenue, Olympia. Fountain plays 9–12, 1:30–5, and 6:30–9:30 daily in summer; 10–9:30 in winter. Feel free to splash in the 47-spout fountain at this waterside park just below the capitol campus.

Millersylvania State Park (360-753-1519; www.parks.wa.gov), 10 miles south of Olympia; from I-5 take exit 95. The Miller family donated their 842-acre property for park use in 1921. There are still traces of a small-gauge railroad and skid roads from 19th-century logging. With old-growth cedar and half a mile of shoreline on Deep Lake, the park offers boating, swimming, and hiking and biking trails. Camping is available year-round (see *To Do—Camping*).

Percival Landing Park (360-753-8380), Fourth Avenue and Water Street, Olympia. Just up Budd Inlet and contiguous to Heritage Park (see above), Percival Landing was the site of harbormaster Sam Percival's office from 1860 to 1877, when he handed it over to his son. A mile-long boardwalk with explanatory plaques details the history, while an observation tower at the boardwalk's north end provides panoramic harbor and mountain views. The park offers overnight mooring, restrooms, and showers.

Priest Point Park (360-753-8380), 2600 East Bay Drive NE, Olympia. Open dawn to dusk. Free. A Catholic mission on this wooded shore closed in 1860. Today 314 acres of mature forest slope to Puget Sound, offering a mile of shoreline, meandering trails along woods and water, picnic facilities, a playground, and a rose garden. Birds like it, too.

Tenino City Park (360-264-2368), 309 Park Avenue East, Tenino. Passengers bound for Olympia used to have to change trains at the depot within this park. Built of Tenino sandstone, it's now a historical museum displaying railroad and other artifacts of Tenino's past.

Tolmie State Park (360-456-6464; www.parks.wa.gov); from I-5 take exit 111 and head north, following the signs, for about 5 miles. Open 8 AM–dusk daily in spring, summer, and fall; Wed.–Sun. in winter. Tolmie offers 105 acres of old forest, salt marsh, and beach on a quiet inlet of Puget Sound. It has picnic tables and trails, and you can moor your boat (from $10 per night) or scuba dive in the park's marine area.

Tumwater Falls Park (360-943-2550), Deschutes Way and C Street, Tumwater; from I-5 take exit 104 and follow the signs. Open 8–6. The 15-acre riverside park offers picnic tables and plaques explaining the salmon cycle. Despite declining salmon populations, fall runs of chinook salmon make their primeval way up the Deschutes River. Many of them find themselves in holding tanks at Tumwater Falls, where their eggs are taken for hatchery use. October and early November are the best times to see the fish swimming upstream or using fish ladders. Stand on the footbridge over the falls and watch the salmon leap as they have done from time immemorial.

Tumwater Historical Park (360-754-4160), 777 Simmons Road SW, Tumwater; from I-5 take exit 104 and follow the signs. Open 1–4 Thurs., Fri., and Sun. Free. This setting beside a waterfall was a natural spot for early mills, homes, and industry, but Tumwater's historic district was mostly razed when the freeway came through in 1957. This 17-acre enclave was preserved. The white clapboard **Crosby House** (ca. 1860) stands at the far end of the parking lot, with the **Henderson House** (1905) at the near end. In between is a hand-built replica of a **pioneer cabin.** Most of the park is green lawn, with paths meandering to and along the Deschutes River, several interpretive plaques, and a view of the old Olympia brewery, which operated from 1906 to 1934.

Watershed Park (360-753-8380), on Henderson Boulevard near I-5, Olympia. The wells of this 153-acre park provided the city of Olympia with water for more than 50 years. Today 2 miles of trails wind through the cool rain forest of Moxlie Creek Springs Basin.

WILDLIFE REFUGES Nisqually National Wildlife Refuge (360-753-9467), 100 Brown Farm Road, 8 miles east of Olympia; from I-5 take exit 114 and follow the signs. Refuge open dawn to dusk (some trails seasonal); visitors center open 9–4 Wed.–Sun. $3 per (broadly defined) family. The Nisqually River rushes just 78 headlong miles from Nisqually Glacier on Mount Rainier to enter, suddenly, a respectable delta emptying into Puget Sound. The 3,000 protected acres of woods and wetlands around the river mouth shelter clouds of wintering waterfowl and nearly two hundred other bird species. The seascapes of salt marsh, islands, and the not-so-distant Olympic Mountains aren't bad either. There's a 5.5-mile loop trail and shorter spurs—some wheelchair-accessible. A visitors center has wildlife dioramas and a model of the Nisqually's path to the sea.

Woodard Bay Preserve (360-577-2025); drive north on East Bay Drive, which becomes Boston Harbor Road, then turn right on Woodard Bay Road and drive to the entrance. This former Weyerhaeuser log dump is now a 600-plus-acre wildlife sanctuary protecting flocks of waterfowl and shorebirds, seals, eagles, and otters, all observable from trails and viewpoints. It's also home to one of the state's largest great blue heron rookeries.

NISQUALLY NATIONAL WILDLIFE REFUGE IS ON PUGET SOUND EAST OF OLYMPIA.

✳ Lodging
BED & BREAKFASTS
Olympia
Inn at Mallard Cove (360-491-9795; www.theinnatmallardcove.com), 5025 Meridian Road NE. If you want to get away from it all, you can in this rambling Tudor-style mansion on the shores of Puget Sound. With the forest at your back and water views in front, who's to disturb you? Roam the woods and gardens or borrow a kayak. You can, of course, use your room's high-speed Internet connection if you must. $169–199.

Swantown Inn (360-753-9123 or 877-753-9123; www.swantowninn.com), 1431 11th Street SE. Now a quiet neighborhood east of the city center, Swantown was once an independent settlement on an inlet that has since been filled in. The dignified Queen Anne–Eastlake house was built by lumberman William G. White in 1887, just two years before statehood. Four guest rooms, a dining room, and a sitting room reflect period taste in furnishings without the excess so often characteristic of Victorian restorations—though one large bathroom has an antique

foot-soaking tub (especially welcome to those who overdo the sight-seeing), as well as a claw-foot tub. Owners Nathan and Casey Allan fix a three-course breakfast that includes their signature scones, fruit, and a "main course" such as French toast or pancakes; they gladly accommodate dietary differences. A free guest computer is available in the lounge; wireless Internet access is available, too. Children over 12 are welcome. $119–179.

CAMPGROUNDS
Olympia
American Heritage Campground (360-943-8778; www.olympiacampground.com), 9610 Kimmie Street SW. Open fall–spring. Ninety-five wooded campsites with and without hook-ups. This privately owned, family-oriented, 40-acre campground has a game room, convenience store, movies, wagon rides, and more. Campsites $20–30; cabins $40.

Olympic Campground (360-352-2551), 1441 83rd Avenue SW. Open year-round. American Heritage Campground's sister facility has 95 sites with hook-ups and some cabins. Reservations recommended. Campsites $19–28; cabins $40.

GUESTHOUSES

Olympia

✍ 🐾 **Puget View Cottage** (360-413-9474; www.bbonline.com/wa/puget view/), 7924 61st Avenue NE. If the weather is good, your shoreside 1930s log cabin will have views of the serrated Olympics as well as Puget Sound, with its islands, seals, and migratory waterfowl. You might want to paddle a complimentary-use kayak or walk the beach to Tolmie State Park. The one-bedroom cottage has a queen-sized bed, a living room with a foldout couch, a refrigerator, a dining area, and a deck. $150; check for discounts and weekly rates.

HOTELS

Olympia

✍ **Phoenix Inn Suites** (360-570-0555 or 877-570-0555), 415 Capitol Way North. Olympia isn't known for its hotels; they are mostly chains that cater to businesspeople or legislators. If you don't like bed & breakfasts, the Phoenix is likely your best bet, with 102 clean, standard rooms and some family suites. There is a complimentary continental breakfast. Children under 17 free. From $139; check for specials.

✳ Where to Eat
DINING OUT

Olympia

Adesso (360-705-2529; www.adesso olympia.com), 109 Legion Way SE. Open for lunch and dinner Mon.–Sat. Any restaurant offering king salmon glazed with Scotch can't be all bad. Adesso concentrates on traditional Mediterranean dishes with a gracious nod to the Northwest. Reasonable, too.

The Mark (360-754-4414; www.the markolympia.com), 407 Columbia Street SW. Open for dinner Thurs.–Sat. Chef Lisa Owen proudly serves rustic Italian cuisine made nearly entirely of organic ingredients in a small, intimate setting. The full bar is locally famous for its cocktails.

Sorrento Ristorante (360-352-9915), 430 Legion Way. Open 11:30–2:30 and 4:30 to closing Mon.–Fri.; 4:30 to closing Sat.–Sun. Cinzano umbrellas brighten Olympia's gray sidewalks in summer, when Sorrento opens up its sidewalk dining. Franco Cannava's traditional Italian menu, featuring fresh pasta, has a devoted following around town.

Trinacria Ristorante Italiano (360-352-8892), 113 Capitol Way North. Open for lunch and dinner Tues.–Sat. Sicilian food from Sicilian chef-owner Eugenio Aliotto. Trinacria has been a cozy favorite with locals and legislators since 1989. Reservations recommended.

EATING OUT

Olympia

Anthony's Homeport (360-357-9700; www.anthonys.com), 704 Columbia Street NW. Open 11:30–9:30 Mon.–Thurs., 11:30–10:30 Fri.–Sat., 10–2 and 3–9 Sun. Anthony's is a Northwest chain that chooses waterfront locations and is generally reliable for fish and seafood.

The Bread Peddler (360-325-1175; www.breadpeddler.com), 222 North Capitol Way. Open 7–6 Mon.–Fri., 7–5 Sat.–Sun. Old-world breads, made by hand from scratch, plus traditional French and American pastries. Breakfast and lunch, too.

Budd Bay Café (360-357-6963; www.buddbaycafe.com), 525 North Columbia. Open for breakfast, lunch, and dinner daily. Situated on Budd Inlet, the marine gateway to Olympia, this café specializes in, naturally, seafood, from Dungeness crabcakes to king salmon to Northwest oysters, Alaska halibut, and more. For variety, there are various cuts of steak and several vegetarian dishes on the menu. On clear days, you can dine on the deck and see the Olympic Mountains; otherwise, you can at least see the capitol. "Sunset Dinners," 4–6 Sun.–Thurs., offer a choice of three-course meals for $17. Monday nights, all bottles of wine are half price.

Fish Tale Brewpub (360-943-6480), 515 Jefferson Street East. Open 11 AM–midnight Mon.–Fri., 9 AM–midnight Sat., 9 AM–10 PM Sun. Over 21 only. Across from an actual brewery, the Fish Tale features lots of local microbrews and organic pub food in a low-key, homey setting.

Lemon Grass Restaurant (360-705-1832), 212 Fourth Avenue East. Open for lunch and dinner Mon.–Sat. This is a favorite among the several Thai restaurants in Olympia.

Ramblin' Jack's (360-754-8909; www.ramblinjacks.com), 520 Fourth Avenue East. Named for guitarist-singer Ramblin' Jack Elliott, Ramblin' Jack's tries to be all things to all people—and very nearly succeeds. Choices range from radicchio-wrapped goat cheese to a 16-ounce grilled porterhouse to fried catfish, with kids' and vegetarian choices as well. There's really no excuse for going hungry here. It can be crowded on weekends but is convivial at any time, and attentive staff keep things running smoothly.

The Spar Café (360-357-6444), 114 Fourth Avenue East. The Spar has been an Olympia fixture since 1935, and if its clientele is now fewer longshore workers than state employees, it still has the wood paneling and bar stools of its straight-talking past (which is not to cast aspersions on state employees). Its maroon-tiled storefront and J-shaped lunch counter bespeak its art moderne origins, and it actually still has a tobacco counter. Steaks, burgers, milk shakes, and other homemade luncheonette fare are served.

Wagner's European Café and Bakery (360-357-7268; wagnersbakery cafe.com), 1013 Capitol Way South; also 3000 Pacific Avenue (360-292-7497) and at the Olympia Farmers Market (see *To See—Farmers' Markets*). Just a block from the state capitol offices, this is a bustling place at breakfast and lunch. And rightly so. Homemade soups, hearty sandwiches and salads, and daily specials at bargain prices make Wagner's irresistible. And that's not even to mention the pastries of every variety, from baklava, brioche, and brownies to fruit tartlets, chocolate mousse cake . . . well, I won't go on.

✳ Entertainment

MUSIC Olympia Chamber Orchestra (360-866-7617; www.olympia chamberorchestra.org), Box 2637, Olympia 98507. The consort is dedicated to producing concerts for adults and children at accessible prices.

Olympia Symphony Orchestra (360-753-0074; www.olympiasymphony .com), 3400 Capitol Boulevard South, Olympia. The symphony plays six concerts a year at the Washington Center for the Performing Arts.

Opera Pacifica (360-458-7477; www .operapacifica.org), 10841 Aero Lane, Yelm (mailing address). Two operas are produced in communities around northwestern Washington. Its local venue is the Fox Theatre in Centralia, half an hour south of Olympia (see the Mount Rainier Area chapter in part 5, Line of Fire: The Cascades).

THEATER **Capitol Theater** (360-754-6670), 206 Fifth Avenue SE, Olympia. This is the "art cinema" in town, featuring foreign and independent films, both first-run movies and classics.

Harlequin Productions (360-786-0151), 202 Fourth Avenue East, Olympia. Here you'll see classic and experimental plays and experimental productions of classics.

✳ Selective Shopping

BOOKS **Fireside Bookstore** (360-352-4006), 116 East Legion Way, Olympia. Open daily. Step in out of the rain and browse. Literature, plus regional and children's books from the obscure to best-sellers, are all found in a couple of cozy rooms.

FOOD **Aunt Kate's Chocolates** (360-264-2884), 296 Sussex Avenue West, Tenino. Open till 7 daily. Kate Donohue's homemade truffles and creams are worth a trip down Tenino's curving main street. Her shop includes some original specialties, too (one, which I didn't try, is called Tenino Sandstone).

The Tea Lady (360-786-0350; www.tea-lady.com), 2828 Capitol Boulevard SE, Olympia. Open 10–6:30 Mon.–Fri., 10–6 Sat., 12–5 Sun. Here you'll find all things tea—pots, strainers, cups, and blends plain and fancy. In a corner of the shop, you can sit and sip some really excellent tea, unfortunately served in Styrofoam cups.

✳ Special Events

July: **Capital Lakefair** (360-943-7344; www.lakefair.org), Olympia. Mid-July.

The five-day carnival beside Capitol Lake features food concessions, arts and crafts, races, and games. Proceeds go to youth- and senior-oriented charities.

Pacific Northwest Mushroom Festival (pnwmushroomfest.com), Regional Athletic Complex, Lacey. Third weekend in July. The festival celebrates all things mushroom (well, almost all things) with food vendors, cooking lessons by local chefs, games, and activities.

Tenino Oregon Trail Days (360-264-4609), Tenino City Park, Tenino. Fourth weekend in July. Celebrate with a parade and festivities.

Thurston County Fair (360-786-5453; www.co.thurston.wa.us/fair), Thurston County Fairgrounds, Lacey. Five days of agricultural, domestic, hobby, and crafts displays are accompanied by, of course, food, music, and carnival rides.

September: **Nisqually Watershed Festival** (Nisqually River Council, 360-438-8715), Nisqually National Wildlife Refuge. Last Saturday in September. Events celebrating the natural and cultural history of the Nisqually Basin include a salmon bake, music, tribal and folk music (the nearby Nisqually Reservation administers some refuge lands), and games.

Olympia Harbor Days (360-566-0498; www.harbordays.com), Percival Landing, Olympia. First weekend in September. Vintage tugboat races as well as food and entertainment are featured on Labor Day weekend.

TACOMA AREA

In the late 1800s, Tacoma was one of those Washington towns that lived in hopes of greatness if only it could get a transcontinental railroad terminus. In Tacoma's case, this actually happened: The Northern Pacific came in 1874, tempted by a deepwater port, and Tacoma boomed. Thenceforth it modestly called itself the City of Destiny. Wharves, mills, and factories bloomed, but when the Depression came, it hit hard. Some of those factories are now pilings on Commencement Bay. Those industries that came back made the bay a ring of smoke. Tacoma declined and became something of a backwater on Puget Sound.

However—and this shows what can be done with will and spirit—within the past decade, the town has acquired a first-class museum district anchored by the Museum of Glass, a jazz scene, free local light rail, and a train to Seattle. It has also renewed its art deco theaters and generally made itself an exciting, habitable, and, not least, child-friendly town. The port is still here, sixth largest in the nation and a veritable constellation at night; you can watch comings and goings from an observation tower.

Tacoma, by the way, is how the settlers heard the word *Takhoma* or *Tacobet*—the local Indians' name for Mount Rainier. It means "source of waters." If you make a visit to what locals call simply "the Mountain," you'll pass small towns such as Puyallup and Sumner in Tacoma's hinterland. They're quickly being swallowed by suburban sprawl but often still have centers with pretty historic homes, grading into fields of daffodils, one of Pierce County's premier crops. And 5 miles west of downtown Tacoma, just before the Tacoma Narrows Bridge, is the town of University Place (though the intended university was never built). To the south are Lakewood, Steilacoom, and Fort Lewis; to the north, Federal Way. Over it all shines the mountain.

GUIDANCE Puyallup/Sumpter Chamber of Commerce (253-845-6755; www.puyallupchamber.com), 323 North Meridian, Puyallup 98371.

Tacoma Regional Convention and Visitor Bureau (253-284-3258 or 800-272-2662; www.traveltacoma.com), in Marriott Hotel, 1515 Commerce Street, Box 1754, Tacoma 98401.

GETTING THERE I-5 is the main freeway connecting Fort Lewis, Lakewood, Tacoma, and Federal Way; **I-705** is a short spur freeway north into downtown

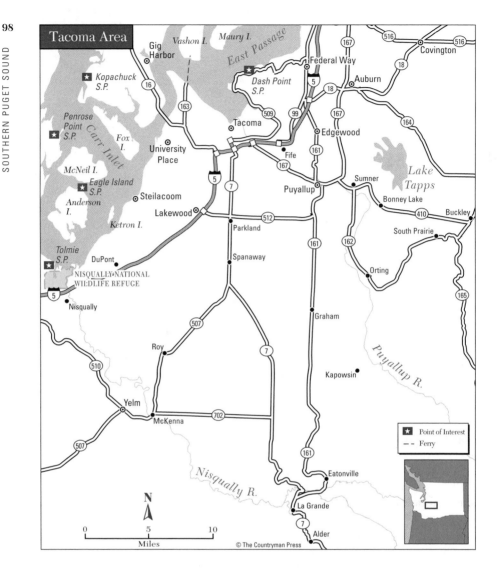

Tacoma. From I-5 at Lakewood, **WA 512** heads east to Puyallup. From I-5 just south of downtown Tacoma, **WA 16** heads north through town across the Tacoma Narrows to the Kitsap Peninsula. Other I-5 exits near downtown Tacoma include **WA 7** south through Puyallup to Elbe (gateway to Mount Rainier) and **WA 167** east to Puyallup, where it morphs into **WA 410** heading east through Buckley and Enumclaw to Mount Rainier and points east. From I-5 between Tacoma and Federal Way, **WA 161** heads south through Puyallup to Eatonville; **WA 18** heads northeast through Auburn to **I-90** near Snoqualmie; and **WA 164** heads south to connect Auburn with WA 410. It's a confusing tangle of highways, with all roads, it seems, leading to Puyallup.

Seattle-Tacoma International Airport (206-787-5388 or 800-544-1965; www .portofseattle.org) is just 25 miles north of Tacoma; from I-5 take exit 154B.

AMTRAK (253-627-8141 or 800-USA-RAIL; www.amtrakcascades.com) stops in Tacoma at 1001 Puyallup Avenue.

Greyhound (253-383-4621 or 800-231-2222; www.greyhound.com) has a station in Tacoma at 510 Puyallup Avenue.

GETTING AROUND Pierce Transit (253-581-8000 or 800-562-8109; www .piercetransit.org) runs 47 bus routes in and around Tacoma and environs, including Gig Harbor on the Kitsap Peninsula and express weekday service to Olympia.

Sound Transit (206-398-5000; www.soundtransit.org), 401 South Jackson Street, Tacoma, provides rail and bus service around Pierce, King, and Snohomish counties, including the popular Sounder, a commuter train running weekdays from the Tacoma Dome Station in Tacoma to downtown Seattle; express buses; and Tacoma Light Rail, a free 1.6-mile line running daily every 10–20 minutes from the Tacoma Dome to downtown Tacoma.

MEDICAL EMERGENCY St. Joseph's Hospital (253-426-4101), 1717 South J Street, Tacoma.

Tacoma General Hospital (253-403-1000), 315 Martin Luther King Way, Tacoma.

✳ To See

CULTURAL SITES Chihuly Bridge of Glass, connecting Pacific Avenue to the Museum of Glass (see *Museums*) across I-705, Tacoma; entrance on Pacific Avenue side is through Washington State History Museum gate (see *Museums*); from Dock Street, just walk upstairs by the Museum of Glass. Open 24 hours daily. Free. This rather astonishing 500-foot bridge displays three major Dale Chihuly works: the *Crystal Towers*, made actually of a polymer Chihuly invented when he realized glass would be too heavy; the *Venetian Wall*, 109 Venetian-inspired glass

THE MUSEUM OF GLASS, CHIHULY BRIDGE OF GLASS, AND HOT SHOP ON TACOMA'S WATERFRONT

vessels displayed in a sort of huge translucent shadow box; and the *Seaform Pavilion,* which you see from below as if you were under the seabed—1,500 pieces like shells, like seaweed, like yet undiscovered sea creatures, in all colors you can think of and then some.

DALE CHIHULY'S SEAFORM PAVILION ON THE BRIDGE OF GLASS MIMICS SEA LIFE FOUND IN PUGET SOUND.

Outdoor sculpture. From the eager commuter (or is he a new immigrant?) outside Union Station (see below) to the proud fishing couple with their salmon at 30th and Carr streets, bronze reminders of Tacoma's history and development are scattered around town. Smaller neighboring towns have picked up on the idea. Puyallup in particular has a lot of public art for a little town, with both permanent and rotating displays downtown; from I-5 take exit 135 onto WA 167 east, then go south on WA 512 and exit at Pioneer Avenue.

Union Station (253-863-5173), 1717 Pacific Avenue, Tacoma. Open 10–4 Mon.–Fri. Free. The copper-domed railway station with its swooping arches was built in 1911 during Tacoma's boom period and used till 1983. Now passengers arrive next door, and the station is yet another site of Dale Chihuly installations. Bright orange poppies have invaded the huge semicircular window; a large, complicated glass chandelier hangs over the main lobby; and another exuberant multiform sculpture stands to one side—really, it seems Dale Chihuly and Dr. Seuss had similar muses.

FARMERS' MARKETS Des Moines Waterfront Farmers' Market (www.dmfm.org), South 227th and Dock streets, Des Moines. Open 10–2 Sat. June–Oct.

Proctor Farmers' Market (253-961-3666), North 27th and Proctor streets, Tacoma. Open 9–2 Sat. late Apr.–Sept. Fresh produce is offered at the Proctor shopping district of Old Town.

Puyallup's Farmers' Market (253-840-2631), in Pioneer Park, Meridian Avenue and Second Avenue NW, Puyallup. Open 9–2 Sat. mid-Apr.–mid-Oct. and 9–2 Sun. May–Labor Day.

Tacoma Farmers' Market (253-272-7077; www.tacomafarmersmarket.com). Three locations: Sixth Avenue and North Pine Street, open 3–7 Tues. May–Sept.; Broadway and South Ninth Street, open 10:30–4 Thurs. May–Oct.; the South Tacoma Market, at South 56th and Washington streets, open 11–3 Sun. June–Sept.

T.H.E. Farmers' Market (253-884-2496), 3501 Bridgeport Way, University Place. Open 9–2 Sat. May–Oct.

FOR FAMILIES ✍ **Children's Museum of Tacoma** (253-627-6031; www .childrensmuseumoftacoma.org), 936 Broadway, Tacoma. Open 10–5 Mon.–Sat.

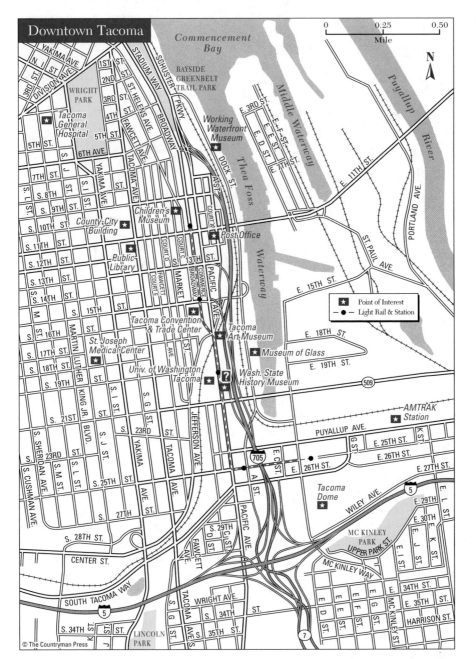

Downtown Tacoma

and 12–5 Sun. $6 over age 1; $3 weekdays 3–5. Playhouses, soapbox derby cars, and an art room allow kids to pick an amusement their own size.

✒ **Point Defiance Zoo and Aquarium** (253-591-5337; www.pdza.com), 5400 North Pearl Street, Tacoma. Open 8:30–6 daily in summer, 9:30–6 June, 9:30–5 May and Sept., 9:30–4 Oct.–Jan; closed Tues.–Wed. in winter except for Christmas break. $15.25 adults, $14.25 seniors, $11.75 children 5–12, $7.75 children 3–4.

A "RUINED TEMPLE" HABITAT AT POINT DEFIANCE ZOO AND AQUARIUM IN TACOMA

This 100-year-old zoo occupies only 29 acres but feels much bigger. Creatures from around the Pacific Rim have large, appropriate habitats: Musk oxen range a tundra of cropped grass; beluga whales disport themselves obligingly in chilly tanks; Sumatran tigers lounge beside a ruined "temple." Walk-around aquariums contrast the Puget Sound environment with that of the South Pacific. Set on a knoll above salt water, the zoo's views span the sound from the Olympic Mountains to Mount Rainier. The only disadvantage is that the rolling terrain can mean a strenuous workout for those pushing strollers or wheelchairs. See also *Wilder Places—Parks*.

GARDENS Lakewold Gardens (253-584-4106; www.lakewold.org), 12317 Gravelly Lake Drive SW, Lakewood; from I-5 take exit 124 west and follow the signs. Open 10–4 Wed.–Sun. Apr.–Sept. (10–8 Wed. Aug.); 10–3 Fri.–Sun. Oct.–Mar. $7 adults; $5 seniors, military, and students; children under 12 free. A dozen formal gardens by landscape architect Thomas Church include boxwood parterres; rose, rock, and woodland gardens; a knot garden; and more, all surrounding a Georgian Revival mansion. Naturally, in this climate, something is blooming year-round.

Point Defiance Park (253-305-1000; www.metroparkstacoma.org), 5400 North Pearl Street, Tacoma. This extensive park includes rose, dahlia, fuchsia, rhododendron, and herb gardens, as well as gardens focused on native Northwest plants and Japanese gardens.

Rhododendron Species Botanical Garden (253-924-5206), 33663 Weyerhaeuser Way South, Federal Way; from I-5 take exit 142A onto WA 18 east and follow the signs. Open 10–4 Fri.–Wed. Mar.–May; 11–4 Sat.–Wed. June–Feb. $3.50 adults, $2.50 seniors and students 12–17; free Nov.–Feb. This 22-acre garden at Weyerhaeuser headquarters is dedicated to the appreciation and cultivation of rhodies.

Weyerhaeuser Bonsai Gardens (253-924-5206), 33663 Weyerhaeuser Way South, Federal Way; from I-5 take exit 142A onto WA 18 east and follow the signs.

Open 10–4 Tues.–Sun. Free. Weyerhaeuser's 60-plant collection includes a coastal redwood that your eye can take in from top to bottom.

W. W. Seymour Botanical Conservatory (253-591-5330; www.metroparks tacoma.org), 316 South G Street, Tacoma. Open 10–4:30 Tues.–Sun. Suggested donation $5. This small but elegant 1908 conservatory in Wright Park (see *Wilder Places*) is one of only three remaining Victorian conservatories on the West Coast. Seasonal entryway displays lead into the hothouse's tropical heart; there is also a small gift shop.

HISTORIC HOMES **Job Carr Cabin** (253-627-5405), 2350 North 30th Street, Tacoma. Open 1–4 Wed.–Sat.; 12–4 Wed.–Sat. in summer; closed Jan. Free. Having judged this the most promising spot for a rail and shipping hub, Job Carr filed the first Tacoma claim near here, in 1864 (10 years after Steilacoom, down the road, was incorporated). He was right about shipping, for a while. Then the railroad decided to build its terminus at the foot of Commencement Bay, a couple of miles south of Carr's claim. Carr's settlement became "Old Tacoma" (now Old Town), and the boomtown to the south became "New Tacoma." The current cabin is a replica. Period-costumed docents will tell you the story.

Meeker Mansion (253-848-1770), 312 Spring Street, Puyallup. Open 12–4 Wed.–Sun. Mar.–mid-Dec. $4 adults, $3 students and seniors, $2 children. When Ezra Meeker, pioneer and promoter of the Oregon Trail, retired, he built himself this huge Italianate Victorian mansion. I guess after all that pioneering, he figured he deserved some comforts. It's open for tours in what is now Puyallup's historic downtown.

HISTORIC SITES **Johnson Farm Museum,** 9306 Otso Point Road, Anderson Island; via ferry ride from Steilacoom (see below). Open 12–4 Sat.–Sun. and Mon. holidays Apr.–Dec. Donation requested. This was actually an egg farm, and its appurtenances, from ram pump to chicken coops, are not unlike those described in Betty MacDonald's book *The Egg and I.*

Old City Hall, 625 West Commerce Street, Tacoma. Tacoma called itself the City of Destiny after the railroad came, and with the Old City Hall it claimed an echo of Italian Renaissance glory. The enormous 1893 brick structure with its square campanile-style tower functioned as city hall until 1959. Financial distress and water damage have left it vacant, but you can admire its faded glory from the outside. Nearby are several other noteworthy buildings, such as the **Northern Pacific Headquarters** (1888) and the **Winthrop Hotel** (1925).

Stadium High School (253-571-3100), 111 North E Street, Tacoma. Because this is an active public school, it can only be viewed from the outside. The Northern Pacific Railroad and Tacoma Land Company intended this structure to be a luxury hotel. The winning architectural bid, for a fanciful French Renaissance–style château much like the Frontenac in Quebec, came from Hewitt and Hewitt in Philadelphia. Building started enthusiastically in 1891—Tacoma was going to be the City of Destiny, after all—but the panic of 1893 brought construction to an abrupt end, as it did so many great Northwest plans. The shell stood sadly on its bluff until gutted by fire in 1898, at which point the financiers gave up. Luckily the city, seeing an opportunity to relieve its overcrowded schools, purchased, refurbished, and opened the building as a high school in September 1906. Though it's been enlarged over the years, it retains its fortresslike appearance and is on the National Register of Historic Places. You may have seen it in the movie *Ten Things I Hate About You.*

Steilacoom, on the Puget Sound shoreline 10 miles southeast of Tacoma; from I-5 take exit 129 west to Steilacoom Boulevard and follow it west to the water. This was Washington's first incorporated town (1854). The whole town is on the National Register of Historic Places. Its library and jail date from 1858, and its Protestant church from 1853. Other sites include the following:

Bair Drug and Hardware (253-588-9668), 1617 Lafayette Street. Open 9–4 Tues.–Fri., 8–4 Sat., 8–2 Sun. Opened in 1895, it is now a restaurant, the Bair Bistro, with a 1906 soda fountain.

The Nathaniel Orr Homesite, 1811 Rainier Street. Open 1–5 Sat.–Sun. Ap.–mid-June and mid-Sept.–Oct., plus 2–5 Wed. mid-June–mid-Sept. $2; includes entry to Steilacoom History Museum. This 1857 homestead stayed in the Orr family till 1974; now it displays original furnishings.

Steilacoom History Museum (253-584-4133), 1801 Rainier Avenue. Open same hours as Nathaniel Orr Homesite (above). A collection of historic photos depicts Steilacoom's birth and evolution.

Steilacoom Tribal and Cultural Center and Museum (253-584-6308), 1515 Lafayette Street. Open 10–4 Thurs.–Sat. $3 adults, $1 seniors and students, $8 families; children under five free. Learn about the Steilacoom tribe, past and present, and grab some chowder and fry bread at the café.

Tacoma Narrows Bridge, WA 16 between Tacoma and Kitsap Peninsula. The first Tacoma Narrows Bridge opened in 1940, but cost-cutting measures had created a peculiar phenomenon: The high transverse winds common in the narrows resonated with vertical vibrations, resulting in violent undulations. Even during construction, the bridge was nicknamed Galloping Gertie. One windy day the frantically waving bridge began to writhe and twist. (The event, captured on film, is enough to give you gephyrophobia.) Luckily, it was closed to traffic as it began to bounce, because it eventually broke up and fell into the narrows below. The resulting artificial reef is as big as five *Titanics* and has, somewhat ironically, been placed on the National Register of Historic Places. The current lovely bridge, opened in 1950, has been a model of respectability; a second span next to it was recently built to accommodate increased traffic.

Union Station (253-863-5173), 1717 Pacific Avenue, Tacoma. Open 8–5 Mon.–Fri. Free. This looks every bit the proud nation-building railroad terminus it was meant to be. Sober brick echoes the neighboring warehouses, while the copper-clad dome and heavy arches proclaim "Empire!" Built in 1911, it was converted to a federal courthouse in 1994 and incidentally houses some of Dale Chihuly's glass creations (see *Cultural Sites*).

University of Washington Tacoma campus (253-692-4000), Pacific Avenue between South 17th and South 24th streets, Tacoma. Tours at 3 PM Mon.–Fri.; meet at Mattress Factory Building, room 206. The UW has won recognition for its preservation of these old warehouses lining Pacific Avenue. Now there are up-to-date university classrooms and offices inside, while the street still looks like old downtown Tacoma, only better.

MUSEUMS Fort Lewis Military Museum (253-967-7206; www.lewis.army.mil), 4820 Main Street, Fort Lewis; from I-5 take exit 120 onto Fort Lewis Military Reservation. Open 12–4 Wed.–Sun. Free; nonmilitary vehicles must get a pass at main gate. Set on an active military reservation, the museum traces the history of the military in the area, from Lewis and Clark onward. Though closed for renovation at the time of this writing, it is scheduled to reopen in early 2012.

✔ **Fort Nisqually Living History Museum** (253-591-5339; www.fortnisqually .org), in Point Defiance Park, 5400 North Pearl Street, No. 11, Tacoma. Open 11–5 daily Memorial Day–Labor Day; 11–4 Wed.–Sun. Jan.–Apr. and Sept.–Dec.; 11–5 Wed.–Sun. Apr.–May. $6 adults; $5 active military or spouse, seniors, and students; $4 children 4–17; $22 families. Fort Nisqually was built for the fur trade in 1833 by the ubiquitous Hudson's Bay Company—but not here. The original fort was located 17 miles south in the rich Nisqually River delta, with easy river access for shipping supplies in and furs out. Abandoned in 1869, the structure gradually fell into ruin. In the 1930s, the state decided to preserve the two remaining buildings and move them to Point Defiance Park, where gradual restoration and reconstruction have been going on ever since. Today the old factor's house looks as if Dr. Tolmie and his family had just stepped out. Likewise, the granary, built in 1850 and one of Washington's oldest buildings, is full of sacks and barrels. The store, kitchen, smithy, and dormitories are faithfully furnished reconstructions. Extremely well-versed docents in period costume explain each facet of life at the fort in as much detail as you'd like.

Harold LeMay Car Museum (253-272-2336 or 877-902-8490; www.lemay museum.org), 325 152nd Street East, Tacoma. Open only by guided tour 10–5 Tues.–Sat. $15. Harold LeMay started by building a garbage-hauling empire, but his passion was cars. He amassed an amazing number of them—nearly three thousand. According to the *Guinness Book of World Records,* it's the biggest vehicle collection in the world. The museum expresses America's embrace of the car through lovingly maintained rare and vintage vehicles, from a 1910 flatbed truck to your great-aunt's 1958 Buick. At the moment, four hundred of the vehicles are on display; the rest are awaiting transfer to their new home in vastly expanded quarters near the Tacoma Dome, slated to open in 2012.

Karpeles Manuscript Library Museum (253-383-2575; www.rain .org/~karpeles), 407 South G Street, Tacoma. Open 10–4 Tues.–Sun. Free. Contemplatively located across from Wright Park and the Seymour Conservatory (see *Gardens*), the Karpeles is a quiet treasure. David Karpeles's encyclopedic collection of a million or so original manuscripts cover every conceivable historical topic, and a few inconceivable ones. "If my kids recognized it or its historical context, I'd buy

FORT NISQUALLY, AN EARLY PUGET SOUND SETTLEMENT, WAS LATER MOVED TO TACOMA'S POINT DEFIANCE PARK.

it," he once said, realizing that a tangible fact is worth a thousand words in the history books. Exhibits rotate among Karpeles's eight museums "dedicated to cultural literacy" nationwide. Thus a visitor may see a letter from Ben Franklin on peace negotiations, a Mendelssohn score for *A Midsummer Night's Dream,* an 18th-century map of the Northwest, or correspondence from Amelia Earhart—and see something completely different a few months later.

Museum of Glass and Hot Shop (253-284-4750 or 866-4MUSEUM; www .museumofglass.org), 1801 Dock Street, Tacoma. Open 10–5 Mon.–Sat., 12–5 Sun. in summer; 10–5 Wed.–Sat., 12–5 Sun. Labor Day–Memorial Day; 10–8 third Thurs. each month. $12 adults; $10 seniors, military, and students; $5 children 6–12; $36 families; free 5–8 third Thurs. each month. The tiered horizontal terraces of glass and concrete rising from the Tacoma waterfront beside the steel Hot Cone have quickly become iconic. Opened in 2002 under the inspiration of Tacoma's glass artist Dale Chihuly, the Museum of Glass is a striking artistic step into the 21st century. Three main galleries present changing and challenging exhibits of things you never thought glass could do, from Chihuly's vegetative tendrils to younger artists' transparent visions to the history of glass. In the conical **Hot Shop** (see *To Do—Unique Adventures*), you can watch the artists at work. The museum's **café** is quite good, and in summer you can eat on the terrace overlooking the Thea Foss Waterway.

Tacoma Art Museum (253-272-4258; www.tacomaartmuseum.org), 1701 Pacific Avenue, Tacoma. Open 10–5 Wed.–Sun.; 10–8 third Thurs. each month. $10 adults; $8 seniors, military, and students; $25 families; children under five free; free 5–8 PM third Thurs. each month. The Tacoma Art Museum emerged into this glass and steel space from a vastly smaller cocoon as another anchor of Tacoma's new art district and essentially a new museum. *Leroy,* a 10-foot-tall cardboard dog by artist Scott Fife, presides in the lobby. Built around a parabolic courtyard of ancient Chinese paving stones scattered with Chihuly glass spheres, the galleries focus mainly on modern and Northwest art. Upstairs, O pioneers, you can create your own works in the **Open Art Studio.** The **"Untitled"** café is open for lunch.

THE VENETIAN WALL IN TACOMA'S BRIDGE OF GLASS

✒ **Washington State History Museum** (253-272-9747 or 888-238-4373; www.washingtonhistory.org), 1911 Pacific Avenue, Tacoma. Open 10–5 Wed.–Sun. (10–8 Thurs.). $8 adults, $7 seniors, $6 military and students; children five and under free; free 5–8 PM Thurs. The intent of this museum is to provide a walk through the state's history as ordinary people experienced it. The Great Hall, which occupies an entire floor, takes you from Washington's geological origins up to today through its Native history, lumber camps, coal mines, farms, and labor struggles. Lots of the exhibits are interactive: You can quiz the plaster characters in a Walla Walla general store or eavesdrop on conversations between a Salish girl and her grandmother (or, more annoyingly, on a hectoring speech by territorial governor Isaac Stevens to the Indians). You can also delve into many aspects of local history via computers. Ezra Meeker's taxidermied oxen Dave and Dandy, a Tacoma fixture for decades, can be visited upstairs in the History Lab. Also upstairs is the new 25-foot-by-95-foot model of the Southern Puget Sound's railroad system circa 1950.

Note: On Wednesdays, a single ticket will get you into the above three museums: $22 adults, $20 seniors and military, $18 students and children.

Working Waterfront Maritime Museum (253-272-2750; www.fosswaterway seaport.org), 705 Dock Street, Tacoma. Open 10–5 Mon.–Fri., 12–4 Sat.–Sun. (12–5 during daylight saving time). $7 adults; $4 seniors, military, and children; $15 families. Tacoma remains firmly anchored in its commercial and seafaring heritage: The Port of Tacoma handles almost as much cargo as does the Port of Seattle. This museum records the town's working history through photos, artifacts, boats, and boatbuilding. And it does so where that history took place: on the Thea Foss Waterway in a wheat warehouse built in 1900. A 2007 expansion has allowed for larger exhibits and docking for tour boats and tall ships.

NATURAL WONDERS The Tacoma Narrows, Puget Sound between the city's west side and the Kitsap Peninsula; from I-5 west of downtown Tacoma, take WA 16 west to the bridge. Site of the 1940s Tacoma Narrows Bridge disaster (see *Historic Sites*), the narrows funnel not only the wind but also the tides. At tidal changes, water rushes through the constricted passage at an average of 3.5 miles per hour, or the pace of a brisk walker. Feasibility studies are being conducted here for one of the first experiments nationally in harnessing the tides for energy production.

SCENIC DRIVES Five Mile Drive, Point Defiance Park (253-305-1000; www .metroparkstacoma.org), 5400 North Pearl Street, Tacoma. Winding through tall Douglas firs and providing peekaboo views across Puget Sound of Vashon Island, the Cascades, and the Olympics, this bucolic road around Point Defiance is just minutes from the city.

✳ To Do

BICYCLING Foothills Trail (253-841-2570), 15 miles from Buckley to Puyallup. This trail runs through miles of farmland near Puyallup (see also *Hiking*). It will eventually be extended and connected to a trail network covering Pierce County.

Ruston Way, 2 miles along Commencement Bay waterfront, Tacoma; from I-5 take exit 133 and follow I-705, then Schuster Parkway north. This path shared with walkers and joggers connects several waterfront parks on the shoreline below Old Town. Past waterfront restaurants, past the fire station and retired fireboat, past old pilings that used to support mills or docks, past sculptures and sundials, you cycle toward the shining Olympic Mountains. It's not uncommon to see bald eagles overhead. Naturally, this is a favorite urban exercise corridor. A planned extension will reach to Point Defiance Park.

CAMPING **Dash Point State Park** (800-CAMPOUT; www.parks.wa.gov), on WA 509 across Commencement Bay from Tacoma and around Browns and Dash points; from I-5 near Tacoma take exit 134 north to WA 509 west and north 8 miles. Open year-round. One hundred fourteen tent sites and 27 RV sites in two campgrounds.

CANOEING AND KAYAKING **Commencement Bay.** The sheltered waters of Tacoma's large bay draw paddlers, who can put in at the marina in **Point Defiance Park,** 5400 North Pearl Street, and along **Ruston Way** (see *Bicycling*). Nearer town, watch out for larger craft headed for Tacoma's docks—mostly they pass east of Vashon Island.

Don's Ruston Market and Deli (253-759-8151), 5102 North Winnifred Street, Ruston. This place, just north of downtown Tacoma, rents kayaks.

DIVING **Bandito Charters** (253-973-0370; www.banditocharters.com), Box 9456, Tacoma 98409. This outfitter will take you to dive sites around southern Puget Sound, including the narrows and Point Defiance.

Lighthouse Diving Center (253-627-7617; www.lighthousediving.com), 2502 Pacific Avenue, Tacoma. This dive shop also offers classes and organizes diving trips.

Ruston Way; from I-5 take exit 133 and follow I-705, then Schuster Parkway north. At any time of year, this area may reveal wetsuit-clad marine mammals equipped with tanks or snorkels. Divers can just walk into the water here. For such cold waters, Puget Sound has abundant and various marine life, from anemones to wolf eels, with nudibranchs and giant octopuses in between.

Titlow Beach, on the narrows, Tacoma; from I-5 take WA 16 west, exit onto 19th Street, and continue west. Divers can just walk into the water here, but consult a tide table and beware of strong currents, especially at the narrows.

CANOEING HAS LONG BEEN A MEANS OF TRANSPORTATION AROUND PUGET SOUND, AS THIS DUGOUT CANOE AT FORT NISQUALLY ATTESTS.

FISHING Carbon River, from Mount Rainier down to Puyallup. Fish in this river are said to reach 20–30 pounds.

Tacoma Narrows (see *To See—Natural Wonders*). During the fall runs, thousands of migrating salmon squeeze through the narrows, and fishermen line **Titlow Beach** (see *Diving*) trying to snag one.

GOLF Chambers Bay Golf Course (253-460-4653 or 877-295-4657; www .chambersbaygolf.com), 6320 Grandview Drive West, University Place; from I-5 take WA 16 west. A 250-acre, 18-hole course on the site of an old gravel pit, designed in the Scottish style by Robert Trent Jones II. Walking only. **Eagles Pride Golf Course** (253-967-6522), Mounts Road, Fort Lewis; from I-5 take exit 116. Twenty-seven holes (18 in winter).

Lake Spanaway Golf Course (253-531-3660; www.lakespanawaygc.com), 15602 Pacific Avenue South, Tacoma. Eighteen holes.

Meadow Park Golf Course (253-473-3033; www.metroparkstacoma.org), 7108 Lakewood Drive West, Tacoma. Run by Tacoma's city parks department, this tree-lined course has twenty-seven holes.

North Shore Golf Course (253-927-1375), 4101 Northshore Boulevard NE, Tacoma. Eighteen holes.

Pacific Lutheran University Golf Course (253-535-7393), 754 124th Street South, Tacoma. Nine holes.

HIKING Dash Point State Park (800-CAMPOUT; www.parks.wa.gov), on WA 509 across Commencement Bay just northeast of Tacoma (see *Camping*); 11 miles of trails. The park's paths wind along forests and shoreline.

Foothills Trail (253-841-2570), 15 miles from Buckley to Puyallup. This rail-to-trails corridor near Puyallup currently runs through farmland and along the rushing Carbon River. Extensions will connect the trail to a network running from Mount Rainier to Commencement Bay.

Point Defiance Park (253-305-1000; www.metroparkstacoma.org), 5400 North Pearl Street, Tacoma; 14 miles of trails. Walk through old growth and along beaches; especially enjoyable when Five Mile Drive (see *To See—Scenic Drives*) through the park is closed to traffic: till 1 PM Sat.

Ruston Way, 2 paved miles along Tacoma's waterfront below Old Town; from I-5 take exit 133 and follow I-705, then Schuster Parkway north. It can get crowded with both foot and bike traffic, but the views are spectacular.

Spanaway Lake Park (253-531-0555), 14905 Gus G. Breseman Road South, Spanaway; off WA 7 south of Lakewood; 3 miles of trails. Gentle forested and wetland trails wind through this park.

UNIQUE ADVENTURES Hot Shop (253-284-4750 or 866-4MUSEUM; www .museumofglass.org), 1801 Dock Street, Tacoma. Open 10–5 Mon.–Sat., 12–5 Sun. in summer; 10–5 Wed.–Sat., 12–5 Sun. Labor Day–Memorial Day; 10–8 third Thurs. each month. $12 adults; $10 seniors, military, and students; $5 children 6–12; $36 families; free 5–8 third Thurs. each month. The 90-foot-tall brushed stainless steel cone set at a 17-degree angle next to the Museum of Glass (see *To See—Museums*) is actually a chimney for the Hot Shop's glass furnace. The cone's

VISITORS CAN WATCH ARTISTS BLOWING GLASS AT THE MUSEUM OF GLASS HOT SHOP IN TACOMA.

shape is intended to remind us of the sawmill wood burners that were ubiquitous here until recently, and incidentally (or not) it echoes the view of the WA 509 bridge and Mount Rainier, visible in repeating cones from the museum's rooftop terrace. But it's the amphitheater inside that provides the unique experience of observing the firing, blowing, and shaping of glass pieces accompanied by expert commentary. The theater seats 180, but there is also a ramp for viewing the process from above and some glass installations on display.

Tacoma Dragon Boat Association (253-588-5174; www.tacomadragonboat.org), 1118 East D Street, Tacoma. Paddling practice sessions 3 PM Sun., 5:30 PM Mon. and Wed., 8 AM Sat.; must be over 18 years old. Free; all equipment provided. If you've ever wanted to paddle a dragon boat, here's your chance. The competitive organization takes out interested visitors on their practice paddles. Meet at **Johnny's Dock Restaurant and Marina,** 1900 East D Street, Tacoma. The association also sponsors dragon boat races, a Chinese tradition, and various other fun things you can do with such craft.

✳ Wilder Places

PARKS Dash Point State Park (253-661-4955; www.parks.wa.gov), Dash Point Road, Federal Way; from I-5 east of Tacoma, take WA 509 east and follow it about 8 miles. The park has more than a half mile of Puget Sound shoreline along Commencement Bay for strolling, kayaking, or canoeing, with abundant shorebirds, 11 miles of hiking and biking trails (see *To Do—Hiking*), and a campground (see *To Do—Camping*).

Point Defiance Park (253-305-1000; www.metroparkstacoma.org), 5400 North Pearl Street, Tacoma. Open sunrise to one-half hour past sunset. With 702 acres, the point has had something for everyone since its inception in 1905. Beaches, a marina, and 14 miles of hiking trails (see *To Do—Hiking*) offer up the Northwest in a nutshell. Five Mile Drive (see *To See—Scenic Drives*) is closed to cars Saturday mornings for joggers and cyclists; Japanese, herb, native Northwest, and other gardens gladden the eye; a go-cart and miniature golf park are tucked into one corner; and picnic opportunities and panoramic Puget Sound views abound. Here, too, are Point Defiance Zoo and Aquarium (see *To See—For Families*) and Fort Nisqually (see *To See—Museums*).

Rogers Park (253-305-1041), 3300 East L Street, Tacoma. This is the city's first off-leash dog park.

Spanaway Lake Park (253-531-0555), 14905 Gus S. Breseman Road South, Spanaway. Offers boating, swimming, picnicking, hiking, and a playground.

Tacoma Nature Center (253-591-6439; www.metroparkstacoma.org), 1919 South Taylor Street, Tacoma. Grounds open 8 AM–dusk; visitors center open 8–5 Tues.–Fri., 10–4 Sat. Fifty-four acres, 3 miles of wooded trails, and an educational center make this urban park popular with schools and families.

Wright Park (253-305-1054; www.metroparkstacoma.org), 501 South I Street, Tacoma. This 27-acre city park is graced by 350 varieties of trees, including a giant sequoia planted to commemorate the 150th anniversary of the adoption of the U.S. Constitution. Donated to the city in 1886 by Charles Wright, president of the Tacoma Land Company, the park offers ponds, sculpture, free Wi-Fi, and a playground.

✳ Lodging

BED & BREAKFASTS

Tacoma
Chinaberry Hill Bed and Breakfast (253-272-1282; www.chinaberryhill .com), 302 Tacoma Avenue North. Lucius Manning, builder of Chinaberry Hill in 1889, was an investor instrumental in getting Tacoma the Northern Pacific terminus and thus facilitating the port city's trade with China. The gift of an antique Chinese fan still hangs in his mansion as a quiet reminder. Many other things hang in the mansion. Owners Cecil and Yarrow Wayman are eclectic collectors, so the decor is an unexpected Victorian-Pacific, rustic-modern concerto. Three suites in the house have bay or garden views and private baths, while two suites in the separate Carriage House sleep six. Common areas include a stocked guest kitchen, living room, parlor, and veranda; two dining rooms with fireplaces; and the garden where Manning's mature trees and century-old rhododendrons provide a shady retreat just north of downtown. Cecil is the breakfast cook, and if you are lucky, he may sing you a song written in honor of his blueberry pancakes. Children are welcome in the Carriage House. Suites $139–245; entire Carriage House $325.

DeVoe Mansion (253-539-3991; www.devoemansion.com), 208 East 133rd Street; just southeast of Parkland. In 1910 Emma DeVoe was influential in the women's suffrage movement. She and her husband, Henry, bought this farmhouse and set about enlarging it so she could host meetings and discussion groups. One wonders if she didn't overdo it—all 5,600 square feet of it—a bit. The extremely elegant Neo-Colonial home comes complete with tall columns, parklike grounds, spacious rooms, and lots of common areas. Current owners Cheryl and Dave Teifke have furnished it with appropriate sumptuousness, from the 1860s rosewood piano down to the silver tea service. The common areas and four large, bright guest rooms are decorated with period antiques. Of course, it's on the National Register of Historic Places. Children over 12 are welcome. No pets. $115–149.

Geiger Victorian Bed and Breakfast (253-383-3504; www.geiger victorian.com), 912 North I Street. On a street of opulent old Victorians north of downtown, the 1889 Geiger is distinguished by its more sober Eastlake style and its red and green trim. Indoors, the theme continues with a lustrous three-story balustrade, Eastlake queen beds, silk-screened Victorian wallpaper, and period decor—the Virginia Mason Suite even has hand-painted allegories on the ceiling, plus a fireplace. Since 1889, its expansive view of Commencement Bay has been cut off by an apartment block, but you can still enjoy the veranda and lush garden. All three guest rooms have antique furniture and private baths. Children over 12 welcome. No pets. $129–179.

Green Cape Cod Bed and Breakfast (253-752-1977 or 866-752-1977; www.greencapecod.com), 2711 North Warner. This cozy 1929 Cape Cod with its deep porch could be anyone's house, but it's Mary Beth King's, and she will take care of you. One guest room on the ground floor and two under the eaves offer pillow-top beds, down comforters, either en suite or adjacent private bathrooms, and elegant but unfussy furniture. Plus, you get Mary Beth's homemade breakfast, a quiet Proctor District neighborhood, and warm hospitality. Children over 12 welcome. No pets. $135–165.

Plum Duff House (253-627-6916 or 888-627-1920; www.plumduff.com), 619 North K Street. This Foursquare house has stood calmly on K Street since 1901. It's in a North Tacoma neighborhood of similarly dignified homes, and its archways, gardens, and fireplaces make for a comfortable retreat. Three bedrooms and a four-person suite all have private baths and a blend of antique and contemporary furnishings. Please consult about bringing children. No pets. $90–180; ask about special rates.

Villa Bed and Breakfast (253-572-1157; www.villabb.com), 705 North Fifth Street. When Mr. McCormack, owner of the Mason Department Store, built his mansion just north of downtown in 1925, his neighbors likely thought, "There goes the neighborhood." Victorian and Colonial were passé by then; he would have an Italian villa. The tile roof and white stucco still stand out, and mathematical Italian-style gardens surround a hopeful palm tree out front. The interior design follows suit, with tile floors and several private verandas. McCormack built a modest 12,000-square-foot home, so each of the five guest rooms has its bathroom, and common areas include a living room, sunroom, salon, loggia, dining room, office, and exercise room. New owners Kristy and Aaron House took over enthusiastically in 2005, and Kristy's breakfasts have already earned a reputation. No children or pets. $150–250.

HOTELS

Tacoma

Courtyard by Marriott (253-591-9100; www.courtyard.com), 1515 Commerce Street. Through the long years of its eclipse, Tacoma has been short of hotels, leaving the field to a nice crop of bed & breakfasts. In the last few years, however, Marriott made a splashy downtown entrance, with 162 rooms, a pool, a fitness center, and lots of meeting space. No pets. $169–249.

Hotel Murano Tacoma (877-986-8083; www.hotelmuranotacoma.com), 1320 Broadway Plaza. $149–359. This new luxury hotel in downtown Tacoma seems geared more to the business than the pleasure traveler—it enjoys no less than seven meeting and event rooms. But it's also practically an art gallery in itself, with commissioned works everywhere you look (especially glasswork, this being Tacoma); pillow, "spiritual," and iPod menus (does my iPod get room service, too?); a salon, spa, and fitness room; and views of Puget Sound. Pets allowed in some rooms. $149–359; oddly, Wi-Fi costs extra.

Silver Cloud Inn (253-272-1300 or 866-820-8448; www.silvercloud.com), 2317 North Ruston Way. All 90 rooms at the Silver Cloud have water views, because the Silver Cloud is built on pilings over Commencement Bay near Old Town. (Though the ads say you can fish from your room, they really would prefer that you fish from the adjacent pier.) Silver Cloud is a regional 11-hotel chain with reliable upscale motel-style accommodations ranging from rooms with one king or two queen beds to suites with a Jacuzzi and/or fireplace. Amenities include complimentary guest laundry, a boat dock, and complimentary continental breakfast. $159–289.

✳ Where to Eat
DINING OUT

Tacoma
Europa Bistro (253-761-5660; www.europabistro.net), 2515 North Proctor. Open 11–2 Mon.–Sat., 4–10 Sun.–Thurs., 4–10:30 Fri.–Sat. The Europa is part of the Proctor District minirenaissance. It gets rave reviews for its Italian cuisine, intimate atmosphere, and chef Alfredo, who greets guests when he isn't in the kitchen concocting classic Italian dishes (*pollo saltimbocca, capellini puttanesca*) with Northwest touches (*salmone alla griglia*). And reasonable withal.

The Lobster Shop (253-759-2165; www.lobstershop.com), 4013 Ruston Way. Open for lunch Mon.–Sat, dinner daily, and brunch 9:30–1:30 Sun. The

Old Town location would almost be enough, right on the clear waters of Commencement Bay with views of the port in one direction and Vashon Island in the other. But the menu matches it, point for point. Chef Jim Belisle allows the Northwest's bounty of fresh seafood to speak for itself through simple and elegant preparation. Grilled Alaska wild salmon and garlic mashed potatoes speak volumes, and the seared ahi tuna with wasabi sounds pretty good, too. There are equally fine pasta, steak, and poultry options for the non-seafood-eating public, and the "Twilight Menu" is a good deal at $16.99 for a three-course meal or $14.99 for two courses, ordered before 5:45. There's another location at Dash Point, 6912 Sound-view Drive NE (253-927-1513), open for dinner daily and breakfast 9–1 Sun. Reservations recommended.

Primo Grill (253-383-7000; www .primogrilltacoma.com), 601 South Pine Street, Suite 102. Open for lunch 11–3 Mon.–Fri.; dinner 4–10 Mon.–Thurs., 4–11 Fri., 5–11 Sat., 4:30–9 Sun. Chef-owner Charlie McManus is Irish but, strangely, prefers Italian cuisine. Not so much your cheese-and-tomato-sauce Italian cuisine, though he does make pizza in the wood-fired oven, but dishes such as ravioli stuffed with artichokes and mascarpone in shallot broth, or saffron risotto with scallops and prawns (just so you remember you are in the maritime Northwest). Charlie presides over the copper-countered open kitchen, while his wife and co-owner, Jacqueline Plattner, makes sure the guests are happy. The servers are exceedingly friendly and knowledgeable, the wines are heavenly, and the food is paradisiac. The mostly local clientele thinks so, too: The triangular space with its brightly painted tables is full and lively well before 6 PM.

SOUTHERN PUGET SOUND

Puyallup

HG Bistro (253-845-5747; www.hg bistro.com), 1618 East Main Avenue. Open for lunch 11:30–2:30 Mon.–Fri., dinner from 5 PM daily, and brunch 9–2:30 Sat.–Sun.; happy hour 2:30–6 daily and all day Sun. Also known as the Hungry Goose. Creative cooking, a sort of Northwest-Asian fusion, surprises travelers who manage to find their way to downtown Puyallup, sandwiched between suburban sprawl and subvolcanic farmland. Live music most weekends, too.

Mama Stortini's Ristorante and Catering (253-845-7569; www .mamastortinis.com), 3207 East Main Avenue. Open for lunch 11–4 daily; dinner 4–9:30 Mon.–Thurs., 4–10:30 Fri.–Sat., 4–9 Sun. Here you'll find homemade pasta and pizza, plus sandwiches, fish-and-chips, and salads.

Toscano's (253-864-8600; www .toscanospuyallup.com), 437 29th Street NE. Open 11:30–9:30 Mon.– Thurs., 11:30–10 Fri., 3–10 Sat., 3–9:30 Sun. Reservations recommended Friday and Saturday. Seafood, soups, salads, and pasta, with a Tuscan flavor. You can get gluten-free pasta, too.

Tacoma

Anthony's Restaurant (253-752-9700; www.anthonys.com), 5910 North Waterfront Drive. Open for lunch and dinner Mon.–Sat., 10–9:30 Sun. Drive or boat up to Anthony's; it sits on the water, literally, just below the Point Defiance Zoo. Anthony's is a chain of a dozen or so casual waterfront restaurants specializing in seafood. They're big and can get crowded, but they are very reliable for seafood, and the location is pretty hard to beat. Another location, Harbor Lights (253-752-8600), is at 2761 Ruston Way.

✐ Antique Sandwich Company (253-752-4069), 5102 North Pearl Street. Just south of Point Defiance Park, in Tacoma's ungentrified north end, stands the Antique Sandwich Company. Its marquee (for it was once a movie theater) might read OPEN MIC TUES., SUNDAY CLASSICAL MUSIC AT 3, POETS FOR PEACE, or DEMOCRACYNOW .ORG. Since 1973 it's been a coffeehouse with a point of view. Inside, people of all ages linger over hot drinks or eat lunch at venerable wooden tables while toddlers remain remarkably mellow at the play area on the podium. Large aviform kites, kimonos, and other varied products of the café's fairtrade affiliate adorn the walls. Order soup, a sandwich, or a pastry from the chalkboard menu and settle in.

Café Divino (253-779-4226), 2112 North 30th Street. Open 11–10 Mon.–Thurs., 11:30–11 Fri., noon–11 Sat. Across from the Spar in Old Town, Café Divino is a microcosm of New York serving hot pastrami sandwiches, gyros, sausage lasagna, and other comfort foods.

Harbor Lights Restaurant (253-752-8600), 2761 Ruston Way. Harbor Lights opened in 1959 amid lumberyards along a very different waterfront. Anthony's bought it in 2000, and it's now smoke-free, like all other Washington restaurants, but still serves gargantuan portions of steaks and seafood.

Katie Downs Tavern and Eatery (253-756-0771), 3211 Ruston Way. Open 11–11 Sun.–Thurs., 11 AM–midnight Fri.–Sat. Before Ruston Way was a park, before the elegant eateries came, there was Katie Downs. Founded in 1982, its turret rises proudly over the water like a castle's; you even enter over a bridge. This is where you go if you feel like having a decent pizza and beer while watching the game on plasma TV, though you can also get burgers, steak, soups, and similar tavern dishes. The waterfront location doesn't hurt either. For those over 21 only.

The Old House Café (253-759-7336; www.theoldhousecafe.com), 2717 North Proctor Street. Open for lunch 11:30–3 Tues.–Sat.; dinner 5–8 Wed.–Thurs., 5–9 Fri.–Sat.; brunch 10:30–2 Sun. With six scallop dishes, four prawn dishes, and two oyster dishes on the menu here, you know where you are. Meat, chicken, and salad dishes are also served in this restored 1907 tea broker's home—and you can get your order to go, too. Reservations recommended.

A Renaissance Café (253-572-1029), 1746 Pacific Avenue. Open for breakfast and lunch daily. Just across from Union Station and handy to the Tacoma branch of the University of Washington, the Renaissance serves breakfast all day as well as Italian sodas, coffee, sandwiches, and barbecue—all at student prices.

The Spar Tavern (253-627-8215; www.the-spar.com), 2121 North 30th Street. Open 11–10 Mon.–Wed., 11 AM–midnight Thurs.–Fri., 9 AM–midnight Sat.–Sun. The Spar bills itself as the oldest saloon in Tacoma. Although the Old Tacoma Saloon was dismantled in 1916, the Spar opened on the same corner site in the 1920s as a soda fountain, restaurant, and (after Prohibition) tavern. And so, more or less, it remains. Historic photos of Old Town hang on the walls, and cheerful diners pack the tables. Good food at reasonable prices is the motto, and in fact the soups, salads, and sandwiches go for a dollar or two less than the local average. Everything's available for take-out for "two bits" additional charge. Live blues on Sunday night. Arrive early for a weekend breakfast; the place fills up fast.

✳ Entertainment

NIGHTLIFE Jazzbones (253-396-9169; www.jazzbones.com), 2803 Sixth Avenue, Tacoma. From 5 PM Sun.–Fri.,

from 6 PM Sat. This is one of Tacoma's new jazz bars, with live music nightly by local and national bands—and dinner, too.

THEATER The Blue Mouse Theatre (253-752-9500; www.bluemouse theatre.com), 2611 North Proctor Street, Tacoma. They've been showing movies here since 1923. Now they show only one movie at a time, but it's probably something you actually want to see, and the marble terrazzo, decorated columns, and Tiffany-style glass sure beat the multiplexes. And that neon mouse running across the marquee? Yep—another of Dale Chihuly's creations. Adults $4–5; all seats $3 every Mon.

Broadway Center for the Performing Arts (253-591-5890; www.broadwaycenter.org), 901 Broadway, Tacoma. The center comprises three theaters that constitute Tacoma's reborn Theater District:

Pantages Theater (253-591-5890), 901 Broadway, Tacoma. Hosts the Tacoma Opera, Tacoma Symphony, City Ballet, and Tacoma Philharmonic. Dating from Tacoma's glory days, it was beautifully restored in the 1980s.

The Rialto (253-591-5894), 310 South Ninth Street, Tacoma. Hosts smaller musical companies such as the Northwest Sinfonietta and the Puget Sound Revels. Also restored in the 1980s.

Theater on the Square (253-591-5890), 915 Broadway, Tacoma. This modern structure is home to the Tacoma Actors Guild.

✳ Selective Shopping

GIFTS AND MORE Freighthouse Square (253-305-0678; www.freight housesquare.com), 430 East 25th Street, Tacoma. Open 10–7 Mon.–Sat., 12–5 Sun. When Tacoma was for a time the terminus for the major northwestern railway lines, this long, green, wooden building beside the tracks held freight for the Milwaukee Railroad. Still green, its several floors have been refurbished to house a large antiques mall, gift and jewelry shops, an art gallery, and more. The hungry will find an international food court (who would have thought of Thai fish-and-chips?) and several small restaurants—not to mention Peggy's Cinnamon Rolls.

The Harp and Shamrock (253-752-5012), 2704 North Proctor Street, Tacoma. Open 10–6 Mon.–Fri., 9–5 Sat. Browse for Irish sweaters, Irish oatmeal, Irish tea, and even instruction books for the Irish tin whistle.

The Pacific Northwest Shop (253-752-2242 or 800-942-3523; www.pacificnorthwestshop.com), 2702 North Proctor Street, Tacoma. Open 10–6 Mon.–Sat., 11–5 Sun. Here you'll find everything Northwest, from local products such as aplets, cotlets, and almond roca to Native American art to wines.

✳ Special Events

April: **Daffodil Festival** (253-840-4194; www.daffodilfestival.net), Tacoma. Floral parades from Tacoma wend up the bulb-producing Puyallup Valley; also a daffodil regatta in the bay.

Puyallup Spring Fair, third weekend in April. $8 adults, $6 children; free parking. This shorter version of the Puyallup Fair (see below) includes a garden show and a science fair.

June: **Meeker Days Festival** (253-848-1770; www.puyallupmainstreet.com), Puyallup. This street fair in honor of pioneer Ezra Meeker has music, crafts, classic cars, and children's games.

July: **Fourth of July,** Tacoma. Fireworks over Commencement Bay conclude the celebration.

Taste of Tacoma (425-295-3262; www.tasteoftacoma.com), Point Defiance Park, 5400 North Pearl Street, Tacoma. No admission fee; all food items under $7. "The ultimate family picnic" celebrates local and exotic flavors with food booths. Pierce Transit (253-581-8080) runs a free shuttle bus.

August/September: **Commencement Bay Maritime Fest** (253-318-2210; www.maritimefest.org), Thea Foss Waterway, Tacoma. Most events free. In the heart of Tacoma's busy waterfront, the Maritime Fest features a boatbuilding contest, dragon boat races, boat tours of the container port, and the chance to ride vessels such as a Coast Guard cutter or Bantry Bay rowing gig. Fireworks and a salmon bake round out the celebration of Tacoma's maritime heritage.

Puyallup Fair (888-559-3247; www.thefair.com), Puyallup Fairgrounds, 110 Ninth Avenue SW, Puyallup. Open 10–10 Sun.–Thurs., 10 AM–11 PM Sat.–Sun. for 17 days in mid-Sept. $9–11 adults, $7.50–9 seniors and children; rides and concerts extra; parking $5–20. (Pierce Transit's "fair express" bus from Tacoma [253-581-8080] may be a better bet.) Held nearly continuously since 1900, it's the biggest agricultural fair in Washington and the sixth biggest in the United States, with about 1.5 million visitors a year. Livestock, produce, arts and crafts, a rodeo, food vendors, carnival rides—it's all here, plus some big-name entertainers such as Willie Nelson and Kenny Rogers.

October: **Apple Squeeze** (253-584-4133), downtown Steilacoom. First Sunday in October. Free. Festivities include 20 cider presses, apple products for sale, and music by local and regional groups.

KITSAP PENINSULA AND BAINBRIDGE ISLAND

The Tacoma Narrows Bridge runs like a gossamer web from Tacoma over the churning narrows to Gig Harbor on the Kitsap Peninsula. But it was not ever thus. The Kitsap Peninsula, largely isolated from the outside world by Puget Sound and its dissecting bays and inlets, remained practically pioneer territory well into the 1900s. Trips to the mainland, or indeed to different parts of the peninsula, were possible only on the web of Mosquito Fleet ferries.

Today you can catch the ferry from Seattle to Bremerton, then drive or take the bus across the Kitsap Peninsula to the Hood Canal Bridge and be in the Olympic Mountains all within a couple of hours. That's what many do. The modest Kitsap Peninsula, low-lying and often rain-lashed, tends to be overlooked as a mere way station to its larger cousin to the west. Which is not a bad thing. The Kitsap, with more than 300 miles of saltwater shoreline and large tracts of forest, remains largely rural. Just about every part of this fertile peninsula has its regular farmers' market. Its "big town" is Bremerton, and its small ones hug the coast because for many years there were no interior roads. Early settlers here were Finns and Serbs, especially in Gig Harbor, and Norwegians to the north; Poulsbo, now several generations removed, still celebrates its Norwegian heritage.

A naval station since 1901, when numerous installations were created to protect this fluid corner of the country, Bremerton became a major shipyard during World War II and is now a U.S. Navy home port. With a submarine base at Bangor on Hood Canal, this makes the military a large employer on the peninsula. Tourism is growing, though, as people are realizing that the water and mountain views are as spectacular here as anywhere on Puget Sound; farms convert to B&Bs, while rustic resorts hidden along Hood Canal continue to draw longtime patrons.

Though Bainbridge Island, between the Kitsap Peninsula and the mainland at Seattle, is now practically a suburb of Seattle, with commuters and weekend vacationers, I include it in this chapter because it's functionally and geographically part of the Kitsap, connected by a bridge over the narrow channel of Agate Passage. The island is also a frequent route onto both the Kitsap and Olympic peninsulas,

Kitsap Peninsula and Bainbridge Island

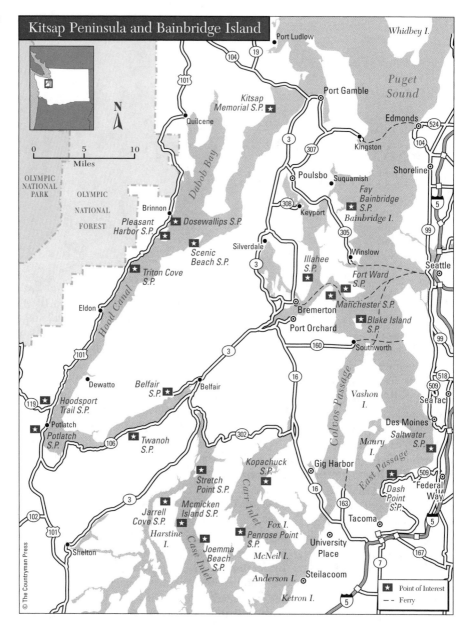

another way station on the journey to places west. Yet visitors find plenty to discover on this green isle just west of the big city, from galleries to farmers' markets and bright gardens to exurban cafés.

GUIDANCE **Bainbridge Island Chamber of Commerce** (206-842-3700; www .bainbridgechamber.com), 395 Winslow Way East, Bainbridge Island 98110.

Bremerton Area Chamber of Commerce (360-479-3579; www.bremerton chamber.org), 286 Fourth Street, Bremerton 98337.

Gig Harbor–Peninsula Area Chamber of Commerce (253-851-6865; www .gigharborchamber.com), 3125 Judson Street, Gig Harbor 98332.

Greater Poulsbo Chamber of Commerce (360-779-4848 or 877-768-5726; www.poulsbochamber.com), 19351 Eighth Avenue, Poulsbo 98370.

Kitsap Peninsula Visitor and Convention Bureau (800-337-0580; www.visit kitsap.com), 9481 Silverdale Way NW, Silverdale 98383.

Port Orchard Chamber of Commerce (360-876-3505 or 800-982-8139, www .portorchard.com); 1014 Bay Street, Suite 8, Port Orchard 98366.

Silverdale Chamber of Commerce (360-692-6800; silverdalechamber.com), 3100 NW Bucklin Hill Road, Suite 100, Silverdale 98383.

GETTING THERE You can drive to the peninsula by taking **WA 16** north from Tacoma over the Tacoma Narrows Bridge, to **WA 3** near Port Orchard, or by taking **US 101** north from Olympia, exiting 20 miles north at Shelton onto WA 3. It's about one and a half hours either way, via WA 3, to the northern tip of the peninsula.

More romantically, you can take one of four **Washington State Ferries** (206-464-6400 or 888-808-7977; www.wsdot.wa.gov/ferries/) onto the peninsula: a 40-minute ferry from Fauntleroy (West Seattle) to **Southworth,** where **WA 160** connects west to WA 16; a one-hour ferry from downtown Seattle to **Bremerton;** a 30-minute ferry from downtown Seattle to **Bainbridge Island,** where **WA 305** connects north to WA 3; or a 30-minute ferry from Edmonds to **Kingston,** where **WA 104** connects west to WA 3.

Seattle-Tacoma International Airport (206-787-5388 or 800-544-1965), 17801 International Boulevard, Seattle.

AMTRAK (253-627-8141 or 800-USA-RAIL; www.amtrak.com), 1001 Puyallup Avenue, Tacoma.

GETTING AROUND **Kitsap Transit** (360-373-2877 or 800-501-7433; www .kitsaptransit.org) provides local transportation within Kitsap County—the northern two-thirds of the peninsula—as well as service for the disabled by reservation.

MEDICAL EMERGENCY **Gig Harbor Multicare Urgent Care** (253-530-3800; www.multicare.org), 4545 Point Fosdick Drive NW, Gig Harbor.

Harrison Medical Center (www.harrisonmedical.org) is the main civilian hospital on the peninsula, with three branches:

Harrison Bremerton (360-744-3911), 2520 Cherry Avenue, Bremerton.

Harrison Silverdale (360-744-8800), 1800 NW Myhre Road, Silverdale.

Harrison Port Orchard (360-744-6275), 450 South Kitsap Boulevard, Port Orchard.

✳ To See

FARMERS' MARKETS **Bainbridge Island Farmers' Market** (206-855-1500), 280 Madison Avenue, Bainbridge Island. Open 9–1 Sat. Apr.–Oct.

Gig Harbor Farmers' Market (www.gigharborfarmersmarket.com). Two locations: 4701 Point Fosdick Drive, Gig Harbor, open 8:30–2 Sat. Apr.–Sept.; Skansie Brothers Park (on the waterfront), Gig Harbor, open 12–5 Wed. June–Sept.

Kingston Farmers Market (360-297-7683; kingstonfarmersmarket.com), Central Avenue and Washington Boulevard, Kingston. Open 9–2 Sat. May–mid-Oct. Even this little town has its own farmers' market.

Peninsula Farmers' Market (360-698-1678; www.silverdalefarmersmarket.com), Old Town Silverdale Port parking lot, Silverdale. Open 11–4 Tues. mid-Apr.–Sept.

Port Gamble Sunday Market (360-779-6720), WA 104 and Puget Way, Port Gamble. Open 11–4 Sun. Apr.–Sept. This market includes antiques.

Port Orchard Farmers' Market (360-710-9931), on the Waterfront Boardwalk at Marina Park, Port Orchard. Open 9–3 Sat. May–Oct.

Poulsbo Farmers' Market (360-779-6720), Seventh and Iverson, Poulsbo. Open 9–1 Sat. mid-Apr.–mid-Dec.

FOR FAMILIES ✿ **Aurora Valentinetti Puppet Museum** (360-373-2992; www.ectandpuppets.org), 257 Fourth Street, Bremerton. Open 11–4 Wed.–Sat. Donation requested. Do you think computer-generated images represent the highest form of animation? The Puppet Museum, a partner of **Evergreen Children's Theater** (which produces four or five children's shows per season), is a fascinating display of what might be called "analog" animation: the puppeteer's art. Indonesian shadow puppets, Chinese marionettes, and a magnificent cast of characters from *Alice in Wonderland* (beware the Jabberwock, hanging from the ceiling) form only part of the impressive collection.

THE JABBERWOCK AT BREMERTON'S
AURORA VALENTINETTI PUPPET MUSEUM

✿ **Kids' Discovery Museum** (206-855-4650; www.kidimu.org), 301 Ravine Lane, Bainbridge Island. Open 10–4 Mon.–Sat., 12–4 Sun. $6 adults and children over 13 months, $5 seniors and military. Having moved and grown since its enthusiastic 2005 debut, the museum features active themed play spaces for all ages, with the aim of entertaining and educating kids about nature. A squad of energetic, enthusiastic docents will facilitate if desired. From the pirates' lair to "Fun with Physics," it's a handy spot for a rainy day.

GARDENS **Bainbridge Gardens** (206-842-5888; www.bainbridgegardens.com), 9415 Miller Road NE, Bainbridge Island. Open 9–5:30 Mon.–Sat., 10–5:30 Sun. Prior to World War II, Bainbridge Island had a thriving Japanese American population. Many were strawberry farmers—Bainbridge was the setting for David Guterson's *Snow Falling on Cedars*—but Zenhichi Harui, who arrived in 1908, preferred flowers and trees. Over the years, he created 20 acres of Japanese gardens. It all fell into ruin when he and his family were interned in eastern Washington during the war. In 1990, though, Zenhichi's son Junkoh began restoring part of the garden. Some of the old elements are still here, including a tree that Zenhichi had trained in the shape of a pear. Lush gardens, Japanese and American, thrive once more, nursery plants are for sale, and the **New Rose Café** serves light refreshments.

The Bloedel Reserve (206-842-7631; www.bloedelreserve.org), 7571 Dolphin Drive, Bainbridge Island. Open 10–7 Tues.–Sat., 10–4 Sun.; 10–4 Tues.–Sun. in winter. $13 adults, $9 seniors and military, $5 students age 13 through college. Wheelchairs available at no charge; pets other than service animals excluded, even in parked vehicles. Bloedel has been called "sublime" by a Japanese garden website, and so it is. Not just its Japanese garden, either. From the Bloedels' former mansion—the image of a small French château—down to Port Madison Bay, half the 150 acres include natural second-growth cedar and fir. Two miles of trails wind through forest and immaculate, varied gardens. There's a rhododendron glade surrounding a waterfall, a wetland moss garden, a reflecting pool, and a Japanese garden complete with Japanese guesthouse. The overarching impression is one of serenity, which was the Bloedels' purpose; to keep it so, visitor numbers are controlled by reservation.

THE JAPANESE GARDEN AND TEAHOUSE
AT THE BLOEDEL RESERVE ON BAINBRIDGE ISLAND

Elandan Gardens (360-373-8260; www.elandangardens.com), 3050 West WA 16, Bremerton. Open 10–5 Tues.–Sun. Apr.–Oct.; 10–5 Fri.–Sun. Nov.–Mar. $8 adults, $1 children 6–12. "You must have a lot of élan, Dan," observed owner Dan Robinson's wife as he set about reclaiming an old dump for his bonsai collection. And that, according to Dan himself, is how Elandan Gardens got its name. It's not the most obvious spot for a bonsai garden. Dan's lifelong passion has landed this former landscaper and firefighter on several acres of former landfill between the highway and the harbor in full view of Bremerton's industrial dis-

BONSAI AT ELANDAN GARDENS IN BREMERTON

trict. But the hundreds of lovingly tended, gnarled miniature trees are astonishing. A Sierra juniper dating from A.D. 700 rubs shoulders with an upstart 245-year-old black pine. The silver bark of Korean hornbeam contrasts with venerable ever-greens. Some are in pots and some planted directly on rock. For good measure, Dan has interspersed his little masterpieces with great cedar snags from nearby forests, curiously shaped lava rocks from Hawaii, and basalt boulders from the desert. The shop, run by his wife, Diane, is an eclectic collection of objets d'art from everywhere you can think of, and some of their son Will's sculpture is displayed on the grounds.

HISTORIC SITES Bainbridge Island Japanese American Exclusion Memorial (206-842-5649), Taylor Avenue just north of Eagle Harbor Drive, Bainbridge Island. On March 30, 1942, 227 men, women, and children departed this island from a ferry dock here. Not voluntarily. They were the first of many Japanese Americans to be herded into internment camps not quite four months after the attack on Pearl Harbor. The memorial commemorating this event opened in August 2011—a long wood and stone wall, perforated at intervals to stand for the holes punched in people's lives, along a walkway leading to the dock. Future elements will include a 150-foot pier, for the 150 who managed to return; a Japanese-style pavilion and gates; and an interpretive center.

Chief Seattle's Grave, cemetery behind St. Peter's Mission Church, Suquamish. Chief Seattle's grave looks out over his homesite in what is now Old Man House Park (see below). In 2011, two carved and painted story poles, created by Squaxin artist Andrea Wilbur-Sigo, replaced the timbers and canoes that had framed the simple tombstone and cross. (Seattle, or Sealth, was an early Catholic convert.) Born about 1786, he reportedly saw Captain George Vancouver's ships pass and became a leader after heading up successful campaigns (or defenses, depending on whom you read) against enemy tribes. Some of his tribe looked askance at his friendship with Seattle's founders, Arthur Denny and "Doc" Maynard. But as history decreed he would preside over the subjugation of his people, his accommodation probably earned him better terms than he might otherwise have gotten. Today his memory is honored with the Chief Seattle Days powwow and memorial service (see *Special Events*) and with the gifts of twig bundles, beads, stuffed toys, and even dream catchers that continue to materialize at his grave.

Old Man House Park, Suquamish. Recently returned to the Suquamish tribe by the state, this 1-acre shoreline park facing Seattle across Puget Sound was once the site of one of the largest longhouses on record: 60 feet wide by some 700 feet long. Thought to have been built about the time of Captain Vancouver's visit (1792), it housed hundreds of individuals, most notably Chief Seattle, until it was burned in 1870 by an Indian agent who considered the communal living insalubrious. Chief Seattle's daughter, Angeline, came paddling furiously back across Puget Sound when she saw her father's house going up in flames—but she was too late to save it. The permanent winter settlement had occupied, naturally, far more than an acre, and in any case the land was part of the Suquamish Reservation, but 70 shoreline acres were appropriated by the U.S. government in 1904 for military installations that were never built (and are now residential developments). The park remains open to all, and the 2005 property return gives added impetus to the tribal canoeing and canoe-building revival.

Port Gamble (360-297-7251; www.portgamble.com), on WA 104 near junction with WA 3. The entire town is a 120-acre National Historic Landmark. Founded by two enterprising lumbermen from East Machias, Maine, in 1853, its lumber mill was the longest operating in the country until it closed in 1995. At that point, the company-owned town had to reinvent itself. The 1879 church and clapboard homes along the maple-shaded main street have been scrubbed, renovated, and brightly painted, giving the town a cheerful but slightly Potemkin-village air. Most houses are now shops or galleries, but the **General Store** still has a straightfor-ward café and snack bar downstairs, while upstairs is the Of Sea and Shore Museum (see *Museums*), housing a large seashell collection. The Port Gamble Historic Museum (see *Museums*), located in the old post office, gives a skillful

HISTORIC PORT GAMBLE ON THE KITSAP PENINSULA

rendering of the town's story. Ask at the visitors' bureau (see *Guidance*) for a **walking tour** brochure.

MUSEUMS Bainbridge Island Historical Society and Museum (206-842-2773; www.bainbridgehistory.org), 215 Erickson Avenue NE, Bainbridge Island. Open 1–4 Wed.–Mon., 10–4 Sat. in summer. $4 adults, $3 seniors and students, $6 families. Exhibits in a 1908 schoolhouse and annex showcase the island's economic history, the experience of Japanese settlers on Bainbridge, and how world events affected local life.

Gig Harbor Peninsula Historical Society and Museum (253-858-6722; www .harborhistorymuseum.org), 4121 Harborview Drive, Gig Harbor. Open 10–5 Tues.–Sun. $6 adults, $5 seniors and military, $4 children 7–17. Documents, photos, and memorabilia show how the Native Americans and early settlers of the area lived up to about 1935. A 2007 expansion includes an entire schoolhouse, fishing vessel, artifact gallery, and more.

& **Kitsap Historical Society Museum** (360-479-6226; www.kitsaphistory.org), 280 Fourth Street, Bremerton. Open 10–4 Tues.–Sat. year-round, plus 12–4 Sun. May–Sept. Suggested donation $2 adults, $1 children 7–17, $5 families. Sometimes small really is beautiful. This pocket-sized museum packs some 100,000 years of history—from Kitsap's Ice Age foundations to the changes World War II wrought on the isolated region—into a snug (but growing) space. Carefully selected artifacts and skillfully composed dioramas illuminate daily life in this watery zone. The "stump farm," a typical smallholding carved out after logging, makes you wonder how people got by at all. And did you know that Kitsap County became the egg capital of the United States during the Second World War, as described in Chimacum Valley and Vashon Island resident Betty MacDonald's *The Egg and I*? Egg farming was promoted throughout northwestern Washington in prewar days.

Puget Sound Navy Museum (360-627-2270; www.pugetsoundnavymuseum.org), 402 Pacific Avenue, Bremerton. Open 10–4 Mon.–Sat., 1–4 Sun.; closed Tues. Oct.–Apr. Free. The shipyard in Bremerton and the submarine base at nearby Bangor have created a naval culture locally. This museum, one of two devoted to this heritage, has been expanded and renovated; its exhibits cover the Puget Sound Naval Shipyard and naval history in general. One fascinating object is a 14th-century wooden cannon from Korea.

Naval Undersea Museum (360-396-4148; www.navalunderseamuseum.org), One Garnett Way, Keyport. Open 10–4 daily June–Sept.; 10–4 Wed.–Mon. Oct.–May. Free. The second of the naval museums is dedicated to the technology of undersea warfare and exploration, from antiquity to the present.

✍ **Of Sea and Shore Museum** (360-297-7636; www.ofseaandshore.com), General Store, 32400 Rainier Avenue NE, Port Gamble. Open 9–5 daily except Christmas. Free. This must be where beachcombers go when they die. Upstairs in the General Store are displays from one of the country's largest private seashell collections: a celebration of cowries, clams, cone shells, and all their ilk. Owner, native son, and mollusk enthusiast Tom Rice lives in Thailand now, but his beautiful, eerie shell world lives on in historic Port Gamble (see *Historic Sites*).

Port Gamble Historic Museum (360-297-8078), in back of the General Store (see above), 32400 Rainier Avenue NE, Port Gamble. Open 9:30–5 daily

May–Sept.; 11–4 Fri.–Sun. Oct.–Apr. $4 adults; $3 seniors, military, and students; children six and under free. This jewel of a local history museum far outstrips the usual collections of memorabilia. A series of painstaking reconstructions includes the ship's cabin bringing founders Pope and Talbot to Puget Sound, the lobby of the 1903 Puget Hotel, and a San Francisco lumber office, as well as rooms from the founders' homes with their own (extremely solid) antique furniture. Original artifacts include the company's silver safe: Pope and Talbot's employees were paid in silver rather than the scrip commonly used in other company towns.

Suquamish Museum (360-394-8496; www.suquamish.nsn.us), 15838 Sandy Hook Road, Poulsbo. Open 10–4 daily. $4 adults, $3 seniors (55 and older), $2 children 12 and under. Like other Puget Sound tribes, the Suquamish have always been water people. Their museum details Suquamish history and traditional ways with historic photos, explanatory plaques, canoes and paddles, fishing equipment, and baskets of all sizes.

USS *Turner Joy* (360-792-2457), 300 Washington Beach Avenue, Bremerton. Open for tours 10–5 daily Mar.–late Oct.; 10–4 Wed.–Sun. late Oct.–Feb. $12 adults, $10 seniors, $7 children 6–12, military and children under 6 free. This restored Vietnam War–era destroyer stands in Bremerton harbor. Among its tours of duty was the Gulf of Tonkin in 1964, including the incident that escalated American involvement in the war.

NATURAL WONDERS Hood Canal, extending from Port Gamble southwest some 40 miles to Hoodsport, where it turns sharply northeastward. Nomenclature in the area is a bit Humpty-Dumptyish: Hood "Canal" is actually a hook-shaped natural fjord that forms one of the Kitsap Peninsula's larger lobes. Whatever it's called, Hood Canal's origin can be traced to the last Ice Age, when a long tongue of ice from Canada scooped out Puget Sound and dumped piles of gravel (such as the peninsula) along its edge when it receded. Today Hood Canal separates the Kitsap from the overshadowing Olympic Peninsula, making for some world-class views when the clouds disperse. Since 1961 the **Hood Canal Bridge** (Washington State Department of Transportation, 360-357-2703)—two approach spans and a floating pontoon—from Port Gamble has connected the Kitsap Peninsula with the Olympic Peninsula via WA 104. Occasionally the bridge is closed in rough weather or to allow the passage of ships; call for information.

SCENIC DRIVES Along Hood Canal. It's hard to go wrong once you leave the main highways, WA 16 and WA 3. Winding roads along the canal offer tremendous views of the Olympics across the blue fjord. Take Anderson Hill Highway from WA 3 at Silverdale to Seabeck Highway leading to Scenic Beach State Park (see *Wilder Places—Parks*), about 8 miles. The perversely named North Shore Road loops around the southern end of the peninsula, hugging Hood Canal the whole time from WA 3 at Belfair to Dewatto, about 10 miles.

Key Peninsula loop, 50 miles. The **Key Peninsula Historical Society** (253-884-3272) has a self-guided historical auto loop connecting sites of interest around the Key Peninsula. From WA 16 at Gig Harbor, head north to Purdy and exit onto WA 302 westbound, then exit onto Key Peninsula Highway, a back road wandering down this lobe of the Kitsap with water views on both sides. The Key Peninsula (also called the Longbranch Peninsula) extends south past Johnson Point, just north of Olympia, with McNeil and Anderson islands just offshore.

Port Gamble ramble, about 14 miles. From WA 3 in Poulsbo, take Bond Road north to WA 104, which runs along the oval Port Gamble harbor up to Port Gamble itself at the entrance to Hood Canal.

WALKING TOURS Gig Harbor Waterfront History Walk. A self-guiding brochure is available from the **Visitor Information Center,** 3302 Harborview Drive, Gig Harbor. This tour takes you to 50 sites around downtown Gig Harbor, including the early ferry landing, pioneer homes, and the one-room schoolhouse. Explanatory plaques detailing the history of Croatian and Scandinavian settlement abound. If you are particularly energetic and the day is clear, the View Climb at the north end of the harbor provides impossibly perfect views of the harbor, surmounted by towering Mount Rainier.

✳ To Do

BICYCLING Key Peninsula Trails System (www.keypen.org), nearly 30 miles of secondary roads. Back roads constitute these looping bike routes linking water views, rural countryside, and the dominating presence of Mount Rainier. Camping is available at parks along the way.

Port Gamble trails, more than 15 miles. Olympic Resource Management, the company that owns the town of Port Gamble, also owns and manages the surrounding 4,300 timbered acres. Its logging roads and paths are open to bikers, hikers, and horses. Maps are available at the Kitsap Peninsula Visitor and Convention Bureau (see *Guidance*) in Port Gamble and at the Port Gamble General Store (see *To See—Historic Sites*).

CAMPING Belfair State Park (reservations 888-226-7688), near Belfair at the far end of Hood Canal's hook. One hundred twenty tent sites and 47 utility sites.

Fay Bainbridge State Park, at the northeastern corner of Bainbridge Island. Ten walk-in tent sites, 36 standard sites, and 20 RV sites with sweeping views of Puget Sound and the Cascade Range. First come, first served.

Illahee State Park (360-902-8844; www.parks.wa.gov), 1 mile east of Bremerton. Twenty-three tent sites and two utility sites in a 75-acre marine camping park with 0.25 mile of shoreline. No reservations.

Joemma Beach State Park, at the south end of Key Peninsula. Nineteen tent sites, two water trails sites, and two hiker-biker sites. No reservations.

Kitsap Memorial State Park, on Hood Canal south of Port Gamble; from WA 3 at Poulsbo, drive 5 miles north, exit, and follow the signs. Twenty-one tent sites, 18 utility sites (only 2 with hook-ups), and 4 cabins; reservations 888-226-7688. The **Hospitality House** (reservations 360-779-3205) is a vacation cabin that can be rented.

Kopachuck State Park, 5 miles west of Gig Harbor. Forty-one quiet tent sites among Douglas firs. No reservations.

Manchester State Park (reservations 888-226-7688), on Rich Passage, 6 miles east of Port Orchard. Thirty-five tent sites and 15 utility sites can be reserved in summer; 3 hiker-biker sites are nonreservable.

Penrose Point State Park (reservations 888-226-7688), on Key Peninsula. Eighty-two tent sites in the woods a short walk from the beach (you can also sleep in your boat at the dock).

Dewatto River campground (360-372-2755; www.dewattoport.com), 1001 Dewatto-Holly Road, Dewatto. Sixty sites and a covered community kitchen; 37 sites have electricity. There are toilets but no showers, and you must bring your own water. This riverside campground amid tall firs is on the southwestern Kitsap Peninsula. Reservations recommended. You can also launch boats 0.75 mile away at Dewatto Bay.

Scenic Beach State Park (reservations 888-226-7688), down Hood Canal near Seabeck. Fifty-two tent sites and 18 RV sites in a somewhat hilly campground.

Tahuya State Forest campgrounds (360-825-1631), off WA 300, north of Belfair 8 miles southwest of Bremerton. Many campsites in this working forest have been turned into day-use areas. **Tahuya River Horse Camp,** with 10 sites, is still open and requires reservations.

Twanoh State Park, on WA 106 on Hood Canal's "hook." Twenty-five tent sites and 22 utility sites. No reservations. The water here is warm enough that you may actually want to swim.

CANOEING AND KAYAKING Cascadia Marine Trail, from Olympia to Canada (where it becomes the British Columbia Marine Trail). Five marine trail campgrounds lie on the Kitsap Peninsula, for marine trail navigators only: two on the Key Peninsula at Joemma Beach State Park and Penrose Point State Park (see *Camping*), two near Gig Harbor at Kopachuck State Park and Narrows State Park, and one on the eastern shore at Fay Bainbridge State Park (see *Camping*). Fort Ward State Park, 4 miles south of Winslow on Bainbridge Island, also has one non-reservable marine trail site.

Key Peninsula sea-kayak trail (Key Peninsula Trails System, www.keypen.org), nearly 40 miles long, southwest of Gig Harbor. This extremely scenic trip takes you to otherwise inaccessible island parks and circumnavigates the scalloped perimeter of the peninsula (a southern extremity of the Kitsap Peninsula). Camping is available at parks along the route; care must be taken in the currents around Devil's Head at the southern tip and in crossing the Herron Island ferry route.

Rentals

Gig Harbor Rent-a-Boat (253-858-7341; gigharborrentaboat.com), 8829 North Harborview Drive, Gig Harbor. Kitsap's myriad bays and inlets invite you to the water; try this outfitter for rentals and classes.

North Bay Kayak and Water Sports (360-535-2198; www.allynkayak.com), 18350 WA 3, Allyn. This outfitter at the southern end of the peninsula provides rentals and instruction.

Olympic Outdoor Center (800-592-5983; www.olympicoutdoorcenter.com), 18971 Front Street, Poulsbo. Here you can rent kayaks and take classes.

DIVING Kitsap Memorial State Park and **Scenic Beach State Park** (see *Camping*) have access to diving in Hood Canal.

Sunrise Beach Park, 10015 Sunrise Beach Drive NW, Gig Harbor. This beach on Colvos Passage is popular with divers.

GIG HARBOR RENT-A-BOAT IS ON THE TOWN'S SCENIC WATERFRONT.

GOLF Gold Mountain Golf Complex (360-415-5432; www.goldmt.com), 7263 West Belfair Valley Road, Gorst. This little community at the foot of Sinclair Inlet between Bremerton and Port Orchard has two courses of 18 holes each.

Horseshoe Lake Golf Course (253-857-3326; www.hlgolf.com), 1250 SW Club-house Court, Port Orchard. Eighteen holes.

McCormick Woods Golf Course (800-323-0130; www.mccormickwoodsgolf .com), 5155 McCormick Woods Drive SW, Port Orchard. Eighteen holes.

Trophy Lake Golf and Casting (360-874-8337; www.trophylakegolf.com), 3900 SW Lake Flora Road, Port Orchard. Eighteen holes and 7,206 yards.

Village Greens Golf Course (360-871-1222), 2298 Fircrest Drive SE, Port Orchard. Eighteen holes and 45 acres.

HIKING Green Mountain State Forest (360-801-5097), on Holly Road off Seabeck Highway, about 5 miles west of Bremerton; 13 miles of multiuse trails, though they may be rerouted when trees are being cut. Open year-round. Green Mountain and adjacent Gold Mountain are the highest points on the Kitsap. The 6,000-acre state forest covers Green Mountain.

Hansville Greenway County Park (360-337-5350), off Buck Road, Hansville; from WA 104 just west of Kingston, take Hansville Road north. Moderate 1- to 3-mile trails wander through meadow and woodland.

Key Peninsula Trails System (www.keypen.org), 25 miles of hiking trails around the Key Peninsula southwest of Gig Harbor. This ambitious trail network has designated separate trails for hikers, cyclists, horses, and kayakers. The 20-mile walking trail, with 5 miles of spur trails, connects parks and points of interest along the scenic, rural peninsula. Camping is available at several state parks along the way. This trail is for pedestrians only!

Kitsap Volkssporters (360-871-3150), Box 2142, Silverdale 98315. They have a list of varied 10-kilometer (about 6.25-mile) walks around the Kitsap Peninsula.

Mosquito Fleet Trail (800-337-0580; www.visitkitsap.com), under development, will be a 57-mile walking and cycling trail along the waterfront connecting old Mosquito Fleet docks in Port Orchard, Bremerton, Poulsbo, and Kingston.

Port Gamble trails, a network of trails in 4,300 acres of timberland open to horses, hikers, and cyclists (see *Bicycling*). For maps or information, contact the Kitsap Peninsula Visitor and Convention Bureau (see *Guidance*) in Port Gamble or the Port Gamble General Store (see *To See—Historic Sites*).

Rocky Creek Conservation Area (253-884-9240; www.keypenparks.com), at WA 302 and 150th Avenue on the Key Peninsula. Several short trails wind through the 224 acres of woods and wetlands. A salmon-spawning stream is on the property.

Tahuya State Forest (360-825-1631), off WA 300, 8 miles southwest of Bremerton; 200 miles of trails. This multiuse, 23,100-acre working forest has other users, including off-road vehicles, so hike early or on weekdays and check for closures.

See also *Wilder Places*.

✳ Wilder Places

NATURE PRESERVES Foulweather Bluff Preserve, near the northernmost tip of Kitsap Peninsula; from Hansville, take Two Spits Road 2.8 miles northwest and park on the left between two signs reading NO PARKING DAWN TILL DUSK. Open dawn to dusk. No pets. The Nature Conservancy acquired this 101-acre site because of its pristine wetlands and in order to foster regrowth of the red-cedar climax forest. A trail runs from the parking area through the preserve to the beach. With brackish wetlands, 0.66 mile of shoreline, and both alder and coniferous forests, the preserve shelters a large number of plant and animal species; wintering ducks are particularly abundant.

&. **Hood Canal Theler Wetlands and Community Center** (360-877-2021; www.explorehoodcanal.com), at the south end of Belfair. Open dawn to dusk daily. No pets. The Theler Wetlands are 135 acres of tidelands and swamp where the Union River flows into salty Hood Canal. Four miles of wheelchair-accessible trails wind through the various habitats; a wheelchair can be borrowed at the ranger station. The number of bird species here varies; the number of mosquitoes is often more than you might like.

PARKS Belfair State Park (360-275-0668; www.parks.wa.gov), on WA 300, 3 miles from Belfair. Besides camping (see *To Do—Camping*), this park has a swimming lagoon and both fresh- and saltwater shorelines, tidal flats, and wetlands.

Fay Bainbridge State Park (206-842-3931; www.parks.wa.gov), on Bainbridge Island. This shoreline park of 17 acres is on the northeast corner of the island, with mooring for boats plus picnicking and camping (see *To Do—Camping*). Views across the sound encompass Seattle and Mount Rainier.

Fort Ward State Park (206-842-2306; www.biparks.org), on Bainbridge Island. Fort Ward's 137 acres are thickly forested, with picnicking and walking trails. It has an underwater area for divers and one nonreservable campsite for Cascadia Marine Trail voyagers in human-powered craft (see *To Do—Canoeing and Kayaking*). Views across Rich Passage are of Kitsap Peninsula shoreline and waterways.

Illahee State Park (360-478-6460; www.parks.wa.gov), 1 mile east of Bremerton. The tall forests here slope steeply toward the water, where ducks, grebes, and loons bob on the bay. This is a 75-acre marine camping park with 0.25 mile of shoreline.

Joemma Beach State Park (253-844-1944; www.parks.wa.gov), south end of Key Peninsula. Here you'll find camping (see *To Do—Camping*), crabbing, fishing, and boating.

Kitsap Memorial State Park (360-779-3205; www.parks.wa.gov), 6 miles north of Poulsbo near Hood Canal Bridge. You'll find canal and mountain views as well as fishing, diving (see *To Do—Diving*), camping (see *To Do—Camping*), hiking, and boating.

Kopachuck State Park (253-265-3606; www.parks.wa.gov), 5 miles southwest of Gig Harbor. Facing west, Kopachuck is famous for its sunsets and sandy beaches, as well as camping (see *To Do—Camping*), crabbing, fishing, and boating.

Liberty Bay Waterfront Park (360-779-9898; www.cityofpoulsbo.com), Poulsbo. A greensward dipping to Liberty Bay and the Poulsbo Marina, its boardwalk, and a bandstand make a pleasant venue for a picnic or a town festival. Not to mention the statue of the Unknown Norwegian, er, Viking.

Manchester State Park (360-871-4065; www.parks.wa.gov), 6 miles east of Port Orchard. On the shores of Puget Sound, this park has 111 acres of woods with campsites (see *To Do—Camping*).

Penrose Point State Park (253-884-2514; www.parks.wa.gov), 16 miles southwest of Purdy. Two miles of forest-backed beach are home to plentiful birds and wildlife, campers (see *To Do—Camping*), and boaters.

Point No Point Lighthouse and Park (360-337-5350; www.kitsapgov.com /parks), 9001 Point No Point Road, Hansville. This tidy lighthouse with spectacular Puget Sound views in three directions has been guiding ships since 1879. You can walk along the beach or on a wood-and-wetland trail; the county park abuts timber property with bike and walking paths.

PAVILION IN LIBERTY BAY WATERFRONT PARK, POULSBO

&. **Scenic Beach State Park** (360-830-5079; www.parks.wa.gov), near Seabeck on Hood Canal. Wheelchair-friendly paths wind through planted gardens strewn with wild native rhododendrons and offer views of the Olympic Mountains. Crabs and oysters may be gathered in season. See also *To Do—Camping* and *Diving*.

Sunrise Beach County Park (253-798-4176), 10015 Sunrise Beach Drive NW, Gig Harbor. Just outside town on the southern peninsula, these 82 undeveloped acres have forested paths and

POINT NO POINT LIGHTHOUSE AND PARK ON THE KITSAP PENINSULA

views of the harbor and Mount Rainier. The park's 2,400-foot waterfront also attracts divers (see *To Do—Diving*).

Twanoh State Park (360-898-6006; www.parks.wa.gov), on Hood Canal, 8 miles southwest of Belfair. This marine camping park (see *To Do—Camping*) has 200 feet of moorage, relatively warm salt water, and more than 0.5 mile of shoreline. Smelt run along the shore in winter, and crabs and oysters can be gathered in season.

✴ Lodging

BED & BREAKFASTS

Bainbridge Island

Fuurin-Oka Futon Bed and Breakfast (206-914-9704; www.futonand breakfast.com), 12580 Vista Drive NE. This place is a bit of a splurge, but it's certainly different—a traditional Japanese *ryokan*, except, of course for the cable TV and entertainment system. It's a little reminder of the Japanese presence on Bainbridge Island that began in the 1880s and the fact that many Japanese Americans were dispossessed and interned during World War II. The private guesthouse has its own Japanese garden and Japanese-style bath, architecture, and Olympic Mountain views. You have your choice of a full Japanese or American breakfast, too. $185 Apr.–Aug., $140 Sept.–Mar., including taxes.

Bremerton

Illahee Manor (360-698-7555 or 877-698-7555; www.illaheemanorbandb .com), 6680 Illahee Road NE. Not your ordinary manor, Illahee was modeled on a Russian country house in 1926 by Russian friends of the owners. Two balconied stories and a tower soar above a wraparound veranda, the whole grandly overlooking Port Orchard Bay. In winter, with snow on the tall firs, you could imagine yourself in Siberia; in summer, roses and fruit trees run riot. The five suites are all different but exquisite; my hands-down favorite is the hexagonal Tower Room with its antique Eastlake bed, Wedgwood-blue walls, and 270-degree views. Illahee is close to parks and attractions, but you'll really feel like just cocooning and gazing at the view. $120–220.

Gig Harbor

Bear's Lair Bed and Breakfast

(253-857-8877 or 877-855-9768; www.bearslairbb.com), 13706 92nd Avenue Court NW. Where the buzz of Gig Harbor fades off into the undeveloped southern Kitsap Peninsula, you'll find the Bear's Lair (or maybe an actual bear—they're fairly common in these wooded hills). Planted solidly among the firs, this B&B looks as if a European hunting lodge had somehow migrated to Puget Sound. In fact, it's the labor of love of Giulio and Jen Santori, who built it from the ground up. Giulio is a professional woodworker from Lucca, Italy. This becomes even more visible indoors in the cabinets, carved trim, and bathroom tiling—that fine Italian hand. Roses and azaleas billow around the house. Three guest rooms range from the spacious Dahlia Room to the airy Rose Room (Jen is a gardener) and the cozy Patio Room. Across the way, a 1,000-square-foot carriage house with all amenities welcomes groups or families with children. Rooms $115–155; Carriage House $195–215; inquire about weekly rates.

Poulsbo

Foxbridge Bed and Breakfast (360-697-4875; www.foxbridge.com), 30860 WA 3 NE. Foxes are the theme here; you'll find plush stuffed foxes on the beds and ceramic ones around the grounds. But there are also real foxes on the undulating, wooded 5 acres, which together with the neighbors' 11 acres make up a federally recognized backyard wildlife refuge. Coyotes, deer, and otters roam here, too, not to mention songbirds galore. The 1985 Colonial-style house was built as a bed & breakfast, so it's like a larger-than-average American home where hosts Hilary and Gray invite you to chat in the living room and browse the library. Or you might feel like just relaxing under a down comforter or on a settee in your room. All three guest rooms come with private bath and breakfast; to call the breakfast "hearty" would be an understatement. $115.

Green Cat Guest House Bed and Breakfast (360-779-7569; www.green catbb.com), 25819 Tytler Road NE. In the quiet countryside 4 miles from Poulsbo, the Green Cat occupies the top two floors of a large Norwegian-style home. The four snug bedrooms and three baths can be rented separately or together for families or groups; the kitchen and dining area are shared. Rates include breakfast. Children over 10 welcome. No pets. $115–139.

COTTAGES AND CABINS

Poulsbo

Kitsap Memorial Sleeper Cabins (360-779-3205), 202 NE Park Street. Four new cabins in Kitsap Memorial State Park on Hood Canal (see *Wilder Places—Parks*) each sleep five. Restrooms are outside, and kitchen facilities consist of a fridge and microwave, but the log furniture is cozy, and it's hard to beat for families. Bring your own linens, pots, and pans. $65 in summer, $55 in winter.

Silverdale

Forest Enchantment Cottage (360-692-5148; www.forestenchantment cottage.com), 7448 NW Ioka Drive. The address is Silverdale, but the cottage is some miles back in the country. Restfully located in a stand of Douglas firs, it has amazing views of the Olympics and is steps from Hood Canal. Two bedrooms, with kitchen, bathroom, living room, and a wood-burning stove; sleep up to seven. Children welcome. $100.

GUESTHOUSES

Port Gamble

✒ **Port Gamble Guest Houses** (360-297-5114), 32440 Puget Avenue NE. Set on a bluff at the entrance to Hood Canal, the guesthouse is one of the original mill workers' houses, with three bedrooms and a full kitchen (renovated and updated, of course), and a suite that can be rented separately if desired. Next door, another house has two bed & breakfast rooms. Kites, beach games, and other amusements are provided, and it's just a short walk to the beach. Rates include breakfast. Children welcome. Ask about pets. $200–425.

Poulsbo

Brauer Cove Guest House (360-779-4153), 16709 Brauer Road NE. A stately farmhouse just above the waters of Liberty Bay and a mile from Poulsbo, Brauer Cove offers a two-bedroom apartment with its own kitchenette, bath, and king-sized view. You can even paddle your own canoe (or, rather, theirs). Children welcome. $125.

HOUSEBOATS

Gig Harbor

Pleasure Craft Marina (253-549-6639), 3215 Harborview Drive. The marina rents out six furnished, 40- to 45-foot houseboats by the day or week as overnight accommodations (they must remain docked, however). Each sleeps four to six and has a complete galley and bathroom with shower. Call for rates.

INNS AND HOTELS

Gig Harbor

✒ ♿ **Maritime Inn** (253-858-1818; www.maritimeinn.com), 3212 Harborview Drive. Just across the street from the harbor and public docks, the Maritime Inn is handy for both sailors and landlubbers. The 10-year-old hotel has 15 rooms, 8 with private entrances. Several have carved wooden bedsteads, and they all have fireplaces to help you dry out from the Puget Sound rain. There's one fully handicapped-accessible room. Children welcome. No pets. Rates include a continental breakfast. $129–198.

Waterfront Inn (253-857-0770; www .waterfront-inn.com), 9017 North Harborview Drive. Jan and Steve Denton took on the restoration of their 1918 fisherman's house and turned it into a homey boutique hotel—if that's not a contradiction in terms. The five suites all have a sensible, nautical feeling, with wooden bedsteads and rattan chairs in front of rock fireplaces; one has two bedrooms. Three of the suites open onto a patio 20 feet from the hotel's dock. Rates include a self-serve continental breakfast. Children over 12 welcome. No pets. $141–219.

MOTELS

Poulsbo

Poulsbo Inn and Suites (360-779-3921 or 800-597-5151; www.poulsbo inn.com), 18680 WA 305. Fundamentally, it's a motel, but recent renovations have added warm wood paneling and furniture for a cozy touch. Families with small children may be more relaxed here than in more adult bed & breakfast environments. There's an outdoor pool, a hot tub, and a cheery breakfast room with fireplace. Rooms range from standard singles or doubles to kitchenette and full suites. Rates depend on the season; ask about discounts and weekly rates. $99–116.

RESORTS

Union

✒ ♿ **Alderbrook Resort** (360-898-2145; www.alderbrookresort.com), 10

East Alderbrook Drive. In 1913, when Alderbrook was founded, you had to come by steamer—there were no roads to this spot on the southern end of Hood Canal. The resort has been expanded since then, but the rustic lodge style has been preserved, with rock and natural wood facing. There are 77 rooms, plus 14 two-bedroom cottages and 1 one-bedroom cottage, all with fine linens, down comforters, and views; the cottages also come equipped with kitchens. The on-site **restaurant** features, naturally, local seafood. Like a good resort, it offers recreation, including tennis, golf, spa, fitness center, and pool. Children welcome. Some rooms are pet-friendly. Rooms from $215; cottages from $360.

✔ **Robin Hood Village** (360-898-2163 or 866-225-2119), 6780 East WA 106. This 1930s resort bills itself as a full-service madhouse. In one of the peninsula's remoter spots, the village boasts nine nicely appointed cottages of varying sizes, from snug retreats to family-sized houses, all with full kitchens, most with private hot tub, TV, and DVD, but no phone. In addition to the cottages, there are tent sites and RV sites with full hook-ups, all on the quiet end of Hood Canal. Picnic facilities and a **restaurant** are also on-site. Children welcome. Ask about pets. Cottages $99–245; RVs $38–60; call for camping rates.

✳ Where to Eat
DINING OUT
Gig Harbor
Brix 25 (253-858-6626; www.harbor brix.com), 7707 Pioneer Way. Open 4:30–9 Mon.–Thurs., 4:30–9:30 Fri.–Sat., 4:30–8:30 Sun. This fairly new restaurant takes Northwest cuisine to some creative heights: clams and mussels in saffron; Moroccan lamb meat-

balls; sausage and squash ravioli. Old favorites include wild salmon and filet mignon.

The Green Turtle (253-851-3167; www.thegreenturtle.com), 2905 Harborview Drive. Open for lunch 11–2:30 Tues.–Fri.; dinner 4:30–9 Tues.–Thurs. and Sun., 4:30–10 Fri.–Sat. The turtle looks down benevolently from the ceiling, and the turquoise walls are painted with swirling underwater themes, but the food is serious: halibut with macadamia nuts and mango chutney, salmon with a creative neo-Asian twist. The emphasis is naturally on seafood, fine and fresh. In summer, sit out on the terrace overlooking the harbor and the stately homes of Vashon Island.

Poulsbo
Molly Ward Gardens (360-779-4471; www.mollywardgardens.com), 27462 Big Valley Road. Open for lunch 11–2 Wed.–Sat.; dinner 5:30–9 Wed.–Sun.; brunch 10:30–2:30 Sun. Closed Jan. Five acres supply much of the produce; the rest, owners Sam and Lynn Ward try to buy fresh and organic. The restaurant hides inside a big old barn, the menu changes seasonally, and vegetarian options are usually available. Reservations recommended.

Mor Mor Bistro and Bar (360-697-3449; www.mormorbistro.com), 18820 Front Street. Open 11–9 Mon.–Sat., 10–3 Sun. Poulsbo's upscale eatery honors the owner's maternal grandmother (*mor mor* is the Norwegian kinship term) and serves Scandinavian-Northwest cuisine from a menu that changes with the seasons.

EATING OUT
Bainbridge Island
Café Nola (206-842-3822; www.cafe nola.com), 101 Winslow Way. Open for lunch 11–3 Mon.–Fri.; dinner 5–9

Sun.–Thurs., 5–10 Fri.–Sat.; brunch 9:30–3 Sat.–Sun. Like Bainbridge Island itself, this bustling bistro is snug and stylish at the same time. The menu is ambitious and eclectic, running from old standbys such as Philly cheesesteak to roast rabbit. It doesn't come cheap—an omelet can run you $10—but everything we tried was good.

Gig Harbor

Susanne's Bakery (253-853-6220), 3411 Harborview Drive. Open 7–5 Tues.–Sun. A cheery shoe box with yellow walls, Susanne's is favored by the young and Wi-Fi'd. It's a pleasant place for anyone to sit and sip with or without a pastry, focaccia sandwich, or salad.

Tides Tavern (253-858-3982; www .tidestavern.com), 2925 Harborview Drive. Open 11 AM to closing Mon.–Fri., 9 AM to closing Sat.–Sun. A Gig Harbor fixture, this 1910 building was originally a general store that metamorphosed over the years into a tavern and dance hall. It's still a tavern, now with an expanded pub menu and an air of good times past and yet to come. Unfortunately for families, you must be over 21 to patronize the place.

Poulsbo

J J's Fish House (360-779-6609), 18881 Front Street. Open 11–9 daily. On Poulsbo's marina, J J's is a casual, family-friendly place serving, of course, local fish and seafood.

Poulsbohemian Coffeehouse (360-779-9199; www.poulsbohemian.com), 19003 Front Street. Open 7–5 Mon.–Fri., 8–5 Sat.–Sun. Coffee and pastries, yes, but also poetry readings, writing groups, chess clubs, and what have you.

Sluy's Poulsbo Bakery (360-697-2253), 18924 Front Street. Open 4:30 AM–6:30 PM Mon.–Thurs. and Sun.,

4:30 AM–7:30 PM Fri.–Sat. Yes, they invented Poulsbo bread, and their front window full of Danishes, *lefse,* and other Scandinavian-type goodies tempt the unwary.

♫ **Thatsa Some Italian Ristorante** (360-779-2266), 18881 Front Street. Ignore the name; this friendly, informal restaurant serves not only tasty pizza and pasta but also seafood dishes, including Pacific snapper piccata and honey-ginger salmon. Which only makes sense, sitting as it does a few hundred feet from Liberty Bay. There's a children's menu and a respectable wine cellar—fun for the whole family. John F. Kennedy Jr. and his wife once ate here.

✳ Entertainment

THEATER Bainbridge Performing Arts (206-842-8569; www.bainbridge performingarts.org), 200 Madison Avenue North, Bainbridge Island. Bainbridge is an artistic community, and the arts here include theater, dance, and music, by considerable local talent and at reasonable prices.

The Kitsap Forest Theater (800-573-8484; foresttheater.com), 3000 Seabeck Highway, Bremerton. An outdoor amphitheater designed in 1926, this community theater uses almost no built structures—the grass is the stage, and "backstage" is the woods. The season is timed to coincide with peak wild rhododendron blooms (May–June)—think *A Midsummer Night's Dream.*

✳ Selective Shopping

HOME AND GARDEN Bainbridge Gardens (206-842-5888; www .bainbridgegardens.com), 9415 Miller Road, Bainbridge Island. This is a respected nursery.

Gracey Nursery (360-297-2111), 28154 WA 104 NE, Kingston. Plants and gardening products are big on the peninsula, as you'll see at this place.

Valley Nursery (360-779-3806), 20882 Bond Road NE, Poulsbo. Six acres of supplies and plants that thrive in the great Northwest.

✳ Special Events

January: **Japanese American New Year** (206-842-4772), Bainbridge Island. With its historic Asian connection, the island puts on a celebration that includes drumming and making rice cakes.

February: **The Chilly Hilly** (Cascade Bicycle Club, 206-522-BIKE; www .cascade.org), a 33-mile bike ride around Bainbridge Island that kicks off the bicycling season. Although it's on an island, the cumulative elevation gain is 2,675 feet, so yes, it's hilly . . . and at this time of year, it can be really chilly. Several thousand riders from around Puget Sound participate every year, finishing up with a finish-line— what else?—chili feed.

May: **Viking Fest** (Chamber of Commerce, 360-779-4848), Poulsbo. The town celebrates its heritage with parades, music, and food timed for the weekend nearest Norway's Constitution Day, May 17.

June: **Civil War Reenactment** (360-874-8548), Port Gamble. This is staged the third weekend in June, with such varied events as battles, bread riots, hospital demonstrations, a fashion

show, and a street dance. Tell your children the Civil War did not actually take place here.

St. John's Day (360-779-5209), Waterfront Park, Poulsbo. One of the few American communities to observe St. John's Day, June 24, in the traditional style, Poulsbo, being of Norwegian heritage, calls it St. Hans Day. Folk dances, children's games, and a bonfire enliven this solstitial holiday.

July: **Fathoms o' Fun** (360-876-3505), Port Orchard. This summer festival includes a parade, a carnival, and fireworks.

August: **Chief Seattle Days** (360-598-3311), central Suquamish. The celebration in honor of Chief Seattle on the third weekend in August includes a memorial service at Chief Seattle's grave (see *To See—Historic Sites*), drumming, dancing, a salmon bake, baseball, and canoe races.

Kitsap County Fair and Stampede (360-337-5376), 1200 NW Fairgrounds Road, Bremerton. There's a rodeo, entertainment, 4-H exhibits, and more.

Washington Renaissance Fantasy Faire (-800-359-5948; www.washington renfaire.com), Gig Harbor. Three August weekends feature jousting, costumes, songs, and stories.

November: **Sons of Norway Annual Lutefisk Feed** (360-779-5209), Sons of Norway Hall, Poulsbo. If you like lutefisk—or adventure—try this event in early November.

Seattle
Metropolitan
Area

3

SOUTHERN SUBURBS AND
VASHON ISLAND

SEATTLE

MERCER ISLAND AND
THE EASTSIDE

INTRODUCTION

If you're lucky, you'll fly in on a clear day—it does happen—with the Olympics sparkling gaily off to the west, the rumpled Cascades punctuated by the cones of Mount Baker and Glacier Peak to the northeast, and the great bulk of Mount Rainier to the south. Below you'll see long Vashon Island and the waters of Puget Sound shelving quickly from green-blue along the squiggly shoreline to the inky depths. You know orcas live here, but did you know about the Pacific giant octopuses? They're quite common, though you seldom see them unless you go diving. Occasionally a storm will wash one ashore.

The fir-clad islands beckon, but the plane banks to starboard just past Seattle's container port with its toy ships bustling about below. You're over Elliott Bay. You bank some more, and there's the Space Needle, best seen from a distance, beyond it the blue expanse of Lake Washington with its own Mercer Island, then the schoolyards of South Seattle, the docks—and you're down. It's quite an entry to the Evergreen State and its major metropolis.

You may have missed Alki Point, sticking out like a thumb between Elliott Bay and the sound. That's where the Queen City of the Northwest was founded back in 1851 with the hopeful name New York Alki—*alki* being the Salish word for "someday." The little settlement didn't last long. It huddled against the squalls and torrents of one winter before moving across the bay at the kindly suggestion of some Indians.

Not that the new site was a dream either, being on a tidal marsh under extremely steep hills. Negotiating the streets even today, whether by foot or by car, is often breathtaking, and not just because of the views; the grades can be 15 percent or more. But many of the slopes had a 40 percent grade back then, which was fine for skidding logs, but not for building or getting around. So the city killed two birds with one stone: After the great fire of 1889, the residents took hoses to the hillsides and washed several feet of soil down onto the flats below, thus making the inclines more manageable while adding a considerable amount of fill downtown, which had always had a drainage problem. It incidentally entombed quite a number of ground-floor businesses, but these were in bad shape anyway after the fire, and you can still visit some of them on the popular Underground Tour.

Like many western towns, Seattle followed a boom-bust cycle. It boomed with timber, busted in the collapse of 1893, and boomed again during the Klondike gold rush—not because of an influx of actual gold, but because Seattle positioned itself as the logical outfitting and embarkation point for wishful gold miners bound for

Alaska. Seattle knew a brief moment of glory during the 1960 world's fair, but apart from that, it had many uneventful, even depressed, decades. "When Boeing sneezes, Seattle catches cold" and "Would the last person to leave town please turn out the lights?" were two rather morose jokes of the 1970s.

Until, that is, the strange alignment of a new industry (software), a meteoric music form (grunge), and—some say—the movie *Sleepless in Seattle* put the town back on the map. Today Seattle is a brash Pacific Rim city, all skyscrapers and glass and high-end shopping malls, with an art and restaurant scene to match and the burgeoning Eastside high-tech corridor. There are big-city problems, too—a sizable homeless population, plus panhandlers in a few locations. It's a lot like its antipodean cousin Sydney, Australia—a bright, energetic town on a spectacular inland sea—though Sydney's weather is rather better. But the old Seattle is still there around Pioneer Square and in the various neighborhoods; and the young Seattle, too, in the clubs and coffee shops and the University District.

Traffic is ridiculous and parking is worse, and the prices have shot up higher than the downtown skyscrapers, but still the visitors come. It's now a world-class city, with world-class museums and entertainment within a stone's throw of some of America's most thrilling wilderness. So most Seattleites are glad of their city's rainy reputation (though annual rainfall is actually no worse than in, say, New York; it's just poorly distributed); it keeps the population under control.

SOUTHERN SUBURBS AND VASHON ISLAND

GUIDANCE **Auburn Chamber of Commerce** (253-833-0700; www.auburn areawa.org), 108 South Division Street, Suite B, Auburn 98001.

Kent Chamber of Commerce (253-854-1770; www.kentchamber.com), 524 West Meeker Street, Kent 98035.

Renton Chamber of Commerce (425-226-4560; www.gorenton.com), 300 Rainier Avenue North, Renton 98057.

Seattle Southside Visitor Center (877-885-9452; www.seattlesouthside.com), 3100 South 176th Street, Seattle, 98188.

Vashon–Maury Island Chamber of Commerce (206-463-6217; www.vashon chamber.com), 17141 Vashon Highway SW, Vashon 98070.

GETTING THERE **I-5** runs north-south through the area, as does **WA 99** to the west and **WA 167** to the east, which connects Auburn, Kent, and Renton. **I-405** begins at I-5 in Tukwila and heads east, then north through Renton. Other east-west highways include **WA 18,** from Federal Way northeast to Maple Valley, and **WA 516,** from Des Moines east to Maple Valley.

Seattle-Tacoma International Airport (206-787-5388 or 800-544-1965; www .portofseattle.org) is off I-5 via exit 154B.

AMTRAK (800-USA-RAIL; www.amtrak.com) has three train routes that stop in downtown Seattle.

Greyhound (206-628-5526 or 800-231-2222; www.greyhound.com), 811 Stewart Street, also serves downtown Seattle.

Washington State Ferries (206-464-6400 or 888-808-7977; www.wsdot.wa.gov /ferries/) serve commuters and travelers between Seattle and Vashon Island from the Fauntleroy dock in West Seattle.

GETTING AROUND **Metro Transit** (206-553-3000; www.metro.kingcounty .gov), 201 South Jackson Street, Seattle, offers user-friendly bus service through Seattle and all of King County, including Sea-Tac Airport.

From the airport, **Shuttle Express** (425-981-7000; shuttleexpress.com) goes to Seattle suburbs, and the **Vashon Shuttle** (206-463-2664 or 877-721-1411; www .vashonshuttle.com) serves Vashon Island. Reservations recommended for Shuttle Express and required for Vashon Shuttle.

202 North Division Street, Auburn.

Valley Medical Center (425-228-3450), 400 South 43rd Street, Renton.

✴ To See

BOAT TOURS Tillicum Village Tours (206-623-1445; www.tillicumvillage.com), 1101 Alaskan Way, Seattle. Operates one or two tours daily mid-Mar.–Oct. $79.95 adults, $72.95 seniors, $30 children 5–12. This four-hour excursion includes a boat ride from Seattle's Pier 55 to Blake Island, where a salmon dinner is prepared in tribal Northwest fashion and served in a longhouse, and a dance performance incorporates stories and mythology from the various tribal traditions. In your free time, you can stroll the island or browse the Native American art gallery. You can also visit the island without the dinner performance ($40 adult).

FARMERS' MARKETS AND FARM STANDS Green Man Farm (360-567-4548), 8800 SW Dilworth Road, Vashon Island.

Hogsback Farm (360-436-1896), 16530 91st Avenue SW, Vashon Island.

Vashon Island Farmers' Market (360-567-5492), at the Village Green, on Vashon's main intersection at Vashon Highway and Bank Road. Open 10–2 Sat. Apr.–mid-Nov.

HISTORIC SITES Fort Dent Park (206-768-2822), 6800 Fort Dent Way, Tukwila. Near this inoffensive-looking plot, now a picnic and play area, Governor Isaac Stevens ordered a fort to be built. It was one of several constructed in western Washington following an unsuccessful 1856 siege of Seattle by local Indians who had rejected removal to the reservation at Port Madison, across Puget Sound. At that time, the site was at the confluence of two small rivers, with fine natural resources. However, one river dried up in 1916 when nearby White Lake was drained, and the last holdouts evacuated. The park now occupies the former lake bed.

Saltwater State Park (www.parks.wa.gov), south of WA 516, 2 miles south of Des Moines. When this park, which lies halfway between Seattle and Tacoma, was dedicated in 1926, a hatchet was buried somewhere on its 88 acres to demonstrate an end to animosities between the two cities. Nobody claims the competition actually ended back then, but today it's mostly a jocose rivalry.

MUSEUMS Renton History Museum (425-255-2330; www.rentonhistory.org), 235 Mill Avenue South, Renton. Open 10–4 Tues.–Sat. Suggested donation $3 adults, $1 children 8–16; free first Wed. and third Sat. each month. Under the motto COAL WAS KING, this museum explores Renton's contributions to Northwest history, from coal mining to aviation. A small gift shop carries books on local history.

White River Valley Historical Museum (253-288-7433; www.wrvmuseum.org), 918 H Street SE, Auburn. Open 12–4 Wed.–Sun. $2 adults, $1 seniors and children; free every Wed. and first Sun. each month. Permanent exhibits focus on the influences of the Northern Pacific Railroad, the Japanese American heritage, and the Native peoples on Auburn's development, while changing displays examine the intersection of broader historical issues with local ones.

UNIQUE ADVENTURES **All-Merciful Saviour Monastery** (206-463-5918; www.vashonmonks.com), 9933 SW 268th Street, Vashon Island. At the farthest end of the island (technically Maury Island, connected by the thinnest of isthmuses to Vashon), a small, blue onion dome appears through the firs. It tops a wooden church that is the focal point of a tiny monastery—an outpost of Russian Orthodoxy in the recesses of Puget Sound. Since the 1980s, a handful of monks (all American, so no language barrier) have been cultivating this ground, literally as well as figuratively. The few simple but harmonious buildings—cells, refectory, library, and icon-lined church—would look as at home in northern Russia or Scandinavia as they do here (the style is actually Norwegian). Visitors are welcome, including to services, but please call beforehand to check visiting hours and dress modestly.

✳ To Do

BICYCLING **King County Parks and Recreation** (206-296-8687) has information on any of these trails:

Cedar River Trail, 17 miles, the last 3 unpaved, from Renton to Landsburg; access is at several points adjacent to WA 169. This hiker-biker-equestrian trail, formerly a railroad bed, runs along the Cedar River.

Green River Trail, 19 paved miles from Tukwila to Kent; access at Fort Dent Park (see *To See—Historic Sites*) or the Riverbend Golf Complex in Kent. Currently rather industrial, this trail will eventually reach Alki Point and Auburn Narrows Park; it now joins the Interurban Trail (see below).

A BIT OF ORTHODOX RUSSIA AT ALL-MERCIFUL SAVIOUR MONASTERY ON VASHON ISLAND

Interurban Trail, access from Fort Dent Park (see *To See—Historic Sites*) and Brannon Park in Auburn. This 14-mile, straight-as-an-arrow rail trail is also open to all nonmotorized use.

Vashon Island, more than 30 miles of country roads. Bring your bike on a ferry ride to the island and explore its hilly terrain and shoreline. A 20-mile network of mountain-bike trails starts 0.2 mile from the village of Vashon.

Vashon Island Bicycles (206-463-6225; www.vashonislandbicycles.com), 9925 SW 178th Street, Vashon. They can rent you a bike and advise you on places to ride on the island.

CAMPING AYH Ranch Hostel (206-463-2592; www.vashonhostel.com), 12119 SW Cove Road, Vashon Island. For a bucolic experience in summer, take the ferry to Vashon Island and stay at the only legal place to camp on the island. Tents only; rates include free use of cruiser bikes. Adults $13, teens $10, children $5. Or choose a tepee, covered wagon, or dorm bed: adults $23, teens $10, children $5. Private room $65/75, double occupancy.

Saltwater State Park (www.parks.wa.gov), south of WA 516, 2 miles south of Des Moines. Forty-seven standard and one primitive tent site. This park lies directly under Sea-Tac Airport's flight path, so it's not the most peaceful camping experience.

Seattle-Tacoma KOA (253-872-8652 or 800-562-1892), 5801 South 212th Street, Kent. One hundred twenty-nine sites with full hook-ups, 14 with water and electricity only, and 10 tent sites, plus all the usual amenities and a heated swimming pool. Reservations recommended.

DIVING Saltwater State Park (www.parks.wa.gov), south of WA 516, 2 miles south of Des Moines. On the Puget Sound shore halfway between Seattle and Tacoma, this park has an artificial reef offshore that is often visited by divers.

GOLF Foster Golf Links (206-242-4221; www.fostergolflinks.com), 13500 Interurban Avenue, Tukwila. Eighteen holes.

Jade Greens Golf Course (253-931-8562), 18330 SE Lake Holm Road, Auburn. Nine holes.

HIKING Soos Creek Trail (www.kingcounty.gov), about 6 miles, from Gary Grant Park in Kent to Lake Meridian Park in Renton; several access points. This trail, which runs through a greenbelt in eastern King County, is to be extended.

Vashon Island trails tend to be short—it's a small island—and a hike here is more of a saunter, of which Thoreau would approve. **Fisher Pond Preserve**, in the middle of the island, offers 2 miles of forested trails around the bird-friendly pond. **Island Center Forest and Natural Area** is a county forest managed for maximum sustainability and has 9 miles of winding trails. **Dockton Forest and Natural Area**, on Maury Island, has 3 miles of trails. Maps can be picked up at the Vashon–Maury Island Chamber of Commerce (see *Guidance*).

HORSEBACK RIDING Heavenly Gaits Trail Rides (206-940-4422; www .heavenlygaitsvashon.com), 118th Avenue SW, Vashon Island. Meander the island's woods, meadows, or beaches on one of Julie Sharpe's saddle horses. Custom, guided rides for riders of all skill levels. $50 for 90 minutes.

KAYAKING Vashon Island Kayak Center (206-463-9257; www.vashonpark district.org), Jensen Point, Vashon Island. Rentals, guided tours, and lessons, all offered by the county park service.

✳ Wilder Places

PARKS Blake Island State Park (360-731-8330; www.parks.wa.gov), between Bainbridge and Vashon islands; reached only by tour or private boat. This boat-in-only park has some primitive campsites plus a standard campground with 51 tent sites; no reservations. Several sites on the west side are designated for canoers and kayakers on the **Cascadia Marine Trail** (www.wwta.org), the nonmotorized boaters' route from Olympia to Canada. You can also sleep on your own boat: 21 mooring buoys are available, and 1,500 feet of linear moorage are rented out, too.

⚓ **Ed Munro Seahurst Park** (206-988-3700; www.burienparks.net), 140th Avenue SW and 16th Avenue SW, Burien. This 185-acre park enjoys a 2,000-foot saltwater beach backed by a seawall, with a play area and picnic tables. Recent improvements include an environmental science center and activities such as free family beach walks and bonfires.

⚓ **Fort Dent Park** (206-768-2822), 6800 Fort Dent Way, Tukwila. This park has picnic tables and a play area next to the Duwamish River.

Saltwater State Park (www.parks.wa.gov), south of WA 516, 2 miles south of Des Moines. In addition to camping and diving, this park offers picnicking, swimming, and beachcombing on Puget Sound.

✳ Lodging

BED & BREAKFASTS

Kent
Victorian Gardens Bed & Breakfast (888-850-1776; www.victorian gardensbandb.com), 9621 South 200th Street. Only 2.5 acres remain of the original 80-acre property, but the 1888 house, be-gabled and much rehabilitated, sits proudly upon it amid restored Victorian gardens. Three rooms and a suite each offer a sitting area, private bath, balcony, and antiques; there's also a TV and VCR. Rates include full breakfast. No small children or pets. $135–155.

Vashon Island
Artist's Studio Loft (206-463-2583; www.vashonbedandbreakfast.com), 16529 91st Avenue SW. Owner Jacque-

line Clayton has lived and traveled widely, and it shows in the individual decor of each room, as well as in the elegant yet soothing gardens. Set on 5 lush acres, the place certainly reflects an artist's eye, though it's hardly a loft. Four cottages offer ample sofa space to sprawl, a kitchen or kitchenette, rocking chairs, and all the amenities, including a continental breakfast in the fridge. B&B rooms have no kitchen but come with a full breakfast served in the main dining area. No children or pets. Rooms $119–139; cottages $159–215.

COTTAGES AND CABINS

Vashon Island
AYH Ranch Hostel (206-463-2592; www.vashonhostel.com), 12119 SW Cove Road. In winter the hostel rents

out its log cabin lodge as a whole or as three separate suites. Each suite has private bath and can sleep up to seven (cozily). Fix your breakfast (or lunch or dinner) in the kitchen. Entire cabin $300; suite $65–75.

Betty MacDonald Farm (206-567-4227 or 888-328-6753; www.betty macdonaldfarm.com), 11835 99th Avenue SW. Betty MacDonald, author of *The Egg and I*, moved here after quitting her farm near Port Townsend. Six acres are left, with some artifacts from those days. The barn loft has been converted into a two-person suite with kitchen, bath, and deck, while a fully equipped cottage sleeps four. Both have lovely water views. Rates include continental breakfast. $125–160.

Lavender Duck (206-463-2592; www .vashonhostel.com), 16503 Vashon Highway SW. Owned by the AYH Ranch Hostel (see above), this 1896 farmhouse has been updated for comfort while retaining its character. Four bedrooms all have private baths and share a full kitchen and living room. $75.

Swallow's Nest Guest Cottages (206-463-2646 or 800-ANY-NEST), 6030 SW 248th Street. Eight cottages range in size from a cozy two-person "nest" to a two-floor house (you can rent one floor or both). Children welcome in larger units. Pets welcome in certain cottages; call to consult. $105–245.

GUESTHOUSES

Vashon Island
Belle Baldwin House (206-463-9602; www.vashonparkdistrict.org), Fern Cove Nature Preserve, 11408 Cedarhurst Road. This 1912 house was the home of Washington's first female doctor, Belle Baldwin. Situated in a nature preserve on the island's northwest cor-

ner, it offers comfort with a view: three bedrooms, one bath, and fully furnished for six. $1,580 per week in summer; $1,200 Labor Day–Memorial Day.

Madrona Meadows Bed and Barn (206-295-6233; www.madrona meadowsbedandbarn.com), 21828 Monument Road SW. Do you and your horse need some bonding time? While you relax in the comfortable guesthouse, your horse rests in his own 12-by-12-foot stall, unless he's munching on grass in the meadow. Then you can explore the trails or practice jumps in the arena. The cozy house sleeps four and comes complete with kitchen, dining area, and Wi-Fi, while the barn stalls are rubber-matted; a wash stall has hot and cold water. $150 per night; two-night minimum.

Point Robinson Keepers' Quarters (206-463-9602; www.vashonpark district.org), Point Robinson Light Station, 3705 SW Point Robinson Road, Dockton. Really on the western tip of Maury Island, the lighthouse (now automated) is one of many guiding ships among the bays and straits of Puget Sound. Today its two keepers' bungalows welcome guests: one, with three bedrooms, two baths, kitchen, and living room, sleeps six; the other, with two bedrooms, one bath, kitchen, and living room, sleeps four. $1,380–1,580 per week in summer; $975–1,200 Sept.–May; weekends only available in low season.

✳ Where to Eat
DINING OUT

Vashon Island
Quartermaster Inn Restaurant (206-463-5355; www.backbayinn.net), 24007 Vashon Highway. Open 5–9 Fri.–Sun. Overlooking the harbor, the Quartermaster serves up reliable Northwest favorites, featuring lots of

seafood and fish but also rib-eye steak and vegetarian options such as the shiitake mushroom tart.

EATING OUT

Kent

Spiro's Greek Island (253-854-1030; www.spirosgreekisland.com), 215 First Avenue South. Open 11–9 Mon.–Sat. A favorite with locals as well as guests, Spiro's serves reliably mouthwatering, affordable Greek dishes in a casual setting.

Wild Wheat Bakery, Café & Restaurant (253-856-8919), 202 First Avenue South. Open 7–3 Mon.–Fri., 7:30–3 Sat., 8–3 Sun. Not only breakfast and dessert pastries, but home-baked breads are on luscious display here, together with sandwiches made therefrom. The lunch menu is supplemented with salads and burgers, while breakfast features omelets, blintzes, and other goodies.

Vashon Island

Café Luna (206-463-0777; www.cafe luna.com), 9924 SW Bank Road. Open 7–7 Mon.–Thurs., 7 AM–10 PM Fri.–Sat., 8–6 Sun. In the best coffeehouse tradition, Luna offers not only a variety of coffees, and teas from actual tea leaves, and not only pastries, sandwiches, soups, and salads (mostly from organic ingredients), but also art displays, live music, and a spot where locals gather to discuss anything and everything. Oh, and "Luna" was a German shepherd belonging to one of the original owners.

The Hardware Store (206-463-1800; www.thsrestaurant.com), 17601 Vashon Highway SW. Open 8 AM–8:30 PM Sun.–Thurs., 8 AM–9:30 PM Fri.–Sat. In "downtown" Vashon, the Hardware Store is the oldest commercial building

on the island—now a restaurant–art gallery. The menu includes old favorites (crabcakes, Penn Cove mussels, fried chicken breast) and newer ones (Havarti shrimp), plus vegetarian dishes and tempting desserts. Between meals, you can belly up to the espresso bar or even the real bar.

Pure (206-463-1442), 9925 SW Bank Road. Open 11–5 Mon.–Wed., 11–5 Sat., 11–3 Sun. A gluten-free, vegan café seems almost a contradiction in terms, but Pure manages to please with salads, juices, chili, and even pizza, not to mention other items that change seasonally.

SELECTED SHOPPING DK Market (425-277-5055), 720 Lind Avenue SW, Renton. Open 8–8 daily. Fulfill your hankering for Asian spices, Turkish jams, Chinese teas, Russian deli food, and many more international necessities here, at reasonable prices. You'll also find a large section containing fresh produce both familiar and exotic.

Great Wall Shopping Mall (425-251-1600; www.greatwallmall.com), 18230 East Valley Highway, Kent. Open 9 AM–10 PM daily. A hypermarket dedicated to foods of East Asia, the mall serves the area's large Asian community and other lovers of Asian food. Besides the actual market, you'll find small restaurants, video stores, and a game arcade here.

✳ Special Events

July: **Vashon Island Strawberry Festival** (206-463-6217), Ober Park, Vashon Island. Classic cars, street dancing, food, music, and art celebrate the berries.

SEATTLE

GUIDANCE **Chinatown–International District Business Improvement Association** (206-382-1197; www.cidbia.org), 507 South King Street, Seattle 98104.

Greater Seattle Chamber of Commerce (206-389-7200; www.seattlechamber .com), 1301 Fifth Avenue, Suite 2500, Seattle 98101.

Seattle's Convention and Visitors Bureau (206-461-5800 or 866-732-2965; visitseattle.org), One Convention Place, 701 Pike Street, Suite 800, Seattle 98101. Also serves as the Citywide Concierge Center.

GETTING THERE **I-5** is the primary north-south highway; **WA 99** parallels I-5 to the west. **I-90** is the primary east-west route, and **WA 520** parallels it to the north; both cross Lake Washington on bridges to the Eastside. **WA 522** heads northeast from I-5 through north Seattle to Bothell and eventually US 2 at Monroe.

Seattle-Tacoma International Airport (206-787-5388 or 800-544-1965; www .portofseattle.org) is half an hour south of Seattle, off I-5 at exit 154B. From Sea-Tac Airport, **Gray Line Downtown Airporter** (206-626-6088 or 800-426-7532; www.graylineofseattle.com) runs twice an hour to downtown hotels, 5:30 AM–midnight; **Shuttle Express** (425-981-7000) goes to Seattle suburbs.

AMTRAK (800-USA-RAIL; www.amtrak.com) has three routes that serve Seattle from its Pioneer Square depot at 303 South Jackson Street: Coast Starlight, which runs south to Los Angeles; Empire Builder, which runs north to Everett, then east to Spokane and Chicago; and Cascade Express, which runs between Eugene, Oregon, and Vancouver, British Columbia.

Greyhound (206-628-5526 or 800-231-2222; www.greyhound.com) serves Seattle from the AMTRAK station as well as a downtown station at 811 Stewart Street.

Washington State Ferries (206-464-6400 or 888-808-7977; www.wsdot.wa.gov /ferries/) serve commuters and travelers between Seattle and Vashon Island, Bremerton, and Bainbridge Island. Most tickets are available at Colman Dock, Pier 52, on the waterfront; call for seasonal schedules.

GETTING AROUND **Central Link** (888-889-6368; www.soundtransit.org), Seattle's new light rail, runs between downtown Seattle and Sea-Tac Airport, with a dozen or so stops in between. This speedy and clean line quickly gained

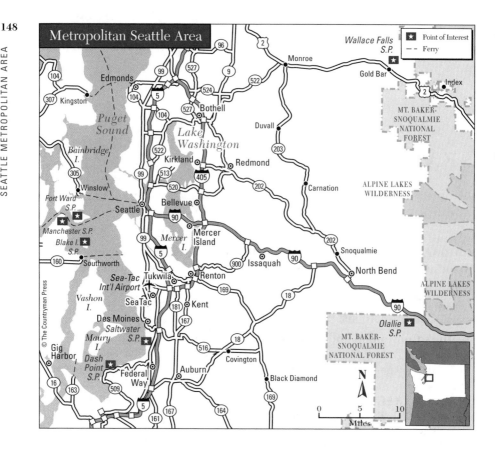

acceptance and is a handy way to navigate between the southern suburbs, the International District, Pioneer Square, and the city center. Runs 5 AM–midnight.

Metro Transit (206-553-3000; www.kingcounty.gov), 201 South Jackson Street, Seattle. User-friendly bus service runs through Seattle and all of King County, including Sea-Tac Airport; downtown Seattle is a free-ride area. If you plan to stay within the city, it's hardly worth bringing a car. The **Seattle Monorail** (206-905-2600) runs from the Westlake Center, downtown at Fourth and Pine streets, north to the Seattle Center.

MEDICAL EMERGENCY Harborview Medical Center (206-731-3000), 325 Ninth Avenue, Seattle.

Northwest Hospital and Medical Center (206-364-0500), 1550 North 115th Street, Seattle.

Swedish Medical Center (206-386-6000 or 800-SWEDISH; www.swedish.org), 747 Broadway, Seattle.

University of Washington Medical Center (206-598-3300), 1959 NE Pacific, Seattle.

Virginia Mason Medical Center (206-624-1144), 925 Seneca Street, Seattle.

There are a couple of ways to take the edge off Seattle's price tag.

Go Seattle Card (800-887-9103; www.goseattlecard.com) gets you into more than 30 attractions, including the Space Needle and some listed below, plus provides discounts at some shops and restaurants. You can buy versions good for one, two, three, five, or seven days; $50–135 adults, $38–95 children. Or choose a **Go Select Pass,** which allows you to choose the attractions you want and essentially gives you discounted entry rates. Go Seattle is available online or at the **Pacific Place Concierge Desk** (206-405-2655), 600 Pine Street, Seattle; at the Space Needle (see *To Do—Unique Adventures*); or in summer at the **Pioneer Square Information Kiosk** (206-667-0687), South Main Street and Occidental Avenue, Seattle. Go Select is available online.

Seattle CityPass (707-256-0490; www.citypass.com) lets you visit the following six attractions for $59 adults, $39 children 4–12 (valid for nine days): Space Needle, Seattle Aquarium, Pacific Science Center, harbor cruise, EMP Museum, and either Woodland Park Zoo or Museum of Flight. This is a substantial savings if these are places you want to go. It's available online, at the Seattle's Convention and Visitors Bureau (see *Guidance*), and at each of the above attractions.

BOAT TOURS Argosy Cruises (206-888-1445; www.argosycruises.com), 1101 Alaskan Way, Suite 201, Seattle. Argosy offers several boat tours of Seattle, including a one-hour harbor cruise with live commentary that is included on the CityPass card (without the card: $17.50–22.50 adults, $15–19.75 seniors, $8.50–9.75 children 4–12). Or you can cruise Seattle's lakes or Chittenden Locks.

CRUISE SHIPS AND STORY POLES IN SEATTLE

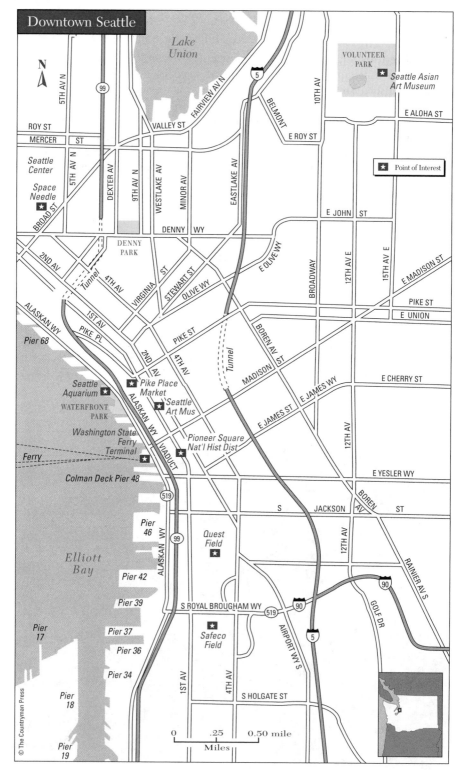

Downtown Seattle

N

Lake Union

VOLUNTEER PARK

Seattle Asian Art Museum

ROY ST

MERCER ST

5TH AV N

99

DEXTER AV

9TH AV N

WESTLAKE AV

MINOR AV

VALLEY ST

FAIRVIEW AV N

5

BELMONT

10TH AV

E ALOHA ST

E ROY ST

Point of Interest

Seattle Center

Space Needle

5TH AV N

BROAD ST

DENNY WY

E JOHN ST

DENNY PARK

2ND AV

Tunnel

4TH AV

VIRGINIA ST

STEWART ST

OLIVE WY

EASTLAKE AV

E OLIVE WY

BROADWAY

12TH AV E

15TH AV E

E MADISON ST

PIKE ST

E UNION

ALASKAN WY

Pier 68

1ST AV

PIKE PL

PIKE ST

2ND AV

4TH AV

Tunnel

BOREN AV

MADISON ST

E CHERRY ST

Seattle Aquarium

WATERFRONT PARK

Pike Place Market

Seattle Art Mus

ALASKAN WY

E JAMES WY

E JAMES ST

12TH AV

Washington State Ferry Terminal

VIADUCT

Pioneer Square Nat'l Hist Dist

Ferry

Colman Deck Pier 48

E YESLER WY

519

BOREN AV

S JACKSON ST

Elliott Bay

Pier 46

99

ALASKAN WY

Quest Field

12TH AV

Pier 42

90

RAINIER AV S

Pier 39

S ROYAL BROUGHAM WY

519

90

5

GOLF DR

Pier 17

Pier 37

Safeco Field

AIRPORT WY S

Pier 36

Pier 34

1ST AV

4TH AV

S HOLGATE ST

Pier 18

Pier 19

© The Countryman Press

0   .25   0.50 mile

Miles

Ride the Ducks (206-441-3825 or 800-817-1116; www.ridetheducksofseattle
.com), 516 Broad Street, Seattle. Tours every half hour in summer, every hour in
winter. $28 adults, $17 children 2–13, $1 children under 2. The Ducks will show
you around town in World War II amphibious vehicles, from Pioneer Square to
Lake Union, with running commentary. These "surf-and-turf" tours last 90 minutes. Tours depart from Fifth Avenue and Broad Street or from the Westlake Center. Reservations recommended.

CULTURAL SITES Fremont Troll, under the Aurora Bridge at North 36th
Street, Seattle. This 18-foot-tall kooky sculpture has been holed up under a bridge
since 1990. In his concrete hand, he holds, and is evidently about to munch, an
actual Volkswagen Beetle. Definitely worth a look, though parking is a bit dicey on
the busy street.

Olympic Sculpture Park (206-654-3100; www.seattleartmuseum.org), 2901
Western Avenue, Seattle. Free. A project of the Seattle Art Museum (see *Muse-
ums*), the sculpture park has transformed 9 acres of former industrial waterfront
into public art. Trees and lawns complement works by Alexander Calder and
Robert Serra, among others, along Elliott Bay in the Belltown neighborhood.
There are several access points, but the main entrance is on Broad Street between
Western and Elliott avenues. Good views over the bay, too.

FARMERS' MARKETS Pike Place Market (206-624-8082; www.pikeplace
market.com), First Avenue and Pike Street, Seattle. Open 9–6 Mon.–Sat., 10–5

MAKING WAVES AT OLYMPIC SCULPTURE PARK IN SEATTLE.

Sun. The granddaddy of Seattle's public markets, Pike Place Market is the one with the PUBLIC MARKET sign in big red letters standing against the western sky. The several floors of the old market building cascade down the bluff to Western Avenue near the waterfront; other market buildings line the sidewalks between First Avenue and Pike Place. It's all filled with a—well, marketplace—of flowers, fruits, vegetables, fresh meats, fish (if you've seen the vendors tossing large salmon on TV, now you can see them in the flesh), breads, crafts, wines, you name it—all mostly homegrown. You can spend an entertaining hour or two completely free of charge and then replenish your energy at one of the several eateries in the market. And although it's become a tourist attraction, it is what it always has been: a place for people to purchase their daily needs.

Ballard Farmers' Market (206-250-0609), 5300 Ballard Avenue NW, Seattle. Open 10–3 Sun. year-round.

Broadway Sunday Farmers' Market (206-547-2278), in front of Seattle Central Community College at Broadway and Pine Street. Open 11–3 Sun. mid-May–mid-Dec.

Columbia City Farmers' Market (206-547-2278), South Edmunds Street at 37th Avenue. Open 3–7 Wed. late Apr.–mid-Oct.

Fremont Street Market (206-781-6776), at the north end of the Fremont Bridge. Open 10–5 Sun. year-round. This one has become quite a happening, with clothes, antiques, junk, imports, and much more besides fresh produce.

Lake City Farmers' Market (206-547-2278), NE 125th Street and 28th Avenue NE. Open 3–7 Thurs. June–early Oct.

Magnolia Farmers' Market (206-547-2278), 33rd Avenue West and West McGraw Street. Open 10–2 Sat. mid-June–early Oct.

Phinney Farmers' Market (206-547-2278), 67th Street and Phinney Avenue North. Open 3–7 Fri. June–early Oct.

University District Farmers' Market (206-547-2278), NE 50th Street and University Way NE, Seattle. Open 9–2 Sat. year-round.

West Seattle Farmers' Market, 44th Avenue SW and SW Alaska Street. Open 10–2 Sun. year-round, except Christmas and New Year's Day.

FOR FAMILIES *✶* **Center for Wooden Boats** (206-382-2628; www.cwb.org), 1010 Valley Street, Seattle. Open 10–6 daily May–Dec.; 10–6 Tues.–Sun. Sept.–Apr.; rentals 12–6. Admission free, but donation accepted. At the south end of Lake Union, the center's collection of classic wooden craft is a treat for your inner sailor. Not only can you admire these beautiful boats, but you can also learn the skills involved in making them and take one out on the lake; if you don't know how, you can take lessons (open to adults and kids). On Sunday afternoons, there are free rides. A branch at Cama Beach on Camano Island offers boat rentals, educational programs, and the chance to stay in one of the restored 1930s cabins.

✶ **Children's Museum** (206-441-1768; www.thechildrensmuseum.org), 305 Harrison Street, Seattle. Open 10–5 Mon.–Fri., 10–6 Sat.–Sun. $7.50 adults and children over one, $6.50 grandparents, $6 active military. Join your kid on a journey to far shores or through Seattle's backyard. Changing and permanent exhibits exercise the imagination, mind, and even muscles through (miniature) mountain climbs, sea voyages, artwork, and more.

Hiram Chittenden Locks (206-783-7059; www.nws.usace.army.mil), 3015 NW 54th Street, Seattle. Open 7 AM–9 PM daily May–Sept.; 10–4 Thurs.–Mon. Oct.–Apr.; guided tours Mar.–Nov. Free. Dedicated in 1917, the locks allow ships entry from Elliott Bay to Lakes Union and Washington through the Ship Canal. Cross the walkway, watch the boats moving through the locks, and check the fish ladder to see if the salmon are running—the latter presciently put in the plans in 1910. Run by the U.S. Army Corps of Engineers, the grounds include a visitors center, a historical home, the fish ladder, and a botanical garden. It's a surprisingly well-visited destination, where families can picnic while watching the ships come and go.

Pacific Science Center (206-443-2001; www.pacsci.org), 200 Second Avenue North, Seattle. Open 10–5 Mon.–Fri., 10–6 Sat.–Sun.; closed Tues. in low season. Admission to exhibits only, $14 adults, $12 seniors, $9 children 6–15, $3 children 3–5; IMAX extra. Friendly to children and adults as well, the science center has a bit of everything, from live animal exhibits to a tropical butterfly house (nice to visit in winter) to robotic dinosaurs and insects (be warned)—and occasional blockbusters, such as the 2012 Tutankhamun exhibit. IMAX movies take you to the deep ocean or through the eruption of Mount St. Helens, while planetarium shows (add $3 to museum admission) open your eyes to the night sky.

✪ **Seattle Aquarium** (206-386-4300; www.seattleaquarium.org), 1483 Alaskan Way, Pier 59, Seattle. Open 9:30–5 daily. $19 adults, $12 children 4–12, $5.50 children under 4. Tanks display marine creatures and their ecosystems, from Puget Sound's marine mammals to Pacific Ocean corals. Observe fish from an underwater dome, feel starfish in a touch tank, check out orca skeletons, and watch the sea otters play. The "wall of water," a Pacific fish habitat, leans into the lobby and is especially intriguing when feeding time comes and the feeder answers visitors' questions from underwater.

& ✪ **Seattle Central Library** (206-386-4636; www.spl.org), 1000 Fourth Avenue, Seattle. Open 10–8 Mon.–Thurs., 10–6 Fri.–Sat., 12–6 Sun.; call for tours. Seattle's downtown public library sits among the skyscrapers like a tropical bird in the forest. Definitely not a Carnegie library, or any old-fashioned library with "sequester'd nooks / And all the sweet serenity of books" (as Longfellow put it in "Morituri Salutamus"), it looks out on the world through vast, angled windowpanes making up virtually the entire 11-floor building's exterior. The inner spaces are equally vast, with one level wanting to be the city's living room and another housing 140 computers in rows. And yet it seems to work. The Rem Koolhaas design has been a hit with the citizens of Seattle, who in fact can be seen lounging about the huge main level or staring concentratedly at computer screens. The stacks radiate from a four-floor spiral

A VISITOR CONTEMPLATES CORALS AT THE SEATTLE AQUARIUM.

SEATTLE CENTRAL LIBRARY'S MAIN-FLOOR "LIVING ROOM"

ramp with Dewey decimal floor mats at each level (accessible, of course, by elevator and escalator). And, naturally, there are wonderful things such as a map room, genealogy collections, and a large, friendly children's room and activities—even a coffee and sandwich cart. Somehow, despite the large spaces and numbers of people, sound is muted.

Theo Chocolate (206-632-5100; www.theochocolate.com), 3400 Phinney Avenue North, Seattle. Open 10–6 daily, with scheduled tours four or five times a day (reservations recommended) and a walk-in tour at 2:30. Tours $6. "Theo" is for *Theobroma*, the genus to which the cacao plant belongs, and this is an actual chocolate factory. So satisfy your inner Charlie with a tour. Your lively guide will delineate the process of creating their organic, fair-trade chocolates, with plenty of free samples along the way. And if that's not enough, or you don't have the time, buy from their retail space in the lobby.

Woodland Park Zoo (206-684-4800; www.zoo.org), 601 North 59th Street, Seattle. Open 9:30–6 daily May–Sept.; 9:30–5 daily Oct.–Apr. $17.50 adults, $15.50 seniors and disabled, $11.50 children 3–12 in summer; $11.50, $9.50, and $8.50, respectively, in winter. More than three hundred species, from African elephants to zebras, await your visit (no aardvarks, apparently). Arranged by bioclimatic zones, "naturalistic" exhibits place the animals in environments resembling their natural habitats—tundra, tropical forest, and the like—some indoors and some out, so there are enough covered exhibits to entertain a child on a rainy day.

GARDENS Kubota Garden (206-684-4584; www.kubota.org), 9817 55th Avenue South, Seattle. Open dawn to dusk daily. Free. Though now run by the Seattle Department of Parks and Recreation, these 20 acres were the lifetime's labor of

Fujitaro Kubota, who came to America in 1907. A self-taught gardener, he built a successful landscape business, cultivating his own garden in his free time. His work was interrupted when he was interned during World War II; luckily, he was able to return afterward and lived to be 94. Also luckily, the 20 acres were rescued from development and preserved so that the public can enjoy Kubota's reflecting pools, waterfalls, and exquisite plantings.

Volunteer Park Conservatory (206-332-4112; www.volunteerparkconservatory .org), 1402 East Galer Street, Seattle. Open 10–4 Tues.–Sun. Free. The Victorian-style greenhouse in venerable Volunteer Park is divided into five climate-controlled areas featuring bromeliads, palms, ferns, cacti, orchids, and much more. It's fun for plant lovers and a nice place to escape the winter rains!

& **Washington Park Arboretum** (206-543-8800; depts.washington.edu/uwbg /gardens), 2300 Arboretum Drive East, Seattle. Grounds open dawn to dusk daily; visitors center open 9–5 daily. Free. More than 4,600 species of trees and shrubs are found on the extensive grounds of the arboretum. Displays concentrate on Northwest species, although there are trees here from around the world. Come to learn or just to walk among beautiful, beloved trees; paths include a 1,700-foot shoreline trail and wheelchair-accessible trails. The grounds also include a **Japanese Garden** (206-684-4725), open 10–7 daily in summer, Tues.–Sun. the rest of the year; $6 adults, $4 seniors, disabled, students, and children.

Woodland Park Rose Garden (www.seattle.gov/parks), 601 North 59th Street, Seattle. Open 7 AM–dusk. Free (though there's a parking fee if the zoo is open). More than five thousand rose plants are grown on 2.5 acres adjacent to the zoo.

GUIDED TOURS Chinatown Discovery (206-623-5124; www.seattlechinatown tour.com), 719 South King Street, Seattle. Standard tours $17.95 adults, $15.95 seniors, $12.95 students, $10.95 children. The International District is a hodge-podge of Chinese, Japanese, Laotian, Vietnamese, Cambodian, and other Asian cultures. Chinatown Discovery guides you through the sights, sounds, and foods; specialized tours focusing on music, herbs, art, etc., are available on request.

✄ **Underground Tour** (206-682-4646; www.undergroundtour.com), 608 First Avenue, Seattle. $16 adults, $13 seniors and students, $8 children 7–12—all cash only! Local history buff Bill Speidel started this tour in the 1960s, about the time Pioneer Square was saved by citizens from being turned into a parking lot. His tour became a rousing success. It's underground because, following the fire of 1889, the district was rebuilt an entire floor above what was then ground level. As your guide will explain, perhaps more graphically than you might wish, this was in part to solve the recurrent sewage disposal problem in a tidal marsh. Anyway, numerous offices and businesses were abandoned in situ, and you can take a ghostly peek at Seattle's early life while hearing pedestrians pass overhead. At one and a half hours, the tour is a bit longer than the material really warrants, but you learn some "underground" history, and the guides' ebullient patter keeps even children's attention.

HISTORIC HOMES Dearborn House (206-622-6952), 1117 Minor Avenue, Seattle. Open 9–5 Mon.–Fri. Currently the headquarters of **Historic Seattle,** the 1907 house was built for Henry Dearborn, an eastern banker influential in much of Seattle's development. His house was one of many large homes to go up in the swanky First Hill neighborhood; it's now one of only four left among the skyscrapers and hospitals.

Stimson-Green Mansion (206-624-0474; www.stimsongreen.com), 1204 Minor Avenue, Seattle. Financier Charles Stimson came to Seattle in 1889, just in time to rebuild the city—with some help, of course. His house on First Hill, built from 1899 to 1901, is an enormous Tudor Revival mansion with three stories and plenty of gables and half-timbering. In 1914 he sold it to Joshua Green, another influential businessman, who lived in the house till his death at the age of 105. Tours may be arranged by calling the Washington Trust for Historic Preservation, 206-624-2410.

HISTORIC SITES Alki Point, Alki Avenue SW, Seattle. A pylon marks the spot, or thereabouts, where the Denny party—4 families and 4 single adults, including no one over the age of 34, but 12 children, of whom 3 were infants—landed on November 13, 1851. They had come out along the Oregon Trail but found the Willamette Valley filling up, so they searched for elbow room and ended up on this inhospitable point that is now in West Seattle. Why they chose a site facing incoming storms and surrounded on three sides by cold salt water is not clear, but after one winter, they moved into the recesses of Elliott Bay.

Arctic Building, 306 Cherry Street, Seattle. There were apparently enough Seattleites who struck it rich in the Klondike to start their own club. In 1916 the Arctic Club commissioned this building as their new home. It was a fine and exclusive thing in its day, with Alaskan marble, frescoed ceilings, chandeliers, tearooms, and dining rooms. Today it's given over to office space, but the row of walrus heads around the third-floor exterior mark it as something out of the ordinary.

✌ **Gas Works Park** (206-684-4075; www.seattle.gov/parks), 2101 North Northlake Way, Seattle. From 1907 to the 1950s, this plant produced gas from coal. The property, with its half-ruined buildings, now constitutes a city park, where the boiler room is a picnic shelter and the exhauster-compressor building surreally houses a children's play barn. The park seems to attract nonmainstream events, from peace concerts to the annual Naked Bike Ride protesting oil dependence.

Occidental Park, at Occidental Avenue South and South Main Street, the center of the historic district's grid of four or five streets, is somewhat seedy: Full of small restaurants and galleries, it is also the outdoor home to a seasonally variable number of people. The city has tried to curb panhandling and other irregular occupations in the neighborhood, but it pays to be careful here at night. That said, it's the heart of old Seattle, home of the Underground Tour (see *Guided Tours*), Klondike National Park (see *Museums*), the Smith Tower (see below), a bronze bust of Chief Seattle, several historic totem poles, and a lively music scene. The art galleries sponsor an **art walk** the first Thursday evening of every month.

Pioneer Square, Seattle's birthplace, is really a triangle, at First Avenue and Yesler Way, marked by an elaborate pergola. Most of the buildings here are Victorian and Edwardian brick and stone, dating from after the 1889 fire that destroyed most of the city. A decidedly mixed boom zone, the square became derelict during the Depression, emerging only in the 1960s with a movement for historical preservation.

Pioneer Square Historic District, bounded by Alaskan Way, Yesler Way, Third Avenue South, and South King Street, Seattle. This is where the Denny party settled after fleeing Alki Point (see above). Their new home was no Ritz either, being a tidal marsh with steep hillsides at its back, though several Duwamish villages dotted the neighborhood. The settlers made the best of it, and from this unlikely group sprang a busy hub that, with its plentiful timber and eventual port, soon became the powerhouse of the Northwest.

Smith Tower (206-622-4004; www.smithtower.com), 506 Second Avenue, Seattle. Observation deck open 10–5 daily Apr. and Oct.; 10–8:30 daily May–July; 10–8 daily Aug.; 10–7:30 Sept.; 10–4 Sat.–Sun. Nov.–Mar. Observation deck: $7 adults, $6 seniors and students, $5 children 6–12. This is the Smith of Smith-Corona typewriters and Smith & Wesson guns. The 522-foot-tall building that Smith opened in 1914 was the first skyscraper in Seattle and one of the first in the world. A 21-story tower was set on top of a 21-story base, the whole framed mostly in steel and covered in white terra-cotta—an in-your-face challenge to a brash timber town. It had 540 offices, an observation deck (as the tallest building west of the Mississippi for many decades, it couldn't *not* have one), and the elaborate Chinese Room, named for the blackwood furniture and wood and porcelain ceiling given by the Chinese empress to Mr. Smith. The array of elevators you see on entering the building today mostly still have their original motors, except those operated manually. And the open-air, wraparound observation deck is still accessible via a manual elevator.

Starbucks (206-448-8762), 1912 Pike Place, in Pike Place Market, Seattle. This is the world's first Starbucks shop, opened in 1971 and still in operation. (There's a town called Starbuck in far southeastern Washington, but apparently it has nothing to do with coffee.)

THE SEATTLE WATERFRONT, OLD AND NEW

Yesler Way, from Elliott Bay and Pioneer Square east to Lake Washington, Seattle. In 1852, Henry Yesler was persuaded to choose the nascent settlement of Seattle for his new sawmill. The "city" donated a waterfront lot and a corridor for his lumbermen to skid logs in from the forested hills—a "skid road." The corridor, first named Mill Street, is now Yesler Way, though the neighborhood was long known as a "skid row."

MUSEUMS Burke Museum of Natural History and Culture (206-543-5590; www.burkemuseum.org), 17th Avenue NE and NE 45th Street. Open 10–5 daily, 10–8 first Thurs. each month. $10 adults, $8 seniors, $7.50 students and children over 5; free first Thurs. each month. Parking $15, with prorated refund for less than four hours; parking free Sat.–Sun. (There's also metered neighborhood on-street parking.) On the University of Washington campus, the Burke is the state's oldest museum, dating from 1885. In it you'll find a grand repository of the natural and cultural history of the Pacific Northwest, with tendrils reaching around the Pacific Rim. Ongoing and changing exhibits include fossils from around the region (who knew that the remains of a 12,000-year-old giant ground sloth had been found at Sea-Tac Airport?), all aspects of nature in Washington, Native American art old and new, and an ethno-botanical garden. A research museum with large archaeological, botanical, and zoological collections, it is the current custodian of Kennewick Man (see the Tri-Cities Area chapter in part 6, Southeastern Washington).

KILLER WHALE SCULPTURE AT SEATTLE'S BURKE MUSEUM OF NATURAL HISTORY AND CULTURE

& **EMP Museum** (206-770-2700; www.empmuseum.org), 325 Fifth Avenue North, Seattle. Open 10–5 daily. $18 adults ($15 if you buy online), $15 seniors and military, $12 students and children over five Mon.–Thurs.; $2 more Fri.–Sun. Formerly the Experience Music Project and the Science Fiction Museum. The two have now become one, with a friendlier price tag. Frank Gehry's wavy, metallic creation opened in 2000, the brainchild of Microsoft cofounder Paul Allen and one of the splashier additions to Seattle's architectural scene. The main hall seems to suggest a garage, but maybe that's intentional—this was conceived as a rock museum, after all. There are both hands-on and hands-off exhibits: The Sound Lab is a studio where you can create music on computerized instruments and learn musical basics; there's a digital lab for researching rock arcana and a Sky Church for performances. In the galleries, you'll find a whole hall devoted to native son Jimi Hendrix, as well as instruments, a history of the Northwest music scene, rotating exhibits (a rather academic deconstruction of hip-hop on one visit), and a nifty centerpiece: a floor-to-roof tower of instruments tracing the history of American popular music.

The smaller Science Fiction wing displays Klingon swords and lots of other extraterrestrial artifacts, including some of the most famous spaceships in the fictional universe. Changing exhibitions in 2011 included real materials from *Battlestar Galactica* and special effects from the movie *Avatar.* Beyond artifacts, though, the museum examines the literary borders of science fiction—the social, philosophical, and scientific questions it addresses; once and future technology; and the evolution of sci-fi as a genre. All this and some actual science, too. Elevators make the whole building handicapped-accessible.

& **Frye Art Museum** (206-622-9250; www.fryemuseum.org), 704 Terry Avenue, Seattle. Open 10–5 Tues.–Sun., 10–7 Thurs. Free. Charles Frye did quite well for himself as a meatpacker during the Klondike gold rush and in subsequent ventures. He and his wife began collecting art in the 1890s and amassed more than two hundred pieces, which they willed, with funds, to create a museum of art that would remain forever free to the public. The original collection consists of 19th- and 20th-century European and American works, while rotating exhibitions focus more on modern art. Wheelchair-accessible.

Henry Art Gallery (206-543-2280; www.henryart.org), 15th Avenue NE and NE 41st Street, Seattle. Open 11–4 Wed., Sat., and Sun., 11–9 Thurs.–Fri. Suggested donation $10 adults and children 14–17, $6 seniors; free for students with ID and children 13 and under; free first Thurs. each month. The "other" museum at the University of Washington (the first being the Burke; see above), the Henry displays art on the cutting edge, from the beginnings of photography to 21st-century media.

Klondike Gold Rush National Historical Park (206-220-4240; www.nps.gov), northwest corner of Jackson Street and Second Avenue, Seattle. Open 9–5 daily. Free. If you've ever seen Charlie Chaplin's *Gold Rush,* you have some idea what this place is about. Historic photos, archives, and artifacts record the Klondike gold rush of 1897–1898, when thousands of prospectors streamed north to the Klondike goldfields, many of them taking the arduous route through Canada. The stampede was set off in July 1897 when gold-laden ships docked in San Francisco and Seattle, claiming to carry tons of Klondike gold. Thereafter Seattle positioned itself as the logical supply station for gold miners, who were required by the Canadian government, fearing mass starvation among the prospectors, to carry a year's worth of supplies. This small museum-park is actually the smaller half of the Klondike Gold Rush National Historical Park; the larger half is in Skagway, Alaska.

Log House Museum (206-938-5293; www.loghousemuseum.org), 3003 61st Avenue SW, Seattle. Open 12–4 Thurs.–Sun. Suggested donation $3 adults, $1 children; tours $2. Originally the carriage house of an early (1904) Alki estate, the Log House now contains changing exhibits on the birth of Seattle and the history of the Duwamish Peninsula.

& **Museum of Flight** (206-764-5720; www.museumofflight.org), 9404 East Marginal Way South, Seattle. Open 10–5 daily, 10–9 first Thurs. each month. $16 adults, $14 seniors, $9 children 5–17; free 5–9 first Thurs. each month. It's been almost a century since Bill Boeing came west and decided he could build a better aircraft. The museum, a tribute to him and the major Seattle employer that the company he founded became, is near the spot where he did it. The Red Barn, Boeing's original assembly plant and the oldest aircraft production facility in the United States, is on the grounds, with a history of the company and mock-up of an assembly floor. The first piece in the collection was a 1929 Boeing aircraft someone found in an Alaska landfill. That plane is now the centerpiece of the Great Gallery, where 23 historic planes by Douglas, de Havilland, and, yes, Boeing hang from the ceiling above another 20 that are displayed on the floor. From the Wright brothers to NASA, the history of flight takes off, so to speak. Outdoors you can visit the Concorde and the first *Air Force One;* visit an air traffic control tower—the museum is at Boeing Field, a general aviation airport, so it's not all for show; and stroll around some of the Boeing giants. Some wheelchairs are available, and there are elevators to all floors.

❧ **Museum of History and Industry** (206-324-1126; www.seattlehistory.org), 2700 24th Avenue East, Seattle; scheduled to move to the Naval Reserve Armory, 860 Terry Avenue North, in November 2012. Open 10–5 daily, 10–8 first Thurs. each month. $8 adults, $7 seniors and students, children 5–17 free; free first Thurs. each month. Entirely dedicated to the history of Seattle, this museum's exhibits bring out lost details such as Seattle life before the fire of 1889, a whole garden of historic objects, and a diorama of the foundational scene: the landing of the Denny party at Alki Point in 1851. Lots of exhibits have aspects geared to children.

Nordic Heritage Museum (206-789-5707; www.nordicmuseum.org), 3014 NW 67th Street, Seattle. Open 10–4 Tues.–Sat., 12–4 Sun. $6 adults, $5 seniors and students, $4 children 5–17. The Ballard district of northern Seattle was heavily populated by Scandinavian immigrants in the late nineteenth and early twentieth centuries. They came in waves, some directly from the mother countries and some as "secondary immigrants" from the Midwest, drawn by opportunities in logging, fishing, and, later, farming (apparently the Finns dominated logging and the Norwegians fishing). The museum traces this migration: the ground floor is dedicated to the impetus for and experience of emigration, with appropriate sound effects (birdsong on the home farm, crying babies and tumult on Ellis Island), while the top two floors are dedicated to Scandinavians in the various industries to which they gravitated and their cultural evolution in the United States. There are some fine examples of folk art, a student-built replica of a Viking boat, and intriguing artifacts of the immigrant experience—which, the museum points out, is a universal American experience, not just a Nordic one.

Seattle Art Museum (206-654-3100; www.seattleartmuseum.org), 1300 First Avenue, Seattle. Open 10–5 Wed., Sat., and Sun.; 10–9 Thurs. and Fri. Suggested donation $15 adults, $12 seniors and military, $9 students, children under 12 free; free for all first Thurs. each month; free for seniors first Fri. each month; free for teens with ID 5–9 second Fri. each month. Reopened after a major renovation, the museum has 118,000 square feet of new space, with room to grow. This allows for some surprising exhibits, such as a hall whose walls are completely covered in European and Asian porcelains. The permanent collection constitutes an artistic world tour, with creations from aboriginal Australia, Africa, and North America, as well as classical and modern Asian and European works.

Seattle Asian Art Museum (206-654-3100; www.seattleartmuseum.org), Volunteer Park, 1400 East Prospect Street, Seattle. Open 10–5 Wed.–Sun., 10–9 Thurs. Suggested donation $7 adults, $5 seniors and students, children under 13 free; free for all first Thurs. each month; free for seniors first Fri. each month; free for families first Sat. each month. A branch of the Seattle Art Museum, SAAM displays an exquisite collection of Korean, Chinese, Southeast Asian, and Japanese works, from Neolithic ceramics to modern art; its Japanese collection is said to be one of the best outside Japan.

Wing Luke Asian Museum (206-623-5124; www.wingluke.org), 719 South King Street, Seattle. Open 10–5 Tues.–Sun., 10–8 first Thurs. and third Sat. each month. $12.95 adults, $9.95 seniors and students, $8.95 children 5–12; includes a guided tour of an early immigrant guesthouse and Chinese store. In the middle of Seattle's Chinatown–International District, this dream of immigrant and civil rights lawyer Wing Luke preserves the history, culture, and stories of Seattle's East Asian immigrants.

✳ To Do

BICYCLING Burke-Gilman Trail, 27 paved miles from Eighth Avenue NW in Seattle to Kenmore. This rail trail goes along the Ship Canal, through the University District, and up Lake Washington's west shore to the mouth of the Sammamish River, with seven access points. Among the King County park system's more than 175 miles of hiking and biking trails, this is a regional favorite.

Green Lake Park, 7201 Green Lake Drive North. In northern Seattle, this 2.8-mile loop around Green Lake is an easy, family-friendly ride.

Lake Washington Boulevard (www.cityofseattle.net/parks), 4 miles from Colman Park to Seward Park. This is a favorite scenic ride; add the 2.5-mile partially paved loop trail around **Seward Park** for a 6.5-mile spin. On 10 summer days a year, the boulevard stretch is closed to traffic for a quiet, pollution-free bicycling experience.

Clubs
Cascade Bicycle Club (206-522-3222; www.cbcef.org), Box 15165, Seattle 98115. This organization has trail information and classes for all levels.

Seattle Bicycle Club (www.seattlebicycle.org), Box 31423, Seattle 98103. Another source of trail information and group rides at all levels.

CAMPING Seattle is an urban area, obviously, so what camping there is will be found mostly outside the city and fairly RV-oriented; see the Southern Suburbs and Vashon Island chapter and the Mercer Island and the Eastside chapter.

Camp Long (206-684-7434), 5200 35th Avenue SW, Seattle. Want to take the family camping in the city? This forested, 68-acre park in the middle of West Seattle offers 10 rustic cabins for rent, each with six double bunk beds—quite a deal at $50 per cabin per night. Bring your own bedding. Picnic tables and fireplaces are outside; restrooms are a short walk away.

THE SEATTLE SEAHAWKS' OPEN-AIR STADIUM SOUTH OF DOWNTOWN

CANOEING AND KAYAKING Elliott Bay. As a maritime city, Seattle can bring a gleam to a water lover's eye. Sea kayaking in the bay is an up-close-and-personal way to experience Puget Sound. For launch points, see *Wilder Places—Parks*.

Lakes-to-Locks Water Trail (www.wwta.org). This urban water route, inaugurated in 2000, goes through the above-mentioned lakes via Chittenden Locks to Lake Sammamish (see the Mercer Island and the Eastside chapter).

Lake Union and **Lake Washington** offer flatwater paddling; you can launch your canoe or kayak from several **city parks** on their shores (www.seattle.gov/parks), including **Madrona Park,** 853 Lake Washington Boulevard; **North Passage Point Park,** 600 NE Northlake Way; and **Seward Park** (see *Wilder Places—Parks*).

Rentals and Tours
Alki Kayak Tours (206-953-0237; www.kayakalki.com), 1660 Harbor Avenue SW, offers guided sea kayaking, plus sea kayaking classes and rentals.

Center for Wooden Boats (see *To See—For Families*) offers boats to rent if you don't have your own.

Moss Bay Rowing Center (877-682-2031; www.mossbay.net), 1001 Fairview Avenue North, Seattle, rents boats—kayaks, sailboats, rowing shells, and paddle boards—on Lake Union. They also offer classes and summer camps.

Outdoor Odysseys (206-361-0717 or 800-647-4621; www.outdoorodysseys.com), 12003 23rd Avenue NE, Seattle. For the serious paddler, these folks offer guided sea kayaking trips in the San Juan Islands.

GOLF Interbay Golf Center (206-285-2200), 2501 15th Avenue West, Seattle. Driving range and miniature golf.

Jackson Park Golf Club (206-363-4747), 1000 NE 135th Street, Seattle. One 18-hole and one 9-hole course.

Jefferson Park Golf Course (206-762-4513), 4101 Beacon Avenue South, Seattle. Eighteen-hole and nine-hole courses.

Premier Golf Centers (206-285-2200; www.seattlegolf.com), 2501 15th Avenue West, Seattle, runs the four municipal golf courses listed here. For more golf in the metropolitan area, check online (www.seattlegolfguide.com).

West Seattle Golf Course (206-935-5187), 4470 35th Avenue SW, Seattle. Eighteen holes.

HIKING Alki Beach Trail (206-684-4075; www.seattle.gov/parks), 2.5-mile paved path around Alki Point. How about a beach walk in this popular park (see *Wilder Places—Parks*)?

Burke-Gilman Trail, 27 paved miles from Fremont to Kenmore (see *Bicycling*). Great for longer ventures.

Golden Gardens Park (206-684-4075; www.seattle.gov/parks), 8498 Seaview Place NW, Seattle. For something a bit more rugged, try walking from the woods down to sandy beaches.

Myrtle Edwards Park (www.seattle.gov/parks), 3130 Alaskan Way, Seattle; 1.25 paved miles along Elliott Bay. An urban stroll on scenic paths.

& **Washington Park Arboretum trails,** 2300 Arboretum Drive East, Seattle. Paths include a 1,700-foot shoreline stroll and wheelchair-accessible trails (see *To See—Gardens*).

Waterfront Park (www.seattle.gov/parks), 1301 Alaskan Way, Seattle; about 0.25 mile from Pier 57 to Pier 58. This urban park along the shoreline, with benches, shade trees, and picnic tables, offers a restful stroll with views of ships, Elliott Bay, and the Olympic Mountains.

See also *Wilder Places—Parks*.

UNIQUE ADVENTURES Space Needle (206-905-2100; www.spaceneedle .com), 400 Broad Street, Seattle. Open 9 AM–11 PM Sun.–Thurs., 9 AM–11:30 PM Fri.–Sat.; sometimes closed for special events. Observation deck: $18 adults, $16 seniors and military, $11 children 4–12; day-and-night ticket (enter twice in 24 hours) $24, $22, and $15, respectively. Built for the 1962 world's fair, the Space Needle is, of course, a Seattle icon, and you will probably feel obliged to take the elevator up to the 520-foot-high observation deck. It's true there is a very nice view. There are even telescopes. On a good day, you can see all over the city, south to Mount Rainier, and west over Puget Sound and the islands. But the lines are long, the price is high, and don't bother if it's foggy. The **SkyCity Restaurant** just below the observation deck, the second revolving restaurant in the world when built, is definitely a special spot. It's as expensive as you might think, with a minimum food charge of $30 per person, but if you have a reservation, your elevator ride is free.

WHALE-WATCHING ♪ **Mosquito Fleet** (800-888-2535; www.whalewatching .com), 1724 West Marine Drive, Everett. Open Apr.–Oct., weather permitting. Named for the informal fleet of small boats that used to provide transportation on Puget Sound, the Mosquito Fleet offers whale-watching tours to the San Juan Islands out of Seattle. Since they have farther to go than boats based in the northern sound, they are correspondingly more expensive. On the bright side, you get a full day's trip.

✳ Wilder Places

PARKS Alki Beach Park (206-684-4075; www.seattle.gov/parks), 1702 Alki Avenue SW, Seattle. Open 6 AM–11 PM. This is where the party of settlers headed by Arthur and David Denny landed in 1851, determined to found a great city (which they eventually did—elsewhere). The park is a narrow strip of beach popular with walkers, cyclists, sunbathers, and the like, with fine views of Elliott Bay and the Seattle skyline.

Camp Long (206-684-7434), 5200 35th Avenue SW, Seattle. A forested, 68-acre park in West Seattle (see *To Do—Camping*).

Carkeek Park (206-604-0877; www.seattle.gov/parks), 950 NW Carkeek Park Road, Seattle. Open 6 AM–10 PM. In northwestern Seattle, with views of Puget Sound and the Olympic Mountains, this 220-acre beach park has a creek where salmon runs have been restored, 6 miles of trails, and an environmental learning center.

Denny Park (206-684-4705; www.seattle.gov/parks), 100 Dexter Avenue North, Seattle. Open 4 AM–11:30 PM. Seattle's first park was originally donated by city father David Denny and his wife for a cemetery. In 1883 they changed their minds and rededicated it as a public park. Its 6.4 acres, planted with azaleas, rhododendrons, and tall trees, are now a haven in the midst of the busy city (and also house the city's parks department offices).

Discovery Park (206-386-4236; www.seattle.gov/parks), 3801 Discovery Park Boulevard, Seattle. Open 6 AM–11 PM; visitors center open 8:30–5 Tues.–Sun. Formerly Fort Lawton, this promontory site overlooking Puget Sound and Shilshole Bay is now Seattle's biggest city park, at 534 acres. Just northwest of downtown, the park has 12 miles of trails, 2 miles of tidal beaches, cliffs, forest, and dramatic views that make it a near-wilderness oasis in the city. Also in the park is **Daybreak Star Cultural Center,** a project of the United Indians of All Tribes Foundation.

♪ **Gas Works Park** (206-684-4075; www.seattle.gov/parks), 2101 North Northlake Way, Seattle. A city park with a picnic shelter and a children's play barn (see *To See—Historic Sites*). People come here to fly kites. Although it's on the lake, no water sports are allowed due to hazardous materials in the sediment.

🐾 **Golden Gardens Park** (206-684-4031; www.seattle.gov/parks), 8498 Seaview Place NW, Seattle. Open 6 AM–11:30 PM. This 88-acre park has a spectacular waterfront near the Chittenden locks, with sandy beaches, forest trails, and an off-leash dog area. A renovated 1930s bathhouse can be rented for events.

Myrtle Edwards Park (www.seattle.gov/parks), 3130 Alaskan Way, Seattle. This shoreline park along Elliott Bay is a pleasant way to get from downtown to the

Magnolia neighborhood via a paved bike and pedestrian path. Myrtle Edwards Park is next to the Olympic Sculpture Park (see *To See—Cultural Sites*).

Occidental Park, between Occidental and Second avenues and Washington and Main streets (see *To See—Historic Sites*).

Olympic Sculpture Park (206-654-3158; www.seattleartmuseum.org), 2901 Western Avenue, Seattle (see *To See—Cultural Sites*).

Seattle Center (206-684-7200; www.seattle.gov/parks), 305 Harrison Street, Seattle; bounded by Denny Way, Mercer Street, First Avenue North, and Fifth Avenue North. The 1962 world's fair was staged on this site—almost as audacious an act for the backwater that Seattle was then as Spokane's successful 1974 bid was for that smaller city. It was called the "jewel box fair" because of the relatively tiny site overlooking Puget Sound. Today its 87 acres just north of downtown conserve many of the fair pavilions as theaters, concert halls, and event centers. Among the Seattle Center's many tourist attractions are three museums: Children's Museum, Pacific Science Center (see *To See—For Families* for both), and EMP Museum (see *To See—Museums*).

Seward Park (206-684-4396; www.seattle.gov/parks), 5895 Lake Washington Boulevard South, Seattle. Open 6 AM–11 PM. Perhaps because of opposition from citizens who thought the proposed park in 1892 was too far from town to be useful, the city named it after William Seward (the U.S. secretary of state responsible for "Seward's folly"—the purchase of Alaska). This 300-acre park on Lake Washington, southwest of downtown, offers old-growth forest, an art studio, a native-plants garden, and a swimming beach. A 2.5-mile paved trail is open to walkers and cyclists. Nature and history walks are offered the first Saturday of each month.

❀ **Warren Magnuson Park** (206-684-4946; www.seattle.gov/parks), 7400 Sand Point Way NE, Seattle. Open 4 AM–11:30 PM May–Labor Day; 4 AM–10 PM in winter. Magnuson, originally a naval air station on Lake Washington, conserves numerous military buildings dating from the 1930s and 1940s. But with 350 acres, this park also has outdoor art installations, beaches, an off-leash dog area, 4 miles of walking trails, even wind surfing.

& **Washington Park Arboretum** (206-543-8800; www.wparboretum.org), 2300 Arboretum Drive East, Seattle. See *To See—Gardens*.

& **Waterfront Park** (www.seattle.gov/parks), 1301 Alaskan Way, Seattle. Open 6 AM–11:30 PM. This urban park between Piers 57 and 59 consists of a sidewalk, viewing platforms, benches, picnic tables, and a fountain. Wheelchair-accessible.

❀ **Westcrest Park** (206-684-4075; www.seattle.gov/parks), 9000 Eighth Avenue SW, Seattle. Open 4 AM–11:30 PM. Surrounding West Seattle Reservoir, this 81-acre park used to belong to the water district. Mostly wooded, it has an off-leash dog area and panoramic views of the city.

✑ ❀ **Woodland Park** (206-684-4075; www.seattle.gov/parks), 1000 North 50th Street, Seattle. Open 4 AM–11:30 PM. Most of Woodland's 91 acres are taken up by the Woodland Park Zoo (see *To See—For Families*) and the Woodland Park Rose Garden (see *To See—Gardens*), but the acreage east of Aurora Avenue contains playgrounds, picnic areas, tennis courts and other game areas, and a 2-acre off-leash dog area.

✳ Lodging

BED & BREAKFASTS

Ballard

9 Cranes Inn (206-855-5222; 9cranes inn.com), 5717 Palatine Avenue North, Seattle. A new and upscale B&B graces the Ballard area, handy to the zoo, Woodland Park, and Chittenden Locks. Three rooms (to be four) in a comfy old house have been remodeled to an elegant hipness. All have private baths. Rates include a full breakfast. Children over 12 welcome. No pets. $139–209.

Capitol Hill

The Bacon Mansion (800-240-1864; www.baconmansion.com), 959 Broadway East, Seattle. This is an American stately home: You can see Cecil Bacon's red and white coat of arms in the stained-glass windows. The 1909 Tudor Revival mansion near Volunteer Park and the arboretum boasts a huge chandelier, marble fireplaces, a garden patio, and 11 elegant guest rooms ranging from a "cabin" under the eaves to large suites. Most, but not all, have private baths. Rates include a full breakfast. $99–234; minimum-stay requirements weekends, holidays, and in summer.

11th Avenue Inn (206-720-7161 or 800-720-7161; www.11thavenueinn .com), 121 11th Avenue East, Seattle. Like many Capitol Hill houses, this one is around a hundred years old but neither Victorian nor Craftsman— rather, an elegant "box," or Foursquare house. The eight guest rooms have private baths, polished wood floors, and Persian rugs. Common areas include a spacious living room and dining room, plus a den with high-speed Internet access. Rates include a full breakfast. Free on-site parking and Wi-Fi throughout. Children over 12 wel-

come. No pets. $89–149; minimum-stay requirements often in effect.

Gaslight Inn (206-325-3654; www .gaslight-inn.com), 1727 15th Avenue, Seattle. The Gaslight celebrated its centennial in 2006. One of the many solid Capitol Hill homes, its eight guest rooms sleep one or two; several have views and period oak furnishings, and most have private baths. The owners also have quite an art collection, running from Native American works to glass art. Rates include a continental breakfast, free Wi-Fi, and access to the swimming pool. No children or pets. $98–168.

Hill House (206-323-4455 or 866-417-4455; www.seattlehillhouse.com), 1113 East John Street, Seattle. This understated 1903 B&B just east of downtown consists of two houses with four inviting guest rooms (two with shared bath), all featuring down comforters, Oriental rugs, and some antiques. Guests have the run of the parlor in each house and the dining room, porch, and garden in the main house. Capitol Hill is a varied, active district with plenty of restaurants on nearby Broadway. Rates include a full breakfast. No children or pets. $79–199; two-night minimum in summer.

♪ Mildred's Bed and Breakfast (206-325-6072 or 800-327-9692; www.mildredsbnb.com), 1202 15th Avenue East, Seattle. A rambling 1890 Victorian on Capitol Hill, this is one of the few B&Bs that accept children. And it's right across from Volunteer Park, with the Seattle Asian Art Museum, so those children can run free. Four guest rooms with private baths are all properly decorated for the period, and the living room has a grand piano and fireplace. Rates include fruit, biscotti, and coffee for breakfast.

No pets. $99–155; three-night minimum on weekends.

Fremont
Chelsea Station Inn (206-547-6077 or 800-400-6077; www.bandbseattle .com), 4915 Linden Avenue North, Seattle. At the northern end of the eccentric Fremont district, 4 miles north of downtown, gay-friendly Chelsea Station is across from 92-acre Woodland Park, with its zoo and rose garden. The B&B is a large brick house with four guest suites, each with private bath, kitchen, and dining room. Rates include a full breakfast brought to your room. $225.

Queen Anne
Inn of Twin Gables (206-284-3979 or 866-INN-3979; www.innoftwingables .com), 3258 14th Avenue West, Seattle. A comfortable arts and crafts home with lots of the original woodwork, this inn has three snug guest rooms with private baths. Sit by the living room fireplace or look out over Puget Sound; you're not far from tourist attractions but away from some of the crowds. Rates include a full breakfast. $100–250; $15 surcharge for one-night stay.

University District
Chambered Nautilus Bed and Breakfast (800-545-8459; www .chamberednautilus.com), 5005 22nd Avenue NE, Seattle. This neoclassical home was built for a University of Washington professor of Oriental studies in 1915. It's been through a few permutations since, notably as a residence for WAVES (women serving in the U.S. Navy) in the 1940s, but it has been a B&B for nearly 30 years. Six cozy guest rooms look out on gardens or the mountains, while cottages in the back offer comfortable one- or two-bedroom apartments. Rates include a full breakfast. Children over 8 and pets welcome in the cottages (please mention them at the time of reservation). $104–199.

GUESTHOUSES

University District
The College Inn (206-633-4441; www.collegeinnseattle.com), 4000 University Way NE, Seattle. Neither hostel nor hotel, the College Inn occupies the top two floors of a four-story 1909 mansion and caters to the budget traveler—round-the-world ticket holders of all ages, University of Washington applicants, an eclectic and adventurous bunch. It's simple but friendly. Twenty-seven modest single and double rooms manage to be cozy with queen-sized beds, desks, windows, carpets, phones, sinks, and a few antiques here and there. There's a common breakfast room and separate men's and women's bathrooms on each floor, but no elevator or wheelchair access. The building, conveniently located in the University District, also houses Cafe Allegro (see *Where to Eat*) and the **College Inn Pub.** Rates include a continental breakfast. $55–95.

HOSTELS

Downtown
Seattle is not an inexpensive city. For the frugal trying to stay on a budget, there are two hostels (open to all ages; they're no longer called "youth hostels"), both downtown.

The Green Tortoise Hostel (206-340-1222; www.greentortoise.net), 105 Pike Street, Seattle. Right across from the Pike Place Market, the Green Tortoise could hardly be more centrally located. Rates include a continental breakfast and—get this—dinner on Sunday, Tuesday, and Thursday. Advance reservations a must. Dorm beds $29–33; queen dorm beds

$56–58. Some small rooms may be rented as private or family rooms for $70.

The HI-Seattle at the American Hotel (206-622-5443; www.hiusa.org /seattle), 520 South King Street, Seattle. Hostelling International is now located at the historic American Hotel, with 286 beds in four- to six-bedded dorms as well as private rooms. Near the International District and train station, it has convenient access to public transportation to most parts of town. Common areas include a kitchen, library, TV room, and computer room. Reserve early! HI membership is required; you can purchase daily membership on-site for a few bucks. Breakfast is included. Dorm beds $26–32; private or family rooms $80–96 (some with private baths).

HOTELS

Airport

The southern reaches of Seattle and nearby suburbs offer accommodations that are often cheaper than in town, albeit more homogeneously American—that is, hotels that could be near any major airport. However, the difference in price may be worth it (especially when you consider the free parking), and most of them have shuttle service to the new light rail (Link), so you can get downtown without fighting the traffic. That may be incentive enough to stay here.

Cedarbrook Lodge (877-515-2176; www.cedarbrooklodge.com), 18525 36th Avenue South, Seattle. The 18 acres of restored wetlands give you some elbow room. All the rooms have views of water and greenery (okay, you could call it swamp) instead of concrete and freeways. All the amenities plus an on-site restaurant. Dogs allowed in some rooms for a $50 fee per stay. $159–189; ask about specials.

Seattle Tukwila Homewood Suites (206-433-8000; www.homewoodsuites1 .hilton.com), 6955 Fort Dent Way, Tukwila. Though near both the airport and a freight train line, the sound-proofing keeps you nearly unaware of them. All rooms are one- or two-bedroom suites, some with fireplaces. And while the decor is "chain business hotel," the suites are family-friendly, with kitchens, a swimming pool, a fitness room, and free Wi-Fi. Rates include breakfast. Some handicapped-accessible rooms are available. $169–284.

Capitol Hill

Silver Cloud Hotel—Seattle Broadway (206-325-1400 or 800-590-1801; www.silvercloud.com), 1100 Broadway, Seattle. Silver Cloud Inns, a regional chain, all have swimming pools, clean and comfortable rooms, and complimentary breakfast, with an at-home friendliness that sets them apart from the larger chains. $139–189.

Downtown

The Ace Hotel (206-448-4721; www.acehotel.com), 2423 First Avenue, Seattle. The Ace is a "design" hotel, which apparently is the next generation of boutique: small and art-oriented, but edgy. A 100-year-old rooming house in Belltown has been made over, with 28 high-ceilinged rooms, starkly white but for the unusual artwork (murals of Northwest forests or Warholesque faces; *Time* called it a "super-aesthetic barrack"). Cube lighting softens the edges, and platform beds allow a roomy feeling. Standard rooms share a bathroom; "deluxe" rooms have private baths behind secret doors, which could be a problem. Rates include a continental breakfast. Pets welcome. $109–199.

Alexis Hotel (206-624-4844 or 866-356-8894; www.alexishotel.com), 1007 First Avenue, Seattle. "You're supposed to feel you're in an art gallery," says former manager Jeremy Strober. And you kind of do. A large, intricate work by glass artist Dale Chihuly graces the lobby, and the halls feature rotating exhibits by local artists. You could hold an art opening in the double rooms, which are roughly the size of a football field (in one of the building's previous incarnations, many of the rooms were individual apartments); the large desk, armoire, and bed vanish in the room's depths. This is a Kimpton hotel, and all the luxury amenities are here—wonderful beds, a fitness center, a private steam room— but for some reason you can't open the windows. Off the lobby, the **Bookstore Bar,** whose gleaming shelves are full of bottles and books, is a popular spot for an evening drink, and the **Library Bistro** is open for breakfast and lunch. $225–635.

Belltown Inn (206-529-3700 or 866-525-4704; www.belltown-inn.com), 2301 Third Avenue, Seattle. Here you're in the thick of Belltown's action—cozy restaurants, friendly cafés—without a hefty price tag. Opened in 2008, the inn was formerly an apartment block, and all the units, though completely refurbished, have kitchenettes. It's often used for long-term stays, and there is a laundry, fitness center, and business center on the premises. $89–169; $485–685 per week.

☙ ♿ **Hotel Monaco** (206-621-1770 or 800-715-6513; www.monaco-seattle .com), 1101 Fourth Avenue, Seattle. Another Kimpton hotel, the Monaco's exterior looks like the telephone switching center it was in 1972. The inside has obviously undergone a transformation. The four-star hotel opened in 1997 with lobby frescoes inspired by Knossos (dolphins disport themselves above a frieze of interlocking spirals); a cheery Greek-isles color scheme based

on blues, white, gold, and earth tones; and striped wallpaper. It's a pleasant conceit, though the twice-weekly readings by the resident (Delphic?) fortune-teller may be taking it a bit far. The place certainly warms you up if your stay coincides with a Seattle wet spell. However, the windows don't open here either. Oh, and the Monaco is kid- and pet-friendly: Not only can they arrange on-site pet-sitting, but they'll bring a goldfish in a bowl to look after you if you didn't bring your own pet. $219–349.

✿ ♿ **Mayflower Park Hotel** (206-623-8700 or 800-426-5100; www .mayflowerpark.com), 405 Olive Way, Seattle. Two grand lobbies, a player piano by a gas fire, a blend of antique and contemporary furnishings—one of Seattle's oldest grand hotels. The independently owned Mayflower Park has operated more or less continuously since opening in 1927. Birney and Marie Dempcy bought it in decline in 1973, and it has been under loving renovation ever since, though somehow the place keeps humming along as graciously as if nothing were happening. The 171 rooms (three are wheelchair-accessible) are comfortably insulated from the world at large. Move effortlessly from one of the original deep bathtubs to your soft yet firm bed; pull aside the curtains for a city view. If you were Eloïse in New York, you might consider moving here from the Plaza Hotel. The dark-beamed **Oliver's Bar** is a favorite with locals and guests, famous for its martinis. Andaluca (see *Where to Eat*) has rapidly made a name for itself on the Seattle fine-dining scene. Reasonably behaved children are welcome (guess that excludes Eloïse). No pets. $149–289.

✿ **Pioneer Square Hotel** (206-340-1234 or 800-800-5514; www.pioneer square.com), 77 Yesler Way, Seattle.

This, one of the last remaining hotels of Seattle's pioneering era, offers a little more affordability downtown. It's been acquired by Best Western but still looks like an ambitious frontier establishment. The interior has been updated, of course, but it tries to retain some old-time atmosphere with period-style furniture, brass fixtures, and tile floors. Rooms tend toward the small side. Some have street or even water views, while others look out on an air shaft. Still, for the location it's hard to beat. Rates include a continental breakfast. Children are welcome. Consult about pets. $100–179.

Queen Anne

Inn at Queen Anne (206-282-7357 or 800-952-5043; www.innatqueenanne .com), 505 First Avenue North, Seattle. This renovated 1929 hotel, originally built as a residence for retired clergy, is in a lower Queen Anne neighborhood—north of downtown but convenient to Seattle Center, from which you can take the Monorail downtown. All 68 rooms, running from studio-sized to a modest suite, have kitchenettes and service for four. Though some of the decor is a little frayed around the edges, antiques, a shady courtyard, and a complimentary breakfast make this a comfortable, affordable Seattle stay. No elevator, though. And no pets. $89–119.

The Mediterranean Inn (206-428-4700 or 866-525-4700; www .mediterranean-inn.com), 425 Queen Anne Avenue North, Seattle. What is it about the Mediterranean—Puget Sound isn't good enough? Well, the lemon and white building with the tower on the corner does stand out. Because the inn is intended for longer stays, all rooms have kitchenettes, and amenities include an exercise room, Starbucks, and on-site parking (extra charge). There's a terrific view from the rooftop terrace. $129–179; $695–805 per week.

South Lake Union

Silver Cloud Inn—Seattle Lake Union (206-447-9500 or 800-330-5812; www.silvercloud.com), 1150 Fairview Avenue North, Seattle. The hotels in this chain are usually on or near the water. This one on Lake Union has fine marina views. $129–219.

University District

Silver Cloud Inn—University (206-526-5200; www.silvercloud.com), 5036 25th Avenue NE, Seattle. This is a mile from the University of Washington's main campus. $129–219.

University Inn (206-632-5055 or 866-866-7977; www.universityinnseattle .com), 4140 Roosevelt Way NE, Seattle. The rooms here come in three sizes, with a standard, motel-type decor. It's a convenient, adequate, and, for Seattle, reasonable place to stay if you're visiting the university, and there's a shuttle to local attractions and hospitals. Rates include a breakfast buffet and afternoon snack. Pets allowed in some rooms. $104–219.

Watertown (206-826-4242 or 866-866-7977; www.watertownseattle.com), 4242 Roosevelt Way NE, Seattle. Also near the university, the Watertown is a little more upscale, offering wine tastings on weekday evenings, loaner bikes to try out on the nearby Burke-Gilman Trail, and—get this—a complimentary themed cart upon advance request. This may be an art cart, with art supplies for your inner Miró; a child's cart with games, books, glue, and construction paper; a spa cart with bath salts and other pampering products; or any of a number of carts to keep you busy and/or relaxed. $139–249; discounts often available for stays of two or more nights.

✳ Where to Eat

DINING OUT

Capitol Hill

Lark (206-323-5275; www.larkseattle
.com), 926 12th Avenue, Seattle. Open
5–10:30 Tues.–Sun. Lark joins the
trend toward serving a series of small
portions rather than a main dish—fine
if you find most restaurant portions
overly large, although meals don't necessarily cost less. The cuisine and
ingredients here are definitely unusual,
in some cases so untraditional they're
"nouvelle": farro, grilled quail, even
Landjäger, a German sausage I've
never seen before on an American
menu, although my nonagenarian
father still manages to find it in New
Jersey. The mix of European cheeses,
tempting local vegetables, and
thoughtful recipes makes for a unique,
pleasurable evening.

Osteria la Spiga (206-323-8881),
1429 12th Avenue, Seattle. Open 5–10
Mon.–Thurs., 5–12 Fri.–Sat., 5–9 Sun.
A *spiga* is an ear of wheat. La Spiga
started out selling Emilia-Romagna flat
bread and sandwiches. The place is
unobtrusive, and the food is simple,
bordering on rustic, in the best sense:
homemade pasta, soups, salads, and
antipasti. Self-effacing as it is, it's been
a Seattle favorite for years.

Downtown

Andaluca (206-382-6999; www
.andaluca.com), in the Mayflower Park
Hotel, 407 Olive Way, Seattle. Open
for breakfast daily; lunch 11:30–2
Tues.–Fri.; dinner 5–9 Sun. and
Tues.–Thurs., 5–10 Fri.–Sat. The
brown and terra-cotta decor comple-
ments the Spanish-accented Mediterranean cuisine. Everything is the
freshest of the fresh, from the salads to
the seafood, and inventive, too: scallops with prosciutto and manchego
cheese; a medley of vegetable dishes.

Cheap it's not, but you're quite free to
go just with appetizers. It's the tapas
tradition, after all.

Assaggio Ristorante (206-441-1399;
www.assaggioseattle.com), 2010 Fourth
Avenue. Open for lunch 11:30–2:30
Mon.–Fri.; dinner 5–10 Mon.–Sat.;
happy hour 3–6:30 Mon.–Fri. Seattle
has no shortage of Italian restaurants,
so there's room to specialize. Chef
Mauro Golmarvi focuses on northern
Adriatic cuisine, which of course
includes seafood but also pizza, pasta,
main dishes from various regions, and
interesting appetizers that make up
nearly half the menu. Assaggio has gar-
nered awards for being among the best
restaurants in town and even in the
country. "The best compliment I've
gotten is that the salt and pepper never
get touched," says Golmarvi.

**Brasserie Margaux Restaurant and
Bar** (206-777-1990; www.margaux
seattle.com), in the Warwick Hotel,
401 Lenora Street. Open for breakfast
6:30–11 daily; lunch 11–2 Mon.–Fri.;
brunch 11–1:30 Sat.–Sun.; dinner 5–10
daily. The brasserie aims for Northwest
cuisine "with French overtones"; this
means, among other things, you have a
choice of *boeuf bourguignon* or rib-eye
steak. You can come for tapas at the
bar or a full breakfast, lunch, or dinner.
Choosing the daily prix fixe menu will
get you three courses for $28.

Campagne (206-728-2800; www
.campagnerestaurant.com), in Pike
Place Market, 86 Pine Street. Open
4:30–midnight daily. This has always
been the place to find French cuisine
for the French, including dishes not
often found in the Pacific Northwest—
when was the last time you ate sweetbreads or steak tartare? Over its two
decades, Campagne has received many
laurels for the care and authenticity of
its cuisine and has become one of
Seattle's most esteemed restaurants,

with a wine list including more than 150 vintages, French as well as Northwest. However, chef-owner Daisley Gordon has done a makeover: Campagne has become Marché, with offerings from French and other cuisines. If you want to stay faithful to your French muse, its sister restaurant, **Café Campagne** (206-728-2233), 1600 Post Alley, is just downstairs and around the corner. Open for lunch 11–5 Mon.–Fri.; dinner 5 or 5:30–10 or 11 daily; brunch 8–4 Sat.–Sun. Here you can get a *croque monsieur* for $13 or the prix fixe menu for about $30.

Etta's Seafood (206-443-6000; tom douglas.com), 2020 Western Avenue. Open 11:30–9:30 Mon.–Thurs., 11:30–10 Fri., 9–3 and 4–10 Sat., 9–3 and 4–9 Sun. One of Tom Douglas's five Seattle restaurants, Etta's focuses on—naturally—seafood, for which it gets consistently good reviews.

Le Pichet (206-256-1499; www.le pichetseattle.com), 1933 First Avenue. Open for lunch and dinner daily. Opened in 2000, Le Pichet has become a much-appreciated addition to the Seattle French cuisine scene, not seeming to suffer from competition with nearby Campagne. Then again, chef Jim Drohman came here from Campagne, and Le Pichet's less formal atmosphere, combined with its quality food, has allowed it to create its own niche. The place stays cheerful and bustling till all hours—with live music on Sundays—and why not? Reservations recommended.

Eastlake

Serafina (206-323-0807; www.serafina seattle.com), 2043 Eastlake Avenue East. Open for lunch Mon.–Fri., dinner daily, and brunch Sun. On the east side of Lake Union, you'll find this cheerily rustic restaurant with ocher walls, plumes of dried flowers, and good Italian food. Menus vary season-

ally, but of course there's plenty of fine seafood on which to base, say, a Sicilian fish soup. If you possibly can, try the gnocchi with wild mushroom sauce and baby pea vines. If you don't feel like a complete dinner, come for the happy hour (weekdays) or late-night (all week) menu. Or pick up a fresh sandwich for lunch from the sandwich window, open 11:30–2:30 Mon.–Sat. There's live jazz on weekend evenings and wine tasting the first Saturday of the month.

Queen Anne

Racha Noodles and Thai Cuisine (206-281-8883; www.rachathai.com), 23 Mercer Street. The locals know where to go for authentic Thai food—Racha, in lower Queen Anne. They season it perfectly, they treat you right, and the price is right. Branches have opened in Woodinville (425-481-8833) and Tukwila (425-271-4219).

West Seattle

✍ **Salty's on Alki Beach** (206-937-1600; www.saltys.com), 1936 Harbor Avenue SW. Open for lunch Mon.–Fri., dinner daily, and brunch Sat.–Sun. People come for the postcard view of Seattle across Elliott Bay as much as for the famous steaks and seafood (and lots of it). There's a children's menu, too, and live music some nights.

EATING OUT

Ballard

The Hi-Life (206-784-7272; www .chowfoods.com), 5425 Russsell Avenue NW. Open for "blunch" 8:30–3, snacks 3–5, and dinner from 5 PM daily. This Chowfoods outlet displays the same fun attitude toward food as their other restaurants. It's in an old firehouse, focusing half on American favorites and half on varying regions of the world. On weekdays between 8:30 and 11 AM, you can get breakfast for $5.55, and the daily happy hour (3–6:30) offers some really good deals, too.

Capitol Hill

Café Presse (206-709-7674; cafe presseseattle.com), 1117 12th Avenue. Open 7–2 daily. Jim Drohman and Joanne Herron, of Le Pichet (see above), opened Café Presse in 2007 as a relaxed, low-key French alternative modeled on your everyday French café. Same style, in fact some of the same dishes, plus French "fast food" such as *croque monsieur* and baguette sandwiches—everything from breakfast bites to a full meal.

Coastal Kitchen (206-322-1145), 429 15th Avenue East. Open for breakfast, lunch, and dinner daily. This homey restaurant, although it's on Capitol Hill, has the air of an old-fashioned beach place, with blue walls, wood floors, and various nooks and crannies. The fish is fresh (and so are the non-fish dishes), the service is friendly, and the restrooms offer foreign-language instruction.

Dilettante (206-329-6463; www .dilettante.com), 538 Broadway East, Seattle. Open 5–11 Mon.–Thurs., 5 PM–1 AM Fri., 10 AM–1 AM Sat., 10 AM–11 PM Sun. There are five other locations: Sea-Tac Airport, 1300 Fifth Avenue, 818 Stewart Street, 514 Ramsey Way in Kent, and Westlake Mall at 400 Pine Street. When I walked in, it was like walking into a dream. I had last seen *Rigó Jancsi* about 40 years earlier, in an Austro-Hungarian café on New York's West Side, and here it was again, staring me in the face. Round this time, rather than the traditional square, but so what? The first chocolaty, creamy morsel on my palate was like Proust's madeleine, except a sight tastier. Owner and pastry chef Dana Davenport is the third of three generations of confectioners and pastry chefs

whose line originated with one Julius Franzen, born in Hungary and one-time pastry chef to Franz Josef, emperor of, yes, Austria-Hungary. Davenport offers a whole array of truffles, dragées, coffees, and luscious cakes in tempting display. A grand café in the Viennese tradition has been translated into the Seattle idiom, and it's probably the best place for dessert in town.

Downtown

Anthony's Pier 66 and **Bell Street Diner** (206-448-6688; www.anthonys .com), 2201 Alaskan Way, Seattle. Anthony's is generally reliable for a pleasant dining experience that doesn't exclude the kids. At this one, you'll get a view of the Seattle skyline and, weather permitting, "the Mountain." Open for dinner daily; reservations recommended. The **Bell Street Diner** is more casual; open for lunch and dinner daily. For even more informality, walk up to the **fish-and-chips bar** downstairs and eat on the deck, spring and summer.

Belltown Pizza (206-441-2653; www .belltownpizza.net), 2422 First Avenue, Seattle. Open 4–11 daily. If you need a

DELICIOUS OFFERINGS AT DILETTANTE IN SEATTLE

pizza fix, this is the place to get it, right in cozy Belltown just north of Pike Place Market. It gets busy, but what pizza place worth its sauce doesn't? And the price is right.

Ivar's Acres of Clams (206-624-6852; www.ivars.net), at Pier 54 on the waterfront, Seattle. Open 11–10 Mon.–Sat. Ivar's has been a Washington fixture since 1938. Try their signature clam chowder, oysters, or any of the many seafood dishes at this original, casual location and watch the ships go by. Early-bird specials Mon.–Thurs.: three courses for 20 clams (er, dollars).

Macrina Bakery (206-448-4032; www.macrinabakery.com), 2408 First Avenue, Seattle. Open 7–6 daily. Macrina hums, and with good reason— luscious coffee cakes, scones, rustic breads, and cakes—and if that isn't enough, you can also sit down for a brilliant brunch or lunch. Go early, though; it gets crowded. Named for the fourth-century mystic Saint Macrina, who founded a community of prayer and simple living.

The Pink Door (206-443-3241; the pinkdoor.net), in Pike Place Market, 1919 Post Alley, Seattle. Open 11:30– 10 Mon.–Thurs., 11:30 AM–1 AM Fri.– Sat., from 4 Sun. Definitely for those in the know: There's no sign, just a pink door on Post Alley in the market. But it's a tremendously popular place among the younger crowd—and crowded; reservations are a must. The food is Italian, but people come mostly for the show and ambience; the view over Elliott Bay is good, too. Every night but Monday, there's some kind of performance, from music to dance to trapeze artistry . . . yes, it's a little unusual.

Piroshky Piroshky (206-441-6068), 1908 Pike Place, Seattle. Open 7:30 or 8–6 or 7 daily, depending on season.

For a snack or quick lunch, try some *piroshky*—Russian pastries stuffed with savory or sweet fillings such as spinach, potato, or cheese.

Sichuanese Cuisine Restaurant (206-720-1690; sichuaneserestaurant .com), 1048 South Jackson Street, Seattle. Open 11–9 daily. A hole-in-the-wall in Chinatown, it always seems to be full, mostly with Chinese customers. The food is delicious, copious, and cheap, featuring, of course, Sichuan (Szechuan) specialties, but not exclusively. In the suburbs, you can find another branch at 15005 NE 24th Avenue, open 11–10 daily.

Wild Ginger (206-623-4450; www .wildginger.net), 1401 Third Avenue, Seattle. Snack at the satay bar or have a regular sit-down dinner in the long dining room across from Benaroya Hall. The cuisine comes from East and Southeast Asia, all with delicate, individual flavors. There are several vegetarian choices and seven kinds of satay.

Fremont
Brouwer's Café (206-267-2437), 400 North 35th Street, Seattle. Open 11 AM–2 AM daily; happy hour 3–6 daily. Not just for beer (although the list is long and venerable, and that's not to mention the whiskeys), the café draws foodies, too, with bar food taken up a notch—or two. When's the last time you went to a pub for local mussels in white wine cream sauce? Or quality steak (Oregon grass-fed beef, in this case)? Homemade sausage; healthy, creative salads (this is the Northwest); crème brûlée—why, you can go for a real dinner. Over 21 only, unfortunately.

Madison Park
Café Flora (206-325-9100; www.cafe flora.com), 2901 East Madison Street, Seattle. Hours vary seasonally, but generally open for breakfast and lunch

Mon.–Fri., dinner daily, brunch Sat.–Sun. Seattle vegetarians have a choice, but they particularly appreciate Café Flora's gourmet vegetarian approach. Simple, light, and airy decor belies an imaginative use of ingredients and sauces, often with vegan options.

Queen Anne
5 Spot (206-285-7768), 1502 Queen Anne Avenue North, Seattle. Open for breakfast, lunch, and dinner daily. On a busy corner in Queen Anne, the 5 Spot looks like the auto showroom it used to be from the outside. Inside, the walls are decorated with Americana (kitsch, some may call it, but with personality), and it's bustling and cheery. Cheery because folks are tucking into heavenly breakfasts such as *crespelle* with fig sauce or some of the American regional cuisine the place specializes in—regular melting-pot meals from five "spots" across the country or varying dishes from varying places.

University District
Ivar's Salmon House (206-632-0767; www.ivars.net), 401 NE Northlake Way, Seattle. Open for lunch Mon.–Sat., dinner daily, brunch Sun. The Native American theme features Indian art on the walls and the design of an Indian longhouse, with a deck overlooking Lake Union. The salmon is pit-smoked over alder; the menu includes Ivar's seafood classics, wild salmon several different ways, and even steak.

COFFEE In case you haven't noticed, coffee is to Seattleites as rivers are to salmon: everywhere, and essential. Of course, the chains are ubiquitous— **Starbucks, Seattle's Best,** and **Tully's** are on practically every corner, and you may want to look at the original Starbucks in Pike Place Market (see *To*

See—Historic Sites), although it looks like all the others. However, there are plenty of new and independent coffee-houses, too, creating an actual 21st-century café culture. Here are a few.

Cafe Allegro (206-633-3030), 4214 University Way NE, Seattle. Open 6:30 AM–10 PM Mon.–Fri., 7:30 or 8 AM–10 PM Sat.–Sun. Seattle's original espresso bar and U District hangout.

Caffé Vita (206-709-4440; www.caffe vita.com), 1005 East Pike Street, Seattle. Open 6 AM–11 PM Mon.–Fri., 7 AM–11 PM Sat.–Sun. A roaster on Capitol Hill; buy your beans here or at the several other outlets in Queen Anne, Seward Park, Fremont, Phinney Ridge, and Pioneer Square.

El Diablo Coffee (206-285-0693; www.eldiablocoffee.com), 1811 Queen Anne Avenue North, Seattle. Open 5:30 AM–10 PM Mon.–Thurs., 5:30 AM–11 PM Fri., 6:30 AM–11 PM Sat., 6:30 AM–10 PM Sun. Cuban brews and tropical desserts make this place unique.

Espresso Vivace (206-860-2722; www.espressovivace.com), 532 Broadway East, Seattle. Open 6 AM–11 PM daily. Another Capitol Hill fave, with satellite locations at 227 Yale Avenue North (206-388-5164) and 321 Broadway East (206-860-5869).

✳ Entertainment

MUSIC **Benaroya Hall** (206-215-4747 or 866-833-4747; www.seattle symphony.org), 200 University Street, Seattle. Opened downtown in 1998, Benaroya is the home of the Seattle Symphony and hosts visiting performers such as the Kirov Orchestra and Pinchas Zukerman.

McCaw Hall (206-389-7676; www .seattleopera.com), 321 Mercer Street, Seattle. If you're an opera buff, you may want to visit Queen Anne's McCaw Hall, the city's glass-walled opera venue at Seattle Center.

NIGHTLIFE Belltown Billiards (206-420-3146; www.belltownbilliards .com), 90 Blanchard Street, Seattle. Pool and pub? Billiards and brew? Take a cue from the clientele: Enjoy supper and a game. You can even take lessons if you don't know how to play. Live DJ and dancing nightly.

Dimitrou's Jazz Alley (206-441-9729; www.jazzalley.com), 2033 Sixth Avenue, Seattle. This downtown restaurant and club features performances by legendary artists.

Purple Café and Wine Bar (206-829-2280; www.thepurplecafe.com;), 125 Fourth Avenue, Seattle. Open 11–11 Mon.–Thurs., 11 AM–midnight Fri., 12–12 Sat., 12–11 Sun. With typical Seattle coolness, a spiral staircase embraces a floor-to-ceiling cylinder packed with wine bottles in the center of the establishment. Wine, wine, and more wine, obviously (the list runs to 70 pages), from just about everywhere, but also fine cuisine for lunch and dinner. And a children's menu, too. Check the website for hours and addresses of the Bellevue, Kirkland, and Woodinville locations.

THEATER ACT (206-292-7676; www .acttheatre.org), 700 Union Street, Seattle. A Contemporary Theatre (ACT) is committed to producing contemporary works (and newer versions of older works) in various modes— drama, dance, cabaret, comedy, and more—by well-known and lesser-known artists.

5th Avenue Theatre (206-625-1900; www.5thavenue.org), 1308 Fifth Avenue, Seattle. A grand old theater dating from 1926, the 5th Avenue was beautifully restored to its former intricate glory—a sort of Chinese-themed jewel box replete with dragons, chrysanthemums, and other imperial elements. Just being inside is worth the price of a ticket. The 5th Avenue specializes in musical theater, especially American musicals.

✳ Selective Shopping

In the past two decades, downtown Seattle has striven to become the Northwest's version of Fifth Avenue in New York, bringing the nation's upscale chains to gleaming new buildings such as downtown's **Westlake Mall.** Here are some other best bets.

BOOKS Elliot Bay Book Company (206-624-6600 or 800-962-5311; www .elliottbaybook.com), 1521 Tenth Avenue, Seattle. Open 10–9, 10, or 11 daily. Moved (but not far) from its venerable location on Main Street, this labyrinth of cedar bookshelves continues to host writers and readers as it has for more than 30 years. Within, the **Elliott Bay Café** serves breakfast and dessert.

FOOD Chocolopolis (206-282-0776; www.chocolopolis.com), 1527 Queen Anne Avenue North, Seattle. Open 11–7 Mon.–Wed., 11–9 Thurs.–Sat., 11–6 Sun. If your palate will tolerate only the finest of chocolates, they're here—fair trade, organic, what have you—from the world's premier cacao regions. Don't expect Hershey bar prices.

Kress IGA Supermarket (206-749-9500; kressiga.com), 1423 Third Avenue, Seattle. Open 7 AM–10 PM daily. If you have sensibly reserved a room with a kitchen for your stay, shop here: It's the only supermarket in downtown Seattle, and it's actually a pleasant place to shop. Located in the basement of the former Kress department store, it's on a human scale, with orderly, artistic displays and friendly clerks. And the prices are no higher than at any other supermarket.

Pure Food Fish Market (800-392-FISH; www.freshseafood.com), in Pike Place Market, Seattle. This is a place to pick up fresh or smoked seafood. They'll ship anywhere.

Uwajimaya (206-624-6248; www.uwajimaya.com), 600 Fifth Avenue South, Seattle. Open 8 AM–10 PM Mon.–Sat., 9–9 Sun. This is a recently remodeled Asian shopping center in the International District, featuring the venerable grocery store as well as a pan-Asian food court.

OUTDOOR GEAR REI (206-223-1944; www.rei.com), 222 Yale Avenue North, Seattle. For a quintessential Seattle experience, visit the regional flagship store of this recreational equipment giant. Landscaping features a waterfall and trails for testing hiking boots and mountain bikes. There's an indoor climbing rock, too.

MORE Sur la Table (206-448-2244; www.surlatable.com), 84 Pine Street, Seattle. Open 9–6:30 daily. Everything you could possibly need or want for the kitchen, and then some.

✷ Special Events

February: **Têt Festival** (www.tetinseattle.org), Seattle Center House. Celebrate the Vietnamese New Year with firecrackers, food, games, and performances.

May: **Maritime Festival** (206-787-3163; seattlepropellerclub.org), Pier 66, Seattle waterfront. This weekend bash features tugboat races, a chowder cook-off, a boatbuilding contest, children's activities, free admission to the Seattle Aquarium (see *To See—For Families*) and Odyssey Maritime Discovery Center (see *To See—Museums*), and much, much more.

Northwest Folklife Festival (206-684-7300; www.nwfolklife.org), Seattle Center. On Memorial Day weekend, this event focuses on cultural traditions of the Pacific Northwest with musical performances, workshops, discussion, poetry readings, and films.

Seattle Cheese Festival (206-622-0141; www.seattlecheesefestival.com), Western Avenue at Pike Place Market, Seattle. Cheese-making demonstrations, seminars, and most of all free samples of the world's best cheeses, whether from far-flung regions or the Pacific Northwest, which produces some very respectable artisanal cheeses.

June: **Fremont Fair** (206-632-1500; www.fremontfair.org), Fremont district, Seattle. The Fremont neighborhood is known for its eclecticism, and this summer solstice parade and fair is a natural outgrowth of that. Proceeds benefit local antipoverty programs.

July: **Lake Union Wooden Boat Festival** (206-382-2628), Center for Wooden Boats, 1010 Valley Street, Seattle. There are free boat rides, boatbuilding demonstrations, Indian paddle carving, boat races, and more.

September: **Bumbershoot** (206-673-5060; www.bumbershoot.org), Seattle Center. This is Seattle's huge Labor Day weekend music and arts festival—music, theater, film, visual arts, food, you name it. Advance tickets $35 per day or $90 for the weekend; children under 10 free with adult.

MERCER ISLAND AND
THE EASTSIDE

GUIDANCE **Bellevue Chamber of Commerce** (425-454-2464; www.bellevue chamber.org), 302 Bellevue Square, Bellevue 98004.

Explore Kirkland (425-587-3000; www.explorekirkland.com), 123 Fifth Avenue, Kirkland 98033.

Greater Redmond Chamber of Commerce (425-885-4014; www.redmond chamber.org), 16210 NE 80th Street, Redmond 98052.

Issaquah Chamber of Commerce (425-392-7024; www.issaquahchamber.com), 155 NW Gilman Boulevard, Issaquah 98027.

Mercer Island Chamber of Commerce (206-232-3404; www.mercerisland chamber.com), 7605 SE 27th Street, Mercer Island 98040.

GETTING THERE **I-405** is the primary north-south highway; **I-90** and **WA 520** are the main east-west highways. **WA 202** links Woodinville to Snoqualmie; **WA 203** a bit farther east links Duvall and Carnation to Snoqualmie.

Seattle-Tacoma International Airport (206-787-5388 or 800-544-1965; www .portofseattle.org) is at exit 154B off I-5. From Sea-Tac Airport, **Shuttle Express** (425-981-7000) goes to Seattle suburbs, including the Eastside.

AMTRAK (800-USA-RAIL; www.amtrakcascades.com) serves Seattle at 303 South Jackson Street.

Greyhound (206-628-5526 or 800-231-2222; www.greyhound.com) also serves Seattle at 811 Stewart Street.

GETTING AROUND **Metro Transit** (206-553-3000; www.metro.kingcounty .gov), 201 South Jackson Street, Seattle. User-friendly bus service operates through Seattle and all of King County, including Sea-Tac Airport.

MEDICAL EMERGENCY **Evergreen Hospital Medical Center** (425-899-1000; www.evergreenhospital.org), 12040 NE 128th Street, Kirkland.

Overlake Hospital Medical Center (425-688-5000), 1035 116th Avenue NE, Bellevue.

Overlake 24-Hour Urgent Care Center at Issaquah (425-688-5777), 5708 East Lake Sammamish Way, Issaquah.

FARMS AND GARDENS **Bellevue Botanical Garden** (425-452-2750; www
.bellevuebotanical.org), 12001 Main Street, Bellevue. Open dawn to dusk daily;
visitors center open 9–4 daily. Free. Thirty-six carefully tended acres include an
alpine garden, a Japanese garden, a perennial border, and other gardens of earthly
delights—a restorative stroll at any time of year.

Mercer Slough Blueberry Farm and Produce Stand (425-467-0501), 2380
Bellevue Way SE, Bellevue. Open 9–7 daily mid-Apr.–Oct. The Seattle burbs are
home to Costco (Kirkland) and Microsoft (Redmond), but here's an attempt to
preserve a bit of the agricultural past. The 1940s farm is now owned and managed
by the Bellevue Parks District. U-pick organic blueberries late June–mid-Sept.,
and U can also buy apples, peaches, pears, and raspberries in season.

MUSEUMS **Bellevue Arts Museum** (425-519-0770; www.bellevuearts.org), 510
Bellevue Way, Bellevue. Open 11–5 Tues.–Sun., 11–8 first Fri. each month. $10
adults, $7 seniors and students over six, $25 families; free first Fri. each month.
This dramatic museum in downtown Bellevue features changing design and decorative arts exhibits in all sorts of media, from glass to textiles to beads, on themes
ranging from Islamic calligraphy to teapots.

Northwest Railway Museum (425-888-3030; www.trainmuseum.org), 38625 SE
King Street, Snoqualmie. Open 10–5 daily. Free. The museum consists of the 1890
Snoqualmie Depot (complete with turret, just like the Queen Anne houses of the
period), 5.5 miles of track, numerous train cars and maintenance equipment, and
other artifacts conveying the joys and intricacies of trains. The depot now houses
the museum and historic displays, but on weekends you can still buy a ticket for a
half-hour **train ride** to North Bend ($12 adults, $10 seniors, $8 children).

Rosalie Whyel Museum of Doll Art (425-455-1116; www.dollart.com), 1116
108th Avenue NE, Bellevue. Open 10–5 Mon.–Sat., 1–5 Sun. $10 adults, $9 seniors, $5 children 5–17. Established in 1992, the museum is dedicated to what we
may not think of as an art form: the doll. With 1,200 dolls of all kinds and ages
from around the world, from an ivory Eskimo doll to the first Barbie, there's ample
artistry to admire. There's a store as well, of course!

NATURAL WONDERS ♿ **Snoqualmie Falls,** on WA 202 near Snoqualmie;
from I-90 take exit 25 onto Snoqualmie Parkway, then left on WA 202. Where the
Snoqualmie River drops 270 feet at the edge of the Cascades is one of the most
popular natural sites in the Seattle area. A 2-acre park and wheelchair-accessible
viewing platform are open around the clock (though not to pets).

✷ To Do

BICYCLING **East Lake Sammamish Trail,** 11 miles from Issaquah to Redmond. Seven access points lead to this trail along an old railroad bed. The current
crushed-rock surface is being replaced with pavement and a soft shoulder, and
parts of the trail may be closed till the work is finished.

Lake Washington loop, 26 miles around the southern end of the lake and across
Mercer Island. The route starts and ends at Gene Coulon Park, 1201 Lake

Washington Boulevard North, Renton. Loop north to the outskirts of Bellevue, across Mercer Island's north end, over a floating bridge to Seattle, and down Lake Washington Boulevard past Seward Park to return. It's now been extended around the entire lake, skipping the Mercer Island crossing, which is an option if you're up for a 53-mile ride.

Marymoor Velodrome (206-675-1424; www.velodrome.org), at Marymoor Park, 6046 West Lake Sammamish Parkway NE, Redmond. Call for hours. The velodrome hosts bike races and sponsors classes in track bike riding and racing, but it is also open to public riding. You can rent a track bike at the velodrome or just bring your road bike.

Mercer Way, 15-mile paved loop around Mercer Island. Start at **Luther Burbank Park,** 6046 West Lake Sammamish Way, Renton. This route connects several parks on the island.

Snoqualmie River Valley Trail, 31.5 miles of crushed-rock surface beside the river. From Tolt MacDonald Park (see *Camping*), wind your way through an agricultural valley.

BOATING Lake Sammamish State Park (425-455-7010; www.parks.wa.gov), 2000 Sammamish Road, Issaquah. This day-use park is popular with boaters.

CAMPING Issaquah Village RV Park (425-392-9233 or 800-258-9233), 650 First Avenue NE, Issaquah. Issaquah sits in the Cascade foothills 14 miles west of Seattle. One hundred twelve sites, nice views, and all amenities, but just off the freeway; no tents. $43–55. Reservations recommended.

Tolt MacDonald Park and Campground (206-205-5434), 31020 NE 40th Street, Carnation; from I-90 take exit 22, Preston–Fall City Road, to WA 203, then drive 5.7 miles north. Seventeen tent sites, 16 utility sites, and six yurts on 574 acres at the confluence of the Tolt and Snoqualmie rivers. Tent and utility sites $20–30; yurts $50.

Vasa Park Resort (425-746-3260), 3560 West Lake Sammamish Parkway SE, Bellevue. Twenty-two tent and RV sites with full or partial hook-ups on the west shore of Lake Sammamish, with a playground, showers, restrooms, water, and a boat launch. $26–32. Reservations accepted.

GOLF Bellevue Municipal Golf Course (425-452-7250), 5500 140th Street NE, Bellevue. Eighteen holes.

Willows Run Golf Club (425-883-1200), 10402 Willows Road NE, Redmond. Three 18-hole courses and one 9-hole course.

HIKING Issaquah Alps Trail Club (425-641-3815; www.issaquahalps.org) leads hikes in the Issaquah Alps east of Seattle.

Mount Si, 4 miles. Trailhead is outside North Bend, 28 miles southwest of Seattle; from I-90 take exit 31. This hike in the Cascade foothills takes you up 4,167 feet. This is a Department of Natural Resources site. As at state parks and other state recreation sites, a Discover Pass is required: $10 per day; $30 one-year pass. Available at most state parks and online at discoverpass.wa.gov.

Sammamish River Trail (www.kingcounty.gov/recreation), 11 miles from Bothell to Marymoor Park, Redmond. This path extending from the Burke-Gilman Trail (see the Seattle chapter) is open to bikes as well.

See also *Wilder Places—Parks*.

✳ Wilder Places

PARKS **Bridle Trails State Park** (425-307-3578; www.parks.wa.gov), off 116th Avenue NE at NE 53rd Street, Kirkland; from I-405 take exit 17. This day-use park features a small riding arena and lots of trails for hikers and equestrians.

Cougar Mountain Wildland Park (206-296-8687; www.kingcounty.gov), 18201 SE Cougar Mountain Drive, Bellevue. Open 8 AM–dusk. On the edge of the Eastside's sprawl, Cougar Mountain's 3,000-plus acres are a heavily forested wilderness in the Issaquah Alps. With 36 miles of hiking trails and 12 miles of equestrian trails, it's a real escape.

Gene Coulon Park (425-430-6400; www.rentonwa.gov), 1201 Lake Washington Boulevard North, Renton. Picnicking, swimming, and lake access.

Lake Sammamish State Park (425-455-7010; www.parks.wa.gov), 20606 SE 56th Street, Issaquah. Open 6:30 AM–dusk in summer; 8 AM–dusk in winter. On the southern end of Lake Sammamish, this 512-acre day-use park offers kayak rentals in summer, swimming, picnicking, and a boat launch.

Luther Burbank Park (206-296-2966; www.mercergov.org), 2040 84th Avenue SE, Mercer Island. Picnicking on Lake Washington shoreline and an off-leash dog area.

♪ **Marymoor Park** (206-205-3661; www.kingcounty.gov), 6046 West Lake Sammamish Parkway NE, Redmond. Open 8 AM–dusk. A popular and diverse park, Marymoor hosts concerts, movies, and bike races but also has community gardens, the 1904 **Clise Mansion,** and a 40-acre off-leash dog area. If your kids have you climbing the walls, there's a climbing wall right here.

St. Edward State Park (425-823-2992; www.parks.wa.gov), 14445 Juanita Drive NE, Kenmore. Formerly a Catholic seminary, this day-use park on Lake Washington in Kirkland has trails for hiking and mountain biking, picnic areas, and playing fields.

Tiger Mountain State Forest (360-825-1631); from I-90 take exit 20 and follow the signs to the Tradition Lake trailhead. With 13,000 acres and 80 miles of hiking, biking, and equestrian trails just half an hour from Seattle, forested Tiger Mountain is a magnet for outdoor urbanites. Corridors now connect Tiger Mountain to Squak Mountain and Cougar Mountain, which together with the Mountains to Sound Greenway enable you to walk from Lake Washington to Cle Elum. Trail maps are available from the Issaquah Chamber of Commerce (see *Guidance*).

Tolt MacDonald Park and Campground (206-205-5434), 31020 NE 40th Street, Carnation; from I-90 take exit 22, Preston–Fall City Road, to WA 203, then drive 5.7 miles north. At the confluence of the Tolt and Snoqualmie rivers, there's access to fishing and the Snoqualmie River Valley Trail.

✳ Lodging

HOTELS

Bellevue

Red Lion Bellevue (425-455-5240), 11211 Main Street. The Red Lion has 181 king and queen rooms in downtown Bellevue, with landscaped gardens and an outdoor pool. $84–129.

Silver Cloud Inn–Bellevue Downtown (425-637-7000), 10621 NE 12th Street. Silver Cloud Inns, a regional chain, all have swimming pools, clean and comfortable rooms, and complimentary breakfast, with an at-home friendliness that sets them apart from the larger chains. $99–199.

Silver Cloud Inn–Bellevue Eastgate (425-957-9100 or 800-571-9926), 114632 SE Eastgate Way. Another Eastside location. $89–169.

Redmond

Silver Cloud Inn–Redmond (425-746-8200 or 800-205-6934), 2122 152nd Avenue NE. Like the other two Eastside locations, this is business-oriented, being in Washington's high-tech corridor, just three blocks from the Microsoft campus. $89–179.

LODGES

Woodinville

🐾 **Willows Lodge** (877-424-3930), 14580 NE 145th Street. A rustic luxury lodge, if such a thing is possible, the Willows sits within a stone's throw of Woodinville's wineries and in the midst of its own gardens. Built of Douglas fir logs salvaged from the Port of Portland, plus ash and slate (some recycled from old bars), the place has a two-story lobby with a huge fireplace and 86 large rooms, many with balconies and/or fireplaces. Your dog can stay, too, and even get room service (as well he or she might, at these rates). The on-site **Herbfarm Restaurant** serves nine-course meals, equally pricey. $179–669; ask about holiday specials.

MOTELS

Redmond

Redmond Inn (800-634-8080), 17601 Redmond Way. The Redmond Inn has 150 commodious motel rooms (king or double queen) and suites. You can also rent a bike. Rates include a continental breakfast. No pets. $139–149.

✳ Where to Eat

DINING OUT

Kirkland

Café Juanita (425-823-1505; www.cafejuanita.com), 9702 NE 120th Place. Open 5–10 Tues.–Sat., 5–9 Sun. Contrary to what you'd expect, this venue features fine northern Italian cuisine—*fonduta,* fava beans, white truffles, whatever the season brings—and, of course, pasta. Reservations recommended.

Purple Café and Wine Bar (425-828-3772; www.purplecafe.com), 3223 Park Place Center. First-class wines (and second-class ones for lower budgets) and dinners (see *Where to Eat* in the Seattle chapter).

Woodinville

Barking Frog (425-424-2999; www.willowslodge.com), 14580 NE 145th Street. Open for breakfast 6–10:30 Mon.–Fri., 6–2:30 Sat.–Sun.; lunch 11:30–2:30 Mon.–Fri.; dinner 5–10 daily. At the luxurious Willows Lodge (see *Lodging*), the Barking Frog is more casual than the Herbfarm (see below), also on premises. Its ambitious, seasonally changing menu may feature roast pheasant, braised oxtails, or actual frog's legs; fine cuisine but pricey. Reservations recommended.

The Herbfarm (425-485-5300; www.theherbfarm.com), 14590 145th Street. Open for dinner Thurs.–Sun. No guidebook to Washington would be complete without a reference to the nationally renowned Herbfarm. Sprung in 1986 from Lola Zimmerman's roadside herb stand in Fall City, it's become a sort of Tour d'Argent of the Northwest. It started with six-course "educational luncheons"— educational about food and wine, that is—run by Lola's son Ron and his wife, Carrie. Expansion was followed by a disastrous fire. The restaurant reopened in Woodinville four years later and continues to get rave reviews. That said, it's not a place to stop by with the family, unless your family consists entirely of adult foodies, preferably employed at Microsoft. Dinners are strictly nine-course affairs, matched with five or six wines, on a different theme each week, and based almost entirely on local products (some from the gardens on the premises). Prepared by virtuoso chefs Chris Weber and Tony Demes, they run $179–195. There are one or two sittings per evening, at 7 and sometimes at 4:30. Don't even think of taking in a movie afterward.

Kirkland

Hoffman's Fine Cakes and Pastries (425-828-0926; www.hoffmansfine pastries.com), 226 Park Place Center. Open 7–6 Mon.–Wed., 7–7 Thurs.–Fri., 8–7 Sat., 8–5 Sun. Mouthwatering breads, cakes, and pastries all day, plus quiche at breakfast and soups and salads for lunch.

✳ Selective Shopping

Bellevue Square (425-454-8096; www.bellevuesquare.com), 575 Bellevue Square, Bellevue. There are two hundred stores and restaurants—all the mallgoers' favorites.

Redmond Town Center (425-867-0808; www.redmondtowncenter.com), 16495 NE 74th Street, Redmond. This mall includes two hotels, 17 restaurants, movies, and even live theater.

✳ Special Events

July: **Bellevue Festival of the Arts** (206-363-2048; www.bellevuefest.org), just north of Bellevue Square, Bellevue. There are juried artist booths, free entry to the Bellevue Arts Museum, jugglers, clowns, and food.

October: **Salmon Days Festival** (425-392-0661; www.salmondays.org), Issaquah. Celebrate the return of the salmon with art, food, and salmon viewing.

Northern Puget Sound

4

INTRODUCTION

The light changes rather suddenly as you drive north from Seattle on a narrow coastal strip of inlets and river deltas squeezed between the North Cascades and the Salish Sea. Somewhere between the Skagit Valley and Bellingham, you get the odd feeling of being in another country—and, of course, you almost are: Vancouver, British Columbia, is barely half an hour away. You might catch yourself wondering whether you have the right currency before you're even across the border. In fact, the border wasn't always clear; remember "54-40 or fight"?

While the 49th parallel, agreed upon as the boundary between the United States and Canada in 1846, was all very well for the mainland, the archipelago offshore was quite another story. The line was intended to jog around the south end of Vancouver Island, but who could tell through which of several channels it should run? Britain and the United States almost came to blows over this in the San Juan Islands in what is known today as the Pig War. The matter wasn't settled till 1872, when the chosen arbiter—Kaiser Wilhelm of Germany, for some reason—decreed that the boundary passed through Haro Strait to the west of the nearly two hundred San Juan Islands and islets, and therefore they were American.

Still, it's an artificial boundary. The orcas don't recognize it, any more than the minke and gray whales that forage in these waters—or the tides. Properly speaking, "Northern Puget Sound" isn't even Puget Sound, which officially extends from Olympia to Port Townsend; up here, it's the Strait of Georgia, the Strait of Juan de Fuca, or the confluence of the two. Some have taken to calling the whole waterway, from Olympia north to Vancouver and west almost to Neah Bay, the Salish Sea, after the tribes who still inhabit its perimeter and for whom, before the modern age, it was undoubtedly mare nostrum—a trade corridor and rich food source, though subject to occasional depredations by coastal raiders from the north.

The islands spattering the sea's surface today are either resistant rock (the San Juans) or glacial till (Whidbey), products of the ice sheet that carved deep canyons out of the bedrock and then flooded them. You could easily drive up to Canada in a couple of hours, but you'd be missing a lot. Most of the small towns you'll see along the way were built by fishing and timber. Only Everett, with Boeing and a naval base, and Bellingham could be called cities.

From the coastal fringe, under the benign gaze of Mount Baker, you can reach some of the islands by bridge. The outer isles, requiring a trip on the Washington

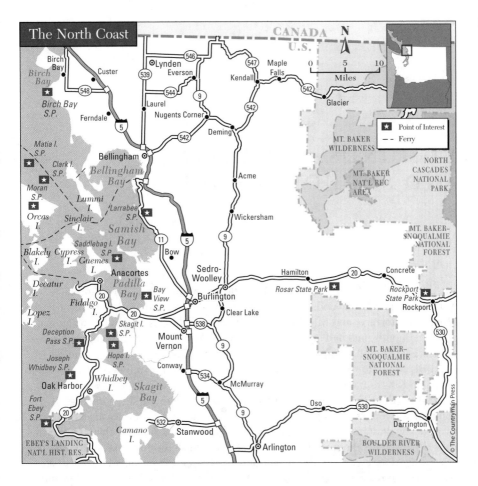

The North Coast

State Ferries or a private boat, are well worth a visit. To sail the broad blue waters among islands whose tall forests reach to the waterline, with the horizons bounded by the peaks of the Cascades and Olympics, is to experience one of the world's great places. And all for the price of a ferry ride.

EDMONDS, EVERETT, AND SNOHOMISH AREA

Along the I-5 corridor north of Seattle are suburbs including Shoreline, Alderwood, and Lynnwood; inland nearer Lake Washington are Lake Forest Park, Mountlake Terrace, and Mill Creek. Seattle's sprawl begins to thin out when you get to Edmonds, just half an hour north of the city's downtown. A couple of miles west of I-5, Edmonds might almost be an English seaside town but for the serrated Olympic Mountains staring at you across the water. From here you can catch a ferry to Kingston on the Kitsap Peninsula.

A bit north of Edmonds is Mukilteo, also on the water and the jumping-off point for the ferry to Whidbey. Mukilteo's edges merge into the naval city of Everett, the western terminus of cross-state highway US 2. Along this, the Stevens Pass Highway, sits the quaint little town of Snohomish; farther east is Monroe, now expanding as an Eastside suburb. But once you reach the farmland on its outskirts, you're well into the Cascade foothills, where the hamlets of Sultan, Startup, and Gold Bar lie to the east and Lake Stevens to the north.

GUIDANCE **Greater Edmonds Chamber of Commerce** (425-776-6711; www .edmondswa.com), 121 Fifth Avenue North, Edmonds 98020.

Snohomish Chamber of Commerce (360-568-2526), 127 Avenue A, Snohomish 98290.

Snohomish County Tourism Bureau (888-338-0976; www.snohomish.org), 909 SE Everett Mall Way, C-300, Everett 98208.

GETTING THERE **I-5** north of Seattle and **US 2** east of Everett are the major access routes. North-south **WA 9** links Woodinville to Snohomish and Lake Stevens (and points farther north).

Shuttle Express (425-981-7000; www.shuttleexpress.com) goes north from Sea-Tac Airport to this area via I-5.

AMTRAK (800-USA-RAIL; www.amtrak.com) stops in Edmonds at 211 Railroad Avenue.

Greyhound (425-252-2143 or 800-231-2222; www.greyhound.com) stops in Everett at 3201 Smith Avenue and in Monroe at 19916 Old Owen Road.

Washington State Ferries (206-464-6400 or 888-808-7977; www.wsdot.wa.gov /ferries) operate between Edmonds and Kingston, on the Kitsap Peninsula, and between Mukilteo and Clinton, on Whidbey Island.

GETTING AROUND Community Transit (425-353-RIDE; www.community transit.org), 20110 46th Avenue West, Lynnwood, provides bus service around Snohomish County and south to Seattle and the Eastside.

MEDICAL EMERGENCY Providence Everett General Hospital (425-261-2000), 1321 Colby Avenue, Everett.

✳ To See

FARMERS' MARKETS Edmonds Museum Summer Farmers' Market (425-742-4512), Fifth Avenue North and Bell Street, Edmonds. Open 9–3 Sat. May–Oct.

Everett Farmers' Market (425-258-3356), 1600 West Marine View Drive, Everett. Open 11–4 Sun. June–Sept.

Everett Friday Farmers' Market (425-773-3233), North Broadway and Tower Street, Everett. Open 10–3 Fri. late May–Sept.

Monroe River Valley Farmers' Market (425-750-2473), Monroe-Duvall Road south of Lewis Street Bridge, Monroe. Open 11–5 Sat.–Sun. May–Sept.

Monroe Tuesday Market (360-863-3521), at Traveler Park, US 2 and Main Street, Monroe. Open 2–7 Tues. June–Sept.

Snohomish Farmers' Market (360-348-2674), Cedar Street between First and Pearl streets, Snohomish. Open 3–7 Thurs. May–Sept.

FARMS AND GARDENS The Skykomish and Snoqualmie rivers merge to form the Snohomish River, whose fertile bottomlands bring forth plentiful fruits, flowers, and vegetables. Snohomish County puts out a **Farm Trail Guide** (888-338-0976) with more complete listings. Here are some places you can find this bounty.

Antique Rose Farm (360-568-1919; www.antiquerosefarm.com), 12220 Springhetti Road, Snohomish. An antique-rose nursery.

Bailey Vegetables (360-568-8826; www.baileyveg.com), 12711 Springhetti Road, 2 miles south of Snohomish. This produce stand and U-pick has green beans, beets, and more. Open 8–6 daily mid-July–Oct.

Bob's Corn (360-668-2506; www.bobscorn.com), 10917 Elliott Road, 6 miles south of Snohomish. Here you'll find corn, squash, pumpkins, potatoes, honey, cider, and a corn maze in season. No pets, please. Open 10–7 daily in season.

Ed's Apples (360-793-1996), 13420 339th Avenue SE, Sultan. East of Snohomish is a Jonagold apple orchard. Call with your order; they'll call you when it's ready.

The Farm (425-334-4124), 7301 Rivershore Road, Snohomish. The Farm has a putting green and hayrides, a corn maze, and pumpkins in season, plus fresh seasonal produce including sweet corn. Open 8–6 daily late Sept.–Oct.

FOR FAMILIES ✐ **Imagine Children's Museum** (425-258-1006; www.imagine cm.org), 1502 Wall Street, Everett. Open 9–5 Tues.–Wed., 11–5 Thurs.–Sat., 11–5

Sun. $7.95, $4 3–5 Thurs., children under one free. Opened in 2004 and aimed at children ages 1 to 12, ICM flaunts its lighthouse at the corner of Wall Street and Hoyt Avenue in Everett. The building used to be a bank and presumably conceived the lighthouse as a way of attracting customers. Whatever shoals it might have betokened, the model tower really is more appropriate for a children's museum. At 20,000 square feet, ICM is one of the biggest and most ambitious in the state. Does your kid want to milk a cow? She can (the cow actually produces water). Climb a tree house or run a café? He can do that, too. Climb a rock face or play vet? Yep. He can even play on the jungle gym on the carefully fenced rooftop. There are puzzles and a book room, themed to complement the exhibits, for quieter play. There's a lot to do and a lot of kids doing it, but it's pretty orderly for all that, has the latest safety standards, and is a nice way to do something just for the kids. It does seem there ought to be a family admission fee, though, as at some other museums.

✎ **The Serpentarium** (360-805-5300; www.reptileman.com), 22715-B US 2, 1 mile east of Monroe. Open 10–8 Mon.–Thurs., 10–6 Fri.–Sat. in summer; 10–5 Mon.–Thurs., 10–6 Fri.–Sat. in winter. $5 adults, $3 children 3–17. If you or your children are reptile fans, this is the place. Tortoises, terrapins, cobras, an anaconda, and a rare albino alligator inhabit this rambling frame residence. Each reptile has its own enclosure except for some free-running (well, running is an exaggeration) tortoises. Owner and collector Scott Peterson started by demonstrating his scaly friends to school science classes, and when the children kept demanding visiting rights, he decided to build the Serpentarium.

HISTORIC HOMES Snohomish was founded in 1859, and a fair number of the early homes escaped its 1911 fire. A self-guiding tour brochure available at the chamber of commerce (see *Guidance*) takes you to many of these houses and early businesses. Here are a couple of points of interest.

Blackman House (360-568-5235), 118 Avenue B, Snohomish. Open 12–3 Sat.–Sun. Donation accepted. Hyrcanus Blackman, who owned several shingle mills and was Snohomish's first mayor, had this house built in 1878. The rather restrained Victorian still has many furnishings that belonged to the family, although the house is now owned by the Snohomish Historical Society.

E. C. Ferguson Cottage, 17 Avenue A, Snohomish. This was the first dwelling in this town, which was originally called Cadyville. The cabin was delivered by steamer in 1859.

HISTORIC SITES Historic Everett (425-530-2722; www.historiceverett.org), 2625 Colby Avenue, Everett. This organization periodically offers historic **walking tours** of both Everett and Snohomish.

Lynnwood Heritage Park (888-338-0976), 19921 Poplar Way, Alderwood. Puget Mill began selling off parcels of its land in 1917 and created a demonstration farm on 30 acres to encourage buyers. The development became known as Alderwood Manor and later incorporated as Lynnwood. In its early days, Alderwood was a curious combination of bedroom community, from which many residents commuted on the Interurban Railway to Seattle, and egg factory. As it did in several northwestern Washington communities, the federal government promoted egg production here because the hens would lay virtually year-round. Most of the farms failed during the Depression. The park includes an eclectic collection of historical artifacts such as an Interurban trolley car, the restored Superintendent's Cottage, the original water tower, and several other restored buildings. There's a small museum and visitors center, too.

Mukilteo Light Station, west of the ferry dock, Mukilteo. Open 12–5 Sat.–Sun. and holidays Apr.–Sept.; grounds open dawn to dusk daily. Tours available from the **Mukilteo Historical Society** (425-513-9602). The 1906 lighthouse rises 40 feet over the shoreline facing Whidbey Island and the busy channel between. It gleams white above the tide, as a lighthouse should, although it's dwarfed now by the ferry docks. The keeper's house contains a small museum and gift shop.

Oxford Saloon (360-568-3845; www.theoxfordsaloon.com), 913 First Street, Snohomish. This was originally the Blackman Grocery Store but has been a tavern and eatery since 1910. It's said to be occasionally haunted—by the ghost of a local policeman or by those of the prostitutes and their clients who consorted on the second floor while still alive. The latter is the version put out by the **Washington State Ghost Society** (www.washingtonstateghostsociety.com), also located in Snohomish, which should know, it would seem.

MUSEUMS Edmonds–South Snohomish County Historical Society Museum (425-774-0900; www.historicedmonds.org), 118 Fifth Avenue North, Edmonds. Open 1–4 Wed.–Fri., 10–2 Sat., 1–4 Sun. $2 adults, $1 students. A reincarnation of a 1910 Carnegie library, this museum depicts local history through things such as a diorama of Edmonds in 1910, a working model of a shingle mill, a photo gallery, and a room for changing exhibits.

Future of Flight Museum (800-464-1476; www.futureofflight.org), 8415 Paine Field Boulevard, Mukilteo. Open 8:30–5:30 daily; Boeing tours hourly 9–4. Gallery plus Boeing tour: $20 adults, $14 children 15 and under Apr.–Sept.; $18 and $10, respectively, Oct.–Mar. ($2 less if you reserve ahead). Gallery visit only: $8. This museum really should be called the "future of Boeing flight"—you don't see projects by Lockheed, for instance. Let's stipulate that Boeing is a major employer in the Seattle area, and its manufacturing operations are based in Seattle and Everett. The attractions at this museum come in two parts. The first is the gallery, where you can compare cockpits and systems on older planes with newer ones; learn what goes on under an airplane's "skin" and how much fuel a 737 uses on an average flight (a lot); ride the XJ5 flight simulator (but that costs extra); and take a gander at Boeing's finally forthcoming fuel-efficient 787. Design buffs can digitally create their own aircraft; computer stations around the gallery allow you to select specs for your plane and get a printout at the end. Tickets for the gallery only can be bought at the door without reservations.

Second, but more emphasized, is the tour of the nearby Boeing production facility. It is in fact impressive to see the 737s, 747s, and 767s in various stages of assembly lined up in what is said to be the biggest building in the world, the workers scurrying around like ants under and over the great machines. The downsides are that tours are in English only, even though they draw many international visitors; you must reserve your tour ahead of time; and, for security, you can take absolutely nothing with you—no handbags, cell phones, cameras, zilch (a preview of commercial flight security requirements in the near future?). Lockers are provided, however.

Snohomish County Museum of History (425-259-2022), 1913 Hewitt Avenue, Everett. Open 1–4 Wed.–Sat. Donation accepted. Changing exhibits highlight aspects of local history—or how national trends played out locally. Recent exhibits have included "Making Tracks," on the building of the Seattle to Everett Interurban Railway.

NATURAL WONDERS American chestnut tree, corner of Fifth Street and Avenue B, Snohomish. An enormous 21 feet 5 inches in circumference at chest height, with branches buttressed by other branches, this tree is truly mammoth, and it produces a huge yearly crop that has been eagerly scooped up by the neighborhood for generations. George Hendrie, a pharmacist who built the house on the corner in 1902, brought the tree out from New Hampshire as a seedling. In 1904 the chestnut blight that killed billions of American chestnuts appeared in New York, but it never reached this corner of the United States, and the tree survived, as it were, as a refugee. It's among the biggest in the state. The house, by the way, built by local architect Nels Peter Hansen, is sometimes on the fall Tour of Historic Homes (see *Historic Homes*).

Salmon runs. You can see the Northwest's iconic fish at these locations: **Lake Stevens spawning channel,** on Mitchell Road off Lakeshore Drive, Lake Stevens, in winter; **Pilchuck River,** at Pilchuck Park, off Second Street, Snohomish, in fall and winter; **Sultan River,** at the river's mouth off US 2, Sultan, in fall in odd-numbered years; and **Wallace River,** at a rest area on the south side of US 2 west of Gold Bar, in winter.

✳ To Do

BICYCLING Centennial Trail, 17.5 paved miles from Snohomish to Arlington. This trail's nearly level surface along a former railroad right-of-way draws walkers and in-line skaters as well as cyclists, but at 14 feet wide, there's room for all. It makes for a pleasant ride past farmland and the occasional small town. Several parks on the route provide water, restrooms, and benches. Access is from various points, including Machias Road north of Snohomish.

Interurban Trail, about 15 mostly paved miles from Seattle to Everett. This route runs along the old trolley line from Seattle to Everett (see *To See—Historic Sites*); open to nonmotorized transport.

BIRDING The 3.5-mile **Spencer Island loop trail** in the Snohomish River Estuary (see *Wilder Places—Nature Preserves*), has been washed out, but a smaller loop trail and short paths let you observe the birds. This restored wetland and major wildlife area attracts bald eagles and myriad waterfowl. From Everett take WA 529 across the river, turn right onto Smith Island Road, and follow it to Langus Waterfront Park.

CAMPING Flowing Lake County Park (360-568-2274), 17900 48th Street SE, Snohomish. Thirty tent or trailer sites, most with hook-ups (no water in winter). There are also four rustic cabins(). Tent or trailer sites $18–25; cabins $41–45.

Kayak Point Regional County Park (360-652-7992), 15610 Marine Drive, Stanwood. This shoreline park offers 28 standard sites, 10 yurts, and 1 cabin, some ADA-accessible. Standard sites $23–25; yurts $41–68; cabin $139.

River Meadows County Park (360-435-3441), 20416 Jordan Road, Arlington. Meadows, an old orchard, and riparian forest compose this park on the banks of the Stillaguamish River. Camp in the meadows or rent a yurt; 10 campsites without hook-ups and 6 yurts. Standard sites $18; yurts $45–74.

Squire Creek Park (360-435-3441), 41415 State Road 530, Arlington. An old-growth forest shelters 33 non-hook-up sites along Squire Creek.

Wallace Falls State Park (360-793-0420), off US 2, 2 miles northeast of Gold Bar; take US 2 east from Monroe 12 miles and follow the signs. Nearly 5,000 acres, plenty of wildlife, and room to hike, swim, fish, or kayak. Two walk-in tent sites 50–150 feet from parking; one restroom and no showers. No reservations. Five cabins, one open to pets, may be reserved (888-226-7688). See also *Wilder Places—Parks*.

CANOEING AND KAYAKING Snohomish River Estuary Water Trail (Snohomish County Parks and Recreation, 425-388-6600). This is a work in progress to establish a 14-mile paddling trail in the network of channels that make up the Snohomish River delta.

DIVING Edmonds Underwater Park (425-771-0227), access from Brackett's Landing Park (see *Wilder Places—Parks*). In this marine park's 27 acres, you can scuba dive amid schools of fish in an artificial reef.

GOLF Golf Club at Echo Falls (360-668-3030), 20414 121st Avenue SE, Snohomish. Eighteen holes.

Kayak Point Golf Course (800-562-3094), 15711 Marine Drive, Stanwood. Eighteen holes.

Kenwanda Golf Course (360-668-1166), 14030 Kenwanda Drive, Snohomish. Eighteen holes.

Lynnwood Municipal Golf Course (425-672-4693), 20200 68th Avenue West, Lynnwood. Eighteen holes.

Snohomish Public Golf Club (360-568-2676), 7806 147th Avenue SE, Snohomish. Eighteen holes.

HIKING Centennial Trail, 23 paved miles from Snohomish to Bryant. This multiuse trail for nonmotorized transport runs along an old railroad bed. There are seven access points; the southern end is on Machias Road just north of Snohomish.

Lord Hill Regional Park, 12921 150th Street SE, 4 miles southwest of Snohomish. Six miles of hiking and equestrian trails roam this park (see *Wilder Places—Parks*); an easy one is the 2.2-mile **Beaver Lake Loop** through woods to a marshy lake and back. Longer trails take you to views of Mount Baker.

&. **Marsh Wildlife Sanctuary Trail,** Edmonds (425-771-0230). In this 23 acres of wetland, a wheelchair-friendly interpretive walkway tells you about the history and wildlife of the marsh, which attracts more than two hundred species of birds, such as marbled murrelets, auklets, shorebirds, and Eurasian vagrants.

BRACKETT'S LANDING PARK IS A SANDY BEACH NORTH OF THE EDMONDS-KINGSTON FERRY DOCK.

✳ Wilder Places

PARKS Brackett's Landing Park, just north of the Edmonds-Kingston ferry dock. Has a pleasant sandy beach and jetty.

Jetty Island, accessible by free ferry from 10th Street and West Marine View Drive, Everett. Open 10–5:30 Wed.–Sat., 11–5:30 Sun. (summer only). Tickets at kiosk. This artificial 2-mile-long island with sandy beaches and shallow, abnormally warm water is a place to go with kids or if you just have to get into the water.

Lord Hill Regional Park, 12921 150th Street SE, Snohomish. Mitchell Lord's 1879 homestead is the nucleus of what is now a 1,300-acre evergreen forest just outside Snohomish. The farm is gone, but you can wander the trails by foot (see *To Do—Hiking*), horse, or mountain bike and take in Cascade and Olympic views from the hilltops.

Wallace Falls State Park (360-793-0420), off US 2, 2 miles northeast of Gold Bar; take US 2 east from Monroe 12 miles and follow the signs. The 4,735-acre park sprawling along two forks of the Wallace River and three lakes (Shaw, Jay, and Wallace) harbors abundant wildlife, a 265-foot waterfall, and old-growth forest. Nonmotorized boats are welcome. There are 12 miles of hiking trails and 5 miles of bike trails, plus a secluded campground.

NATURE PRESERVES Snohomish River Estuary. Otters, coyotes, eagles, and peregrine falcons haunt the sloughs of the largest wetland on Puget Sound, at 1,900 acres. You might spot them from a kayak or the viewing platforms on **Spencer Island,** which has a trailhead accessible by road (see *To Do—Hiking*).

✳ Lodging

BED & BREAKFASTS

Edmonds

The Maple Tree Bed and Breakfast
(425-774-8420), 18313 Olympic View
Drive. There's just one guest room in
this older home, so you have the patio,
gardens, and Olympic views to yourself. Children welcome. No pets. $100.

Mukilteo

The Hogland House (888-681-5101;
www.hoglandhouse.com), 917 Webster
Street. Though the 4,700-square-foot
mansion has had a number of uses in
its hundred-year history—it's served as
an army hospital and convent as well as
a private home—it retains much of its
original design: a Craftsman sporting,
unusually, not only columns but also
elaborate woodwork. Trails on 5 acres
wind down to the creek or beach. Two
guest rooms have private baths and
antique bedsteads. $125 ($95 without
breakfast).

Snohomish

Countryman Bed and Breakfast
(360-568-9622 or 800-700-9622;
www.countrymanbandb.com), 119
Cedar Avenue. This renovated 1896
Victorian has three guest rooms with
private bath; breakfast is included if
desired. $95–135; tiered pricing lets
you choose among full, continental, or
no breakfast.

HOTELS

Edmonds

**Best Western Plus Edmonds Har-
bor Inn** (425-771-5021), 130 West
Dayton Street. A reliable Best Western
with all the usual—free Wi-Fi, free
continental breakfast, outdoor pool,
etc. Pet-friendly, too. $110–190.

Everett

Inn at Port Gardner (888-252-6779;
www.innatportgardner.com), 1700
West Marine View Drive. Everett's
working waterfront is carefully gentri-
fying, with a cluster of restaurants and
the Inn at Port Gardner, which was
built in a "New Northwest" style. The
curved roof and siding suggesting cor-
rugated iron are intended to evoke the
neighborhood's industrial heritage,
which they do, but in the lobby, polished wood armchairs stand on an Oriental rug by the fireplace, and vast
windows overlook the marina. The
rooms are similarly understated but
comfortable. Continental breakfast is
brought to your room in a little basket.
$109–220.

Mukilteo

Silver Cloud Inn (425-423-8600 or
800-311-1461; www.silvercloud.com),
718 Front Street. One of a chain of
eight Silver Clouds around the Northwest, this one is a convenient block
from the ferry to Whidbey Island. Seventy calm, comfortable rooms, some of
which have fireplaces, look out onto
the island. Rates include breakfast.
$139–269.

✳ Where to Eat

DINING OUT

Edmonds

Café de Paris (425-771-2350), 109
Main Street. Open for lunch 11:30–2
Mon.–Fri.; dinner from 5:30 daily. It
really does look like a nice, relaxed
Paris café. Clearly this is the place to
get your escargot fix, or perhaps your
poulet à l'estragon if you don't do
snails.

Everett

Emory's Lake House (425-337-7772;
www.emorys.com), 11830 19th Avenue
SE. Open for lunch Mon.–Sat.; dinner
from 4 daily; brunch 10–2:30 Sun.
Emory's offers fine American food on
the shore of Silver Lake, just off I-5. A
plethora of salads; expertly prepared

fresh seafood, poultry, and meats; and fine desserts have made this an Everett favorite. Check for early-bird dinner specials. Live jazz on the weekend.

EATING OUT

Edmonds

✐ **Anthony's Homeport** and **Beach Café** (425-771-4400), 456 Admiral Way. This Anthony's location is two in one: a regular Homeport upstairs for a full-service restaurant (open 11–9:30 Mon.–Thurs., 11–10 Fri.–Sat., 11:30–midnight Sun.), and the Beach Café downstairs for comfortable family meals (open for lunch 11–4 Mon.–Sat.; dinner daily from 4). Four hours of free moorage while dining are offered at the **Edmonds Marina** (425-775-4588).

Everett

Anthony's Homeport (425-252-3333), 1726 West Marine View Drive. Open for lunch daily; dinner from 4:30 daily; brunch Sun. Anthony's has not one but two locations on Everett's Port Gardner Bay: the Homeport and the Woodfire Grill (see below). The Homeport gives you six hours of free moorage at the **Everett Marina** (425-259-6001) next door. Like all the Anthony's, it features seafood from their own seafood company, water views, and Northwest beers and wines.

Anthony's Woodfire Grill (425-258-4000), 1722 West Marine View Drive. Open for lunch 11:30–3:30 Wed.–Sun.; dinner from 3:30 daily. More Northwest seafood, this time prepared over applewood in their special oven, grill, or rotisserie. And six hours of free moorage, as at the Homeport (see above).

✐ **Scuttlebutt Brewing Company** (425-257-9316; www.scuttlebutt brewing.com), 1205 Craftsman Way. Open 11–9 Sun.–Thurs., 11–11

Fri.–Sat. The happy buzz here may be due to Scuttlebutt's own brews—it is an actual working brewery visible from the dining room—but the pub fare is fine, too. Choose among burgers, pizza, soups, sandwiches, and, of course, fish-and-chips. It's an informal, family-friendly brewery with informal, enthusiastic servers.

Mukilteo

Ivar's Mukilteo Landing (425-742-6180; www.ivars.com), 710 Front Street. Open for lunch and dinner daily. If you had been dining here one day in 2003, the seafood would have come in through the window—storms sent waves crashing through the picture windows, resulting in months of repairs (and reinforcements). Now it's cozy again with gleaming wood beams and new carpeting, and the fish appear decently, via the kitchen. Located on the waterfront next to the ferry, Ivar's is reliable for seafood in both classic and experimental recipes; you can enjoy halibut in blackberry-lavender sauce or, just as easily, Dungeness crab Louie. The three-course early-bird dinner is a good value.

Snohomish

The Cabbage Patch (360-568-9091; www.cabbagepatchrestaurant.com), 111 Avenue A. Open 10–PM Mon.–Fri., 8 AM–10 PM Sat.–Sun. Set in a humble 1905 house, the Cabbage Patch has been serving homestyle meals since 1975 in a homelike atmosphere of vintage furniture and works by local artists. Dinner choices run from beef stroganoff to pecan chicken to fettuccine Alfredo, with plenty of seafood, too.

✐ **Collector's Choice** (360-568-8623), 120 Glen Avenue. Open 7 AM–10 PM daily. This place is known for its ribs and steaks. No surprises here, but they do have a children's menu, plus pasta and seafood.

Snohomish Pie Company (360-568-3589), 915 First Street, Suite C. A local if not regional favorite for pies, this bakery has been pleasing residents, shoppers, cyclists, and just about everyone since 1997.

✳ Entertainment

THEATER Everett Performing Arts Center (425-257-8600; www.village theatre.org), 2710 Wetmore Avenue, Everett. Dedicated to live theater, especially musicals, the center offers a crowded calendar of both classic and new works.

Historic Everett Theatre (425-258-6766 or 800-838-3006; www.everett theatre.org), 2911 Colby Avenue, Everett. Built in 1901, the theater was a grand opera house with a capacity of 1,200 till it burned down in 1923. It was rebuilt immediately but, with competition from TV and film, closed in 1989. Now it's open again, offering classic films, plays, and concerts.

✳ Selective Shopping

ANTIQUES Snohomish calls itself the **"Antiques Capital of the Northwest,"** and its Main Street (about three blocks long) is in fact lined with antiques malls representing several hundred dealers.

BOOKS Rick Steves' Europe Through the Back Door (425-771-8303; www.ricksteves.com), 130 Fourth Avenue North, Edmonds. Open 9–5 Mon.–Wed. and Fri.–Sat., 9–8 Thurs., except holidays and Aug. 24. If you are a Rick Steves fan, stop by his store, where you'll find guidebooks from his Back Door series, European rail passes, travel equipment, videos, travel classes and workshops (how about Italian for Travelers?), and a book and video library.

✳ Special Events

June: **Edmonds Art Festival** (425-771-6412; www.edmondsartfestival .com), 700 Main Street, Edmonds. This three-day celebration of the visual and performing arts has been running since 1957, with exhibits, seminars, workshops, and entertainment.

July: **Kla Ha Ya Days** (360-493-7824; www.klahayadays.com), various locations around Snohomish. Just about every kind of small-town event you can imagine—from a Civil War reenactment to a baby-crawling race to, ahem, a cherry-pit-spitting contest—augments a frog-jumping contest, bike rodeo, and much, much more.

RICK STEVES' EUROPE THROUGH THE BACK DOOR HEADQUARTERS IN DOWNTOWN EDMONDS

WHIDBEY ISLAND

Is Whidbey the longest island in the Lower 48, as some Washington sources claim? For that matter, how long is it? Some sources say 40-odd miles, some as much as 55. It depends how you count and who is doing the counting.

First, there's the little matter of Long Island. New Yorkers all know their island is the longest, at 118 miles. To the naysayers who would make Long Island a peninsula, one can ask, is it surrounded by natural waterways? Yes. Case closed. But which is prettier?

Now, Whidbey. It's shaped approximately like a snail extracted from its shell: curly. If you draw a line along its main axis, it is more than 55 miles long. Those 55 miles happen to constitute a scenic highway that will bear you over 170 gently rolling square miles of farms, woodlands, state parks, and villages.

It does have two unofficial divisions: North Whidbey, home of the Air Naval Base at Oak Harbor, and South Whidbey, a somewhat eclectic mix of longtime islanders, conservationists, retirees, and ex-urbanites. Summer people have come to Whidbey for generations for its quietude, beauty, and easy access—it's a 20-minute ferry ride from Mukilteo to the south or a scenic drive over the Deception Pass Bridge at the north end.

GUIDANCE **Central Whidbey Island Chamber of Commerce** (360-678-5434; www.centralwhidbeychamber.org), 905 NW Alexander, Coupeville 98239.

Greater Oak Harbor Chamber of Commerce (360-675-3755; www.oakharbor chamber.org), 32630 WA 20, Oak Harbor 98277.

Langley Chamber of Commerce (360-221-6765; www.visitlangley.com), 208 Anthes Avenue, Langley 98260.

Whidbey and Camano Islands Tourism (www.whidbeycamanoislands.com), Box 365, Coupeville 98239.

GETTING THERE Whidbey Island can be reached from the south by a 20-minute ferry ride via **Washington State Ferries** (206-464-6400 or 888-808-7977; www.wsdot.wa.gov/ferries) from Mukilteo, 30 miles north of Seattle; there's also the Keystone ferry from Port Townsend on the Kitsap Peninsula to Ebey's Landing on Whidbey.

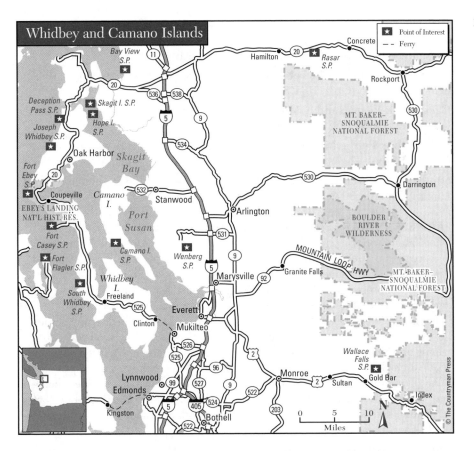

From the north, Whidbey can be reached by **WA 20** and the bridge over Deception Pass; from **I-5** at Burlington, head west on WA 20, which continues south down Whidbey to Ebey's Landing. From there south to Clinton, the main route is **WA 525.**

From Seattle-Tacoma International Airport, the **Whidbey–Sea-Tac Shuttle** (877-679-4003) serves all of Whidbey Island.

GETTING AROUND Island Transit (360-678-7771 or 800-240-8747; www .islandtransit.org) offers free bus service all around Whidbey Island.

MEDICAL EMERGENCY Whidbey General Hospital (360-678-5151 or 888-903-2345; www.whidbeygen.org), 101 North Main Street, Coupeville.

✳ To See

FARMERS' MARKETS Naturally, with all its horticultural activity, Whidbey has some venerable farmers' markets.

Bayview Farmers' Market (360-321-4302; www.bayviewfarmersmarket.com), on WA 525 at Bayview Road, Bayview. It's held outdoors in summer; inside the Bayview Community Hall in spring and fall. Open 10–2 Sat.–Sun. May–Oct.

Coupeville Farmers Market (360-678-4288), 788 Alexander Street, Coupeville; behind the library. Open 10–2 Sat. Apr.–early Oct.

Greenbank Farm Sunday Market (360-678-7710), at WA 525 and Wonn Road, Greenbank. Open 10–3 Sun. May–Sept.

Oak Harbor Public Market (360-678-4288), on WA 20 next to the visitors center, Oak Harbor. The only evening market. Open 4–7 Thurs. mid-May–Sept.

South Whidbey Tilth Farmers' Market (360-579-2892), 2812 Thompson Road, Langley. Open 11:30–3:30 Sun. May–Oct.

FARMS AND GARDENS ✔ **Chocolate Flower Farm** (360-221-2464; www .chocolateflowerfarm.com), 5040 Saratoga Road, Langley. Open 10–5 Sat.–Sun. and occasional weekdays May–Sept. It's hard to resist a place with *chocolate* and *flower* in the same name. Gardening addict Marie Lincoln and chocolate addict Bill Schlicht broke ground here in 2005. Their 8 lush acres feature plants with dark brown or purple flowers and foliage, from chocolate soldier *Aquilegia* (columbine) to chocolate *Zantedeschia*. Marie propagates and sells many of these rare and unusual plants, or you can just buy some cocoa mulch, a soil cover containing crushed cocoa beans, to add fragrance to your garden. Children enjoy the resident chicks, ducks, horses, and dogs, and there's a children's garden just for them, though they might be disappointed that they can't actually eat the "chocolate" flowers. The farm's shop on First Street in Langley, the **Garden Shed** (360-221-4464), does sell specialty chocolates, body products, candles, teas, coffees, and seeds; open 10–6 daily.

Cultus Bay Nursery and Garden (360-579-2329; www.cultusbaynursery.com), 7568 Cultus Bay Road, Clinton. Open 10–5 Thurs.–Mon. Apr.–Sept.; 10–5 Sat.–Sun. Mar. Tucked under a hill along a lush back road, Mary Fisher's profusely flowering garden has gained a reputation mostly by word of mouth during the 20 years since she turned the first spade. (Her husband, Tom, built the Victorian-style farmhouse.) Box hedges, a pond, an aisle of espaliered apple trees, and varied beds create a little Eden—and flowers for many local weddings.

Greenbank Farm (360-678-7171; www.greenbankfarm.com), at WA 525 and Wonn Road, Greenbank. Open 10–5 daily June–Sept.; 11–4 Mon.–Fri., 10–5 Sat.–Sun. Oct.–May. When owner Château Ste. Michelle threatened to sell the 522-acre farm for development, Whidbey residents rose up in outrage and promptly rearranged the sale. It went to a consortium of the Nature Conservancy, Island County, and the Port of Coupeville, which runs it as an organic farm and retail outlet for local crafts, specialty foods, regional wines, and antiques. Owned by the Philips family until the 1970s, it was at one time the largest loganberry farm in the United States. It still produces loganberries, and its signature loganberry wine is for sale in the wine shop.

The on-site **Whidbey Pie Café** (360-678-1288) offers homemade pies and yummy soups, salads, and sandwiches. The farm sits on Whidbey's narrow waistline, and a **trail** wandering up the ridge leads you to views east, north, and west, from the Olympics to Mount Rainier. (Just across the road, **Coupe's Greenbank Store** has been providing residents with gas and necessities for more than a hundred years.)

Hummingbird Farm Nursery and Gardens (360-679-5044; www.humming birdfarmnursery.com), 2319 Zylstra Road, Oak Harbor. Open 10–6 Wed.–Sun. and by appointment. Hummingbird's display gardens include a wild rose garden, a bog, a moon garden, and a shade garden, not to mention hummingbird and butterfly areas.

Lavender Wind Farm (360-678-0919 or 877-242-7716; www.lavenderwind.com), 2530 Darst Road, Coupeville. Open 9–5 daily in summer; 10–4 Mon.–Sat., 12–4 Sun. in fall and spring. Washington's inland sea may seem almost exactly unlike Provence, but many of Puget Sound's islands—including parts of long, thin Whidbey Island—are in the rain shadow of the Olympic Mountains. Lavender Wind is in one such microclimate: 20 inches of rain a year combine with marine breezes to make Mediterranean plants such as lavender feel almost at home here. The small farm's harvest goes into soaps, lotions, sachets, and other handmade lavender goodies available in the shop. And you can walk a **lavender labyrinth** with views of the Olympics and Vancouver Island.

Meerkerk Rhododendron Gardens (360-678-1912; www.meerkerkgardens.org), 3531 Meerkerk Lane, Greenbank. Open 9–dusk daily in summer; 9–4 Wed.–Sun. in winter. $8 adults; children under 16 free with adult. Planted in the 1960s by Ann and Max Meerkerk, who were influenced by both Asian and English gardens, the 53 acres here are a haven for both flower and forest lovers. Ten acres of forest gardens, of rhododendrons plain and fancy interspersed with beds of daffodils and bluebells, are enchanting in late spring, lovely all season. Forty-three acres of woodlands, with 5 miles of walking **trails,** enclose the gardens. Dogs are allowed on leash; please pick up after your dog.

FOR FAMILIES ✍ **Blue Fox Drive-in** (360-675-5667; www.bluefoxdrivein .com), 1403 Monroe Landing Road, Oak Harbor. For a nostalgic experience, try one of the few functioning drive-in movie theaters left in the country and experience life before the cineplex. $6.50 adults, $1 children 5–10.

✍ **Brattland Go-Karts** (360-675-2794; www.bluefoxdrivein.com), 1403 Monroe Landing Road, Oak Harbor. Give your kids an experience of driving their own vehicles for a change.

HISTORIC HOMES So many sea captains retired to **Coupeville** in the late 1800s that the county seat is dotted with their late-Victorian homes. A self-guiding brochure to the many historic homes and sites in Coupeville is available from the **Island County Historical Society** (360-678-3310; www.islandhistory.org), 901 Alexander Street, Coupeville.

Captain Coupe House, 504 NE Ninth Street. The oldest is this house built for the intrepid captain and his wife in 1854, of redwood shipped from San Francisco; it's been moved inland twice because of beach erosion.

Captain Joseph Clapp House, 307 NE Front Street. Captain Clapp built his elegant Queen Anne house upon retiring in 1886 and died at 97, the last of the Coupeville captains.

Captain Kinney House, 207 NE Front Street. The original house dates from 1871, though much of the current structure was added later.

Compass Rose B&B, 508 Main Street. A Jenne brother lived a block away from Jacob and Berthe Jenne (see below), in a house built in 1890; it is now a B&B (see *Lodging*).

Dentist's office, behind 602 North Main Street. In back of the Blue Goose Bed and Breakfast (see *Lodging*) is a simpler but false-fronted building that belonged to the dentist Berthe Jenne married after Jacob died (see below); the dentist had it brought up from Front Street.

Jacob and Berthe Jenne House, 602 North Main Street. These farmers who did well built their lovely Italianate Victorian house in 1889 (it's now the Blue Goose Bed and Breakfast; see *Lodging*), notable for its decorated friezes and carved brackets.

HISTORIC SITES

Coupeville

The entire town of Coupeville, which lies within **Ebey's Landing National Historic Reserve** (see below), has nearly 100 buildings on the National Register of Historic Places. Founded in 1853 by Captain Thomas Coupe, it's Washington's second-oldest town and preserves many old homes, several of which are now bed & breakfasts (see *Historic Homes*). A self-guiding brochure from the **Island County Historical Museum,** 901 Alexander Street, leads you around the historic district.

Alexander Blockhouse, 908 NW Alexander Street (next to the historical museum). Pioneer John Alexander built this in 1855. In that year, Governor Isaac Stevens managed to cajole, intimidate, or force the various Washington tribes into

THE COMPASS ROSE, A HISTORIC HOME IN COUPEVILLE, IS NOW A B&B.

giving up most of their lands—he called it "extinguishing Indian claim"—and set-tlers, fearing backlash, built structures such as this; mostly the backlash didn't come.

Commercial buildings, along Front Street. Many of these date from the late 19th and early 20th centuries, false fronts and all, though what was a general store then might be a tavern now, and vice versa.

Coupeville wharf, at the western end of Front Street. This is the oldest wharf still standing on Puget Sound; the local whale-watching boat ties up here. The skeleton of Rosie the gray whale welcomes you near the ticket counter.

Glenwood Hotel, 1 NW Front Street. Of interest is this building, now a private residence above commercial space. The Italianate hotel with two-story bay windows was built in 1890.

Greenbank Store (360-678-5326), 25189 WA 525, Greenbank. Coupe's descendants are still in the area; some of them own the historic plank-floored general and convenience store dating from 1904.

Ebey's Landing

Ebey's Landing National Historic Reserve comprises **Fort Casey State Park, Fort Ebey State Park,** the town of **Coupeville** (see above), and a lot of territory in between. Created in 1978, the reserve's somewhat quixotic purpose is not to preserve a particular historic moment but the aspect of a land in transition. Thus the lands protected include homesteads that are still working farms, plus woodlands and wetlands, as well as old military installations, the town, and Penn Cove itself. The few thousand people living in the preserve live normal, modern lives in countryside where the 21st century is evident mostly as paved roads and, overhead, the jets associated with the naval station at Oak Harbor. A stroll or drive around the 17,400-acre preserve yields pastoral views, century-old homes, and wayside interpretive sites. A self-guiding tour brochure can be had at the museum in Coupeville (see *Museums*).

Admiralty Head Lighthouse (360-240-5584), in Fort Casey State Park. Open 11–5 daily June–Aug.; 11–4 or 5 Sat.–Sun. Sept.–Apr.; 11–5 Thurs.–Mon. May; closed Jan.–Feb. Tours by appointment. This was built in 1903 to replace an 1860 light that was removed to make way for the gun emplacements of Fort Casey in 1900. An interpretive center is in the lighthouse.

Blockhouses, at Sunnyside Cemetery outside Coupeville (see below); near museum in Coupeville (see *Museums*); and on Fort Casey Road (see below). These three structures dating back to the 1850s recall the fairly brief period of Indian and settler hostilities.

Fort Casey, on WA 20 in Fort Casey State Park (see *Wilder Places—Parks*). Forts Flagler and Worden on Kitsap Peninsula across Admiralty Inlet, along with Fort Casey on Whidbey, were built as a "triangle of fire" guarding the entrance to Puget Sound, which officially is defined as a line connecting the Fort Worden and Admiralty Head lights.

Fort Ebey, off Libbey Road in Fort Ebey State Park (see *Wilder Places—Parks*). During World War II this fort was added, with 6-inch guns; you can still explore the batteries and concrete bunkers.

Sunnyside Cemetery, on Sherman Road south of WA 20. This is the resting place of many pioneers, including settler Isaac Ebey, who was killed a few years after filing his claim, by Haida Indians on a retaliatory raid from the north. A raid by settlers against the Haidas had resulted in some Haida deaths; Ebey wasn't involved, however, and was later killed by mistake.

Langley

The Dog House, 230 First Street. Around the corner from the museum (see below), this was built in 1908 as a sports club. It was then a general store and later for many years a bar and restaurant.

South Langley Historical Society Museum, 314 Second Street. The white clapboard structure was originally built in 1902 as a bunkhouse for loggers. Their cordwood provided fuel for Puget Sound steamers, while brush went for landfill during Seattle's building boom.

Oak Harbor

City Beach Park, off Pioneer Way on City Beach Avenue. A historical marker in this 28-acre park tells how the first white settlers landed here in 1850 to claim land that would become the town of Oak Harbor.

Neil's Barn, 100 East Whidbey Avenue. This was built by James Neil about 1910, as was the nearby wooden water tower in which a little **museum** is sometimes open.

Oak Park, aka **Smith Park,** Midway and SE Ninth Avenue. This park, by whatever name, preserves a grove of the Garry oaks that gave their name to the town.

Windmill, in City Beach Park (see above). This structure recalls the wave of Dutch settlement around 1900.

MUSEUMS Island County Historical Museum (360-678-3310; www.island history.org), 908 NW Alexander Street, Coupeville. Open 10–5 Mon.–Sat., 11–5 Sun. May–Sept.; 10–4 Mon.–Sat., 11–4 Sun. Oct.–Apr. $3 adults; $2.50 seniors, active military, and students; $6 families. Whidbey Island really only entered the modern world with the opening of the Deception Pass Bridge in 1935. This homey museum details the island's history through displays that include the first car to brave Whidbey's "roads," a 1902 Holsman; prehistory in the form of mammoth bones, teeth, and tusks; an eclectic collection of tools, clothes, and artifacts; and themed exhibits using items from the museum's collection. Carved cherrywood doors by local artist Glen Russell depict scenes from Whidbey's early settlement.

South Whidbey Historical Society Museum (360-221-2101), 312 Second Street, Langley. Open 1–4 Fri.–Sun. in summer; 1–4 Sat.–Sun. in winter. Donation accepted. Located in a former bunkhouse, this little museum features lovingly detailed reconstructions of a pioneer kitchen, parlor, and school, as well as historical photos and memorabilia.

NATURAL WONDERS Deception Pass, on WA 20 at the north end of Whidbey Island. When Captain George Vancouver sailed by here in 1792, Whidbey at first appeared to be an extension of nearby Fidalgo Island. It was only on closer inspection that he could see the narrow channel separating the two. He named the channel Deception Pass and the island Whidbey after his lieutenant. Much later, Captain Thomas Coupe became the first to sail a fully rigged sailing vessel through the pass. The foolhardiness of his act is clear when you look down at the boiling waters of a channel a mere 500 feet wide, bounded on both sides by steep, rocky headlands with a tidal rip that can reach 8 knots. Deception Pass kept the island effectively isolated till the bridge was opened in 1935. From the headlands or from the 182-foot-high bridge are impressive views of the Strait of Juan de Fuca and the San Juan Islands—all, like the entire Salish Sea, carved out by the glaciers of the last Ice Age.

SCENIC DRIVES **Whidbey Island Scenic Way,** 49 miles of WA 525 and WA 20 running along the island's spine. This constitutes the only National Scenic Byway on an island. From south to north, the road traverses a surprising variety of scenery, from the bluffs at Clinton to rolling farmland to village to forest and, finally, to the cliffs and panoramas of Deception Pass. On a clear day, you'll also have memorable views of the Olympics, the Cascades, and island-spattered Puget Sound.

WALKING TOURS The town of **Coupeville,** founded by the Coupe family in 1853, lies within **Ebey's Landing National Historic Reserve** (see *Historic Sites*). Its central district, along First and Main streets, contains a concentration of **Victorian homes** (see *Historic Homes*), as well as the **Alexander Blockhouse.** A self-guiding brochure is available from the **Island County Historical Museum,** 908 Alexander Street.

✳ To Do

BICYCLING Whidbey Island's softly rolling terrain makes it a pleasant cycling venue with lots of scenic itineraries.

Dean's Sports Plus (360-679-6145), 730 North Oak Harbor Street, Oak Harbor. For routes, contact this shop.

Deception Pass State Park, about 16 miles of mountain bike trails; on WA 20, 9 miles north of Oak Harbor. These are steep at times but beautiful.

Half Link Bicycle Shop (360-331-7980), 5603 Bayview Road, Langley. This place rents bikes and offers maps of suggested back-road and trail routes around South Whidbey for both road and mountain bikes.

Kettles Park, just west of WA 20 between Coupeville and Fort Ebey State Park. A network of both easy and more challenging trails link up with the Fort Ebey trails system for some very scenic riding.

Oak Harbor to Crockett Lake loop, 30 miles, in the heart of spectacular Ebey's Landing (see *To See—Historic Sites*).

Oak Harbor to Silverlake loop, 12 miles. Up north, this back-road loop takes you past views of Saratoga Passage and the Cascades.

Saratoga Woods Trail System, off Saratoga Road, slightly north of Langley. On southern Whidbey, this forest preserve totaling more than 600 acres has miles of forest trails for bikers and hikers.

Tour de Whidbey, circuits of 25, 50, and 100 miles. Serious cyclists might want to try this, an annual event raising funds for Whidbey General Hospital (see *Special Events*).

BIRDING Some 60 pairs of **bald eagles** nest on Whidbey Island, which is inspiring in itself. But the coasts, tidal flats, fields, and forests attract many species, some as migrants, some as summer or winter residents. Some propitious locations include the following:

Ala Spit County Park, off Troxell Road north of Oak Harbor. A mile of beach and tidelands make this park a haven for shorebirds and waterfowl in season.

Bluff Trail and **Perego's Lake,** near Fort Ebey State Park (see *Wilder Places—Parks*). The draw here is warblers, finches, owls, and shorebirds.

Crockett Lake, in Fort Casey State Park (see *Wilder Places—Parks*). Here you may see shorebirds such as black-bellied plovers and numerous waterfowl.

Dugualla Bay and Lake, east of WA 20 north of Oak Harbor. Peregrine falcons and ospreys can be seen here, as well as the rare trumpeter swan.

Fort Casey State Park (see *Wilder Places—Parks*). The surf here has auklets, murrelets, oystercatchers, and more.

Fort Ebey State Park (see *Wilder Places—Parks*). Visit this park to see the endangered marbled murrelet, ducks, and forest species including pileated woodpeckers.

BOAT EXCURSIONS *Cutty Sark* (800-366-4097). Call for schedules and rates. If you neglected to bring your own boat, consider a sail on the 52-foot ketch named for the famous British clipper and owned by John Colby Stone, proprietor of the Captain Whidbey Inn (see *Lodging*), for a day, afternoon, or overnight trip.

BOATING Boat launches. You can launch your small boat from many state parks (see *Wilder Places—Parks*) for $7; from **Captain Thomas Coupe Park,** Coupeville; from **Dave Mackie County Park** (360-687-5111), on Maxwelton Road on the island's southwestern side; or from **Freeland Park** (360-331-1980), on Holmes Harbor.

Coupeville Wharf. If you arrive by boat, this historic marina invites you to dock day or night; if you do, you're already downtown.

Deception Pass Marina (360-675-5411), 200 West Cornet Bay Road, Oak Harbor. Overnight moorage space; also offers chartered wildlife cruises.

Oak Harbor Marina (360-279-4575), in City Beach Park, 1401 SE Catalina Drive, Oak Harbor. Lots of guest moorage space is within walking distance of central Oak Harbor.

South Whidbey Marina (360-221-1120), on Wharf Street, Langley. Some guest moorage space is available here.

CAMPING Deception Pass State Park (360-675-2417, reservations 888-226-7688; www.parks.wa.gov), on WA 20, 9 miles north of Oak Harbor. Three campgrounds offer 167 tent sites and 143 trailer sites, plus 5 hiker-biker sites. With its lovely forests and stunning views (see *Wilder Places—Parks*), it can get busy; call for reservations. Caution: Proximity to the naval air base can create unpredictably noisy conditions.

Fort Casey State Park (www.parks.wa.gov), within Ebey's Landing National Historic Reserve, mid-island. Thirty-five campsites next to the Keystone ferry termi-

DECEPTION PASS SEPARATES WHIDBEY ISLAND FROM ANACORTES ON FIDALGO ISLAND.

nal; popular with divers, families, and fishermen but not particularly quiet or private (see *Wilder Places—Parks*). No reservations.

Fort Ebey State Park (888-226-7688; www.parks.wa.gov), within Ebey's Landing National Historic Reserve, mid-island (see *Wilder Places—Parks*). Thirty-nine standard sites and 11 full-hook-up sites near the end of the famous Bluff Trail and Lake Pondilla (see *Hiking*).

Rhododendron County Park, on Patmore Road about 2 miles east of Coupeville, within Ebey's Landing National Historic Reserve; entrance 1 mile south of Coupeville's traffic light on WA 525. Eight rustic campsites (see *Wilder Places—Parks*).

South Whidbey State Park (888-226-7688; www.parks.wa.gov), on Smuggler's Cove Road, 7 miles north of Freeland. Forty-six tent sites and eight utility sites among ancient trees (reservable); also a few primitive water-trail campsites (see *Kayaking*). See *Wilder Places—Parks*.

Windjammer Park (360-679-5551), off Pioneer Way on City Beach Avenue, Oak Harbor. Fifty-six RV sites; first come, first served.

DIVING With many sunken ships and tire reefs, the water around Whidbey teems with sea life from wolf eels to giant Pacific octopuses, sponges, abalone, and more. Most of these waters have strong currents and tides with little slack time, so it's wise to consult with dive shops or have a guide. Favorite spots include those below.

Deception Pass State Park, north of the WA 20 bridge. Two popular sites are rife with sea creatures. Collecting is generally forbidden.

Ebey's Landing, on Ebey Road south of Coupeville. A large kelp bed has concomitant wildlife.

Keystone Underwater Park, just south of the Keystone ferry terminal. This park has very rich marine life.

Langley Tire Reef, at Langley Boat Harbor (see *Boating*). Here you may see Dungeness crabs, sea cucumbers, and sea urchins, but be careful of fishing lines.

Whidbey Island Dive Center (360-675-1112; www.whidbeydive.com), 1020 NE Seventh Avenue, Oak Harbor. You must be certified to rent equipment here.

GOLF Gallery Golf Course (360-257-2178), 3065 North Cowpens Road, Oak Harbor. Eighteen holes.

Island Greens Golf (360-579-6042; www.islandgreens.com), 3890 East French Road, west of Cultus Bay Road, south of Clinton. Nine holes set in bucolic gardens and open woods. No need to call for tee times; just come.

Lam's Links (360-674-3412), 597 Ducken Road, Oak Harbor. Nine holes; 18-hole miniature golf course.

HIKING

Mid-island

Ebey's Landing National Historic Reserve (see *To See—Historic Sites*). This area offers trails past historic Sunnyside Cemetery and around Perego's Lake.

Fort Ebey State Park, in Ebey's Landing National Historic Reserve. Trails here link to others in the reserve for many miles of enjoyable rural walking.

Kettles Park, west side of WA 20 east of Fort Ebey State Park. This trail system starts with easy paved trails that grade into dirt forest trails.

Point Partridge Beacon trail, about 1.5 miles; Fort Ebey State Park (see *Wilder Places—Parks*). The most spectacular trail in this area is from the southern end of Point Partridge Road up to the top of the 200-foot bluff, with views of the Strait of Juan de Fuca all the way.

North Whidbey

♿ **Deception Pass State Park,** 38 miles of trails; on WA 20, 9 miles north of Oak Harbor. Hikers of all fitness levels enjoy rugged cliff paths, beach walks, forest trails, and a 1.2-mile wheelchair-accessible trail. The views are almost unparalleled, which on this island is saying something.

♿ **Joseph Whidbey State Park,** A couple of miles of hiking-biking trails and a 0.5-mile wheelchair-accessible trail are set amid beautiful wildlife and scenery.

South Whidbey

Double Bluff Beach (Park), 3 miles of beach; off WA 525 at the end of Double Bluff Road. Enjoy the tidal flats and tremendous views as you walk this beach. Mount Rainier looms over the tiny towers of Seattle.

♿ **Possession Point County Park ADA trail,** about 3 paved miles round-trip; off Possession Road near the southernmost tip of the island. In addition to this paved ADA path along the beach, there's a strenuous **forest trail** inland to a hilltop.

Saratoga Woods Trails Complex, just north of Langley. This preserve has miles of hiking and biking trails through 600-plus acres of woods and wetlands.

South Whidbey State Park, on Smuggler's Cove Road 7 miles north of Freeland. Gentle trails take you through old-growth forest; there's also a beach walk.

KAYAKING Adventure Marine (360-675-9395), at Oak Harbor Marina (see *Boating*). Rentals are available here.

Cascadia Marine Trail, running from Olympia to Canada. Water-trail campsites for long-distance kayakers are available on the island at Deception Pass State Park, Joseph Whidbey State Park, and City Beach Park in Oak Harbor (see *Camping*).

State parks (see *Wilder Places—Parks*). For a day or afternoon, you can put in at almost any state park, though novices should stick to the sheltered east side of the island; the west side has strong winds and currents.

Whidbey Island Kayaking Company (360-661-5183; www.whidbeyisland kayaking.com), 2724 Evening Glory Court, Clinton. If you've never kayaked but want to try, this outfitter will take you out for a two-hour adventure and provide instruction. Or they'll rent you a kayak if you want to go on your own.

UNIQUE ADVENTURES **Chinook Center at Whidbey Institute** (360-341-1884; www.whidbeyinstitute.org), 6449 Old Pietila Road, Clinton. Mostly the institute caters to ecologically or spiritually oriented group retreats, but if you catch them at a low period, you might be able to rent a cabin for the cost of a donation. The rustic **cabins** require a walk to the bathhouse or communal kitchen, but they're cozy, and the setting amid 70 acres of pasture, woods, and blooming fruit trees is a treat. Even if you don't stay, you're welcome to walk the **trails** or **labyrinth,** and a strikingly simple sanctuary invites **meditation.** Children are welcome, though pets are not—the place is also a wildlife preserve.

✳ Wilder Places

PARKS **Deception Pass State Park** (360-675-2417; www.parks.wa.gov), on WA 20, 9 miles north of Oak Harbor at the northern tip of the island. Straddling the roiling narrows separating Whidbey from Fidalgo (see *To See—Natural Wonders*), this park has more than 4,000 acres of forest, cliffs, and beaches; miles of hiking and equestrian trails; both lake and saltwater boating; and smashing views of the Strait of Juan de Fuca with all its islands. It's a favorite camping (see *To Do—Camping*) and outdoor activity spot. Many of the trails, buildings, and bridges were built by the Civilian Conservation Corps in the 1930s. Other attractions are weekend lectures and slide shows, a historical interpretive center, and a story pole at Rosario Beach, which tells the tale of how a Samish girl became the bride of the sea spirit.

🐾 **Double Bluff Park,** off WA 525 at the end of Double Bluff Road. With access to miles of beach on Useless Bay and views extending from the Olympics to Seattle and Mount Rainier, this is a favorite spot for kite flying, shellfish gathering (with a license), walking, and running your dog—a portion is a designated off-leash area. Erratic Canadian boulders and layers of peat exposed in the eroded bluffs sloping to the beach bear mute testimony to the mile-thick ice that once covered the Northwest.

Fort Casey and Fort Ebey state parks (www.parks.wa.gov), in **Ebey's Landing National Historic Reserve** (see *To See—Historic Sites*). The interest here is mainly historic, with gun emplacements and fortifications dating back to 1890, but both have remarkable Strait of Juan de Fuca views that at any time might include whales, seals, ships, or seabirds. Keystone Spit and its associated lagoon are particularly favored birding spots (see also *To Do—Birding*). Hikers and scuba divers, too, favor the parks (see *To Do—Diving* and *Hiking*).

Rhododendron County Park, on Patmore Road about 2 miles east of Coupeville. A nice public-sector companion to Meerkerk Gardens (see *To See—Farms and Gardens*), this 42-acre park includes picnic and recreation areas, a rustic campground (see *To Do—Camping*), and 10 acres of wild rhododendron (Washington's state flower) understory in a second-growth forest. Peak bloom is usually in the first half of May. A **loop trail** around the park connects with other Island County hiking trails. A sign on WA 20 indicates the northern entrance to the park; signage on the Patmore Road (south) side is cryptic.

& **Possession Point Waterfront Park,** off Possession Road near the southernmost tip of the island. Run by the Port of South Whidbey, this park has 700 feet of waterfront with paved, wheelchair-friendly paths and picnic areas. Behind the beach, the park rises steeply through woods; a new hiking trail runs with switchbacks from the shoreline to the viewpoint.

Seawall Park (Langley Chamber of Commerce, 360-221-6765), Langley. For access, go down the flight of stairs next to the Whidbey Inn to the beach and enjoy views of Saratoga Passage and, maybe, a picnic.

South Whidbey State Park (www.parks.wa.gov), Smuggler's Cove Road, 7 miles northwest of Freeland. Walking trails through old-growth red cedar, Douglas fir, and Sitka spruce take you down to 2 miles of beach and panoramic views. The park's 327 acres include a campground and ample opportunities for bird-watching, crabbing, beachcombing, and even (they say) swimming. Among many scenic parks, this one stands out for its ancient forest and beach.

NATURE PRESERVES ∂ **Whidbey Watersheds** (360-579-1272; www.whidbey watersheds.com), 7015 South Maxwelton Road, Clinton. Maxwelton Creek rises from springs just behind South Whidbey Intermediate School and meanders a few miles to Maxwelton Beach, near Whidbey's southwestern tip. This modest waterway had salmon runs as late as the 1970s, and even now a few salmon return every year to spawn. Small as it is, the creek floods: In the heavy rains of 1996, salmon were seen swimming across the road. You might miss this spot but for the sculpted wooden salmon leaping at the entrance. This 6-acre watershed sanctuary is a joint project of the school district and Maxwelton Salmon Adventure, whose mission is to restore the creek's salmon runs through stream protection and restoration, research, and public education. You're welcome to stroll through the pleasant secondary forest and follow a **self-guided trail** explaining salmon habitat and protection; pets must stay in cars or at home. An outdoor classroom and native plant **garden** round out the offerings. And yes, it was named by Scots settlers in memory of "Maxwelton's braes."

✴ Lodging

BED & BREAKFASTS

Coupeville
Blue Goose Bed and Breakfast
(360-678-4284 or 877-678-4284; www
.bluegoosecoupeville.com), 702 North
Main Street. Sue and Marty McDaniel
are your hosts at two handsome vintage houses—the 1887 Kineth House
and the 1891 Coupe-Gillespie House.
The gaily painted Victorian ladies have

six guest rooms between them (eight in summer) and several common areas, all furnished with period furniture. You're in the heart of historic Coupeville here, with easy access to the museum, wharf, and restaurants. Rates include full breakfast. Children over 12 welcome. $99–159.

Compass Rose Bed and Breakfast
(360-678-5318 or 800-237-3881;

www.compassrosebandb.com), 508 South Main Street. After a lifetime of embassy postings around the world, Captain Marshall and Jan Bronson (his first name is Marshall; his title is captain) retired to the 1890 Jenne house (see *To See—Historic Homes*), packed it with art and antiques they had amassed, and opened their home to guests. The difference between this Queen Anne and many other restored Victorian B&Bs is that it feels comfortably lived-in—Oriental rugs, Victorian furniture, and all—and your amiable hosts will soon make you feel at home, too. Two guest rooms each have private bath and come with a full breakfast. Consult about children. $115.

Inn at Penn Cove (360-678-3598), 602 North Main Street. Now on the former premises of the Blue Goose (the Blue Goose is now where this inn used to be), the Inn at Penn Cove is an imposing blue Victorian with four guest rooms (one is a separate cottage). Unusually, it houses a Thai restaurant on the ground floor. They don't actually serve breakfast, but they will give you a breakfast voucher to use at the nearby Knead & Feed (see *Where to Eat*). Children in cottage only. No pets. $99–139.

Greenbank

✐ **Smuggler's Cove Haven and Roost** (360-678-7100 or 800-772-7055; www.smugglerscove.com), 3258 Smuggler's Cove Road. Expansive views of Puget Sound with its shipping lanes, eagles, and occasional orcas are all yours from either of the suites: the Haven, on the ground floor of Dick and Dee Fulcher's home, or the Roost, a cottage that has two bedrooms. Both have private entrances, woodstoves, kitchens, and living rooms; great vistas; and the run of the sweeping lawn. Down a wiggly forest road and backed by blue waters, this spot has all the pri-

vacy you could want. Cook your own breakfast from ingredients provided. Children welcome. No pets. $125–175.

COTTAGES AND CABINS

Coupeville

Fort Casey Inn (866-661-6604; www.fortcaseyinn.com), 1124 South Engle Road. If you've visited Fort Casey (see *Historic Sites*), you know it was one of numerous defense stations built in the early 20th century. The 10 white-painted houses here were home to officers from about 1909 till the fort was decommissioned. Nicely renovated and furnished, each house sleeps four and has two bedrooms, a large kitchen, a living room, a gas fireplace, and a bathroom (except for the Eagles Nest, which is smaller but still self-contained). $145–185.

Freeland

Cliff House and Cottage (360-331-1566 or 800-297-4118; www.cliffhouse .net), 727 Windmill Drive. Everything's elegant in this contemporary cliff-top house with its sunken living room, full kitchen, breakfast nook, and two bedrooms—from the natural weathered wood inside and out to the designer furniture and cathedral ceilings. Architect Arnie Bystrom has won awards for this 1980 creation. And that's not to mention the 14 acres and view of Admiralty Inlet and the Olympic Mountains. It comes with a hefty price tag, though—$495 per couple, $595 for two couples (by special request). Little Seacliff Cottage ($210), on the same forested cliff top, has a living room with a fireplace, a small kitchen, one bedroom, and a bath. It's furnished with plump armchairs and carved wooden furniture; deer look in the windows—you could almost be in the Black Forest. No children or pets. Two-night minimum for house or cottage.

Greenbank

Guest House Log Cottages (360-678-3115 or 800-997-3115; www.guest houselogcottages.com), 24371 WA 525. Five cottages are scattered amid 25 wooded acres, each individually and warmly designed with touches including stained-glass windows, skylights, exposed wood or brick, and fireplaces. Or if you want to splurge, there's the luxury lodge over the pond: two floors built entirely of logs, with a wraparound deck, large picture windows, and all comforts, including one bedroom and bath and a kitchenette (for one couple only). Either way, natural seclusion is the order of the day. No children or pets. Cottages $165–235; lodge $350; inquire about midweek specials.

Langley

♂ 🐾 **Country Cottage of Langley** (360-221-8709 or 800-713-3860; www.acountrycottage.com), 215 Sixth Street. Six romantic one-bedroom, one-bath cottages dot the gardens of this 1920s farmstead. Most are placed so you can see Puget Sound and the Cascades from your cozy bed. Should you want to get out of that bed, you can relax in a wicker chair by your fireplace, loll on your deck, or stroll the few blocks to Langley's shops and restaurants. After one of ebullient owner Jacki Stewart's breakfasts in the central dining room, though, you're not likely to need lunch. Children and pets welcome. $139–189.

GUESTHOUSES

Langley

Sea Breeze (360-221-8568; www.seabreeze.ws), 309 Noblecliff. Ruth and Duane Den Adel's beach house sits just above Langley's little (but soon to be enlarged) marina. Two balconies overlook Saratoga Passage,

Camano Island, and frequently passing whales. Three bedrooms sleep two to six people, and the kitchen comes with all the conveniences. $250; $1,100–1,500 per week.

HOTELS ♂ ♿ **Saratoga Inn** (360-221-5801 or 800-698-2910; www.saratogainnwhidbeyisland.com), 201 Cascade Avenue. The Saratoga is part of a trend of new-old inns. Built 12 years ago in Nantucket style, with unpainted shingle siding and a sprawling wraparound porch, it's an imposing presence in little Langley. Each of the 16 rooms comes with a fireplace and a teddy bear; most have a window seat; and many have a fine water view. Oh, and you can use the inn's bicycles. Rates include a buffet breakfast and afternoon hors d'oeuvres. One ground-floor room is handicapped-accessible. Children are welcome. No pets. $155–375.

INNS

Coupeville

Anchorage Inn (360-678-5581 or 877-230-1313; www.anchorage-inn .com), 807 North Main Street. It looks *almost* like a late Victorian—gables, tower, wraparound porch—but it's just a bit shiny, which can be forgiven since it was actually built in 1989 to conform with Coupeville's architectural codes. Indoors, seven rooms plus the living and dining rooms are comfortably furnished partly with antiques, partly with look-alikes—most also have Wi-Fi. Rates include full breakfast. Children over 10 welcome. No pets. Next door, historic **Calista Cottage** really does date from 1883. It's been fully refurbished; with two cozy bedrooms, a parlor, kitchen, dining room, and bathroom, it's great for families with children over 10. A continental breakfast is provided on the first day. Rooms

$95–155; cottage $180 (two-night min-imum), $1,000 per week.

Captain Whidbey Inn (360-678-4097; www.captainwhidbey.com), 2072 Captain Whidbey Inn Road. At Whid-bey Island's pinched waist, this stone and log hotel was built in 1907 of trees cut on-site. Overlooking lovely Penn Cove, it was an obvious place of resort for tired but well-heeled Seattleites brought in by ferry. Today the hotel is much as it was then (even to the shared bathrooms), with its cozy lobby warmed by the original rock fireplace and 12 log-walled rooms. Updates include high-speed Internet. The original cabins are gone, replaced with more modern ones, and along the shoreline the Lagoon Rooms—modern, condolike units—shelter devotees of the 21st century. The hotel restaurant, Ship of Fools, concentrates on the many varieties of local seafood (see *Where to Eat*). Inn rooms $93–170; Lagoon Rooms $162–180; cabins $192–230.

Langley

✍ **Boatyard Inn** (360-221-5120; www.boatyardinn.com), 200 Wharf Street. Its promotional material says the structure and corrugated-metal roofing make it "reminiscent of an old cannery." But if you didn't want to stay in an old cannery, that's okay; it's been completely made over into 10 comfort-able studio and loft apartments, all of which have kitchenettes, gas fireplaces, and views across Saratoga Passage to the Cascades. One room is handi-capped-accessible. Since it's right on the water, you can sail up if you've a mind to. The marina is a few steps away. Children are welcome. One pet-friendly room. $195–295; ask about specials.

Coupeville

& **Countryside Inn** (360-678-5610), 19777 WA 20. Screened by its own forested grounds a mile south of town, the Countryside has 18 rooms and suites, including one that's ADA-accessible, around a landscaped court-yard. Some units have kitchenettes, and guests are invited to use the sev-eral outdoor grills. Clean, cozy rooms, a warm welcome, and a spacious prop-erty make this a quiet retreat that's also family-friendly. The whole property is within Ebey's Landing National Histor-ical Reserve, with access to the reserve's trail system (see *To See—Historic Sites*). No pets. $90–195.

Freeland

Harbour Inn Motel (360-331-6900; www.harbourinnmotel.com), 1606 East Main Street. These calm motel rooms are simple but clean, comfortable, and even tasteful. A continental breakfast is included. Your pet can stay, too, for $15 a night. $79–110; children under 10 free.

Langley

🐾 **Langley Motel** (360-221-6070 or 866-276-8292; www.langleymotel.com), 526 Camano Avenue. The Langley Motel's four old-timey beach units pro-vide pleasant, reasonable accommoda-tions on an often pricey island. Each unit has a full kitchen, patio, and sepa-rate living area (though not all have phones); queen-sized beds are equipped with down comforters. You'll be welcomed with flowers and choco-lates. The motel sits on a bluff above the marina within walking distance of Langley and the beach. Pets allowed in some rooms. $95–135.

✒ **Coachman Inn** (360-675-0727 or
800-635-0043; www.thecoachmaninn
.com), 32959 WA 20. With a swimming
pool, play area, sunny breakfast room,
and on-site laundry, the Coachman is
convenient for active families or
groups. Units range from standard
queens to a town house. $89–209.

✳ Where to Eat
DINING OUT
Coupeville
Christopher's on Whidbey (360-678-
5480; www.christophersonwhidbey),
103 NW Coveland Street. Open for
lunch and dinner daily. After cooking
around the world (literally—he was a
chef on cruise ships as well as at fine
land-based restaurants), Austrian-born
chef Andreas Wurzrainer took over
Christopher's Café in 2002. The menu
could be called Northwest with a hint
of central Europe—fresh seafood, of
course, in a variety of incarnations,
but also filet mignon and chicken
paprikash—all slightly more affordable
than usual on this island. Reservations
recommended.

Ship of Fools (360-678-4097), 2072
Captain Whidbey Inn Road. Open for
dinner 5–8 Thurs.–Sun.; brunch 11–2
Sun. I'm not sure this is the greatest
name for a seaside restaurant, but
that's beside the point. Ship of Fools is
the restaurant at the Captain Whidbey
Inn (see *Lodging*) and offers one of
the island's fine dining experiences,
starting with Penn Cove mussels, naturally, and moving on to more of the
abundant local seafood. You can also
choose steak or pasta, if you prefer.
Much of the produce comes from
nearby Willowwood Farms, an organic
producer. Fresh seafood, fresh greens,
and a little creativity—it would be hard
to go wrong. Reservations recommended.

Freeland
Gordon's on Blueberry Hill (360-
331-7515), 5438 Woodard Avenue.
Open 11:30–2 and 5 to closing
Tues.–Fri.; 4 to closing Sat.–Sun.;
closed Mon. Chef Gordon Petrie
knows how to please 'em. On a Friday
night, his restaurant is full of happy
people who have tracked the cuisine
down the back roads to this country
locale. Dishes range from the tried-
and-true (linguine with mussels and
clams; filet mignon) to daring (tan-
doori-style game hen; prawns over
ravioli in sambuca cream sauce), all
tasty and surprisingly reasonable.
Reservations recommended.

EATING OUT
Coupeville
Knead & Feed (360-678-5431;
www.kneadandfeed.com), Four NW
Front Street. Open 9–3 Mon.–Fri., 8–4
Sat.–Sun. It evolved from a bakery
opened in 1974 and is still owned by
its founding family, the Kroons, and
still popping out hearty breads and
pastries, plus breakfast dishes, sandwiches, soups, and salads. A local
favorite, like Mosquito Fleet (below);
Coupeville seems to breed them.

Mosquito Fleet Chili and Pies (360-
678-2900), 12 Front Street NW. Open
7–4 Mon.–Sat. Not just chili. Not even
just chili and pies. This little family-run
place radiates comfort, as in happy
comfort food, whether it's homemade
corn bread, homemade quiche, homemade mussel chowder—everything
here is homemade. Often busy (with
good reason), the owner-operators
manage to be exceedingly helpful and
friendly as well.

Langley
Garibyan Brothers Café Langley
(360-221-3090), 113 First Street. Open
for lunch 11:30–2:30 Mon.–Fri.,
11:30–3 Sat.–Sun.; dinner 5–8 daily;

closed Tues. in winter. Mediterranean cuisine jostles Northwest seafood in this snug eatery, with some interesting results, such as Penn Cove mussels cooked with saffron. Here "Mediterranean" covers all bases, from mixed grill Anatolia to Macedonian chicken breast, and from moussaka to Andalusian flank steak. Well, if they don't do it, who will?

❧ **Mike's Place** (360-221-6575), 219 First Street. Open for breakfast, lunch, and dinner Thurs.–Mon. Families in the know come here for Mike's bounteous meals. One section has been made over into an ice cream parlor and game room, good for a snack on a rainy afternoon. Take-out is available, too.

Prima Bistro (360-221-4060; www .primabistro.com), 201½ First Street. Open for lunch and dinner daily. Formerly the Star Bistro, this place is located over the Star Store. It used to serve Mediterranean/Northwest cuisine but has switched to a more Francophile stance, with dishes you won't easily find elsewhere, such as roast marrowbone, sweetbreads, and steak tartare. Of course, there are the ubiquitous mussels and other solid Northwest fare. Vegetarian items and a children's menu complete the appeal.

❧ **Village Pizzeria** (360-221-3363), 108 First Street. Open for lunch and dinner daily. This is where locals meet to take out or eat in. In summer you can eat in the garden overlooking Saratoga Passage. Enjoy comforting pizzas, pasta dishes, salads, and sandwiches.

✳ Entertainment

THEATER Clyde Theater (360-221-5525; www.theclyde.net), 217 First Street, Langley. The Clyde has been showing movies, one screen at a time, since 1937. It's still family-owned and still a community fixture, showing first-run and art-house films.

Whidbey Island Center for the Arts (360-221-8268 or 800-638-7631; www.wicaonline.com), 565 Camano Avenue, Langley. The center stages classical, modern, and children's theater; concerts by local musicians; and DjangoFest (see *Special Events*).

Whidbey Playhouse (360-679-2237; www.whidbeyplayhouse.com), 730 SE Midway Boulevard, Oak Harbor. This old church turned playhouse presents live theater spring and summer.

✳ Selective Shopping

ANTIQUES Antiques became practically a cottage industry around Whidbey Island, with entire antiques districts in both **Langley** and **Coupeville.** The bottom has fallen out of the market, but some outlets remain.

Mutiny Bay Antique Mall (360-331-3656), 5550 Vanbarr Place, Freeland.

Red Rooster Antique Mall (360-331-0150), 1635 Main Street, Freeland.

DESPITE A DECLINE IN THE ANTIQUES MARKET, LANGLEY'S MAIN STREET STILL OFFERS A FEW OUTLETS.

Shady Ladies Antiques (360-679-1902), 656 SE Bayshore Drive, Oak Harbor.

FOOD Seabolt Smokehouse and Fish Market (800-574-1120; www .seabolts.com), 31640 WA 20, Oak Harbor. Here you'll find naturally smoked wild salmon and albacore in season. They will also custom-smoke.

✳ Special Events

February: **Langley Mystery Weekend** (360-221-6765), Langley. If you ever felt like playing a life-sized game of Clue, try this. Clues are distributed around town the last weekend of February, and the whole town participates in solving the (hypothetical) murder mystery.

March: **Penn Cove Mussel Festival** (360-678-5434), at Coupeville Recreation Hall. The mussels of Penn Cove are celebrated and shipped around the world. The first weekend of March, this festival features a mussel-eating contest, mussel chowder cook-off, and more.

May: **Penn Cove Water Festival** (360-678-5434; www.penncovewater festival.com), Coupeville. This revival of Native canoe races on the Coupeville waterfront also includes food, performances, and environmental displays.

July: **Loganberry Festival** (360-678-7700), Greenbank Farm. In late July there's plentiful food, music, and art, plus wine tasting and a pie-eating contest. It's a huge block party without the block; free admission.

August: **Island County Fair** (360-221-4677), Langley. Takes place the third week of August.

September: **DjangoFest Northwest** (800-638-7631; www.djangofest.com), Whidbey Island Center for the Arts, Langley. This is a five-day international celebration of gypsy jazz, Django Reinhardt–style.

Tour de Whidbey (360-678-7656, ext. 4020; www.whidbeygen.org), throughout the island. This annual cycling event is dedicated to raising funds for the Whidbey General Hospital Foundation. All riders are welcome to sign up for 100-, 50-, or 25-mile circuits starting at Greenbank Farm; registration includes a pancake breakfast, chili feed, and plentiful camaraderie.

✇ **Whidbey Island Kite Festival** (360-678-9358; www.whidbeykites .org), Camp Casey Conference Center at Fort Casey (866-661-6604), near Coupeville. You'll see competitions and displays, kite making and lessons.

CAMANO ISLAND AND ARLINGTON AREA

C amano Island is hardly known. Hidden in plain view just east of Whidbey, it hugs the mainland; you hardly notice you're crossing the bridge at Stanwood before you're on an island right enough. Almost completely logged a century ago, it's since been left to its own devices, so it has island seclusion and scenery but no glitzy tourism. A couple of lovely state parks, a few bed & breakfasts, no fancy restaurants—just people making an island living. You can have it practically to yourself for biking, bird-watching, and beach walking.

To the east, along the WA 9 corridor, are the burgeoning towns of Marysville and Arlington, surrounded by farmland. Granite Falls (just east of Marysville) and Darrington (inland on WA 530 east of Arlington) anchor either end of the Mountain Loop Highway, which stretches deep into forested wilderness on the wet side of Glacier Peak. You'll find lots of woods to explore in these parts.

GUIDANCE **Camano Island Chamber of Commerce** (360-629-7136; www .camanoisland.org), 578 North Camano Drive, Camano 98282.

City of Arlington (360-403-3421; www.arlingtonwa.gov), 238 North Olympic Avenue, Arlington 98223.

Snohomish County Tourism Bureau (888-338-0976; www.snohomish.org), 909 SE Everett Mall Way, C-300, Everett 98208.

GETTING THERE **I-5** is the major north-south route in this area, with **WA 9** to the east. **WA 92** leads east from WA 9 to Granite Falls and the southern portion of the Mountain Loop Highway; **WA 530** leads east from I-5 through Arlington to the northern part of the Mountain Loop Highway. Reach Camano Island from I-5 via exit 212 and follow **WA 532** west.

Shuttle Express (425-981-7000) goes north from Sea-Tac Airport to this area via I-5.

The nearest **AMTRAK** and **Greyhound** stops are in Everett and Mount Vernon; see the chapters that cover those cities.

GETTING AROUND Community Transit (425-353-RIDE; www.commtrans .org), 20110 46th Avenue West, Lynnwood, provides bus service around Snohomish County.

Island Transit (360-387-7433 or 800-240-8747; www.islandtransit.org) has a connection from Whidbey Island to the northwestern end of Camano.

MEDICAL EMERGENCY Camano Community Health Clinic (360-387-5398), 127 NE Camano Drive, Camano. This clinic provides primary care.

Cascade Valley Hospital (360-435-2133), 330 South Stillaguamish Avenue, Arlington.

Skagit Valley Hospital (360-424-4111; www.skagitvalleyhospital.org), 1415 East Kincaid, Mount Vernon.

✳ To See

FARMERS' MARKETS Marysville Farmers' Market (360-651-9470), Fifth and State, Marysville. Open 9–3 Thurs. May–Sept.

FARMS AND GARDENS Dues Berry Farm (360-659-3875), 152nd Street NE, Marysville. Open mid-June–mid-July. Acres and acres of U-pick strawberries.

Schuh Farms (360-629-6455), 9828 WA 532, Stanwood. Open 9–6 daily Apr.–Dec. A branch of Schuh Farms in Mount Vernon, this Schuh Farms carries flowers, fruits, baked goods, jams, even Christmas trees.

White Picket Perennial and Herb Farm (360-629-6196), 30900 68th Avenue NE, Stanwood. Open 10–7 Thurs.–Sun. Apr.–Oct. Yes, herbs and perennials can be found here, but also lavender, soaps, and candles.

HISTORIC HOMES D. O. Pearson House (360-629-6110), 27112 102nd Avenue NW, Stanwood. Open 1–4 Wed., Fri., and Sun. Mr. Pearson, the first mayor of Stanwood, had this rather forbidding Second Empire–style house built in 1890. It's one of the few French-inspired buildings in the state, mansard roof and all, and now serves as a local historical museum exhibiting mainly old photographs.

Gehl House (360-659-5808), 6915 51st Avenue, Marysville. Open 12–5 Sat.–Sun. Memorial Day–Aug. This simple 1884 home of hand-hewn cedar was moved to Jennings Park and furnished as a farmhouse of the period.

HISTORIC SITES Camano Lutheran Church (360-629-4592), 850 Heichel Road, Camano Island. This is the home of an active Lutheran congregation that was founded in 1890. The small, steepled church was dedicated in 1906 and is on the State Register of Historic Places.

MUSEUMS Stillaguamish Valley Pioneer Museum (360-435-7289; www.stilly museum.org), 20722 67th Avenue NE, Arlington. Open 1–4 Wed. and Sat.–Sun. $5 adults, $2 children 12 and under. Strikingly new with solar panels covering one side, it's nevertheless a work of preservation, with lots of old photos, household items, and logging and farm equipment. In the outbuildings you'll find vintage trucks, farm vehicles, and printing presses.

from Granite Falls to Darrington. Storms may cause washouts; for road conditions, call the Darrington Ranger Station (360-436-1155). FR 20 is a two-lane paved road except for 14 miles of single-lane graded road. Allow a morning or afternoon to pull over and enjoy the sights along this route as it winds up through the hills past ice caves (dangerous; do not enter), ghostly mining towns, and the wild and scenic Sauk River.

✻ To Do

BICYCLING **Arlington Velo Sport** (360-629-6415; stanwoodvelosport.com), 401 North Olympic Avenue, Arlington. This store conducts weekly bike rides as well as classes on things such as fixing a flat tire.

Camano Island's quiet back roads invite a little spin through small farms and along Port Susan to the east and Saratoga Passage to the west. There are no bike rental outlets as of this writing, though—Camano is still a low-key spot that doesn't think of itself as a tourist attraction.

Centennial Trail (425-388-6600), 17.5 paved miles from Snohomish to Arlington. This path along an old railroad bed has rest areas and parks en route.

BIRDING **Camano Island State Park** (360-387-3031), at the end of Lowell Point Road, 14 miles southwest of Stanwood. This park welcomes woodland species such as warblers and pileated woodpeckers; from the shoreline, you may see harlequin ducks and loons. See *Wilder Places—Parks.*

English Boom Historical County Park, off Moore Road, Camano Island. At this spot on the island's north end, overlooking Skagit Bay, look for nesting eagles, ospreys, and purple martins, as well as loons and waterfowl. See *Wilder Places—Parks.*

Four Springs Lake Preserve (360-387-1418), 585 Lewis Lane, off Camano Hill Road, Camano Island. The quiet grounds of this preserve (see *Wilder Places— Nature Preserves*) are home to wood ducks, songbirds, and woodpeckers.

Iverson Spit Waterfront Preserve, at the north end of Iverson Road, off Sunrise Boulevard, Camano Island. This spit that overlooks miles of tidal flats, beach, and shrubland is one of the state's premier spots for birds. Of the nearly 200 bird species known to nest on or to visit Camano Island, 130 species have been observed here.

CAMPING **Camano Island State Park** (360-387-3031), at the end of Lowell Point Road, 14 miles southwest of Stanwood, Camano Island. Eighty-eight tent sites, some of which will accommodate an RV, and five cabins. No reservations.

Kayak Point Park (360-652-7992), 15610 Marine Drive, Stanwood. Thirty standard campsites and 2 ADA-accessible sites; 10 yurts with screens, electric heat, and beds; and a three-bedroom vacation house. All Snohomish County parks are alcohol-free. Campsites $23–25; yurts $41–68; house $73–139.

Mount Baker–Snoqualmie National Forest campgrounds (206-470-4060 or 800-627-0062; www.fs.fed.us/r6/mbs) are scattered along the Mountain Loop Highway: Bedal, Boardman Creek, Clear Creek, French Creek, Gold Basin, Perry Creek, Red Bridge, River Bar, Turlo, Verlot, and White Chuck.

River Meadows Park (360-435-3441), 20416 Jordan Road, Arlington. Thirty-five sites without hook-ups and six yurts along a mile of the Stillaguamish River. Campsites $18; yurts $40–74.

Squire Creek Park (360-435-3441), 41415 WA 530, Darrington. Thirty-three campsites without hook-ups near national forest land. $18.

Wenberg County Park (360-388-6600), on Lake Goodwin, 18 miles northwest of Everett; from I-5 take exit 206. Forty-five tent sites and 30 RV sites in this 46-acre park.

CANOEING AND KAYAKING **Cama Beach State Park** (360-387-9361), 1880 SW Camano Drive, Camano Island. The Center for Wooden Boats, based in Seattle, has a branch here and rents kayaks, rowboats, and sailboats.

Camano Island Waterfront Inn (888-718-0783) and **Blue Moon Beach House** (360-387-6666) rent kayaks to guests. The waters around Camano are fairly sheltered.

Cascadia Marine Trail, from Olympia to Canada. Camano is on this trail, with a marine trail campsite at the south end of Point Lowell in Camano Island State Park (see *Camping*).

GOLF **Battle Creek Public Golf Course** (360-659-7931), 6006 Meridian Avenue North, Marysville. An 18-hole course and a 9-hole course.

Camaloch Golf Course (360-387-3084 or 800-628-0469; www.camalochnews .org), 326 NE Camano Drive, Camano Island. Eighteen holes.

Kayak Point Golf Course (360-652-9676), 15711 Marine Drive, Stanwood. Eighteen holes with Olympic views.

HIKING **Camano Island State Park,** 5 miles of trails (see *Wilder Places— Parks*). Pleasant forest and beach paths wind through this park on Saratoga Passage. The 2.5-mile **perimeter loop** takes in several dramatic water and mountain views. A 2-mile **woodland path** connects the park with **Cama Beach State Park** to the north (see *Wilder Places—Parks*).

Camano Ridge Forest Preserve, 3 miles of trails; via Canku Road off Camano Drive, Camano Island. More trails are in the works for this 400-acre preserve.

Friends of Camano Island Parks (focip11@gmail.com), Box 1385, Stanwood, 98292. E-mail or write for a list of guided walks; it's a gentle island with, mostly, gentle walks.

Island County Elger Bay Preserve, 2.5 miles of trails; on Elger Bay Road 0.1 mile north of Dry Lake Road, Camano Island. Trails take you through an old logging area, some brushy and some second growth.

Lime Kiln Trail, 7 miles round-trip; trailhead on Waite Mill Road—from Granite Falls, proceed south on South Granite Avenue, then left on Pioneer Street and left again on Waite Mill Road. In the Cascade foothills, this trail leads you along the green canyon of the rushing Stillaguamish River to an abandoned town site and ruined lime kilns—debris such as old bricks and bed frames must be left for others to enjoy.

Mount Baker–Snoqualmie National Forest (206-470-4060 or 800-627-0062; www.fs.fed.us/r6/mbs), 367 miles of trails for hikers in the Darrington Ranger District. Caution: Proximity to the Seattle metro area means heavy use, not always by hikers. In 2006 two women were shot on a trail near Mount Pilchuck. This is not a usual occurrence, but be as prudent as possible.

✳ Wilder Places

PARKS Cama Beach State Park (360-387-9361), 1880 SW Camano Drive, Camano Island. Unusually for a state park, this one is on the National Register of Historic Places. It was the site of an 1890s logging camp. Then, from 1934 to the 1980s, these 31 cottages and surrounding acreage were the Cama Beach Resort, everyman's auto court and fishing destination. Eventually the state acquired it. When construction began on the park, archaeological remains dating back 1,600 years were found—mostly food-processing remains, but some burials, too. The Washington Parks and Recreation Commission worked with local tribes while developing the park, which includes renovated **cabins,** a retreat **lodge,** and a branch of the Center for Wooden Boats.

Camano Island State Park (360-387-3031), on Lowell Point Road, 14 miles southwest of Stanwood, Camano Island. Unlike Rome, this park was built in a day. Back in 1949, the South Camano Grange, as part of a national grange service contest, hit on the idea of creating a park on school district land. Sites were marked out, volunteers were called for, and on July 27 armies of citizens materialized with tools, trucks, tractors, and even a first-aid station. The grange ladies served chowder, and by the end of the day a park, including picnic areas, campsites, and trails, was in place. They won first prize. Today the park comprises 134 acres, with more than a mile of beachfront, a boat launch, a campground, miles of trails, and a new covered kitchen at the beach picnic area. Beautiful views, shoreline access, and forest trails have made this a favorite with families—both local and visiting—for generations.

English Boom Historical County Park, at the end of Moore Road, Camano Island. The "boom" held floating logs in place when this was a busy lumber mill on the north shore, run by one Mr. English. Lumbering came early and fast to Camano, stripping much of the surface (most forest is now second growth) and keeping the harbors bursting a century ago. Largely undeveloped, the 7.5-acre park preserves the waterfront site and is a favored bird-watching point (see *To Do—Birding*).

Kayak Point Park (360-652-7992), 15610 Marine Drive, Stanwood. Besides camping, yurts, and a three-bedroom vacation house to rent, there's picnicking, fishing, and wind surfing.

River Meadows Park (360-435-3441), 20416 Jordan Road, Arlington. Camping along a mile of the Stillaguamish River, plus picnicking, hiking, fishing, and boating.

Squire Creek Park (360-435-3441), 41415 WA 530, Darrington. Camping and picnicking on 53 acres of old-growth forest.

Wenberg County Park (360-388-6600), on Lake Goodwin; from I-5 take exit 206. A 46-acre park with camping, boating, and fishing.

NATURE PRESERVES Camano Ridge Forest Preserve (360-387-3443), on Canku Road off Camano Drive, Camano Island. This 400-acre preserve has hiking trails.

⅃ Four Springs Lake Preserve (360-387-1418), 585 Lewis Lane, Camano Island. Formerly the home of the Natoli family, these 50 peaceful acres of meadow and forest were purchased by Island County Parks in 1998 to preserve natural habitat. The house is reserved for retreats and events, but the grounds are open to the public dawn to dusk, with a pond and trails (some paved) winding through the woods.

Island County Elger Bay Preserve (360-387-3443), on Elger Bay Road, 0.1 mile north of Dry Lake Road, Camano Island. This old logging area, some parts brushy and some second growth, has hiking trails.

Iverson Spit Waterfront Preserve, on Iverson Beach Road, off Sunrise Boulevard, Camano Island. This is also known for its variety of birds (see *To Do—Birding*); a short trail along the dike offers viewing of mudflats and wetlands.

✳ Lodging

BED & BREAKFASTS

Camano Island

⌔ Blue Moon Beach House (360-387-6666; www.bluemoonbeachhouse.com), 3267 Shoreline Drive. The secluded hamlet at the southern end of the island consists mainly of decades-old beach houses, but this one has been refurbished to a chic yet comfy waterfront B&B. Three warmly contemporary guest rooms all have private baths and water views, two have balconies, and one has a wood-fired hot tub. Young hosts Samantha and Andy Egloff will rent you a kayak or lend you a bike, or you can walk the gravel beach—but you will be sorely tempted just to lounge in your room gazing at Puget Sound. Rates include a full homemade breakfast. Children are welcome. No pets. $95–195.

Camano Blossom Bed and Breakfast (360-629-6784 or 866-629-6784; www.camanoblossombandb.com), 1462 Larkspur Lane. Besides running her B&B, Melissa Mei teaches Chinese cooking; if you ask her, she'll cook you a Hunan, Szechuan, Mandarin, or Cantonese dinner (breakfasts are American-style). Four guest rooms with views and private baths combine American and Asian decor, and 5 landscaped acres provide a peaceful setting outside. Rates include breakfast and afternoon snacks. One child okay. No pets. $159–209; two-night minimum most summer weekends.

INNS

Camano Island

⅃ Camano Island Inn (360-387-0783 or 888-718-0783; www.camanoisland inn.com), 1054 SW Camano Drive. A hundred years ago, Camano Island had one of the busiest lumber ports in the Northwest. What is now the Waterfront Inn was then a boardinghouse for workers at a shingle mill. Soon enough, the island was logged off and the mill closed, and the lodgings became a hotel. Today the six rooms are modern and spacious, discreetly decorated with a blend of antiques and Northwest art. Owners Jon and Kari Soth try to combine the privacy of a hotel with the friendliness of a bed & breakfast: You can eat breakfast in the dining room or have it delivered to your door. One room is fully ADA-compliant, and in general the building is wheelchair-friendly. $125–230; check for specials and packages.

Inn at Barnum Point (360-387-2256 or 800-910-2256; www.innatbarnumb point.com), 464 South Barnum Road. You just can't escape the views here. On a bluff on the east side of the island, the inn is half-surrounded by water, the snowy peaks of the Cascades, and abundant wildlife. All three guest rooms have fireplaces. Carolin, whose grandfather homesteaded here, fixes a hearty breakfast or stocks your fridge if you're in the large loft suite. Rates include breakfast (self-serve in the suite). $115–225.

Granite Falls
Country Cedar Inn (360-691-3830; www.countrycedarinn.com), 5732 Robe Menzel Road. Up in the foothills past Lake Stevens, as you head away from Puget Sound and toward the scenic Mountain Loop Highway, you're near Pugetopolis yet far from the madding crowd. This lodge-style building (the cedar siding was milled on the property) has four comfy guest rooms, all with private baths, on 5 acres of trees and gardens with views of Mount Pilchuck. Rates include a full breakfast. No pets. $99–149.

✴ Where to Eat
EATING OUT

Camano Island
Brindles (360-387-8614; www.brindles market.com), 848 North Sunrise Boulevard, Building C. Mainly an outlet for fresh Pacific seafood and meats from Washington and Oregon, Brindles also serves fish-and-chips, salmon chowder, and (startlingly) Nathan's hot dogs in its seating area.

✑ **Elger Bay Café** (360-387-2904), 1994 Elger Bay Road. Open 6 AM–9

PM daily. Elger Bay Café is locally famous for its extensive and hearty breakfast menu. Lunch concentrates on burgers, sandwiches, and salads; dinner includes pot roast, salmon, prime rib, and similar meat-and-potatoes fare.

Island Custard and Gelato (360-722-7486), in Camano Commons. Local ice cream connoisseurs come here for flavors such as chocolate chili pepper.

Islander's Restaurant and Bar (360-722-7470; www.islandersrestaurant andbar.com), 848 North Sunrise Boulevard. Open 11–9 daily. This casual restaurant serves burgers, soups, sandwiches, and pizzas.

✴ Special Events
February: **Port Susan Snow Goose and Birding Festival** (www.snow goosefest.org), various locations around Camano Island and in Stanwood. This festival takes advantage of the island's phenomenal population of wintering birds, especially snow geese.

May: **Mother's Day Studio Tour** (425-235-6921; www.camanoarts.org), Camano Island. Visit studios and gardens of participating local artists.

July: **Pilchuck School Open House** (360-445-3111; www.pilchuck.com), 1201 316th Street NW, Stanwood. Usually held the last Sunday in July; you can tour the glass studios of the Pilchuck School, watch demonstrations, and see glass artwork. $20.

August: **Stanwood-Camano Community Fair** (360-629-4121; www .stanwoodcamanofair.org), at Stillaguamish Fairgrounds just outside Stanwood. Enjoy livestock exhibits, food, games, and rides.

LA CONNER, MOUNT VERNON, AND ANACORTES AREA

T his region extends from Skagit Bay to Samish Bay west of I-5. But get off the interstate and follow the daisy chain of back roads through the tulip fields of the Skagit Valley, and you'll find little towns such as La Conner, an artists' colony since the 1930s. To the west of La Conner is Skagit Island, just offshore of the Swinomish Indian Reservation.

To the north in the I-5 corridor are Mount Vernon and Burlington, the latter the gateway to WA 20. To the east, WA 20 leads to Sedro-Woolley and the North Cascades Scenic Highway; the town with the funny name was formed from the merger of two logging towns—one named for its founder and the other for the giant cedars.

To the west, WA 20 leads to Anacortes and Whidbey Island's north end. Anacortes, itself on an island (Fidalgo), is the jumping-off point for visiting the San Juan Islands; except for Guemes Island just north of Anacortes, the San Juans are covered in another chapter. A five-minute ferry ride from Anacortes, little Guemes Island is home to a few hundred people and 15 miles of quiet roads.

At the north end of this region are the tiny hamlets of Bow and Edison, tucked west of I-5 in the shadow of the Chuckanut Mountains.

GUIDANCE **Anacortes Chamber of Commerce** (360-293-7911), 819 Commercial Avenue, Suite F, Anacortes 98221.

Burlington Chamber of Commerce (360-757-0994; www.burlington-chamber .com), 111 South Cherry Street, Burlington 98233.

La Conner Chamber of Commerce (360-466-4778), 606 Morris Street, La Conner 98257.

Mount Vernon Chamber of Commerce (360-428-8547; www.mountvernon chamber.com), 105 East Kincaid Street, Mount Vernon 98273.

Sedro-Woolley Chamber of Commerce (360-855-1841; www.sedro-woolley .com), 714-B Metcalf Street, Sedro-Woolley 98284.

GETTING THERE The primary north-south route is **I-5; WA 9** to the east connects Arlington to Mount Vernon and Burlington (and beyond). From I-5 at Burlington, take exit 230 onto **WA 20,** the primary east-west route. From Burlington, **WA 11** heads north along the shoreline of Samish Bay.

Shuttle Express (425-981-7000) goes north from Sea-Tac Airport to this area via I-5.

AMTRAK (800-USA-RAIL; www.amtrak.com) stops in Mount Vernon at 105 East Kincaid Street.

Greyhound (360-336-5111 or 800-231-2222; www.greyhound.com) also stops in Mount Vernon.

Washington State Ferries (206-464-6400 or 888-808-7977) provide service from Anacortes to the San Juan Islands as well as Victoria, British Columbia.

GETTING AROUND Skagit Transit (360-757-4433; www.skagittransit.org), 105 East Kincaid Street, Mount Vernon. Eleven fixed routes connect the Skagit Valley from Anacortes to Concrete, 7 AM–9 PM Mon.–Fri.

MEDICAL EMERGENCY Island Hospital (360-299-1300), 1211 24th Street, Anacortes.

Skagit Valley Hospital (360-424-4111 or 360-629-4583), 1415 East Kincaid Street, Mount Vernon.

United General Hospital (360-856-6021), 2000 Hospital Drive, Sedro-Woolley.

✳ To See

CULTURAL SITES La Conner Sculpture Walk, 20 pieces of public art around downtown La Conner. For La Conner's art scene, you might want to check this out; guide maps are at the chamber of commerce (see *Guidance*).

The Scott Collection (www.scottcollection.com), 512 South First Street, La Conner. This is one of numerous galleries that feature Northwest art in various media.

FARMERS' MARKETS Anacortes Farmers' Market (360-293-7922; www .anacortesfarmersmarket.org), at Depot Center for the Arts, 611 R Avenue, Anacortes. Open 9–2 Sat. mid-May–mid-Oct.

Mount Vernon Farmers' Market (360-540-4066; www.mountvernonfarmers market.org), at Gates and Main streets, Mount Vernon. Open 9–1 Sat. late May–early Oct.

Sedro-Woolley Farmers' Market (360-202-7311), at Metcalf and Ferry streets, Sedro-Woolley. Open 3–7 Wed. June–Oct.

FARMS AND GARDENS Butterfly Garden, on Second Street across from the quilt museum, La Conner. This little spot is planted with flowers butterflies love.

Christianson's Nursery (360-466-3821; www.christiansonsnursery.com), 15806 Best Road, Mount Vernon. Find bulbs, roses, and more here; it's also the home of the oldest one-room schoolhouse in northwestern Washington, which is now used for garden clubs and classes.

La Conner Flats, 15920 Best Road, Mount Vernon. Gardens open dawn to dusk daily; $3. This 230-acre farm has 11 acres of rhododendrons, bulbs, annuals, and perennials; afternoon tea, too.

Roozengarde (866-488-5477; www.tulips.com), 15867 Beaver Marsh Road, Mount Vernon. Founded by the Roozen family in 1985, this is the largest producer of tulips, daffodils, and irises in the world. Its 1,200 acres are among those that turn the Skagit Valley into a Mondrian painting in spring. Three acres of display gardens and a store mean fun for flower lovers.

Schuh Farms (360-424-6982), 15565 WA 536, Mount Vernon. Open Apr.–Dec. Here you'll find berries, berries, and more berries; also fruits, flowers, corn, cider, pies, and breads.

✍ **Skagit Display Gardens,** 16602 WA 536, Mount Vernon. Self-guided tours sunrise to dusk. This Washington State University research station includes herbs, roses, vegetables, perennials, a children's garden, a native plant area, and various test gardens.

Snow Goose Produce (360-445-6908), 15170 Fir Island Road, Mount Vernon. Open daily, more or less, Apr.–Oct. Snow Goose Produce sells, naturally, fresh fruits and veggies but is renowned for its generous homemade ice cream cones. You can also find local wines, cheeses, and seafood in this landmark barn.

Tulip Town (360-424-8152), 15002 Bradshaw Road, Mount Vernon. Open daily in season. Here you'll find tulip fields, an indoor flower show during tulip season, bulbs in the fall, and fountains.

HISTORIC HOMES Cannery worker cottage, 1106 Fourth Street, Anacortes. When its railroad dreams went bust, Anacortes turned to milling lumber, fishing, and canning. Of the many cottages built for cannery workers, only this one, built in 1898, is left. It still has its original cedar siding.

Gaches Mansion (360-466-4288; www.laconnerquilts.com), 703 South Second Street, La Conner. Open 11–4 Wed.–Sun. $7; $5 military and students. This yellow gingerbready house on the hill now houses the quilt museum (see *Museums*). But a century ago, brothers George and James Gaches bought Mr. Conner's mercantile store. George and his wife, Louisa, assured of prosperity, built this home in 1891. In 1900, though, the couple moved to Seattle, and the house suffered the slings and arrows of many such bereft mansions, becoming a hospital, then apartments, and finally burning down in 1973. Luckily, the citizens were able to restore it, and you can now visit it. The ground floor is decorated in Victorian style, while the second is dedicated to quilt exhibits.

J. A. Matheson House, 1205 Fifth Street, Anacortes. Matheson, who came to Anacortes to start the first codfish cannery, bought this appropriately respectable house in 1899. With its solid, sober proportions, gables, and two-story columned porch, it would not look out of place in New England.

HISTORIC SITES ♿ **W. T. Preston Snagboat and Heritage Center** (360-293-1916), 713 R Avenue, Anacortes. Open 10–4 Mon.–Sat. June–Aug.; 10–4 Sat. and 11–4 Sun. Apr.–May and Sept.–Oct. $3 adults, $2 seniors, $1 students 8–16. This is a reminder of days not so long gone. From the 1880s, "snagboats" were commissioned to keep the Puget Sound shipping lanes free of navigational hazards—

floating logs, derelict boats, etc. (called, generically, "snags"). The wooden *W. T. Preston* came into service in 1939 and worked the sound from Blaine to Olympia, clearing, dredging, even breaking ice. Retired in 1981, it was the last stern-wheeler to work on Puget Sound. You can board the boat by a wheelchair-accessible ramp. The heritage center has displays and artifacts tracing a century of local snagboats.

MUSEUMS **Anacortes Museum** (360-293-1915; www.anacorteshistorymuseum .org), 11305 Eighth Street, Anacortes. Open 10–4 Mon.–Tues. and Fri.–Sat., 1–4 Sun.; closed Wed. Donation welcome. This stately, white-columned 1910 Carnegie library has been the home of the town's historical museum since 1967. Exhibits, on the second floor, display articles from the pre- and early-settlement periods, the heyday of the fishing and canning industries, and historical photos, maps, and charts.

La Conner Quilt Museum (360-466-4288; www.laconnerquilts.com), 703 South Second Street, La Conner. Open 11–4 Wed.–Sun. $7 adults, $5 military and students. Today the Gaches House (see *Historic Homes*), an imposing yellow Queen Anne mansion, houses the only quilt museum in the Pacific Northwest. Exhibits change every few months; you might see quilts from Japan or exhibits on quilts and travel or quilts and poetry.

Museum of Northwest Art (360-466-4446; www.museumofnwart.org), 121 South First Street, La Conner. Open 10–5 Tues.–Sat., 12–5 Sun.–Mon. $5 adults, $4 seniors, $2 students, children under 12 free. Artists began congregating in the village of La Conner back in the 1930s and 1940s, drawn by the shimmering northern marine light and probably the isolation. Back then, before the freeway and microchips, this coast was practically the edge of the known world. Regionally well-known artists, including Mark Tobey and Guy Anderson, still remembered by some neighbors here, are featured in this modern, 12,000-square-foot museum, along with contemporary artists of the Skagit Valley.

Sedro-Woolley Historical Museum (360-855-2390), 725 Murdock Street, Sedro-Woolley. Open 12–4 Wed.–Thurs., 9–4 Sat., 1:30–4:30 Sun. Donation accepted. This place contains old logging and farming equipment. A self-guiding brochure is available from the Sedro-Woolley Chamber of Commerce (see *Guidance*).

Skagit County Historical Museum (360-466-3365), 501 Fourth Street, La Conner. Open 11–5 Tues.–Sun. $4 adults, $3 seniors and children 6–12; $8 families. Skagit County extends from the mountains to the shore, and this museum documents the history of the varied Skagit Valley through the eclectic stuff of daily life, from Indian baskets to tools to doll collections.

SCENIC DRIVES **Tulip Route,** about 20 paved miles on back roads between Mount Vernon and La Conner. In spring, follow this colorful route; a map and brochure are available from **Skagit Valley Tulip Festival** (360-428-5959; www .tulipfestival.org).

WALKING TOURS **Historic Walking Tour of Anacortes.** Available from the Anacortes Museum (see *Museums*) or Anacortes Chamber of Commerce (see *Guidance*). This tour guides you past many homes and businesses dating from the 1890s and 1900s, when Anacortes had railroad terminus fever: the 1911 **Great Northern Depot,** now an art gallery; **cannery buildings** from the 1890s; and

City Hall, built in 1914 as an Elks lodge and now displaying historical photos (open 8–5 Mon.–Fri.).

Mural Project, Anacortes. Local artist Bill Mitchell, an Anacortes native, has painted the town with murals of local historical worthies and events (including himself). Get a guide to the 100-plus images chronicling Anacortes's history from the chamber of commerce (see *Guidance*).

Sedro-Woolley Walking Tour. This self-guided tour takes you past strategically placed pieces of early logging equipment, several hundred-year-old homes, and a 1904 standing eight-day clock. For information, contact the Sedro-Woolley Chamber of Commerce (see *Guidance*) or Sedro-Woolley Historical Museum (see *Museums*).

✳ To Do

BICYCLING Anacortes forestland trails. These 3,000 acres are undeveloped but for hiking trails, which are also open to mountain bikes. A map, $10 from **Anacortes Parks and Recreation** (360-293-1918), is recommended (see *Hiking*).

Guemes Island, via Skagit County ferry from the dock at Sixth Street and I Avenue, Anacortes. This island five minutes from Anacortes is a favorite for road biking on its rolling country roads.

Thompson Parkway Trail, 3.1 paved miles from 22nd Street to Weaverling Spit, Anacortes. This level and paved road is a nice alternative to biking WA 20.

Tulip field roads, east of La Conner. These flat roads are easy and pleasant in bloom season.

Washington Park Loop Road, 2 miles (see *Hiking*), Anacortes. This offers nice views.

BIRDING Bay View State Park (on Padilla Bay just north of WA 20), **Bowman Bay** (on Rosario Road just north of Deception Pass Bridge), and **Washington Park** (at the end of Sunset Avenue, Anacortes). Alcids, loons, and other wintering waterfowl can be found in the lakes and bays off these places.

Hayton Reserve, on Fir Island Road southwest of La Conner. Innumerable trumpeter and tundra swans and snow geese descend on the fields of the Skagit River delta in the fall and spend the winter feasting on agricultural leavings. This is a good place to see them. In turn, they draw raptors, including peregrine falcons.

BOATING This is water world, and several parks and marinas offer guest moorage; you'll also find boat rentals and tours. Moorage is available at the following:

Bowman Bay (360-675-3767), in the north unit of Deception Pass State Park, on Rosario Road just north of Deception Pass Bridge. Moorage and boat launch.

Cap Sante Boat Haven (360-293-0694), 1019 Q Avenue, Anacortes.

La Conner Marina (360-466-3118), 613 North Second Street, La Conner.

Skyline Marina (360-293-5134), 2011 Skyline Way, Anacortes.

CAMPING Bay View State Park (888-226-7688), on Padilla Bay just north of WA 20. Forty-six tent sites and 29 utility sites, as well as 6 **cabins.**

BOATS AT THE LA CONNER MARINA

Marine state parks (360-675-2417). Three campgrounds accessible only to boats are on small islands near Anacortes: **Hope Island,** in the north end of Skagit Bay; five campsites, toilets, no drinking water. **Saddlebag Island,** in Padilla Bay just east of Guemes Island; five campsites, restrooms, more than a mile of beach. **Skagit Island,** between Similk and Skagit bays east of Deception Pass; two mooring buoys, primitive campsites, and toilets.

&. **Rasar State Park** (reservations 888-226-7688), off WA 20, 19 miles east of Burlington (follow the signs). Eighteen standard sites, 20 utility sites, and 3 primitive sites; 3 ADA-compliant restrooms.

Washington Park (360-293-1927), at the end of Sunset Avenue, Anacortes. Seventy-five campsites, plus showers, restrooms, and a playground.

CANOEING AND KAYAKING Anacortes Kayak Tours (360-588-1117; www .anacorteskayaktours.com), 1801 Commercial Avenue, Anacortes. Day tours out of Anacortes and longer tours off Cypress Island (west of Guemes Island) are offered.

Sea Kayak Shop/Island Outfitters (360-299-2300; www.seakayakshop.com), 2515 Commercial Avenue, Anacortes. Contact this shop for instruction, sales, and rentals, as well as tours.

GOLF Avalon Golf Club (360-757-1900), 19345 Kelleher Road, Burlington. Twenty-seven holes; free golf on your birthday.

Eaglemont Golf Club (360-424-0800), 4127 Eaglemont Drive, Mount Vernon. Eighteen holes.

Overlook Golf Course (360-422-6444), 17523 WA 9, Mount Vernon. Eighteen holes.

Sauk Mountain View (360-856-0315), 839 Fruitdale Road, Sedro-Woolley. Eighteen holes.

Similk Beach Golf Course (360-293-3444), 12518 Christianson Road, Anacortes. Eighteen holes.

HIKING

Fidalgo Island

Cranberry Lake and Whistle Lake forest areas (Anacortes Parks and Recreation, 360-293-1918), west and south of town. These comprise 3,000 acres of land undeveloped but for trails; a trail map is recommended.

Heart Lake (Anacortes Parks and Recreation, 360-293-1918), a city park in Whistle Lake Forest (see above). Loop trails of 2–4 miles around this lake lead through old-growth forest.

Rotary Park (Anacortes Parks and Recreation, 360-293-1918), Market Street and T Avenue, Anacortes. The 1.5-mile shoreline promenade to this park makes a pleasant stroll, with possible wildlife viewing.

Thompson Parkway Trail, 3.1 paved miles from 22nd Street, Anacortes, south to Weaverling Spit.

Washington Park (360-293-1918), at the end of Sunset Avenue, Anacortes. The 2-mile loop road offers island views, birds (see *Birding*), and wildflowers.

Mount Vernon Area

Boardwalk, 0.25 mile along the riverfront west of Main Street, Mount Vernon.

Kulshan Trail, 4 miles from downtown Mount Vernon to the east side. This multipurpose path through town goes through residential neighborhoods, natural areas, and a park.

Little Mountain Park, the south end of Mount Vernon. A 1.5-mile trail leads to views from the Skagit Valley across to the Olympics.

Padilla Bay Area

Padilla Bay Shore Trail, 2 miles along Padilla Bay, halfway between Mount Vernon and Anacortes. This easy walk has mountain views and a large population of wintering peregrine falcons.

Padilla Bay Upland Trail, 0.8 mile, half paved, along Padilla Bay slightly north of the shore trail (see above). This trail leads from the interpretive center (see *Wilder Places—Nature Preserves*) through meadow and forest.

Sedro-Woolley Area

Cascade Trail, 22 gravel miles from Sedro-Woolley to Concrete. This rails-to-trails right-of-way paralleling the Skagit River and WA 20 is open to horses, ambitious walkers, and bikers. Good news: If you start at Concrete, it's all downhill.

WHALE-WATCHING Mystic Sea Charters (800-308-9387; www.mysticsea charters.com), 819 Commercial Avenue, Anacortes (boarding at 710 Seafarers' Way). Tours May–Oct.; reservations required. $89 adults, $79 seniors over 65, $49 students and children 2–17. In spring, the eastern Pacific population of gray whales makes its way from Baja Mexico's limpid waters to cold Alaskan seas. Some of them detour into Puget Sound to fatten up on ghost shrimp, and they are often observed even from shore. For a closer look as the giants dive, breach, and disport themselves, Mystic Sea Charters offers whale-watching cruises in sheltered

Saratoga Passage, between Whidbey and Camano islands, the whales' favorite hangout. You can spy on them from the deck or the comfortable cabin of the 100-foot, 78-passenger boat. Outside gray whale season (spring), you're almost guaranteed a view of orcas. The boat is wheelchair-accessible.

✳ Wilder Places

PARKS Bay View State Park (360-757-0227), on Padilla Bay just north of WA 20. Camping and picnicking near the Padilla Bay National Estuarine Reserve; great bird-watching, too (see *To Do—Birding*).

Cap Sante Park (360-293-1918), on V Street south of Fourth Street, Anacortes. A viewpoint overlooks Fidalgo Bay.

Maiben Park (360-755-0531), Washington and Greenleaf avenues, Burlington. This city park contains a senior and community center, water park, and playground. It's also the site of the annual Berry Dairy Days (see *Special Events*).

Mount Erie Park (360-293-1918), on Mount Erie Drive in Whistle Lake Forest south of Anacortes. Walk, bike, or drive to this 1,300-foot peak, where you can see the Skagit Valley and neighboring islands.

♿ **Rasar State Park** (360-826-3942), off WA 20, 19 miles east of Burlington (follow the signs). This 168-acre park lies along the Skagit River as it tumbles down from the North Cascades. Eagles abound, especially in winter. Camping and 4 miles of hiking trails, including 1 mile wheelchair-accessible.

Washington Park (360-293-1918), at the end of Sunset Avenue, Anacortes. On 220 acres on Fidalgo Island's westernmost point, this park's scenic loop road offers magnificent views of sunset over the San Juans (see *To Do—Bicycling* and *Birding*). There are trails, beaches, a picnic area, and camping.

NATURE PRESERVES ♿ **Padilla Bay National Estuarine Reserve** (360-428-1558), 10441 Bayview-Edison Road, Mount Vernon. Trails open daily. Interpretive center open 10–5 Wed.–Sun. This is where many migratory birds spend the winter. Reserve trails and a wheelchair-accessible observation deck are frequented by birdwatchers.

Sharpe Park (360-336-9414), on Rosario Road 1 mile north of Deception Pass. This 75-acre environmental preserve has a 0.75-mile trail leading to a beach and Puget Sound views.

✳ Lodging

BED & BREAKFASTS

Anacortes
Autumn Leaves Bed and Breakfast (360-293-4920 or 866-293-4929; www.autumn-leaves.com), 3201 21st Street. This one is definitely for the special occasion, with solid carved-wood bedsteads, antiques, and gas fireplaces in all three rooms (one is actually called the King Louis Room). Each has a private bathroom and TV, too. Relax in the garden after a day of touring. Not handicapped-accessible, as all rooms are upstairs. Children over 14 welcome. No pets. $160.

La Conner
🐾 **Katy's Inn** (360-466-9909; www.katysinn.com), 503 Third Street. This 1882 Victorian is the oldest house in town; it became a B&B more than a

century later. The four guest rooms are simple and homey, all with private baths. Plenty of porch space invites you to sit and relax. Rates include full breakfast. Small pets allowed for a fee. $99–149.

COTTAGES AND CABINS

Anacortes

✔ ☻ **Guemes Island Resort** (360-293-6643 or 800-965-6643; www .guemesislandresort.com), 4268 Guemes Island Road. Three houses, eight cabins, and five yurts sit on 20 beachfront acres on the north side of this lesser-known San Juan island. All but the yurts come with a kitchen, bathroom, linens, and a picnic table; guests also have use of the sauna and rowboats or kayaks. Cabins sleep 2–4; houses sleep 4–12; yurts (16 or 20 feet in diameter) sleep 2–8. Well-behaved pets allowed for a fee. Cabins $137–225; houses $198–440 (weekly rates available); yurts from $75.

✔ **Pioneer Trails RV Resort** (360-293-5355; www.pioneertrails.com), 7337 Miller Road. True, it's geared to RVs, but it also has more rustic options: one- and two-bedroom log cabins, each with a full-sized bed and a set of bunk beds. A small house on the premises also is available. Shared showers and toilets. RVs $32–49.50; cabins $47.50–59 (bring your own bedding); house $89–129.

The Ship House Inn (360-293-1093; www.shiphouseinn.com), 12876 Marine Drive. Is it a boat? Is it a house? Hard to say, but the shipshape wood-paneled quarters make you think you're far out at sea. Four rooms with assorted sleeping arrangements. Rates include continental breakfast. $89–159.

INNS AND HOTELS

Anacortes

& **Anaco Bay Inn** (360-299-3320 or 877-299-3320; www.anacobayinn.com), 916 33rd Street. Classier than your average motor court, with its two-story stone front and dormer windows, the Anaco Bay is a reasonably priced family option. Just 18 guest rooms and 4 suites keep it intimate; a hot tub, library, and continental breakfast are nice extra touches. Several rooms have gas fireplaces; two rooms are handicapped-accessible. $64–139.

☻ **Anaco Inn** (360-293-8833 or 888-293-8833; www.anacoinn.com), 905 20th Street. In the same style as the Anaco Bay Inn (see above), this inn has 11 comfortably equipped rooms and 2 suites plus a library, hot tub, and breakfast. Priced like a motel, its size and attitude make it more like an inn. Small pets allowed, but consult first. $59–149.

The Islands Inn (360-293-4644 or 866-331-3328; www.islandsinn.com), 3401 Commercial Avenue. Fundamentally a motel, this inn has freestanding fireplaces in many rooms, and its pool and reasonable prices make it convenient for families. The welcome is friendly, and the complimentary continental breakfast is quite edible, thanks perhaps to the Dutch owners, Fien and Bela Hulscher. An additional attraction is the on-site wine bar (see *Where to Eat*). $79–149.

Majestic Inn (360-299-1400 or 877-370-0100; www.majesticinnandspa .com), 419 Commercial Avenue. A boutique hotel in little Anacortes! The Majestic was a hotel about a century ago; the exterior has been preserved, while inside it's been renovated to meet today's demands. Twenty-one rooms of various sizes have luxuriously plump beds and flat-screen TVs. The on-site spa and restaurant are additional draws. Rates include a breakfast buffet. $169–399.

The Nantucket Inn (360-333-5282); www.nantucketinnanacortes.com),

3402 Commercial Avenue. It's about 3,000 miles from Nantucket, but the solid 1925 house looks the part. The eight queen- and king-sized rooms all have private baths, and you have access to the spacious living room (nice to curl up in front of the fire), as well as the kitchen and dining room. Rates include continental breakfast. $99–$159.

La Conner

The Heron Inn (360-399-1074; www .theheroninn.com), 117 Maple Avenue. Within walking distance of galleries and shops, the Heron is a large, 12-room inn that invites you to relax in its own day spa or with a book by the slate fireplace. The rooms are cozy, too, with plush bedding and antique-style furnishings; lots of decks take in the view. Rates include full breakfast. Children welcome. Pets allowed in some rooms for a $50 fee. $109–159.

Hotel Planter (360-466-4710 or 800-488-5409; www.hotelplanter.com), 715 First Street. Right in downtown La Conner, this National Historic Inn has a private garden courtyard. The rooms are upstairs; all 12 have private baths and are decorated to recall the early 1900s. Consult about children. No pets. $99–169.

✍ ♿ ❀ **La Conner Country Inn** (360-466-3101 or 888-466-4113), 107 South Second Street. Of the inn's 28 rooms, 22 have two beds, and all have gas fireplaces. There's 1 ADA room and several wheelchair-accessible rooms at ground level, but no elevator. Rates include continental breakfast. Children and pets welcome. $119–289.

Wild Iris Inn (360-466-1400 or 800-477-1400; www.wildiris.com), 121 Maple Avenue. Opened in 1992, the Wild Iris is a small, plush inn surrounded by gardens and fruit trees. Most of the 16 rooms have fireplaces and jetted tubs; the house has a long porch from which to appreciate the gardens. Rates include full breakfast. $119–199.

✳ Where to Eat

DINING OUT

Anacortes
Petite Wine Bar (360-293-4644), 3401 Commercial Avenue. Open 4–9 daily. The brainchild of Bela Berghuys, co-owner of the Islands Inn, the Petite opened in July 2011. It's a stroke of genius: relaxed but elegant wining and dining. Adjoining the inn, it offers a short but well-chosen list of mostly Northwest wines and an innovative small-plate menu dreamed up and created by chef Matt McVay, which can easily make a very satisfying dinner. We shared salmon pâté, spanakopita, hummus, curry-carrot soup and salad, and chocolate mousse—with Matt's own particular take on it all.

EATING OUT

Anacortes
Adrift (360-588-0653; www.adrift restaurant.com), 510 Commercial Avenue. Open 8 am–9 pm Mon.–Thurs., 8 am–10 pm Fri.–Sat. Used books line one brick wall as young waitstaff bustle about and equally young cooks brew up a variety of dishes, which may include Vietnamese sandwiches, creative soups, and always fresh local seafood and produce. Satisfying, relaxed, yet energetic—and Anacortes isn't even a college town.

5th Street Bistro (360-299-1400; www.majesticinnandspa.com), 419 Commercial Avenue. Open 4–9 Sun.–Mon., 4–10 Tues.–Thurs., 4–12 Fri.–Sat. This restaurant at the Majestic Inn serves rib-eye steak, salmon, southern fried chicken, and other such comforting dishes at fairly reasonable prices. And talk about reasonable, how about the three-course meal for two ($25)?

Gere-a-Deli (360-293-7383; www .gereadeli.com), 502 Commercial Avenue. Open 7–4 Mon.–Sat. The sandwiches, quiche, and soups here are approved by the locals.

Il Posto Ristorante Italiano (360-293-7600), 2120 Commercial Avenue. Open 4:30 to closing Wed.–Mon. Chef Marcello Giufrida serves Italian country cuisine, including but not limited to homemade pasta and daily risotto specials.

Naung Mai Thai Kitchen (360-588-1183), 3015 Commercial Avenue. Open 11–9 Mon.–Sat., 12–9 Sun. Like a taco stand, except Thai. Naung Mai serves a selection of hearty dishes.

Rockfish Grill/Anacortes Brewery (360-588-1720; www.anacortesrock fish.com), 320 Commercial Avenue. Open from 11 AM daily. There's something for everybody here, whether it's a portobello mushroom sandwich, cedar-plank salmon, fish-and-chips, or pork schnitzel (and a children's menu, too). As the name implies, it's also a brewery, with an astonishing list of its own beers and ales.

Guemes Island
Anderson's General Store and Café (360-293-4548; www.guemesisland store.com), Mangan's Landing. Open 8–7 Mon.–Fri., 8–8 Sat.–Sun. This store down by the ferry landing serves hefty hot and cold sandwiches, salads, oysters, and more. "If we don't have it, we'll explain how you can get along without it." Live music some Fridays.

La Conner
Calico Cupboard Café and Bakery (360-466-4451; www.calicocupboard cafe.com), 720 South First Street. Open 7:30–5 daily. There are lots of dishes here for vegetarians, plenty of vegetables for meat eaters, and fresh

pastries for everyone. The Calico Cupboard has been accommodating food allergies, diets, and preferences—and just plain cooking healthy food—since 1981. Other branches: Anacortes (360-293-7315), 901 Commercial Avenue, open 7–4 daily; Mount Vernon (360-336-3107), 121-B Freeway Drive, open 7–5 daily.

La Conner Fruit and Produce Market (360-466-3018), 116 South First Street. Open 8:30–6 in summer; 8:30–5 in winter. Buy your fresh produce and eat breakfast or lunch—soups, salads, and sandwiches—at the market.

Seeds: A Bistro and Bar (360-466-3280; www.seedsbistro.com), 623 Morris Street. Open 11–9 daily. In the old Tillinghast Seed Company building, Seeds concentrates on produce of the fertile Skagit Valley for lunch and dinner.

✳ Selective Shopping

FOOD Seabear Smokehouse and Store (800-645-3474; www.seabear .com), 605 30th Street, Anacortes. Open daily. You're in the Northwest, so you should eat smoked fish. Here you'll find both fresh and smoked seafood, soups, and chowders. Perhaps best of all, Seabear also offers smoke-house tours and free tastings. If you like what you taste, you can ship some home.

SPECIAL SHOPS The Lime Dock, on North First Street, La Conner. This old red warehouse on the waterfront has been made over to contain art galleries, a wine shop, a bakery, and gift shops.

✳ Special Events

April: **Skagit Valley Tulip Festival** (360-428-5959; www.tulipfestival.org), various locations around the lower Skagit Valley. For the entire month, view blooming tulips, daffodils, or irises; ride bikes along the fields; and take in art shows and a salmon barbecue.

June: **Berry Dairy Days** (360-757-0994; www.burlington-chamber.com), Maiben Park (see *Wilder Places—Parks*), Burlington. Celebrate two of the great regional products with music, a parade, and, of course, strawberry shortcake.

July: **Loggerodeo** (360-770-8452; www.loggerodeo.com), Sedro-Woolley.

This festival combining logging and cowboy contests has been going on since the 1930s.

August: **Shakespeare Northwest** (360-770-7748), Edgewater Park, Mount Vernon. Performances are given for about four weeks.

September: **La Conner Classic Yacht and Car Show** (360-466-4778), La Conner Rotary Club. View classic boats and cars, then enjoy barbecue and a beer. $3.

Oyster Run Motorcycle Rally (360-435-9103), Anacortes. Ten thousand bikers show up for this event.

THE SAN JUAN ISLANDS

Even before the British arrived, Spanish ships roved up here on exploratory forays from their bases in Mexico and California. Deeming the Northwest a damp, unprofitable wilderness, they showed surprisingly little interest in staking a claim. Only when they noticed how the Hudson's Bay Company was digging in, and making a tidy profit, too, did they establish a small, unsuccessful settlement off Vancouver Island. When departing shortly thereafter, they left behind a scattering of place names such as Lopez, Fidalgo, and, of course, San Juan.

It's easy to recover that exploratory feeling today. On the border between land and ocean, the United States and Canada, the San Juan archipelago consists of 172 named islands and many unnamed rocks and islets. Washington State Ferries serve four—Orcas, San Juan, Lopez, and Shaw—from Anacortes, itself on Fidalgo Island. Lummi Island is served by county ferry from Bellingham (see the Bellingham, Blaine, and Lynden Area chapter) and Guemes by county ferry from Anacortes, while Fidalgo, barely separated from the mainland, is reached by bridge (see the La Conner, Mount Vernon, and Anacortes Area chapter).

Others offer a real marine wilderness experience if you have your own boat or take an excursion from Orcas Island. Virtually all services are concentrated on Orcas, Lopez, and San Juan. Shaw is the smallest inhabited island, but there are no commercial amenities except a small grocery. Unlike many transportation experiences today, getting to these islands *is* half the fun—the comfortable and convenient ferries allow you to slow down to island time.

And that dampness? Illusory. The islands are in the rain shadow of the Olympic Mountains and Vancouver Island. They get rain enough in winter but otherwise tend to be glorious.

GUIDANCE Lopez Island Chamber of Commerce (360-468-4664; www.lopez island.com), Box 102, 6 Old Post Road, Lopez 98261. Open 10–2 Wed.–Sat.

Orcas Island Chamber of Commerce (360-376-2273; www.orcasislandchamber .org), 65 North Beach Road, Eastsound 98245. Open 10–4 daily in summer; 10–2 Tues.–Sat. in winter.

San Juan Island Chamber of Commerce (360-378-5240; www.sanjuanisland .org), 135 Spring Street, Friday Harbor 98250. Open 10–4:30 Mon.–Fri., 10–4 Sat.–Sun.

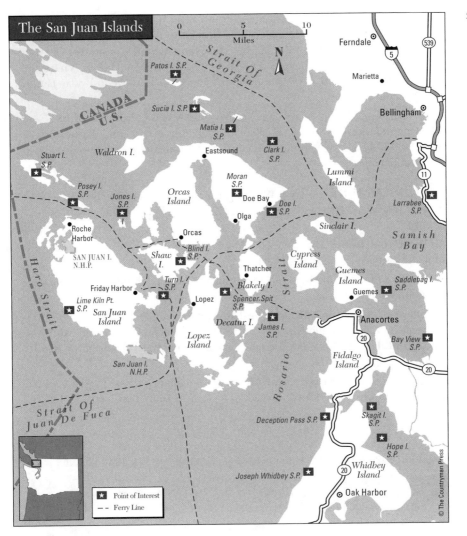

The San Juan Islands

San Juan Islands Visitors' Bureau (888-468-3701; www.visitsanjuans.com), 640 Mullis Street, Box 1330, Friday Harbor 98250.

GETTING THERE

By boat: **Washington State Ferries** (206-464-6400 or 888-808-7977; www.wsdot .wa.gov/ferries) sail from Anacortes 15–18 times a day; from **I-5** at Burlington, take **WA 20** west into Anacortes and follow the signs to the ferry dock. In summer the lines of cars waiting for a ferry may be several hours' long. If you take only a bicycle or simply walk on, you can board immediately, and your ride will be cheaper. Long-term parking is available at the ferry dock. Tickets can be bought online or at the dock.

Some private boat lines offer seasonal service to San Juan Island: **Puget Sound Express** (360-385-5288; www.pugetsoundexpress.com), from Port Townsend on the Olympic Peninsula to Friday Harbor; **San Juan Island Commuter** (800-443-4552; www.islandcommuter.com), from Bellingham to Friday Harbor; **Victoria Clipper** (800-888-2525; www.victoriaclipper.com), from Seattle to Friday Harbor (and Vancouver Island).

By air: Air service, from Seattle and smaller nearby cities, is offered by the following: **Island Air** (888-378-2376; www.sanjuan-islandair.com); **Kenmore Air** (866-435-9524; www.kenmoreair.com); **San Juan Airlines** (800-874-4434; www.sanjuanairlines.com).

GETTING AROUND *By boat:* **Washington State Ferries** (see *Getting There*) provide interisland transportation among Lopez, San Juan, Orcas, and Shaw islands.

By bus: **Orcas Island Shuttle** (360-376-7433; www.orcasislandshuttle.com) offers some bus service around Orcas Island.

San Juan Transit (800-887-8387; www.sanjuantransit.com) offers some bus service around San Juan Island.

Rentals and cabs: **Susie's Mopeds and Rental Cars** (800-532-0087; www.susies mopeds.com), with locations at Friday Harbor and Roche Harbor, and **M&W Auto Rentals** (360-378-2794; www.sanjuanauto.com) give you wheels on San Juan Island.

All three major islands have several taxi services, including these: **Lopez Cab** (360-468-2905); **Orcas Island Taxi** (360-376-TAXI); **San Juan Taxi** (360-378-TAXI).

WASHINGTON STATE FERRIES PROVIDE PASSAGE AMONG THE SAN JUAN ISLANDS.

MEDICAL EMERGENCY The nearest emergency room is at Island Hospital in Anacortes (see the La Conner, Mount Vernon, and Anacortes Area chapter). Clinics in the San Juans:

InterIsland Medical Center (360-378-2141 or, after hours, 360-378-4151), 550 Spring Street, Friday Harbor (San Juan Island).

Lopez Island Medical Clinic (360-468-2245), Washburn Place and Village Road, Lopez Island.

Orcas Family Health Center (360-376-7778), 1286 Mount Baker Road, Suite B-102, Eastsound.

San Juan Healthcare Associates (360-378-1338), 689 Airport Center, Suite B, Friday Harbor.

✳ To See

CULTURAL SITES **Westcott Bay Sculpture Park and Nature Reserve** (360-370-5050; www.wbay.org), Wescott Bay, San Juan Island. Open dawn to dusk daily. Donation requested. Dozens of sculptures are artistically disposed around a meadow overlooking a wetland and Westcott Bay, at the northwest end of San Juan Island. In many materials and styles, sometimes idiosyncratic, all of the work is by regional artists, a project of the **Island Museum of Art** in Friday Harbor.

FARMERS' MARKETS **Eastsound Farmers' Market** (360-317-8342; www .orcasislandfarmersmarket.org), on the Village Green on North Beach Road, Orcas Island. Open 10–3 Sat. May–Sept.

Lopez Farmers' Market, next to Lopez Community Center, Lopez Island. Open 10–2 Sat. May–Sept.

San Juan Farmers' Market, Brickworks Plaza, Friday Harbor, San Juan Island. Open 10–1 Sat. May–mid-Oct.

FARMS AND GARDENS ✐ **Krystal Acres Alpaca Farm** (360-378-6125; www.krystalacres.com), 3501 West Valley Road, Friday Harbor, San Juan Island. Open 10–5 daily Apr.–Dec.; 11–4 daily Jan.–Mar. You may not want to buy your child a souvenir T-shirt at the end of this farm tour, but the cuddly, liquid-eyed alpacas are natural kid attractants. Here, 50-odd of the fuzzy creatures roam green pastures studded with old oaks. Alpacas, together with lavender, are the latest regional specialty crops in the San Juans, preserving open space while creating their own niche markets.

Pelindaba Lavender Farm (360-378-4246 or 866-819-1911; www.pelindaba lavender.com), 33 Hawthorne Lane, Friday Harbor, San Juan Island. Open 9:30–4:30 daily May–Oct. Lavender is not an obvious crop to grow in the Northwest. It needs alkaline soil, a dry climate, good drainage, and altitude—as in the south of France, for example. This did not deter Susan and Stephen Robins, who thought they had found a retirement occupation. Carting in loads of lime and putting drains under their fields, they planted their first lavender in 1999 and now have more than 12,000 plants, all grown organically. More than a hundred lavender products, from soaps to cookies, come from these acres. And when you see the rows and rows of silver-green plants cascading down the slope, it does put you in mind of Provence—even more so when they're in bloom. Take a self-guided tour through the fields and visit the gift shop, or buy the products at the Pelindaba store downtown (see *Selective Shopping*) 150 First Street, Friday Harbor.

FOR FAMILIES ✐ **The Funhouse Discovery Center** (360-376-7177; www.the funhouse.org), 30 Pea Patch Lane, Eastsound, Orcas Island. Open 3–5:30 Mon–Fri. (plus 6–11 PM Fri.–Sat. for teens) Sept.–June; 11–5 Wed.–Sat. (plus 6–11 PM Fri.–Sat. for teens) July–Aug. Free. Designed for children from preschoolers through high schoolers, the Funhouse also appeals to adults with its imaginative exhibits. Figure out how kinetic sculptures work; see yourself as an animated, computer-generated "painting" as you move about the room; and otherwise tease your brain.

HISTORIC HOMES Many older homes on the islands now are guest accommodations (see *Lodging*).

Rosario, on Orcas Island. In 1906, when Seattle politician Robert Moran was told he had a year to live, he built his ideal mansion in an idyllic spot overlooking Rosario Strait. Today it's the heart of **Rosario Resort** (see *Lodging*), but the residential area has been preserved as a museum where you can admire Moran's concert room with its 1,972-pipe Aeolian organ, the huge fireplace in what is now the lounge, fantastic woodwork, and more. It seems the mansion reinvigorated Moran, who lived on for quite a number of years.

HISTORIC SITES **American Camp** and **English Camp,** at southern and northern ends, respectively, of San Juan Island; the two camps now form **San Juan Island National Historic Park** (see *Wilder Places—Parks*). These sites are vestiges of the period when the British and Americans jointly and often amicably occupied the Northwest, 1818–1846. Eventually the parties agreed to separate along the 49th parallel, which is why we now have such a long, straight border with Canada. However, the Oregon Treaty of 1846 stipulated a southward jog once the parallel reached the middle of the "channel" between Vancouver Island and the mainland, and another jog northwestward up the Strait of Juan de Fuca.

A BLOCKHOUSE AT ENGLISH CAMP, PART OF SAN JUAN ISLAND NATIONAL HISTORIC PARK

These jogs probably looked nice on paper, but the fact is, the waters are liberally strewn with islands; where exactly was that "channel" located? The upshot was that both nations claimed San Juan Island. Although only about 25 Americans had settled there by 1859, one of them, angry because a pig belonging to the Hudson's Bay Company kept rooting in his garden, managed to shoot the pig. The British threatened to arrest him, the Americans called for military protection, and

66 men under Captain George Pickett came and dug in by the Hudson's Bay wharf (what is now American Camp). The British then sent in three warships. Escalations of men and ships followed, and the British established a garrison to the north (what is now English Camp), till 461 Americans faced 2,140 British troops.

This absurd buildup came to be known as the Pig War, though happily it was only a Pig Cold War. and the two sides never actually came to blows (aside from the pig). Both sides' armed forces occupied the island till the case was, for obscure reasons, referred to Kaiser Wilhelm of Germany. He ruled in 1872 that the border lay to the west; therefore San Juan Island was American. The British withdrew in 1874, and everyone lived happily ever after.

Roche Harbor, on San Juan Island's northwest corner. This quiet inlet was the site of a Hudson's Bay post. After cession of the island to the United States, a couple of brothers started a small lime operation, which was soon bought out by attorney John S. McMillin, who had discovered a huge limestone deposit. His Tacoma and Roche Harbor Lime Company transformed the site into a company town almost overnight, with the **Hotel de Haro** (see *Lodging*) quickly erected for important guests, as well as company housing, a company store, schools, churches, a warehouse, docks, and the lime works itself. It quickly became one of the largest lime works in the nation, and like the archetypical company town, it was all-encompassing, with its own water, phone, and electric systems; workers were generally paid in scrip usable only at the company store.

Things continued this way till 1956, when the town was sold. It's still a company town, now run by a shipping consortium, but as a resort. It's probably a sight pleasanter now, with the white hotel and McMillin's restored home gleaming over the water, plus restaurants, lovely gardens, and pleasure boats coming and going. A stroll with a historical map available at the hotel desk reveals some early kilns and a large, columned monument serving as McMillin's mausoleum.

MUSEUMS Crow Valley School Museum (360-376-4849), Crow Valley Road, Orcas Island; 3 miles southwest of Eastsound. Open 12–4 Wed. and Sat. Memorial Day–Sept. 15. Donation requested. For a glimpse of pioneer school days, visit this one-room schoolhouse dating from 1888, with the original desks, woodstove, and other furnishings.

Lambiel Museum (360-376-4544; www.lambielmuseum.com), Olga Road, Olga, Orcas Island. By appointment only. $10. Hidden in the dense woods of Orcas Island, the Lambiel is a private collection of eclectic, sometimes eccentric, artwork of 100-plus artists, created exclusively in San Juan County.

Lopez Island Historical Museum (360-468-2049), 450 Price Street, Lopez Island. Open 12–4 Wed.–Sun. May–Sept. Donation requested. Island life is detailed through farming tools, photos, and genealogical charts.

Orcas Island Historical Museum (360-376-4849; www.orcasmuseum.org), 181 North Beach Road, Eastsound, Orcas Island. Open 11–4 Wed.–Mon. $5 adults, $4 seniors, $3 students and children under 12. John and Rachel Boede raised nine children in the 425-square-foot cabin at the heart of this museum. Several other cabins, moved from various points on the island, trace the history of Orcas through artifacts of early Anglo-Indian contact, homesteaders' possessions, replicas of early stores, and evidence of the development of tourism.

San Juan Island Historical Museum (369-378-3949; www.sjmuseum.org), 325 and 405 Price Street, Friday Harbor, San Juan Island. Open 10–4 Wed.–Sat., 1–4 Sun. May–Sept.; 1–4 Sat. Apr. and Oct. $5 adults, $4 seniors over 60, $3 children 5–18, $10 families. For a glimpse of life on a remote island, don't go to the movies—go to this homestead dating from 1894, when only 550 people lived on all the San Juans. Here are the original farmhouse and appurtenances, plus other early evidence of settlement, such as the first county jail.

✇ **Whale Museum** (360-378-4710; www.whalemuseum.org), 62 First Street North, Friday Harbor, San Juan Island. Open 10–5 daily. $6 adults, $5 seniors over 65, $3 students and children 5 and over. Recorded whale songs accompany you up the stairs of this 1892 Odd Fellows hall to fascinating exhibits on whale life. Learn about the latest research on topics from whale myths to morphology to social life. The museum and its affiliated **Center for Whale Research** pioneered whale study in Puget Sound. Pick up a phone and listen to vocalizations or study the family trees of the resident orcas; the more morbid enjoy the preserved whale parasites.

NATURAL WONDERS The Salish Sea, from slightly east of Cape Flattery at northwest edge of the Olympic Peninsula east and south to Olympia and back north through southern coastal British Columbia and around southern Vancouver Island. Deep blue spattered with emerald islands in the sun or gray and wave wracked, this inland sea is 10,000 square miles of flooded canyons and deltas, gouged out by glaciers and filled at the end of the last Ice Age. Its water is remarkably clear at the northern end around the San Juan Islands, and a glance down can reveal starfish, eelgrass, and even coral before the sea shelves off to its depths. Even today, after a hundred years of industrialization and decimated salmon runs, the inland waterway supports amazing flora and fauna, from mussels, oysters, and clams to whales and otters. This is not to mention the majestic birdlife—eagles, auklets, guillemots, ospreys, puffins—most easily visible from the ferries. The "boundaries" of the Salish Sea coincide with zones where Coastal Salish languages were spoken and where the waters have a slightly lower salinity than the Pacific Ocean. Besides, "Salish Sea" is easier to say than the alternative (see below). To rest within it, framed by the Cascades to the east and the Olympics to the west, is to have as fine a view as any in the world.

Salish Sea orcas. Three pods of the black and white "killer whales" (actually the largest of the dolphin family) inhabit the waters of Puget Sound, the Strait of Georgia, and the Strait of Juan de Fuca, now often collectively called the Salish Sea. Designated J, K, and L pods, these residents subsist entirely on fish—mostly salmon, which makes you wonder about their future. Today the three pods number nearly a hundred individuals living in matrilineal family groupings that stay together for life. K and L pods seem to depart for the winter and have been observed as far away as Monterey, California, while J pod stays year-round. Sometimes all three pods come together in a sort of superpod jamboree, during which they seem to have a lot to communicate because they squeak and click incessantly.

Little studied until the past 30 years, the orcas are yielding fascinating information to the Center for Whale Research on San Juan Island (see *Museums*) and the network of lay observers around the islands. For instance, orcas commonly live to their 40s and 50s; one matriarch is estimated to be more than 90 years old. Different populations of orcas seem to have different dialects and even languages—the small groups of transient orcas that occasionally appear in the area have quite different vocalizations and eat only marine mammals. And did you know that marine mammals, including orcas, have to make a conscious decision to breathe, and that therefore only one half of their brain sleeps at a time? The 30-foot-long orcas are an unforgettable sight as they forage and frolic in these waters, and it's well worth a whale-watching trip (see *To Do*) to see them.

SCENIC DRIVES **Lopez Island Historical Tour.** This self-guided tour includes significant buildings and sites from Lopez's development, such as the 1889 Community Hall, 1912 phone switchboard, and several early schools, farmsteads, and churches. Information is available at the Lopez Island Historical Museum (see *Museums*).

West Side Road, along San Juan Island's western bluffs overlooking Haro Strait. It's hard not to find a scenic drive on these island roads, but perhaps this is the most impressive. You might even see some whales.

✳ To Do
BICYCLING
Road Cycling
The islands are small, and virtually all roads are scenic, so they're ideal for biking. In general, narrower roads have bike turnouts for stopping safely.

Crow Valley Road and **Enchanted Valley Road,** Orcas Island. These are very pretty, though narrow, routes. Eastern Orcas is fairly hilly.

Lopez Island. This is a favorite with cyclists because of its fairly level topography and low traffic volume. Visit Lopez Bicycle Works (see *Rentals*) for details.

Roche Point Road and **Cattle Point Road,** San Juan Island. These have wide shoulders for cyclists.

Mountain Biking
Gravel roads, between White Beach Bay, at West Sound, and Dolphin Bay, Orcas Island. These lightly traveled roads are fun.

Moran State Park, Orcas Island. Mountain bikes do best on certain trails in this park; get a trail map at the chamber of commerce (see *Guidance*).

Rentals
Island Bicycles (360-378-4941; www.islandbicycles.com), 380 Argyle Avenue, Friday Harbor, San Juan Island. You can get rentals and further information here.

Lopez Bicycle Works (360-468-2847), 2847 Fisherman Bay Road, Lopez Island. Rentals and repairs are offered here.

Wildlife Cycles (360-376-4708), 350 North Beach Road, Eastsound, Orcas Island.

BOAT EXCURSIONS Several islands, such as **Sucia and Patos,** lie off the larger San Juans. Some are wildlife preserves that are off-limits to humans, but others are marine state parks, affording campsites and hiking trails. A trip to one of these, whether in your own boat or with a guide service, is an experience of wilderness seclusion in the huge inland waterway straddling the United States and Canada.

Gnat's Nature Hikes (360-376-6629), Box 272, Deer Harbor, Orcas Island 98243. This outfitter will take you to boat-only islands in an inflatable boat for a half-day tour.

See also *Canoeing and Kayaking.*

CAMPING

Lopez Island

Lopez Farm Cottages and Tent Camping (800-440-3556; www.lopezfarm cottages.com), 555 Fisherman Bay Road, Lopez Island. Open mid-Apr.–Oct. Ten wooded, private tent sites with bathrooms, water, showers, and coffee. For greater luxury, you can get an 8-by-10-foot tent complete with queen-sized bed. No RVs, no children under 14, and no pets. Tent sites $40–45; tent with bed $75.

Odlin County Park (360-378-1842), Ferry Road; 1 mile from ferry landing. Thirty wooded or beach sites and six hiker-biker sites, plus water and toilets; no showers. $20–25. Note: As of this writing, the water system is under repair and water must be boiled; inquire before using.

Spencer Spit State Park (360-468-2251 or 888-226-7688), 521 Bakerview Road; about 1 mile southwest of ferry landing. Thirty-seven tent sites plus seven hiker-biker sites and Cascadia Marine Trail sites. Moorage, toilets, and water; no showers or hook-ups. $12–36.

Orcas Island

Doe Bay Resort and Retreat (360-376-2291; www.doebay.com), Box 437, Olga 98279. Eleven drive-in and 17 walk-in campsites and 8 yurts, most with water views. See *Lodging* for on-site amenities. Campsites $45–55; yurts $85–120.

Moran State Park (888-226-7688), 5 miles south of Eastsound. This park has 151 tent sites in five campgrounds, mostly on or near various lakes and often among impressive trees, with water and handicapped-accessible bathrooms and showers. Some sites can accommodate RVs up to 45 feet long. Fifteen primitive hiker-biker sites are off the road up Mount Constitution (see *Wilder Places—Parks*). $12–36.

Obstruction Pass State Park (360-376-2326), just over 2 miles from Olga; past Olga, turn left on Doe Bay Road, then in 0.5 mile turn right on Obstruction Pass Road and right again on Trailhead Road. This property is administered by the state Department of Natural Resources. Ten secluded walk-in (or boat-in) sites with pit toilets and picnic tables, some mooring; no water or showers. No reservations. $14.

San Juan Island

Lakedale Resort (800-617-2267), 4313 Roche Harbor Road, Friday Harbor. Open mid-Mar.–mid-Oct. Seventy-one campsites—64 standard sites, 5 hiker-biker sites, and 2 RV sites. There are also tent cabins with sleeper sofas and chairs. This private resort on 82 wooded acres with three spring-fed lakes also has a rather upscale lodge and cabins. Standard sites $36–52; hiker-biker sites $24–30; RV sites $45–59; tent cabins $159–259.

San Juan County Park (360-378-8420), 50 San Juan Park Drive, 2.5 miles north of Lime Kiln Point. Twenty sites with water and toilets, plus a hiker-biker-kayaker group site on Haro Strait, one of the world's great whale-watching beaches. Reservations recommended in summer. Standard sites $30–42; hiker-biker-kayaker group site $10.

South Beach County Park (360-378-8420), about 2 miles south of ferry landing. Eleven wooded, beachside campsites in a quiet, bucolic setting; with water (except in winter) and toilets. Reservations in summer only. $12–16.

CANOEING AND KAYAKING **Orcas Island Kayaks** (360-376-2472; www .orcasislandkayak.com), at Lieber Haven Marina near Obstruction Pass, Orcas Island. They rent kayaks and rowboats.

Outdoor Odysseys (360-378-3533 or 800-647-4621; www.outdoorodysseys.com), 86 Cedar Street, Friday Harbor, San Juan Island. Paddle out of San Juan County Park to kayak among eagles and whales.

Shearwater Adventures (360-376-4699; www.shearwaterkayaks.com), across from Island Market in Eastsound, North Beach Road, Orcas Island. This shop offers half-day, whole-day, and custom trips.

DIVING **Diver's Dream Charters** (360-202-0076; www.lujacsquest.com), at Skyline Marina, Anacortes. These clear, chilly waters support a surprising array of corals, giant octopuses, pink and purple starfish, and other underworldly creatures. But if you're not familiar with the conditions and strong currents, it's better to go with someone who is. This outfitter helps you visit them safely.

GOLF **Lopez Island Golf Course** (360-468-2679), 589 Airport Road, Lopez Island. Nine–eighteen holes.

Orcas Golf and Country Club (360-376-4400), 2171 Orcas Road, Eastsound, Orcas Island. Nine–eighteen holes.

San Juan Golf and Country Club (360-378-2254; www.sanjuangolf.com), 806 Golf Course Road, Friday Harbor, San Juan Island. Nine–eighteen holes.

HIKING
Lopez Island
Department of Natural Resources trails. Isolated trails wander over Department of Natural Resources lands, some accessible via private property; directions are available from the chamber of commerce (see *Guidance*).

Otis Perkins County Park; from Lopez Village, drive south on Fisherman's Bay Road to the south end of the bay and turn north. There's a nice beach walk here, especially at low tide.

Shark Reef Sanctuary, 7.7 miles south of Lopez Village on Shark Reef Road. A short stroll through woods leads to a rocky shore with lots of marine mammals.

Spencer Spit State Park, 2 miles of trails; on Bakerview Road; about 1 mile southwest of the ferry landing. Wander through the woods and out along the spit beside a lagoon.

Orcas Island
Gnat's Nature Hikes (360-376-6629; www.orcasislandhikes.com), Box 272, Deer Harbor 98243. Interpretive walks are led by naturalists who will guide you around Moran State Park or nearby uninhabited islands.

Madrona Point, five minutes from downtown Eastsound to the point. For a nice stroll, follow this dirt path that meanders from the parking area out to the rocky point, with side trails offering other views.

Moran State Park (360-376-2326). Of the 30-plus miles of trails, you can choose among the ones listed here, and many in between; interpretive walks are led by park rangers.

Cascade Lake nature trail, 0.3 mile. A short but rewarding walk.

Lakes loops, 2–4 miles. Trails loop around Cascade and Mountain lakes.

Mount Constitution loop, 6.7 miles. You'll have unparalleled panoramas of the Salish Sea, islands, Cascades, and Olympics.

A TRAIL LEADS FROM EASTSOUND TO MADRONA POINT ON ORCAS ISLAND.

Obstruction Pass State Park trail, 0.5 mile from parking area to beach. Walk through thick forest to the campground. A 0.5-mile trail parallels the shoreline.

San Juan Island

American Camp trails, at the southern end of the island. Paths wind along the sandy beaches and windy grasslands. The rabbits you'll see here are European—the kind that dig warrens, so watch your step—brought in by the English in the mid-1800s. When the rabbits became too numerous, foxes were imported. Just like in Australia. You might also see bald eagles pouncing on the bunnies.

MOUNT CONSTITUTION, IN MORAN STATE PARK ON ORCAS ISLAND, HAS A COMMANDING VIEW.

English Camp trails, two 0.5-mile trails from the parking lot at the northern end of the island. Pleasant paths lead from the former military post down to Bell Point or up to the English Cemetery.

Lime Kiln Point State Park trails, on the western shore of the island, about 10 miles west of Friday Harbor. Rangers lead nature walks on trails with views.

San Juan County Park trails, 50 San Juan Park Drive, 2.5 miles north of Lime Kiln Point. Also trails with views here.

WHALE-WATCHING Five species of cetaceans inhabit or pass through these waters, and outfitters can help you see them. Summer tours mostly involve orcas, minke whales, and Dall's porpoises; spring brings gray whales; fall, the occasional humpback. You'll also see seals and seabirds at any time.

Lime Kiln Point State Park, also known as Whale Watch Park, on the western shore, about 10 miles west of Friday Harbor; and nearby **San Juan County Park,** 50 San Juan Park Drive, 2.5 miles north of Lime Kiln Point; both on San Juan Island. Of course, you could just go to these parks and watch from the bluffs for free. In summer the orcas cavort through Haro Strait, passing quite close to the shore.

Orcas Island Eclipse Charters (360-376-6566; www.orcasislandwhales.com), Box 353, Orcas Village 98280, at ferry landing, Orcas Island. Operates half-day, family-friendly boat excursions.

San Juan Excursions (800-809-4253; www.watchwhales.com), next to the ferry landing at Friday Harbor, San Juan Island. They "guarantee" whale sightings.

Western Prince Whale Watching (360-378-5315 or 800-757-6722; www.western prince.com), One Spring Street, Friday Harbor, San Juan Island. Offers afternoon trips daily, plus morning trips on weekends.

✳ Wilder Places

PARKS Lime Kiln Point State Park (360-902-8844), on the western shore, about 10 miles west of Friday Harbor, San Juan Island. Day-use only. Besides being a prime whale-viewing point (see *To Do—Whale-Watching*), the park is the site of a functioning 1919 lighthouse that also houses the Center for Whale Research (see *To See—Museums*). The point and park get their name from a lime operation active from the 1860s to the 1920s; limestone was quarried from adjacent deposits, and much of the island's forest was cut to fire the kilns that processed it into lime. Rangers are on-site in summer to lead nature walks and lighthouse tours.

Moran State Park (360-376-2326), 5 miles southeast of Eastsound, Orcas Island. In 1921 shipbuilder Robert Moran, who built Rosario (see *To See—Historic Homes*), donated some of his huge forest holdings to the state. The gift has since been expanded to 5,252 acres, by far the largest public tract in the islands. This jewel contains several lakes; Mount Constitution, at 2,407 feet the highest point in the San Juans; campgrounds; a bathing beach; 33 miles of trails; and luxuriant forest. Most of the tall and healthy forest is actually second growth, but a large tract on Mount Pickett was never logged, and the Mount Pickett Trail walks you among awesome old red cedars and Douglas firs.

KAYAKERS OFF LIME KILN POINT, SAN JUAN ISLAND

Obstruction Pass State Park (360-376-2326), just over 2 miles from Olga, Orcas Island; past Olga, turn left on Doe Bay Road, then in 0.5 mile turn right on Obstruction Pass Road and right again on Trailhead Road. Evergreen and madrona forest run the 0.5 mile from the parking lot to a bluff dropping sharply to a pebble beach at this 80-acre park—and so do you, since the road doesn't enter the park. Amenities consist of a walk-in campground (see *To Do—Camping*) with pit toilets and a mile or so of walking trails, plus eagles, ospreys, the splashing of wavelets on the beach, and pristine views of the islands and channels.

San Juan County Park (360-378-8420), 50 San Juan Park Drive, San Juan Island; 2.5 miles north of Lime Kiln Point. Another good whale-watching spot (see *To Do—Whale-Watching*), this 12-acre park has a campground, trails, a boat ramp, and moorage.

San Juan Island National Historic Park (360-378-2240; www.nps.gov/sajh), two sites on San Juan Island. **English Camp,** off West Valley Road on Westcott Bay, on the northwest end of the island, and **American Camp,** just off Cattle Point Road, on the southeast end, form this national park (see *To See—Historic Sites*). At American Camp, there's a small **visitors center** (360-378-2902) open 8:30–5 daily in summer; 8:30–4 or 4:30 daily in winter. It displays artifacts from the Pig War period that have come to light in archaeological digs.

Spencer Spit State Park (360-468-2251 or 888-226-7688), on Bakerview Road; about 1 mile southwest of the ferry landing, Lopez Island. Woodland trails lead to a spit beside a lagoon that attracts birds. Camping and boat moorage.

See also *To Do—Camping* and *Hiking.*

9778). Of the 172 named islands in the San Juan archipelago, 83 are designated national wildlife refuges, in full or in part. You are free to paddle around them and view the array of seals, sea lions, eagles, porpoises, and other abundant wildlife, but not to disturb the islands. Generally, you cannot land on them. However, several islands, including **Jones, Matia, Sucia, Patos,** and **James,** are state marine parks with trails, campsites, and mooring buoys (see *To Do—Boat Excursions*).

Shark Reef Sanctuary (360-378-8420; www.co.san-juan.wa.us), on Shark Reef Road 7.7 miles south of Lopez Village, Lopez Island. This rocky shore has lots of marine mammals and impressive views of the San Juan Channel and Olympic Mountains. Rough trails wander through the woods backing the shore. The park is one of the few relatively unaltered areas on Lopez.

✴ Lodging
BED & BREAKFASTS
Lopez Island
Aleck Bay Inn (360-468-3535; centurytel.net/abi), 45 Finch Lane. You can't get much more secluded than this place overlooking Aleck Bay and the Strait of Juan de Fuca and still have running water. Four snug guest rooms, some with sunrooms and/or fireplaces (and one with kayaks), look out to sea, inspiring the artists and writers who favor this spot. Rates include goodies on arrival and a full breakfast. Dinner also available for a fee. $149–198.

Edenwild Inn (800-606-0662; www .edenwildinn.com), 132 Lopez Road. Grand house, wraparound porch, gardens, sea . . . no wonder they call it Eden. Eight rooms or suites all have private baths and views; within walking distance of galleries, shops, and restaurants. Rates include expanded continental breakfast. Children over 12 welcome. No pets. $130–195.

Mackaye Harbor Inn (888-314-6140), 949 Mackaye Harbor Road. This renovated 1927 farmhouse overlooks Mackaye Harbor and its sandy beach. A dignified frame house on 4 acres with a wraparound porch, it invites you to sit and enjoy the view, and maybe take out a kayak. The five

guest rooms have water or garden views and private baths Rates include breakfast and use of mountain bikes. Consult about children. No pets. $135–235.

Orcas Island
⚓ **Kangaroo House Bed and Breakfast** (888-371-2175; www.kangaroo house.com), 1459 North Beach Road, Eastsound; 1 mile north of town. This spreading 1907 Craftsman house of wood and fieldstone has a large, lodge-like common room with riotous gardens behind. At one time you might have seen a kangaroo hopping around the premises—it was brought by a sea captain who owned the house in the 1950s. Three guest rooms and two suites have all amenities, including private baths. Rates include full breakfast. Children welcome. No pets. $155–195.

⚓ **Kingfish Inn** (360-376-2500; www .kingfishinn.com), 4362 Crow Valley Road, Eastsound. This out-of-the-way, old waterfront house sits above quiet West Sound—just a few miles from the amenities of Eastsound—but the restaurant downstairs (see *Where to Eat*) and the beach across the street mean you don't have to leave at all if you don't want to. Four guest rooms have king- or queen-sized beds, comfortable furnishings, water views, and private baths. Rates include a full breakfast. Children welcome. No pets. $157–197; two-night minimum in general.

Otter's Pond Bed and Breakfast (888-376-8844; www.otterspond.com), 100 Tomihi Drive, Box 1540, Eastsound 98245. A tranquil venue especially attractive to birders, Otter's Pond sits in the forest on—naturally—Otter's Pond, whose rushy margins are a magnet for herons, eagles, waterfowl (including the rare trumpeter swan), and numerous songbirds. The large neotraditional home has five big guest rooms, comfortable without being frilly, all with private baths and two with Wi-Fi. Owners Carl and Susan Silvernail live in a smaller home next door and will tell you all they know about the island, which is a considerable amount. They also offer delicious breakfasts (included in rates); the lemon soufflé pancakes are light and heavenly. No children or pets. $125–235; ask about specials.

☙ **Turtleback Farm Inn** (800-376-4914; www.turtlebackinn.com), 1981 Crow Valley Road, Eastsound; about 4 miles west of Eastsound. Secluded on its own farm, the imposing late-1800s house has seven elegantly relaxing guest rooms, while a second house out in the orchard has four even more luxurious king-bedded rooms. All have woolen comforters made from the sheep out in the pasture—you can actually buy a sheepskin if you want. Rates include full breakfast. Children welcome. No pets. $110–195 farmhouse rooms; $225–260 Orchard House.

San Juan Island
Dragonfly Inn (360-378-4280 or 877-378-4280; www.thedragonflyinn.com), 4770 Roche Harbor Road, Friday Harbor. Tucked into the woods halfway down the island's east side, there's something completely different. Wend your way up the driveway (*up* is the operative word), and you'll come face-to-face with a Japanese *ryokan*, or traditional inn. Owner Robert Butler spent years living and working in Japan and gained a deep appreciation for Japanese culture and esthetics. Com-

THE POND AT OTTER'S POND BED AND BREAKFAST, ORCAS ISLAND

ing back to the United States, he meticulously created his dream: a hostelry in the Japanese style, from architecture to interior decor. Of course, there are some concessions: You get your own bath rather than sharing one, and breakfast is Asian fusion. (Potato–smoked salmon galette? I think we can live with that.) Four rooms with your own *yukata* (robe) and exquisite furnishings. $175–230; closed Nov.–Jan.

🐾 **Harrison House Suites** (360-378-3587 or 800-407-7933; www .harrisonhousesuites.com), 275 C Street, Friday Harbor. A 1905 restored Craftsman house has been redone into very comfortable (as in Persian rugs and crystal chandeliers) suites sleeping 4–10. All have private baths and kitchens. Friendly owners Anna Maria de Freitas and David Pass are avid outdoors enthusiasts, and besides caring for your comfort, they will advise you on diving, kayaking, and other active options. Rates include full breakfast, which is taken in the shared dining room of the Tucker House Bed and Breakfast (see below). Children welcome. Pets allowed for a fee. $100–400.

Olympic Lights Bed and Breakfast (360-378-2783 or 888-211-6195; www .olympiclights.com), 146 Starlight Way, Friday Harbor. Sitting in a field looking out to sea, this 1895 frame house could be a lighthouse minus the tower. In fact, it was Andy and Isabelle Johnson's farmhouse, where they raised 11 children. Their homestead of 320 acres and a mile of waterfront was very successful. But gone are the hardscrabble days; the four guest rooms (three upstairs) are arranged for your comfort with king or queen beds, down comforters, private bathrooms, and hair dryers (which the Johnsons certainly never dreamed of). The views, of

course, are magnificent. Rates include full breakfast. No children or pets. $105–165.

&. *♪* **Tucker House Bed and Breakfast** (360-378-2783 or 800-965-0123; www.tuckerhouse.com), 275 C Street, Friday Harbor. Right next door to Harrison House Suites (see above) and also owned by Anna Maria de Freitas, this renovated Victorian home in downtown Friday Harbor has six guest rooms, two suites, and two cottages, all spacious and impressively furnished. Quiet and private, it has several common areas, including gardens, a patio, a sunroom, a living room, and a computer available to guests. Breakfasts (included in the rates) are huge and delectable. Children welcome. Pets allowed in cottages. $100–400.

COTTAGES AND CABINS

Lopez Island
Bay House and Garden Cottages (360-468-4889), Box 602, Lopez Island 98261. A two-bedroom house is on Fisherman's Bay, and two cozy wood cottages in Lopez Village will remind you of a captain's cabin. Pets allowed for a fee. House $200; cottages $150.

Blue Fjord Cabins (888-633-0401), 862 Elliott Road. Two comfortably furnished chalets are in the woods on Jasper Bay. $150; ask about extended-stay discount.

Lopez Farm Cottages and Tent Camping (800-440-3556; www.lopez farmcottages.com), 555 Fisherman Bay Road. Five "Northwest Scandinavian" cottages come with continental breakfast. No children under 14. No pets. $170–215. See also *To Do—Camping.*

Lopez Village Properties (360-468-5057 or 888-772-9735; www.lopez villageproperties.com), Box 550, Lopez Island 98261. Contact them for more choices.

Orcas Island

Coho Lodge (360-376-2242; www .bartwoodlodge.com), 178 Fossil Bay Drive, Eastsound. Formerly the Bartwood Lodge, the Coho is on the quiet northern shore of Orcas. It offers 16 motel rooms either on the waterfront or the patio. Simple but clean and affordable. No pets. $99–189.

♪ Orcas Hotel (360-376-4300 or 888-672-2792; www.orcashotel.com), Box 369, 8 Orcas Hill Road, Orcas Landing. You can't miss it. It's the white frame house with the red roof looking out at you when you arrive on the ferry. On the National Register of Historic Places, it's been a hostelry since 1904. Twelve cozy rooms furnished with antiques overlook either the harbor or the village. Some rooms have shared baths. An on-site restaurant (see *Where to Eat*) serves breakfast and dinner. Children welcome. No pets. $89–218.

Outlook Inn (360-376-2200 or 888-688-5665; www.outlookinn.com), Main Street, Eastsound. As the Seattle area "settled up" after statehood, wealthier Seattleites sought out the seclusion of the islands as a respite from the labors of empire building. The Outlook Inn was one of their early havens—a 22-room hotel built in 1891 with a terrific view down Eastsound. They would come up by steamer or paddleboat from Seattle and enjoy venison steaks and the view from the veranda. Renovated and updated, the rooms still have Victorian simplicity—in-room sinks and shared baths—but with pillow-top mattresses and down comforters (and the same bay views, of course). The whole has the calm air of an English seaside hotel, with an on-site restaurant (see *Where to Eat*). Two new buildings have dignified motel-style rooms and luxury suites, all with private baths. Rates are among the most reasonable on the island. No pets. Original hotel rooms $59–99; motel-style rooms $89–209; suites $129–309.

San Juan Island

Friday's Historic Inn (800-352-2632; www.friday-harbor.com), 35 First Street, Friday Harbor. Friday's is another early island retreat, dating from 1891. Nice touches are the garden courtyard and in-floor radiant heat—not, probably, an original feature. Fifteen rooms range from simply but tastefully appointed economy and standard rooms (some share baths) to luxury suites, all including continental breakfast. Rooms $59–129; suites $159–269.

Hotel de Haro (360-378-2155 or 800-451-8910; www.rocheharbor.com), 248 Reuben Memorial Drive, Roche Harbor. John McMillin built this fine clapboard hotel with three floors and balconies in 1886 next to his newly acquired cement company. It's still taking guests. Though some of the walls are alarmingly canted and floors have a list, the rooms are cozy in a 19th-century frontier way—small but well furnished, with shared baths. Teddy Roosevelt even stopped here. In the lobby, you can still see the logs of the old Hudson's Bay cabin around which the hotel was built. There are also suites with private baths and 9 two-bedroom cottages, originally built to house kiln workers. Rooms $70–100; suites $121–183; cottages $130–250.

HOSTELS

Orcas Island

♪ Doe Bay Resort and Retreat (360-376-2291; www.doebay.com), Box 437, Olga 98279. Formerly a Hosteling International hostel, this resort has been upgraded, although it still retains some of its renowned "alternative" character. Thirty acres of wild Salish

Sea waterfront, including a small beach and hidden waterfall, hold a choice of accommodations—cabins, yurts, dorms, and campsites—though at the time of this writing, the dorm rooms, both communal and private, definitely lagged behind the bright new cabins and organic café (see *Where to Eat*), and the shared guest kitchen lacked all but the barest utensils. (There's a larger common kitchen in one of the bathhouses.) People come for the breathtaking location and the added availability of a sauna, outdoor hot tubs fed by deep hot springs, a massage, yoga, and kayaking. Cabins $80–200; yurts $85–120; dorms $45–55; campsites $45–55.

San Juan Island

Juniper Lane Guest House (360-378-7761 or 888-397-2597; www .juniperlaneguesthouse.com), 1312 Beaver Valley Road, Friday Harbor. Juniper Maas backpacked around the world before coming home and buying this property, which she then proceeded to renovate and decorate in the manner of guesthouses she had stayed in worldwide. (It sounds easy but involved virtually complete reconstruction.) When you come up the hill and see the cedar-shingled house flying a PLANET EARTH flag, you're there. It's now more boutique than backpacker: Gone are the dorm rooms, but the decor remains colorful and international. Accommodations range from private doubles to family rooms sleeping six or seven to a cabin that sleeps four. Like a hostel, it has a common kitchen and living room, except they're prettier than most. Although almost everything was made of salvaged materials, much energy has gone into art and decor, one room having a Mexican design, another African, and so forth. If you can imagine boutique democratized, this is it. Rooms $65–135 (discount for more than one night); cabin $185–199.

Wayfarer's Rest (360-378-6428; www.rockisland.com/~wayfarersrest), 35 Malcolm Street, Friday Harbor. A budget option within walking distance of the ferry landing, Wayfarer's has hostel beds and rustic guest cabins (one of which is half cabin, half sailboat). Clean and orderly, with a common kitchen and shared baths, its atmosphere is cheery, and in season you can have fresh greens from the garden. Walk-ins are welcome; all the same, it gets tight in the summer, so it's best to call ahead. Children welcome. Dorm beds $30 (linens provided); private rooms from $80.

MOTELS

San Juan Island

Orca Inn (360-378-2724 or 877-541-6722; www.orcainn.com), 770 Mullis Street, Friday Harbor. Okay, so it isn't hip, chic, or elegant; in fact it looks more like a series of barracks, which is not unlikely. But it's the cheapest place for a private room on an expensive island, and while the rooms are tiny, they all have private baths and even TVs. Rooms come in full, queen, king, and double-queen size (14 by 11 feet and 14 by 22 feet), so you can bring the kids. And so what if it's near the island airport: The planes are tiny, and they stop running at night. $49–99, with frequent specials.

RESORTS

Orcas Island

Rosario Resort and Spa (360-376-2222; www.rockresorts.com), 1400 Rosario Road, Eastsound. As the dream home of Seattle city councilman Robert Moran (and quite a dream home it is, worth a tour in itself; see *To Do— Historic Homes*), Rosario is on the National Register of Historic Places. The 1906 mansion no longer houses guests—today's accommodations are in the 127 rooms and cabins scattered on the nearby grounds and hillsides—but you can still enjoy the same wooded shoreline and magnificent views that drew Moran to the spot. The mansion is now partly a museum but also contains a restaurant, lounge (check out the fireplace), and spa. Children under 18 free. No pets. $89–359.

✷ Where to Eat

DINING OUT

Lopez Island

Bay Café (360-468-3700; www.bay -café.com), 9 Old Post Road. Open from 5:30 PM Wed.–Sun. The Bay Café is Lopez's ambitious dining venue, featuring traditional island favorites such as clams, prawns, and fish—all from lovely local waters—and quality meats. Reservations recommended.

Orcas Island

New Leaf Café (360-376-2200; www.newleafcafeorcas.com), Main Street, Eastsound. Open for breakfast and dinner daily. The glassed-in veranda of the Victorian Outlook Inn (see *Lodging*) is the quintessential seaside dining room. Chef Steve Debaste composes meals from organic produce, free-range meats, and fresh regional seafood as the seasons allow, and he does an artistic job both gastronomically and visually. Reservations recommended.

Octavia's Bistro (360-376-4300 or 888-672-2792; www.orcashotel.com), Orcas Landing. In the venerable Orcas Hotel (see *Lodging*), you can dine on Octavia's Northwest steaks and seafood while looking out over the English gardens and the water. The **Orcas Hotel Café** is another option.

San Juan Island

Backdoor Kitchen (360-378-9540), 400 A Street, Friday Harbor. Open from 5 PM Wed.–Sat., 11:30–2:30 Mon. This locally popular café experiments with eclectic choices—on a given day, you may find curries, Vietnamese noodles, chalupas, and smoked salmon

EASTSOUND, VIEWED FROM MADRONA POINT ON ORCAS ISLAND, OFFERS SEVERAL FINE RESTAURANTS.

with goat cheese on the same menu. In summer, you can eat in the garden. Dinner reservations recommended.

Duck Soup Inn (360-378-4878; www.ducksoupinn.com), 50 Duck Soup Lane, Friday Harbor. Open 5–10 Tues.–Sun. in summer, Wed.–Sun. in June, Sat.–Sun. in spring and fall. It ain't cheap, but it is creative, based on mostly island produce and local seafood and meats, all artistically combined by chef-owner Gretchen Allison (who also offers cooking classes). Set in the woods 4 miles from town, it's definitely the spot for an elegant, leisurely dinner. And with the painting of Groucho Marx at a bowl of duck soup in the entryway, what's not to like? Reservations recommended.

McMillin's (360-378-5757), 248 Reuben Memorial Drive, Roche Harbor. Open 5–10 daily. Like Lime Kiln Point down the coast, Roche Harbor was the site of busy lime kilns a hundred years ago. This white gingerbread house was the home of the company's owner, John McMillin, who became quite a magnate—at one point the company owned 4,000 acres and 12 miles of shoreline. Today the restaurant sitting right on the harbor offers a traditional menu of prime rib, steaks, and seafood as the boats come in and go out. Reservations recommended.

The Place (360-378-8707; www.the placefridayharbor.com), One Spring Street, Friday Harbor. Open from 5 PM Thurs.–Tues. Right on the waterfront (maybe it should have been called The Plaice?), and priced accordingly, this restaurant serves a balanced selection of marine, terrestrial, and vegetarian dishes, often with an Asian touch and mostly from local sources. Well, except for the New Zealand lamb chops. Reservations recommended.

Orcas Island

Café Olga and Artworks (360-376-4408), 11 Point Lawrence Road, Olga. Open 9–4 daily in summer; 9–3 Thurs.–Tues. in fall and winter; closed Jan. It's at a country crossroads seemingly in the middle of nowhere, in an old strawberry-processing barn that looks the part, but the gravel lot is usually full, and you may have a (brief) wait. If so, you can browse the art gallery and shop (open 10–6 daily), which occupy most of the airy, renovated space. Like many Orcas cafés, Olga prides itself on fresh, wholesome foods tastily prepared. The black bean soup and salad are just piquant enough. The lox and cream cheese plate are also tempting, but leave room for homemade pie, which takes full advantage of local succulent berries and sells like, er, hotcakes.

Chimayo (360-376-6394), 123 North Beach Street, Eastsound. Open 11–3 and 5–9 Mon.–Sat. If you want a change from seafood, little Chimayo is ready to serve you fresh New Mexican cuisine for lunch or dinner. At the moment. Owner Bill Patterson, who bought the place in 2010, has a passion for Tuscan dishes and has been surreptitiously slipping them into the menu. Which does up the price a bit. Homemade pasta! Crab ravioli! And, actually, seafood. His goal is to transition gracefully to a Tuscan menu, but he'll probably serve a few tamales or quesadillas for old times' sake.

Doe Bay Café (360-376-2291; www .doebay.com), 107 Doe Bay Road, Doe Bay. Open for breakfast, lunch, and dinner daily in summer, Fri.–Mon. in spring, and Sat.–Mon. in winter (but always for pizza on Thurs.). The resort is upwardly mobile funky (see *Lodging*), but the café has arrived. With organic food produced in its own garden, local farms, or the bay out back, its menu changes daily, and it's all good "slow food"—also all vegetarian or seafood. Three meals daily; desserts are to die for.

Inn at Ship Bay (360-376-5886; www.innatshipbay.com), 326 Olga Road, Eastsound. Open from 5:30 PM Tues.–Sat. This restaurant at a posh new bed & breakfast offers Northwest cuisine, both new and experimental, with some Asian touches and a great view. Reservations recommended.

Kingfish Inn–Westsound Café (360-376-4440; www.westsoundcafe.com), 4362 Crow Valley Road, West Sound. Open for breakfast and dinner Wed.–Sun. The café, with its deck overlooking West Sound, serves as the breakfast room for guests at the inn (see *Lodging*), but you can sup here even if you're not an overnight guest. Breakfasts are hearty, and dinners are informal, with burgers, sandwiches, and fish.

Luna's (360-376-2335), 325 Prune Alley, Eastsound. Open 1:30–9 Mon.–Sat. This is the latest incarnation of a string of businesses on this site, having opened in 2010; still basic Italian. So far reviews have been mixed, but it's family-friendly and offers gluten-free options, which you don't always find.

Portofino (360-376-2085; www .portofinopizzeria.com), 274 A Street, Eastsound. Open 11:30–8:30 Mon.–Sat., 4:30–8 Sun. Just like the real Portofino, this place also has a water view, although the waters here are markedly cooler. A casual favorite of bicyclists and other active types, it serves 11 generously topped varieties of pizza, with thick or thin crust, for lunch and dinner. The aromas floating into the street will draw you inexorably in.

San Juan Island

The Bean Café (360-370-5858; www.thebeancafe.com), 150B First Street, Friday Harbor. Open 7–5 daily. Is your pocketbook tired of expensive haute cuisine? Pop into the Bean, a spacious but comfortably homey café, for perfectly edible soups, sandwiches, cookies, or just a cup of coffee. Stay as long as you like; there's free Wi-Fi. Outdoor seating in summer.

Cannery House (360-378-6505), 174 First Street North, Friday Harbor. Open 7–4 daily. Here's another option for good, simple, affordable food, in an old cannery overlooking the harbor. It serves mostly chowder and a variety of sandwiches (and breakfast). Order at the counter and take a seat, preferably on the terrace.

✎ **Downriggers** (360-378-2700), 10 Front Street, Friday Harbor. Open for lunch and dinner daily, breakfast Sat.–Sun. Downriggers has a straightforward menu of regional fish and other seafood, plus beef and pasta dishes for landlubbers. Not as chic as the nearby Place, but it has been a dining landmark for ages and is kid-friendly.

✎ **Lime Kiln Café** (800-451-8910), 248 Reuben Memorial Drive, Roche Harbor. Open 7–4 daily. Eat homemade doughnuts, burgers, sandwiches, and fish-and-chips on the patio overlooking busy Roche Harbor.

Maloula (360-378-8485; www.maloula .com), One Front Street, Friday Harbor. Open 11:30–3 and 5:30–9 Thurs.–Tues. Apr.–Sept. Adnan Nasrullah has been serving Middle Eastern food here since 1992, from kibbeh and falafel to rack of lamb and tofu souvlaki (vegetarians, how's that?), with an occasional salmon thrown in for those who have to eat Northwest.

✳ Entertainment

THEATER Island Stage Left (360-378-5649; www.islandstageleft.org), 1062 Wold Road, Friday Harbor. Performances of traditional and experimental plays are staged outdoors. Free.

Orcas Center (360-376-2281; www .orcascenter.org), 917 Mount Baker Road, Eastsound. This 213-seat theater plus gallery is the venue for Orcas's lively performing arts lineup, which runs the gamut from the Orcas Chamber Music Festival to Cashore Marionettes to national and international performers such as Cantabile. The center also offers many and varied workshops for practicing and aspiring artists.

San Juan Community Theatre (360-378-3210), 100 Second Street, Friday Harbor. Offers traditional and experimental plays.

✳ Selective Shopping

POTTERY Orcas has been a haven for artists since the mid-20th century, when nobody wanted to live in its isolation and long, dark winters.

Crow Valley Pottery (360-376-4260 or 877-512-8184; www.crowvalley .com), 2274 Orcas Road, Eastsound. Open 10–5 daily in summer. This place has been around since 1959, housed in an 1866 log cabin. The work of 70 creators—mostly potters but also glass and jewelry artists—covers the walls and shelves of the tiny cabin in a dizzying variety of styles and colors.

Orcas Island Pottery (360-376-2813; www.orcasislandpottery.com), 338 Old Pottery Road, Eastsound. Open 10–5

daily. This place goes back even further, nearly 70 years. Getting here is half the experience, involving a couple of miles of narrow dirt roads through tall cedar forest. Suddenly the forest opens onto a little cabin complex with dazzling pots everywhere—on picnic tables, on interior and exterior walls, on shelves, and in studios. The location on a bluff plunging to President Channel doesn't hurt either.

SENSE AND SCENTS **Griffin Bay Bookstore** (360-378-5511; www .griffinbaybooks.com), Friday Harbor. While away an hour or an afternoon browsing a fine collection or attend an author reading.

Pelindaba (866-819-1911), 150 First Street, Friday Harbor. Here you can browse the fragrant items handcrafted at Pelindaba Lavender Farm (see *To See—Farms and Gardens*).

✳ Special Events

June: **San Juan Island Artists' Studio Tour** (artists@sanjuanislandartists .com; www.sanjuanislandartists.com), various studios around the island.

July: **San Juan Lavender Festival** (www.pelindaba.com), Pelindaba Lavender Farm and other locations on San Juan Island.

August: **Orcas Island Chamber Music Festival** (360-376-6636; www .oicmf.org), Orcas Center (see *Entertainment*), Eastsound.

BELLINGHAM, BLAINE, AND LYNDEN AREA

Drive along Chuckanut Drive with views worthy of Big Sur and up through newly chic Bellingham to the Peace Arch at the Canadian border, a route always accompanied by unparalleled expanses of salt water and salt air, with wild islands offshore. One of those islands is Lummi, officially one of the San Juan Islands, though a lesser-known one; it is reached by ferry from Bellingham.

North of town along I-5 are Ferndale and Blaine, at the border. East of Bellingham are Maple Falls and Glacier, on the Mount Baker Highway. At the edge of the national forest on the road to Mount Baker, the tiny village of Glacier is a natural base for exploration, with several types of accommodations. Also inland but right up against the border are Lynden and little Everson, amid farmland and dairies in the Nooksack River valley.

GUIDANCE **Bellingham–Whatcom County Tourism** (360-671-3990 or 800-487-2032; www.bellingham.org), 904 Potter Street, Bellingham 98229.

Blaine Chamber of Commerce (360-332-4544 or 800-624-3555), 728 Peace Portal Drive, Blaine 98230.

Lynden Chamber of Commerce (360-354-5995), 518 Front Street, Lynden 98264.

GETTING THERE At the northern reaches of the **I-5** corridor are Bellingham, Ferndale, and Blaine. Prettier back roads include **WA 542** east toward Mount Baker, with Maple Falls and Glacier en route; north-south **WA 9** connecting Sedro-Woolley with Lynden; and other smaller highways in between.

Bellingham International Airport (360-676-2500), 4255 Mitchell Way, has several daily connections to Seattle and Salt Lake City.

AMTRAK (800-USA-RAIL; www.amtrak.com) serves the Seattle–Vancouver, British Columbia, corridor with a stop in Bellingham. The train terminal is at the **Fairhaven Station,** 401 Harris Avenue, Bellingham.

Greyhound (360-733-5251 or 800-231-2222; www.greyhound.com) runs four times daily between Seattle and Vancouver, British Columbia, stopping in

Bellingham. The bus terminal is at the **Fairhaven Station,** 401 Harris Avenue, Bellingham.

Alaska State Car Ferry (800-382-9229; www.akferry.com) runs to southeast Alaska twice a week in summer and once a week in winter from **Bellingham Cruise Terminal,** adjacent to Fairhaven Station (see AMTRAK and Greyhound above).

Border crossings to or from Canada can involve a longish wait, especially in summer, especially returning south. Remember that passports are required for entering or reentering the United States from Canada by land, sea, or air.

GETTING AROUND Airporter/Bellair Baker Shuttle (866-235-5247; www .airporter.com), 1416 Whitehorn Street, Ferndale. This runs from Bellingham up to Mount Baker daily in ski season; reservations recommended.

Whatcom Chief (360-676-6692), from Gooseberry Point, Bellingham, to Lummi Island. The six-minute ferry ride operates daily, with 38 runs Mon.–Fri. and morning runs Sat.–Sun. $4 per pedestrian, $10 per car.

Whatcom Transportation Authority (360-676-RIDE; www.ridewta.com), 4111 Bakerview Spur, Bellingham. Serves Bellingham and Whatcom County as far north as Blaine and Lynden.

MEDICAL EMERGENCY St. Joseph Hospital (360-734-5400), 2901 Squalicum Parkway, Bellingham.

✳ To See

FARMERS' MARKETS Bellingham Farmers' Market (360-647-2060; www .bellinghamfarmers.org). Two locations: at Railroad and Chestnut streets, Bellingham, open 10–3 Sat. Apr.–Dec.; at Village Green, Fairhaven, open 12–5 Wed. June–Sept. Produce, crafts, and street musicians.

Lummi Island Farmers' Market (360-758-2711), 2106 South Nugent Road, outside Islander Store. Open 10–1 Sat. May–Sept.

HISTORIC HOMES Every Northwest town seems to have its advantageously located neighborhood where wealthy city boosters settled on the principle of first come, first served. In Bellingham, this is the **Eldridge Avenue District,** with its terrific bay views and many fine homes built between 1885 and 1920 in a variety of (often vernacular) Victorian styles. About 50 city blocks in the neighborhood consist mainly of fine and/or historic homes, which makes for a nice stroll. The district was originally the land donation claim of city fathers Edward Eldridge and Henry Roeder. The **Eldridge Historical District Map** (www.cob.org) is available online. Here are some highlights.

George Bacon House, 2001 Eldridge Avenue, Bellingham. Particularly notable is this home, designed by George's cousin Henry Bacon in 1906. Henry was an eminent architect who also designed the Lincoln Memorial in Washington, D.C., and the Bacon House does have a sort of translated neoclassical look—what a Greek temple might look like if it had a wood frame. George had done quite well himself in the real estate and home loan business since coming to Whatcom as a young man, and the house stayed in the family till 1938. It is still a private home.

Pickett House (360-734-1827), 910 Bancroft Street, Bellingham. Open 1–4 second Sun. each month or by appointment. Donation requested. Captain George Pickett of the Ninth Infantry was sent up here to reassure settlers who feared raids by the coastal Indians of British Columbia, and he built this stockadelike house in 1856 in what was then known as Fort Bellingham. Although it's seen some additions since its beginnings as a 15-by-25-foot house, its essential structure is the same, and its undressed planks give us an idea of the city's earliest appearance. It is the oldest house standing in Bellingham. Pickett left the area in 1861, joined the Confederate army, and led Pickett's charge at the Battle of Gettysburg.

Roland Gamwell House, 1001 16th Street, Bellingham (Fairhaven). This is surely one of the most fantastical homes a Bellingham businessman could have conceived—a graduate of MIT and an insurance agent, no less. Actually he capitalized on the real estate boom and brought out a pair of Boston architects to build his nine-room, three-story, gabled, porched, columned, even cupola'd abode. Inside, a hand-carved oak staircase spans all three floors, relieved by stained-glass windows. It's still a private residence, so admire it from the outside.

Victor Roeder Home (360-733-2900), 2600 Sunset Drive, Bellingham. This home was completed in 1908 by the son of one of Bellingham's founding fathers. The very solid, imposing house with its outer stone chimney, inside oak paneling, murals, and central vacuum-cleaning system (!) is now used as an arts center by Whatcom County.

HISTORIC SITES Black Mountain Forestry Center (360-599-2776), at Silver Lake County Park, 9006 Silver Lake Road, Maple Falls. Grounds open 12–4 Sat.–Sun. Memorial Day–Labor Day; tours 1 PM Sun. Free. This is a joint venture of Whatcom County and Crown Pacific. The grounds outside display massive early logging equipment, while seven buildings focus on various aspects of forestry, from reforestation to forest products. The Gerdrum Museum (see *Museums*) is a centerpiece building here.

Fairhaven Carnegie Library, 1117 12th Street, Bellingham. Open 2–6 Tues–Sat. Free. This is one of several Carnegie libraries around the state that still serve as public libraries. Step in here for the familiar library hush or to use the computers.

Mount Baker Theater, 104 North Commercial Street, Bellingham. The red-lettered white tower stands over the Eldridge Avenue District like a beacon, calling the citizens to entertainment since 1927. Built by 20th Century Fox and designed by architect R. C. Reamer, who designed the Old Faithful Lodge in Yellowstone National Park, it's been in continuous theatrical use since then.

MV *Plover* (360-332-4844), Blaine Visitors' Dock, Blaine. Donation accepted. This is not exactly a place, but it's on the National Register of Historic Places. The 32-foot wooden boat used to ferry workers from Blaine to the cannery on Semiahmoo Spit. Now it's the oldest working foot ferry in the state, carrying up to 17 passengers at a time across Semiahmoo Bay. It looks rather like an old lobster boat. Use it to commute from what is now Semiahmoo Resort (see *Lodging*) to town or to view seals and seabirds.

Nelson Building, opposite the Mount Baker Theater, (see above). Currently private offices, this was a bank from 1900 to the early 1930s. During renovations in the 1970s, a skeleton was found in the foundation, testimony perhaps to the less savory aspects of the Wild West.

Old City Hall, 121 Prospect Street, Bellingham. This massive town landmark dwarfs the surrounding buildings. Completed in 1892, just before the worldwide financial collapse, its red brick and square turrets reflected the ambition and optimism not only of the Gay Nineties but of the Northwest as the last episode of American empire building (there's a reason why AMTRAK's Chicago-to-Seattle run is called the Empire Builder). Despite all vicissitudes, it remained City Hall for 40 years before the city moved to new quarters. In 1941 it became the local history and art museum, and it's still part of the now larger Whatcom Museum complex (see *Museums*).

Peace Arch (360-332-8221), Blaine; from I-5 take exit 276 just before the Canadian border. The 67-foot white concrete arch on the U.S.-Canada border was the brainchild of the same Sam Hill who built the Stonehenge replica in the Columbia Gorge (see part 5, Line of Fire: The Cascades). Just as Hill, a Quaker, had built his Stonehenge as a monument to Klickitat County's World War I dead, so he conceived the Peace Arch to frame, as it were, the happy post-1812 treaties providing for a nonmilitarized border between the United States and Canada. These treaties were signed in 1814 and 1817, but the arch wasn't built until 1920–1921; evidently Hill was the first to have thought much about it. In summer, a juried sculpture exhibition adorns the lawns, gardens, and picnic tables surrounding the arch.

Pioneer Park (360-384-4302), 2002 Cherry Street, Ferndale. Open 11:30–4 Tues.–Sun. mid-May–mid-Sept. Fourteen original log cabins from locations around Whatcom County are furnished with pioneers' objects of daily life.

Richards Building, 1308 E Street, Bellingham. This brick structure was thrown up as a general store and bank during the Fraser gold rush of 1858; the barely existent town was a prospectors' jumping-off place. However, the rush stopped almost as soon as it started, and this place was sold to Whatcom County, which used it for a time as a courthouse; now it houses a private business. It's not a terribly prepossessing building, being a simple frontier block, but it was placed on the National Register of Historic Places in 2003.

Terminal Building, northeast corner of 11th and Harris, Bellingham. The oldest surviving commercial building in Fairhaven dates from 1888. Fairhaven was yet another town that, having sprung nearly full-blown from the soil in 1889, bid fair to become the next railroad terminus and thus the "next Chicago." In the frenzy, like the other towns it vied with, it became a schizophrenic frontier town, with respectable trading families at one end, saloons and bordellos at the other, and a weekly cattle drive through town. Like the other towns, too, it was disappointed in its ambitions and sank into somnolence. The Terminal Building served first as a saloon and pool hall, then a drugstore, and since the 1930s as a bar or restaurant.

MUSEUMS ✍ **American Museum of Radio and Electricity** (360-738-3886; amre.us), 1312 Bay Street, Bellingham. Open 11–4 Wed.–Sat., 12–4 Sun. $5 adults, $2 children under 12. Begun from the collections of co-curators and radio enthusiasts Jonathan Winter and John Jenkins, this fun, homegrown museum has expanded to occupy an entire downtown storefront and is taking over the adjacent space, too. Rare antique radios; thousands of vacuum tubes; original Marconi transmitters; a reproduction of Ben Franklin's lab, including some of his own equipment; and many more devices jostle one another to follow the thread linking the exploration of electricity to radio communications. It's a fascinating jaunt from 17th-century parlor tricks through the golden age of radio—there's even a 1930s living room set up with recordings of *The Green Hornet*. Did you know a wireless phone was offered for sale in 1909? The mission of the museum is to show or remind people "how things work"; to this end, several exhibits are hands-on. It's helpful to take a guided tour for full benefit.

✈ **Bellingham Railway Museum** (360-393-7540; www.bellinghamrailway museum.org), 1320 Commercial Street, Bellingham. Open 12–5 Tues. and Thurs.– Sat. $4 adults, $2 students, $7 families, children under two free. Although the major railroad termini went to Tacoma and Seattle, trains did come to Bellingham, carrying coal for Canada, wood to the docks, and construction equipment to dam sites. The museum is a small but eager space, with a photo presentation of railway history in Skagit and Whatcom counties, plus several toy train collections and lay-outs of various model trains. There's even a Thomas the Tank Engine play area for younger enthusiasts and a high-tech train simulator—why settle for flight simula-tors when you could "drive" a locomotive? For the real hobbyists, the museum presents lectures, history walks, and trips focused on all aspects of Washington's railroads.

Drayton Harbor Maritime Museum/Alaska Packers' Association Museum (360-371-3558), Semiahmoo Spit, Blaine. Open 1–5 Fri.–Sun. May–Sept. Semiah-moo made its fortune, for a time, canning fish. This museum details this marine legacy.

Gerdrum Museum (360-599-2623), in Silver Lake County Park, 9006 Silver Lake Road, Maple Falls. Open 12–4 Sat.–Sun. in summer. Norwegian immigrant Embert Gerdrum built this house of a single cedar he felled in 1894. Inside, it's furnished as a prosperous homestead would have been back then—pots and pans on the kitchen wall, solid bedstead in the bedroom—though the track lighting makes it clear that this is a museum.

Lynden Pioneer Museum (360-354-3675; www.lyndenpioneermuseum.com), 217 Front Street, Lynden. Open 10–4 Mon.–Sat., 1:30–5 Sun. $7 adults, $4 seniors and students, free Sun. A hundred or so years ago, contingents of Dutch immi-grants converged, for some reason, on this far corner of the country and took a large part in building its dairy and berry industries. Here, 5 miles south of Canada, this museum celebrates the community's pioneer, especially Dutch, heritage. A large (28,000-square-foot) museum in a small town, it showcases western pre–World War II rural life through life-sized replicas of Lynden's downtown circa 1900, a farmhouse, and a milking parlor, as well as antique buggies, cars, and farm implements. In true Amsterdam spirit, the museum also lends out bikes for those who wish to explore this cycle-friendly town on two wheels!

Mindport Exhibits (360-647-5614; www.mindport.org), 210 West Holly, Belling-ham. Open 12–6 Wed.–Fri., 10–5 Sat., 12–5 Sun. $2. This is a private, experimen-tal museum. Why experimental? Well, you get not only to look at the works but often to interact with them as well, at the intersection of art and science—creating rhythms by rearranging magnets, for example. In addition to the interactive gallery, the "regular" gallery features contemporary Washington art.

Whatcom Museum of History and Art (360-778-8390; www.whatcommuseum .org), 121 Prospect Street, Bellingham. $10 for all buildings. Centered in the grandiose Old City Hall (see *Historic Sites*), the museum actually occupies four buildings along Prospect Street: the Lightcatcher, a new, translucent arc housing most of the museum's fine arts collection, plus the Family Interactive Gallery, where kids and parents can get involved with exhibits; the Old City Hall itself, three floors of red brick and square turrets, with permanent and changing exhibits on local and regional architecture and history; and the Syre Education Building, whose photographic archives alone run to 150,000 historic images, and which contains ethnographic and historic exhibits. Lightcatcher is open 12–5 Thurs.–Sun.; Old City Hall, 12–5 Tues.–Sun; Syre Education Building, 1–4:45 Wed.–Fri. The fourth building, the ARCO exhibits building (360-676-6981), at 206 Prospect Street, houses large art installations. Open 12–5 Tues.–Sun. Free.

NATURAL WONDERS Point Roberts, about 10 miles due west of Blaine. When the U.S.-Canada border was drawn along the 49th parallel, nobody thought about this landform. It extends south from British Columbia into the Strait of Georgia and happens to reach about 2 miles south of the said parallel. So the little 5-square-mile point is actually part of the state of Washington, though since there's no ferry service to it, you can reach it only through Canada. And though it's only about 20 miles by road from the Peace Arch at Blaine, the trip involves two border crossings each way, a process that can be cumbersome and time-consuming in these times. It's even more so for the residents who have to make such trips to attend school, visit the doctor, and do many other humdrum tasks.

SCENIC DRIVES Chuckanut Drive, 21 paved miles from Burlington north to Bellingham's Fairhaven District. Winding along the undulating coast, sometimes along tidal flats and sometimes under cliffs, WA 11 offers panoramas of Puget Sound and the San Juan Islands. You'll pass inns and oyster bars on the way, as well as Larrabee State Park (see *Wilder Places—Parks*). The drive began as a logging road when most transportation in the area was by water, for good reason: The coastline was rugged, muddy, and densely forested. It took 16 years to pave the 10 miles from Fairhaven south to Blanchard; it opened in 1921 and by 1929 had put the Interurban Railway, which ran alongside it, out of business.

Mount Baker Highway, 58 paved miles from Bellingham to Mount Baker. WA 542 starts at sea level and rises through the Nooksack River valley through farmland and cedar forest to the rugged slopes of 10,775-foot Mount Baker, one of the few volcanoes of the North Cascades. Mount Baker is surrounded by lesser but still impressive peaks. The end of the road is at Artist's Point—so named for obvious reasons—at about 5,000 feet, though the road may not be fully cleared of snow till mid-July.

WALKING TOURS Fairhaven Walking Tour Map, available from the **Old Fairhaven Association,** 1106 Harris Avenue, Fairhaven. This tour takes you past the buildings listed under *Historic Sites* and more, as well as a series of historical markers. These detail where, for example, a battle between Spaniards and Indians took place in the 1600s and where a Spanish silver chalice was found; the site of an Indian campground from 1500 B.C.; where the railroad was that shipped coal from nearby mines to Canada; and a couple of dozen other points of interest.

✳ To Do

BICYCLING

Road Biking

Mount Baker Bicycle Club (360-734-8540; www.mtbakerbikeclub.org) organizes weekly rides and suggests these routes for road bikes:

Aldrich Road Loop, 20 miles.

Bellingham-Ferndale Loop, 18 miles.

Gooseberry Point Loop, 30 miles.

Lake Samish Loop, 16 miles.

Mountain Biking

Bellingham trails. Several are shared with hikers. The **Visitors Bureau,** 904 Potter Street, Bellingham, has maps for sale.

Galbraith Mountain trails, near Whatcom Falls Park. Miles of logging trails and 5 miles of single track connect with the **Lake Padden Park Trail** (see *Hiking*).

Interurban Trail, 9 miles from Fairhaven to Larrabee State Park.

Railroad Trail, 3.5 miles from King Street to Alabama and Vining, Bellingham.

Whatcom Falls Park trails, 3.5 miles (see *Hiking*).

BIRDING Several spots are particularly reliable for catching Puget Sound's rich variety of birdlife. For more information, check online (northcascadesaudubon.org).

Deming Homestead Eagle Park, east on WA 542 past WA 9, then right on Truck Road. Bald eagles are seen here.

Lake Padden This large Bellingham city park has many resident songbirds.

Larrabee State Park (see *Wilder Places—Parks*). Seabirds frequent this park, especially in winter, and several owl species live in the uplands backing the shore.

Marine Park and **Birch Bay State Park,** Blaine (see *Wilder Places—Parks*). These are both great for saltwater ducks, geese, and shorebirds in season.

Mosquito Lake Road, east on WA 542 for 16 miles, then right on Mosquito Lake Road and drive 1 mile to a bridge. Bald eagles can often been seen here in winter.

CAMPING ♿ **Birch Bay State Park** (888-226-7688), on Point Whitehorn, about 8 miles south of the Canadian border. Has 147 tent sites and 20 RV sites in a wooded campground, with ADA restrooms and showers.

Larrabee State Park (888-226-7688), on Chuckanut Drive about 10 miles south of Bellingham. Has 51 tent sites, 26 utility sites, and 8 primitive sites. Note: A functioning train track runs through the park west of the campground.

Lighthouse Marine County Park (360-945-4911; www.co.whatcom.wa.us/parks), 811 Marine Drive, Point Roberts. Has 30 standard sites, plus restrooms, shower, boardwalk, and whale-watching. Note: Accessible only by going through Canada!

Silver Lake County Park (360-599-2776; www.co.whatcom.wa.us/parks), 9006 Silver Lake Road, Maple Falls. Has 89 sites, some with hook-ups; a 28-site horse camp; 7 cabins (1 ADA-compliant); and a handicapped-accessible overnight lodge for groups. Call for rates.

See also *Wilder Places—Parks*.

GOLF Baker's Edge (360-599-2416), 432 Sprague Valley Drive, Maple Falls; off Mount Baker Highway, halfway to the mountain. Nine holes.

Birch Bay Golf Club (360-371-7933; www.birchbaygolfclub.com), 7878 Birch Bay Drive, Blaine. Eighteen holes.

Homestead Golf Course (800-354-1196), 115 East Homestead Boulevard, Lynden. Eighteen holes.

Lake Padden Municipal Golf Course (360-738-7400), 4882 Samish Way, Bellingham. Eighteen holes.

Loomis Trail Golf Club (360-332-8138), 4342 Loomis Trail Road, Blaine, at Semiahmoo Resort. Eighteen holes.

North Bellingham Golf Course (360-398-8300 or 888-322-NBGC; www.north bellinghamgolf.com), 205 West Smith Road, Bellingham. Eighteen holes.

Semiahmoo Golf Course (360-371-7012), 8720 Semiahmoo Parkway, Blaine. Eighteen holes.

Shuksan Golf Course (360-398-8888), 1500 East Axton Road, Bellingham. Eighteen holes.

Sudden Valley Golf Course (360-734-6435), 4 Clubhouse Circle, Bellingham. Eighteen holes.

HIKING

Bellingham
The National Park Service has called Bellingham a "Trail Town USA," meaning it's one of the hiker- and biker-friendliest places around. Pleasant hikes in and around Bellingham include these:

Boulevard Park and South Bay Trail, 2 miles from Fairhaven District to downtown Bellingham. Access this waterfront connector from 10th and Mill Street, Fairhaven.

Cornwall Park, 1.5 miles of trail; on Meridian Street at Birchwood Avenue. This wooded trail is on Squalicum Creek. There's also a rose garden in this park.

Interurban Trail, 9 miles from Fairhaven to Larrabee State Park, mostly beside Chuckanut Drive. Trailheads and parking are found in Fairhaven Park, Old Fairhaven Parkway, Old Samish Highway, and Chuckanut Drive.

Sehome Hills Arboretum, 5 miles of trails next to Western Washington University. An observation tower at the summit provides views of Bellingham Bay.

Squalicum Harbor, 1 paved mile from Hotel Bellwether to Zuanich Point Park. More bay views here.

Whatcom Falls Park, 5.5 miles of trails on Lakeway Drive 2 miles east of Bellingham. Walk beside Whatcom Creek in woods, past a waterfall, and over a stone bridge.

Ferndale
Hovander Homestead Park trails, Ferndale; from I-5 take exit 262. Several short wetland trails wind along the Nooksack River.

Whatcom County
Chuckanut Ridge Trail, 4 miles; from Fairhaven take WA 11 (Chuckanut Drive) south 4 miles and turn left onto Highline Road for about 3 miles. South

of Bellingham, this hike follows the ridge of Chuckanut Mountain between WA 11 and I-5, with nice views.

Semiahmoo Spit Trail, 0.75 paved mile, at Semiahmoo Resort near Blaine (see *Lodging*). Follow the spit with an easy trail along one side or on the beach on the other side. You'll have good views and birds.

Stimpson Family Nature Reserve loop trail, 3 miles, in Sudden Valley, slightly southeast of Bellingham. The trail loops through forest and over streams. Cougars have been seen here, so watch your family.

See also *Wilder Places—Parks*.

✳ Wilder Places

PARKS ✿ **Berthusen Park** (360-354-2424), 8837 Berthusen Road, Lynden. Hans Berthusen came to America at age 4 and went west at 19—you could say he grew up with the country. At 23, he filed a homestead claim, farmed it, and lived on it till he died in 1944, bequeathing the 263 acres to the city of Lynden. You can still see his huge barn and the 20 acres of great cedars he refused to cut, remembrance of how it all used to be. Paths wind through the old- and second-growth forests, and picnic tables are scattered in the shade. A children's playground and a campground round out the park's amenities. And maybe it's the Dutch heritage, but it's kept extremely tidy and well cared for.

Birch Bay State Park (360-902-8844), on Point Whitehorn, about 8 miles south of the Canadian border. Perched on the southern tip of crescent-shaped Birch Bay, this park has old growth and expansive views, and the shallow bay between park and town warms up enough that you can actually go in the water, though the beach itself is narrow and gravelly.

Larrabee State Park (360-902-8844), on Chuckanut Drive (WA 11) about 10 miles south of Bellingham. This large 2,683-acre park slopes from Chuckanut Mountain down to Samish Bay, where the tide goes way out, leaving tidal pools with starfish and anemones. When it comes back, the scuba divers and kayakers head out. There are hiking trails for all ages, freshwater lakes, and campgrounds in the woods behind the beach, plus glorious views of the San Juans.

& **Silver Lake County Park** (360-599-2776; www.co.whatcom.wa.us/parks), 9006 Silver Lake Road, Maple Falls. In this 411-acre park with its 180-acre lake, you'll find camping, six rustic **cabins** built by the original owners in the 1940s (one ADA; no pets), and the three-bedroom **Overnight Lodge,** which sleeps eight, plus the Gerdrum Museum (see *To See—Museums*) and Black Mountain Forestry Center (see *To See—Historic Sites*).

See also *To Do—Camping* and *Hiking*.

NATURE PRESERVES Stimpson Family Nature Reserve (360-733-2900), in Sudden Valley, slightly southeast of Bellingham; from I-5 take Laneway Drive about 3.5 miles to Lake Louise Road, turn right, and continue 1.6 miles. Cougars have been seen in the forest and riparian areas here.

☀ Lodging

BED & BREAKFASTS

Bellingham

♪ **DeCann House Bed and Breakfast** (360-734-9172; www.decannhouse.com), 2610 Eldridge Avenue. This 1902 home in the historic Eldridge Avenue District (see *To See—Historic Homes*) has two guest rooms, each with private bath, on the second floor, plus an elegant 1930s-style billiard room—take a cue! All rooms are nicely furnished with antiques, and owners Barbara and Van Hudson can tell you all about them. They completely refurbished the house when they bought it in 1984; it had gone through several families and 20 years as a nursing home. Rates include a full breakfast. Children welcome. No pets. $115–125; discount for more than one night.

Everson

Kale House Bed and Breakfast (360-966-7027; www.kalehouse.net), 201 Kale Street; 7 miles north of Mount Baker Highway via WA 9. Kale House, a country home in an old apple orchard in the heart of the rural Nooksack Valley, has three guest rooms, one with a queen-sized bed, one with twin beds, and the third a tiny room with a bed that can be rented with the twin-bedded room. Rates include a full breakfast. No children or pets. $95; nominal charge for the tiny room alone.

Glacier

Inn at Mount Baker (360-599-1776; www.theinnatmtbaker.com), 8174 Mount Baker Highway. Positioned for views of Mount Baker and the Nooksack River, this inn was expressly built as a B&B. Five guest rooms have all the luxury amenities: down pillows and duvets, 6-foot-long tubs, views from all rooms, heated floors. Rates include a full breakfast. $149–165; discount for more than one night.

Mount Baker Bed and Breakfast (360-599-2299; www.mtbakerbedandbreakfast.com), 9447 Mount Baker Highway. Three rooms with Mount Baker staring you in the face and a wraparound deck make up this chalet-style B&B (two of the rooms share a bath). The chalet sits on 4 acres amid gardens and peak views. Rates include a continental breakfast. Owners Jacques and Vel Massie also rent out nearby cabins, some of which accept dogs. Rooms $80–110; cabins $149–329.

Lummi Island

The Willows Inn (360-758-2620 or 888-294-2620; www.willows-inn.com), 2579 West Shore Drive. Six minutes from Bellingham by boat, this is a sought-after retreat with an on-site "slow food" restaurant (see *Where to Eat*). Five guest rooms in a vintage home all have private baths and restful, homey decor. The living room has a wood-burning fireplace; the dining room has water views. There's also a romantic cottage that sleeps two with a bath, kitchenette, and private garden, and a guesthouse that sleeps six: two bedrooms and a futon in the living room, plus two baths, a fully equipped kitchen, and lots of exposed wood. One ADA room. Small dogs allowed in some rooms. $165–625.

INNS AND HOTELS

Bellingham

&. ☎ **Fairhaven Village Inn** (360-733-1311 or 877-733-1100; www.fairhavenvillageinn.com), 1200 10th Street. Just a couple of blocks from the harbor, this choice small hotel looks out over Bellingham Bay on one side and the Village Green (an urban park) on the other—a boutique hotel, really, without the pretension. It's right in the middle of things in Fairhaven. Twenty-two quietly elegant rooms come with king- or queen-sized beds, plump arm-chairs, down comforters, and all the amenities; many have balconies and gas fireplaces. Two wheelchair-accessible rooms are located by the elevators. Rates include breakfast. Rooms $189–259; suites $209–289.

HOSTELS

Birch Bay

Birch Bay Hostel (360-371-2180; www.birchbayhostel.org), 7467 Gemini Lane. A project of the local Lions Club, the Birch Bay Hostel sits in a forested county park on a bluff above the crescent of summer shacks that is Birch Bay. If hostels are your cup of tea, you can beat the somewhat inflated local prices and still get clean, safe accommodations, plus a friendly welcome. Dorm beds $27.50; private rooms with bath $60; family rooms sleeping four $65.

LODGES

Glacier

Glacier Creek Lodge (360-599-2991 or 800-719-1414; www.glaciercreek lodge.com), 10036 Mount Baker High-way. Here, between two rushing streams, you can choose between motel-type rooms and rustic but cozy studio, one-bedroom, or two-bedroom cabins—there are even duplex cabins for family gatherings. All cabins have kitchens or kitchenettes; one has a fire-place. Use the hot tub after a day of exploring, or prepare your day's catch on one of the barbecues. It's relaxed and affordable, and rates include a continental breakfast. Motel rooms $60–95; cabins $85–135 (duplex $155).

RESORTS

Blaine

Ġ **Semiahmoo Resort and Golf Spa** (800-770-7992), 9565 Semiahmoo Parkway. Probably the luxury venue on this northern stretch of coast, big, glitzy Semiahmoo Resort imposes on the landscape: Its two golf courses and 198-room hotel are right on the shore. Options run from classic king and queen rooms to expansive suites; the decor is standard modern plush (stuffed furniture, armoires, some fire-places), but all spacious. And, of course, the resort includes musts such as a swimming pool, a fitness center, trails, restaurants (see *Where to Eat*), a spa, and more. From $199.

✳ Where to Eat

DINING OUT

Bellingham

The Table and **Bellingham Pasta Company** (360-594-6000; www .bellinghampasta.com), 100 North Commercial Street. Open for lunch only Mon., lunch and dinner Tues.–Sat. A new venture in 2008, the Table was invented by young pasta fanatics Katie Hinton and Anna Rankin and features, naturally, fresh homemade pasta in many guises. Have them cook and serve it in one of their many recipes, or take it home and cook it yourself. Thursday is ravioli night. Reasonable.

Blaine

Stars Restaurant (360-318-2000 or 800-770-7992; www.semiahmoo.com), 9565 Semiahmoo Parkway. Open for breakfast daily, dinner Thurs.–Sat. Stars is Semiahmoo Resort's fine-dining venue (see *Lodging*). The view is fine and the menu ambitious: filet mignon with port demi-glace, duck breast with blackberry coulis, fish of the season, and more. While not cheap, the prices have come down in the past couple of years.

Bow

Chuckanut Manor Seafood and Grill (360-766-6191; www.chuckanut

manor.com), 3056 Chuckanut Drive. Open for lunch and dinner Tues.–Sat., brunch and dinner Sun.; no lunch Tues.–Thurs. in winter. A fixture for three decades, this low, rambling building set in gardens takes full advantage of Samish Bay, both visually and gastronomically. The seafood is always wild, and the very copious Friday buffet and Sunday brunch have made the place regionally famous. Reservations recommended. If you want to stay, there is a two-bedroom **suite** ($160) with continental breakfast.

The Oyster Bar on Chuckanut Drive (360-766-6185; www.theoyster bar.net), 2578 Chuckanut Drive. Open for lunch and dinner daily. It started life as an oyster shack during the Great Depression, selling to tourists along Washington's first scenic highway, and has evolved into an elegant shingled restaurant overlooking Samish Bay. Today you'll still find several kinds of oysters plus all the other fresh seafood inhabiting the Northwest coast, prepared with aplomb. Definitely upscale, this one's for a splurge or special occasion. Reservations recommended.

Oyster Creek Inn (360-766-6179; www.oystercreekinn.com), 2190 Chuckanut Drive. Open 11:30–9 daily. The northernmost of the three dowager restaurants on Chuckanut Drive, and with a view equally as majestic as that at its sister places, this one goes back 70 years. Oysters, oysters, oysters, but also duck, filet mignon, and local fish with some creative twists: duckling in sweet-and-sour apricot sauce; thyme-and-juniper-berry-cured pork tenderloin.

Lummi Island
The Willows Inn Restaurant (360-758-2620; www.willows-inn.com), 2579 West Shore Drive. One dinner seating 7 PM summer, 6:30 PM winter. The dining room of the Willows Inn (see *Lodging*) has a spacious deck, so you can spot whales in Rosario Strait while munching your organic salad. Most of the food served here comes from their own Nettles Farm or from other organic sources close by. Dinner is prix fixe with five courses ($105); the seasonally changing menu usually features meat, poultry, seafood, and vegetarian choices. The inn also owns the **Taproot Espresso Bar** and the **Beachfront Café** on the island, both with the same suppliers.

EATING OUT
Bellingham
The Abbey Garden Tearoom (360-752-1752), 1312 Harris Street (in Fairhaven). Open 11–5 daily. When the hour comes that you just have to have a cup of tea, stop in here, where you can also have a light lunch.

Avenue Bread and Café (360-676-1809; www.avenuebread.com), 1135 11th Street (in Fairhaven). Open 7–5 daily. All artisan, all the time—20 kinds of bread, including gluten-free, plus pastries, soups, salads, and sandwiches. There's another location at 1313 Railroad Avenue in downtown Bellingham.

The Bagelry (360-676-5288), 1319 Railroad Avenue. Open 7–4 Mon.–Fri., 7:30–4 Sat., 8–3 Sun. Here you'll find 12 kinds of bagels, plus bialys, which shows they know a thing or two; 14 cream cheese spreads; and a variety of deli meats and fish, which open all kinds of possibilities. And then you can have an omelet.

The Black Drop (360-738-3767; www.blackdropcoffeehouse.com), 300 West Champion Street. Open 7–7 Mon.–Fri., 8–5 Sat., 8:30–4 Sun. You might want to "drop" in here after visiting the wine bar next door. Opened in 2002 by a pair whose avowed aim was to serve "coffee that curls your toes," it was soon recognized as having the best coffee in Bellingham. An example of revived coffeehouse culture, it draws people to sip and read, sip and talk, sip and blog, or sip and tap—free Wi-Fi, of course.

Colophon Café (360-647-0092; www.colophoncafe.com), 1208 11th Street (in Fairhaven). Open 9–8 Mon.–Thurs., 9 AM–10 PM Fri.–Sat., 10–8 Sun. You can eat outdoors facing either the Village Green or the street—or even indoors, where you'll notice lots of cows peering from the walls. That is because originally the café served only ice cream, lattes, and bagels with cream cheese, naturally making visions of Holsteins dance in the owners' heads. However, it's become famous since then for its creative soups and "Northwest" French bread, hearty sandwiches, and quiche. Oh, yes—did I mention dessert?

Dirty Dan Harris (360-676-1087), 1208 11th Street (in Fairhaven). Open from 5 PM daily. Dan Harris was one of Fairhaven's biggest promoters in the glory days before the Great Northern terminus went to Seattle. He was nicknamed "Dirty," apparently, because of his substandard personal hygiene and possibly also his variegated career as land speculator, developer, rumrunner, and gold smuggler. He built a hotel and wharf in Fairhaven and made a considerable fortune in both his legal and his underground enterprises. At 59, he surprisingly married and moved to California, where his wife soon died and he shortly followed, penniless, having been conned out of his money by a "friend." All this is by way of introduction to a restaurant specializing in high-quality steaks, prime rib, and seafood, which he probably would have liked seeing: As a medium-sized

guy, he weighed 200 pounds. Harris Street is named after him.

✔ **Dos Padres** (360-733-9900), 1111 Harris Avenue (in Fairhaven). Quiet colonial decor and down-home Mexican cooking have made this family-oriented restaurant a local favorite for 30 years and counting.

Harris Avenue Café (360-738-0802), 1101 Harris Avenue (in Fairhaven). Open 8–2 daily. Comfort food old and new and a cozy environment keep customers contented. Eat in or on the leafy patio.

La Vie en Rose French Bakery (360-715-1839), 111 East Holly Street. Tempting cakes, pastries, and breads.

Mount Bakery (360-715-2195; www.mountbakery.com), 308 West Champion Street. Open 8–3:30 Sun.–Tues., 8 AM–9 PM Wed.–Sat. BELGIAN DESSERT read a sign in the window. SLOW FOOD read another. It was late in the day when I came in, and not much was left, but I picked up a truffle and was transported back to my student days in Europe. Belgian born and bred chef-owner Olivier Vrambout produces a full line of fine pastries; there are also breads by sidekick Sean Hughes, plus breakfast, lunch, and dinner. This is the place to pick up your morning *pain au chocolat* or a cake for dinner, or just to relax with a cup and a croissant.

Skylark's Hidden Café (360-715-3642; www.skylarkshiddencafe.com), 1308 Harris Street (in Fairhaven). Open 8 AM–midnight Mon.–Fri., 7 AM–midnight Sat.–Sun. A café and wine room "hidden" down a cobblestone alley, tiny Skylark's has been a Fairhaven favorite for a decade, with lines out to the street some weekends. The owner has described the look as "upper-class bordello," with its carved mahogany fireplace and chandeliers. This address was formerly in Fairhaven's rough district, with plenty of actual bordellos, though maybe not upper-class. A weekday "budget bailout" menu at all three meals is a real deal: $7.99 for your choice of dinner entrée with salad and bread.

The Temple Bar (360-676-8660; www.templebarbellingham.com), 306 West Champion Street. Open 11 AM to closing Mon.–Fri., 3 PM to closing Sat.–Sun. This is not, as you might expect, a Dublin-style brewpub—which would not be amiss in the microbrewery culture of the Northwest—but a new wine bar also serving panini, salads, and soups. This makes sense, too, given the heady rise of Washington's wine industry.

Glacier
Graham's Restaurant (360-599-3663), 9989 Mount Baker Highway. Open 11 AM to closing. A store since the 1930s, Graham's has had a restaurant since the 1970s, one of just two in this last outpost before starting up the mountain in earnest. Well, there was one interruption—two months in 2011 when the place closed for lack of funds, then reopened after a massive outpouring from the community. The current incarnation has preserved the cracker-barrel look with old wooden tables and bar, but it includes dishes such as Thai fried rice and curries as well as burgers and steaks—international home cooking, they call it.

Milano's (360-599-2863), 9990 Mount Baker Highway. Milano's is just across the road from Graham's (see above). Open for breakfast, lunch, and dinner daily. A glass-enclosed deck and an open deck overlook the creek, or you can sit in the inner dining room if it's cold. Pasta and other Italian American

cuisine will help you carb up for your adventures in the mountains.

✳ Entertainment
Fairhaven's Village Green, Mill Avenue and 10th Street, Bellingham. Summer Saturday evenings find moviegoers sitting on blankets watching **free movies** at 7:45. Monday evenings at 5, come and **play bocce!**

✳ Selective Shopping
BOOKS Village Books (360-671-2626; www.villagebooks.booksense .com), 1200 11th Street, Bellingham (in Fairhaven). Open 10–10 Mon.–Sat., 11–8 Sun. This 26-year-old independent bookstore has lots of events involving local and regional authors. It's a fine place to browse if the weather's not so good—or even if it is—and there's a café upstairs.

GIFTS Drizzle (360-392-8838), 1208 11th Street, Bellingham (Fairhaven). An olive oil tasting room? Well, why not? Olive oil is a kitchen staple of many varieties and terroirs, so why not taste before you buy? Ross and Dana Driscoll opened the store in 2011 after a stint in California and offer not only oils but vinegars, salts, and other items.

The Silvery Moon (360-715-1393), 1010 Harris Avenue, Bellingham (in Fairhaven). Open 10–6 Tues.–Sun. The Fairhaven District is also good for original jewelry, such as this place's pieces from the Northwest and worldwide.

✳ Special Events
May: **Holland Days** (360-354-5995), Lynden. Come enjoy Dutch food, costumes, street scrubbing, and Klompen dancers.

July: **Raspberry Festival** (360-354-5995), Lynden. This harvest festival for a major local product is observed with wine and raspberry tasting, berry farm tours, jazz, and lots of small-town razzle-dazzle.

August: **Bellingham Festival of Music** (360-201-6621; www.bellingham festival.org), Box 818, Bellingham 98227. Two weeks of jazz, classical, opera, and international music take place at several area locations.

Northwest Washington Fair (360-354-4111; www.nwwafair.com), Lynden. This is one of the biggest agricultural fairs in the Northwest, with regional and national entertainers.

Line of Fire: The Cascades

5

INTRODUCTION

"Vancouver! Vancouver! This is it!"

—*David Johnston, May 18, 1980*

This was the young geologist's last radio message to the U.S. Geological Survey station in Vancouver, Washington, which he sent as he observed the incipient eruption of Mount St. Helens from the ridge now bearing his name. Neither his remains nor his equipment was ever found.

Most of the time, the Cascade Range looks green and snowcapped and inviting. Running north and south from British Columbia to northern California, it catches the plentiful precipitation driven in from the Pacific, dividing Washington and Oregon into two neat sections: the moist west, still holding some of the world's few temperate rain forests; and the arid east, marked by blowing dust, bare basalt cliffs, and the great blue snake of the Columbia River. Its shoulders are crossed by hikers and climbers, its clear rivers are fished and rafted, its forests are camped in and, sometimes, cut: Apart from two national parks, three national recreation areas, one national scenic area, and of course the national volcanic monument, most of the acreage is national forest. But sometimes all hell breaks loose.

As North America slides inexorably west, the Pacific Ocean floor is forced underneath it. Eventually it melts and, becoming lighter, tries to force its way back up. Unfortunately, it is now under miles of rock. But the terrific pressure cooker pushes itself even through rock, till it bursts through and becomes a volcanic eruption. Lassen, Shasta, Hood, St. Helens, Rainier, and myriad lesser peaks—all are volcanoes, mostly young and active into recent geological times, even historical times: Lassen erupted in 1912, St. Helens several times in the 19th century. As I write this, a mysterious bulge has been forming in the Three Sisters Wilderness, 20 miles west of my Oregon home. It's an active landscape.

Mountains usually give birth to rivers, and the abundant rain and snow here provide plenty of those, with a multitude of waterfalls, for which the range is named. For obvious reasons, rivers rarely cross mountain ranges, but it happens here, and that is another volcanic story, both older and newer. Perhaps 14 million to 16 million years ago, lava began pouring out of fissures in the ground—thin, runny lava that did not pile up into mountains, but formed sheets on the ground, eventually becoming thousands of feet thick and covering an astonishing amount of territory. Now it's known as the Columbia Plateau, extending over most of eastern

Washington and Oregon and parts of Idaho. Much, much later, as the latest Ice Age came to an end, an ice dam imprisoning huge glacial Lake Missoula in Montana broke, and hundreds of cubic miles of water tore at breakneck speed over the plateau and down the course of the Columbia, tearing out soil and bedrock and cutting the Columbia Gorge. Now the river winds its stately way between the cones of Mount Adams and Mount Hood at the bottom of 1,000-foot-high basalt cliffs.

The North Cascades, beginning roughly between I-90 and US 2 and extending north into Canada, are another animal entirely. They are not well-spaced volcanic cones but jumbled masses of granite overlain in places with sandstone, steep faces hacked and serrated by glaciers, like the Alps or the Sierra Nevada. The latest theory is that they arrived in America in the dim past as a minicontinent, approaching slowly across the Pacific (or America approached it) till it docked ungently against our continent's then western edge near what is now Wenatchee. This created unseen faults that still rumble occasionally. The theory actually describes several such islands jamming up against North America in succession like a train wreck. However they came to be, the North Cascades remain nearly an island unto themselves, rugged enough to stay eternally remote and, with their granite faces and seven hundred glaciers, majestic as John Muir's Range of Light.

COLUMBIA RIVER GORGE

Lewis and Clark canoed down it, David Douglas botanized along it, Oregon Trail emigrants were awed by its rapids, and, of course, Columbia Plateau tribes lived, fished, and traded along it for eons. In those days, the Columbia was a dangerous river punctuated with thunderous falls and rapids. Today it's much more placid, held back by huge dams, but its canyon is still an awe-inspiring sight—basalt cliffs up to 4,000 feet high, columnar rock, waterfalls, and forests, all backed by the monstrous volcanic cones of Mount Hood, Mount Adams, and Mount St. Helens. A railroad that once transported grain from the interior and lumber from the mountains runs along both banks, and so do highways—I-84 on the Oregon side, WA 14 in Washington.

It's just the route for a leisurely drive. East of Vancouver, settlements dwindle to far-flung, fading timber towns sprinkled with occasional galleries, wineries, fruit stands, and wind surfing beaches. These little towns include Camas, Washougal, North Bonneville, Stevenson, Carson, White Salmon, Bingen, Lyle, and Wishram.

The Columbia Gorge National Scenic Area officially runs from Washougal 80 miles east to The Dalles, Oregon, a spot that on the Washington side is some 12 miles east of Lyle. I include Vancouver in this section, since it's the western gateway city to the gorge, located on I-5 and I-205. This section's eastern end is at Wishram. The Washington side of the gorge tends to be quieter and less discovered; the state highway, small and winding—just right for a modern pace of discovery.

GUIDANCE Columbia River Gorge National Scenic Area (541-308-1700; www.fs.usda.gov), 902 Wasco Avenue, Hood River, OR 97031.

Columbia River Gorge Visitors' Association (800-98-GORGE; www.crgva.org), Box 324, Corbett, OR 97019.

Mount Adams Chamber of Commerce (509-493-3630; www.mtadamschamber .com), One Heritage Plaza, White Salmon 98672.

Skamania County Visitor Information Center (509-427-8911 or 800-989-9178; www.skamania.org), 167 NW Second Street, Stevenson 98648.

Vancouver USA Regional Tourism Office (360-750-1553 or 877-600-0800; www .visitvancouverusa.com), 101 East Eighth Street, Vancouver 98660; **Visitor Information Center** (877-224-4214), 1501 East Evergreen Boulevard, Vancouver 98661.

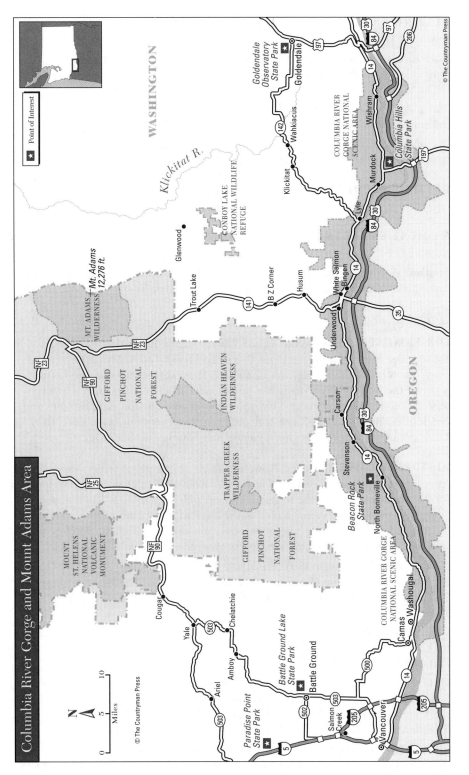

Columbia River Gorge and Mount Adams Area

N

0   5   10
Miles

© The Countryman Press

□ Point of Interest

WASHINGTON

OREGON

MOUNT ST. HELENS NATIONAL VOLCANIC MONUMENT

MT. ADAMS WILDERNESS — Mt. Adams 12,276 ft.

GIFFORD PINCHOT NATIONAL FOREST

INDIAN HEAVEN WILDERNESS

TRAPPER CREEK WILDERNESS

GIFFORD PINCHOT NATIONAL FOREST

CONBOY LAKE NATIONAL WILDLIFE REFUGE

Klickitat R.

COLUMBIA RIVER GORGE NATIONAL SCENIC AREA

COLUMBIA RIVER GORGE NATIONAL SCENIC AREA

Columbia Hills State Park

Goldendale Observatory State Park

Beacon Rock State Park

Battle Ground Lake State Park

Paradise Point State Park

Goldendale

Glenwood

Trout Lake

B Z Corner

Husum

White Salmon

Bingen

Underwood

Carson

Stevenson

North Bonneville

Washougal

Camas

Vancouver

Salmon Creek

Battle Ground

Amboy

Chelatchie

Yale

Ariel

Cougar

Wahkiacus

Klickitat

Lyle

Murdock

Wishram

Wishram

© The Countryman Press

NF 23

NF 23

NF 90

NF 25

NF 90

141

142

84

30

14

197

35

30

14

84

30

84

14

500

502

503

503

503

205

5

205

5

30

97

84

206

97

GETTING THERE **WA 14** runs along the Washington side of the gorge; I-84 serves the Oregon side.

Portland International Airport (503-460-4040 or 877-739-4636; www.portof portland.com) is off I-5 at 7000 NE Airport Way, Portland, OR—just minutes from the gorge.

The gorge is served by **AMTRAK** (800-USA-RAIL; www.amtrak.com), which stops in Wishram and Bingen.

The gorge is also served by **Greyhound** (800-231-2222; www.greyhound.com), which stops in The Dalles and Hood River on the Oregon side.

GETTING AROUND Several gorge hotels have airport shuttles, but it's better to have a car if you want to be mobile within the gorge.

MEDICAL EMERGENCY **Skyline Hospital** (509-493-1101; www.skylinehospital .com), 211 Skyline Drive, White Salmon.

Southwest Washington Medical Center (360-256-2000; www.swmedicalcenter .com), 3400 Main Street, Vancouver; and 400 NE Mother Joseph Place, Vancouver.

✳ To See

FOR FAMILIES ✍ **Bonneville Dam** (509-427-4281), River Mile 146.1 on WA 14, 40 miles east of Vancouver. Open 9–5 daily. Free. Of record-breaking size when it was built in the 1930s, the Bonneville Dam was expanded in the 1970s; it is one of the series of huge dams that power much of the Northwest. Visitors centers on both the Washington and Oregon sides let you view the giant turbines and watch fish climb the fish ladders; biologists have been counting them since 1938. Look around on your own or take a guided half-hour or one-hour tour.

HISTORIC HOMES **Officers' Row,** north side of Evergreen Street, Vancouver. After the Hudson's Bay Company left Fort Vancouver in 1860, it didn't take long for the Americans to turn the fort area into a sizable military site. The fine houses along Evergreen Street were erected in the last half of the 19th century to house officers and their families. These homes are quite ornate, with large porches, turrets, bay windows, and elegant woodwork. Many today contain offices.

George Marshall House (360-693-3103), 1301 Officers' Row, Vancouver. Open 9–5 Mon.–Fri., 11–6 Sat.–Sun.; tours available. Free. This 1886 home is where Secretary of State George Marshall, of the Marshall Plan, spent two years in the 1930s.

Grant House (360-906-1101), 1101 Officers' Row, Vancouver. This home named for Ulysses S. Grant, who visited but ultimately did not live in it, is now a restaurant (see *Where to Eat*).

O. O. Howard House (360-992-1800), 750 Anderson Street, Vancouver. Open 8–5 Mon.–Fri. Free. This home now contains offices of Washington's senators and the **Vancouver National Reserve Trust** (360-992-1800). General Howard, who lived here for a time, later founded Howard University in Washington, D.C.

Slocum House (360-696-2427), 65 Esther Street, Vancouver. The colonnade of this 1867 Italianate house juts out onto a neat lawn. Built by Charles and Laura Slocum, with a cupola and a widow's walk—the better to see loved ones returning across the treacherous Columbia River—it's now home to a theatrical company, which stages several plays a year in the old house.

HISTORIC SITES **Apple Tree Park,** near Columbia Walkway trailhead (see *To Do—Hiking*), across from Beaches Restaurant (see *Where to Eat*), just east of I-5 in Vancouver. Here, lovingly tended, is an gnarled apple tree planted in 1826. The story is that an early Fort Vancouver man was given some apple seeds to plant in the New World by his girlfriend before he left England, and this tree was one of those shoots.

✒ **Captain William Clark Park** (360-835-2196), Cottonwood Beach, Washougal; from WA 14 take 32nd Street exit. The Corps of Discovery camped here for six days on their homeward journey in 1806. Their journal entries sound almost jovial, as well they might, considering the miserable, wet winter the group had just spent on the Oregon coast. The park features a beach, playground, and 4-mile dike trail along the Columbia.

Esther Short Park, between Esther, Columbia, Sixth, and Eighth streets, downtown Vancouver. The Short family staked the first Vancouver claim here, in 1847. Trouble was, it was smack next to Hudson's Bay Company lands at Fort Vancouver, and the company's policy was to discourage Americans. But the Shorts defended their farm against lawsuits and forcible evictions, even killing a couple of Fort Vancouver men in the process. Remarkably, Esther dug in even after her husband drowned in the Columbia while returning from a market trip to San Francisco. The British eventually left, and Esther deeded this property to the city. She is memorialized here with shade trees, a rose garden, and the 35-bell **Salmon Run Glockenspiel,** which not only plays tunes but also retells a Chinook Indian legend complete with revolving images. It's the oldest park in Washington, having been dedicated in 1853. Across from the southwestern corner, a bronze statue of **Captain George Vancouver** stands contemplating a bronze globe.

✒ **Fort Vancouver National Historic Reserve** (360-816-6230) includes several points of interest clustered around the old fort in Vancouver:

✒ **Fort Vancouver National Historic Site,** just south of Columbia Way. Open 9–5 Mon.–Sat. in summer; 9–4 Mon.–Sat. winter. $3 adults, $5 families; ticket good for seven days. At this restored site, you can borrow a headset (available for a donation) for a guided tour—there's one for children, about 45 minutes long, and another for adults, 60 minutes long. Although it was called a fort, just in case, it was really a large, glorified trading post. Within the stockade, you can visit the Factor's House, where the factor and his family lived in respectable British style and entertained officers. The factor supervised the company's trapping, farming, and trading operations over an unimaginably vast area and essentially ruled the Northwest for several decades. The quarters for ordinary people were rather more austere. The bakehouse, washhouse, blacksmith shop, warehouse, and other scrupulously refurbished sites explain the roles of various employees, from clerks to laborers; several buildings focus on the life of children at the fort, of whom there were quite a number. The place wonderfully interprets why these people were there (furs) and how they lived (hard).

Officers' Row (see *Historic Homes*), above the fort on Evergreen Street. This area came later, when Washington Territory was firmly in American hands and the fort neighborhood had become a military site.

✒ **Pearson Air Museum** (360-694-7026; www.fortvan.org), 1115 East Fifth Street. Open 10–5 Wed.–Sat. This is next to the fort (see *Museums*).

Visitors center (360-816-6230), 1501 East Evergreen Boulevard. Open 9–5 daily in summer; 9–4 daily in winter. The historic reserve's visitors center features exhibits on daily life at the fort, with porcelain dishes such as officers used, trappers' equipment, and tools.

✒ **Water Resources Education Center** (360-487-7111), on Columbia Way about 3 miles east of the fort. The national historic reserve also operates this site (see *Museums*).

Marine Park, SE Marine Parkway and Columbia Way, Vancouver. Lewis and Clark camped near this spot in March 1806. The park, which has a boat launch and views of Portland, is part of the Lower Columbia River Water Trail—a 146-mile nonmotorized boat trail, from Bonneville Dam to the sea, that opened in 2004, with dedicated boat launches and campsites. The park also connects with the Vancouver Waterfront Renaissance Trail, a 4-mile path along the river starting at Columbia Avenue just east of I-5.

She-Who-Watches National Historic Site (509-767-1159), in Columbia Hills State Park, on WA 14 at milepost 85. Open to nontribal members by guided tour only, 10 AM Fri.–Sat. Apr.–Oct.; reservations required. Free. Tsagaglalal (She-Who-Watches) was a chief until Coyote came by announcing that women would no longer be chiefs. In the ensuing altercation, Coyote flung She-Who-Watches into the rock wall, where she remained watching over her people. Her image is the best-known and one of the most striking of the many pictographs and petroglyphs near Horsethief Lake. This location is not the original home of the rock art, however—that was a mile or so away in a canyon that was flooded when The Dalles dam was completed in 1957. Of the thousands of images in the canyon, those here were carefully removed on their rock slabs, then stored near the dam for nearly 50 years until being affixed to these cliffs, where they look almost natural. If you can't get on

TSAGAGLALAL, OR SHE-WHO-WATCHES, A PETROGLYPH AT COLUMBIA HILLS STATE PARK

one of the excellent ranger-led tours, a series of very impressive petroglyphs can be seen before the trailhead, complete with interpretive plaques.

Stonehenge replica, on WA 14, 4 miles east of Maryhill Museum (see *Museums*). Sam Hill built this full-scale replica of Stonehenge, to honor the young men of Klickitat County who were killed in the First World War. Unlike the original, it's made of concrete, and all the plinths are properly upright, rising impressively from the bare plateau.

MUSEUMS **Clark County Historical Society Museum** (360-993-5679; www .cchmuseum.org), 1511 Main Street, Vancouver. Open 11–4 Tues.–Sat. Suggested donation $5 adults, $2 children 6–18, $10 families. Located in a 1909 Carnegie library, this museum has, naturally, military memorabilia, a Native American collection, a Lewis and Clark library, and exhibits on the railroad in Clark County history.

Columbia Gorge Interpretive Center Museum (800-991-2338; www.columbia gorge.org), 990 SW Rock Creek Drive, Stevenson. Open 10–5 daily. $7 adults, $6 seniors over 60 and students, $5 children 6–12. This ambitious museum opened in 1995 and quickly became a must-see. With room for both intimate and spacious displays, its 11,000 square feet sweep through the natural and cultural history of the gorge, from its geological beginnings (depicted in a fine 12-minute film) through its role as food supply and marketplace for the plateau tribes, the coming of the railroad, and, finally, hydroelectric dams. A sculpted Indian with a dip net beside a two-floor indoor waterfall recalls the longest human use to which the gorge has yet been put. Exhibits on view include a huge fish wheel, several steam engines, delicate Native basketry and spear points, and much more. There's room for a few eccentricities, too, such as the more than 4,000 rosaries from around the world, donated by a local collector.

Gorge Heritage Museum (509-493-3228), 202 East Humboldt, Bingen. Open 12–5 Fri.–Sun. $5; children under 16 free. Inside this old Congregational church, you'll find tools, furniture, and possessions of the town's early inhabitants, such as a pair of beaded deerskin gloves made by a granddaughter of Chief Chenowith. Not wheelchair-accessible.

Maryhill Museum (509-773-3733; www.maryhillmuseum.org), 35 Maryhill Museum Drive, Goldendale. Open 10–5 daily Mar. 15–Nov. 15. $9 adults, $8 seniors over 65, $3 children 7–18. *Eclectic* and *eccentric* are two words that come to mind here. This is an improbable site for an art museum to begin with: on a desiccated, windy bluff 100 miles from the nearest city (though it has a Goldendale address, it's actually down on the river). But then founder Sam Hill, son-in-law of Jim Hill, who owned the Great Northern Railway, was an unusual man. Trained as a lawyer, he moved west at the turn of the 20th century with his children and wife, Mary. There he made a great deal of money in utilities—this was, after all, the last frontier—giving much of it away and directing the rest to personal projects. Sam was a Quaker, and the Maryhill property was intended to be a Quaker farming community. But there were no Quaker takers, as it were, and other farmers who did come were quickly bankrupted by the scant rain and plentiful wind and isolation. Eventually the queen of Romania (Sam was a well-traveled man) persuaded him to turn the place into a museum. The result is a room full of royal Romanian furniture, a huge and stunning collection of Native American artifacts from all parts of the country, paintings by English and American impressionists, a sizable Rodin sculpture collection, a gallery devoted to dancer Loïe Fuller, a collection of unique chess sets . . . well, you get the idea. It is a remarkable trove. The gardens and shade trees, too, make a pleasant oasis in the high desert.

✎ **Pearson Air Museum** (360-694-7026; www.fortvan.org), 1115 East Fifth Street, Vancouver. Open 10–5 Wed.–Sat. $7 adults, $5 seniors over 55 and military, $5 children 6–17. Pearson Field is the oldest continuously operating airfield in the United States today, and its adjacent museum traces the history of flight, particularly in the Northwest. For instance, the Portland area began airmail service in 1912, and Andrei Chkalov, for whom a Vancouver thoroughfare is named, completed the first transpolar flight in 1937 by leaving Moscow and landing at Pearson (he had meant to land in San Francisco but ran out of fuel). There is a plethora of antique planes, a children's hands-on room, and a summer day camp where your kid can learn to fly.

Two Rivers Heritage Museum (360-835-8742; 2rhm.com), One Durgan Street, Washougal. Open 11–3 Tues.–Sat. $3 adults, $2 seniors over 60, $1 children and students, $8 families of five or more. The Washougal and the Columbia are the two rivers in question here, and the seven-room museum traces the ebb and flow of history at this confluence through Native American and pioneer artifacts, reconstructions of early homes (including a 1940s kitchen), and an extensive research room.

✎ **Water Resources Education Center** (360-487-7111), 4600 SE Columbia Way, about 3 miles east of Fort Vancouver (see *Historic Sites*). Open 9–5 Mon.–Sat. Free. This water sciences center has two aquariums, a lab, hands-on activities, and a multimedia theater designed mainly for children.

NATURAL WONDERS Beacon Rock, on WA 14 at milepost 3. Here explorers Lewis and Clark first noticed tidal shifts as they descended the Columbia. The

THE MARYHILL MUSEUM

865-foot-tall basalt rock rises nearly sheer from the river, but a trail was put in by Henry Biddle, a former owner, and later improved by the state as part of a state park (see *Wilder Places—Parks*). Today it's a rigorous climb rewarded by 360-degree views of the gorge.

Bridge of the Gods, across the Columbia River near Bonneville. This is now a man-made steel affair named for a natural feature that no longer exists. Indian legends tell of a stone bridge that spanned the river here and then was destroyed by fighting between two mountain spirits, Mount Hood and Mount Adams. In fact, 400–500 years ago, Table Mountain, on the northern bank, split in half; the resulting landslide did block the river, creating a land bridge. Erosion eventually washed it away, leaving only legends and a visibly broken Table Mountain.

Celilo Falls, underwater 12 miles upstream of The Dalles, Oregon. This waterfall is no longer here either, having being flooded in 1957 by The Dalles dam, but it deserves a mention nonetheless. For thousands of years, it was the largest salmon fishery on the Columbia, where multitudes would gather during the runs to spear or net fish from rough platforms and preserve them, incidentally courting, socializing, and trading. Trade items included shells and cedar from the coast, buffalo skins from the plains, and obsidian from Oregon. As Captain William Clark observed in 1806, Celilo Falls was the trading place of the country. The loss of the falls was, and still is, traumatic; for an account, see Robert Clark's *The River of the West*.

Columbia River Gorge, 80 miles of canyon from Washougal to Wishram. In places 4,000 feet deep, this deep bed along one of the continent's mightiest rivers was carved in remarkably short order, geologically speaking. As the last Ice Age waned, ice dams that had held back the waters of gigantic prehistoric Lake Missoula, in Montana, broke, creating a flood that is estimated to have exceeded the flow of all the rivers in the world today (however such things are estimated). This unimaginable flood tore through central Washington, creating the Channeled Scablands, and burst into the mid–Columbia River. Such floods may have occurred once or several times, but the inconceivable force of the mass of water laden with rock and debris ground the basalt of the Columbia Plateau down nearly to sea level. The river looks peaceful now, lined with lush forest and waterfalls along its western stretch and bare cliffs to the east. The Columbia Interpretive Center Gorge/Museum in Stevenson (see *Museums*) shows an excellent film on the subject.

SCENIC DRIVES WA 14, about 80 paved miles from Washougal to Wishram. All of this highway is a scenic drive; that's the point of the Columbia River Gorge National Scenic Area. From Washougal, where the urban spread thins out, to Wishram, you look up or down the river canyon, backed by either green forest or austere brown hills and the extraordinary expanse of water. Even the hills are washed in green early in wheat season. The national scenic area runs along the Oregon side, too, where the views are just as good, but the road there is I-84, which lacks the rural pace of WA 14.

WALKING TOURS Downtown Vancouver historic walking tour. Pick up a brochure at the Clark County Historical Society Museum (see *Museums*) or the **Vancouver National Historic Trust** (360-992-1800), 750 Anderson Street, Vancouver.

A VIEW OF THE COLUMBIA RIVER NEAR MARYHILL

WINERY TOURS Since 2004, the Columbia Gorge has had its own appellation. Twenty or so wineries and some actual vineyards are scattered along both the Oregon and Washington sides of the gorge, making for a very scenic wine tour. For maps and information, contact the **Columbia Gorge Winegrowers' Association** (866-413-9463; www.columbiagorgewine.com), 515 East Second Street, The Dalles, Oregon.

✳ To Do

CAMPING **Beacon Rock State Park** (509-427-8265 or 999-226-7688), on WA 14 at milepost 3. Campground closed mid-Oct.–Mar. Twenty-six tent sites in a forested setting; five sites near boat moorage that are open year-round. No reservations.

Columbia Hills State Park (509-767-1159), on WA 14 at milepost 85. Campground closed Nov.–Mar. Four standard sites, eight partial utility sites, and six primitive sites for hikers and cyclists. No reservations.

&. **Maryhill State Park** (reservations 888-226-7688), off US 97, 12 miles south of Goldendale along the Columbia. Twenty tent sites and 50 RV sites; ADA restrooms and showers. Most water turned off in winter.

GOLF **Beacon Rock Golf Course** (509-427-5730), 102 Grenia Road, North Bonneville. Nine holes.

HIKING **Columbia Walkway,** 4 paved miles east from Beaches Restaurant (see *Where to Eat*), just east of I-5 in Vancouver. For an urban hike, stretch your legs along this 14-foot-wide path running along the river. Part of an attempt to rejuvenate the city's waterfront, it features ospreys, historical markers, benches, and a larger-than-life bronze statue of Illchee, a daughter of Chinook chief Comcomly.

Dog Mountain Trail, 3.7 miles; trailhead on WA 14 between mileposts 53 and 54, east of Stevenson. This is a rigorous but popular hike: rigorous because it rises 2,900 feet and popular for its wildflowers and panoramic views of the gorge and three volcanoes. The 7-mile loop can be broken into smaller trips; for a shorter ascent, try **Puppy Dog Mountain,** only 2,500 feet high. Brochures are available from Mount Adams Chamber of Commerce (see *Guidance*), on the highway just east of the Hood River Bridge.

HOT SPRINGS Bonneville Hot Springs (866-459-1678; www.bonnevilleresort .com), 1252 East Cascade Drive, just north of North Bonneville. These mineral-rich waters have attracted the ailing since presettlement times. Today it is a highly developed resort (see *Lodging*), but the mineral pool is also available to nonguests. Rates for three hours: $25 adults, $18 seniors Fri.–Sun.; $15 and $12, respectively, Mon.–Thurs.; children under two free.

Carson Mineral Hot Springs (509-427-8296; www.carsonhotspringresort.com), 372 St. Martin's Springs Road, Carson. This spring slightly upriver of Bonneville Hot Springs was modestly developed in about 1900 and remained a budget traveler's watering spot till the resort's renovations of 2006 (see *Lodging*), but the bathhouse is also open to nonguests. Call for rates.

KAYAKING AND RAFTING Zoller's Outdoor Odysseys (800-366-2004; www.zooraft.com), 1248 WA 141, White Salmon.

WIND SURFING On almost any day other than in winter, you can see bright sailboards skimming across the river's surface like water striders. The gorge's strong winds have drawn wind surfers for the past 20 years, contributing to a rebirth of some of the struggling river towns: Bingen on the Washington side and Hood River in Oregon have become meccas, but surfers are independent sorts, and you'll find them at various river beaches. For surfing information, check with the **Columbia Gorge Windsurfing Association** (541-386-9225; www.windsurf.gorge.net).

Doug's Beach State Park, on WA 14, 3 miles east of Lyle. This undeveloped day-use park under towering basalt cliffs is a favorite launch point for advanced wind surfers and wind surfing observers.

✳ Wilder Places

PARKS Beacon Rock State Park (509-427-8265), on WA 14 at milepost 35. A mecca for rock climbers, who like to scale the nearly sheer face of the 800-foot-tall volcanic plug, and for hikers who prefer a safer though still strenuous route to the top, Beacon Rock was so named by Lewis and Clark. It is a practical landmark and also the spot where they first noted tidal influences, though it's still 100 miles from the mouth of the Columbia. (It nearly became Biddle Rock, after an owner who built the trail to the top.) With a prime location on the Columbia, the 4,650-acre park is popular for fishing, boating, camping, and climbing. Climbing is restricted to certain faces to protect nesting raptors and sensitive areas; check with park rangers for information. A boat launch, moorage, and 9 miles of hiking trails are provided.

Columbia Hills State Park (509-767-1159), Box 426, Dallesport 98617; on WA 14 at milepost 85, 2 miles east of US 97. Closed Nov.–Mar. The prime attraction here is the Indian rock art (see *To See—Historic Sites*). But it's also good for beginning wind surfers, who enjoy the protected lake (actually created by river overflow when the dam was built a few miles downstream); for fishermen; and for rock climbers, who like to challenge the basalt walls of Horsethief Butte. Campsites, picnic tables, and 12.5 miles of hiking trails are also available.

PETROGLYPHS ARE VISIBLE AT COLUMBIA HILLS STATE PARK.

Doug's Beach State Park, on WA 14, 3 miles east of Lyle (see *To Do–Wind Surfing*). There are picnic tables but no water.

Maryhill State Park (509-773-5007), off US 97, 12 miles south of Goldendale. With nearly a mile of waterfront along the Columbia River, Maryhill draws boaters, swimmers, and water-skiers during the Columbia Plateau's hot, dry summers. A mile east is Sam Hill's Stonehenge replica, and to the west is his Maryhill Museum, both open to the public (see *To See—Historic Sites* and *Museums*). The park offers two boat ramps, a dock, and camping.

See also *To See—Historic Sites*.

WILDLIFE REFUGES Franz Lake, Steigerwald, and Pierce national wildlife refuges, in a chain along the Columbia just east of Washougal, are administered from Ridgefield National Wildlife Refuge (see the Mount St. Helens Area chapter). Designated to preserve wetlands for migrating waterfowl, they are

SAM HILL'S STONEHENGE REPLICA SITS ABOVE THE COLUMBIA RIVER NEAR MARYHILL STATE PARK.

fairly small, and only Steigerwald offers public access, via the Columbia Dike Trail; the trailhead is in nearby Captain William Clark Park (see *To See—Historic Sites*).

✳ Lodging

BED & BREAKFASTS

Bingen

Joslyn House (509-493-4888; www .joslynhouse.com), 706 West Steuben Street. Mary and Erastus Joslyn built their house in 1860 and settled down to grow fruits and vegetables for the burgeoning population. Subsequent owners added two imposing turrets and a double porch, so that it sits now rather startlingly on Bingen's small-town main street. Seven guest rooms come with shared bath and continental breakfast. $86–107.

Lyle

Morning Song Acres (509-365-3600; www.morningsongacres.com), 6 Oda Knight Road. Just north of Lyle, Morning Song is a contemporary structure sitting on 40 acres with views. Wildflowers, elbow room, and Wi-Fi— just about perfect, if you consider you can get dinner for an extra $10. Rates include full breakfast. $75–95; owners Myrin and Audrey Bentz invite negotiation.

HOSTELS

Bingen

Columbia River Gorge Hostel (509-493-3363; www.bingenschool.com), Box 155, corner of Cedar and Humboldt streets, Bingen. The Civilian Conservation Corps built this place, and it served as a school for many years; naturally, it draws the young and young at heart in its present incarnation as a hostel. Like most hostels, it's fairly spartan, with shared bathrooms and kitchen facilities, but it's clean, friendly, and convenient to downtown. Dorm beds $19; private rooms with linens and towel $49.

HOTELS

Camas

Camas Hotel (360-834-5722), 405 NE Fourth Avenue. Just a few miles from Portland and Vancouver, Camas's downtown is a small but cozy other-world, and the hotel is in the midst of it. The 1908 boardinghouse remained a residential and budget hotel until it was renovated a few years ago. Now all the rooms are stylish and have private baths. There's even an on-site restaurant, Oliver's. Shops, cafés, and movie theaters are a few steps away, and so is the Georgia Pacific plant that long supported the town. Rates include continental breakfast. $79–135.

Lyle

Lyle Hotel (800-447-6310; www.lyle hotel.com), 100 Seventh Street. The trains don't stop in Lyle anymore, but the 1905 railroad hotel is still here, with 10 simply but comfortably furnished rooms (bed, night table, chair, mirror) with shared baths and period wallpaper. What's not period, though, is free Wi-Fi. There's a small bar and restaurant downstairs (see *Where to Eat*), which may go a long way toward revitalizing the small town. Note: Live music at the restaurant may last till 10 or so. And trains do run past the hotel, though they don't seem to bother guests much. Rates include continental breakfast. $75–95.

Stevenson

Skamania Lodge (509-427-2547 or 800-221-7117; www.skamania.com), 1311 SW Skamania Lodge Way. Designed to remind us of the great lodges of a century ago, Skamania Lodge does the job with huge timbers taken from dismantled buildings, a grand stone fireplace, and pitched roofs—upsized, though, for the 21st century. It has 254 rooms, a conference center, a golf course, a spa, a fitness center, and all the amenities that were never dreamed of a hundred years ago. Its restaurant, the **Cascade Room,** is open for breakfast, lunch, and dinner, serving Northwest cuisine. $176–306.

Vancouver

The Heathman Lodge (360-254-3100; www.heathmanlodge.com), 7801 NE Greenwood Drive. The Heathman's native softwood and stone construction make it a modern take on the classic Northwest lodge, though its situation in a business park somewhat mutes the effect. Indian blankets and Inuit-style kayak frames decorate the lobby and mezzanine. The 142 guest rooms, on-site restaurant (see *Where to Eat*), spa, swimming pool, and fitness center make it a comfortable base for exploring Vancouver and surrounding areas. (They'll even bring a Bowflex exercise machine to your room.) $104–149.

&. ❦ **Hilton Vancouver Washington** (360-993-4500; www.vancouver washington.hilton.com), 301 West Sixth Street. This 226-room Hilton's very contemporary design is dominated by earth tones and fluid lines to evoke the Columbia River and Gorge. Art by Northwest artists decorates the rooms and halls, and efforts have been made to use regional talent, materials, and so forth—part of a "green" hotel, which also includes water and energy conservation, site design, and more. The spacious rooms, running from one bed to two beds to suites, have all the usual amenities—robes, flat-screen TVs, and more; those overlooking Esther Short Park (see *To See— Historic Sites*) have balconies. There's

a pool and fitness room as well. Some rooms are handicapped-accessible. Small pets allowed with a deposit. From $99.

White Salmon

♨ ❦ **Inn of the White Salmon** (509-493-2335 or 800-972-5226; www.white salmoninn.com), 172 West Jewett Boulevard. The stolid brick block, riotous back garden, and dignified 1930s furnishings give this place something of the air of a small-town English hotel. A parlor at one end of the building sports a piano, burgundy carpeting, and cushy chairs; the sunny breakfast room at the other is all china and lace tablecloths. The 16 rooms come with a groaning (breakfast) board. There is a tidy dorm room for those on a budget. Rooms $85–149 ($77 for stays of seven days or more); dorm beds $25–40.

RESORTS

Carson

&. **Carson Hot Springs** (509-427-8292 or 800-607-3678), 372 St. Martin's Springs Road. These mineral-laden springs were developed in the early 1900s, with a rustic hotel built in 1901 and rustic cabins added in 1923. For a century, this was a simple place to "take the waters" by soaking in an old bathtub and/or sipping them from a cup. That age has passed: A 2006 renovation eliminated the cabins and turned the old hotel into offices, adding a 28-room motel. The bathhouse, though, is still as it was, with individual tubs and separate areas for men and women. Definitely no frills and in need of some maintenance, it may not be for everyone, but it offers a budget hot-spring stay. $75–85.

North Bonneville

Bonneville Hot Springs Resort (866-459-1678; www.bonnevilleresort.com),

1252 East Cascade Drive. Hot springs bubble invitingly throughout the volcanic Cascade Range, and during settlement they were seized upon as much for their commercial as their healing properties. The first hotel at the Bonneville springs was constructed in 1882. Today's sleek resort opened in 2002 with a three-story Great Hall and fireplace, 6,000-square-foot spa, lap pool, hot tubs, and soaking pools—not to mention 78 geothermally heated rooms. Massage and spa treatments are available. Overall, the other end of the spectrum from Carson Hot Springs (above). Rooms $179–249; suites with hot tub, $499.

✳ Where to Eat
DINING OUT

Camas

Oliver's (360-210-4037; oliversatthe camashotel.com), 401 NE Fourth Avenue. Open for lunch and dinner Wed.–Sun. A welcome addition to the renovated Camas Hotel, Oliver's has branched out from river-town fare to become an upscale, experimental eatery. It's not every day that you see Muscovy duck breast on a menu, or veal with a Grand Marnier–cranberry glaze. Not so easy on the pocketbook, but intriguing.

Lyle

Lyle Hotel (509-365-5953 or 800-447-6310; www.lylehotel.com), 100 Seventh Street. Open 5:30–8 Thurs.–Sat., 9–1 Sun. A surprising find in tiny Lyle, the hotel's (see *Lodging*) restaurant offers fine seasonal menus at reasonable prices and an extensive, award-winning list of regional wines. The half-dozen dinner entrées are all carefully and wonderfully made. Polished wood floors, light yellow walls, and seating for perhaps 30 create a cozy atmosphere, and you may even catch a live flamenco guitar performance. It always seems busy despite being way off the beaten track. There's also a lunch barbecue on summer weekends.

Stevenson

Skamania Lodge (800-221-7117; www.skamania.com), 1131 Skamania Lodge Way. Open for breakfast, lunch, and dinner Mon.–Sat., brunch and dinner Sun. The Cascade Dining room is the lodge's formal dining venue, serving steak, game, seafood, and vegetarian dishes overlooking the Columbia River Gorge.

Vancouver

Hudson's Bar and Grill (360-816-6100; www.hudsonsbarandgrill.com), 7801 NE Greenwood Drive. Open for breakfast, lunch, and dinner Mon.–Fri., brunch and dinner Sat.–Sun. Hudson's is located in the Heathman Lodge (see *Lodging*), where head chef Ray Delgado brings you seasonal menus emphasizing fresh, local Northwest ingredients. The cuisine is complemented by nouveau Northwest decor featuring log accents and a dugout canoe over the fireplace. Reservations recommended.

The Grant House (360-906-1101; thegranthouse.us), 1101 Officers' Row. The historic Grant House, with its several rooms, woodwork, and high ceilings (see *To See—Historic Homes*), makes a fine spot for a leisurely lunch or dinner. The menu is hearty Northwest fare, featuring seafood, meats, and fresh greens.

EATING OUT

Bingen

Beneventi's Pizza (509-493-2177), 201 West Steuben Avenue. Open 10:30–9 Mon.–Fri., 12–9 Sat., 12–8 Sun. A handy lunch spot for surfers and families, Beneventi's serves 8-inch to 20-inch pizzas using their own dough and tomato sauce; a variety of sandwiches is also available.

🖉 **Big River Diner** (509-493-1414), 740 East Steuben Avenue. This comfortable place serves family fare for breakfast, lunch, and dinner: homemade soups, salads, sandwiches, and meat-and-potatoes staples (with some pasta dishes for good measure).

Vancouver
Beaches Restaurant and Bar (360-699-1592), 1919 South Access Road. Open for lunch 11–4 daily; dinner 4–9 Sun.–Mon. and 4–10 Tues.–Sat. It's big and busy and offers plate-glass views of the Columbia. The eclectic menu ranges from pub fare to Chinese to Mexican.

The Jerusalem Café (360-906-0306; www.thejerusalemcafe.com), 106 West Evergreen. Open 11–9 Mon.–Fri., 12–9 Sat. This small family restaurant attracts a steady stream of lunch and dinner regulars with its informal atmosphere and homemade Middle Eastern dishes—*shawarma*, falafel, meze, and more. A second location is at 516 SE Chkalov Drive.

Little Italy's Trattoria (360-737-2363; www.littleitalystrattoria.com), 901 Washington Street. Open 11–9 Mon.–Thurs., 11–10 Fri.–Sat., 1–9 Sun. Another downtown lunch and dinner treasure, Little Italy's has the red and ocher walls and plastic checked tablecloths of an old-time Italian restaurant, and the cuisine takes you back to old immigrant neighborhoods, too. Pizzas come in both American and Neapolitan versions, splendid with marinara sauce and mozzarella; pasta and antipasti come in various shapes and sizes, all tempting. Reasonable, too. They have another location at 204 SE Park Plaza Drive.

McMenamin's on the Columbia (360-699-1521), 1801 SE Columbia River Drive. Open 11–11 Sun.–Thurs., 11–1 AM Fri.–Sat. McMenamin's is a quirky Northwest fixture that started in the 1970s, with pubs and hotels dotting small-town Washington and Oregon. "Brew with a view," they call this one: There's a viewable brewery on-site, but the main view is the Columbia, whether through the windows or on the patio. Choose from a selection of two hundred ales and pub fare for lunch or dinner. They're known for their burgers, fish-and-chips, and black-and-tan brownies.

Tommy O's Aloha Café (360-694-5107; www.tommyosaloha.com), 801 A Washington. This local dinner favorite specializes in Hawaiian and Pacific Rim cuisine, from Korean *kalbi* ribs to slow-roasted pork to (of course) halibut and salmon. Another location at 4101 SE 192nd Street.

White Salmon
Everybody's Brewing (509-637-2774; www.everybodysbrewing.com), 151 East Jewett Boulevard. Open for lunch and dinner Tues.–Sun. This is the Northwest, where almost everybody really is brewing, especially here in wind surfer territory. A family-friendly, polished-wood pub with the proper reverence for beer, Everybody's is also a handy place for lunch or dinner with a mixture of regular pub food (chips and salsa) and exotica (Kerala curried eggplant).

✳ Selective Shopping
ART White Salmon Glassworks (509-493-8400; www.whitesalmon glass.com), 105 East Jewett, White Salmon. Call for hours. Part of the town's revival through art, the glassworks took over a former grocery store to produce and showcase creations in glass by local artists. The public is invited to glassblowing demonstrations on Friday nights.

BOATS White Salmon Boat Works (509-637-4393; www.raysdreamboats .com), 230 East Jewett Boulevard, White Salmon. Call for hours. Okay, so you don't really want to buy a wooden canoe, much less build one, as owner Ray Klebba would urge, but I bet your spouse does. Or will. Klebba has won awards for his kayaks, rowboats, and canoes and can sell you plans, kits, classes, or an entire boat. And even if a boat's not on your shopping list, it's fun just to look at his beautiful craft.

OUTLET STORES Pendleton Mill Outlet Store (360-835-1118 or 800-568-2480; www.pendletonmillstore .com), Two 17th Street, Washougal. Tours at 9, 10, 11, and 1:30 Mon.–Fri. Closed two weeks in Dec. and two weeks in Aug. (call ahead). Remember the Pendleton blankets that became a major trading item among American Indians just about the time the frontier closed? Well, Pendleton Woolen Mills is still alive and well and producing blankets, not to mention men's and women's wear and fabric by the yard. It started in 1863, when the Oregon Country was being opened up to sheep (much to the disgust of cattle ranchers), and Englishman Thomas Kay was brought in to oversee the weaving. He later moved the mill to Pendleton, Oregon, and opened other mills around the Northwest—the one in Washougal dates from 1912. Most of the wool is still domestically produced and woven, though the sewing may be done elsewhere (some garments are labeled "Made in China"). You can tour the mill to learn about the process, then browse the shop for the signature blankets (there's a line devoted to Indian themes) and other fine wool products.

✳ Special Events

June: **White Salmon Spring Festival** (509-637-2869), White Salmon. Enjoy works by local artists, music, square dancing, and bratwurst.

September: **Huckleberry Festival** (509-493-3607), Daubenspeck Park, at the west end of Bingen. Besides huckleberries, you'll find beer and bratwurst.

MOUNT ADAMS AND GOLDENDALE AREA

Mount Adams is a giant standing 50 miles north of the Columbia River, not easily accessed from anywhere, but a presence guarding the river opposite Oregon's Mount Hood. Contemplative side trips up narrow roads lead to the skirts of Mount Adams. Goldendale provides otherwise scant visitor services near this area's eastern end.

GUIDANCE **Klickitat County Visitor Center** (509-773-7060; www.klickitat county.org), 205 South Columbus Avenue, Goldendale 98620.

Mount Adams Chamber of Commerce (509-493-3630; www.mtadamschamber .com), One Heritage Plaza, White Salmon 98672.

Mount Adams Ranger District (509-395-3400), **Gifford Pinchot National Forest,** 2455 WA 141, Trout Lake 98560.

GETTING THERE **WA 14** runs along the Washington side of the Columbia between **WA 141** and **US 97.** WA 141 heads north from WA 14 through Husum and B Z Corner to Trout Lake. US 97 heads north from Maryhill to Goldendale (and beyond to connect with **I-82** at Toppenish). **WA 142** runs west from Golden- dale to WA 14 at Lyle. Between WA 142 and WA 141 at Trout Lake, back roads go through Glenwood.

Portland International Airport (503-460-4040 or 877-739-4636; www.portof portland.com) is off I-5 at 7000 NE Airport Way, Portland, OR, about an hour southwest of this area.

AMTRAK (800-USA-RAIL; www.amtrak.com) stops in Bingen and Wishram, both on WA 14.

Greyhound (800-231-2222; www.greyhound.com) stops in The Dalles and Hood River in Oregon.

GETTING AROUND It's preferable to have a car if you want to be mobile in this area.

Skyline Hospital (509-493-1101; www.skylinehospital .com), 211 Skyline Drive, White Salmon.

✳ To See

HISTORIC HOMES **Whitcomb-Cole Log House** (509-546-8300), near the headquarters of Conboy Lake National Wildlife Refuge (see *Wilder Places— Wildlife Refuges*), 6 Hansen Road, Glenwood; 5 miles southwest of Glenwood off the Glenwood–Trout Lake road. Open dawn to dusk. Free. Visitors can see a reminder of pioneer life in the shadow of remote Mount Adams at this log house, built by settler John Cole in 1891. Originally located 2 miles away from its present location, it housed his family of seven for several years. Today, restored, the chinked-log home on the National Register of Historic Places stands starkly against the sky.

MUSEUMS **Presby Mansion** (509-773-4303), 127 West Broadway, Goldendale. Open 10–4 daily Apr. 15–Oct. 15; otherwise by appointment. $5 adults, $1 children 6–12. This 1902 dentist's mansion resembles a gigantic wedding cake, all gables and gingerbread and spindles, with the requisite wraparound porch and turret. There's even what looks like a widow's walk, though the nearest ocean is a safe 200 miles away. The house doubles as a historical museum: The downstairs is furnished as a typical prosperous home of the period, with some original pieces and lots of donated ones. Particularly intriguing are several early vacuum cleaners, in which the vacuum is created by vigorous pumping, or in one case by a bellows. The upper rooms variously depict a schoolroom, local church, general store, and more. One even houses a collection of coffee grinders. Since the house was built with 20 rooms, there's plenty of space.

Whoop-n-Holler Museum (509-896-2344), 1 Whitmore Road, Bickleton; off East Road 11 miles south of Bickleton. Hours variable; call ahead. $3. The Whitmores' private museum consists partly of family memorabilia—they've been in the area more than a hundred years—partly of eclectic acquisitions such as an old schoolhouse, and partly of Lawrence's antique car collection, which fills a good-sized barn. This place is definitely off the beaten path.

NATURAL WONDERS **Mount Adams.** Standing 30 miles east of the general crest of the Cascades, Adams is an outlier among volcanoes and splendid in its isolation. At 12,276 feet it's the second-highest peak in Washington, but it's bigger in volume than champion Mount Rainier and a solemn presence towering over the Yakima Valley and dry plains. Indians call Mount Adams "Pahto," one of the sons of the Great Spirit who fought with his brother, Wyeast (Mount Hood), over the beautiful Loowit (Mount St. Helens; see Mount St. Helens Area chapter) with fire and brimstone. Pahto was a sacred mountain nonetheless, being the source of waters, especially for the lands to the east. It hasn't erupted recently, but fumaroles indicate that it probably will again. Forest roads access its south and west sides from Trout Lake, north of White Salmon; the largely inaccessible east side is part of the Yakama Reservation.

PLANETARIUMS **Goldendale Observatory State Park** (509-773-3141), 1602 Observatory Drive, Goldendale. Open 2–5 and 8–midnight Wed.–Sun. Apr.–Sept.;

MOUNT ADAMS RISES ABOVE THE PLAIN NORTH OF THE COLUMBIA GORGE.

2–5 and 7–10 Fri.–Sun. Oct.–Mar. Donation requested. It was a case of a telescope looking for a home. The clear, dry skies and relatively low (though increasing) light pollution of Goldendale would make it a logical place for an astronomical observatory. But apparently no one had thought of it till 1964, when four amateur astronomers at Clark College in Vancouver built the 24.5-inch reflector and offered to donate it to anyone who would build it a home. The city of Goldendale volunteered, and the Goldendale Observatory was born. The official site for observing the solar eclipse of 1979, it draws thousands of viewers to major events such as the passage of the Hale-Bopp comet and the 2003 perigee of Mars. Besides the reflector there are 3-inch and 6-inch refractors. Evening programs include talks on astronomy and viewing various celestial objects. In the afternoon, you can tour the telescope room and grounds, which include seven types of sundials made by director Stephen Stout.

SCENIC DRIVES Glenwood Loop, about 100 miles from Bingen to Trout Lake to Glenwood to Lyle and back to Bingen. This tour starts in the Columbia Gorge and takes you up WA 141 along the wild White Salmon River to Trout Lake. There you turn east onto back roads to Glenwood and on to the Klickitat, another wild and scenic river, at WA 142. This highway takes you back to the gorge at Lyle, and WA 14 returns west back to Bingen. For a shorter trip of about 70 miles, you can turn south at Glenwood, take in the Conboy Lake National Wildlife Refuge (see *Wilder Places—Wildlife Refuges*), and return to WA 141 at B Z Corners. The longer trip takes about four hours, the shorter trip two.

UNIQUE ADVENTURES St. John the Forerunner Greek Orthodox Monastery (509-773-7141; www.stjohnmonastery.org), 5 Timmer Lane, Goldendale. Open 9–2 and 4–6 daily; shop open 9–6 Mon.–Sat. Call to arrange a one- or two-day monastic retreat. As you head north on US 97 from the Columbia Gorge, the views as you wind up the cliffs are stunning. Soon you enter a welcome forest, and at milepost 24, a clearing reveals the Greek Orthodox monastery of St. John. Three Greek nuns founded the community in 1995. Now 16 nuns support themselves with traditional religious crafts and a Greek bakery; visitors are welcome to stop by the gift shop. Modest dress is expected.

WALKING TOURS A **self-guided historic tour** of Goldendale takes in the older homes and public buildings of this Old West town; information is available at the Presby Mansion (see *Museums*).

✷ To Do

BICYCLING **Gifford Pinchot National Forest**'s (see *Guidance*) roads and trails are mostly open to mountain bikes, except in wilderness areas.

Hardtime Loop, 11 miles, at the Oldman Pass Sno-Park, 24 miles north of Carson. This trail for cross-country skiers in winter has rolling terrain with mountain views; in summer the ski-trail system offers bike rides of varying levels of difficulty.

Klickitat Trail (www.klickitat-trail.org), 31 miles from Lyle to near Goldendale. Check the website regarding washouts or other barriers on this hiker-biker trail.

Trout Lake country roads. For road bikes, the area around this hamlet offers low traffic, level roads, and fine views; contact the Mount Adams Chamber of Commerce (see *Guidance*) for information.

CAMPING **Brooks Memorial State Park** (509-773-5382), 2465 US 97; 140 miles north of Goldendale. Has 22 tent sites, 23 RV sites, and 2 primitive sites, plus a group camp; restrooms, cabins, and tepees, too. No reservations.

Guler Trout Lake County Park (509-773-3900), 18 Park Road, Trout Lake. Forty-five sites; restrooms and showers. No reservations.

Gifford Pinchot National Forest (reservations 877-444-6777; www.recreation .gov). Camping is plentiful in the national forest surrounding Mount Adams. Some campgrounds require fees; some don't.; In addition, it's usually permissible to camp fee-free outside an official campground, away from bodies of water and leaving no trace; check for regulations. Forest Service campsites include the following, open summer only:

&. **Blue Lake Creek,** on FR 23 south of North Fork. Eleven sites; water, picnic tables, and ADA toilets. It's small but near off-road-vehicle trails. Reserve at 877-444-6777; www.recreation.gov.

Council Lake, on FR 2334 just west of FR 23. Seven sites.

Crest Horse Campground, on FR 60; from WA 14 at Carson, take FR 63 north to FR 60. Four unimproved sites; one toilet.

Cultus Creek, on FR 24 just west of Little Goose. Fifty sites; restrooms but no water.

Forlorn Lakes, on FR 6035 north of Carson-Guler Road (FR 24). Twenty-five sites; toilet.

Goose Lake, on Carson-Guler Road (FR 24) west of Forlorn Lakes Road. Eighteen walk-in sites; toilet. Reservations required in summer.

Little Goose, on FR 24 north of South Prairie Road. Six sites; toilet.

Morrison Creek, on FR 500 north of Mount Adams Recreation Road. Twelve sites; restrooms. Access road is rough.

Moss Creek, on Oklahoma Road north of Willard. Seventeen sites; water and toilets. Reserve at 877-444-6777; www.recreation.gov.

North Fork, on FR 23 east of FR 25; from US 12 at Randle, turn right on FR 25 (Woods Creek Road), then left on FR 23 (Cispus Road) for 10 miles. Thirty-three sites; water, toilets, and picnic tables. Largish campground along the Cispus River.

Oklahoma, on FR 18 north of South Prairie Road. Twenty-two sites; water and toilets. Reserve at 877-444-6777; www.recreation.gov.

Peterson Prairie, on Carson-Guler Road (FR 24) just west of the end of WA 141. Twenty-seven sites; water and toilets. Reserve at 877-444-6777; www .recreation.gov.

Saddle, off FR 24 northeast of Tillicum. Twelve sites; no water or toilet.

Takhlakh, on FR 2329 north of FR 23. Fifty-four sites. Reservations required July–Sept. Reserve at 877-444-6777; www.recreation.gov.

Tower Rock, on FR 2306 south of Cispus Road; from US 12 at Randle, take FR 25 (Woods Creek Road) south, then turn left on FR 23 for 8 miles, right on FR 28, and right again on FR 76 to FR 2306. Twenty-one sites; water, toilets, and picnic area. On the Cispus River between Mount Adams and Mount St. Helens. Store nearby. Reserve at 877-444-6777; www.recreation.gov.

Walupt Lake, on FR 2160 east of FR 21. Forty-two sites; water and toilets.

FOREST SERVICE CABIN RENTALS Peterson Prairie Guard Station (reservation required: 877-444-6777; www.recreation.gov), on FR 24 about 15 miles northwest of Mount Adams Ranger Station at Trout Lake. Built for fire guards in 1926, it sleeps four; there's one bedroom, two futon beds, a kitchen, and a living room. It's in the middle of huckleberry country. The cabin is available year-round, although the plumbing is outdoors; access by snowmobile in winter. $50.

GOLF Husum Hills Golf Course (509-493-1211), 820 WA 141, Husum. Nine holes.

HIKING Klickitat Trail (www.klickitat-trail.org), 31 miles from Lyle to near Goldendale. This former railway corridor follows the wild and scenic Klickitat River for 11 miles before rising through remote Swale Canyon. The trail is open to hikers and mountain bikers; dogs must be on a leash. Much adjacent land is private property, but a two-day trip could be broken at a campground or motel in Klickitat. Check the website for closures due to washouts or fire hazard.

Pacific Crest Trail (916-285-1846; www.pcta.org), 5325 Elkhorn Boulevard, 1331 Garden Highway, Sacramento, CA 95833. About 500 of the Pacific Crest Trail's 2,650 miles pass through the state of Washington. In this region, the PCT passes through the **Indian Heaven and Mount Adams wilderness areas** (see *Wilder Places—Wilderness Areas*) for a total of 150 miles between Cascade Locks and White Pass.

Weldon Wagon Trail, 3 miles from Indian Creek Road, off WA 141 in Husum (marked by a sign), to Sanborn Road. The trail follows a former wagon roadbed, built by landowners east of Husum in 1908 to get their apples to market. But the local profitability of apples was short-lived. The road was abandoned after 1923 and has mostly reverted to (state) forest. The trail climbs through an area rich in shade and birdsong.

Willard Springs Trail, 2-mile loop at Conboy Lake National Wildlife Refuge (see *Wilder Places—Wildlife Refuges*); 5 miles southwest of Glenwood off the Glenwood–Trout Lake road. This easy, level (but not paved) loop goes through open marsh, lake edge, and pine forest habitat, with abundant wildlife, including sandhill cranes, bald eagles, elk, otters, deer, and more.

KAYAKING AND RAFTING Wet Planet Whitewater (877-390-9445; www.wet planetwhitewater.com), 860 WA 141, Husum. Several Wild and Scenic–designated rivers flow from the Mount Adams region into the Columbia, offering some exciting white-water rafting and kayaking. This outfitter and guide service will take you there.

✳ Wilder Places

PARKS Brooks Memorial State Park (509-773-5382), 2465 US 97; 140 miles north of Goldendale. Just south of 3,149-foot Satus Pass, this 700-acre park on the Little Klickitat River has camping, picnicking, fishing, hiking, and an environmental learning center with cabins and tepees.

WILDERNESS AREAS About a third of Mount Adams lies on the Yakama Reservation. The rest is part of **Gifford Pinchot National Forest** (see *Guidance*) and is in or near several wilderness areas:

Goat Rocks Wilderness, 105,600 acres; between US 12 at White Pass and the north side of Mount Adams. These remains of an extinct volcano are named for the mountain goats you can still sometimes see.

Indian Heaven Wilderness, 20,600 acres on the southwest side of Mount Adams; accessible in summer by FR 24 west of WA 141 at Trout Lake. These acres and acres of wild huckleberries were a traditional Native area for berry picking and drying. Part of it is still reserved for Indian use only, but other areas are open for picking by the general public seasonally.

Mount Adams Wilderness, 46,353 acres comprising most of the mountain's higher elevations. These are quite remote, untrammeled areas where you won't find crowds, but you will find wildlife, views, and extreme beauty.

WILDLIFE REFUGES Conboy Lake National Wildlife Refuge (509-546-8300), 5 miles southwest of Glenwood off the Glenwood–Trout Lake road; office at 6 Hansen Road, Glenwood. Open dawn to dusk; closed during hunting season. The lake is now a wetland since settlers set about draining it in the late 1800s. By the 1960s, the claims were abandoned, and 6,532 acres of marsh, forest, and grassland became a refuge managed for the many species of wildlife, from migrating ducks and swans to elk, coyotes, beavers, and more. Refuge roads and a 2-mile trail (see *To Do—Hiking*) provide observation opportunities, while sweeping mountain and prairie views and a pioneer home (see *To See—Historic Homes*) are further attractions.

✳ Lodging

BED & BREAKFASTS

Husum

Husum Highlands Bed and Breakfast (509-493-4503 or 800-808-9812; www.husumhighlands.com), 70 Postgren Road. Leaving the White Salmon River, you climb and climb some more, the last 3 miles on gravel (which does get plowed in winter), till you come to a gate marked WELCOME. Suddenly the woods open up, and if you're lucky, you're staring at the ice cream cone of Mount Hood across the Columbia, seemingly at eye level. You're at Husum Highlands B&B, built and furnished by Carol and Jerry Stockwell to look remarkably like an old farmhouse, on 22 acres of meadow, garden, and forest. You want quiet? You've got it—plus friendly hosts, comfortable rooms, and a hearty breakfast. Five guest rooms each have a private (sometimes adjacent) bath. Dinner available on request. $150–175.

Trout Lake

Kelly's Trout Creek Inn Bed and Breakfast (509-395-2769; www.kellys bnb.com), 25 Mount Adams Road. This is a modest 1940s farmhouse with three guest rooms, right by the creek. Rates include full breakfast; dinner available on request (when making your reservation). $75–100.

COTTAGES AND CABINS

Trout Lake

Serenity's Cabins (509-395-2500 or 800-276-7993; www.serenitys.com), milepost 22.5 on WA 141. Five handcrafted chalets in the woods on the way to Mount Adams sleep two to six. Most have "lite-cooking" kitchens; there's a restaurant on the premises. $89–259; ask about midweek discounts.

HOTELS

Trout Lake

Trout Lake Country Inn (509-395-3667; www.troutlakeinn.com), 15 Guler Road. Four rooms, two with private baths, occupy the attic above this 1904 dance hall. The spreading front porch and stepped false front suggest a colorful and ongoing history. In fact, it continues to be an informal but lively community gathering place (see *Where to Eat*), and in the spirit of pioneer networking it's a Wi-Fi hot spot. The restaurant below has live music Thurs.–Sun. nights; if you prefer a quieter night, come midweek. $50.

Trout Lake Valley Inn (509-395-3200; www.troutlakevalleyinn.com), 2300 WA 141. A rustic board-and-batten motel, with log furniture and wide lawns, the inn opened in 2002. A porch extends the full length of the building, offering chairs and a table for each unit, so you can contemplate the gardens over your morning coffee or after a day's outdoor recreation. Rates include continental breakfast. $90–110.

LODGES

Glenwood

🏃 **Flying L Ranch** (509-364-3488; www.mt-adams.com), 25 Flying L Lane. The snowy dome of Mount Adams seems to rise right behind this 100-acre ranch with a choice of cabins, a six-room lodge, or a five-room guesthouse. All facilities have kitchens, and the lodge has a large living room and library available to all guests. Rates include continental breakfast. Families welcome. No cell service, Wi-Fi, TVs, or DVDs. Come on down! Rooms $95–150; cabins $165–190.

✳ Where to Eat

EATING OUT

B Z Corners

✐ **The Logs** (509-493-1402), corner of
WA 141 and the Glenwood Road. If
you like broasted chicken, or even if
you don't, this log house might be an
atmospheric lunch or dinner stop. It
first opened in the 1920s and is said to
have been a Wild West kind of place—
it was pretty out of the way back then,
and the only spot for eating (drinking,
gaming, and so forth) for miles around.
It's a family place now, and though
they do serve about a dozen chicken
dishes—including chicken potpie,
chicken gizzards, and chicken livers—
there are also burgers, pizzas, salads,
sandwiches, and a children's menu. It's
being renovated as of this writing but
plans to reopen in 2012.

Trout Lake

Trout Lake Country Inn (509-395-
3667; www.troutlakecountryinn.com),
15 Guler Road. Open for breakfast,
lunch, and dinner Thurs.–Mon. in
summer. The rustic inn was a merry
eatery and drinkery for the farmers
and loggers who hung out here in
1904. It's still a pretty active place,
with live music by regional bands three
nights a week in summer. Local wines
and beers are served, along with burgers, tacos, and pizza anytime and larger
meals for dinner.

✳ Special Events

July: **Trout Lake Festival of the
Arts** (509-395-2448), Trout Lake.
Juried artists from around the gorge
display their work in the barn at the
former Farm Bed and Breakfast.
There's food and music, too.

MOUNT ST. HELENS AREA

T he beauty of the West is that so much of its geological history is right out there for all to see, and nowhere more so than at Mount St. Helens. You catch only glimpses of the mountain from I-5, but on either of the western access roads, you'll round a bend and there it is, reflected tranquilly in Silver Lake if it's not hidden in the clouds. The jagged, truncated peak graphically reminds you of what happened not so long ago. Until 1980, St. Helens was one of the most symmetrical cones in the Cascades, a mountain whose beauty was noted both in Indian legends and by early explorers. Today it's a demonstration area of volcanic destruction and recovery.

The mountain is set in a national monument within a national forest. Although plenty of facilities will explain the mountain to you, food and lodging are scant beyond the interstate, where the offerings are hardly inspiring. This chapter's I-5 communities include Ridgefield, Battle Ground, and Woodland just north of Vancouver; the larger towns of Longview and Kelso; and Castle Rock, Vader, and Toledo to the north. If you leave the interstate and head east to find some of the simple accommodations along the back roads, you'll be rewarded by quiet forest, friendly service, and maybe some elk. Towns such as Amboy, Ariel, Yale, and Cougar are south of the mountain; Silver Lake, Toutle, and Kid Valley lie due west of the mountain between it and I-5. On the way up to Mount St. Helens, which is surrounded by visitors centers, make sure you have gas in your tank.

GUIDANCE Cowlitz County Visitor and Community Services (360-577-3137; www.co.cowlitz.wa.us), 207 Fourth Avenue, Longview 98632.

Gifford Pinchot National Forest Headquarters (360-891-5000; www.fs.fed.us /giffordpinchot), 10600 NE 51st Circle, Vancouver 98682. Rangers are also stationed in the **Cowlitz Valley Ranger District** (360-497-1100), 10024 US 12, Randle 98377.

Kelso Longview Chamber of Commerce (360-423-4800; www.kelsolongview chamber.org), 1563 Olympia Way, Longview 98632.

Kelso Visitor and Volcano Information Center (360-577-8058), 105 Minor Road, Kelso 98626.

Mount St. Helens National Volcanic Monument Headquarters (360-449-7800), 42218 NE Yale Bridge Road, Amboy 98601. This center for visitor information is not actually located within the monument.

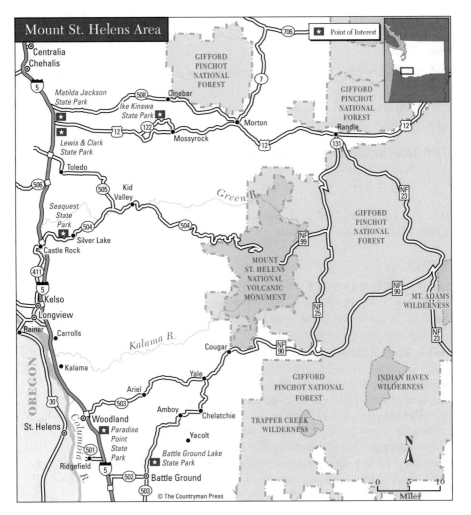

Mount St. Helens Area

★ Point of Interest

Centralia
Chehalis
Matilda Jackson State Park
Ike Kinswa State Park
Lewis & Clark State Park
Toledo
Seaquest State Park
Silver Lake
Castle Rock
Kelso
Longview
Rainer
Carrolls
Kalama
Ariel
Woodland
Paradise Point State Park
Ridgefield
Battle Ground
St. Helens

GIFFORD PINCHOT NATIONAL FOREST
Cinebar
Mossyrock
Kid Valley
Morton
Randle
GIFFORD PINCHOT NATIONAL FOREST
Green R.
GIFFORD PINCHOT NATIONAL FOREST
MOUNT ST. HELENS NATIONAL VOLCANIC MONUMENT
MT. ADAMS WILDERNESS
Kalama R.
Cougar
Yale
Amboy
Chelatchie
Yacolt
Battle Ground Lake State Park
GIFFORD PINCHOT NATIONAL FOREST
INDIAN HAVEN WILDERNESS
TRAPPER CREEK WILDERNESS
OREGON
Columbia R.

N

0   5   10
Miles

© The Countryman Press

Woodland Chamber of Commerce and Tourist Center (360-225-9552; www
.woodlandwachamber.com), 900 Goerig Street, Woodland 98674.

GETTING THERE I-5 is the major corridor in this region. **WA 501, WA 502,**
and **WA 503** connect towns near Vancouver. **WA 503** from I-5 at exit 21 parallels
the Lewis River from Woodland east to Cougar on the southern edge of the
national monument. It connects with **FR 90,** leading east to **FR 25,** which takes
you north along the remote eastern side past **FR 99,** the road west up to the
Windy Ridge Viewpoint, as close as you can or would want to get to the crater. The
latter route is closed in winter. FR 25 continues north to US 12 at Randle. **WA
504,** off I-5 at exit 48, winds 52 scenic miles east past the Silver Lake Visitor Center and up the Toutle River to the Johnston Ridge Observatory, passing several
educational experiences on the way. **WA 505** leaves I-5 at exit 59 to join WA 504
from the north.

Portland International Airport (503-460-4234 or 877-739-4636; www.portof portland.com) is off I-5 at 7000 NE Airport Way, Portland, OR, north of the monument.

AMTRAK (800-USA-RAIL; www.amtrak.com) stops in Kelso at 501 South First Avenue.

Greyhound (360-423-7380 or 800-231-2222; www.greyhound.com) also stops in Kelso at 200 Kelso Drive.

GETTING AROUND Community Urban Bus Service (360-442-5663; www .cubs-bus.com) runs five routes in the Longview-Kelso area. Beyond the I-5 corridor there is no public transit, so you'll want a car.

MEDICAL EMERGENCY St. John Medical Center (360-414-2000 or 800-438-7562), 1615 Delaware, Longview.

✳ To See

FARMS AND GARDENS Holland America Bulb Farms (360-225-4512), 1066 South Pekin Road, Woodland. Farm open seasonally; shop open 9–5 Tues.–Sat. year-round. In the proud tradition of Dutch bulbs, this farm is a blaze of tulips and daffodils in the spring.

Hulda Klager Lilac Gardens (360-225-8996; www.lilacgardens.com), 115 South Pekin Road, Woodland. Gardens open 10–4 daily; house open only for special events (see *Historic Homes*). $2 adults, children under 12 free. Hulda Klager immigrated from Germany as an infant and ended up in Woodland in 1877, at the age of 14. Always a lover of plants, she began to experiment with creating hybrids in the early 1900s (especially apples—she liked to bake pies). But she soon found her vocation growing and creating lilac hybrids and became renowned for her gardens, even starting over from scratch after a flood wiped them out in 1948. In two years, she had replanted and continued her work and her yearly open houses till her death in 1960 at the age of 96. The 4.5-acre property is now run by the Hulda Klager Lilac Society. Besides lilacs, the grounds include a Victorian garden.

HISTORIC HOMES Hulda Klager House (360-225-8996; www.lilacgardens .com), 115 Southern Pekin Road, Woodland. Open only on special occasions. The house was built by Hulda's German immigrant family in the 1880s. She lived in it, tending and propagating her lilacs, till death in 1960. A dignified, gabled farmhouse, it has been restored by the Hulda Klager Lilac Society, along with its water tower, windmill, and woodshed. The whole property is a National Historic Site. The gardens can be visited all year (see *Farms and Gardens*).

Judge Columbia Lancaster's House, 32410 NW Lancaster Road, Ridgefield. Not open to the public (the house is still a private residence). This fine house, with its porches and white columns, could hardly fail to impress. Built in 1850, it is among the oldest frame houses in the state. Lancaster's original name was Thomas; he was renamed as a child in honor of the river. Supreme judge of the Oregon Territory, he helped work out the separation of Oregon from Washington that was finalized in 1853. It's said that Ulysses S. Grant, among others, slept in this house.

Pomeroy Living History Farm (360-686-3537), 20902 SE Lucia Falls Road, Yacolt. Open 10–5 Sat., 1–5 Sun. in summer. $5 adults, $3 children 3–11. The farm dates from 1910, though the two-story house, built with logs from the property, is slightly younger. Today it houses exhibits and living-history demonstrations on early farm life in the area.

HISTORIC SITES Cedar Creek Grist Mill (360-225-5832; www.cedarcreek gristmill.com), Box 1404, Woodland 98674; from Woodland take NW Hayes Road, which becomes Cedar Creek Road, and after 8 miles turn left onto Grist Mill Road. Open 1–4 Sat., 2–4 Sun. Donation accepted. Volunteers at this restored 1876 mill grind flour, cornmeal, and even apples for cider, using only waterpower and millstones. The only mill still doing so in Washington, it is on the National Register of Historic Places.

Longview (www.mylongview.com), on I-5 between Woodland and Castle Rock. The town was built in the 1920s as one of the nation's first planned communities. The person responsible for this was lumber baron Robert A. Long, who, like many in his day, had great plans for the state, or at least for his corner of it. A **walking tour guide** available from the city's website includes these historic structures:

Columbia River Mercantile Building, 1339 Commerce Street, Longview. The Merk, as it's called, contained company stores and still is a retail center.

Library, 1600 Louisiana Street, Longview. This was a gift to the city from Long himself, with a cupola, balustrade, and arched windows.

Monticello Hotel, 1405 17th Avenue, Longview. One of the first city buildings, this imposing hotel opened in 1923 for businesspersons and others expected to flock to the new city's opportunities. Next, logically, was the train station, which is no longer standing.

MUSEUMS Cathlapotle Plank House (360-887-3046, www.plankhouse.org), at Ridgefield National Wildlife Refuge (see *Wilder Places—Wildlife Refuges*); from Ridgefield, take Main Street north 1 mile to the refuge. Open 12–4 Sat.–Sun. Apr.–Oct. Free. Opened in March 2005, the plank house is a careful reproduction of the cedar houses built by the Chinookan and other tribes of the region. Lewis and Clark mentioned a village of 14 such houses containing perhaps 900 individuals when they camped near here in 1805. Excavations have revealed the traces of 6 dwellings, the largest about 200 feet long. Built of cedar planks stuck vertically in the ground, the Cathlapotle Plank House (named for a local tribe) measures 78 feet by 37 feet and could have housed many families. Enthusiastic docents are happy to explain how each family was allocated its "booth" based on social standing, how cooking was done in common cooking pits in the middle of the house, and how smoke was released by adjusting a sort of skylight. Sculptures and paintings by modern tribal members, based on description and tradition, adorn both interior and exterior. Future plans for the site include a museum and venue for tribal events.

Cowlitz County Historical Museum (360-577-3119), 405 Allen Street, Kelso. Open 10–4 Tues.–Sat., 10–9 first Thurs. each month. Donation requested. Through memorabilia, replica frontier buildings, a restored 1913 Harvester, and an original settler's cabin, this little museum guards the county's history.

Lelooska Living History Museum (360-225-9522; www.lelooska.org), 165 Merwin Village Road, Ariel. Open 11–3 Sat. Memorial Day–Labor Day. Donation requested. Lelooska was a Cherokee who came west and was adopted into several other tribes; it was the Nez Perce who gave him the name that stuck. Mindful of how Native traditions were dying out, he devoted his life to preserving Indian art and artifacts, especially those from the Northwest, and was a prolific sculptor himself. The museum features his own work plus Native art from around the country: dresses, tomahawks, pipes, baskets, and other daily or ceremonial objects. The Lelooska Foundation also offers traditional performances and classes in Native American crafts.

North Clark Historical Museum (360-247-5800), 21416 NE 399th Street, Amboy. Open 12–4 Sat. Free. This small museum in a former United Brethren church is devoted to developing exhibits on the Native, pioneer, and logging heritage of Clark County. The austere clapboard building dates from about 1900.

NATURAL WONDERS Ape Cave. From WA 503 at Cougar, continue east 6.8 miles to FR 83 and turn left; after 2 miles, turn left on FR 8303 and drive 1 mile to the Ape Cave parking area (Northwest Forest Pass required; see *Wilder Places—Parks*). When low-silica lava flows downhill, often its surface forms a crust, while the lava below continues to flow. This is what happened here. About two thousand years ago, the mountain erupted, spilling fluid *pahoehoe* lava down its slopes. Some of it was funneled into a streambed, where its surface quickly cooled, but the lava inside continued to run downhill like toothpaste from a tube. And *voilà*—a lava cave. Such tubular caves are not uncommon in the volcanic Northwest, but this one, at 4.2 miles long, is the longest one known in North America. It's possible, though strenuous, to hike the length of the cave (see *To Do—Hiking*).

Coldwater Lake, on WA 504 at milepost 45. Like several lakes on Mount St. Helens's flanks, Coldwater is new, formed when an avalanche during the 1980 eruption dammed a tributary of the Toutle River. There's a 0.25-mile interpretive trail beside the lake, plus a picnic area and boat launch.

Mount St. Helens. Before 1980, St. Helens was a deceptively smooth, symmetrical white cone—deceptive because that smooth symmetry meant that nature had not had time to erode it since its last (and therefore recent) eruption. In fact, over the past four millennia, Mount St. Helens has erupted more often than any other Northwest volcano. Its rise began only about 40,000 years ago, making it a mere baby in mountain terms, with major mountain-building episodes within the past 2,500 years. A major eruption apparently occurred in 1800, and others were documented off and on between 1831 and 1857. Then the mountain put itself into sleep mode.

But geological memory was there in Indian legends about the mountains. One story is that two sons of the Great Spirit, who were named Pahto and Wyeast, fell in love with the girl-spirit Loowit. The brothers fought, hurling rocks and liquid fire at each other and incidentally breaking the Bridge of the Gods that crossed the Columbia River (see the Columbia River Gorge chapter). The Great Spirit was not pleased and turned them all into mountains. Pahto is now known as Mount Adams, and Wyeast as Mount Hood. Since Loowit was so beautiful, she became the lovely Mount St. Helens. Loowit Latkla, one of the mountain's original names, means Fire Mountain.

A VIEW OF MOUNT ST. HELENS

In May 1980 the mountain awoke, surprising even geologists with its ferocity. David Johnston, a young geologist observing the cone from a nearby ridge, was killed in the blast and never seen again. Fifty-six others—some scientists, some outdoorspeople who had decided to ignore the Forest Service's cordoned-off zone (which was far smaller than the blast zone turned out to be), some campers who were not even aware of the danger—perished. One was Harry Truman, 84-year-old owner of the Spirit Lake Lodge, who had spent 50 years of his life on the mountain and refused to leave.

The beginning of the end came on the morning of May 18. Yielding to pressure from below, the north slope finally gave way in an enormous landslide. The rubble and mudflows roared through Spirit Lake and continued into the Toutle River, whose course was buried in mud and debris 45–150 feet deep. Picking up trees, bridges, and buildings as it went, the flow charged on to the Columbia River, where it blocked the shipping channel. Meanwhile, the famous mushroom cloud of ash began to blanket the region, and the less visible but deadlier incandescent gases vaporized the forest for miles around, flattened it into toothpicks for further miles, and seared trees 17 miles away.

A visit today shows how life is returning remarkably rapidly, carried on the wind or on the feet of birds. But a lava dome within the cracked and broken crater continues to grow, the crater continues to emit steam, and occasional fireworks since 2004 keep the surrounding communities on their toes.

Spirit Lake, north of FR 99; only legal access is via Harmony Trail (see *To Do— Hiking*); closed to fishing and boating. Visible from the Windy Ridge Viewpoint, this lake used to be a limpid mirror of the volcanic cone. It always had a reputation, though—tribes knew it as a place where rock (pumice) floated, while wood (dense, waterlogged hemlock) sank. But it's no longer the lake it once was. In 1980 the north side of the mountain collapsed and slammed into Spirit Lake, over a 1,300-foot ridge, and down the Toutle River valley. The forests surrounding the lake were ripped away and the lake itself filled with debris—rock, mud, dead trees. Its water level also rose: The lake bottom is nearly 300 feet higher than it was before the eruption, and since its outlet to the Toutle River was blocked, the water level is higher, too. And though all the fish in it were killed, wild fish have reappeared, possibly washed down from higher lakes that were frozen at the time of eruption.

Trail of Two Forests, on FR 90, 6 miles east of Cougar. This 0.25-mile boardwalk takes you through a lava-cast forest—molds of tree trunks encased in lava during an eruption two thousand years ago. These ghost trees contrast with the living forest that has since grown up over the black basalt.

SCENIC DRIVES Lewis River Highway (WA 503), 31 miles from I-5 at exit 21 (Woodland) to just past Cougar. This is definitely the road less traveled. Winding along the Lewis River (yes, *that* Lewis), it approaches Mount St. Helens from the southwest, a side that was nearly unaffected by the eruption of 1980 and is largely lush forest. Dams along the way create several lakes made available to the recreating public by Pacific Power (see *Wilder Places—Parks*). Past Cougar, the road becomes FR 90, also very scenic.

Spirit Lake Memorial Highway (WA 504), 52 miles from I-5 at exit 49 (Castle Rock) to Johnston Ridge Volcanic Observatory. Once the way to the resort at Spirit Lake, this rebuilt and rerouted road is now unique in the continental United States for observing an active volcano—steam can often be seen rising from the cone, and it occasionally spews ash. What you also observe is devastation and recovery. The road passes shining Silver Lake and the few settlements in the Toutle River valley, traversing the blast zone on its way to the observatory at the end of the road. Besides several visitors centers en route (see *Wilder Places—Parks*), the route offers several turnoffs for viewing the mountain, elk, devastated forest, and regenerating forest. It's not to be missed if the weather's good, and if the weather isn't, the visitors centers are still worthwhile.

Wind River Highway, 54 miles from WA 14 at Carson in the Columbia River Gorge to Cougar on WA 503. A more remote approach from the south to Mount St. Helens is via this two-lane road running north into Gifford Pinchot National Forest. After about 20 miles on the Wind River Highway, turn left on Curly Creek Road and stop at the McClellan Viewpoint (yes, George McClellan of Civil War fame—he passed through in 1853 scouting for a railway route and declared the valley "useless") for spectacular views of the cone emerging from a forest wilderness. Then continue west to join FR 90, which runs west along the Swift Reservoir to Cougar.

✳ To Do

BICYCLING Lewis River Trail, 14.4 miles; from WA 503 at Cougar, take FR 90 east beyond the end of Swift Lake and turn left on FR 9039. This trail takes you through lowland old-growth forest, past five waterfalls.

Old Man Pass Trails, series of loops 1–13 miles long; access via McClellan Meadows Sno-Park on FR 3053 or opposite Oldman Pass Sno-Park on FR 30. These 50-foot-wide ski corridors offer moderate bike rides and good views.

CAMPING **Battle Ground State Park** (reservations 888-226-7688), off WA 503, 3 miles northeast of Battle Ground. Has 25 standard sites, 6 hook-up sites, and 15 primitive sites; also 4 cabins with bunk beds, heat, grills, and lighting.

Gifford Pinchot National Forest (see *Guidance*) campsites include the following:

Beaver, off Wind River Road a few miles north of Stabler. Twenty-three sites; toilets and water.

Canyon Creek, on FR 37 east of Amboy. Sixteen sites; restrooms but no water.

Falls Creek Horse Campground, on FR 57 east of Wind River Road. Four unimproved sites; toilet.

Iron Creek Campground (reservations 877-444-6777; www.recreation.gov), near junction of FR 25 and FR 76 northeast of Mount St. Helens. Ninety-eight sites; toilets and drinking water.

Kalama Horse Camp, on FR 81 about 5 miles north of Merrill Lake along the Kalama River. Twenty-eight campsites; toilets, corrals for horses, and access to equestrian and hiking trails in old-growth forest; no water.

Lower Falls Recreation Area, on FR 90 north of Curley Creek Road. Forty-four sites; drinking water and showers.

Panther Creek, off Wind River Road. Thirty-three sites; restrooms and drinking water.

Paradise Creek, off Wind River Road north of Little Soda Springs. 42 sites; water and restrooms. Reservations required in summer.

Swift, on FR 90, 1 mile west of Pine Creek Ranger Station. Ninety-three sites; not ADA.

PacifiCorp (503-813-6666; www.pacificpower.net) runs several campgrounds on its lakes along WA 503; all are popular for fishing:

Beaver Bay, 2 miles east of Cougar. Seventy-eight sites on Yale Lake.

Cresap Bay, south of Yale. Fifty-eight sites on Lake Merwin, some ADA-compliant; water, toilets, and showers.

Cougar Park, just east of Cougar. Forty-five tent sites on Yale Lake; water, toilets, and showers.

Paradise Point State Park (360-902-8608; reservations 888-CAMPOUT), off I-5 at exit 16 and 1 mile east. Fifty-eight tent sites, 18 RV sites (no hook-ups), 9 primitive sites, and 2 yurts; some ADA restrooms and showers.

⚓ ♿ **Seaquest State Park** (360-274-8633), on WA 504 just across from Mount St. Helens Visitor Center at Silver Lake. Fifty-five tent sites, 33 utility sites, and 5 yurts; water, showers, and toilets in a quiet wooded setting.

Washington Department of Natural Resources (360-902-1004; www.dnr.wa .gov) campground: **Merrill Lake,** along FR 81 north of WA 503 at Cougar. Eight primitive sites; outhouses and drinking water in a lakeside forest.

CANOEING AND KAYAKING **Coldwater Lake Recreation Area,** on WA 504 in Mount St. Helens National Volcanic Monument. Beside the lake is a short interpretive trail, picnic tables, and a fish-cleaning area.

Merrill Lake, on FR 81 just northwest of WA 503 at Cougar. This still lake is surrounded by steep hills inside a state forest. There's a primitive campground onshore (see *Camping*).

CLIMBING Mount St. Helens, 8,366 feet. For information, contact **Mount St. Helens National Volcanic Monument Headquarters** (360-449-7800; www.fs .fed.us/giffordpinchot); for permits, contact **Mount St. Helens Institute** (360-449-7826), 42218 Yale Bridge Road, Amboy. Within the monument, climbing permits ($22) are required to hike or climb above 4,800 feet and must be bought in advance. Much of the zone above 4,800 feet is a restricted area where scientific observation is the priority and camping, fires, pets, and straying from the trails are prohibited. The crater is off-limits. During the high season (mid-May–Oct.), only one hundred climbers a day may be on the mountain. The climbing season may be suspended at any time due to volcanic activity.

FOREST SERVICE CABIN RENTALS Government Mineral Springs Guard Station (reservations 877-444-6777), off Wind River Highway about 13 miles north of Carson. The renovated cabin was built by the Civilian Conservation Corps in 1937. It sleeps nine and has two bedrooms, a kitchen, and a living room. Available year-round, though there's no indoor plumbing. $65.

GOLF Lewis River Golf Course (360-225-8254; www.lewisrivergolf.com), 3209 Lewis River Road, Woodland. Eighteen holes.

Three Rivers Golf Course (360-423-4653), 2222 South River Road, Kelso. Eighteen holes.

HIKING Gifford Pinchot National Forest (see *Guidance*) has uncountable (well, nearly) trail miles; among the more accessible are these:

Cedar Flats Nature Loop, 0.9 mile; from Cougar take WA 503, then FR 90, east 18.6 miles to FR 25; turn north another 2.9 miles to the trailhead. This trail through mossy old-growth forest is easy but drops steeply in places to the river.

✍ **June Lake Trail,** 1.4 miles; take WA 503 through Cougar to FR 83 and turn left, continuing about 6.5 miles to the trailhead. The trail climbs gently along June Creek to the lake and waterfall—great for kids.

Woods Creek Watchable Wildlife Loops, 2.4 miles; trailhead is across from Woods Creek Information Station on FR 25, 55.2 miles from Cougar. The forest here is mostly deciduous. You'll see big-leaf maple, vine maple, alder, and ash.

Mount St. Helens National Volcanic Monument (see *Wilder Places—Parks*) trails include these:

Ape Cave (see *To See—Natural Wonders*); from FR 90 take FR 83 and FR 8303 to Ape's headquarters and the descent into the cave; turn left at the bottom of the stairs. **Lower cave trail,** 0.85 mile: The lower cave is fairly level except in a few places, but it becomes low and narrow toward the end; use caution so as not to get stuck. **Upper cave trail,** 1.75 miles: This much rougher route involves boulder scrambles and a rock-face climb—it's only for the fit and experienced. Once you reach the upper entrance, you can exit and return aboveground, which is safer than returning through the cave.

Coldwater Lake, 10.8-mile loop; from milepost 46 on WA 504. More demanding is this loop along the **Lakes Trail** and **South Coldwater Trail.** It includes a climb of 1,380 feet and is entirely within the blast zone.

Goat Marsh Trail, 1.4 miles; from the Kalama Ski trailhead on FR 8123 north of Cougar. This easy trip takes you to small lakes formed by mudflows 300–600 years ago. The forest is lush, but mosquitoes can be thick in summer.

Harmony Trail, 1.2 miles; on FR 99, 13.5 miles west of FR 25. This hike brings you to the shore of Spirit Lake through a ravaged but regenerating landscape.

Hummocks Trail, 2.3-mile loop; off WA 504, 0.25 mile past the turnoff to Coldwater Lake. This is an easier but representative hike through part of the Debris Avalanche. Lupine and alder have colonized the mess, and elk are often seen.

Loowit Trail, 28 miles around the mountain; access via 6-mile trail from Windy Ridge or 3-mile Ptarmigan Trail from FR 830. This strenuous hike involves several days and about 6,000 feet of elevation gain through zones ranging from devastated to nearly unaffected.

Mount Margaret Backcountry (360-449-7800), access only by trail. Within the northern end of the monument is this primitive area of lakes, ridges, and rugged trails. Camping is allowed only on designated sites, and a permit is required; no pets or stock.

Redrock Trail, 3.8 miles; from WA 503 just before Cougar, turn onto FR 81 and continue for 13.5 miles. This hike to the **Loowit Trail** (see above) takes you through forest and lava beds, with an elevation gain of 1,640 feet.

✳ Wilder Places

PARKS Battle Ground State Park (360-687-4621), 3 miles northeast of the town of Battle Ground; from I-5 take exit 9 and follow the signs. The battle expected between Indians and the U.S. Army in 1855 never took place, but the name stuck. In 280 forested acres surrounding a small lake, visitors enjoy fishing, swimming, boating, and camping; interpretive programs include night-sky observation.

Mount St. Helens National Volcanic Monument Headquarters (360-449-7800; www.fs.fed.us/gpnf/mshnvm), 42218 NE Yale Bridge Road, Amboy. When the dust settled after the 1980 eruption, Mount. St. Helens's shattered cone and the immediate surroundings were set aside as a 110,000-acre national volcanic monument. Unlike most national monuments, this one is administered by the Forest Service rather than the National Park Service, and it still lies almost entirely within Gifford Pinchot National Forest—indicating different goals, uses, and management styles. Several overlooks and visitors centers were constructed, the Spirit Lake Highway (WA 504) was rebuilt, trails were reconfigured, and observation stations were set up for ongoing monitoring. Biological research also continues as the blast zone recovers. Visitor services include the following:

✎ **Charles W. Bingham Forest Learning Center** (360-274-7750), on WA 504 at milepost 33. Open 10–6 daily mid-May–Sept.; 10–5 daily Oct. Free. The center is run jointly by the Washington State Department of Transportation, the Rocky Mountain Elk Foundation, and Weyerhaeuser Corporation, which operated on many national forest acres in and around the blast zone and has replanted extensively. Viewpoints often allow elk sightings along the riverbed below. Exhibits simulate forests before, during, and after the eruption, explaining Weyerhaeuser's forest management practices. Hands-on exhibits let children manage their own woodlots.

Hoffstadt Bluffs Visitor Center (360-274-5200), on WA 504 at milepost 27. Open 9:30–6 daily. Free. Cowlitz County owns this facility, which has a gift shop, restaurant, demonstrations of glassblowing using volcanic ash, and outdoor trails.

Johnston Ridge Observatory (360-274-2140), on WA 504 at milepost 52 (end of the road). Open 10–6 daily May–Oct.; closed in winter. $8; Northwest Forest Pass also accepted. This is as close as you can get to the crater by car, which at 5 miles is quite close enough: The lava dome stares you in the face. Young geologist David Johnston radioed his last message—"Vancouver, this is it"—from near this spot on May 18, 1980. A spectacular 0.5-mile walk has views of the crater, pumice plain, and landslide. Indoors, view monitoring equipment and learn how geologists continue to study the mountain.

Mount St. Helens Visitor Center (360-274-2131), on WA 504 at milepost 5, by Silver Lake outside Castle Rock. Open 9–5 daily June 1–Sept. 15. $5 adults, $2.50 children 7–17. This center dwells on the social history of the area via artifacts and vintage photos of the earliest inhabitants, miners, loggers, and tourists. There's also a walk-through mock-up of the mountain, with the various geological layers explained, and a mural chronology of the 1980 eruption. Outside, a 1-mile board-walk trail has a nice view over the wetlands of the truncated cone.

Windy Ridge Viewpoint, from US 12 via FR 25 and FR 99. Closed in winter. Northwest Forest Pass required. On the mountain's east side, this viewpoint overlooks a desolate landscape and Spirit Lake, still matted with logs downed in the blast. The eruption, with its avalanche and mudflows, filled the original lake, so the water level is 200 feet higher than it was previously. In summer, rangers explain the events.

Paradise Point State Park (360-263-2350), on the Lewis River just east of I-5 at exit 16. It's not so paradisiac since the coming of the freeway, but it's still pretty with its firs and hardwoods reflected in the Lewis River. There's a dirt boat ramp and camping.

⚓ ♿ **Seaquest State Park** (360-274-8633), on WA 504, 6 miles east of Castle Rock. Originally the homestead of Alfred Seaquest, who deeded his land to the state on the condition that liquor would never be sold on it, the 475-acre park now includes the Mount St. Helens Visitor Center across the road (see above). A 1-mile ADA trail along Silver Lake, which was formed when an ancient eruption dammed Silver Creek, offers wetland and wildlife views, while 6 miles of trails wander among tall red cedars and western hemlocks. With forested campsites, ADA restrooms, and play and picnic areas, this can be an excellent base for exploring Mount St. Helens.

WILDERNESS AREAS Trapper Creek Wilderness, 6,050 acres; off Wind River Highway just north of Government Mineral Springs. This old-growth and second-growth Douglas fir forest is administered by Gifford Pinchot National Forest (see *Guidance*). Several trails meander through it, including one up to Observation Peak, a former fire lookout with sweeping views of the region's volcanoes. Fields of wild huckleberries grow at the higher elevations. There are plenty of streams and waterfalls, and mineral water is available at nearby Government Mineral Springs.

WILDLIFE REFUGES Ridgefield National Wildlife Refuge, 5 miles north of Ridgefield. Check gate for hours. $3 per vehicle. This 5,150-acre refuge where the Lewis River flows into the Columbia was established in 1965 to protect wetland habitat for migrating birds. Apparently it's always been a major stop on the Pacific Flyway: In 1805 Captain William Clark noted the Corps of Discovery barely slept for the constant gabbling of waterfowl, which was "horid." Six miles of trails meander along the marsh and through upland oak and fir forest, offering views of the river and an environment not greatly changed since prediscovery times. Bring insect repellent.

✳ Lodging

BED & BREAKFASTS

Castle Rock

Blue Heron Inn (360-274-9535; www .blueheroninn.com), 2846 Spirit Lake Highway (WA 504). This contemporary country inn has seven guest rooms with private baths and balconies overlooking beautiful Silver Lake, with Mount St. Helens beyond. There's also a library focusing, naturally enough, on Mount St. Helens literature, and a fireplace in the parlor. Rates include a full breakfast. $170–215; lower in winter.

Cougar

Monfort's Bed and Breakfast (360-238-5229), 132 Cougar Loop Road Monfort's is the traditional mom-and-pop operation—people sharing their extra space. The Monforts built their two-bedroom guest cottage in 1992 on a side street in this one-gas-station hamlet and have been hosting climbers, cyclists, and just regular people from around the world ever since. It's quiet and simple; you'll recognize it by the tree-root art in front. The cottage has a living room and kitchen; both bedrooms have private baths. Rates include a self-serve continental breakfast. $60–90.

Woodland

Lewis River Bed and Breakfast (360-225-8630; www.lewisriverbedand

breakfast.com), 2339 Lewis River Road. With its deck overlooking the Lewis River, spacious common room for less clement weather, and five rooms with private baths, this is a spot for a restful stay. Stay put and read a book or explore the river, the volcano, the forest, or even nearby Portland, Oregon. One room handicapped-accessible. $125–150.

MOTELS

Woodland

Lewis River Inn (800-543-4344; www.lewisriverinn), 1100 Lewis River Road. In Woodland itself, this place is convenient to stores and restaurants, plus it backs onto the river and overlooks its own garden. $60–93; pet room $97–113.

RESORTS

Cougar

⚲ 🐾 **Lone Fir Resort and RV Park** (360-238-5210; www.lonefirresort .com), 16806 Lewis River Road. Dating from the 1940s, the Lone Fir offers a mix of "motel" rooms, bungalows, RV sites, and tent sites in tiny Cougar, on the southern flanks of Mount St. Helens. Eighteen units, furnished with locally made pine-stick chairs and tables, are divided among several buildings on several grassy acres. Some have kitchens, and most have balconies where you can sit and watch the occasional car go by. A café serves burgers and fried chicken. Children and controlled pets welcome, except for pit bulls or pit mixes. Tent sites $20; RV sites $30; motel rooms or bungalows $70–85.

✳ Where to Eat

Mount St. Helens is fairly out of the way; the only food you'll find on the mountain is fast, at the Hoffstadt Bluffs visitors center (see *Wilder Places—Parks*). Options even in the neighboring towns (and "neighboring" can mean 20–50 miles distant), beyond chain eateries, are few.

DINING OUT

Longview

Rutherglen Mansion (360-425-5816; www.rutherglenmansion.com), 420 Rutherglen Road. Open for dinner from 5 PM Wed.–Sat., brunch 10–2 Sun. This enormous 1927 Douglas fir and red cedar house was the home of John Tennant, vice president of Long-Bell Lumber Company, of which Longview was the company town. Today it's a bed & breakfast and elegant restaurant serving dinner and brunch, with a focus on steaks and the region's abundant seafood.

EATING OUT

Cougar

🍴 **Cougar Bar and Grill** (360-238-5252), 16849 Lewis River Road. A pleasant hole-in-the-wall, this place serves up country breakfasts, sandwiches and salads for lunch, and meat-and-potatoes (or fish-and-potatoes) dinners.

Ridgefield

Pioneer Street Café (360-887-8001), 207 Pioneer Street. A small café in a town that's definitely off the beaten track, this place, with its plain ocher walls and green booths, doesn't cry out for attention. But it does offer three meals a day of fresh, homemade comfort food—pasta, pork loin—with some updated touches. In 2006 it hosted the regional slow-food forum. Live music on Sundays.

Vinnie's Pizza (360-887-7200; www.vinniespizzainc.com), 206 North Main Street. Open for lunch and dinner Mon.–Sat. They serve great pizza as well as soups, sandwiches, and salads. Have a slice for $2.25 or their biggest, fanciest pizza for $28.99.

Toutle

Patty's Place at 19 Mile House (360-274-8779), 9440 Spirit Lake Highway. Open for lunch and dinner daily. A welcome addition to the St. Helens scene, such as it is, Patty's serves homemade cobbler, elk burgers, chicken and dumplings, and more American comfort food.

✳ Special Events

April: **Lilac Festival** (360-225-8996; www.lilacgardens.com), Woodland. Mid-Apr.–mid-May at Hulda Klager Lilac Gardens (see *To See—Farms and Gardens*). See lilacs at their peak of bloom, plus lilac sales, an open house, and more.

Tulip Festival (360-225-4512), Woodland. Free. For two weeks in mid-Apr., Holland America Bulb Farms (see *To See—Farms and Gardens*) features blooming display gardens, tulip fields, food, and music.

September: **Highlander Festival** (360-577-3301; www.highlander.kelso.gov), Kelso. The town celebrates its Scottish heritage with music, games, golf, and a parade.

MOUNT RAINIER AREA

Though not far from the Seattle-Tacoma metropolis—indeed, it looms over those cities like a tutelary spirit—Mount Rainier and its environs are a different world, where the frontier is not long gone. An approach through farmland and daffodil fields quickly gives way to logging towns such as Morton and Elbe or old mining towns with names such as Carbonado, whose coal deposits once fueled Seattle and young British Columbia.

Centralia and Chehalis on I-5 are gateway towns for the US 12 corridor on the mountain's south side. Mossyrock, Morton, Randle, and Packwood lead the way up to White Pass. Enumclaw on WA 410 is the gateway on Rainier's north side, with Greenwater the only settlement on the way to Chinook Pass. Connecting the two highways is Cayuse Pass on WA 123, a short bit of highway on the mountain's east side that's almost entirely within the national park.

On the mountain's west side, WA 7 leads south from Puyallup to Elbe and Mineral, then to US 12 at Morton. At Elbe, WA 706 heads east through Ashford to the park, and Eatonville is just north of Elbe on WA 161. Services for visiting the national park are concentrated in Ashford, just short of the park's southwestern entrance. "Concentrated" is a relative term. The town's several restaurants and lodgings are strung discreetly along WA 706, their shingle walls blending nicely into the surrounding forest. In summer, it pays to reserve ahead. For an even more remote experience, try the few resorts east of the mountain—the views are just as good or better, for that is the dry side of the Cascade Range. For a day trip, you can visit from Tacoma, but "the Mountain" deserves more than a day. So do you.

GUIDANCE **East Lewis County Chamber of Commerce** (360-983-3778; www.eastlewiscountychamber.com), 118 State Street, Mossyrock 98356.

Eatonville Visitor Center (360-832-4000), 220 Center Street East, Eatonville 98304.

Gifford Pinchot National Forest (360-891-5000; www.fs.usda.gov), 10600 NE 51st Circle, Vancouver 98682.

Lewis County Convention and Visitor Bureau (800-525-3323; www.tourlewis county.com), 500 North Chamber Way, Chehalis 98531.

Mount Baker–Snoqualmie National Forest (800-627-0062; www.fs.fed.us.gov), 2930 Wetmore Avenue, Everett 98201.

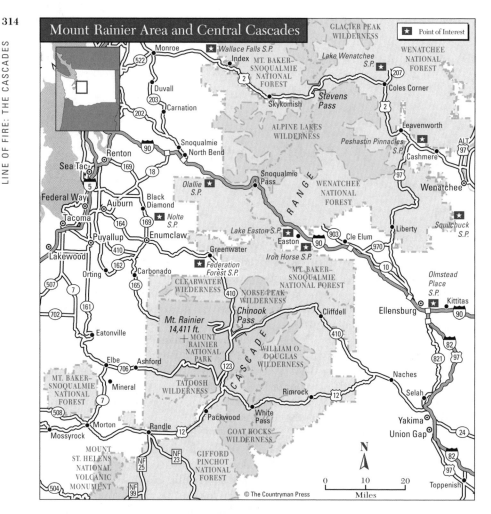

Mount Rainier Area and Central Cascades

Mount Rainier Guest Services (360-569-2275; www.mtrainierguestservices .com), 55106 Kernahan Road East, Ashford 98304.

Mount Rainier Visitor Association (360-569-0910 or 877-617-9951; www.mt-rainier.com), Box 214, Ashford 98304.

Okanogan-Wenatchee National Forest—Naches Ranger District (509-653-1401; www.fs.usda.gov), 10237 US 12, Naches 98937.

GETTING THERE This remote area is more or less encircled by **US 12** to the south, which crosses White Pass at 4,500 feet; **WA 410,** which crosses Chinook Pass at 5,430 feet, and **WA 123,** which crosses Cayuse Pass at 4,675 feet, to the north and east; and **WA 7** to the west, with **WA 706** leading directly east to the main entrance to Mount Rainier National Park (see the Mount Rainier National Park chapter).

Seattle-Tacoma International Airport is about 75 miles north.

Gray Line Tours (800-426-7532; www.graylineseattle.com) runs daily trips from Seattle to Mount Rainier May–Sept.; $85 adults, $65 children.

Paradise Shuttle. The Park Service runs a shuttle on summer weekends from Ashford, outside the park entrance, up the mountain to Paradise via Longmire and Cougar Rock. Free.

AMTRAK's (800-USA-RAIL; www.amtrak.com) Coast Starlight route between Los Angeles and Seattle stops in Centralia at 210 Railroad Avenue.

Greyhound (360-736-9811 or 800-231-2222; www.greyhound.com) stops in Chehalis at 1232 Mellen Street.

GETTING AROUND There is no public transport in this region.

MEDICAL EMERGENCY St. Elizabeth Hospital (360-802-8800; www.fhs health.org), 1455 Battersby Avenue, Enumclaw.

Providence Centralia Hospital (360-736-2803), 914 South Scheuber Road, Centralia.

✳ To See

CULTURAL SITES Recycled Spirits of Iron Sculpture Park (360-569-2280; www.danielklennert.com), 22410 WA 706 East, Ashford. Its creator, Dan Klennert, calls it "Ex Nihilo." He collects old bits of metal and reorganizes them into lively representations of birds, fish, dinosaurs, even people. The whimsical works have been displayed at venues as varied as the Thoroughbred Breeders' Association Equine Art Show and the Harley riders' rally in Sturgis, South Dakota. Dan invites you to drop by his 4-acre grounds in Ashford and look around.

A VIEW OF MOUNT RAINIER FROM WA 706 NEAR ASHFORD

FARMERS' MARKETS Eatonville Farmers' Market (253-879-5535), 104 Washington Street, Eatonville. Open 10–2 Sat. June–Sept.

FARMS AND GARDENS De Goede Bulb Farms (360-983-9000; www.degoede bulb.com), 409 Mossyrock Road West, Mossyrock. Call for hours. Candy-striped fields of golds, pinks, and reds might startle the driver along quiet US 12. De Goede principally supplies bulbs to the retail market, with the nice side effect of blooming tulips and daffodils in spring. The public is welcome to stroll the garden paths and visit the greenhouses and garden shop, where bulbs, perennials, cut flowers, and garden supplies are for sale.

FOR FAMILIES ✔ Mount Rainier Scenic Railroad (360-492-5588 or 888-STEAM11; www.mrsr.com), 54124 Mountain Highway East, Elbe. Open Memorial Day–mid-Oct. $20–25 adults, $18 seniors, $15 children over four; $73 to ride in the cab. Vintage steam locomotives chug out of the old Milwaukee Road Depot in Elbe, pulling passengers on the old freight line to Mineral Lake and back. Formerly, of course, the trains hauled lumber headed to the Tacoma waterfront, and occasionally tourists going to Mount Rainier. The 14-mile round-trip generally lasts an hour and a half. Special events take place year-round.

✔ ♿ Northwest Trek Wildlife Park (360-832-6117; www.nwtrek.org), 11610 Trek Drive East, Eatonville; on WA 161, 35 miles southeast of Tacoma. Open 9:30–6 daily July–Labor Day; 9:30–3 Sat.–Sun. Nov.–mid-Feb., daily during Christmas week; 9:30–3 or 4 Mon.–Fri., 9:30–4 or 5 Sat.–Sun. in fall and spring. $17 adults, $15.50 seniors over 65, $12 children 5–12, $9 children 3–4. This sister facility of Tacoma's Point Defiance Zoo and Aquarium is a safari park focusing exclusively on animals of the Northwest. Guided tram tours take you past herds of bison, bighorn sheep, maybe even moose; then you can view grizzlies, cougars, black bears, wolves, and more from trails through large, habitat-appropriate exhibits. All trails are ADA-accessible.

✔ Pioneer Farm Museum and Ohop Indian Village (360-832-6300; www .pioneerfarmmuseum.org), 7716 Ohop Valley Road, Eatonville. Visits by guided tour only. Homestead tours: 11–5:30 daily Father's Day–Labor Day; 11:15–4 Sat.–Sun. mid-May–mid-June and Sept.–Nov.; $7.50 adults, $6.50 seniors over 60 and children 3–18. Indian village tours: 1 and 2:30 Fri.–Sun. in summer only; $7 adults, $6 seniors and children 3–18. $1 rebate if both tours taken in one day. Children (or adults, for that matter) can milk cows and gather eggs on an 1880s homestead or have their hair curled with a curling iron. Then they can visit a replica Coast Salish village to try out a bow and arrow, work at hollowing out a canoe, or try their hand at weaving on a Salish loom. Lots of hands-on activities bring frontier Washington to life.

HISTORIC SITES Downtown Centralia, off I-5. The city's central district, virtually untouched since the boom of the 1920s, was put on the National Register of Historic Places in 2003; **guided group tours** and a **walking tour** flyer are available from the Lewis County Convention and Visitor Bureau (see *Guidance*). Centralia also features several **murals** depicting scenes from the town's history, including the 1919 Armistice Day Massacre, when parading veterans attacked the local offices of the Industrial Workers of the World (the Wobblies)—one of several such violent confrontations around the state in the early days of the labor move-ment. Four veterans died in the melee; several IWW members were arrested, one of whom was kidnapped from jail and lynched.

Evangelische Lutherische Kirche (253-846-7932), 54222 WA 7, Elbe; beside the railroad tracks. A handful of German immigrants founded a congregation here in 1893. By 1906, they were able to build this church—the polar opposite of today's megachurches, measuring 18 feet by 24 feet with a 46-foot-tall steeple. Among the smallest in the country, it's still a functioning place of worship, with Sunday services at 2:30 PM.

George Washington Park, Main and Pearl streets, Centralia. Not *that* George Washington. *This* George Washington, born of a slave father and white mother, came west in 1850 with the Cochrans, a white family who had raised him, and they settled in Oregon City. A couple of years later, he crossed the Columbia and home-steaded at a river confluence in near wilderness. But Oregon Territory, embroiled in discussions of entering the Union as a slave or a free state, had decided it would allow neither slavery nor black landownership, so the Cochrans held deed to the land, though Washington proved it up. When Washington Territory separated from Oregon, it left behind discriminatory landownership laws, and he obtained the deed to his own land. In 1872 the railroad came through. In 1875 Washington, by then married, platted a town on his 640 acres and named it Centerville, giving away free lots to those who built houses on them. Until his death in 1905, he was a father to his town (soon renamed Centralia), offering free loans after the panic of 1893 and donating land for a church, a cemetery, and the public park that now sits restfully below the Carnegie library with inviting benches, mature trees, and flow-ering shrubs.

MUSEUMS ✐ **Lewis County Historical Museum** (360-748-0831; www.lewis countymuseum.org), 599 NW Front Way, Chehalis. Open 9–5 Tues.–Sat., 1–5 Sun.; 10–5 Tues.–Fri. in winter. $4 adults, $3 seniors, $2 children 4–16. Estab-lished in 1845, Lewis County is practically prehistoric—Washington's oldest. The collection here is eclectic: a Native American room includes baskets and, unusu-ally, a loom; for children, there's a model railroad and mini-rooms depicting old-fashioned stores, a doctor's office, and more; and for everyone, there's an exhibit on old-time medicine, such as Kickapoo Tapeworm Remedy. The slate-roofed building is Chehalis's rather grand former train station; the twin cities of Chehalis and Centralia were important timber towns a hundred years ago.

SCENIC DRIVES Chinook Pass Scenic Byway (WA 410), 87 miles from Enumclaw to Naches. This route runs through damp cedar and Douglas fir forest to the north of Mount Rainier, cuts along the northeast corner of the national park, and crosses Chinook Pass down into open glades of ponderosa pine, sagebrush, and Washington's irrigated fruit and wine country.

White Pass Scenic Byway (US 12), 119 miles from I-5 to Naches. This route also bridges Washington's western and eastern sides. From Mary's Corner, just off I-5, US 12 runs east through the low-lying farmland and tulip fields of Mossyrock and Morton. Then it follows the sparkling Cowlitz River into the national forest, through the hamlets of Randle and Packwood, and up 4,500-foot White Pass, continuing over to the basalt rimrock of the east slope of the Cascades. Overlooks along the way offer views of Mount Adams and Mount Rainier.

WALKING TOURS Eatonville walking tour. Pick up a brochure at the Eatonville Visitor Center (see *Guidance*) for a 3-mile walk around the relics of Eatonville's lumbering heritage, including one of the conical burners once emblematic of the timber industry in the Northwest.

✳ To Do

BICYCLING Crystal Mountain, 35 miles of bike trails; trailhead on FR 510 off Crystal Mountain Road, via WA 410. For skilled riders, a 12.2-mile round-trip up a ridge to the summit is spectacular.

Mount Tahoma Trails (360-569-2451; www.skimtta.com), 20 miles of trails; just east of Ashford. These state forest trails are open to cyclists in summer, with some steep climbs, nice views, and trail shelters (see *Winter Sports*).

Skookum Flats Trail, 6.5 rugged miles in White River Recreation Area; trailhead at WA 410 and FR 73. Due east of Mount Rainier in Mount Baker–Snoqualmie National Forest, this trail runs south along the White River, then continues as the smoother **White River Trail,** 5 miles, on the other side of WA 410.

Sun Top Trail, 8 miles; trailhead at WA 410 and FR 73. This hard 1-mile climb to 3,000 feet is followed by 7 downhill miles; there's a view of Mount Rainier from the top.

CAMPING Camping is plentiful in the **Okanogan-Wenatchee, Gifford Pinchot,** and **Mount Baker–Snoqualmie national forests** (see *Guidance*) surrounding the national park. Sites in many of the campgrounds below can be reserved (877-444-6777; www.recreation.gov). In addition, in national forests it's usually permissible to camp fee-free outside an official campground, away from bodies of water and leaving no trace; check for regulations.

Gifford Pinchot National Forest

Big Creek, on FR 52 near the west entrance to Mount Rainier National Park. Twenty-nine sites; water, toilet facilities, and picnic tables.

La-Wis-Wis, on US 12, 4 miles east of Packwood. One hundred fifteen sites on the Cowlitz River; water, toilets, and a picnic shelter.

Mount Baker–Snoqualmie National Forest

The Dalles, on WA 410, 26 miles east of Enumclaw. Nineteen tent sites and 26 RV sites; tables, water, toilets, and a picnic shelter. Twenty-six sites can be reserved.

Silver Springs, on WA 410, 32 miles east of Enumclaw, 1 mile from Mount Rainier National Park. Fifty-five sites; water, picnic tables, and toilets. Can be reserved.

Okanogan-Wenatchee National Forest

American Forks, on FR 18 just south of WA 410. Sixteen sites; toilets but no water. No reservations.

Bumping Lake, at the end of FR 18. Also Bumping Crossing and Bumping Dam campgrounds nearby. Forty-five sites total, 9 barrier-free at Lower Bumping Lake); water and toilet.

Cedar Springs, on FR 18 just south of American Forks. Fourteen sites; water, toilet, and some ADA-compliant sites.

Cottonwood, on WA 410 east of Cliffdell. Eight sites; water and toilet. No reservations.

Cougar Flat, on FR 18 west of Soda Springs. Twelve sites; water and toilet.

Crow Creek, on FR 19 north of WA 410 at Little Naches. Fifteen sites; toilet but no water.

Dog Lake, off US 12 just east of White Pass. Eight sites; outhouses but no water.

Halfway Flat, on WA 410 just south of Little Naches. Eight sites, dispersed camping; toilet but no water.

&. **Hause Creek,** on US 12 east of Rimrock Lake. Forty-two sites, one ADA; restrooms and water.

Hells Crossing, off WA 410 east of Pleasant Valley. Sixteen sites; water and toilet.

Indian Creek, on US 12 at west end of Rimrock Lake. Thirty-nine sites; water and outhouses.

Kaner Flat, on WA 410 just west of Little Naches. Forty-three sites; water and vault toilets.

Little Naches, on FR 1900 off WA 410, 24 miles east of Mount Rainier. Eighteen tent sites on the Little Naches River; water and vault toilets.

Lodge Pole, on WA 410 at milepost 75.8. Thirty-four tent sites; water and barrier-free vault toilets.

Peninsula, off US 12 along FR 1200-711. Sixty sites; toilets but no water.

Sawmill Flat, on WA 410 just south of Halfway Flat. Twenty-three sites total, 1 barrier-free; water and toilet.

Soda Springs, on FR 18 just south of Cedar Springs. Twenty-six sites; water and toilets.

Willows, on US 12 just east of Wild Rose. Sixteen sites; water and outhouses.

Windy Point, on US 12 west of Naches. Fifteen sites; water and toilet.

CANOEING AND KAYAKING Most lakes here are in the backcountry, and since the Forest Service usually prohibits gas motors on boats, these waters tend to be quiet but not very accessible.

Bumping Lake, at end of Bumping Lake Road, off WA 410 about 20 miles east of Chinook Pass. This reservoir just outside the William O. Douglas Wilderness is surrounded by mountains but accessible by road.

GOLF Maple Grove RV Resort and Golf Course (360-497-2741), 175 WA 131, Randle. Nine holes.

Newaukum Valley Golf Course (360-748-0461), 153 Newaukum Golf Drive, Chehalis. Twenty-seven holes.

HIKING Below is a sampling of the trails on public lands surrounding Mount Rainier, which offer hikes of all lengths and levels of difficulty:

Boulder Cave National Recreation Trail, 2 miles; from WA 410 east of Chinook Pass, turn left on FR 1706 north of Cliffdell, then right toward Camp Roganunda and Boulder Cave. Open Apr.–Oct.; closed in winter to protect hibernating Pacific western big-eared bats. The trail 32 miles west of Naches leads to an unusual cave, formed by water hollowing out friable soil between basalt flows.

Crystal Mountain Loop, 6 miles one way (loop nearly 12 miles); from WA 410 west of Chinook Pass, turn onto Crystal Mountain Road and park in the ski area parking lot. Take chairlift No. 2 (see *Winter Sports*) to the summit, 6,776 feet, enjoy the views of Mount Rainier and the White River valley, then find trail No. 1163 and hike either north or south down the mountain to old mining road No. 184 (FR 7190) and back to the parking lot. It's about 6 miles to the north, a bit less to the south; if you're energetic, skip the chairlift and hike the entire loop. The Summit House Restaurant (see *Where to Eat*) is at the top of the chairlift.

Mount Beljica, 4 miles; from WA 706 east of Ashford, turn left on Copper Creek Road (FR 59), in 5 miles turn right on FR 5920, and 1.5 miles later park at Lake Christine trailhead. This walk in the Glacier View Wilderness west of Mount Rainier has a challenging 1,300-foot elevation gain in just 4 miles but terrific views of Tahoma Glacier on Mount Rainier.

Mount Tahoma Trails (360-569-2451), 20 miles of trails just east of Ashford. This trail system with three generous huts is used mostly by winter sports enthusiasts (see *Winter Sports*); that means summer users have more choice and privacy. The state forestlands are just west of Ashford, in various stages of regrowth but rich in wild birds and views of Mount Rainier.

Noble Knob trail, 3.5 miles; from WA 410, 0.5 mile east of Alta Lodge (before Crystal Mountain turnoff), turn left on FR 7174 and drive steeply upward 6 miles to Corral Pass—trailhead No. 1174 is to the left. This trail along the edge of the Norse Peak Wilderness has 500 feet of elevation gain and offers wildflower meadows the equal of those at Paradise, but without the crowds. These meadows sprang up after a forest fire in the 1920s. After 3 miles, reach a three-way fork and take the middle trail to find the old lookout on top of Noble Knob.

Pacific Crest Trail (916-285-1846; www.pcta.org), 1331 Garden Highway, Sacramento, CA 95833. About 500 of the Pacific Crest Trail's 2,650 miles pass through the state of Washington. Many sections in this area are accessible for day hikes, notably from a trailhead at White Pass (US 12), whence it winds north about 30 miles through the William O. Douglas Wilderness Area, along the eastern edge of Mount Rainier National Park, to Chinook Pass (WA 410)—another good access point; from WA 410 it continues along miles of ridge in the Norse Peak Wilderness Area and over historic Naches Pass. Around three hundred people hike the entire trail yearly, but even a short hike can take you from the highway to the deep wilderness of Cascade crests, mountain meadows, lakes, and canyons.

Sourdough Gap, 3 miles; from WA 410 at Chinook Pass, 0.2 mile east of the national park boundary. This section of the Pacific Crest Trail runs north to Sourdough Gap through brilliant wildflower meadows whose peak bloom is in August; it's a popular trail despite an 1,100-foot elevation gain.

Twin Sisters Lakes, 2 miles; from WA 410, 19 miles east of Chinook Pass, turn right on Bumping River Road and continue 13.5 miles, then drive on FR 1808 another 7 miles to the trailhead at Deep Creek Campground. This hike in the William O. Douglas Wilderness is a trip through a complex volcanic landscape with alpine lakes and just 800 feet of elevation gain. Take a map to find the trailhead.

Union Creek Trail, 4 miles; off WA 410, 9.2 miles east of Chinook Pass. This nice hike goes along the creek and past waterfalls, with a 1,300-foot elevation gain.

WINTER SPORTS Crystal Mountain (360-663-2265 or 888-754-6199; www .crystalmountainresort.com), 33914 Crystal Mountain Boulevard, Crystal Mountain; off WA 410 about 30 miles east of Enumclaw. In the Mount Baker–Snoqualmie National Forest just east of Mount Rainier National Park, this is Washington's biggest ski area, with 50 runs, 10 lifts, and a vertical drop of 3,100 feet. In summer a chairlift runs up to a nearly 7,000-foot viewpoint for panoramas of Mount Rainier and the Cascade Range (see *Hiking*). Several nearby hotels are run by **Crystal Mountain Hotels** (360-663-2262 or 888-754-6400; www.crystalhotels.com).

Mount Tahoma Trails (360-569-2451; www.skimtta.com), Box 206, Ashford 98304; just east of Ashford. State forestlands straddling WA 706 contain 20 miles of trails used by skiers and snowshoers in winter, hikers and mountain bikers in summer (see *Hiking*). But the best part is that the system is sprinkled with huts (actually two huts and a yurt)—not lean-tos, but actual refuges with solar electricity, propane fireplaces, kitchen facilities, and sleeping pads. And they're absolutely free except for a processing fee; just bring your food and sleeping bag. Reservations are required; contact the phone number or website above, or go to **Whittaker Mountaineering,** 800-238-5786, 30027 WA 706 East, Ashford.

White Pass Ski Resort (509-672-3101 or 509-672-3100; www.skiwhitepass.com), 48935 US 12, White Pass; on US 12, 50 miles west of Yakima and 20 miles east of Packwood. This resort averages 350 inches of snow a year. There are five lifts, a 1,500-foot drop, and 32 trails; also 18 kilometers (11 miles) of Nordic trails.

✳ Wilder Places

PARKS Federation Forest State Park (360-663-2207), on WA 410, 18 miles east of Enumclaw. Park open 8 AM–dusk. Interpretive center open 9–4 Wed.–Sun. May–Sept.; also Sat.–Sun. Apr. (hours may vary). This 619-acre day-use park has 12 miles of trails through old-growth Douglas fir, Sitka spruce, and western red cedar forest. It also contains part of the historic Naches Trail and an interpretive center explaining Washington's wet and dry sides, with gardens of native plants from six of the state's nine ecosystems.

Ike Kinswa State Park (800-CAMPOUT), on WA 122, 4 miles north of US 12 just west of Mossyrock. This is a busy park in summer, with lots of boating, fishing, and waterskiing on the lake behind Mayfield Dam. At least there are 8 miles of shoreline to spread out the activity, and it's swimmable. Picnicking and camping are available, too.

WILDERNESS AREAS Several designated wilderness areas managed by national forests (see *Guidance*) cluster around Mount Rainier National Park.

Clearwater Wilderness, 14,300 acres; borders the park on the north. Part of Mount Baker–Snoqualmie National Forest, it contains many small lakes, mature Douglas fir and western hemlock forests, and some hiking trails.

Glacier View Wilderness, 3,080 acres; abuts the park on the west slightly north of the Nisqually entrance. Within Gifford Pinchot National Forest, this comparatively small wilderness area boasts the headwaters of the South Fork of the Puyallup River, astounding views of Mount Rainier, and tons of ripe huckleberries in fall. Watch for bears.

Norse Peak Wilderness, 50,923 acres; between Chinook Pass and Naches Pass slightly east of the park; access via WA 410 (closed in winter). It lies east of the Cascade Divide, so it's jointly administered by the Okanogan-Wenatchee and Mount Baker–Snoqualmie national forests. Its rugged terrain includes 7,000-foot peaks and the canyons of the Greenwater and Naches rivers. Naches Pass, through which settlers streamed to the Puget Sound area, lies just north. A substantial network of trails crosses the wilderness.

Tatoosh Wilderness, 15,800 acres; borders the park to the south. Managed by Gifford Pinchot National Forest, it includes most of the jagged Tatoosh Range. The single trailhead is on FR 52.

William O. Douglas Wilderness, 167,195 acres; slightly east of the park. Managed by the Okanogan-Wenatchee and Gifford Pinchot national forests and named for the Yakima-born Supreme Court Justice, it is a fitting tribute to the tireless conservationist. More than 250 trails, including part of the Pacific Crest Trail, wind through this wilderness where the judge spent many happy years hiking. It includes subalpine meadows, lakes, and cirques.

✳ Lodging

BED & BREAKFASTS

Ashford
Alexander's Country Inn (360-569-2300 or 800-654-7615; www.alexanders countryinn.com), 37515 WA 706 East. Doubtless it was happy coincidence when, in 1899, the main entrance to the newly designated Mount Rainier National Park was placed just a mile from Alexander Mesler's homestead. As tourists quickly lined up to visit the nation's fifth park, Mesler's son drew up grandiose plans for lodgings. It took some time, but in 1912 the 10,000-square-foot inn with a three-story turret opened, with both rooms and restaurant, and prospered till the Depression and Second World War forced the family to give it up. Even so, it continued to be run as a restaurant, with only two changes of ownership

since. In 1984 it opened once more to overnight guests, with renovations including modern plumbing and old English stained glass, and the rambling pale blue Victorian now stands resplendent among its lawns and gardens on Ashford's main drag. The 12 guest rooms have Victorian dimensions— small by current standards but pleasant and quietly furnished—and all have private baths. (Suites, in the tower, are larger.) A sprawling parlor on the second floor has a library, sofas, and a fireplace. Watch hummingbirds from the enclosed porch at breakfast, where you'll have a multitude of choices, since Alexander's is still a restaurant, too (see *Where to Eat*). Across the road, a chalet and guesthouse sleep eight and six, respectively. No pets. Rooms $99–160; suites $135–179; houses $185–235.

◊ **Mountain Meadows Inn** (360-569-2788; www.mountainmeadowsinn.com), 28912 WA 706 East. This comfortable country house was built in 1910 for a Pacific National Lumber Mill superintendent. The sawmills are gone now; instead, guests enjoy 11 acres of lawns scattered with cedar groves and rhododendrons and no disturbance but birdsong and bubbling Eagle Creek. Three bright guest rooms in the main house and three in an adjacent guesthouse are restfully furnished with antiques and puffy feather beds. If you can tear yourself away, there's a 1,000-volume library to browse. Rates include a full breakfast. They'll also pack you a picnic lunch ($10). Children 4 and over welcome. $149–175.

COTTAGES AND CABINS

Ashford
Copper Creek Inn (360-569-2799 or 877-325-5881; www.coppercreekinn.com), 35707 WA 706 East. Founded as a gas station and luncheonette in the 1920s, it was gradually expanded to a full-sized restaurant with lodgings—small but versatile. For the budget-minded, there's a room and two suites above the 1940s restaurant (see *Where to Eat*)—formerly quarters for local workers or restaurant employees, now little rooms that time forgot. Gouges from loggers' corked boots can still be seen in the floors. Seven new or modernized cabins range from a one-bedroom hideaway to a 1919 lumber baron's lodge sleeping 12, all on 8 forested acres with Copper Creek running through it. No pets. Room and suites $59–150; cabins $95–195; lodge $295 for 6 people, $25 per additional person; weekly rates, too.

◊ 🐾 **Mounthaven Resort** (800-456-9380; www.mounthaven.com), 38210 WA 706 East. Ten forest cabins set among tall cedars all have kitchens and private baths. There's also space for 17 RVs, plus volleyball, badminton, and basketball courts and a little kids' playground. Pets allowed in RV area only. Cabins $115–310; RV sites $33.

◊ **Stone Creek Lodge** (360-569-2355 or 800-819-3942; www.stonecreeklodge.net), 38624 WA 706 East. Just a stone's throw from the park's Nisqually entrance, six renovated, 1940s cedar

THE HISTORIC ALEXANDER HOME IN ASHFORD IS NOW A B&B.

cabins sit in a green lawn ringed by tall firs. Each cabin is a snug woodland hideaway with quilts, cast-iron (gas) stove, fridge, and picture window. It's sort of like coming to Heidi's grandpa's cabin, except for the fridge. The two larger units each sleep four and have a range-top stove or microwave. In keeping with owner Sandy Altman's philosophy of a getaway, there are no TVs or phones, but there is plenty of room for kids to play and a ring for a convivial evening campfire. No pets. $95–150.

HOSTELS

Ashford

Whittaker's Bunkhouse (360-569-2439; www.whittakersbunkhouse.com), 30205 WA 706 East. Ashford was a logging town in the early 1900s, and this bunkhouse was built in 1912 to house loggers and mill workers. Renovated in 1990 under the aegis of mountaineer Lou Whittaker (whose brother Jim has climbed Everest, Kanchenjunga, Rainier, and more), it now houses climbers and other mountain devotees in a mix of dormitory rooms and private rooms with baths. A guest library, hot tub, and cheerful café are on the premises. Sister enterprises **Whittaker Mountaineering,** where you can buy or rent mountaineering equipment, and guide service **Rainier Mountaineering Inc.** are conveniently located next door (see *To Do—Climbing* in the Mount Rainier National Park chapter). No pets. Dorm beds $35 (summer only: May–Sept.); private rooms $65–115 depending on season and occupancy.

HOTELS

Packwood

Hotel Packwood (360-494-5431), 104 Main Street. This hundred-year-old hotel of weathered wood with a wraparound porch has been renovated to

the point of having TVs in the rooms but otherwise keeps it simple. The rooms are small but clean and cozy, with quilts, iron bedsteads, and period furnishings, and only two of the nine have private baths. But the welcome is warm, the views are priceless, and the price is right. Some rooms will accommodate four people. $30–50.

LODGES

Ashford

🐾 🏠 **Rainier Overland Lodge and Restaurant** (800-582-8984; www.rainieroverland.net), 31811 WA 706 East. Rainier Overland is a small, longtime operation offering nine motel-type rooms, some of which connect to accommodate families, plus rustic cabins. A restaurant on the premises offers family-friendly dining, too (see *Where to Eat*). Children welcome. Small pets allowed in two units. Rooms $59; cabins $89.

Chinook Pass

Whistlin' Jack Lodge (509-658-2433 or 800-827-2299; www.whistlinjacklodge.com), 20800 WA 410. About 30 miles east of Chinook Pass, Whistlin' Jack sits among tall pines on the Naches River shortly before the highway drops to Washington's eastern desert. Eight motel rooms with bay windows overlooking the river, six cottages with fireplaces, riverside bungalows, and a casual dining room make it a destination for snow chasers in winter and Yakimans escaping the heat in summer. No pets. Rooms $110; cottages and bungalows $160–265; check for midweek or low-season rates.

Elbe

Hobo Inn (888-773-4637; www.rrdiner.com), 51630 WA 706 East. As Elbe is the home of the Mount Rainier Scenic Railroad (see *To See—For Families*), it's only to be expected that someone would think of lodging people on the train. Eight 1916 cabooses, brightly painted red, yellow, or orange, have been refitted as guest rooms complete with bathrooms (and even, in one case, a hot tub). The **Mount Rainier Railroad Dining Company** and **Side Track Room,** both also in retired railroad cars, are conveniently located just steps away. From $115.

Mineral

Mineral Lake Lodge (360-492-LAKE; www.minerallakelodge.com), 195 Mineral Hill Road. Constructed of cedar logs in 1906, this inn drew wealthy Seattleites to soak in the supposedly healthful waters of the lake. It still has very much the look of a wilderness lodge, though a century has brought civilization and, in fishing season, crowds. Guests have shore access along 215 feet of private waterfront. Eight guest rooms are decorated with sporting themes; only three have private baths. Rates include continental breakfast. Children over 12 welcome. No pets. $115–145.

MOTELS

Ashford

Nisqually Lodge (360-569-8804 or 888-674-3554; www.escapetothe mountains.com), 31609 WA 706 East. In the middle of Ashford just a few miles from the park entrance, Nisqually Lodge has large motel-style rooms and a vaulted central common area with a fireplace. Amenities include laundry facilities and a hot tub. $85–125.

Packwood

✍ **Inn of Packwood** (360-494-5500 or 877-496-9666; www.innofpackwood .com), 13032 US 12. Strategically located between Mount Rainier, Mount St. Helens, and the White Pass ski area, these 34 pine-paneled rooms are a reasonable option. There are single, double, and kitchen units, and the

heated indoor pool is a plus. Rates include continental breakfast. $50–145.

RESORTS

Greenwater

✍ **Alta Crystal Resort** (800-277-6475; www.altacrystalresort.com), 68317 WA 410 East. Far from the madding crowd, yet just outside Mount Rainier's back door and below Crystal Mountain Ski Resort, Alta Crystal is a quiet 22-acre property just east of the park, within the national forest. One- and two-bedroom suites, each with a full kitchen and wood-burning stove or fireplace, plus a swimming pool and hot tub on-site, make it especially convenient for families. $199–310; check for extended-stay and other discounts.

✳ Where to Eat

Like most national parks, Mount Rainier is surrounded by public lands in a sparsely settled area where restaurants are thinly spread. For a few more options besides those listed below, try Enumclaw, an hour north of the park, or Eatonville, half an hour west.

DINING OUT

Ashford

Alexander's Country Inn and Restaurant (360-569-2300 or 800-654-7615; www.alexanderscountryinn .com), 37515 WA 706 East. Open for lunch and dinner daily in summer, weekends only in winter except for hotel guests. Ensconced in Ashford's stateliest home, Alexander's not only has guest rooms (see *Lodging*), it also serves the most ambitious cuisine in town, from grilled vegetable and chèvre tart to apricot-glazed halibut to tarte tatin—and, of course, blackberry pie. The trout comes from their pond, and they'll fillet it at your table. The food they serve for three meals a day would be lovely anywhere, but the setting doesn't hurt, and in summer you can dine beside the trout pond.

EATING OUT

Ashford

Copper Creek Inn (360-569-2326), 35707 WA 706 East. Open for breakfast, lunch, and dinner daily in summer; 11–7 Mon.–Thurs., 11–8 Fri., 8 AM–9 PM Sat., 8–8 Sun. in winter. This cheery red house sits right on the highway, as it has since the 1920s, when it began serving breakfast, lunch, and dinner to loggers, tourists, and locals. It's as well liked now as then, the polished-wood dining room seeming to hum with weekending couples and families. The cooking is down-home Northwest: seafood chowder, beef stew, trout, the works; a breakfast special, apparently peculiar to the Mount Rainier area, is blackberry pie with vanilla ice cream. Today, of course, "down-home Northwest" includes a roster of regional wines and microbrews.

❧ **Rainier Overland Lodge and Restaurant** (360-569-0851), 31811 WA 706 East. Open for breakfast, lunch, and dinner daily. Family-friendly food in a chinked-log dining room yields rib-eye steak, baked salmon, pot roast, and homemade soups. Rooms are available, too (see *Lodging*).

Wild Berry Restaurant (360-569-2277), 33718 WA 706 East. Open 7 AM–9 PM daily. Here's a restaurant that has undergone a major makeover. In 2009 a Nepalese couple, Dawa and Pawan Sherpa, bought the place and are now serving Nepalese food. Veterans of the climbing hospitality industry, they owned a resort near the North Face Base Camp at Mount Everest, feeding guests and leading treks. In a stroke of genius, they've transferred their skills to Mount Rainier, where the visitors are just as hungry and can now enjoy Nepalese dumplings, curries, and yak burgers (the yaks come from Colorado). They've made quite a splash in the community. Some concessions to local cuisine remain, such as blackberry pie, without which you can hardly be considered a restaurant in Ashford.

Centralia

Olympic Club Hotel and Theater (360-736-5164 or 866-736-5164), 112 North Tower Avenue. Open 7 AM–midnight Mon.–Thurs., 7 AM–1 AM Fri.–Sat. One of the quirky, home-grown McMenamin's chain, the Oly was actually a "men's club" in the early 1900s, and the long mahogany bar, the rougher wood floors, the woodstove, and the general physical ambience have been carefully preserved. It's still frequented by a jolly crowd, though probably much tamer than the loggers of yesteryear. Many come for lunch or dinner and a movie, simultaneously—you can eat either in the in-house theater or the dining room. The food is pub grub: good fish-and-chips, respected burgers, desirable desserts. The Olympic has **hotel rooms,** too, breakfast included; above the men's club was a railway hotel (the trains still run just behind, several times a night). Anyone who has ever stayed near a provincial European train station knows the type.

Greenwater

Summit House Restaurant (360-663-3003), top of Chinook Express chairlift on Crystal Mountain, off WA 410. Open for lunch and dinner daily, breakfast Sat.–Sun. in winter; lunch daily and dinner Sat.–Sun. in summer. At an elevation of 6,872 feet, it's the highest restaurant in the state, with panoramas of Mount Rainier and the Cascade Range in good weather. Dinner reservations recommended, especially since lift tickets are then free.

✳ Selective Shopping

ANTIQUES Tower Avenue, Centralia, is lined with antiques shops representing hundreds of dealers.

FOOD Suver's General Store (360-569-2377), 30402 WA 706 East, Ashford. If you're self-catering, Suver's is the only stop for groceries in Ashford.

OUTDOOR GEAR Whittaker Mountaineering (800-238-5756; www.whittakermountaineering.com), 30027 WA 706 East, Ashford. Your local source for climbing and outdoor gear.

POTTERY Ashford Creek Pottery (360-569-1000), 30510 WA 706 East, Ashford. Pottery, rustic furniture, and work in various media by local artists are sold here.

✳ Special Events

July: **Antique and Art Fest** (www .jazzartique.com), Centralia. There are free workshops and an appraisal fair.

August: **Morton Loggers' Jubilee** (360-496-6362; www.loggersjubilee .com), Morton. The Loggers' Jubilee is to logging as rodeos are to ranching. You'll see springboard chopping, birling, and more.

September: **Rainier Mountain Fest** (800-238-5756; www.rainiermountain fest.com), Rainier Base Camp, 30027 WA 706 East, Ashford. Free. A trail run, salmon bake, workshops, music, and sale of used mountain gear, including book signings and appearances by climbing stars, are all part of the fun.

MOUNT RAINIER NATIONAL PARK

One could spend years exploring "the Mountain" itself, a great patch of the wild Northwest from rain forest to alpine meadow to rock and ice happily preserved in a state of nature. More than 90 percent of the national park is wilderness; stroll away from one of the several visitors centers, and you soon forget they're there. Lucky for us John Muir and Teddy Roosevelt were around to see that Mount Rainier received proper protection in 1899, though not before some of the meadows had been trampled by thousands of little sheep hooves and some of the lower forests had been cut. Still, having mainly recovered over the century, the meadows present the most spectacular display of alpine flowers in the Northwest—carpets of wildflowers is no hyperbole. And the dense evergreen forests, which cover most of the park at elevations below 5,500 feet, are largely old growth (old, as in 100 to 1,000 years, and large, as in 10–12 feet across). Although what you see at Longmire, inside the main entrance, looks like a little village (and it is), 97 percent of the park's 368 square miles is designated wilderness; the rest is National Historic Landmark.

Plans for a circular road around the park's perimeter never got off the ground. It's just as well. The existing roads—WA 706, WA 410, and WA 123—through the park's southern and eastern flanks offer quite spectacular scenery, visitors centers, and short or long access to the gloriously wild backcountry. Whether you stay near the roads or venture into the interior, opportunities for hiking, climbing, camping, bird-watching, and botanizing abound; in winter, some areas are open to snowshoeing, cross-country skiing, or tubing. Then again, you might just want to sit and contemplate nature.

GUIDANCE Mount Rainier National Park Headquarters (360-569-2211; www.nps.gov/mora), Tahoma Woods, Star Route, Ashford 98304. This is a resource for phone or mail inquiries; for inquiring in person, visit one of the park's information centers. All offer activities such as guided nature walks, talks, and exhibits. Most wilderness permits can be obtained at the Wilderness Information Center at Longmire (360-569-6650) or White River (360-569-6670), or at any ranger station in summer.

Carbon River Ranger Station (360-829-9639), off WA 165 at the northwestern entrance to the park. Open in summer; call for hours.

Jackson Visitor Center (360-569-6581), off Stevens Canyon Road at Paradise. Open 10–5 Sat.–Sun. Oct.–Apr.; 10–6 daily in summer.

Longmire Museum (360-569-6575), east of WA 706 next to the National Park Inn. Open 7:30–5 daily spring–fall; 9–4:30 daily in winter. This is the main entrance.

Ohanapecosh Visitor Center (360-569-6581), off WA 123, in the southeastern corner of the park. Open late May–early Oct.; call for hours.

Sunrise Visitor Center (360-663-2425), off WA 410, in the northeastern corner of the park. Open July–Sept.; call for hours.

GETTING THERE Entry costs $15 per vehicle per week; an America the Beautiful Pass (which replaces the National Park Service, Golden Eagle, and Golden Age passes, although those in circulation are still honored) will also get you in. Several of the roads listed below were washed out by floods in the fall of 2006. Most have been repaired, but weather or road work can always cause closures. Call ahead for current information.

Carbon River entrance, the remote northwest corner; take **WA 410** to Buckley and **WA 165** through Carbonado. Road closed beyond ranger station.

Mowich entrance, also in the northwest corner; take WA 165 to its end. Open only in summer.

Nisqually (main) entrance, the southwest corner. From the Tacoma area: Take **I-5** to exit 142 and follow **WA 161** south to La Grande, about 36 miles; then follow **WA 7** and **WA 706** east through Ashford, 24 miles. From the Olympia area: Take I-5 to exit 111 and follow **WA 510** south, **WA 702** east, then WA 7 and WA 706 east, 58 miles. From the Centralia area: Take I-5 to exit 68 and follow **US 12** east, WA 7 north, and WA 706 east, a scenic 65 miles.

Stevens Canyon entrance (360-569-2211), the southwest corner; from either WA 410 to the north or US 12 to the south, take **WA 123** to the Stevens Canyon Road. Closed in winter and under repair during 2012; call for opening and closing dates.

White River entrance (360-569-2211), middle of the east side; off WA 410 just west of Chinook Pass. Closed in winter; call for opening and closing dates.

GETTING AROUND Limited shuttle service is available within the national park along the main park road on weekends during the summer; otherwise, unless you plan to spend all your time hiking the backcountry or sitting on the National Park Inn's veranda, you must, unfortunately, bring a car. Absurd traffic jams are thus created between Longmire and Paradise, the two most popular tourist sites, during the brief wildflower season (July–Aug.); it's much better to go before or after. Traffic flow elsewhere is generally reasonable, but roads are narrow and winding, so drive with caution.

✳ To See

HISTORIC SITES Mount Rainier National Historic Landmark District includes nearly all the man-made structures in the park, including buildings, roads, and bridges—even the 93-mile Wonderland Trail around the mountain. High points include the following:

Longmire, 6 miles east of the Nisqually entrance to the park (see *Getting There*). Built in the early 1900s as a consciously planned park headquarters community, it included administrative offices, employee housing, lodging, and visitor services. It still serves most of these functions, though the actual headquarters has been moved outside the park. The "Park Service Rustic" style, with its heavy beams, logs, stone, and shingles, was supposed to put you in mind of a European hunting lodge, and so it does—all that's missing is a boar's head on the wall. Which is fine. Across from the National Park Inn, along the 0.7-mile Trail of the Shadows (see *To Do—Hiking*), are the crumbling remains of James Longmire's Medical Springs resort, which predated the park. Longmire had his guests bathe in and drink the waters, and explanatory plaques juxtapose Longmire's claims for the mineral springs' panaceac properties with the Park Service's plea not to drink from them: "It could make you very sick!"

Paradise Inn, 6 miles east of Longmire on Stevens Canyon Road. Open mid-May–Oct. This classic of the park lodge genre is, at 3,000 feet, higher than the Longmire area. It's of a size to match the mountain, and its steeply pitched roof recalls Rainier's profile. The nearby Jackson Visitor Center, opened in 2008, replaces a flying-saucer-shaped structure built in the 1960s. The new building, in what one might call a "Neo–Park Service" style, harmonizes much better with the inn and the mountain.

MUSEUMS Longmire Museum (360-569-6575), WA 706, Longmire. Open 9–5 daily May–Oct.; 9–4:30 daily Oct.–Apr. Free with park entrance fee. This modest cabin across from the historic Administrative Building was the park's first administration building when it was built in 1916. In 1928 it became a museum of nature

THE ADMINISTRATIVE BUILDING AT LONGMIRE IN MOUNT RAINIER NATIONAL PARK

in the park; lots of the exhibits date from the 1930s, including a large number of stuffed animals and birds. Check for some eye-popping Native American baskets over the wildlife displays. They're more than a hundred years old, and the colors are still vibrant.

NATURAL WONDERS Glaciers. More than 70 glaciers give the crest and slopes of Mount Rainier its mantle of eternal white. They have created the deep furrows radiating from the summit and, though generally in retreat since the last Ice Age, continue to fluctuate with changes in climate. Some, such as the Nisqually, Puyallup, Carbon, and Emmons glaciers, are the sources of quite respectable rivers. Six of the biggest glaciers originate at the summit, while the rest, interestingly, are born in the middle zone of 5,000–11,000 feet, where the most snow falls. Emmons is the largest glacier in the Lower 48, while Carbon reaches the lowest elevation—only 3,000 feet. The myriad watercourses born of these ice fields result in many beautiful **waterfalls,** of which **Narada, Christine, and Silver falls** are some of the most accessible.

Grove of the Patriarchs, near the Stevens Canyon entrance on WA 123 (see *Getting There*). A stand of the most impressive and ancient trees in the park is located along the Ohanapecosh River. Enormous Douglas firs, western hemlocks, and western red cedars grow on an island in the river. The largest red cedar in the park is here, but there are also 20 whose circumference is more than 25 feet; one Douglas fir is 35 feet around. Some of these trees are estimated to be a thousand years old and counting. An interpretive trail runs through the grove (see *To Do— Hiking*).

Mount Rainier. No wonder the early inhabitants considered it a god. Rising to 14,410 feet above the surrounding lowlands near sea level, it towers over nearby peaks, its hunched shoulders gazing down at Puget Sound, to which its own waters hasten. You can see it from Yakima in the east and from Port Townsend far to the northwest. In a region not lacking in mountains, it's known simply as "the Mountain." People comment, "The Mountain's out today," whether they see it floating serenely above Seattle's haze, hulking over Gig Harbor, or echoed in Tacoma's new glass and steel waterfront.

Formed by eruptions of basalt, ash, pumice, and andesite only about half a million years ago, it actually rose to 16,000 feet before being cut down to size in the last glaciations. Though its last known eruptions were in the mid-1800s, continual steam from the twin craters at the summit maintains a system of caves in the ice and signals an active mountain—notice the small VOLCANO EVACUATION ROUTE road signs in the communities around its base. A new eruption could make the 1980 Mount St. Helens devastation look like a fire drill. Rainier's shoulders carry the largest mass of glacier and permanent ice in the Lower 48 (see above), much of which would swiftly make its way down to sea level if heated.

Rain forest, Carbon River entrance (see *Getting There*). The northwestern corner of the park gets the brunt of the storms continually driving in from the northern Pacific, and this area has the park's highest rainfall. Here you'll find a rare temperate rain forest that includes Sitka spruce, a coastal species. The whole forest should really be 150 miles to the northwest, in the company of the Bogachiel and Hoh river systems, but *voilà!* here it is, well inland, because Mount Rainier's bulk catches the swirls of Gulf of Alaska cyclones. A 0.25-mile **interpretive trail** starts at the Carbon River Ranger Station (see *Guidance*).

Subalpine meadows. A brief growing season means subalpine flowers have to do a lot in a short time; abundant snowmelt and summer sunshine give them plenty of resources with which to do it. Mount Rainier's meadows are renowned for their glorious wildflower displays, with lupine, columbine, penstemon, glacier lilies, spring beauty, monkey flower, and endless others blooming together and in succession. **Paradise Valley** is the best-known meadow, and crowds have brought a need for nearly constant rehabilitation; other accessible meadows are at **Tipsoo Lake** and **Yakima Park,** near Sunrise. In all these areas, you are begged to stay on established trails and fined if you don't.

SCENIC DRIVES Mather Memorial Parkway (WA 410), about 20 miles from the park boundary south of Greenwater to Chinook Pass. This beautiful highway following the White River offers particularly fine views of the mountain as well as old-growth forest. Call for road conditions in low season.

Park road, 11 miles from Longmire to Paradise. On this ur-scenic drive, you wind past waterfalls and up and up till you're surrounded by peaks and think you're in the Hall of the Mountain King; then you burst into the flowery meadows of Paradise. Or you would if the road were not jammed with cars and tour buses. Outside the flowering season, though, traffic is quite reasonable and the views just as good.

Stevens Canyon Road, about 15 miles from Paradise east to WA 123. This is also a beautiful drive.

WALKING TOURS Longmire walking tour. A flyer is available at the Longmire Museum (see *Museums*). This tour takes you by the log and stone **Administrative Building;** a 1929 **gas station** built in rustic style like everything else here; the **general store,** which is the oldest extant building in the park; and of course the National Park Inn (see *Lodging*).

✷ To Do

BICYCLING Cycling is allowed only on park roads, most of which are not suitable because they are winding, narrow, and heavily trafficked. The following options are, therefore, obviously all for mountain bikes:

Carbon River Road (see *Getting There*), about 5 miles. This road through the rain forest is subject to washouts. No cars are allowed beyond the ranger station, but pedestrians are.

Mowich Lake Road, 5 unpaved miles; at end of WA 165 in the northwest corner of the park. This dirt road leads to a subalpine lake.

West Side Road, 9.25 miles; north of WA 706 just past the Nisqually entrance. This is closed to vehicles 3 miles in, so it has little traffic; the ensuing 6.25 miles are open to bikers and hikers, with some steep climbs and impressive views.

CAMPING

Car-Accessible Campgrounds

♿ **Cougar Rock,** on the park road 2.3 miles north of Longmire. One hundred seventy-three tent or RV sites (four ADA-compliant; no hook-ups); picnic tables,

THE NATIONAL PARK'S MOST-VISITED
AREA IS CALLED, APTLY, PARADISE.

fire grates, water, and flush toilets. Reservations recommended late June–Labor Day (877-444-6777; www.recreation.gov); first come, first served Memorial Day–late June and Labor Day–Columbus Day.

Mowich Lake walk-in campground, a short distance from the end of WA 165. Open July–mid-Oct. if road is open and Carbon River doesn't rise. Free. Ten primitive sites for dispersed camping (no hook-ups); picnic tables and vault toilets but no water or fires. No reservations.

♿ **Ohanapecosh,** off WA 123 in the park's southeastern corner. Open late May–early Oct. One hundred eighty-eight sites (two ADA-compliant; no RV hook-ups); water, flush toilets, picnic tables, and fire grates. Reservations recommended late June–Labor Day (877-444-6777; www.recreation.gov); first come, first served Memorial Day–late June and Labor Day–Columbus Day.

White River, west of WA 410 in the northeastern quarter (see *Getting There*). Open late June–mid-Sept. One hundred twelve sites; water, flush toilets, picnic tables, and fire grates. No reservations.

Backcountry Camping

Numbers of backcountry campers are managed, which is why you have to get a permit first. You can ask to reserve a permit in advance, but it's a cumbersome process: Download the request form from the park website (www.nps.gov/mora) and mail or fax it in; requests are accepted beginning Mar. 15. It can take as much as two months to get a letter confirming your reservation, after which you must pick up your permit in person at the Longmire Wilderness Information Center. Usage is high, and you may actually be denied. Also, your reserved permit may be canceled if you don't show up by 10 AM on the first day of your trip.

The other option is to show up at the information center and request a permit there. Arrive there the day of your trip or the day before (but no earlier).

Seventy percent of permits are allocated to those who reserve in advance, 30 percent to those who just turn up. It's your choice. At least they're free.

Backcountry camping options include designated **trailside campgrounds** with a few tent sites, primitive toilets, and nearby untreated water. These are located beside the longer hiking trails, especially from the Sunrise and Carbon River trailheads (see *Hiking*); the Wonderland Trail has one every 3–7 miles.

It's also permissible to hike **cross-country** and choose your own spot, leaving (naturally) no trace. You still need a permit. Camping in the alpine zones has special rules; consult with the rangers. Be aware, too, that snow is present at most elevations until June or July and may fall at any time of year above 5,000 feet. Be prepared.

CANOEING AND KAYAKING Nonmotorized boats are allowed on all park lakes except Tipsoo, Frozen, Ghost, and Reflection. That said, most lakes are in the backcountry. **Mowich Lake** is the only one really accessible by road (see *Getting There*); it's also the biggest.

CLIMBING Climbing Mount Rainier (360-569-6641; www.nps.gov/mora/climb) is technical and arduous, and it should not be attempted without significant experience and, preferably, a guide (see below). Climbers generally bivouac at one of two high camps—**Camp Muir** or **Camp Schurman,** at about 10,000 feet—and begin their ascent at 1–2 AM to take advantage of firm snow. Both camps have backcountry toilets and a ranger station; Camp Muir has a 25-person shelter. A $43 climbing pass ($30 if you're under 25), valid for one year and an unlimited number of climbs, is required to climb on glaciers or over 10,000 feet. Passes are obtained by submitting an online form and picking up the pass in person. Unfortunately, the location for picking up passes changes; call the number above to find out where to go. In addition, camping reservations are strongly suggested for climbing May–Sept., and they cost an additional $20. Reservation forms can be downloaded from the above website and sent in ahead of time by fax (360-569-3131) or mail (Wilderness Reservations Office, Tahoma Woods Star Route, Ashford 98304). Authorized guide services in the park include the following:

American Alpine Institute (360-671-1505).

Mount Rainier Alpine Guides (360-369-2609).

Rainier Mountaineering, Inc. (360-569-2227 or 888-892-5462; www.rmiguides .com), 30027 WA 706 East, Ashford. This is the park's original guide service, offering climbing instruction and guided climbs.

HIKING The park has hundreds of miles of hiking trails, from short strolls to the 93-mile Wonderland Trail encircling the mountain (see below). Except in the lowlands, the season doesn't begin till June or July due to the heavy snow cover. Some highlights include the following (distances are one way unless noted otherwise).

Longmire Area

Eagle Saddle Trail, 3.6 miles; start from just past Nisqually Bridge at Longmire. High season only due to snow. This strenuous climb of nearly 3,000 feet leads to panoramic views.

Kautz Creek Trail, 4.5 miles; start from the bridge 3 miles east of the Nisqually entrance. Hike a gentle mile to the creek, then climb through venerable cedars to a meadow called Indian Henry's Hunting Ground.

Rampart Ridge Trail, 4.6-mile loop; start from the Trail of the Shadows at Longmire (see below). Hike through forest to views from Rampart Ridge, a 1,339-foot elevation gain.

&. **Trail of the Shadows,** 0.7-mile loop; start at Longmire. James Longmire's old resort (see *To See—Historic Sites*) is now a beautiful wetland bordered by forest. This easy walk is wheelchair-accessible for about half its length.

Wonderland Trail section, 6 miles from Longmire to Paradise. If you want to avoid driving in traffic to Paradise, you can hike there through deep forest, past several waterfalls, and finally to Paradise (Regained), with a 2,700-foot elevation gain.

Mowich Area

Green Lake Trail, 1.8 miles; trailhead 3 miles east of the Mowich Ranger Station. This trail has a side spur to Ranger Falls and an elevation gain of 1,000 feet.

Lake James and Windy Gap Trail, 8.5 miles; start from Ipsut Creek campground at the Carbon River entrance. Cross the Carbon River and head up 3,450 feet. There are several wilderness campsites in this area (permits required).

Mystic Lake Trail, 8 miles; start from Ipsut Creek campground at the Carbon River entrance. For overnight trips, this hike rises 3,900 feet for some fine views.

Rain Forest Loop, 0.25-mile loop; at the Carbon River Ranger Station. Explore a relict temperate rain forest.

Spray Park Trail, 3 miles; start from Mowich Lake campground. There are spurs to two waterfalls on the way to Spray Park; turn back for a 6-mile round-trip, or continue another 7 miles to Ipsut Creek campground for 10 miles one way (car shuttle required).

Tolmie Peak Trail, 2.8 miles; start from WA 165, 5.5 miles east of the park boundary. The trail leads past Eunice Lake to an old lookout, for an elevation gain of 1,010 feet.

Ohanapecosh Area

East Side Trail, 11.5 miles from Ohanapecosh campground to Chinook Pass. You don't have to hike the whole distance, but it's nice to know it's all there.

Grove of the Patriarchs, 1.3 miles; start from the Stevens Canyon entrance station parking lot. Perhaps the favorite in this area, the trail leads you to an island in the Ohanapecosh River where huge Douglas firs and western red cedars, protected by their location from fire and logging, have attained ages of a thousand years.

Silver Falls Loop Trail, 3-mile loop; start from Ohanapecosh campground. Hike up to Silver Falls along one side of the river and come back on the other.

Paradise Area

Bench and Snow Lakes Trail, 1.25 miles; trailhead on Stevens Canyon Road 1.5 miles west of Reflection Lakes. This gently rolling trail is an easy jaunt.

♪ **Nisqually Vista Trail,** 1.2 miles; start from just behind the Paradise Inn (see *Lodging*). This stroller-friendly walk provides views of Nisqually Glacier.

Paradise Inn trails. Several short trails suitable for flower gazing wind through the wildflower meadows just behind the Paradise Inn (see *Lodging*). Stay on the trails; fragile alpine plants can take years to recover from one casual tread.

Reflection Lakes, 3-mile loop; from Stevens Canyon Road just beyond Paradise. Hike around this series of small lakes.

Skyline Trail, nearly 6-mile loop; start from the Paradise Inn (see *Lodging*). For a longer venture, walk past Myrtle Falls and Sliuskin Falls—the latter named after the Indian who guided Hazard Stevens and Philemon Van Trump on the first successful ascent of Mount Rainier. Panoramas include Mount Adams and Mount St. Helens and close-ups of Nisqually Glacier. The elevation change is 1,400 feet.

Sunrise Area

Sunrise Visitor Center is the highest in the park, and its trail network is correspondingly alpine.

Northern Loop Trail, 3.5 miles; start from the visitors center. Follow the Sourdough Ridge Trail west 1.5 miles to Frozen Lake and the Mount Fremont Trail; continue 0.7 mile past this junction and turn onto the Northern Loop Trail to Berkeley Park for a hike with a 1,200-foot elevation gain. There's a wilderness camp here (permit required).

☙ **Pet loop,** 1-mile loop; start from the west end of the parking lot. This is the only trail in the park on which pets are allowed.

Silver Forest Trail, 1 mile; start from the visitors center. This leisurely walk goes through an old burn, with a viewpoint along the way.

Sourdough Ridge Nature Trail, 1.5-mile loop; start from the picnic area. This self-guided walk has nice views of Rainier and the Cascade Range.

Sourdough Ridge Trail east, 2 miles; start from the Sourdough Ridge Nature Trail (see above). Continue east along the ridge to the base of Dege Peak.

Sourdough Ridge Trail west, 3 miles; start from the visitors center. Follow the Sourdough Ridge Trail west to Frozen Lake and then turn north on the Mount Fremont Trail to an old fire lookout.

Throughout the Park

Wonderland Trail, 93-mile loop. This is the mother of all trails, wandering up and down the mountain's many ridges, in and out of forests, alpine meadows, panoramas, creeks, and most other things the mountain has to offer. Most hikers allow 10 or more days to complete the circuit; the terrain is rugged, and elevation changes of 3,000 feet in a day are not uncommon. A free wilderness permit is required for any overnight wilderness stay (see *Guidance*). It's always good to check trail conditions at one of the Wilderness Information Centers, whether your hike is short or long, as there may be downed trees, washouts, or other obstacles at any time.

WINTER SPORTS Mount Rainier gets plenty of snow: Paradise Valley receives about 600–700 inches a year and sometimes nearly twice that.

Sledding and tubing. These are allowed only in the snow play area at the north end of the Paradise parking lot.

Snowboarding. Surprisingly, snowboarding (but not downhill skiing) is allowed when snow is deep; consult the Longmire Museum (360-569-6575).

Snowshoe walks. Start from the Jackson Visitor Center at Paradise at 12:30 and 2:30 PM daily mid-Dec.–early Jan., Sat.–Sun. only early Jan. on; sign up an hour ahead of time. Walk free; $4 donation to rent snowshoes. Ranger-guided walks last about two hours and are open to anyone eight years old or over.

Snowshoeing and cross-country skiing. Several snow-covered park roads are open for Nordic skiing and snowshoeing. Check availability at the Longmire Museum (360-569-6575).

✴ Lodging

Shelter within the park is confined to the two historic lodges listed below. Plentiful, and often cheaper, quarters can be found in nearby Ashford and other communities (see the Mount Rainier Area chapter).

LODGES ♿ **National Park Inn** (360-569-2275; www.mtrainierguest services.com), along WA 706 at Longmire, 6 miles east of the Nisqually (southwestern) entrance. The price for a room with a shared bath might seem a bit steep, especially for those who remember the heady days when you could afford to take your whole family on a national parks vacation. But this lodge is worth a visit even if you don't stay—the inn is a classic of "Park Service Rustic" architecture. The log columns, gables, and weathered shingle exterior bespeak a conscious slowing down in the presence of America's crown jewels, and the living room, with its big stone fireplace and plump chairs, suggests curling up with a book after a day in the great outdoors. From the veranda, guests can exchange long gazes with the mountain. There's a full-service **restaurant** on the premises. The 25 rooms are adequate but fairly plain. Two ground-floor guest rooms and all ground-floor facilities (restaurant, lobby, and lounge) are wheelchair-accessible. Rooms without bath $118–154; rooms with bath $164–200; two-room units with bath $229; handicapped-accessible rooms $163; off-season packages may be available.

Paradise Inn (360-569-2275; www .mtrainierguestservices.com), on WA 706, 6 miles beyond Longmire but considerably higher. The steep-roofed Paradise Inn is swathed in snow through the winter—15 or more feet of it. The 118-room lodge has welcomed summer visitors since 1917 and emerged from a 2008 revamping with its historical looks intact. And some looks—the hand-hewn yellow-cedar lobby furniture, including a piano, grandfather clock, and thronelike chairs, wouldn't look out of place in the halls of Middle Earth. Neither

EVEN IN SPRING, PARADISE INN IS SURROUNDED BY SNOW.

would the huge open-trussed **dining hall.** As for the surrounding meadows in summer, well, there's a reason it's called Paradise. Reserve early. Lodge rooms $114–186; annex rooms with private bath $167–207; two-room units $250–278; handicapped-accessible rooms $167–207.

✳ Where to Eat

EATING OUT Jackson Visitor Center Deli (see *Guidance*). Open daily May–Oct.; Sat.–Sun. rest of the year. You'll find hot dogs, hamburgers, and the like here.

National Park Inn dining room (see *Lodging*). Open for breakfast, lunch,

and dinner daily year-round. There are several restaurants in nearby Ashford (see the Mount Rainier Area chapter), but at present the only restaurant within the park is this casual dining room serving American and Northwest standbys.

Paradise Inn dining hall (see *Lodging*). Open for breakfast, lunch, and dinner daily in summer. Dine by a crackling fire in the famous historic dining hall.

Sunrise Day Lodge cafeteria (see *Guidance*). Open early July–early Sept. This place serves hot dogs, hamburgers, and the like on the park's eastern side.

CENTRAL CASCADES

The Central Cascades extend north from WA 410 north of Mount Rainier to US 2, the Stevens Pass Highway, with the I-90 corridor smack-dab in the middle. From WA 169, WA 18, WA 202, and WA 203 running south to north along the western foothills to a bit west of US 97 along the eastern foothills, the Central Cascades are among the most often visited part of the range. The Cascade Scenic Loop—US 2, US 97, and I-90—makes this mountain playground easily accessible to the populous Puget Sound area, but the recent discovery of a wolf pack near Cle Elum underscores the tangled wildness of the backcountry.

In the western foothills to the south, old mining towns with names such as Black Diamond had coal deposits that once fueled Seattle and young British Columbia. North Bend, western gateway to Snoqualmie Pass, is now bypassed by I-90 but still serves well as an entryway to hikes in the Issaquah Alps—Cougar Mountain, Squak Mountain, Tiger Mountain. On US 2, Index and Skykomish are mountain towns that still draw hikers and climbers out to the peaks.

In the eastern foothills, I-90 drops from Snoqualmie Pass to Roslyn and Cle Elum, more old mining towns being revitalized by television shows and resorts. US 97 between Cle Elum and Leavenworth rises over Blewett Pass, past tiny Liberty and Mineral Springs.

Leavenworth, at the eastern end of US 2's Tumwater Canyon, was a boomtown in the early 1900s but a moribund timber town by the 1960s, when the city fathers had the inspired, if unlikely, idea of resurrecting it by turning it into a Bavarian village. It has succeeded beyond their wildest expectations. True, there are an awful lot of dirndls, not to mention lederhosen, and the oompah music gently blaring from a loudspeaker on the main *Platz* might be a bit much. But architects were brought over from Germany, and the hotel and restaurant owners travel in the other direction to make their lodgings and cuisine as authentic as they can—certainly, here you can get some of the best central European food in the Northwest. It's a peculiarly space-warping experience. And the Cascades backdrop is straight out of *The Sound of Music*.

Just east of Leavenworth are Cashmere and Wenatchee, which bills itself as the apple capital of the world. It's true that this sun-drenched bend in the Columbia River ships millions of apples around the globe; it has the old warehouses along the waterfront to prove it. But which came first, the apple or Wenatchee? Today the town resembles an American freeway town almost anywhere, but it draws

DOWNTOWN LEAVENWORTH, AN AMERICAN BAVARIAN VILLAGE

visitors with attractions such as Ohme Gardens, the Wenatchee Valley Museum, and the Mission Ridge ski area—where the Cascades are snug up against Wenatchee's back door.

GUIDANCE **Cascades Loop Association** (509-662-3888; www.cascadeloop .com), Box 3245, Wenatchee 98807.

Leavenworth Chamber of Commerce (509-548-5807; www.leavenworth.org), 220 Ninth Street, Leavenworth 98826.

Mount Baker–Snoqualmie National Forest (425-783-6000 or 800-627-0062; www.fs.usda.gov), 2930 Wetmore Avenue, Everett 98201.

Okanogan-Wenatchee National Forest Headquarters (509-664-9200), 215 Melody Lane, Wenatchee 98801. District offices are at Lake Wenatchee and in Chelan, Cle Elum, Entiat, Winthrop, Naches, and Leavenworth.

Wenatchee Valley Convention and Visitors' Bureau (800-572-7753; www .wenatcheevalley.org), 5 South Wenatchee Avenue, Wenatchee 98801.

GETTING THERE The Central Cascades are crossed east to west by **I-90,** from North Bend to Cle Elum via 3,022-foot Snoqualmie Pass, and by **US 2,** from Index to Wenatchee via 4,061-foot Stevens Pass. Towns along the eastern slopes are accessed by **US 97,** from Cle Elum to Leavenworth via 4,102-foot Blewett Pass.

Wenatchee Airport (EAT) (509-884-2494) is at One Pangborn Drive, East Wenatchee.

AMTRAK's (800-USA-RAIL; www.amtrak.com) Empire Builder, which runs from Chicago to Seattle, stops in Wenatchee at the corner of Kittitas and South Columbia streets.

Greyhound (800-231-2222; www.greyhound.com) stops in Leavenworth and in Cashmere, at 102 Kitchenal Road, on the way to and from Seattle.

GETTING AROUND Basically, you need a car in these mountains.

✔ **Leavenworth Trolley** (509-662-1155). Mon.–Sat. in summer. If your toddler's feet are tired, this takes you around Leavenworth's sights and neighborhoods. The same goes for your own feet, of course. Cutbacks threaten this service for 2012.

Link Transit (509-662-1155; www.linktransit.com) offers intercity bus service in and among Wenatchee, Cashmere, and Leavenworth (as well as Entiat, Chelan, and Manson—see the North Cascades chapter).

MEDICAL EMERGENCY Cascade Medical Center (509-548-5815), 817 Commercial Street, Leavenworth.

Central Washington Hospital (509-662-1511; www.cwhs.com), 1201 South Miller Street, Wenatchee.

Cle Elum Urgent Care Center (509-674-6944), 201 Alpha Way, Cle Elum.

✳ To See

FARMERS' MARKETS Leavenworth Farmers' Market (509-548-5786), at Lions Club Park. Open 4–8 Thurs. June–Oct.

Wenatchee Valley Farmers' Market has three venues offering local produce and crafts: Riverfront Park in Wenatchee, open 8–1 Wed. and Sat.; Methow Park in Wenatchee, open 3–7 Thurs.; and Wenatchee Memorial Park, open 10–3 Sun., all June–early fall.

FARMS AND GARDENS Ohme Gardens County Park (509-662-5785; www .ohmegardens.com), 3327 Ohme Road, Wenatchee; near junction of US 2 and US 97. Open 9–6 daily Apr. 15–Memorial Day weekend and Labor Day weekend–Oct. 15; 9–7 daily Memorial Day weekend–Labor Day weekend. $7 adults, $3.50 children 5–17. Ruth and Herman Ohme started this project to provide some green relief after arriving on this desolate bluff in 1929. Rock by rock and tree by tree, they planted, irrigated, and leveled by hand—all the while scrabbling a living from their orchard—till the neighbors got curious. Soon there were so many marveling at the Eden in the desert that by 1939 the Ohmes had to control the visitors, and so they allowed it to become a public park. Today you can visit this little bit of subalpine forest in the desert; lawns and ground covers set off wild violets, columbines, buttercups, and other tender flowers peeping out among the rocks or under fir groves. A 1-mile trail winds around the 9-acre site, though due to the rough terrain it's not suitable for wheelchairs or strollers, and the lovely view over the Columbia that the Ohmes must have enjoyed is now unfortunately marred by huge warehouses and the freeway below.

FOR FAMILIES ✔ **Aplets and Cotlets** (509-782-1000 or 800-231-3242; www .libertyorchards.com), 117 Mission Avenue, Cashmere. Open 8–5:30 Mon.–Fri., 10–4 Sat.–Sun. Apr.–Dec.; 8:30–4:30 Mon.–Fri. Jan.–Mar. Tours every 20 minutes. Free. The story goes that an Armenian immigrant here in the 1920s tried to duplicate Turkish delight from memory and ended up (more or less) with Aplets and

Cotlets—a bit more substantial than Turkish delight and, to some, more flavorful. Capitalizing on the Wenatchee Valley's productive orchards, the candy makers first produced apple- and apricot-flavored confections but have now branched out to blackberry and other flavors. Tours of the candy kitchens allow you and yours to follow the candy-making process from boiling to cutting and packaging. Free samples, too.

✒ **Friends in the Making Bear Factory** (509-548-7020), Obertal Mall, 220 Ninth Street, Leavenworth. Open 12:30–8:30 Mon.–Tues. and Thurs., 9:30–5:30 Wed. and Fri. Call for prices. Stuff your own bear at this shop, which also deals in the famous Steiff stuffed animals.

✒ **Icicle Junction Family Fun Center** (509-548-2400; www.iciclejunction.com), on US 2 next to the Best Western (which offers a package deal), Leavenworth. Open 10–10 daily in summer; 3–8 Mon.–Thurs., 3–10 Fri., 10–10 Sat., 10–8 Sun. in winter. Movies $3.50–7.50; miniature golf $4.50–6.50; arcade by game. Available activities include miniature golf, billiards, darts, bumper boats, a video arcade, and other amusements.

✒ **Leavenworth National Fish Hatchery** (509-548-7641; www.fws.gov /leavenworth), 12790 Hatchery Road, Leavenworth; left off Icicle Road. Open 8–4 daily in summer; 8–4 Mon.–Fri., 8–2 Sat.–Sun. in winter. Free. Take a self-guided tour of the hatchery, stop at the visitors center to learn about the problems facing Northwest salmon, and walk the nature trail. Oh, and bring a picnic.

HISTORIC SITES **Iron Goat Trail,** 6 miles of abandoned railroad grade near US 2 (see *To Do—Hiking*). Access to the actual Wellington train disaster site (see below) is along this trail named for the Great Northern railroad's logo of a mountain goat.

Liberty, on US 97 a few miles north of Cle Elum (follow the signs). The gold is long gone—such as it was—from this erstwhile gold-mining town, but the rather well-preserved settlement is on the National Register of Historic Places.

Roslyn cemeteries, Roslyn. More than 24 ethnic groups came to work the Roslyn mines, each burying its dead in its own cemetery. For information, contact the Roslyn Museum (see *Museums*).

Wellington train disaster, on US 2 at milepost 58.3. The Cascades, with their steep grades and abominable winter weather, were one of the railroads' last frontiers. In 1910, 4,016-foot Stevens Pass on US 2 was the site where two Great Northern trains, which had already been held up for two days in Leavenworth due to bad weather, were again stopped by impassable snow on the west side of the Cascade Tunnel. For six days, the trains were stuck at the pass below Windy Mountain. On the seventh day, an avalanche roared down the slope, overturning both trains and sending them to the bottom of a ravine 150 feet below. The official death toll was 96. The right-of-way was eventually moved to a lower route through the new 7.8-mile Cascade Tunnel, which is still in use by Burlington Northern.

MUSEUMS **Cle Elum Historical Telephone Museum** (509-674-5702), 221 East First Street, Cle Elum. Open 12–4 daily Memorial Day–Labor Day. Free. This home of the Cle Elum Historical Society was a Pacific Northwest Bell office building until 1966. Today it displays the old (pre-automated) Cle Elum switchboards and explains the history of the telephone and its role in the town's development.

Historic Museum and Pioneer Village (509-782-3230; www.cashmeremuseum .org), 600 Cotlets Way, Cashmere. Open 10:30–4:30 daily Mar.–Oct. $5.50 adults, $4 seniors and students, $3 children 6–12. Outdoors you can wander through a mining village complete with cabins, school, hotel, church, and assay office, all buildings dating from the late 1800s and brought together here. Inside is one of the most surprising small-town museums you'll find, with a terrific collection of Native American crafts, tools, artifacts, and art spanning thousands of years, including rare stone sculptures.

Nutcracker Museum (509-548-4573; www.nutcrackermuseum.com), 735 Front Street, Leavenworth. Open 2–5 daily May–Oct.; 2–5 Sat.–Sun. Nov.–Apr. $2.50 adults, $1 students, children under five free. If you ever wanted to see five thousand nutcrackers in one place, they're all here, from prehistoric cracking stones to Indian betel nut crackers to exquisitely carved Italian and German pieces. A recent coup was the acquisition of a bronze Roman nutcracker. Sweet.

Rocky Reach Dam Visitor Center (509-663-7522; www.chelanpud.org), on US 97A about 15 miles north of Wenatchee. Open 9–4 daily except in winter. Free. Here you can visit the **Museum of Electricity** and the **Museum of the Columbia**— interconnected, of course, since the Columbia is now the Northwest's powerhouse, but including exhibits on river life over the ages. There's also a fish ladder, garden, and arboretum. For security reasons, the visitors center restricts entry with bags, packages, firearms, etc.; call ahead for details.

Roslyn Museum (509-649-2355; www.roslynmuseum.com), 203 West Pennsylvania Avenue, Roslyn. Open 12–5 Fri.–Mon., 1–5 Tues. Donation accepted. Roslyn was built on mines, and this museum recalls that history with photos and equipment. It also houses souvenirs of the TV series *Northern Exposure*, which was filmed in Roslyn.

Upper Valley Museum at Leavenworth (509-548-0728; www.uppervalley museum.org), 347 Division Street, Leavenworth. Open 11–5 Thurs.–Sun. spring– fall, 11–4 in winter. $5 adults, $3 seniors, $2 children 6–12; free first Fri. each month. Historic photos detail Leavenworth's inception as a lumber town, its near death as same, and its wildly successful resurrection as a "Bavarian" village. There's also exquisite Native American beadwork and more. Its new home, the Barn Beach Reserve (which it shares with the local Audubon chapter), is a hundred-year-old bungalow over the creek, former home of a local banker.

✎ **Wenatchee Valley Museum and Cultural Center** (509-888-6240), 127 South Mission Street, Wenatchee. Open 10–4 Tues.–Sat. $5 adults, $4 seniors over 60, $2 children 6–12; free first Fri. each month. This two-story museum interprets life in the Wenatchee Valley with special emphasis on the apple. Apples put Wenatchee on the map, as you can see from a large wall map detailing where Wenatchee apples go. A big room re-creates a 1920s apple-packing shed with vintage equipment, much of it still operational: an apple wiper, apple sorter, and of course lots of apple crate labels. Another fun exhibit is the detailed model railroad crossing the Cascades. Changing exhibits take an artistic angle, such as the "River of Memory," an extraordinary collection of photos of the Columbia River spanning 1891–1962.

WINERY TOURS Wineries and even vineyards are spreading to Washington's mid-Columbia Basin from Ellensburg to Wenatchee—"about the latitude of Bordeaux," though the bulk of the grapes are grown farther south, in the Yakima or Walla Walla valley. You'll find ample tasting opportunities in Wenatchee and Leavenworth.

Columbia Cascade Wines (509-782-0708; www.columbiacascadewines.com), 301 Angier Avenue, Cashmere. Contact them for a self-guiding brochure.

Icicle Ridge Winery (509-548-7019; www.icicleridgewinery.com), 8977 North Road, Peshastin; 4 miles southwest of Leavenworth. Tastings here, too.

✳ To Do

BICYCLING Blewett Pass (US 97). Many scenic trails with stunning views are around this pass; superior skill required.

Das Rad Haus (509-548-5615), 1207 Front Street, Leavenworth. Contact them for trail information, rentals, and repairs.

Eagle Creek Road, off Chumstick Road in Leavenworth. Wander up a quiet farming valley for miles; eventually the road turns to dirt, with some climbs. (There are many other routes in the nearby hills.)

East Leavenworth Road, 7.5-mile loop from downtown. This flat route gives you spectacular views of the Enchantment Mountains and takes you back downtown via Icicle Road, Riverfront Park, and lush Blackbird Island. Suitable for road or mountain bikes.

Iron Horse or John Wayne Trail, 110 miles from North Bend to the Idaho border (and then some); access from I-90 at exit 38. This easy and scenic old railroad bed runs clear across the state. For details contact the Mount Baker–Snoqualmie National Forest (see *Guidance*). See also the Mid-Columbia Basin chapter in part 6, Southeastern Washington.

Mountain Home Road, 10 miles to Boundary Butte; off East Leavenworth Road. This winds uphill, steeply at times. Mountain bikes only.

BIRDING The Leavenworth area, where leafy trees meet evergreens and the mountains begin to grade into desert, is a Washington birding hot spot; spring bird counts commonly tally more than 150 species.

Barn Beach Reserve (509-548-0181; www.nwaudubon.org), 347 Division Street, Leavenworth. This new home of North Central Washington Audubon is worth a visit. On a bluff above the Wenatchee River, a century-old house built by Leavenworth's founding lumberman sits amid 50 acres of leafy parkland. It's a nature education center as well as a gallery for local artists, and you can find plenty of bird species right here. For more sites and information, pick up the handy guide "The Great Washington State Birding Trail: Cascade Loop" from any visitors center.

Blackbird Island, part of Waterfront Park in downtown Leavenworth. Dozens of songbirds, ospreys, and waterfowl are attracted to this spot.

Leavenworth National Fish Hatchery (509-548-7641), 12790 Hatchery Road, Leavenworth; off Icicle Road about 2 miles from town. More than one hundred species have been recorded here.

Wenatchee Confluence State Park, Wenatchee. Where the Wenatchee River meets the Columbia, vagrant species from as far away as Siberia congregate during the fall migration; two hundred American species also are present.

CAMPING **National forest campsites** require fees; contact the **Okanogan-Wenatchee Ranger Station** (509-664-9200) for information.

Chiwawa River Road Area
Alpine Meadows. Four sites; toilets but no water. No reservations.

Goose Creek, on FR 6100, 4 miles west of Lake Wenatchee via WA 209. Twenty-nine sites; toilets and water. No reservations.

Phelps Creek, at the end of Chiwawa River Road via WA 209. Seven sites; vault toilet but no water.

Icicle River Road Area
These are all west of Leavenworth, and all have water and toilets: **Blackpine Creek Horse Camp,** 10 sites, no reservations; **Bridge Creek,** 6 sites, reserve at 877-444-6777 or www.recreation.gov; **Chatter Creek,** 12 sites, reserve at 877-444-6777 or www.recreation.gov; **Eight Mile,** 45 sites, reserve at 877-444-6777 or www.recreation.gov; **Ida Creek,** 10 sites, no reservations; **Johnny Creek,** 65 sites, no reservations; **Rock Island,** 22 sites, no reservations.

I-90–Cle Elum Area
Most of these require a Northwest Forest Pass or a fee, though reservations (877-444-6777; www.recreation.gov) are taken only for Salmon la Sac and Cayuse.

Cayuse Horse Camp, at the end of Salmon la Sac Road (WA 903). Thirteen sites; water and toilet.

Cle Elum River, on WA 903, 15 miles north of Cle Elum. Twenty-three sites; water and toilet.

Manastash Camp, on FR 3104 off Manastash Road. Fourteen sites.

Owhi, on FR 4616 north of Salmon la Sac. Two walk-in sites and several large group sites; toilet but no water.

Red Mountain, on Salmon la Sac Road just north of Cle Elum River. Ten sites; toilet but no water.

Salmon la Sac Camp, at the end of Salmon la Sac Road (WA 903). Sixty-seven sites; water and toilets.

Taneum, on FR 33 west of I-90 near Thorp. Thirteen sites; water and toilet.

Wish Poosh, on WA 903, 8 miles north of Cle Elum. Thirty-four sites; boat launch, water, and toilet.

US 2–Index Area
Troublesome Creek, on Index-Galena Road east of Index. Thirty sites.

US 2–Leavenworth Area
Glacier View, on FR 6607 on the south side of Lake Wenatchee. Twenty-three sites. No reservations.

Lake Creek, on FR 6701 west of Soda Springs. Several dispersed sites; no water or toilet. No reservations.

Napeequa, on FR 6400 north of Lake Wenatchee. Five sites; toilet but no water. No reservations.

Nason Creek, on WA 207 near Lake Wenatchee. Seventy-three sites; water and toilets. No reservations.

Rainy Creek, on FR 6701 near the Little Wenatchee River off WA 207. Ten rustic sites; toilet but no water. No reservations. (Replaces Riverside, which was flooded out.)

Soda Springs, on FR 6701 near the Little Wenatchee River west of Rainy Creek. Twenty-six sites; water and toilets. Reserve at 877-44-6777; www.recreation.gov.

Tumwater, on US 2 just north of Leavenworth. Eighty-six sites; water and toilets. Reserve at 877-44-6777; www.recreation.gov.

White River Falls, on FR 6400 north of Napeequa. Five sites; toilet but no water. No reservations.

US 97–Blewett Pass Area

Beverly, on North Fork Teanaway Road, north of Cle Elum. Ten sites; toilet but no water. No reservations.

Mineral Springs, on US 97 south of Blewett Pass. Six sites; toilet but no water. Reserve at 877-444-6777; www.recreation.gov.

Swauk, on US 97 just south of Blewett Pass, 30 miles north of Cle Elum. Twenty sites; water and toilet. No reservations.

State Parks

Kanaskat-Palmer State Park (see *Wilder Places—Parks*), on Kanaskat Selleck Road north of Enumclaw. Twenty-five tent sites and 19 RV sites. Reservations required in summer (888-226-7688).

&. **Lake Easton State Park** (see *Wilder Places—Parks*), on I-90 east of Snoqualmie Pass. Ninety-five tent sites and 45 RV sites; ADA restrooms and showers. Reservations accepted (888-226-7688).

Lake Wenatchee State Park (see *Wilder Places—Parks*), on North Shore Drive off WA 207. One hundred fifty-five tent sites and 42 RV sites; all amenities. Reserve at 888-226-7688.

Lincoln Rock State Park, on US 97 just north of Wenatchee. Twenty-seven tent sites, 64 utility sites, and 4 cabins; all amenities. Reserve at 888-226-7688.

Wenatchee Confluence State Park (509-664-6373), Old Station Road, Wenatchee; about 1.3 miles from US 2. Eight tent sites and 51 utility sites; all amenities. Reserve at 888-226-7688.

CANOEING AND KAYAKING The **Green River** near Flaming Geyser State Park (see *Wilder Places—Parks*) has seasonally variable rapids for white-water kayaking.

CLIMBING Cashmere Crags, including **Enchantment Peak,** are favorites among climbers.

Leavenworth Mountain Sports (509-548-7864), 220 US 2, Leavenworth. Contact them to learn more about area climbs and to find guides or equipment.

Peshastin Pinnacles State Park (see *Wilder Places—Parks*) has spires that are a favored climbing destination.

(reservations 877-444-6777; www.recreation.gov), in Okanogan-Wenatchee National Forest near US 2, 10 miles northeast of the Skykomish Ranger Station. Available by reservation; usually open only Sept.–Oct. For further information, call 360-677-2414. The 14-by-14-foot cabin sitting on a mountaintop with views of the surrounding Cascades was a fire lookout from 1934 to the 1980s. It has a propane stove, lanterns, and an outhouse but no water. Access involves a steep 1.5-mile hike. Pets welcome. $40.

Table Mountain Cabin (reservations 877-444-6777; www.recreation.gov), in Okanogan-Wenatchee National Forest on US 97 near Blewett Pass. Available July–Oct. and Dec.–early Apr. This rustic cabin has no water. In winter it's accessible only by skis or snowmobile. $50; sleeps up to 10.

Taneum Cabin (reservations 877-444-6777; www.recreation.gov), on Taneum Creek 20 miles from Ellensburg. This one has running water and propane. $75; sleeps up to four.

Teanaway Guard Station (Cle Elum Ranger District, 509-852-1100, ext. 30; reservations 877-444-6777; www.recreation.gov), 13941 Taneum Road, Thorp. Available May–mid-Nov. and Dec.–Apr. This log cabin has a woodstove, propane cookstove, and toilet, but no drinking water. $40; sleeps two.

GOLF Highlander Golf Course (509-884-4653), 2920 Eighth Street SE, East Wenatchee. Eighteen holes.

Leavenworth Golf Club (509-548-7267; www.leavenworthgolf.com), 9101 Icicle Road, Leavenworth. Eighteen holes.

Sun Country Golf Resort (509-674-2226); 841 St. Andrews Drive, Cle Elum. Eighteen holes.

HIKING

Alpine Lakes Wilderness Trails

Alpine Lakes Wilderness (see *Wilder Places—Wilderness Areas*) can be accessed from I-90 near Snoqualmie Pass, US 97 near Blewett Pass, US 2 south of Stevens Pass, or Icicle Road (FR 7600) west of Leavenworth. **Wenatchee River Ranger District** (509-548-2550), 600 Sherbourne Street, Leavenworth, has maps or information on trails in this largely wild area. For real adventure, explore trails along Icicle Creek:

Eightmile Lake, 3.3 miles; from Icicle Road turn left at Bridge Creek Campground and go 4 miles to the trailhead. It's steep at first, then levels off through mature forest to sparkling Little Eight Mile and Eight Mile lakes.

Icicle Gorge Trail (No. 1555A), about 3.5 miles; on Icicle Creek Road between Chatter Creek and Rock Creek campgrounds. This favorite loops around a section of the creek; it's fairly level with views of the boulder-strewn canyon.

I-90 Area

Iron Horse or John Wayne Trail, 110 miles in Washington. Originally a right-of-way for the Chicago, Milwaukee, St. Paul, and Pacific Railroad, this paved, low-grade 276-mile trail roughly follows I-90 and is shared with cyclists, dogsledders, equestrians, and skiers, depending on the season. The few campgrounds on the

EIGHTMILE LAKE IN THE CASCADES NEAR LEAVENWORTH

trail are all between mileposts 2109 and 2127; some Forest Service campgrounds are near the trail—contact the Mount Baker–Snoqualmie National Forest (800-627-0062) for details—and two park campgrounds are located at Lake Easton and Wanapum state parks.

Mount Si, 4 miles; from I-90 take exit 31 to the trailhead outside North Bend, 28 miles southwest of Seattle. This rigorous hike rewards you with views of the Snoqualmie Valley and beyond (the less energetic can try Little Si, only 1,576 feet but sometimes frequented by mountain goats).

Lake Wenatchee Area
To hike in **Lake Wenatchee State Park** (see *Wilder Places—Parks*) or the adjacent national forest, from US 2, 16 miles west of Leavenworth, go 2 miles north on WA 207.

Phelps Creek Trail, 5 miles; from US 2 take WA 207 north to Chiwawa River Loop Road, go 1.5 miles, and turn left on Chiwawa Valley Road. In spring, this is a favorite for viewing wildflowers.

Twin Lakes, 3.5–4.25 miles; take WA 207 around the north side of Lake Wenatchee, turn right on White River Road, and follow the signs. This trail just northwest of Lake Wenatchee makes a nice hike.

Leavenworth Area
Riverfront Park and **Blackbird Island,** right in town on the Wenatchee River; park at the bottom of Ninth Street. At a river confluence right under the mountains, Leavenworth and environs offer plenty of choices. This easy, pleasant stroll takes in shady paths, tiny beaches, and birdsong.

Ski Hill Trails, just above Leavenworth on Ski Hill Road. This network with nice views is good for wandering after dinner.

Iron Goat Trail (206-517-3019; www.irongoat.org), 9 miles; Martin's Creek trail-head is on US 2 at milepost 55; Wellington trailhead is on US 2 at milepost 64.3. This trail runs along the old Great Northern railroad grade. Besides forests and wildflowers, this trail takes you past the site of the **Wellington train disaster** (see *To See—Historic Sites*) and remains of railroad buildings and equipment. Interpretive walks are offered four times a year. Two segments are barrier-free, one of which leads from now-abandoned Wellington to the wreck site.

Whitepine Trail, on Whitepine Road south of US 2, 22.6 miles northwest of Leavenworth. This lightly traveled path gains slightly in altitude as it goes up a valley. Turn around when you feel like it.

Wenatchee Area

Apple Capital Loop Trail, 10 miles; accessible from Riverwalk Pedestrian Overpass, 19th Street, 27th Street, Confluence State Park, and Walla Walla Point Park, Wenatchee. Walkers, cyclists, and skaters share this path running along both banks of the Columbia through downtown Wenatchee.

Okanogan-Wenatchee National Forest Headquarters (509-664-9200), 215 Melody Lane, Wenatchee, also offers lots of backcountry hiking.

HORSEBACK RIDING Icicle Outfitters and Guides (800-497-3912; www .icicleoutfitters.com), Box 322, Leavenworth 98826. They will get you a horse in the Leavenworth area. Llama packing and sleigh rides, too.

KAYAKING AND RAFTING Several outfitters offer rentals and/or guided trips on the Wenatchee and Kittitas rivers.

THE CASCADES SURROUNDING LEAVENWORTH DRAW HIKERS FROM AROUND THE STATE.

Blue Sky Outfitters (206-938-4030 or 800-228-RAFT; www.blueskyoutfitters .com), 9674 50th Avenue SW, Seattle.

Enchanted Water Tours (509-548-5031), Box 611, Leavenworth 98826.

Osprey Rafting Company (509-548-6800 or 800-548-6850; www.ospreyrafting .com), US 2 and Icicle Road, Leavenworth.

WINTER SPORTS **Leavenworth Ski Hill** (Leavenworth Winter Sports Club, 509-548-5477; www.skileavenworth.com), just north of town. This is where locals have been skiing for generations. Small-town skiing centers on two runs with rope tows, a terrain park, and a 1930s Civilian Conservation Corps lodge. Miles of Nordic trails, too.

Mission Ridge (509-663-6543; www.missionridge.com), Box 1668, 7500 Mission Ridge Road, Wenatchee. In the forest south of Wenatchee, Mission Ridge is a sunny-side ski center with 36 trails, four lifts, and a vertical rise of 2,250 feet.

Stevens Pass (206-812-4510; www.stevenspass.com), Box 98, Summit Stevens Pass, US 2, Skykomish 98288. Stevens gets plenty of snow, about 450 inches a year. With 10 lifts and 3 day lodges, parks, and 28 kilometers (17 miles) of Nordic trails, this is a popular place for Seattleites.

Summit at Snoqualmie (425-434-7669), Box 1068, Snoqualmie Pass 98068. Snoqualmie Pass, on I-90, is positioned to catch winter storms barreling through the Puget Sound area. It gets indecent amounts of snow—one year, enough to block the ski lifts (that was unusual). Just an hour east of Seattle, it also gets a lot of traffic. Four alpine areas, Nordic trails, parks, and pipes provide almost all things to all skiers.

✸ Wilder Places

PARKS ♿ **Flaming Geyser State Park** (253-931-3930), 23700 Flaming Geyser Road, Auburn. Open 6:30 AM–dusk in summer; 8 AM–dusk in winter. Situated on the Green River just south of Black Diamond, the park is popular for tubing and kayaking and has a model airplane–flying area. But its real curiosity is its "geysers." Methane from underground coal seams percolates up through two old test holes; one actually flames, while the other just bubbles. Trails along the river include an ADA salmon interpretive trail.

Kanaskat-Palmer State Park (888-226-7688), on Kanaskat Selleck Road north of Enumclaw. This 320-acre park on the Green River offers camping, picnicking, and technical white-water sports.

♿ **Lake Easton State Park** (360-902-8844), on I-90 east of Snoqualmie Pass. This park has nearly 5 miles of beach access offering swimming and boating, plus 5 miles of trails for hiking or, in winter, cross-country skiing. There's also camping, ADA restrooms, and showers.

Lake Wenatchee State Park (509-763-3101), 18 miles northwest of Leavenworth; from US 2, turn right on WA 207. Five miles of equestrian trails, 1-mile interpretive snowshoe trail, 8 miles of hiking trails, and 7 miles of biking trails, plus 2 miles of stunning lake waterfront, make this a park of many attractions, including camping. Boating, wind surfing, and kayaking are also popular. The north side is more developed for recreation, while the south side, across the Wenatchee River, remains more natural and forested. Bears are present, so exercise proper caution.

Lincoln Rock State Park (360-902-8844), on US 97 just north of Wenatchee. Closed in winter. This 80-acre park under basalt cliffs above Rocky Reach Dam offers swimming, waterskiing, and camping. It gets busy in summer.

Olallie State Park (360-902-8844), on I-90 east of North Bend. Day use. Olallie features old-growth forest, waterfalls, and abundant huckleberries; 6 miles of trails give access to the 110-mile Iron Horse or John Wayne Trail (see *To Do—Hiking*).

Peshastin Pinnacles State Park (360-902-8844), 14 miles west of Wenatchee; from US 2, turn off at North Dryden. Day use. The pinnacles in this 34-acre dry-land park are a formation of sandstone slabs popular for technical climbing. A short but steep hiking trail also leads to the top for views. No drinking water is available.

Squilchuck State Park (509-664-6373), 9 miles southwest of Wenatchee; from Wenatchee, travel south on Wenatchee Avenue and follow the signs up Squilchuck Road. A forested park at 4,000 feet, Squilchuck offers a group camp, a heritage day lodge, and 10 miles of hiking and biking trails. In winter it's open intermittently for sledding, tubing, snowshoeing, and cross-country skiing; call for snow conditions.

Wenatchee Confluence State Park (360-902-8844), Old Station Road, Wenatchee; about 1.3 miles from US 2. Where the Wenatchee flows into the Columbia, this urban park offers swimming, boating, and camping, plus a restored wetland accessible by pedestrian bridge. In spring and fall it's a haven for migrating birds.

WILDERNESS AREAS Alpine Lakes Wilderness, 394,000 acres; straddling the Cascades divide between I-90 and US 2, with acreage on both the east and west sides of the crest. Access at Snoqualmie Pass on I-90 or Deception Falls on US 2. This wilderness includes thick western forest, mountain meadows, and more parklike east-slope forests. Created by glaciers, it contains myriad small lakes and ponds; together with its proximity to Seattle, this puts it among the higher-use wilderness areas. Hiking and climbing at Cashmere Crags in the Enchantments are popular activities.

✳ Lodging

BED & BREAKFASTS

Leavenworth
Pension Anna (509-548-6273 or 800-509-ANNA; www.pensionanna.com), 926 Commercial Street. Sixteen Swiss-chalet rooms with imported *Bauernmalerei* (peasant painting) furniture naturally require a German-style breakfast of sliced cheeses, meats, bread, pastries, and soft-boiled eggs. Rooms, all with private baths, range from single queens to fireplace suites, but they're all immaculate and cozy. You also have the option of the Old

Chapel Suite or Parish Nook, in an old remodeled church on the premises. Rooms $150–230; suites $239–330; Parish Nook $169–250.

Run of the River Inn and Refuge (509-548-7171 or 800-288-6491; www.runoftheriver.com), Box 285, 9308 East Leavenworth Road, Leavenworth. This is definitely a splurge, but the hewn-log lodge makes you forget about sight-seeing and just about everything else. Six guest rooms feature stone fireplaces, plump four-poster beds, and decks over Icicle Creek. You can borrow a bike or snowshoes to enjoy the outdoors if you must, but you might be just as happy watching birds from the deck. Rates include a huge family-style breakfast. Adult-oriented—no children. No pets. $230–265.

Roslyn

✍ **Huckleberry House** (509-649-2900; www.huckleberryhouse.com), 301 Pennsylvania Avenue. Three antiques-furnished guest rooms with private baths in a restored home offer a snug haven in this historic mining town. Each has a view of the town and mountain surroundings, while a wraparound porch offers plenty of room to sit and enjoy the Cascade views. Rates include a full breakfast. Children welcome. No pets. $75–125.

GUESTHOUSES

Leavenworth

Mrs. Anderson's Lodging House (800-253-8990; www.quiltersheaven .com), 917 Commercial Street. When the house opened its doors in 1903, Leavenworth was a scrappy logging town with great expectations. Most of the lodgers were loggers or mill workers. Sharing quarters with a quilt shop, it's still a plain but cozy lodging house whose 10 rooms, some with private and some with shared baths, have simple turn-of-the-20th-century-style furnishings. Part of the mission here is to provide space for Bible-oriented retreats. For rafters, families, and others on a budget, it offers the most reasonably priced accommodations in town and is convenient to everything. Rates include a buffet breakfast. No pets. $43–141.

HOTELS

Leavenworth

Bavarian Lodge (509-548-7878 or 888-717-7878; www.bavarianlodge .com), 810 US 2. This is the very large chalet with the turret visible on US 2.

The lobby is impressive, with finely carved heavy furniture—there's a chandelier of exquisite deer heads—and a fireplace. The 54 rooms are comfortably provided with stuffed armchairs or sofas and village or mountain views. And yes, there are rooms in the tower. Rates include a full breakfast buffet. No pets. $119–395.

♿ **Enzian Inn** (509-548-5269 or 800-223-8511; www.enzianinn.com), 590 US 2. This is the place to stay if you like to be awakened by an alpenhorn. Every morning, owner Bob Johnson or his son Rob plays the horn from a balcony. Bob and Rob built the place themselves in 1983; it has grown to 104 rooms (3 ADA-compliant), with 2 pools, a breakfast room, meeting rooms, an 18-hole golf course, and an impressive lobby with a large stone fireplace and much carved wood. Elegant rooms have hand-carved or hand-painted furniture. Here and there, worked into the design, you'll find the *Enzian,* or blue gentian, an alpine flower for which the hotel is named. Over the golf course is the Alm Hütte, a log house featuring the family's virtuoso craftsmanship. Rates include a full breakfast in the solarium. No pets. Rooms $120–305; house $330–420.

♨ **Obertal Inn** (509-548-5204 or 800-537-9382; www.obertal.com), 922 Commercial Street. The Obertal is a reasonable, family-friendly alternative to the pricier hotels in town. The rooms are like those of a nice motel, with some fireplace and spa suites, and it's right downtown with the restaurants and shops. Rates include a breakfast bar. Pets welcome for a fee ($15). $109–289.

Skykomish

Cascadia Inn (360-677-2030 or 866-677-2030; www.historiccascadia.com), 210 Railroad Avenue East. Between the railroad tracks and the Skykomish

THE OBERTAL INN IN LEAVENWORTH

in 1904, this property became a summer camp in the 1950s and has evolved into a guest ranch. Not that you'll round up cattle here—but you can enjoy trail rides and riding lessons (extra fee). Two cookhouses allow you to cook your own meals. Accommodations include four self-contained cabins sleeping two to six; to nine bunkhouses sleeping eight (no bath); tepees with beds for two; and antique-bedded 14-by-16-foot tents. Tents and tepees $90; bunkhouses $100; wrangler cabins $115; larger cabins $165–275.

River, this 1922 hotel is a budget option for recreationalists in summer or winter. Rooms are simple but snug and free of phones and TV; relax in the parlor in the evening. Two dog-friendly rooms. Family bunk room $40 double occupancy; rooms with shared bath $40–60; rooms with private bath $75–85.

MOTELS

Gold Bar
Stevens Pass Motel (360-793-6633; www.stevenspassmotel.net), 809 Croft Avenue. This renovated 1916 hotel in downtown Gold Bar caters to skiers, hikers, and other lovers of the mountain outdoors; 18 rooms. $54–84; weekly rates available.

Skykomish
🐾 **Skyriver Inn** (360-677-2222 or 800-367-8194; www.skyriverinn.com), 333 River Drive East. This chalet-style motel overlooking the Skykomish River is a family-friendly accommodation with the usual motel amenities. $83–140.

RANCHES

Cle Elum
Flying Horseshoe Ranch (509-674-2366; www.flyinghorseshoeranch.com), 3190 Red Bridge Road. Homesteaded

RESORTS

Leavenworth
Leavenworth Icicle Village Inn (509-961-0162 or 800-558-2438; www.icicleinn.com), 505 US 2. Lodgings here include a Best Western Plus (the Icicle Inn), whose rooms look out on the creek or the jagged faces of the Cascades, and separate condominium rentals. They range from spacious and comfortable to downright luxurious, and the condos have one, two, or three bedrooms, plus living room, dining area, and kitchen. A panoply of activities—game arcade, swimming pool, movie theater, swimming pool, and more—make it popular with families. Rates include a hot continental breakfast. Pets allowed in some of the Best Western rooms. Rooms $150–300; condos $249–419; check for online specials.

✳ Where to Eat
DINING OUT

Leavenworth
Many of the restaurateurs in Leavenworth travel frequently to Germany, Austria, and beyond and put excellent authentic dishes on the table. *Mahlzeit!*

Andreas Keller (509-548-6000; www.andreaskellerrestaurant.com), 829 Front Street. Open for lunch and dinner daily. Literally in the cellar of one of Front Street's half-timbered houses, Andreas is appreciated almost as much for its convivial musical evenings as for its hearty Bavarian food, from pickled herring to *Käse-spätzle* and *Weisswurst* to Wiener schnitzel. Chef Anita Hamilton, who grew up and studied cooking in Germany, brings it all home for lunch and dinner.

Café Mozart (509-548-0600; www.cafemozartrestaurant.com), 829 Front Street. Open for lunch and dinner daily. Owned by the same family that owns the Andreas Keller downstairs (see above), Café Mozart prides itself on its Viennese (the concept of Bavaria has been extended, obviously), as well as French, German, and Pacific Northwest, dishes. Check out the Symphony of Schnitzels. Dinner reservations recommended.

EATING OUT

Leavenworth

⚙ **Café Christa** (509-548-5074), 801 Front Street. Open 11 AM to closing daily. *Gemütlich* is an overused word in

A MARRIAGE OF OLD COUNTRY AND NEW, LEAVENWORTH

Leavenworth, but it does apply here. Originally owned by Heinz Ulbricht, who pioneered the city's redesign in the 1960s (and named his restaurant for his wife, Christa), and now by Jori Delvo, who lived in Europe for two years learning German cooking, the café is on a cozy second floor in a downtown chalet with views over the town. A whole line of homemade sausages awaits you, as well as the requisite schnitzels and goulash, but also salads, salmon fillet, or Icicle Valley chicken for lighter fare. *"Kinder* menu" also available.

⚙ **King Ludwig's Restaurant** (509-548-6625; www.kingludwigs.com), 921 Front Street. Open for lunch and dinner daily. Bavarian and Hungarian food compete with the image of Mad King Ludwig's Neuschwannstein Castle. Bavarian pork hocks are the specialty, and the goulash, veal and pork schnitzels, and sauerbraten transport you thousands of miles away. There's a children's menu, too. On weekends you can enjoy music and dancing in this comfortable, casual setting.

München Haus (509-548-1158; www.munchenhaus.com), 709 Front Street. Open 11 AM to closing daily May–Oct., Fri.–Sun. Nov.–Apr. In summer there's a long line at the counter, where you order from a menu of sausages and beers, then go sit at one of the long tables in the courtyard. It does put you in mind of Bavaria, and attention has been paid to the authenticity of the wurst, but it's not the place for dinner conversation. For live music and the company of youthful beer enthusiasts, though, this is the ticket.

South (509-888-HEAT; www.south leavenworth.com), 913 Front Street. Open 11–9 Sun.–Thurs., 11–10 Fri.–Sat. This busy, new south-of-the-border restaurant offers a great variety of tacos and burritos, plus some regional Mexican dishes and a list of interesting margaritas, too. The enthusiasm is high, but service can be slow, and noise levels can be elevated.

✔ **The Tumwater Inn** (509-548-4232; www.tumwaterinn.com), 219 Ninth Street. Open for breakfast, lunch, and dinner daily in summer; call for hours in winter. A larger restaurant—large enough to accommodate tour groups, which is something to be aware of if you're not in such a group—the Tumwater nonetheless strives for a blend of Bavarian and Northwest themes, with apple-box ends on the walls complementing the old-wood furnishings. The menu, too, is German American and family-friendly.

Uncle Uli's (509-548-7262), 902 Front Street. Open for lunch and dinner Thurs.–Mon. This informal pub always seems to be busy with both local clientele and visitors. There are Northwest wines and microbrews to drink, and soups, salads, and sandwiches to eat—though this is Leavenworth, so there's also fondue. Being a pub, it can get pretty loud. Live music some weekends.

✔ **Viadolce** (509-548-6712), 636 Front Street. Open 11–7 Mon.–Thurs., 11–9 Fri., 10–9 Sat., 10–8 Sun. After too much sight-seeing, try their 20 flavors of gelato, which should soothe everyone. Pastries, espresso, and panini, too, for breakfast, lunch, or a light supper.

Roslyn

The Brick Tavern (509-649-2643), 100 Pennsylvania Avenue. Open for lunch and dinner daily. Dating from 1889, this is said to be the oldest operating tavern in Washington. Its running-water spittoon is still in place and functioning. The tavern offers pub fare and live music on weekends.

Roslyn Café (509-649-2763; www.roslyncafe.com), 201 West Pennsylvania Avenue. Open for lunch and dinner

daily. This was Roslyn's Café in the TV series *Northern Exposure*. It was and is an actual café, though the current owners, who bought it in 2003, have expanded the menu. Lunch still features classic hamburgers and such, while at dinner you can get blackened ahi and other newfangled dishes, but you'll still find prime rib and steaks as well.

Wenatchee

Inna's Cuisine (509-888-4662; www.innascuisine.com), 26 North Wenatchee Avenue. Open 11–9 Tues.–Sat. Inna's offers Italian, Greek, Russian, and Ukrainian cuisine, which is pretty ambitious even if you're not in Wenatchee. Get it by the dish or order a combo plate—several Russian, or Greek, or Ukrainian goodies all at once (pelmeni, stuffed cabbage, *böorek,* and much more). A couple of salmon or halibut dishes may be thrown into the mix out of respect for place. A children's menu is also available.

✴ Selective Shopping

Leavenworth is your place for German doodads. Here are some of the more interesting shops.

BOOKS A Book for All Seasons (509-548-1451), 703 US 2, Leavenworth. Less obsessive types can browse here, where you might find a visiting author and you will find a Starbucks.

FOOD The Cheesemonger's Shop (509-548-9011), 819 Front Street, Leavenworth. Get your European cheeses, sausages, beers, and ales here (in the basement).

Home Fires Bakery (509-548-7362; www.homefiresbakery.com), 13013 Bayne Road, Leavenworth. Open 9–5 Thurs.–Mon. A favorite of cyclists touring the Cascade foothills, Home Fires is in an old log cabin 3 miles from Leavenworth. In keeping with the town's German theme, they bake stollen at Christmastime, and all their bread is made in a German masonry oven. But it's not all Teutonic: You'll find American specialties such as brownies and cinnamon rolls, as well as tortoni, cheesecake, pies, and more. And you don't have to come by bike (though it may be a good idea).

Prey's Fruit Barn (509-548-5771), on US 97 between Leavenworth and Peshastin. Open daily late May–early Nov. Fruits from the orchard are available in season (including free samples), plus juice, cider, honey, jams, and jellies.

Willis Sausage Haus and Euro Markt (509-548-0681), 217 Ninth Street, Leavenworth. Specializes in German sausages, cheeses, and the like.

GIFTS **Die Musik Box** (800-288-5883), 933 Front Street, Leavenworth. More kinds of music boxes than you thought existed.

Gifts from Russia (509-548-2388; www.giftsfromrussia.net), 900 Front Street, Suite F, Leavenworth. They carry Russian goods and crafts.

Kris Kringl (509-548-6867 or 888-557-4645), 907 Front Street, Leavenworth. Predictably, there's a year-round Christmas shop in town.

✴ Special Events

April–May: **Washington Apple Blossom Festival** (509-662-3616), 516 Washington Street, Wenatchee. This 10-day celebration, with its parades, entertainment, and car show at various venues in and around Wenatchee, is the oldest festival in the state.

May: ♿ **Leavenworth Spring Bird Festival** (509-548-5807; www .leavenworthspringbirdfest.com), various locations around Leavenworth. Guided birding trips (some wheelchair-accessible), workshops, art, music, and a barbecue launch the season.

Maifest (509-548-5807), downtown Leavenworth. A Maypole, music, a parade, and flowers celebrate Mother's Day weekend.

June: **International Accordion Festival** (509-548-5807; www.accordion celebration.org), Leavenworth. Accordion artists come from around the world.

July: **Moose Days** (www.moosefest .com), Roslyn. On the last full weekend of July, die-hard fans of the 1980s TV series *Northern Exposure* gather in the town where it was filmed to celebrate the series and the fictional town that Roslyn stood in for. Proceeds benefit local charities.

September: **Quilt Show** (800-253-8990; www.quiltersheaven.com), Leavenworth. Quilts are displayed in shops throughout town and in the Festhalle.

November: **Christkindlmarkt** (509-548-6605; www.christkindlmarkt .projektbayern.com), Front Street Park, Leavenworth. This is a traditional German Christmas market.

NORTH CASCADES

This vast region includes mountainous wilderness from US 2 to the Canadian border, with WA 20—the scenic North Cascades Scenic Highway—smack-dab in the middle. Bordering this region on the west is Darrington, on WA 530, and Mount Baker, on WA 542; on the east is US 97, from Entiat through Chelan to Pateros, and WA 153 north through the Methow Valley to Twisp. Towns along WA 20 include Concrete, Rockport, and Marblemount west of the crest and Mazama and Winthrop to the east.

Where the Chelan River flows out of 55-mile-long Lake Chelan, drowning itself after 3 short miles in the Columbia River, scrappy Camp Chelan grew up in the 1880s to serve loggers and miners. Fruit growers followed. The sunny town on the lake is now mainly devoted to tourism, but the surrounding hills still produce apples and an embryonic wine industry.

Winthrop, a dying western mining town, revived itself as—a western mining town! When gold, silver, and zinc were discovered in the nearby hills, the Indian reservation that had been designated only a few years previously was dismantled, and towns including Winthrop sprang up. Most mines failed to pan out, and the towns slipped toward oblivion. Winthrop, however, was determined to capitalize on the opening of the North Cascades Scenic Highway in 1972, rebuilding itself with plank sidewalks and false fronts. But instead of saloons and assay offices, you'll find art galleries, shops, and restaurants in what is still a low-key little town. Which is just as well. The precious metals, in any case, now come from the pockets of tourists and devotees of the Methow Valley's great outdoors. Nearby Twisp is similar but even smaller, with a vibrant art community and cozy coffee shops.

Just off WA 20 between Winthrop and the North Cascades, Mazama is a tiny hamlet with a store, a gas station, some homes, and a majestic setting. Virtually surrounded by wilderness, Mazama is a recreation paradise offering hiking, biking, access to the Methow Valley's 200-plus kilometers (125-plus miles) of cross-country ski trails, horseback riding, and just about every outdoor activity you can think of. In winter, the North Cascades Scenic Highway is closed, and access to Mazama is only via Winthrop. The centerpiece of this area, of course, is North Cascades National Park, which, including the towns of Newhalem and Diablo, is covered in the next chapter.

GUIDANCE Cascades Loop Association (509-662-3888; www.cascadeloop.com), Box 3245, Wenatchee 98807.

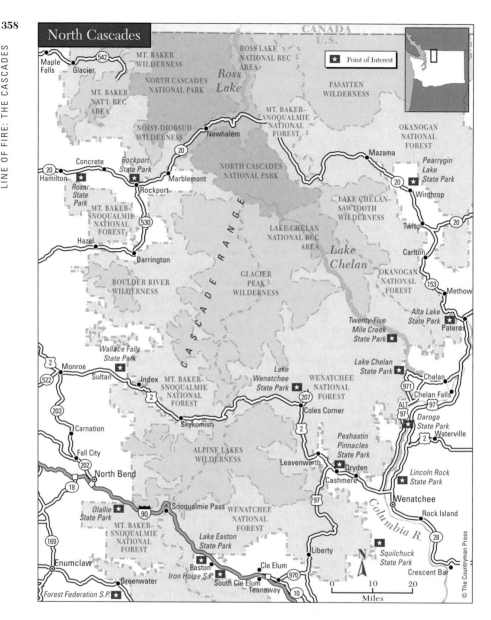

Glacier Public Service Center (360-599-2714), 10091 Mount Baker Highway (WA 542), just east of Glacier. Open 8–4:30 daily in summer; 8–4:30 Thurs.–Mon. late Sept.–mid-Oct.; 9–3 Sat.–Sun. mid-Oct.–mid-Mar.; hours vary late Apr.–Memorial Day; closed mid-Mar.–late Apr. Here you can obtain backcountry permits and maps and see exhibits on the natural and cultural history of the Mount Baker area.

Lake Chelan Chamber of Commerce and Visitor Information Center (800-4-CHELAN), 102 East Johnson Avenue, Chelan 98816.

Methow Visitor Center (509-996-4000), 49 WA 20, Winthrop 98862. Open 8–5 Thurs.–Mon. Memorial Day–Labor Day.

North Cascades Chamber of Commerce (360-873-4150; www.marblemount .com), 59831 WA 20, Marblemount 98267.

Okanogan-Wenatchee National Forest Headquarters (509-664-9200), 215 Melody Lane, Wenatchee 98801. District offices include **Chelan Ranger District** (509-682-4900), 428 West Woodin Avenue, Chelan 98816; **Entiat Ranger District** (509-784-1150), 2108 Entiat Way, Entiat 98822; and **Methow Valley Ranger District** (509-996-4003), 24 West Chewuch Road, Winthrop 98862.

Skagit County Tourism (877-875-2448; www.skagittourism.com).

Twisp Visitor Information Center (509-997-2020; twispinfo.com), 201 South Methow Highway (WA 20), Twisp 98856.

Winthrop Chamber of Commerce (888-463-8469; www.winthropwashington .com), 202 WA 20, Winthrop 98862.

GETTING THERE The North Cascades are crossed east to west by **US 2** and **WA 20.** Towns along the eastern slopes are accessed by **US 97A** (on the west side of the Columbia), **US 97** (on the east side), and **WA 153. WA 530** connects Darrington to WA 20 at Rockport, and **WA 542** connects the Mount Baker area to I-5 at Bellingham.

The closest public airports are in Bellingham and Wenatchee (see the Central Cascades chapter).

AMTRAK (800-USA-RAIL; www.amtrak.com) has a bus link in Pateros at 245 Lakeshore Drive.

Greyhound (800-231-2222; www.greyhound.com) stops in Pateros (served by Northwestern Trailways).

GETTING AROUND Basically, in this vast area you want a car.

The Gabby Cabby (509-341-4650; www.thegabbycabby.com) offers individual and collective shuttle and cab service in and around the Methow Valley.

Link Transit (509-662-1155; www.linktransit.com) offers intercity bus service in and among Entiat, Chelan, and Manson.

Mountain Transporter (509-996-8294) offers shuttle service for wilderness hikers and mountain bikers in and near the Methow Valley.

Special Considerations
Spots around **upper Lake Chelan,** including the village of Stehekin (see North Cascades National Park chapter), are accessible only by boat or floatplane.

Chelan Airways (509-682-5555; www.chelanairways.com), Box W, Chelan 98816, offers flights to upper lake destinations.

Lady of the Lake (509-682-4584; www.ladyofthelake.com), 1418 West Woodin Avenue, Chelan, provides boat service to the upper lake; contact them for rates and schedules.

Stehekin Shuttle (509-682-5555; www.stehekin.biz or www.stehekin.com) offers bus service in season around the isolated community of Stehekin.

MEDICAL EMERGENCY Lake Chelan Community Hospital (509-682-3300), 503 East Highland Avenue, Chelan.

✳ To See

FARMERS' MARKETS Chelan Farmers Market (509-682-4295; www.chelan farmersmarket.org), next to the chamber of commerce in Chelan. Open 8–1 Sat. Memorial Day–Oct.

Twisp Farmers Market (www.methowvalleyfarmersmarket.com), at the Twisp Community Center. Open 9–12 Sat. Apr.–Oct.

FARMS AND GARDENS Cascadian Farm Roadside Stand (800-624-4123; www.cascadianfarm.com), 55749 WA 20, Rockport; at milepost 100.5. Cascadian Farm was bought by General Mills in 2000, but the farm is still there in the Upper Skagit Valley, producing the organic berries and vegetables for which it became famous in the 1970s. In summer you can buy some at their roadside stand. Get some ice cream, too, while you're at it.

FOR FAMILIES North Cascades Smokejumper Base (509-997-9750; www .ncsbsmokejumpers.com), 23 Intercity Airport Road, Winthrop. Open 10–5 daily in summer, Mon.–Fri. in winter. Free. On CR 9129, halfway between Twisp and Winthrop, you can visit the birthplace of smoke jumping. The idea of firefighters parachuting to fires in remote and rugged terrain was conceived and tested here in the North Cascades in 1939 (by hired circus performers, actually) and inaugurated in 1940. Today some 350 trained firefighters around the West are ready to drop into a site at a moment's notice. Drop in and a smoke jumper will explain how it all works, from equipment to the jump.

HISTORIC SITES Concrete, on WA 20 about 10 miles west of Rockport. At the eastern end of town, you'll see the remains of the old Washington Portland Cement site. Operating beginning in 1905, it gave birth to a town called Cement City. In 1908 a competing operation named Superior Portland Cement appeared in next-door Baker. The following year the towns, though not the companies, merged and took the equally descriptive name Concrete. Much of their product went, naturally, to the Seattle City Light dams on the upper Skagit River (see the North Cascades National Park chapter).

St. Andrew's Episcopal Church (509-682-2851), 120 East Woodin Avenue, Chelan. Service 10 AM Sun. This sturdy log church with its steeply pitched roof and square tower wouldn't look out of place in Norway, which is appropriate enough since it sits at the end of a fjord between tall mountains. Conceived when Episcopalians began filtering into the hills around Chelan, the church was designed by famed architect Kirtland Cutter of Spokane and built by an ecumenical group of volunteers. On Christmas Eve 1898, it celebrated its first service and has been an active church ever since.

MUSEUMS Lake Chelan Historical Society Museum (509-682-5644), 204 East Woodin Avenue, Chelan. Open 10–4 Mon.–Fri., 10–3 Sat. in summer; 10–12 and 1–4 Mon.–Fri. in winter. $2 adults, $1 seniors and children. Among the historical photos, you'll find images of the grand old Fields Hotel painstakingly built in

Stehekin in 1927. Sadly, it burned down in 1931, but its box piano stands proudly here beside pioneer and Indian artifacts. Someone has thought to put together a little collection illustrating the history of beads, from medieval Italy to the Pacific Northwest.

Shafer Historical Museum (509-996-2712; www.shafermuseum.com), 285 Castle Avenue, Winthrop. Open 10–5 daily Memorial Day–Labor Day, Sat.–Sun. May and Sept. Suggested donation $2. The vast Indian reservation that once sprawled over this region was promptly abolished when gold was discovered in these hills. Mines and mining towns popped up, most of which disappeared almost as quickly as the reservation had. Much of the old mining equipment is on display at this outdoor museum, with explanations of the process that chewed up rock for gold, silver, and zinc. Also to be seen is a reassembled mining village: the log house built by Guy Waring, first shopkeeper in Winthrop, for his wife, and several other original and replica buildings. A carved-wood relief map indicates the sites of mines, home-steads, and early schools.

NATURAL WONDERS Earthquake Point, on US 97A about 2 miles north of Entiat. A plaque explains that in 1872 an earthquake shook much of Washington and British Columbia, causing half the mountain above this spot to slide down into the Columbia River and stop its flow for several hours. New springs and a tempo-rary, 30-foot-high geyser appeared. The quake's magnitude is estimated to have been 6.8, and it's thought to have been centered south of Lake Chelan. Several lesser quakes have occurred since in the Entiat area. There are no known surface faults, but research suggests "blind faults" that don't reach the surface. Since this is the line where the North Cascades meet the Columbia Plateau—that is, where the North Cascades minicontinent is thought to have "docked" against North America eons ago—some sort of geological slippage zone is not too surprising.

Lake Chelan. Is it natural or unnatural? It's true that when the dam at the south-ern end was built in 1926, it raised the lake level by 21 feet. But as the total depth now is 1,486 feet, such a difference seems hardly worth remarking. Named for the

PASQUEFLOWERS ABOVE RAINY LAKE

Tsillane tribe that inhabited the area when the first white explorers came through, Lake Chelan is really a long inland fjord, 51 miles long by 5 miles wide, set between mountains that are still mostly wilderness. The lake was created by the competing actions of two glaciers, one of which carved out the shallower south end and the other the narrow, deep northern section. Lake Chelan's bottom is nearly 400 feet below sea level. Counting from the top of the tallest neighboring mountain, 8,245-foot Pyramid Peak, to the lake bottom (which may not be entirely fair) only 3 horizontal miles away, this for-mation is the deepest gorge in North America—the Grand Canyon measures a mile in depth, Hells Canyon about 8,200 feet. More precisely, though, Chelan is indeed the third deepest lake in the United States, after Crater Lake (1,932 feet) and Lake Tahoe (1,645 feet), both also in the Cascades. And though Lake Chelan may look placid enough on a calm day, winds funneling down the gorge can slap respectable waves against the beaches and create dangerous boating conditions.

Mount Baker. This symmetrical peak is clearly distinguishable as far away as Port Angeles on the Strait of Juan de Fuca. At 10,788 feet, Baker dominates the surrounding North Cascade pinnacles of 7,000 or 8,000 feet "like a sugar-loaf," as Isaac Stevens, Washington's first governor, put it. Unlike its neighbors, it's one of only two volcanoes in Washington's North Cascades: part of the Pacific's Ring of Fire forced up through the earth's crust by the subduction of the Juan de Fuca tectonic plate, like its more southerly cousins, only here the magma had to push its way through the mountains already in existence. Mount Baker's roots are apparently in a caldera 400,000 years old, but most of the cone seems to have been formed only 30,000–40,000 years ago, making it one of the younger Cascade volcanoes. It's also one of the most active: Several eruptions were recorded in the 19th century, and while it's since been more or less quiescent, increased emissions of steam and new fumaroles in the 1970s make it closely monitored today. Covered in eternal snows, its Nooksack name, Kulshan, means "white steep mountain." Joseph Baker happened to point it out to his captain, George Vancouver, on their 1792 expedition, and so got it named after himself.

SCENIC DRIVES North Cascades Scenic Loop, 400 miles; North Cascades Scenic Highway (WA 20), joined with segments of US 97, I-90, and WA 525. This trip of hugely varied beauty deserves at least several days to take in the small cowboy towns along the Columbia Plateau, two mountain crossings at Snoqualmie Pass (I-90) and Rainy and Washington passes (WA 20), and Whidbey Island in Puget Sound. WA 20's 143 miles of this loop (from Burlington near I-5 on the west to Twisp on the east) make up possibly the most scenic route in the United States.

WA 20, THE NORTH CASCADES SCENIC HIGHWAY

Check for road conditions (see *Guidance*): It's always closed in winter, blocked by 20 feet or more of snow, and may open as early as April or as late as June.

WINERY TOURS Wineries and even vineyards are spreading to Chelan ("about the latitude of Bordeaux," though the bulk of the grapes are grown farther south, in the Yakima or Walla Walla valley). You'll find ample tasting opportunities in Chelan.

Columbia Cascade Winery Association (509-782-0708; www.columbiacascade wines.com). Contact them for a self-guiding brochure.

C. R. Sandidge Wines (509-687-3704; www.crsandidge.com), 145 Wapato Way, Manson. Offers wine tastings.

✳ To Do

BICYCLING **Visitor Information Center** (800-4CHELAN), 102 East Johnson Avenue, Chelan. This place has maps and information.

Echo Ridge Trail System, 18 miles, on WA 150 between Chelan and Manson. Used for skiing in winter, these trails are open to cyclists in summer.

BIRDING **Pearrygin Lake State Park,** off WA 20 just north of Winthrop. This is a good spot for seeing eagles, hawks, and owls.

Skagit River, parallel to WA 20. Since this river still has strong winter salmon runs, hundreds of bald eagles converge on it in one of the greatest concentrations in the United States. Reportedly, many eagles stay on for the summer, too. Good viewing spots include the following:

Marblemount Fish Hatchery (360-873-4241), 8319 Fish Hatchery Lane, off WA 20 near Marblemount.

Milepost 100 Rest Area, on WA 20.

Skagit River Bald Eagle Natural Area (360-445-4441), off WA 530 just south of Rockport.

Bald Eagle Interpretive Center (360-853-7626), at the Fire Hall, Rockport. Open 10–4 Sat.–Sun. Dec.–Jan. Here you'll find programs and guided walks in season.

CAMPING

Baker Lake
In Mount Baker–Snoqualmie National Forest just north of WA 20, there are several campgrounds on the western lakeshore, all accessible via Baker Lake Road. Some sites can be reserved; for these call 877-444-6777 or go to www .recreation.gov.

Boulder Creek. Ten sites; toilets but no water.

Horseshoe Cove. Thirty-four sites; water, toilets, and boat ramp.

Panorama Point. Fifteen sites; water and toilets.

Park Creek. Twelve sites; toilets but no drinking water.

Shannon Creek. Nineteen sites; water and toilets.

Chelan Area

Okanogan-Wenatchee Ranger Station (509-664-9200) and **Chelan Ranger District** (509-682-4900) have information about sites requiring fees. Most of the campgrounds on or near the lakeshore are accessible only by boat or on foot (see *Guidance*).

Beebe Bridge Park (509-661-4551), on US 97A, 5 miles south of Chelan. Forty-six sites; showers, RV dump, water, toilets, boat launch, and trails. No reservations.

Domke Falls, off the south shore via boat only. Four tent sites; toilet but no drinking water. No reservations.

Graham Harbor, south shore via boat only. Five tent sites; floating dock for 10 boats; toilet but no water. No reservations.

Grouse Mountain, off FR 5900, 8 miles west of Twenty-Five Mile Creek State Park. 4 tent sites; toilet but no water. No reservations.

&. **Lake Chelan State Park** (888-226-7688), on South Lakeshore Road, 9 miles west of Chelan. One hundred nine tent sites and 35 RV sites (RVs under 30 feet); ADA restrooms. Reservations required in summer.

Prince Creek, north shore via boat only. Six tent sites; toilet but no water. No reservations.

Refrigerator Harbor, south shore near Lucerne via boat only. Four tent sites; toilet but no water. No reservations.

&. **Twenty-Five Mile Creek State Park** (509-687-3610), on South Lakeshore Road, 19.5 miles west of Chelan. Forty-six tent sites and 21 utility sites; ADA restrooms and showers.

Chewack River Road

Okanogan-Wenatchee Ranger Station (509-664-9200) has information about sites requiring fees. These campgrounds are north of WA 20 at Winthrop.

Buck Lake, on FR 100 west of Chewack River road. Seven sites; boat launch; toilets but no water. No reservations.

Camp 4, on FR 5160 just north of Twentymile Creek. Five sites, not good for trailers; trails; toilets but no water. No reservations.

Chewuch, on FR 5160 north of Falls Creek. Sixteen campsites; toilets and water in season. No reservations.

Falls Creek, on FR 5160 north of FR 5130. Seven sites; trails; toilets and water in season. No reservations.

Flat, on FR 5130 west of Chewack River road. Twelve sites; toilets and water in season. No reservations.

Honeymoon, on FR 5130 west of Ruffed Grouse. Five sites; toilets but no water. No reservations.

Nice, on FR 5130 west of Flat. Three campsites; toilets but no water. No reservations.

Ruffed Grouse, on FR 5130 west of Nice. Four sites; toilets and water in season. No reservations.

Darrington Area

In Mount Baker–Snoqualmie National Forest south of WA 20:

Bedal, on FR 26 south of White Chuck. Twenty-one sites; toilets but no water.

Buck Creek, on FR 26 east of WA 530. Twenty-five sites; toilet but no water.

Clear Creek, on FR 20 south of Darrington. Thirteen sites; toilet but no water.

Sulphur Creek, near end of FR 26. Twenty sites; toilets but no water.

Entiat Area
Okanogan-Wenatchee Ranger Station (509-664-9200) has information about sites requiring fees. Most of these campgrounds are west of US 97A.

Cottonwood, at the end of FR 317. Twenty-three tent sites and two RV sites; water and toilet. No reservations.

Fox Creek, on FR 51 south of Silver Falls. Sixteen sites; water and toilet. No reservations.

Handy Spring, on FR 5900 north of Silver Falls. One tent site; toilet but no water. No reservations.

Junior Point, on FR 5900 northeast of Handy Spring. Five tent sites; toilet but no water. No reservations.

Orondo River Park (509-884-4700), on US 97A, 27 miles south of Chelan. Fourteen tent sites and 13 sites with hook-ups; showers, water, toilets, and swimming.

Silver Falls, on FR 51 west of Fox Creek. Twenty-eight sites; water and toilets.

Three Creek, on FR 317 east of Cottonwood. Three tent sites; toilet but no water; No reservations.

Hart's Pass Road
Okanogan-Wenatchee Ranger Station (509-664-9200) has information about sites requiring fees. Most of these campgrounds are north of WA 20 at Mazama.

Ballard, on FR 5400 west of Mazama. Seven sites; trails; toilets but no water. No reservations.

Hart's Pass, near the end of FR 5400. Five sites; toilets but no water. No reservations.

Meadows, on FR 500 just south of Hart's Pass. Fourteen sites (no trailers); toilets but no water. No reservations.

Riverbend, on FR 050 just west of Ballard. Five sites; trails; wheelchair-accessible toilet but no water. No reservations.

Methow Area
Okanogan-Wenatchee Ranger Station (509-664-9200) has information about sites requiring fees. These campgrounds are off WA 153.

Alta Lake State Park (888-226-7688), just west of US 97. Scenic park with 91 tent sites and 32 utility sites; restrooms (one ADA) and showers.

Foggy Dew, on FR 4340. Twelve sites; wheelchair-accessible toilet and trails—but also rattlesnakes; no water. No reservations.

Mount Baker Highway Area
In Mount Baker–Snoqualmie National Forest east of I-5:

Douglas Fir, on WA 542 just east of Glacier. Twenty-nine sites; water and toilets. No reservations.

Silver Fir, on WA 542 east of Nooksack. Twenty sites, some handicapped-accessible; water and toilets.

Twisp River Area

Okanogan-Wenatchee Ranger Station (509-664-9200) has information about sites requiring fees. These campgrounds are off WA 153.

Blackpine Lake, on FR 300 west of WA 153. Twenty-three sites; water in season, toilets, trails, and boat launch.

Mystery, on FR 44 west of War Creek. Four sites; trails; wheelchair-accessible toilet but no water. No reservations.

Poplar Flat, on FR 44 west of Mystery. Sixteen sites; water, toilets, and trails. No reservations.

Road's End, at end of FR 4440. Four sites; trails; toilets but no water. No reservations.

South Creek, on FR 4440 west of Poplar Flat. Four sites; trails; wheelchair-accessible toilet but no water. No reservations.

Twisp River Horse Camp, on FR 4435, 22 miles west of Twisp. Twelve sites; toilets and trails.

War Creek, on FR 44 west of WA 153. Ten sites; water, trails, and wheelchair-accessible toilet. No reservations.

WA 20 East of the Cascades

Okanogan-Wenatchee Ranger Station (509-664-9200) has information about sites requiring fees.

Early Winters, on WA 20 just west of Mazama. Twelve sites; wheelchair-accessible toilet and water in season. No reservations.

J.R., on WA 20 near Loup Loup Summit. Six sites; wheelchair-accessible toilets but no water. No reservations.

Klipchuck, on WA 20 west of Early Winters. Forty-six sites; water in season, wheelchair-accessible toilet, and trails. No reservations.

Lone Fir, on WA 20 west of Klipchuck. Twenty-seven sites; water in season, ADA toilet, and trails. No reservations.

Loup Loup, just north of WA 20. Twenty-five sites; water in season, ADA toilet, and biking. No reservations.

Pearrygin Lake State Park (888-226-7688), just north of WA 20 near Winthrop. Ninety-two standard sites and 67 full-hook-up sites; all amenities.

WA 20 West of the Cascades

In Mount Baker–Snoqualmie National Forest (see *Guidance*):

Howard Miller Steelhead Park (360-853-8808), 52804 Rockport Park Road, on WA 20 near Rockport. Fifty-nine sites; all amenities, plus the Skagit River Interpretive Center.

Marble Creek, on Cascade River Road east of Marblemount. Twenty-three sites; toilets but no drinking water.

Mineral Park, on Cascade River Road southeast of Marble Creek. Seven sites; toilets but no drinking water.

CLIMBING North Cascades Mountain Guides (509-996-3194; www.nc mountainguides.com), 2 Country Road, Mazama. The North Cascades are mostly granite, steep and lovely, so there are lots of climbing destinations here. Contact this outfitter to learn more and find guides or equipment.

GOLF Bear Mountain Ranch Golf Course (509-682-8200; www.bearmt.com), 1050 Bear Mountain Ranch Road, Chelan. Eighteen holes.

Lake Chelan Municipal Golf Course (800-246-5361), 135 East Johnson Avenue, Chelan. Eighteen holes.

HIKING

Chelan Area

Echo Ridge Trail System, 18 miles; on WA 150, 8 miles from Chelan, between Chelan and Manson. Hikers and cyclists share about 25 miles of varied trails through a recovering burn.

Lake Chelan. For hiking opportunities along the upper lake, see the North Cascades National Park chapter.

Riverwalk Park loop, 1 mile, in Chelan. Saunter along this loop joining two bridges over the Chelan River.

Mount Baker Highway (WA 542)

Many beautiful trails leave WA 542, though those at higher elevations may not be accessible till mid-July. Check the National Park Service newsletter **North Cascades Challenger** at a visitors center or ranger station (see *Guidance*) for more trails and information. Some recommended hikes include these:

Artist Ridge Interpretive Trail, 1 mile; start from the Artist Point parking lot at the end of the Mount Baker Highway. Terrific views.

Chain Lakes Trail, 1 mile; start from the Artist Point parking lot. This level trail with close views of Mount Baker also gives access to other trails.

& **Fire and Ice,** interpretive ADA trail; start from the Heather Meadows Visitor Center on WA 542 at milepost 56.

Heliotrope Ridge, 3 miles; from WA 542 at milepost 34.3, turn right onto narrow FR 39 (Glacier Creek Road) and continue for 8 miles. This path takes you to up-close glacier views, forest, and waterfalls.

Horseshoe Bend, 1.5 miles; trailhead on WA 542 at milepost 35.4, across from Horseshoe Bend campground. This trail along the North Fork of the Nooksack River is usually clear.

& **Picture Lake,** 0.5 mile; parking on WA 542 at milepost 55. This wheelchair-accessible trail has good views of the lake and surrounding peaks.

Pacific Crest Trail

South section, 98 miles, from US 2 at Skykomish to Stehekin. **North section,** 89 miles, from Stehekin to Canadian border. The entire segment is very rugged,

A TRAIL IN THE NORTH CASCADES

though spectacular, with lots of elevation change and potentially severe weather. Pluses: wildflowers, views, wildlife, wilderness.

Rockport Area

River Trail, 1.4 miles; in Howard Miller Steelhead Park, Rockport. This leisurely stroll takes in old-growth Douglas firs, a salmon stream, and meadows with mountain views at the confluence of the Sauk and Skagit rivers.

Winthrop Area

Many great hikes are accessed from the North Cascades Scenic Highway (WA 20), including the Pacific Crest Trail. Check with the **Methow Valley Sport Trails Association** (800-682-5787), 209 Castle Avenue, Winthrop, before setting out; many trails are snow-covered till mid-July. Some options for a lovely afternoon or day hike include the following:

Cedar Creek, 2 miles; start from the end of FR 5310-200, a left turn off WA 20 about 18 miles northwest of Winthrop. Wildflowers and butterflies glow in the open forest in early summer. A climb of 960 feet takes you to Cedar Creek Falls. For an overnight hike, continue 7.7 miles to Abernathy Pass.

Cutthroat Lake, 1.7 miles, trailhead on WA 20, 1.5 miles west of Lone Fir campground. This is a level walk to the peak-surrounded lake.

Cutthroat Pass, 5.2 miles; same trailhead as for Cutthroat Lake (see above). Continue 3.5 miles, gaining 1,300 feet, to glorious panoramas. Or follow the Pacific Crest Trail to Cutthroat Pass, 4 miles; start from WA 20 at Rainy Pass. This northward stretch of the PCT also leads to views of the North Cascades from Cutthroat Pass; elevation gain 1,960 feet.

Goat Peak Lookout, 5 miles round-trip; 8 miles north of Winthrop on WA 20, turn right on Goat Creek Road, then take FRs 52, 5225, and 200 for a total of 14.7 steep, winding, unpaved but well-graded miles to the trailhead. Goat Peak is one of the few remaining staffed fire lookouts in the state. The trail is steep but beautiful, and when you reach the top (after a 1,400-foot elevation gain), the North Cascades and Methow Valley are spread out before you. If you're lucky, you'll meet "Lightning Bill," who mans the fire lookout in season.

⚿ **Rainy Lake,** 1 paved mile, on WA 20 at Rainy Lake Rest Area, about 20 miles west of Winthrop. A flat, wheelchair-accessible trail brings you to sublime mountain views.

Rainy Pass/Maple Pass, 7 miles, on WA 20 at Rainy Lake Rest Area, 20 miles west of Winthrop. From the same trailhead as above, ascend among spectacular wildflowers to end up above the tree line, amid the jagged peaks and incomparable vistas of the North Cascades. This is one of the most sublime trails easily reached by car. It's a loop with an elevation gain of about 2,000 feet; beware of snowfields at higher elevations, which may cover the trail. Also beware of mosquitoes; bring insect repellent.

Twisp Valley Recreational Area, Twisp River valley along FR 44 west of Twisp. The Twisp River Trail parallels the river through forest for about 20 miles; numerous trails fan off it dendritically to reach high-country lakes and connect with long-distance trails such as the Pacific Crest Trail. Contact the Twisp Visitor Information Center (see *Guidance*) for maps and information.

HORSEBACK RIDING Early Winters Outfitting (509-996-2659; www.early wintersoutfitting.com), 18078 WA 20, Mazama. Tucked right under the edge of the Pasayten Wilderness (see *Wilder Places—Wilderness Areas*), Early Winters offers trail rides and pack trips into the wilderness. Trips can be focused on fishing, photography, or just plain recreation.

THE FIRE LOOKOUT AT GOAT PEAK IN THE NORTH CASCADES

RAINY LAKE FROM THE MAPLE PASS TRAIL, OFF WA 20 IN THE NORTH CASCADES

North Cascade Outfitters (509-997-0330), Box 103, Carlton 98814. They lead pack, base-camp, and day trips. Or you can hike in and have your gear brought in by their mules.

KAYAKING AND RAFTING Several outfitters offer rentals and/or guided trips on the Methow River and Lake Chelan. Here are a couple:

Blue Sky Outfitters (206-938-4030 or 800-228-RAFT; www.blueskyoutfitters .com), 61006 WA 20, Marblemount.

Clearwater Kayaking (509-630-7615), Box 688, Manson 98817.

WINTER SPORTS **Loup Loup Summit** (866-699-5334; www.skithe loup.com), on WA 20, 12 miles north-east of Twisp. Open 9–3:45 Wed.–Sun. mid-Dec.–mid-Mar. or later, daily during Christmas break (except Christmas Day). This low-key ski area with 1,240 feet of drop has 10 runs for all levels of skiers, as well as 25 kilometers (15 miles) of cross-country trails.

Methow Valley Nordic trail system (Methow Valley Sport Trails Association, 509-996-3287 or 800-682-5787; www.mvsta.com), 200 groomed kilometers (124 miles) from Winthrop to Mazama, near WA 20. Day pass $10–20. This may be Washington's best-kept secret. In winter, this area along the Cascade Range's northeastern edge really is the end of the road—the pass over WA 20 closes in the fall—so folks from any-where else really have to want to get here. Cross-country ski trails in pristine coun-try, covered with dry and plentiful snow, constitute the champagne of the Nordic experience. Food and lodging can be found in virtually any price range; in fact, one trail area offers hut-to-hut skiing. In summer, many of the trails are open to cyclists, hikers, and equestrians.

Mount Baker Ski Area (360-734-6771; www.mtbaker.us), 1019 Iowa Street, Bellingham. Open daily in season. Lift ticket $52 adults weekends, $46 weekdays. Rising from the Puget Sound shore to 10,778 feet in a mere 62 road miles, Mount Baker breaks records: In the winter of 1998–99, it received 1,140 inches of snow. Located near the end of the Mount Baker Highway (WA 542), it has seven lifts, a vertical drop of 1,500 feet, and a maximum altitude of 5,089 feet. A plethora of Nordic trails are groomed and maintained by the **Nooksack Nordic Ski Club** (www.nooksacknordicskiclub.org), Box 28793, Bellingham 98228.

PARKS **Alta Lake State Park** (360-902-8844), south of WA 153 just west of US 97. Closed in winter. Swimming, camping, and picnicking where the mountains meet the desert.

Beebe Bridge Park (509-661-4897), on US 97A, 5 miles south of Chelan. Camping, boat launch, and trails.

Howard Miller Steelhead Park (360-853-8808), on WA 20 in Rockport. Camping and all amenities; eagle-spotting site in winter.

⚓ **Lake Chelan State Park** (509-687-3710), on South Lakeshore Road, 9 miles west of Chelan. Open daily mid-Mar.–Nov.; Sat.–Sun. Nov.–mid-Mar. The park, which has more than a mile of shoreline and a boat launch, can get crowded on summer weekends. It has nice lawns and sandy beaches for kids to play on.

North Cascades National Park Complex—see the North Cascades National Park chapter.

Orondo River Park (509-784-2556), on US 97A, 27 miles south of Chelan. Camping, swimming, and moorage.

Pearrygin Lake State Park (509-996-2370), just north of WA 20 near Winthrop. Good for birding, swimming, camping, and boating in the Methow Valley.

Rockport State Park (360-853-8461), on WA 20 just west of Rockport. No camping due to unsteady old trees, but a pleasant visit to a pocket of old growth. Closed Nov.–Mar.

Twenty-Five Mile Creek State Park (509-687-3610), on South Lakeshore Road, 19.5 miles west of Chelan. Open Apr.–Oct. Popular for fishing, wading, and especially as a base for boat exploration of upper Lake Chelan. If you don't have your own boat, the *Lady of the Lake* stops here (see *Getting Around*). There's an older campground, too (see *Camping*).

WILDERNESS AREAS **Boulder River Wilderness,** 48,674 acres; south of WA 530 between Darrington and Arlington, and north of the Mountain Loop Highway between Silverton and Verlot. This extremely rough area has only about 25 miles of trails, but it draws climbers to its sharp spires and ridges.

Glacier Peak Wilderness, 570,573 acres; between WA 20 and US 2 east of the crest, accessed from Cascade River Road off WA 20 at Marblemount or Suiattle River Road off WA 530 north of Darrington. Very remote and extremely rugged, this wilderness sprawls around 10,541-foot Glacier Peak, one of the few volcanoes in the North Cascades. People come here to climb or to hike some of the 450 miles of trails, knowing they are sharing habitat with wolverines, bears, and possibly wolves.

Henry M. Jackson Wilderness, 100,356 acres; between the Mountain Loop Highway and Index-Galena Road, accessed via the Pacific Crest Trail at Stevens Pass on US 2. The PCT follows about 30 miles of Cascade crests through this area of remote forest and peaks, joined by several other trails.

Lake Chelan–Sawtooth Wilderness, 145,667 acres; from the lake's northeastern edge almost to Washington Pass along WA 20, accessed only by trail or boat. The wilderness takes in the rugged, uninhabited Sawtooth Range. Lakes, cirques, peaks, and ravines characterize the land, with forest on the lower elevations. This is a wilderness lover's wilderness.

Mount Baker Wilderness, 117,528 acres; south of the Mount Baker Highway (WA 542) nearly to Baker Lake. The wilderness encompasses most of conical Mount Baker: One corner of the peak is reserved for a ski area and another is in the Mount Baker National Recreation Area (see below). Baker, one of only two volcanoes in the North Cascades, is considered the second most active volcano in the state, after Mount St. Helens. It hasn't done much but let off occasional steam for the past few decades, but it's one the geologists watch warily. Heavily forested ridges rise to rock and eternal snows here. Mountain goats inhabit the higher elevations. Hiking trails crisscross the woods and alpine meadows, while climbers take to the heights. Baker, only a short drive from Bellingham and Vancouver, British Columbia, is one of the more heavily used wilderness areas. Luckily, there's a lot of room here.

Noisy-Diobsud Wilderness, 14,133 acres; north of WA 20 and east of Baker Lake. On the western slopes of the North Cascades, this tract is thick with salal, devil's club, ferns, and mosses, and it's very steep. There are several lakes but few trails, so getting around in it is hard. There are no crowds, though. It's named for Noisy and Diobsud creeks.

Pasayten Wilderness, more than 500,000 acres; from north of WA 20 to the Canadian border between Ross Lake and the Chewuch River; access also from Hart's Pass northwest of Mazama. This enormous stretch of wild mountains between the Methow River and Canada has 600 miles of trails, including 32 miles of the Pacific Crest Trail. Lynx, moose, bighorn sheep, mountain goats, and even grizzly bears and gray wolves live here.

RECREATION AREAS Mount Baker National Recreation Area. This southern wedge of the mountain is set aside fundamentally to allow snowmobile use, which is forbidden in the wilderness area that covers much of the rest of the peak. In summer it's for nonmotorized recreation such as hiking and camping. There are four campgrounds and 28 miles of trails, of which 11 miles are for hikers only and the rest shared by horses and hikers. For information call **Mount Baker–Snoqualmie National Forest** (800-627-0062).

✳ Lodging

BED & BREAKFASTS

Concrete

Cascade Mountain Inn (360-826-4333; www.cascade-mtn-inn.com), 40418 Pioneer Lane, Concrete-Birdsview; turn off WA 20 near milepost 83. Amid pastures in the Skagit Valley, this gambrel-roofed inn was built as a B&B in 1984. Five guest rooms each have a private bath and either a queen or twin beds, and there's a more secluded self-catering suite. An enclosed porch makes a nice place from which to view the river valley. Rates include a full breakfast, perhaps Camille's lovely, airy waffles. The inn is oriented toward adults. No pets. (The owners have several of their own, including two mastiffs.) $145–175.

Twisp

Methow Valley Inn (509-997-2253; www.methowvalleyinn.com), 234 East Second Street. In the olden days—that is, back in 1923—the inn sat at the river crossing. There lumbermen and mine owners reaping the riches of the nearby Okanogan Range found handy, comfortable lodging in what was still the Wild West. Today the handsome house, with its gambrel roof and veranda, still offers a home away from home: eight rooms (some with shared baths) and one suite, nicely decorated; a living room complete with a large fireplace; a sunroom and dining room; and a lush garden in summer. In fact, the garden is so luxuriant that your breakfast will likely include fruits and vegetables from the property, as well as homemade jams or preserves. Children over 12 welcome. No pets. Rooms $89–119; suite $149; two-night minimum most weekends.

CABINS

Mazama

☗ **Rolling Huts** (509-996-4442; www.rollinghuts.com), 18381 WA 20, Winthrop. Located 5 miles south of Mazama, these half-dozen modernistic, architect-designed sheds on stilts are styled "the herd"—to evoke perhaps a herd of elk in this valley meadow—and offered as a "modern alternative to camping." They are that, furnished with refrigerators, microwaves, Wi-Fi, modular furniture, sleeping platforms, and fireplaces. Simple, with clean lines, they all have mountain views and were designed with hikers and cross-country skiers in mind. Outside each hut is a portable toilet, picnic table, and water faucet; showers are in a nearby barn. The huts provide an attractive, outdoorsy option, though the price tag may be a bit steep, considering the outdoor plumbing and having to bring your own sleeping bag and linens. Next door, the Wesola Polana Diner (see *Where to Eat*) is a great place to eat. Each hut sleeps four. Children under 12 stay free. Pets allowed for a fee. $125 for two.

Chelan

Riverwalk Inn (509-682-2627; www.riverwalkinnchelan.com), 204 East Wapato Avenue. Just across from green Riverwalk Park in downtown Chelan, this place has been a boardinghouse or motel nearly continuously since it was built in 1918. In 2001 retired naval officer Mike Sherer and first (and apparently last) mate Mary bought and completely remodeled the three buildings. As you would expect, everything is shipshape, from the brass portholes to the berths. The 14 rooms are snug and homey. Amenities include a bright breakfast room, a common room, and use of a small kitchen. It's family friendly—there's even an ice cream bar facing the park. Rates include a full breakfast. No pets. $59–$175.

Stillwater Inn Bed and Breakfast (509-682-3500; www.thestillwaterinn .com), 2205 West Woodin Avenue. You'd think the solid, spreading home had been there forever. In fact it was built in 1906 but moved to a slightly higher elevation in 1927, when the Chelan Dam raised the water levels. The current owners, Don and Patty Forbush, made the home over into a bed & breakfast in 2004. It's a place to sit on the porch and take in the view, or go out exploring and then come back for a homemade snack. $135–185; discount for more than one night.

Winthrop

Duck Brand Hotel and Cantina (509-996-2192 or 800-996-2192; www.methownet.com/duck), 248 Riverside Avenue. Six country-style rooms above the restaurant on Winthrop's Main Street are the lowest-priced accommodations in town. They all have one or two queen beds and private baths, and most have balconies so you can enjoy the priceless view.

They're simple, but the exposed beams and quiet decor make them cozy. No pets. $69–79; special rates during winter holidays and events.

Hotel Rio Vista (509-996-3535; 800-398-0911; www.hotelriovista.com), 285 Riverside Avenue. In keeping with Winthrop's Old West theme, this hotel on Main Street has a fine western facade—beams, false front, and all. It backs onto the rippling Methow River, so each of the 29 bright rooms has a private balcony with its own view. The hotel also owns Aspen Loft Cabin, sleeping six, 20 miles west of Winthrop. No pets. Rooms $75–135; cabin $110–170.

River's Edge Resort (800-937-6621; www.riversedgewinthrop.com), 115 Riverside Avenue. Fifteen cabins beside the rippling Methow River range in size from one bedroom (cozy) to three (family-sized). All are equipped with kitchens, and most have hot tubs, washers and dryers, and virtually all the comforts of home. No pets. $140–205.

Winthrop Inn (800-444-1972), 960 WA 20. Simple but adequate rooms with balconies and one or two queen beds. The inn is a mile or so out of town on 4 acres with picnic grounds and riverfront, giving you room to stretch out. $75–135.

LODGES

Concrete
Ovenell's Heritage Inn (360-853-8494; www.ovenells-inn.com), 46276 Concrete–Sauk Valley Road. A working 500-acre ranch, Ovenell's offers five log cabins each complete with one bedroom, kitchen, and bath; a two-bedroom guesthouse with two baths and a common living room and kitchen, sleeping up to eight; and four rooms (most with shared baths) in the old farmhouse. Views of Mount Baker

and abundant wildlife are included. Cabins $135–145; guesthouse $220; farmhouse rooms $90–110 (add $30 for breakfast).

Winthrop
Chewuch Inn (509-966-3107 or 800-747-3107; www.chewuchinn.com), 223 White Avenue. Sally and Dan Kuperberg escaped the bustle of New York and Chicago to return to their native Northwest and run a lodge. The pine grove near the Chewuch River on the outskirts of nonbustling Winthrop is certainly as much of a contrast as they could wish. Six snug, elegant cabins and eight lodge rooms are a perfect jumping-off point for exploring the Methow Valley's extensive cross-country skiing, biking, and hiking trails or the nearby Pasayten Wilderness. Rates include a full breakfast in the lodge. No pets. Cabins $105–175; lodge rooms $85–200.

MOTELS

Twisp
Sportsman Motel (509-997-2911), 1010 WA 20 East. Okay, so it looks like a Quonset hut—but that's what it is, covered with nice wood siding and cozy wood paneling inside. Quonset huts were in oversupply in the area after an air base closed following World War II, and they were put to various uses by enterprising citizens. This one shortly became a motel and has remained so. Several of the eight units have kitchenettes, and while not fancy they are cozy and pleasant. From $50.

RESORTS

Chelan
Campbell's Resort (509-682-2561 or 800-553-8225; www.campbellsresort .com), 104 West Woodin Avenue It was 1889 when Iowa lawyer Clinton Campbell visited the ragtag settlement

of Chelan and decided to move his family west. They opened a boarding-house and a few years later built the gambrel-roofed hotel that still stands on Woodin Avenue. Perhaps it was happy prescience that made him build on what would become waterfront only later, when the dam came in. Today, still owned by the Campbell family, the hotel has expanded to 173 spacious lakeside rooms and luxury suites with its own beach, moorage, spa, pool, and restaurant. You can paddle a hotel kayak; take swimming, fishing, or art lessons; have a fine dinner; watch the sunset or the night sky from your balcony; or take in some Saturday-night entertainment in the café-bar. The original Campbell house now serves as offices. No pets. $102–330.

Holden Village Retreat Center (registrar@holdenvillage.org; www .holdenvillage.org), HC 0 Box 2, Chelan 98816. Back in the hills west of Lake Chelan, almost but not quite in the North Cascades National Park complex, Holden Village has no telephone. You can only get there by boat—the *Lady of the Lake* runs from Chelan or Fields Point to Lucerne, whence you must get a bus—but despite the isolation, it gets about seven thousand visitors annually. The site of a former copper mine has been transformed into an ecumenical retreat center based in the Lutheran tradition, complete with discussions and workshops on topics ranging from simple living to issues of faith and justice. Accommodations are simple but adequate, with rooms sleeping two to four with a shared bath, and meals are provided. If you're looking for a reflective sojourn in the wilderness, this could be it. Rates include meals, programs, sauna, library, and more. $75 adults, $10–60 children; weekly rates available. Reservations recommended in summer.

Mazama

Mazama Country Inn (509-996-2681 or 800-843-7951; www.mazamacountry inn.com), 15 Country Road. The country inn has 18 cozy rooms sleeping two to four, a common room with a big fireplace, a pool, a sauna, and a hot tub—truly an all-inclusive resort! They even have their own restaurant, serving breakfast, lunch, and dinner in winter. Winter room rates include all meals; summer rates include breakfast. Privately owned cabins are also rented. Rooms $75–235; call for cabin rates; check for specials.

Winthrop

& **Sun Mountain Lodge** (509-996-2211 or 800-572-0493; www.sun mountainlodge.com), Box 1000, Winthrop 98862. Set on a 3,000-acre hilltop, Sun Mountain is a top-end, new-western lodge built on enormous Douglas fir beams and Idaho quartz, with its own lake plus hiking, biking, and ski trails. In case that's not enough, it's in the middle of the Methow cross-country ski trail system, one of the most extensive in the country (see *To Do—Winter Sports*). Guest rooms range from pampering singles or doubles to sumptuous suites and lakeside cabins. All the amenities are here, including a spa, heated outdoor pools, fine dining, and—the best things in life really are free—360-degree views of the North Cascades and Methow Valley. No pets. Rooms and suites $160–865; cabins $275–935; check for specials and packages.

✳ Where to Eat

DINING OUT

Mazama

Wesola Polana Diner (509-996-9804; www.wesolapolana.com), 5 miles south of Mazama on WA 20. Open 8:30 AM–10 PM Thurs.–Sat., 8:30–3:30 Sun.–Wed.

THE MAZAMA COUNTRY INN IN THE METHOW VALLEY HOSTS LOVERS OF THE OUTDOORS, SUMMER AND WINTER.

in ski season and high summer; 8:30 AM–10 PM Thurs.–Sat., 8:30–3:30 Sun.–Mon. in slow season. Polish name, Spanish menu, in the sparsely populated Methow Valley—go figure. Or don't; just enjoy an amazingly good assortment of tapas, two or three of which make a quite satisfying dinner. Outside the diner is quite well camouflaged as a typical rural eatery. Fortunately, the prices are more typical of the latter than of a European café, which this is.

Winthrop

Arrowleaf Bistro (509-996-3919; www.arrowleafbistro.com), 253 Riverside Avenue. Open 5–9 Sun.–Tues. and Thurs., 5–10 Fri.–Sat.; closed Wed. This new addition to Winthrop's slender dining scene is pricey but offers cuisine you won't otherwise find here: duck breast with braised cabbage, pheasant, locally sourced greens, all depending on what's in season.

Sun Mountain Lodge (509-996-4705; www.sunmountainlodge.com), 604 Patterson Lake Road. Open for breakfast and dinner daily. Set 1,000 feet above the Methow Valley, the restaurant at Sun Mountain Lodge (see *Lodging*) offers breathtaking Cascade views and distinguished cuisine. Chef J. Russell Bradshaw gets many of his ingredients from local farms and forests. Reservations recommended. **Wolf Creek Bar and Grill,** also at the lodge, offers lighter and less expensive meals from the same kitchen; open for lunch and dinner daily.

EATING OUT

Chelan

Local Myth Pizza (509-682-2914; www.localmythpizza.com), 122 South Emerson Street. Open for dinner daily and lunch Mon.–Sat. This is reputed to be the best pizza in Chelan, and it's true the aromas that waft onto the street are nearly irresistible. Try one of their own combination pizzas, including seven very different vegetarian selections, or build your own on a choice of six sauces.

2nd Floor Pub and Veranda (509-682-2561; www.campbellsresort.com), 104 West Woodin Avenue. Open for breakfast, lunch, and dinner daily. Entrée-sized salads, pasta dishes, seafood, and all-natural steaks greet you when you come in from a day on the beach at Campbell's Resort (see *Lodging*). Also at Campbell's, the Bistro is open spring–early fall, with much the same menu but a quieter atmosphere.

Concrete

Annie's Pizza Station (360-853-7227; www.anniespizza.com), 4468 WA 20. Open for lunch Tues.–Sat., lunch and dinner Tues.–Sun. If you look around at the layout here, you will see that Annie's was originally a gas station, which explains the names for some of the dishes on the menu. Besides a decent pizza, Annie's serves tasty homemade soups, salads, and sandwiches for lunch or dinner in an informal atmosphere.

Manson

Blueberry Hills (509-687-2379; www.wildaboutberries.com), 1315 Washington Street; about 4 miles west of Chelan via WA 150. Open for breakfast and lunch daily. Here you can pick your own berries or have them served at your table—it's a berry farm and café on owner Kari Sorensen's great-great-grandfather's original homestead, which was converted to blueberries after a near century of apples. Come here for breakfast (with lots of room for blueberries), lunch (burgers, salads, and the like), and lots of homemade pies.

Twisp

Cinnamon Twisp (509-997-5030; www.cinnamontwisp.com), 116 North Glover Street. Open 6–3 daily in summer, Mon.–Sat. in winter. Fresh breads, bagels, scones, and all sorts of goodies, plus salads, sandwiches, and more.

Glover Street Market Natural Foods (509-997-1320; gloverstreet market.com), 124 North Glover Street. Open 9–6 Mon.–Sat. "Pretty good groceries," plus bulk foods, health products, produce, and more, in a friendly country store.

✔ **Twisp River Pub** (509-997-6822; www.methowbrewing.com), 201 North Methow Valley Highway. Open for breakfast, lunch, and dinner daily and brunch Sun. Not just pub food. From burgers and steak to Peruvian chicken to curry bowls, there's something for everyone, mostly homemade and all good, real food. Oh, and they make their own beer, too. In summer sit out on the deck over the Twisp River.

Winthrop

Duck Brand Restaurant and Hotel (509-996-2192 or 800-996-2192), 248 Riverside Avenue. Open 7 AM–9 PM daily. Guy Waring started the Duck Brand Saloon soon after founding Winthrop in 1891. Waring is said to have hated liquor and opened his establishment only to control alcohol consumption in the mining boomtown. This restaurant is not in the original building—that, in history's mysterious way, is now the city hall—but those who opened it in the 1960s wished to honor his name. In its own way, it's a rough-and-ready, kicked-back sort of place. The menu runs from the tried and true (steaks and salads) to Mexican (burritos and fajitas) to their own house and daily specials (pesto halibut and garlic Alfredo). They also offer pastries from their bakery.

Sheri's Sweet Shop (509-996-3834), 207 Riverside Drive. Open daily mid-Apr.–Oct., Sat.–Sun. Nov.–mid-Apr. Go ahead, do it—order a cone and take it to one of the wooden tables on the shady deck over the river. Everyone else in town is. About half the flavors are homemade, including a couple of sorbets, and frozen yogurt for the diet-conscious. Good ices at good prices. There's miniature golf on the premises, too.

ENTERTAINMENT The Merc Playhouse (509-997-7529; www.mercplay house.org), 101 South Glover Street, Twisp. Formerly a general store, the Merc is now an intimate theater (99 seats) offering professional productions, music, lectures, and more.

✳ **Selective Shopping**

Winthrop specializes in westerniana.

ART There are several galleries in Winthrop and Twisp.

Ashford Gallery (509-996-2073), 245 Riverside Avenue, Winthrop. The Ashford specializes in fiber art.

Confluence Gallery and Art Center (509-997-2787), 104 Glover Street, Twisp. They showcase regional artists and artisans.

Western Images (509-996-3336), 229-A Riverside Avenue, Winthrop. This is a photo parlor and gallery.

BOOKS Trail's End Bookstore (509-996-2345), 231 Riverside Avenue, Winthrop. Here you'll find field guides, kids' books, history, and more.

GIFTS DJ's Blacksmith Shop (509-996-2703), 236 Riverside Avenue, Winthrop. This shop features hand-forged pieces for your home (not so much for your stable).

OUTDOOR GEAR Outdoorsman (509-996-2649), 170 Riverside Avenue, Winthrop. You can find outdoor supplies here.

Winthrop Mountain Sports (509-996-2886), 257 Riverside Avenue, Winthrop. Or here.

✳ **Special Events**

February: **Upper Skagit River Bald Eagle Festival** (360-853-7626; www .skagiteagle.org), Concrete. Eagle-watching, arts and crafts, dancing, and drumming celebrate the winter concentration of bald eagles.

NORTH CASCADES
NATIONAL PARK

A lthough it's administered by the National Park Service, North Cascades National Park is actually a national park *complex*, because it also includes two national recreation areas where nature had already been altered before the park was declared in 1968: Ross Lake NRA, along the WA 20 corridor and including Ross, Diablo, and Gorge lakes; and Lake Chelan NRA, comprising the northern part of the lake, Stehekin, and the southern Stehekin River drainage. But 93 percent of the 684,320-acre complex is wilderness, with no roads but WA 20 through the middle and few services. Rainy Pass (4,855 feet) and Washington Pass (5,477 feet) are clustered close together near the park's eastern border, and the overlook at Washington Pass offers stupendous vistas. The park just sprawls in all directions, much farther than the eye can see, range after range and peak after jagged peak, glacier upon glacier (more than seven hundred of them). The Alps might have looked like this 2,000–3,000 years ago.

There's not much infrastructure here, no park inns or restaurants, and such services that do exist are concentrated in the preexisting towns of Stehekin and Newhalem. Newhalem is a company town, built and owned by Seattle City Light. Stehekin, at the head of Lake Chelan, is a unique community: 70 households, more or less, all off the grid, and only 23 miles of roads in the entire valley. It began about the turn of the 20th century as a supply depot for miners but sensibly soon turned to tourism and a few hopeful farms. The remote spot with its breathtaking setting acquired stately lodges such as the Field Hotel, and tourists made the two-day boat trip here from Chelan. Each trip burned two cords of wood, which contributed to the somewhat denuded look of the mountains bordering the lake.

Stehekin is still spectacular and a splendid gateway to the North Cascades. There are no phones, other than an emergency satellite phone at the dock for outgoing calls only; no cell phone service; and mostly no TV (the phone numbers listed for Stehekin businesses in this chapter are Chelan offices). Most residents now have e-mail via satellite, but your laptop, if for some reason you bring it, will likely be useless. To enjoy this area, you'll have to unplug.

GUIDANCE **Golden West Visitor Center and Ranger Station** (360-854-7365, ext. 14), above the boat landing, Stehekin 98852. Open mid-Mar.–mid-Oct., 8:30–5 daily in summer, reduced hours spring and fall. Built using salvaged material from the grand old Field Hotel, it includes natural and cultural exhibits, publications, and backcountry permits. Programs and guided walks are offered in summer.

North Cascades National Park Headquarters (360-854-7200; www.nps.gov /noca), 810 WA 20, Sedro-Woolley 98284. Open 8–4:30 daily in summer, 8–4:30 Mon.–Fri. in winter, spring, and fall. This is on the western side of WA 20; information, maps, and publications are available year-round.

North Cascades Visitor Center (206-386-4495, ext. 11), on WA 20 at milepost 120, Newhalem 98283. Open 9–6 daily in summer, 9–5 in spring and fall.

Wilderness Information Center (360-854-7245), 1 mile off WA 20 at milepost 105.3, 7280 Ranger Station Road, Marblemount 98267. Open 8–6 Sun.–Thurs., 7 AM–8 PM Fri.–Sat. in summer; 8–4:30 Sun.–Thurs, 7–6 Fri.–Sat. in spring and fall. Issues backcountry permits and provides wilderness information.

GETTING THERE Unlike most national parks, this one requires no entry fee. There are three ways to enter the park: *by car* via **WA 20,** between Marblemount and Mazama, or via **Cascade River Road,** a narrow, steep gravel road that departs WA 20 at Marblemount and ends a stiff day's hike from Stehekin; *by foot or pack trails* (see *To Do—Hiking*); or *by boat or plane* from Chelan to Stehekin.

Lady of the Lake (509-682-4584; www.ladyofthelake.com), 1418 West Woodin Avenue, Chelan. Ferry service to Stehekin and other points on the lakeshore.

Chelan Air (509-682-5555; www.chelanairways.com), Box W, 1328 West Woodin Avenue, Chelan. Commuter flights to Stehekin and sight-seeing tours.

STEHEKIN, ON THE EDGE OF NORTH CASCADES NATIONAL PARK, IS ACCESSIBLE BY AIR OR ON *THE LADY OF THE LAKE.*

There is, unfortunately, no shuttle service along WA 20, so
you'll need a car in this corridor.

In Stehekin, the **Stehekin Shuttle** (509-682-5555; www.stehekin.biz or www
.stehekin.com) runs along Stehekin Road two to four times a day, approximately
mid-May–mid-Oct., from the ferry landing as far as the road is safe, currently
about 13 miles. This offers access to trailheads, lodging, and services. Check the
schedule or get tickets at the Courtney Log Office at Stehekin Landing.

✳ To See

BOAT EXCURSIONS Skagit Tours (206-684-3030; www.skagittours.com); tours
begin from Skagit Information Center, Main Street, Newhalem, or North Cascades
Environmental Learning Center, Diablo Dam Road, off milepost 127.5 on WA 20.
Ross Lake and Diablo Lake were created by Seattle City Light between 1910 and
1957, as was the smaller Gorge Lake. The dams made Seattle energy independent,
though they drastically changed the landscape in their long, narrow valleys. Afternoon and dinner cruises, offered on Diablo Lake in conjunction with Seattle City
Light, are an easy way to see some remote and bewitching scenery.

CULTURAL SITES *Temple of Power,* in city park adjacent to Skagit Information Center, corner of Main Street and WA 20, Newhalem. This frankly titled work
is a sort of gazebo made of leftover electrical bushings and related matter from the
Diablo switchyards, created by Dan Carson, an artist in residence for Seattle City
Light.

GUIDED TOURS Stehekin Lodge bus tours (509-682-4494), Stehekin. If you
have a short time to visit Stehekin, take a tour from the ferry landing to 312-foot
Rainbow Falls (45 minutes) or a longer lunch tour to High Bridge, with narration
explaining local sites and history. These are not luxury tours—you'll be in a school
bus.

HISTORICAL SITES Golden West Visitor Center (360-854-7635, ext. 14),
above the boat landing in Stehekin. Open mid-Mar.–mid-Oct., 8:30–5 daily in summer, reduced hours spring and fall. Built with salvaged materials from the old
Field Hotel.

Newhalem, on WA 20 west of Diablo. Set prominently beside the highway in
Newhalem is the **Number Six engine** that used to haul equipment 34 miles from
Rockport to Newhalem. At the **Skagit Information Center,** at the corner of WA
20 and Main Street, you'll find the history and background of the Boundary Project that created the dams, plus information on Seattle City Light and a small
museum of hydropower.

MUSEUMS ♿ **North Cascades Visitor Center** (206-386-4495, ext. 11), on WA
20 at milepost 120, Newhalem. Open 9–6 daily in summer; 9–5 daily in spring and
fall. Besides the information center, this building features a gift shop and an illumi-
nating museum on the natural and archaeological history of the North Cascades. A
large relief map of the range orients you, while exhibits arranged by altitude detail
the species and ecology of each zone. Several acres of grounds include short,
wheelchair-accessible interpretive trails, such as one to a rock overhang used as a

shelter for 1,200 years. The adjacent extensive, shady campground is not frequented.

SCENIC DRIVES **North Cascades Scenic Highway** (WA 20), 143 paved miles from Burlington near I-5 to Twisp at WA 153. Opened in 1972 after 12 years of hacking a way through rugged terrain, and not without controversy, this route split in two what was perhaps the most remote, vast wilderness in the Lower 48, much of which was declared a national park in the middle of construction. WA 20 crosses the North Cascades massif with views that are more breathtaking around each curve than the last. Numerous pullouts let you enjoy the panoramas safely; trailheads allow access on foot into the wilderness. It's possibly the most scenic route in the United States. Check for road conditions: It's closed in winter, with Rainy and Washington passes blocked by 20 feet or more of snow, and may open as early as April or as late as June.

✳ To Do

BICYCLING Bikes are not allowed on national park trails, though cycling is permitted within parts of the national recreation areas. Cycling is also allowed on WA 20, but this requires caution because the road is narrow and winding, and traffic, though not heavy, tends to stop and start erratically at each viewpoint.

Discovery Bikes (www.stehekindiscoverybikes.com), Box 8, Stehekin 98852. They rent bikes hourly or daily: $4 per hour, $20 8 AM–5 PM, $25 per day (24 hours). They also offer packages—a Ranch Breakfast Ride or a Pastry Company Lunch Ride (the latter suitable for day-trippers).

BIRDING **North Cascades Visitor Center,** on WA 20 at milepost 120, Newhalem. The center, sitting on a forested site on the western slopes beside the

LIBERTY BELL IS A STRIKING SIGHT ON THE NORTH CASCADES SCENIC HIGHWAY.

Skagit River, is home to numerous warblers, swallows, thrushes, and many other species.

Stehekin, at the north end of Lake Chelan; accessible by boat or floatplane from Chelan (see *Getting There*). Here you might see harlequin ducks and abundant songbirds in summer.

CAMPING Auto-accessible developed campgrounds are mostly in the Ross Lake NRA.

Colonial Creek (360-873-4590), on WA 20 at milepost 130. Open May–mid-Oct. One hundred sixty-one tent and trailer sites on Diablo Lake in old-growth forest; toilets. No reservations.

Goodell Creek (360-873-4590), on WA 20 at milepost 111. Open year-round. Twenty-one campsites in forest along the Skagit River; toilets but no water in winter. No reservations.

Hozomeen Campground (360-873-4590), at the remote north end of Ross Lake with road access only from Canada. Open mid-May–mid-Oct. Seventy-five rustic campsites; water and toilets. Free. No reservations.

Newhalem Creek (877-444-6777), on WA 20 at milepost 120. Open May–mid-Oct. One hundred eleven tent and trailer sites; water. Reservable.

Backcountry Camping
In the backcountry, you may use one of the more than two hundred walk-in or boat-in backcountry sites, which have toilets and tent pads, or you can camp at least 1 mile from other campgrounds and 0.5 mile from trails. Some of those in the Stehekin Valley are served by the **Stehekin Shuttle** (see *Getting Around*). For any overnight backcountry stay, a free permit is required. These are issued on a first-come, first-served basis at ranger stations or the Wilderness Information Center in Marblemount (see *Guidance*). You may also need a Northwest Forest Pass to park at a trailhead outside the national park. Sites on Lake Chelan don't require a permit but do require a dock permit from the Forest Service (about $5). Care must be taken to avoid attracting bears. Pets are not allowed except on the Pacific Crest Trail and in the national recreation areas.

CLIMBING With all those peaks, the North Cascades complex attracts many climbers. Terrain and weather are both severe and require the best in equipment and experience. A free backcountry permit is required for overnight wilderness stays, issued at ranger stations or the Wilderness Information Center in Marblemount (see *Guidance*). Here are two outfitters and guide services.

American Alpine Institute (360-671-1505; www.aai.cc), 1515 12th Street, Bellingham.

North Cascades Mountain Guides (509-996-3194), 50 Lost River Road, Mazama.

HIKING The North Cascades are a hiker's paradise, whether you hike in the park proper, the national recreation areas, or the adjoining national forest. Most of the trails are remote. Pets are not allowed on the national park trails except, leashed, on the Pacific Crest Trail. You can also bring your leashed pet on the recreation area trails. Among the hundreds of choices are these:

MANY ROCK-CLIMBING ROUTES CHALLENGE CLIMBERS ON THE LIBERTY BELL GROUP, NEAR THE WASHINGTON PASS OVERLOOK ON WA 20.

Cascade Pass Trail, 23 miles from Cascade River Road (off WA 20 at Marblemount) to High Bridge, where the Stehekin Shuttle (see above) will bring you into Stehekin. From the western trailhead, a 3.7-mile, 1,800-foot climb to the pass, at 5,400 feet, offers breathtaking wilderness views. From the pass, it's 18 miles downhill to Stehekin. Artifacts eight thousand years old have been found near the pass; the trail was for millennia a trade route between Puget Sound and eastern tribes, who would paddle up 50-mile-long Lake Chelan (altitude 1,100 feet) with their goods, bear them up over the pass, and bring them down the Skagit River. And vice versa.

Horseshoe Basin, 3.5–8 miles, depending where you start. This is another rugged but spectacular hike near Cascade Pass, rising 4,800 feet from the west, 2,200 feet from the east, to a high cirque surrounded by glaciers and waterfalls.

Ladder Falls, 0.5 mile; from Newhalem city park. A short trail leads to a lovely waterfall. Another trail nearby goes through a grove of old cedars.

Newhalem Campground loops, 1–1.8 miles; see *Camping*. These loops take you through deep forest along the Skagit River.

Pacific Crest Trail (www.pcta.org), about 65 miles from the Glacier Peak Wilderness (see *Wilder Places* in the North Cascades chapter) to WA 20 at Rainy Pass, with about 20 miles within the park; also accessible via the Cascade Pass Trail (see above). The Pacific Crest Trail passes through the park's remote interior along the Stehekin River and Bridge Creek.

Pacific Northwest Trail (877-854-9415; www.pnt.org), 60 miles from Lightning Creek west to Hannegan Pass. This 1,200-mile trail runs from Glacier National

Park in Montana to Cape Alava in the coastal part of Olympic National Park, with a section through the North Cascades complex. Accessible by trails in the Pasayten Wilderness in the east and the Mount Baker Wilderness in the west (see *Wilder Places* in the North Cascades chapter). Information is available from the Pacific Northwest Trail Association, 24854 Charles Jones Memorial Circle, Sedro-Woolley 98284.

HORSEBACK RIDING Stehekin Outfitters (www.stehekinoutfitters.com), Stehekin. Half-day and multiday trips out of Stehekin Valley Ranch, on their gentle Fjord horses, take you into the high Cascades. Most trips have a six-person limit. They can take care of most of your recreational needs: They also offer multiday hiking and base-camp trips, kayak tours, and guided rafting on the Stehekin River.

WINTER SPORTS The **Stehekin area** gets a lot of snow—at only 1,100 feet, it can have 4–7 feet on the ground at any one time—but due to its remoteness and protection, activity here is low-key. People bring their snowshoes or cross-country skis to Stehekin and spend a quiet few days enjoying the pristine winter scene. The rest of the North Cascades complex is virtually inaccessible due to deep snow and road closure.

✳ Lodging

In addition to the listings below, several other **private rentals** are also available (stehekinvalley.com).

LODGES

Diablo Area
Ross Lake Resort (206-386-4437; www.rosslakeresort.com), 503 Diablo Street, Rockport. Accessible only by boat or trail: Take WA 20 to Diablo Dam, cross the dam to the Ross Lake Resort parking lot, and catch the boat (8:30–3 daily in summer; $20); then catch the resort truck ($8). Or park on WA 20 at milepost 134, take the Ross Lake Trail about 1.5 miles down to the lake, and call the resort (18-31974 from pole phone) for a short boat ride ($2). Open mid-June–Oct. This resort at the southern end of Ross Lake is the place for wild but comfortable seclusion. A floating cluster of 12 cabins sleeping one to nine people and three bunkhouses for groups come with electricity, water, furnished kitchens, bathrooms, and heat. Here you can rent a boat or hike directly into the backcountry. Fish or bring your own food,

though—there's no shop or restaurant within miles. No pets. Cabins $145–295; bunkhouses $210.

Stehekin
Silver Bay Inn (509-682-2212 or 800-555-7781; www.silverbayinn.com); where the Stehekin River flows into Lake Chelan. Open year-round. Two fully furnished self-catering cabins, a large rental house, plus one private room all have water views and complimentary bikes, canoes, rowboats, and croquet. The resort is very scenic and private. Children over 12 welcome. No pets. $145–355; minimum stay required.

RESORTS

Stehekin
Stehekin Landing Resort (509-682-4494; www.stehekinlanding.com), Stehekin Valley Road; right above the boat landing. Closed in winter. The lodge has 28 rooms as well as cabins, from basic units sleeping two to apartments with lake views. Here you can rent a bike or snowshoes, moor a boat, or buy gas—not that you'll need much; the

ferry is passengers only, and even if you borrow a car, there's not much road. There's a restaurant (see *Where to Eat*), and the convenience store on the premises isn't just for you, but for all the 30-odd Stehekin households. No pets. $82–175.

Stehekin Valley Ranch (509-682-4677 or 800-536-0745; www.stehekin valleyranch.com), Box 36, Stehekin 98852; 9 miles up the valley from the ferry landing. Open June–early Oct. The Courtneys have been running their ranch for a hundred years or so and always get accolades. You can come to enjoy an organized stay, such as the Spinners' Rendezvous, or just do what strikes your fancy—hike, bike, ride horseback, or sit and watch the river go by. There are three types of cabins: ranch, tent, and housekeeping. Five ranch cabins sleep four and have their own bathrooms. Tent cabins, with wooden walls and a canvas roof, are very cozy. Light is by kerosene lamps, and linens are provided for queen, full, or twin beds. Bathrooms are nearby. Two housekeeping cabins come with bathroom, kitchen, and vehicle. Ranch cabin and tent cabin rates are per person and include meals (see *Where to Eat*) and transportation; housekeeping cabin rates do not include meals. Dogs are allowed for a $25 fee. Tent cabins $90–100 (reduced rate for children); ranch cabins $110–120 (reduced rate for children); housekeeping cabins $135–175 for one or two people.

✳ Where to Eat
EATING OUT
Stehekin
Stehekin Landing Resort (509-682-4494; www.stehekinlanding.com), Stehekin Valley Road. Open for breakfast and dinner daily in high season, lunch only in fall on "boat days"; closed in winter. Serves straightforward Ameri-

can food—burgers, barbecued chicken, vegetarian lasagna—overlooking the water. Dinner reservations required.

Stehekin Pastry Company (509-682-7742; www.stehekinpastry.com), Stehekin Valley Road; 1.8 miles from the ferry landing. Open for breakfast and lunch in summer. The day-trippers' tour buses stop here, but that's no reason to avoid it. It's run by the same Courtneys who fix the fabulous dinners at Stehekin Valley Ranch (see above). The bakery's pastries are prized for breakfast by the cyclists, hikers, and other outdoorspeople who know which end of the lake their cinnamon rolls are buttered on. It's good for soups, salads, or sandwiches at lunch, too. They also rent out a couple of cabins behind the bakery ($180–200).

Stehekin Valley Ranch (509-682-4677 or 800-536-0745; www.stehekin valleyranch.com); 9 miles up the valley from the ferry landing. Make dinner reservations at the Courtney Log Office at Stehekin Landing; the free ranch bus leaves the landing at 5:30 PM. Open seasonally. If you stay at the ranch (see *Lodging*), you get to eat here for breakfast, lunch, and dinner. If you stay elsewhere, you can make a reservation and hop on the shuttle for a family-style dinner. Choose the hearty ranch supper of the evening, something from the grill, or a fish or vegetarian option. Maybe it's the setting, maybe a day spent in the great outdoors, maybe several generations of ranch cooking, but everything here seems to satisfy. How about some homemade pie?

✳ Selective Shopping
CRAFTS House That Jack Built, next door to the Golden West Visitor Center (which also has a gallery featuring local artists; see *Guidance*), Stehekin. Carries crafts made by Stehekin residents.

Southeastern Washington

INTRODUCTION

In the Depression, migrant fruit pickers were mostly Okies and other dust-bowl refugees rather than the Latin American migrants of today—but the work is largely the same. The dry, brown hills east of the Cascades are not an obvious Garden of Eden, however. Rainfall can be as little as 8 inches a year. But settlers in the late 1800s found that almost any temperate-climate fruit would grow with irrigation—and there, like a bolt of lightning or an arrow of Manifest Destiny, was the mighty Columbia, with the canyons of southeastern Washington funneling snowmelt to it via the Yakima, Snake, and Walla Walla rivers.

Soon the Yakima Valley was a green band growing peaches, plums, apricots, cherries, and especially apples. Also hops. More recently, fields have been planted in grapes—the Yakima drainage was Washington's first wine-growing area ("about the latitude of Bordeaux," says the literature; this is the claim of appellations from the Columbia Gorge to Lake Chelan, a span of more than 2 degrees of latitude!).

Washington's wine industry, which started with a few tentative shoots in the 1960s, has mushroomed to second place in U.S. wine production. This unlikely preeminence is made possible, of course, by large-scale irrigation. Most of the grapes are grown on Washington's dry side, where precipitation is about 8 inches a year, but the vineyards bloom thanks to the mighty Columbia River, which obligingly flows in great limpid loops across the entire state from Canada to Oregon, and its tributaries.

To the north of Yakima, the Ellensburg and Kittitas valleys merge Cascade foothills into the Mid-Columbia Basin, an area where the Columbia Reclamation Project has turned arid expanses into farms growing hay, potatoes, corn, and much more. Ellensburg was founded in the 1860s with great ambition where the mountains meet the plains. Begun as a trading post, it soon graduated to a natural homestead supplier when the railroad came to town, and it even entertained hopes of becoming the state capital. That hope was dashed; still, its decades of prosperity are attested to by the numerous mercantile buildings still standing. Today it's home to Washington's biggest rodeo and Central Washington University, founded to train teachers for the young state.

Farther east, along the Walla Walla and Snake rivers, wheat, peas, and lentils are the preferred crops: Walla Walla was the home of the Jolly Green Giant. As wheat and vegetable farming becomes harder to sustain, though, wine fever has spread here, too, with Walla Walla producing some fine expensive vintages, and even the Tri-Cities, better known as the domain of nuclear physicists at the Hanford Site than of vintners, getting into the act. Most of this has come as the by-product of dams built primarily for electrification, war industry, and flood control—which, incidentally, eliminated the previous salmon-based economy. Another new crop is wind—along the Washington-Oregon border you'll see rows of windmills undulating over the dry, treeless ridges, supplementing the dams' hydropower, along with the farmers' incomes.

Travel in the arid southeastern valleys can be arduous. The roads are long and empty, blindingly hot in summer and treacherous in winter, and the winds can be excessive. Parts of the region are so inhospitable that they remained nearly uninhabited well after "pacification": There's a reason why the supersecret Hanford nuclear site was built here in the 1940s. But in summer you can refresh yourself with fresh cherries or peaches at a roadside stand, and you can always cool off (or warm up) at one of the many wine-tasting rooms in the Yakima or Walla Walla valley. Inns have sprung up to cater to the wine tourists or those who just want to ride a horse through the sagebrush and look up at the mountains. Looking at the snow-capped peaks of massive Pahto (Mount Adams) or distant Tahoma (Mount Rainier) from the brown plains, you can see why the nearby tribes revere these mountains as the sacred source of waters—which, as far as this region is concerned, they obviously are.

YAKIMA VALLEY

The settlers who drifted into the Yakima Valley in the second half of the 19th century didn't wait around for massive dam projects: The Yakima River brought plenty of cool, clear water down from the Cascades, and they dug canals to take it where they wanted it to go. From Naches to Selah to Union Gap, the entire upper valley was soon lined with orchards. It was never much of a destination, though, till the vineyards went in down in the lower valley; now winery tours are the major tourist draw. Naches is a frontier hamlet in the northern reaches of the Yakima Valley, with easy access to the wine country southward and to skiing on the Cascade flanks upstream. Yakima itself remains a market town, geared more to farms than to tourism despite its convention center.

Just south of Yakima lies the large Yakama Indian Reservation, reaching from the Yakima River west to the eastern slopes of Mount Adams. The excellent tribal museum in Toppenish details the indigenous culture as well as the history of conquest, treaties, and confinement. Continuing downriver, you'll pass through little farm towns such as Zillah, Granger, Sunnyside, and Prosser, reminders that this verdant valley is the state's breadbasket.

GUIDANCE **Prosser Chamber of Commerce** (509-786-3177 or 800-408-1517; www.prosserchamber.org), 1230 Bennett Avenue, Prosser 99350.

Selah Chamber of Commerce (509-698-7303; www.selahchamber.org), 216 South First Street, Selah 98942.

Sunnyside Chamber of Commerce (509-837-5939 or 800-457-8089; www.sunnysidechamber.com), 451 South Sixth Street, Sunnyside 98944.

Toppenish Chamber of Commerce (509-865-3262 or 800-863-6375; www.toppenish.net), 504 South Elm Street, Toppenish 98948.

Yakima Valley Visitors and Convention Bureau (509-575-3010 or 800-221-0751; www.visityakima.com), 10 North Eighth Street, Yakima 98901.

Yakima Visitors Information Center (509-373-3388 or 800-221-0751), 101 Fair Avenue, Yakima 98901.

Zillah Chamber of Commerce (509-829-5055; www.zillahchamber.com), Box 1294, 119 First Avenue, Zillah 98953.

GETTING THERE Yakima and other Yakima Valley communities can be reached by **I-82,** which runs the length of the Yakima Valley, from **I-90** near Ellensburg to

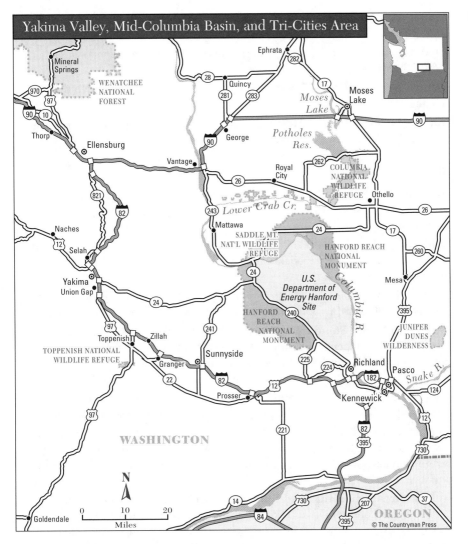

Yakima Valley, Mid-Columbia Basin, and Tri-Cities Area

the Tri-Cities. **US 97** runs north-south from Toppenish through Yakima to Ellensburg. **US 12** and **WA 410** approach from Naches to the west; WA 410 is closed in the winter.

Yakima Airport (509-575-6149), about 4 miles south of the city, serves the area.

Greyhound (800-231-2222; www.greyhound.com) serves Yakima (509-457-5131), at 602 East Yakima Avenue, and Sunnyside (509-837-5344), at 1825 Waneta.

The nearest **AMTRAK** service is in Pasco (see the Tri-Cities Area chapter).

GETTING AROUND Yakima Transit (509-575-6175), 3201 Fruitvale Boulevard, Yakima, serves the city with nine bus routes. In other parts of this region, you'll want a car.

MEDICAL EMERGENCY Medi-Center Valley (509-453-1770), 2 East Valley Mall Boulevard, Union Gap. Open 7:30–6:30 Mon.–Fri., 10–6 Sat.–Sun.

Medi-Center Westside (509-965-1770), 4001 Tieton Drive, Yakima. Open 7:30–7:30 Mon.–Fri., 9–7 Sat.–Sun.

Yakima Regional (509-575-5000; www.providence.org), 110 South Ninth Avenue, Yakima.

Yakima Valley Memorial Hospital (509-575-8000; www.yakimamemorialhospital .org), 2811 Tieton Drive, Yakima.

✳ To See

FARMS AND GARDENS The Yakima Valley is justly famous for its fresh fruit, available at fruit stands throughout the region; some have been in operation for more than a century. Here are a few:

Johnson Orchards (509-966-7479; www.johnsonorchardsfruit.com), 4906 Summitview, Yakima. Open 8:30–5:30 Mon.–Sat., 9–4 Sun. in season. Operated from this location since 1904.

✐ **Jones Farms** (509-829-3002 or 509-829-6024), 2020 Thacker Road, Granger. Open 8–5 daily mid-July–Oct. Includes a straw maze and duck pond.

Residential Fruit Stand (509-453-8827; arlac@aol.com), 1103 South Third Avenue, Yakima. Open 8–4:30 Mon.–Fri., 9–4:30 Sat. June–Oct. Has its own year-round café, the **Magic Kitchen,** besides bushels of delectable produce.

Thompson's Farm (509-949-3450), 9535 Old Naches Road, Naches. Open 10–5 Sat.–Sun. in season. Tours by appointment. You can pick your own or buy fruit ready-picked. The shop next door offers their own jams and a soda fountain.

Washington Fruit Place and Gift Shop (509-966-1275; www.treeripened.com), 1209 Pecks Canyon Road, Yakima. Open 9–6 Mon.–Fri., 9–5 Sat., 11–4 Sun. in season. Standing in its own cherry orchards, it offers fruit-related gifts as well as produce.

Yakima Area Arboretum and Botanical Garden (509-248-7337; www.ahtrees .org), 1401 Arboretum Drive, Yakima. Open dawn to dusk. Few trees can tolerate Yakima's extreme desert climate, where temperatures can range from –25 to 110 degrees, unaided. The 46-acre arboretum provides gentle help to both native and exotic species. Some two thousand kinds of woody plants are nurtured in this restful riverside setting. Unusual trees on display include a dawn redwood and a grove of giant sequoias. Also on the premises are a small Japanese garden and a rose garden. A small **visitors center** houses a library and gift shop. No pets or picnicking.

FOR FAMILIES ✐ **Toppenish murals,** downtown Toppenish; on US 97 just south of I-82 at Zillah. Washington towns seem particularly enamored of murals depicting local life and history, but none more than Toppenish, which boasts 67 murals and counting. Each year since 1989, the **Toppenish Mural Society** (509-865-3262) has sponsored Mural-in-a-Day (see *Special Events*), wherein artists paint the side of a building—in addition to more leisurely mural projects. Themes include "Clearing the Land," "From Horse to Horseless Carriage," the coming of the railroad, and the treaty of 1855, by which the tribes gave up most of their lands. The town has become a colorful outdoor gallery of the changing West.

HISTORIC HOMES H. M. Gilbert Homeplace, 2109 West Yakima Avenue, Yakima. To visit, call the **Yakima Valley Museum** (509-248-0747; see *Museums*). Built in 1989 by the Gilberts, who came out from Illinois to develop land and farm and raise seven children, the spreading Victorian house has since been refurnished with period antiques.

Prosser walking tour of eight historic homes (all privately owned) dating from 1899 to 1907 takes in several popular architectural styles, including Craftsman, Stick-Eastlake, and the ubiquitous Queen Anne. Brochures are available at the Prosser Chamber of Commerce (see *Guidance*). Among the sites is this one:

Goundie bungalow, 962 Court Street, Prosser. This unusual home is made of Leauthier sandstone, an artificial stone made of sand taken from the Yakima River and compressed.

HISTORIC SITES Capitol Theatre (509-853-ARTS; www.capitoltheatre.org), 19 South Third Street, Yakima. Tours 9–4 Mon.–Fri. Free. When it opened in 1920, Yakima's new vaudeville theater was the biggest in the Northwest, with proud arches, ceiling murals, and a vaguely Moorish facade. It was owned by the Mercy family for 50 years, but just after being placed on the National Register of Historic Places, it burned down. Reconstructed using old photos and fiberglass molds, it reopened in 1978 with seats from Constitution Hall and the murals repainted by the same artist, Tony Heinsbergen, who had done them nearly 60 years earlier. It's an active theater again, hosting lectures, concerts, plays, and dance.

Many downtown **retail buildings** date from the early twentieth century. A self-guiding tour brochure is available from the Yakima Visitors Information Center (see *Guidance*).

Yakima, for its size, has an extraordinary number of **historic churches,** including the Episcopal church, 1888, looking like an early English or Irish structure; the Renaissance-style Christian Science church, 1918 (now a theater); the solid stone Baptist church, 1908; and the African Methodist Episcopal church, 1917. Frothy St. Paul's Cathedral, at 15 South 12th Avenue, recalling the Spanish Baroque, is also worth a visit. A self-guiding brochure is available from the Yakima Visitors Information Center (see *Guidance*).

Fort Simcoe State Park (509-874-2372), at the end of Fort Simcoe Road west of Toppenish. Day use only; buildings open 9:30–4:30 Wed.–Sun. Apr.–Sept. This historical site on the Yakama Reservation was a fort in the 1860s, subsequently becoming a boarding school for Indian children. Several military buildings are still standing. Interpretive facilities detail the military and cultural legacy.

Teapot Dome gas station, Zillah; from I-82 take exit 54 and drive 0.4 mile south on the Yakima Valley Highway. Alas, the Teapot stopped pumping gas some years ago (a price of $1.11.9 for regular unleaded is still posted), but it nonetheless stands as a wordless commentary on the Teapot Dome scandal. The gas station stands 15 feet tall, handle, spout, and all. Built in 1922 in Yakima, it was later moved to its present site.

MUSEUMS American Hop Museum (509-865-4677; www.americanhop museum.org), 22 South B Street, Toppenish. Open 10–4 Wed.–Sat., 11–4 Sun.

May–Oct. $3 adults, $2 students, $7 families, children under five free. Since hops were introduced here in the 1860s, the Yakima Valley has come to produce 75 percent of those grown nationally. This homespun museum traces and celebrates the history of the crop in the United States. The building itself, a 1917 creamery, is cheerfully decorated with agriculturally themed friezes and frescoes.

Benton County Historical Museum (509-786-3842), in Prosser City Park, Seventh Street, Prosser. Open 11–4 Tues.–Fri., 12–3 Sat. Donation accepted. Family heirlooms and memorabilia provide a window into pioneer

THE TEAPOT DOME GAS STATION IN ZILLAH

life in the county. A general store, early schoolroom, and 1900 homestead are artfully put together using authentic objects. Most remarkable perhaps is the collection of women's dresses, all displayed on mannequins, dating from the mid-1800s through the 1930s.

Central Washington Agricultural Museum (509-457-8735), 4508 Main Street, Union Gap. Buildings open 9–5 Tues.–Sat., 1–4 Sun. Apr.–Oct.; closed Nov.–Mar. Grounds open dawn to dusk daily year-round. Donation requested. This large indoor-outdoor museum displays large farm equipment and machinery, plus a railroad exhibit and a working windmill.

Northern Pacific Railway Museum (509-865-1911; www.nprymuseum.org), 10 South Asotin Avenue, Toppenish. Open 10–4 Tues.–Sat., 12–4 Sun. May–Oct. $5 adults, $3 children under 18. In a restored 1911 Northern Pacific depot, this museum houses several vintage locomotives and cars to demonstrate the importance of trains to regional history.

Sunnyside Museum (509-837-6010), 704 South Fourth Street, Sunnyside. Open 1–4 Thurs.–Sun. Free. Photos, clothes, books, and other memorabilia provide a glimpse of life in early Sunnyside.

THE AMERICAN HOP MUSEUM IN TOPPENISH

Yakama Nation Cultural Heritage Center Museum (509-865-2800; www.yakamamuseum.com), Spiel-yi Loop, Box 151, Toppenish 98948. Open 8–5 Mon.–Fri., 9–5 Sat.–Sun. $6 adults, $4 seniors over 55 and children 11–18, $2 children under 11, $15 families. This museum, in the shape of an outsized longhouse, offers a stunning look into the lives of the Yakama tribes past and present. The treaty of 1855 herded several different plateau tribes onto what is now the Yakama Reserva-

tion in the shadow of the sacred mountain Pahto (Mount Adams). Dioramas, portraits, tools, and clothing link traditional economy and culture to the present, while
a copy of the 1855 treaty and a hall of chiefs, in full regalia, bring history to life.
The moccasin collection, from tiny beaded baby shoes to tall boots, is itself a tour
de force.

✦ **Yakima Valley Museum** (509-248-0747; www.yakimavalleymuseum.org), 2105
Tieton Drive, Yakima. Open 10–5 Mon.–Sat. Apr.–Oct.; 10–5 Tues.–Sat. Nov.–Mar.
$5 adults, $3 seniors and students, $12 families, children under five and members
free. This museum's eclectic collection sets forth the social and agricultural history
of the Yakima Valley. Exhibits of Indian artifacts, orchard equipment, furniture,
and photos detail the valley's development, but the pièce de résistance is an
astonishing collection of horse-drawn vehicles, from a stagecoach to an 1890s
surrey with a fringe on top, from buckboard phaetons to a horse-drawn hearse—
practically an encyclopedia of life before cars. Native son William O. Douglas is
honored with a reconstruction of his Supreme Court office, with all original furnishings and books. Kids can learn to operate a cherry sorter in the hands-on
exhibits in the **Children's Underground;** all generations enjoy the art deco
Museum Soda Fountain.

SCENIC DRIVES Yakima Valley Highway (US 97 and WA 22), about 53 miles
from Union Gap to Prosser. This winding road running along the north shore of
the Yakima River makes a pleasant alternative to I-82 through the wine country; in
Prosser, it appropriately becomes Wine Country Road. A gentle drive through the
valley hamlets, orchards, and vineyards makes it easy to stop at the many wineries
along the way (see *To Do—Winery Tours*).

✴ To Do

BICYCLING Revolution Cycles (509-452-0063), 3506 Fruitvale Boulevard,
Yakima. Check with them for cycling suggestions.

Wine country roads. The back roads of Zillah, Sunnyside, and Prosser, along the
north side of the Yakima River, are generally quiet—you might encounter a tractor
now and then—and bucolic. Take a spin between vineyards and through the small
towns, stopping if you like at the museums in Sunnyside or Prosser (see *To See—
Museums*), with views of Mount Adams to the west and dry but increasingly vinif-
erous hills to the east.

Yakima Greenway, 10 paved miles through several parks along the Yakima River;
access from the Yakima Area Arboretum and Botanical Garden (see *To See—
Farms and Gardens*) and other points in Yakima. Open to cyclists, walkers, and
skaters, it unfortunately parallels I-82, so it's not exactly a quiet ride, but there are
nice views of Mount Adams, and even Mount Rainier peeps over the horizon.

BIRDING Toppenish National Wildlife Refuge (509-546-8300), 21 Pumphouse Road, Toppenish; on US 97 about 10 miles south of town. Open sunrise to
sunset daily. Twelve parcels (totaling 1,978 acres) of this floodplain are managed
for wildlife, mainly nesting and migratory birds. In fall and winter, clouds of ducks
and geese arrive, while on a June morning the bushes are alive with catbirds, song
sparrows, and red-winged blackbirds.

CAMPING **Crow Butte Park** (509-875-2644), on WA 14 about 25 miles south of Prosser, along the Columbia River. Fifty riverside sites with utilities. Open mid-Mar.–mid-Oct.

&. **Yakima Sportsman State Park** (888-226-7688), just east of Yakima and the river. Thirty tent sites and 37 utility sites; ADA restrooms.

GOLF **Apple Tree Golf Course** (509-966-5877), 8804 Occidental Avenue, Yakima. Eighteen holes.

Fisher Park Golf Course (509-575-6075), 823 South 40th Avenue, Yakima. Nine holes.

River Ridge (509-697-8323), 295 Golf Course Loop, Selah. Nine holes.

Suntides Golf Course (509-966-9065), 201 Pence Road, Yakima. Eighteen holes.

HIKING **Cowiche Canyon,** about 3 unpaved miles; drive Summitview Avenue 7 miles west of 40th Street to Weikel Road and turn right into parking area. A rail trail winds along Cowiche Creek's lush riparian zone; side trails lead up onto the surrounding shrub-steppe habitat, a stark contrast to the creek below. Beware of rattlesnakes above and poison ivy below. For information, contact **Cowiche Canyon Conservancy** (509-248-5065), 302 North Third Street, Yakima.

Yakima Greenway, 10 paved miles, Yakima (see *Bicycling*). A close-in opportunity for a brisk walk.

RAFTING **Lower Yakima Canyon,** along WA 821 north of Selah. A calm float between high cliff walls is especially popular with families and novices.

Rill Adventures (509-964-2520; www.rillsonline.com), Box 102, Thorp 98946. Contact them for information or rentals.

Wet Planet Rafting (877-930-9445), 860 WA 141, Husum, offers unique fall white-water trips on the renowned **Tieton River,** along US 12 just west of Naches.

WINERY TOURS Several dozen **wineries** (509-965-5201; www.wineyakima valley.org) dot the hills from Yakima south to Prosser (and beyond). You can spend a pleasant day meandering down the valley, stopping for a taste here and there; they'll all be glad to see you. If you don't feel like driving yourself, tours are offered by the following:

Moonlit Ride Limousine (509-575-6846).

SUV Tours (509-783-7060).

Top Hat Limousine (509-469-6400).

✴ Wilder Places

PARKS **Crow Butte Park** (509-875-2644), on WA 14 about 25 miles south of Prosser. This park along the Columbia is now run by the U.S. Army Corps of Engineers. It offers camping, swimming, picnicking, and a boat launch.

Fort Simcoe State Park (509-874-2372), at the end of Fort Simcoe Road west of Toppenish. Day use only. This 200-acre park on the Yakama Reservation interprets the history of the site as a fort and, later, an Indian boarding school (see *To See— Historic Sites*). Includes picnic and game areas.

Yakima Sportsman State Park (509-452-5843), just east of Yakima and the river. Formerly a trapshooting club, this park lies along the Yakima River and has an often busy campground.

WILDLIFE REFUGES Oak Creek Wildlife Area (509-653-3290), between Wenas Road and Summitview Extension, west of Selah and Yakima. This 42,000-acre parcel between the Tieton River and Yakima includes evergreen forests and sagebrush steppe, as well as two riparian valleys. It's home to a multitude of creatures, including elk herds, which in winter are fed at two locations along US 12. From a viewing area and interpretive center near the headquarters at 16601 US 12, you may see large concentrations of the critters.

Toppenish National Wildlife Refuge (509-546-8300), 21 Pumphouse Road, Toppenish; on US 97 south of town. Open 5 AM to one and a half hours past sunset daily. These reeded wetlands are a pleasant sight after driving mile after mile of sere hill and plain. Toppenish Creek, a tributary of the Yakima River, is subject to spring flooding, and 12 parcels (totaling 1,978 acres) of this floodplain are managed for wildlife, mainly nesting and migratory birds. A short entrance road off US 97 brings you to a boardwalk and observation blind. In fall and winter, clouds of ducks and geese arrive, while on a June morning the bushes are alive with catbirds, song sparrows, and red-winged blackbirds.

✳ Lodging

BED & BREAKFASTS

Naches

Apple Country B&B (509-972-3409 or 877-788-9963; www.applecountry innbb.com), 4350 Old Naches Highway. Four antiques-furnished guest rooms with private baths occupy this cottage set in quiet gardens among the orchards. There's a porch to sit on and watch the wildlife. Rates include a full breakfast. $79–105.

Sunnyside

🐾 **Sunnyside Inn Bed & Breakfast** (509-839-5557 or 800-221-4195; www .sunnysideinn.com), 804 East Edison Avenue. This 1919 doctor's home now offers 13 cozy, unfussy guest rooms in the middle of the Yakima Valley wine country. Some rooms are pet-friendly. Rates include a full breakfast. $95–119.

Yakima

✐ **Orchard Inn Bed & Breakfast** (509-966-1283 or 866-966-1283; www.orchardinnbb.com), 1207 Pecks Canyon Road. A wing for guests was added to this farmhouse in the cherry orchards above town in 1996. Henner and Karen Krueger bought it in 2004 and run it with gusto and a rural European flair. A deck and pergola look directly into leafy green cherry trees. Breakfast might be *Krabben-kuchen* (from Henner's German recipe bank) or a creation of Karen's, such as savory *clafoutis*. No fussy Victoriana here, just comfortable, homey rooms with some family antiques in all the right places. Four guest rooms all have private, jetted baths. Guests also enjoy a living room with TV, VCR, computer, and library. Supervised children are welcome. Consult about pets. $99–179; group rates available.

Rosedell Bed and Breakfast (509-961-2964; www.rosedellbb.com), 1811 West Yakima Avenue. This huge masonry home with Doric porticoes dominates Yakima's western hillside. Built by a lumber magnate in 1905–1909, it offers three large guest rooms, one in the tower, all with private baths, and a smaller "extra" room that can be rented with a larger room. $120–150; extra room $75.

A Touch of Europe Bed and Breakfast (509-454-9775 or 888-438-7073), 220 North 16th Avenue. This imposing 1889 home sits on sweeping lawns in the middle of Yakima's "mansion district"—the local lumber and sheep barons built here to demonstrate their newly acquired status. It's easily the poshest establishment in Yakima. The three guest rooms reflect Victorian standards of luxury with the happy addition of air-conditioning and private baths. Erika and James Cenci take particular pride in their cuisine: Besides a hearty candlelit breakfast, they'll prepare elaborate, made-to-order lunches and dinners by prior reservation (see *Where to Eat*). $129–137.

Zillah

❦ **Cherry Wood Bed Breakfast and Barn** (509-829-3500; www.cherry woodbbandb.com), 3271 Roza Drive. Terry and Pepper Fewel opened their 80-acre working orchard to guests in 2004. Two guest tepees come with beds, down comforters, and space heaters (or fans) for those who like "almost roughing it." Rates include breakfast and use of the pool. Borrow a bike, sit by the pool, watch the sun set over Mount Adams, or visit Zillah's numerous wineries if you can pull yourself away. Pepper can arrange horseback wine rides or just plain horseback rides on the family's horses; women's and group retreats are also available. No children. Horses welcome; ask about dogs. Open Apr.–Oct. $225.

GUESTHOUSES

Zillah

Hawk Haven Retreat (509-945-6455), 2060 Bailey Road. It looks like an old western storefront, with its awning sheltering a weathered boardwalk, but it's a two-bedroom guesthouse on Chris and Sue Miller's farm. The deck out back gives a 180-degree view of the Rattlesnake Hills; if you prefer, you can enjoy it from the hot tub. Stars and silence reign at night, with only the coyotes for competition. Sue cooks up a luscious breakfast of stuffed Swedish pancakes with fresh fruit and toast. The house, which rents as a single unit, has a full kitchen, two bathrooms (one private), and a living room. A three-bedroom cottage on the property has the same amenities. Consult about pets. $140–175.

INNS AND HOTELS

Naches

✍ ❦ **Natchez Hotel** (509-683-1317 or 888-282-1317; www.nachez-hotel.com), 213 Naches Avenue. Six rooms, one with a Jacuzzi, are available year-round. There's a café next door (see *Where to Eat*). Child- and pet-friendly. $69–139.

Yakima

♿ **Birchfield Manor Inn** (509-452-1960), 2018 Birchfield Road. Originally the "big house" of an enormous sheep ranch, the renovated 1910 manor has five contemporary guest rooms, most with whirlpool baths. Six cottages may include fireplaces and/or a patio or deck; one cottage is wheelchair-accessible. Birchfield caters to business as well as pleasure travelers—all rooms have Wi-Fi—and offers carefully prepared dinners three nights a week. If you want, you can have a private party in the wine cellar. Children eight and over welcome. Rooms $119–159; cottages $139–219.

Hilton Garden Inn (509-454-1111), 401 East Yakima Avenue. Next to the convention center and a few steps from the old downtown core, the

A VIEW OF THE RATTLESNAKE HILLS FROM HAWK HAVEN RETREAT NEAR ZILLAH

Hilton offers its usual quiet and businesslike amenities—111 rooms with high-speed Internet access, a fitness room, a pool, and a restaurant on premises. Rooms have one king or two queen beds. No pets. From $99.

Holiday Inn (800-315-2621; www .holidayinn.com), 802 East Yakima Avenue. The chains have a fair monopoly on accommodations in downtown Yakima. The Holiday Inn may offer few surprises, but it is friendly and reliable. There's a fitness room and pool, and the hotel is close to the 10-mile Greenway, with its paved hiking-biking path along the Yakima River. $81–179.

✔ **Ledgestone Hotel Yakima** (509-543-3151; www.ledgestonehotel.com), 107 North Fair Avenue. The ambience and decor are standard road trip, but all rooms are suites with a bedroom, living room, kitchen, and dining area, so the place is particularly family-friendly. Right by the river and greenway, not far from downtown. $89–139.

RESORTS

Toppenish

Yakama Nation RV Park (800-865-2000; www.ynrv.com), 2800 Buster Road. Next to the Yakama Nation

Museum (see *To See—Museums*), this RV park has 125 sites with full hookups, 10 tent sites, and 14 tepees under the shadow of Mount Adams. Amenities include free computer use, a pool, a sauna, meeting rooms, and an exercise room. Tent sites $20; RV sites $30–32; tepees $25–50.

✳ Where to Eat

DINING OUT

Yakima

Carousel (509-248-6720), 25 North Front Street. Open 4:30–9:30 Tues.–Sat. You don't have to know French to read the menu, but it helps. Choose among such French classics as roast duckling, coq au vin, and marinated rabbit. With new chef-owner Ewa Lichota at the stove, you'll find a touch of Polish cooking as well.

5 North Metropolitan Kitchen and Lounge (509-248-9801; 5north kitchen.com), 5 North Front Street. Open from 5 PM Tues.–Sat. A new haute cuisine venue in Yakima, and well worth the visit. Homemade wild mushroom ravioli, lamb burgers, a bright chickpea salad, and other delectable seasonal dishes are expertly prepared, and the service is stellar.

A Touch of Europe Bed and Breakfast (509-454-9775 or 888-438-7073), 220 North 16th Avenue. You don't have to stay here to eat here (see *Lodging*). Energetic Erika Cenci, author of *A Touch of Europe Cookbook: Bringing Fresh to the Table Naturally,* will cook formal private meals to your order whether you prefer French, German, Italian, or other European cuisine. Meals run about $30–50 per person; book by phone.

EATING OUT

Naches

Sticky-Fingers Bakery and Café (509-653-1370 or 888-282-1317; sticky fingerscafe.net), 217 Naches Avenue, next door to the Natchez Hotel (see *Lodging*). Open for breakfast, lunch, and early supper.

Yakima

Café Mélange (509-453-0571), 7 North Front Street. Open 11–9 Mon.–Thurs., 11–10 Fri.–Sat. A small, bistrolike venue across from the old train depot, Mélange serves steaks, seafood, and poultry that are a cut above the ordinary. Reservations recommended.

Essencia Artisan Bakery and Chocolaterie (509-575-5570), 4 North Third Street. Open 6–4 Mon.–Fri., 7–2 Sat. Yes, you can get real, European-style breads and pastries in the great Northwest desert (should we spell that *dessert*?). Pastry chef Ivone Petzinger whips up delectable cream puffs, fruit tarts, and truffles that wouldn't be out of place on the rue Saint-Honoré—and bread that reminds you why it's called the staff of life.

Gasperetti's (509-248-0628; www .gasperettisrestaurant.com), 1013 North First Street. Open 11–2 Mon.–Fri., 5–10 Mon.–Sat. Named for Angelo Gasperetti, who reputedly invented chicken cacciatore for Pope Pius VII, then immigrated to America and opened a restaurant in Union Gap. His son opened the present restaurant in 1966. The menu reflects a cultural blend of Italy and the far Northwest, with dishes including Dungeness crab cannelloni or a plate combining chicken, ravioli, meatballs, and sausage. It also features a long list of Washington wines.

Santiago's Gourmet Mexican Restaurant (509-453-1644; www .santiagos.org), 111 East Yakima Avenue. Open 11:30–9 Mon.–Thurs., 11:30–10 Fri., 5–10 Sat. This place is much appreciated locally for its house recipes and fresh ingredients.

☙ **Zesta Cucina** (509-972-2000, www .zestacucina.com), 5110 Tieton Drive. Open 11–9 Mon.–Thurs., 11–10 Fri.–Sat. On a Labor Day evening, when Yakima was virtually closed down, Zesta Cucina was open. What a pleasure! A cheerful Northwest ambience combines with northern Italian cuisine for casual, quality dining (risotto to die for) enhanced by local and Italian wines. A children's menu is available. Even its location in the rustic-modern Glenwood Shopping Center west of downtown doesn't detract: Upstairs is Inklings, Yakima's independent bookstore (see *Selective Shopping*) and an atrium where a solitary couple sat playing chess.

✳ Entertainment

THEATER The Capitol Theatre (509-853-ARTS; www.capitoltheatre .org), 19 South Third Street, Yakima. This is Yakima's performing arts center. The new, adjoining 4th Street Theatre is an intimate venue where you can sip a drink while watching the show.

✳ Selective Shopping

BOOKS Inklings Bookshop (509-965-5830; www.inklingsbookshop .com), 5110 Tieton Drive, Yakima. Open 9–9 Mon.–Sat., 12–6 Sun. This independent bookstore serves up espresso and easy chairs as well as books new and old. Poets stop by.

FOOD ✎ **Chukar Cherries** (800-624-9544; www.chukar.com), 320 Wine Country Road, Prosser. This place capitalizes on two fail-safe ingredients: chocolate and local cherries, in countless combinations and permutations. Free samples.

✳ Special Events

April: **Spring Barrel Tasting** (509-965-5201; www.wineyakimavalley.org), throughout the Yakima Valley. Taste wines from the barrel or the bottle and learn about the Yakima appellation.

May: **Cinco de Mayo Festival** (800-457-8089), Sunnyside. The Yakima Valley has a large Mexican population, and Sunnyside hosts the biggest Cinco de Mayo fiesta in the state.

June: **Mural-in-a-Day** (509-865-6516), Toppenish. A dozen artists complete a Toppenish historical mural on the year's chosen facade in eight hours.

July: **Toppenish Powwow and Rodeo** (800-949-5957; www.toppenish.net), Toppenish Rodeo Grounds. Enjoy a rodeo, food, an Indian village, and entertainment.

MID-COLUMBIA BASIN

This vast portion of the Columbia Plateau on the I-90 corridor extends from Ellensburg in the Cascade foothills east to Moses Lake and Ritzville, and from Othello at the junction of WA 17 and WA 26 north to Quincy and Ephrata on WA 28. This is the very heart of Washington State.

GUIDANCE Ellensburg Chamber of Commerce (509-925-3137 or 800-925-2204; www.visitellen.com), 609 North Main Street, Ellensburg 98926.

Ephrata Chamber of Commerce (509-754-4656; www.ephratawachamber.com), 112 Basin Street SW, Ephrata 98823.

Moses Lake Chamber of Commerce (509-765-7888 or 800-992-6234; www.moseslake.com), 324 South Pioneer Way, Moses Lake 98837.

GETTING THERE I-90 is the major highway connecting Thorp and Ellensburg to Moses Lake, crossing the Columbia at Vantage. At Ellensburg, both **I-82** and **WA 821** head south to Yakima. Across the river from Vantage, **WA 243** heads south toward the Tri-Cities and **WA 26** heads east to Othello. From I-90 at George, **WA 281** heads north to Quincy and **WA 283** heads northeast to Ephrata.

The nearest airports are in Yakima and Wenatchee.

AMTRAK (800-USA-RAIL; www.amtrak.com) has a bus connection that stops in Ephrata, at 90 Alder Street, and in Quincy, at 223 F Street NE. Its Empire Builder line from Chicago to Seattle stops in Ritzville at 1503 South Smitty's Boulevard.

Greyhound (800-231-2222; www.greyhound.com) serves Ephrata (509-754-0955) at 90 Alder Street and Moses Lake (509-766-4216) at 1819 Kittelson Road.

GETTING AROUND Grant Transit Authority (509-754-1075; www.gta-ride.com), 8392 West Westover Boulevard, Ephrata. This is the county's bus service, running weekdays only.

MEDICAL EMERGENCY Columbia Basin Hospital (509-754-4631; www.columbiabasinhospital.org), 200 Nat Washington Way, Ephrata.

Kittitas Valley Community Hospital (509-962-9841), 603 South Chestnut Street, Ellensburg.

Quincy Valley Hospital (509-787-3531; www.quincyhospital.org), 908 10th Avenue SW, Quincy.

✳ To See

CULTURAL SITES Wanapum Vista and Echo Vista View Points, I-90 just east of Vantage. The life-sized metal sculpture *Grandfather Lets Loose the Ponies* is visible from the interstate, but there are also pullouts for more leisurely viewing.

FARMERS' MARKETS Ephrata Farmers' Market (509-771-0383), Grant County Court House, Sun Basin Plaza, Basin Street, Ephrata. Open 8–12 Sat. May–Oct.

Kittitas County Farmers Market (509-899-3870; kittitascountyfarmersmarket .com), corner of Fourth and Pearl streets, Ellensburg. Open 9–1 Sat. May–Oct. Besides local produce, vendors sell crafts, baked goods, jewelry, and more.

FARMS AND GARDENS Donald L. Garrity Japanese Garden, at Central Washington University, 400 East Eighth Avenue, Ellensburg. Open 7 AM–dusk except in winter. Rock arrangements, cherry trees, and lanterns create a quiet spot for rest and reflection. Designed by landscape architect Masa Muzano, the garden was dedicated in 1992.

FOR FAMILIES *∂* **Dick and Jane's Spot** (www.reflectorart.com), corner of First and Pearl streets, Ellensburg. View from the sidewalk only, please. "What on earth is this?" might be your first reaction on driving by Dick and Jane Orleman's home of 27 years. It is surrounded by sculptures made of bicycle wheels, electrical bushings, thousands of reflectors, and many other strange things. A huge hand extends from the house's upper wall; it used to belong to a fortune-teller. Besides the couple's own work, the creations of 40 or so artists are featured. Who knew you could be so creative with reflectors?

HISTORIC HOMES Olmstead Place State Park (509-925-1943), 921 North Ferguson Road, Ellensburg. Open 6:30 AM–dusk Apr.–Sept., 8 AM–dusk Oct.–Mar.; interpretive tours 12–4 Sat.–Sun. in summer; seasonal agricultural demonstrations. Free. After waves of settlers had washed westward over the Cascades, a back-wash returned eastward to previously neglected lands. The Olmsteads came over Snoqualmie Pass from Seattle in the fall of 1875 and homesteaded a few miles east of Ellensburg, where the dry but mild climate seemed good for farming. Logs had to be hauled from the Yakima Canyon miles away, but by spring they had a solid,

THE OLMSTEAD CABIN, IN OLMSTEAD PLACE STATE PARK, IS ONE OF KITTITAS COUNTY'S OLDEST HOMES.

unusually spacious cabin with two bedrooms in which the family lived for more than 30 years. It's been lovingly maintained and restored with some of the original furnishings. The farm prospered and finally, in 1908, they built the large house next door. Olmstead granddaughters Leta and Clareta lived out their lives in it. It's been left exactly as it was, from the box piano to the toaster oven, when Clareta died in 1968.

HISTORIC SITES Ellensburg, like so many burgeoning Washington towns, burned down, on July 4, 1889. And like so many others, it had entertained hopes of becoming the state capital, or at least a regional Boston or New York. So it promptly rebuilt, leaving us many imposing brick buildings from the late 1800s and early 1900s. For a guided or **self-guided walking tour** of Ellensburg's historic center, contact the **Kittitas Historical Society** (509-925-3778) or drop in at the Kittitas County Historical Society Museum (see *Museums*). Some of the buildings you'll see include the following:

Bank Saloon Building, on Fourth Street between Main and Pearl streets, Ellensburg. This is so called because the saloon's patrons reportedly used the large safe in the back to store their cash, revealing perhaps a greater trust in their fellows (and their lady friends) than in the frontier banks.

Cadwell Building, 114 East Third Street, Ellensburg. This also dates from the year of the fire and is now the home of the Kittitas County Historical Society. Its history has been checkered; rumors allude to a brothel upstairs.

Davidson Building, corner of Pearl Street and Fourth Avenue, Ellensburg. Perhaps the most exuberant edifice to rise from the ashes, this was completed in 1889 with tinwork around the facade, a grand corner turret, rows of arched windows, and many an architectural flourish, including a carved phoenix high above the street (in case you didn't get it). John Davidson was a local attorney highly commit-

THE 1889 DAVIDSON BUILDING IN DOWNTOWN ELLENSBURG

ted, evidently, to Ellensburg's future. A 1979 restoration added another (painted) phoenix to a street-side wall.

Fitterer Building, on Main Street, Ellensburg. Brothers Frank and Philip Fitterer started their furniture company in 1896. In 1908 they moved into this new building, and the company has been there ever since—to what is now the fifth generation—furnishing the homes of Ellensburg residents.

New York Café, corner of Third and Main, Ellensburg. This was built by Peter Giovanini in 1911 at Ellensburg's bustling center. Today it's a Chinese restaurant, but the old neon sign, intended no doubt to evoke big-city ambitions, is still there. Upstairs, 27 rooms once housed railway workers.

Thorp Grist Mill (509-964-9640; www.thorp.org); from I-90 take exit 101 (about 5 miles west of Ellensburg) and proceed 2 miles through Thorp to the mill. Open dawn to dusk year-round; guided tours Thurs.–Sun. June–Aug. Free. This mill provided grain and meal to the lumber boomers of the 1880s and carried on till 1946; its adjacent ice pond allowed railroad transport of fruit from the nearby orchards to faraway places. The entire mill is still intact, machinery and all, and open for interpretive visits. The surrounding grounds make a nice picnic spot.

MUSEUMS Clymer Museum of Art (509-962-6416; www.clymermuseum.com), 416 North Pearl Street, Ellensburg. Open 10–5 Mon.–Fri., 10–4 Sat.; also 12–4 Sun. in summer. Free. Western artist John Clymer grew up in Ellensburg, so it's fitting that the city has a museum dedicated to his work. More than 80 covers he created for the *Saturday Evening Post,* plus canvases large and small, cover his life's work celebrating the land and history of the West. Included are the well-known *Lewis and Clark in the Bitter Roots* and many lesser-known works. Temporary exhibits feature modern western artists.

Grant County Historical Museum (509-754-3334), 742 Basin Street North, Ephrata. Open 10–5 Mon.–Tues. and Thurs.–Sat., 1–4 Sun. $3.50 adults, $2 children. More than 30 pioneer buildings form a display of pioneer life in the county, while a museum sets forth local history.

Kittitas County Historical Society Museum (509-925-3778; www.kchm.org), 114 East Third Street, Ellensburg. Open 10–4 Mon.–Sat. Donation requested. Housed in a pioneer-era department store (development here was late and rapid), the museum's eclectic collection includes a 1927 Sears catalog, antiques such as a 1903 electric car and an 1899 steam-powered car, and many day-to-day objects from the period.

NATURAL WONDERS Ginkgo Petrified Forest State Park (509-856-2700), 1 mile north of Vantage; from I-90 take exit 136. Hours vary seasonally; call. If a tree dies in a prehistoric forest, does it make an impression? Of course. This desert was a swampy wood 15 million years ago, where dead trees, falling into the acidic water, failed to decay. Subsequently they were covered by basalt, from which minerals slowly percolated into the wood, and then they were partially uncovered by the prehistoric Missoula Floods. Highway construction in the 1930s revealed the world's first examples of petrified ginkgoes, but swamp cypress, walnut, and many other species were found, too. The visitors center has samples of the wood and geological explanations, while an interpretive trail east on the Vantage Highway (see *To Do—Hiking*) leads you to the discovery site and 22 kinds of petrified logs.

Outside the visitors center are some petroglyphs taken from a site flooded by the nearby Wanapum Dam.

Soap Lake, junction of WA 17 and WA 28 just north of Ephrata. This lake with a high mineral content reaches temperatures of 100 degrees Fahrenheit in summer and was used medicinally by Indians and settlers. People locally still use the mud for aches and skin conditions, and the lake for just hanging out.

SCENIC DRIVES Yakima Canyon (WA 821), about 30 paved miles from Ellensburg to Selah. This winding road running along the Yakima River makes a pleasant alternative to I-82. Instead of climbing and dropping over Manastash and Umtanum ridges, it follows the river through a spectacular basalt canyon.

✳ To Do

BICYCLING

Ellensburg Area

Manastash Creek, just south of Taneum off I-90, has countless routes, some challenging.

Old Vantage Highway, 27 paved miles from Ellensburg to Vantage. To the east lies the desert, nice and flat though dangerously hot in summer. Follow this highway or take off along many side roads or trails.

Taneum Creek, off I-90 at the Thorp exit, is rich in trails for mountain bikers of all skill levels.

Rentals

Mountain High Sports (509-925-4626), 105 East Fourth Street, Ellensburg.

Recycle Bike Shop (509-925-3326), 415 North Main Street, Ellensburg.

BIRDING Columbia National Wildlife Refuge (see *Wilder Places—Wildlife Refuges*) hosts thousands of migratory waterfowl in spring and fall. With the **Othello Chamber of Commerce** (www.othellowashington.us), it also cosponsors the Othello Sandhill Crane Festival in March (see *Special Events*).

Quincy Wildlife Area, on WA 28 southwest of Quincy, provides similar habitat with abundant birdlife.

CAMPING ♿ **Cascade Campground** (509-766-9240), Box 1579, Moses Lake 98837. Open Apr.–Sept. This municipal campground has 33 tent sites (1 handicapped-accessible), 41 RV sites, and a large group site; moorage, swimming area, and playgrounds. A waterfront but semi-urban campground. First come, first served.

♿ **Potholes State Park** (reservations 888-226-7688), on WA 262, 17 miles southwest of Moses Lake. Sixty-one tent sites and 60 utility sites; ADA facilities available. See also *Wilder Places—Parks*.

Wanapum Recreational Area (reservations 888-226-7688 May 15–Sept. 15), near Ginkgo Petrified Forest State Park, Vantage. Fifty utility sites (tenters can use them but pay full fee). Subject to high winds, and use is heavy during concert season at the nearby Gorge Amphitheater (see *Entertainment*).

Okanogan–Wenatchee National Forest (509-852-1100) has information on Forest Service campgrounds. Most of the ones listed below require a Northwest Forest Pass or a fee.

Icewater Creek, along Taneum Road between Ellensburg and Cle Elum. Fourteen sites; toilet but no water. No reservations.

Taneum, along Taneum Road between Ellensburg and Cle Elum. Thirteen sites; water and toilet. No reservations.

Taneum Junction, along Taneum Road between Ellensburg and Cle Elum. Fifteen sites; toilet but no water. No reservations.

FOREST SERVICE CABIN RENTALS Taneum Cabin can be reserved through the **Cle Elum Ranger District** (877-444-6777; www.recreation.gov). Summer use only. Sleeps four; running water and propane. $75.

GOLF Colockum Ridge Golf Course (509-787-6206), 17056 Road 5 NW, Quincy. Eighteen holes.

Ellensburg Golf and Country Club (509-962-2984), 3231 Thorp Highway, Ellensburg. Nine holes.

Reecer Creek Golf and Country Club (509-962-5256), 1201 West Umptanum Road, Ellensburg. Nine holes.

Sage Hills Golf Club (509-349-2603), 10400 Sage Hill Road SE, Warden; 14 miles southeast of Moses Lake. Eighteen holes.

HIKING

Ellensburg Area

Ginkgo Petrified Forest State Park (509-856-2700), on the Vantage Highway west of Vantage; from I-90 take exit 136 and follow the signs south 3 miles along Huntzinger Road. Three miles of interpretive trails lead you to 22 kinds of petrified logs.

Iron Horse or John Wayne Trail, 110 paved miles of the total 276 miles are in Washington; access behind Thorp Fruit Stand just off I-90 at exit 101 outside Ellensburg. Originally a right-of-way for the Chicago, Milwaukee, St. Paul, and Pacific Railroad, this low-grade trail roughly follows I-90 and is shared with cyclists, dogsledders, equestrians, and skiers, depending on the season. The few campgrounds on the trail are all between mileposts 2109 and 2127; some Forest Service campgrounds are near the trail. Contact the **Mount Baker–Snoqualmie National Forest** (800-627-0062) for details.

Umptanum Creek Trail, 4 miles in Yakima Canyon; trailhead on the west side of WA 821, 16.5 miles south of Ellensburg. Try the trails of Yakima Canyon, through the flower-strewn meadows of L. T. Murray Wildlife Refuge (see *Wilder Places— Wildlife Refuges*).

Othello Area

Frog Lake Trail, 3 miles, in Columbia National Wildlife Refuge (see *Wilder Places—Wildlife Refuges*); trailhead 8 miles north of Othello. Closed late fall. Sagebrush steppe surrounds ponds amid basalt formations.

Quincy Area

Ancient Lakes Trail, 4 miles, in Quincy Wildlife Area; from Quincy drive 4 miles west on WA 28, turn left on White Trail Road and right on Road 9 NW, and continue for 6 miles. This is an easy walk among desert ponds.

Dusty Lake Trail, 1.5 miles, in the same area. It has a 400-foot elevation gain.

UNIQUE ADVENTURES Chimpanzee and Human Communication Institute (509-963-2244; www.cwu.edu/~cwuchi), Central Washington University, Ellensburg. Home of the famous chimpanzee Washoe until she died in 2007, it still houses several of her colleagues, human and chimp, who all participate in the university's research on chimpanzee behavior and communication. Visitors can attend a "Chimposium"—a one-hour session on chimp life including observation of their conversational abilities: 10:45 AM and 12:45 PM Sat., 12:30 and 2 Sun. $11 adults, $8.50 students. Apprenticeships are also available.

✳ Wilder Places

PARKS Ginkgo Petrified Forest State Park (509-856-2700), 1 mile north of Vantage; from I-90 take exit 136. Hours vary seasonally; call. The visitors center has samples of the wood and geological explanations. An interpretive trail east on the Vantage Highway leads you to the discovery site and 22 kinds of petrified logs (see *To Do—Hiking*). Outside the visitors center are some petroglyphs taken from a site flooded by the nearby Wanapum Dam.

Moses Lake State Park, north of I-90 just west of Moses Lake. Day use only; open daily in summer, Sat.–Sun. in winter. Boat launch, swimming, and picnicking.

Olmstead Place State Park (509-925-1943), 921 North Ferguson Road, Ellensburg. Open 6:30 AM–dusk Apr.–Sept., 8 AM–dusk Oct.–Mar.; interpretive tours 12–4 Sat.–Sun. in summer; seasonal agricultural demonstrations. Free. The Olmstead homestead a few miles east of Ellensburg has a solid, unusually spacious cabin with two bedrooms in which the family lived for more than 30 years.

OLMSTEAD PLACE STATE PARK IN KITTITAS COUNTY

Potholes State Park (reservations 888-226-7688), at Potholes (O'Sullivan) Reservoir, on WA 262, 17 miles southwest of Moses Lake. Just a few miles from the Columbia National Wildlife Refuge (see *Wildlife Refuges*), this lake in the desert offers boating, camping, and wildlife viewing.

RECREATION AREAS Wanapum Recreational Area (360-902-8844), off I-90 south of Vantage. Provides camping adjacent to Ginkgo Petrified Forest State Park (see *Parks*). Both places border Wanapum Reservoir for 5 miles of freshwater shoreline on the Columbia, with boating, waterskiing, and more.

WILDLIFE REFUGES Colockum Wildlife Area (509-663-6260) and **Quilomene Wildlife Area** (509-925-6746), on the west shore of the Columbia River between Ellensburg and Wenatchee. Elk, bighorn sheep, and mule deer abound on these 105,000-plus acres of steppe, as do raptors and game birds. Roads, such as they are, are primitive; for conditions contact the refuge managers.

Columbia National Wildlife Refuge (509-546-8300), office at 64 Maple Street, Burbank. Office open 8:30–4 Mon.–Thurs., 8:30–3 Fri. Refuge open 5 AM–sunset daily Mar.–Sept.; closed Oct.–Feb. except for Frog Lake Trail (see *To Do— Hiking*). Part of the Channeled Scablands that cover much of the state's interior, this refuge was once dry coulees and a few ponds. Then came the Columbia Irrigation Project. The filling of giant reservoirs such as Banks Lake and smaller Potholes Reservoir raised the water table, filling in the depressions so that the 30,000 acres are now a haven for migrating waterfowl. An auto tour allows wildlife and scenery viewing, as do three interpretive trails.

L. T. Murray Wildlife Refuge, between Taneum Road and Wenas Road west of I-82, just west of Ellensburg. Mixed forest, grassland, and trails.

✳ Lodging

BED & BREAKFASTS

Grandview
Cozy Rose Inn (509-882-4669 or 800-575-8381; www.cozyroseinn.com), 1220 Forsell Road. A higher-end getaway for wine country retreats, the Cozy Rose has five luxuriously appointed suites, a cottage, and a "French" villa. Rates include breakfast brought to your room. $189–225.

GUESTHOUSES

Ellensburg
Guesthouse Ellensburg (509-962-3706; www.guesthouseellensburg.com), 606 North Main Street. You don't have to be a wine aficionado to sleep here, but it may add to your enjoyment. Cathy and Gordon Wollen, who also

own the Yellow Church Café (see *Where to Eat*) and happen to be wine enthusiasts who stock a cellar full of Northwest wines, offer wine tastings daily and happily share their enthusiasm. The tall, yellow 1887 house (to match the café?) is a cheery Victorian presence on Main Street, close to the university and downtown Ellensburg. Two private suites come with queen beds, sleeper couches, and a complimentary basket of goodies. Consult about children. No pets. $145–175.

INNS AND HOTELS

Soap Lake
✐ **Inn at Soap Lake** (509-246-1132 or 800-557-8514; www.innsoaplake .com), 226 Main Avenue East. It's historic, having been built as a smithy and

stable in 1905 and turned into a hotel in 1915, evidently in hopes of tourists rushing to the waters of mineral-laden Soap Lake. They trickled rather than rushed, but the hotel hung on somehow and is still in operation (after some renovation). Twenty old-fashioned rooms all have private baths, most complete with tubs for soaking in the local mineral water. Two one-bedroom cottages sleep six and come with the same mineral waters and full kitchens. Children welcome. Consult about pets. Rooms $59–89; bridal suite $100; Jacuzzi suites $110–125; cottages $100–135; check for winter deals.

Notaras Lodge (509-246-0462), 236 East Main Avenue. Built in 1983 and rebuilt after a fire in 1998, Notaras is a log house with 15 idiosyncratically decorated rooms, each with a kitchenette and a choice of regular or Soap Creek bathwater; some have Jacuzzis. $75–135.

LODGES

Quincy

Cave B Inn (509-785-2283 or 888-785-2283; www.cavebinn.com), 344 Silica Road NW. Vince and Carol Bryan opened the nearby Gorge Amphitheater in 1975 (see *Entertainment*). Since then, they have moved onto a 130-acre vineyard and winery and, in 2005, opened Cave B, the first stage of Sagecliffe, a multifaceted resort in the making. Sitting on the high ridges of coulee country, it certainly has a spectacular location. The buildings—a lodge with 3 guest suites, 15 "Cliffehouses," and 12 "cavern rooms"—with their basalt exteriors, manage to blend with the soil while at the same time looking ultramodern. Maybe it's the parabolic roofs. A number of yurts have been added near the edge of the estate vineyards, all with king-sized beds, private baths, and refrigerators.

All accommodations are luxurious, with features including granite-slab bathrooms, private balconies, or sunken living rooms. And the on-site **Tendrils Restaurant** (509-785-3780) must certainly be the most ambitious one for miles around. It's worth a visit just for the setting and innovative architecture, even if you don't stay. Yurts $109–309 (not available in winter); suites $129–259; cavern rooms $169–369; Cliffehouses $209–409; two-night minimum on weekends when there are concerts at the nearby Gorge Amphitheater.

RANCHES

Ellensburg

🐾 **4W Ranch and Guest Cabins** (509-933-2738 or 800-497-2624; www.4wranch.net), 11670 Manastash Road. This is an actual working ranch with two guest cabins, each with a full kitchen, gas fireplace, and porch for viewing the canyon. Dogs and horses welcome. $140–150.

✳ Where to Eat

EATING OUT

Ellensburg

Yellow Church Café (509-933-2233; www.yellowchurchcafe.com), 111 South Pearl Street. Open 11–8 Mon.–Fri., 8–8 Sat.–Sun. This café sits sedately on a residential corner, like a good church, as it has since 1923 when German Lutherans built it. The interior is fittingly simple, with hardwood floors and some original accoutrements, and the food is quite delicious—try the cedar-planked salmon with raspberry-butter sauce. Current owners Gordy and Cathy Wollen both grew up in preachers' households; I guess they must have focused on the loaves and fishes.

✳ Entertainment

MUSIC ♿ **Gorge Amphitheater**
(509-785-6262); from I-90 take exit
143 and follow the signs for about 6
miles. This natural, outdoor concert
venue in the desert overlooks the
Columbia River and seats 20,000. It
brings big-name rock, blues, and other
popular artists to a remote but spectacular location. Services available for
people with disabilities. For scheduling
and ticket information, go to www.live
nation.com.

✳ Special Events

March: **Othello Sandhill Crane Festival** (866-726-3345; www.othellosand
hillcranefestival.org), Columbia
National Wildlife Refuge (see *Wilder
Places—Wildlife Refuges*). In the
spring, thousands of sandhill cranes
move up the eastern edge of the
Pacific Flyway, dropping to rest on the
occasional lakes and wetlands dotting
the desert. View cranes, take a guided
birding tour, or attend a lecture.

June: **Dachshunds on Parade** (509-
925-3137; www.dachshundsonparade
.com), downtown Ellensburg. Dachshunds in and out of costume, a "Stupid
Pet Trick" contest, breakfast, and more
enliven this event.

July: **Jazz in the Valley** (509-889-
3639; www.jazzinthevalley.com),
Ellensburg. This musical weekend fills
up not just with jazz.

September: **Ellensburg Rodeo** (800-
637-2444; www.ellensburgrodeo.com),
Ellensburg Rodeo Arena. This is one
of the West's major rodeo events; book
early.

TRI-CITIES AREA

T he Tri-Cities is the area where the Yakima and Snake flow into the Columbia. But you won't find the name "Tri-Cities" on a map; it's just what everyone calls the agglomeration of Richland, Kennewick, and Pasco. Richland sits between the Yakima and Columbia, Pasco sits between the Columbia and Snake, and Kennewick is just south of the Columbia across from Pasco. There's a lot of water, bridges, and highways here.

The Tri-Cities resemble a piece of Los Angeles suburb thrown down onto the Washington desert—with good reason. Until 1940, nothing was here but farming hamlets and some far-flung ranches. In 1943 a huge tract was evacuated, including the entire village of White Bluffs, to create the Hanford Nuclear Reservation. Here, far from prying eyes but with a handy water source, the process of nuclear weapons fuel production was perfected, in coordination with atomic bomb development at the Los Alamos and Sandia labs. Richland grew up overnight to accommodate the physicists, engineers, construction workers, administrators, and support personnel for the massive project.

Plutonium is no longer produced at Hanford, but the environmental cleanup is ongoing, the cost of which has exceeded $1 billion. Occasionally, though, you can take tours of the formerly top-secret site (see *To See—Unique Adventures*). Meanwhile, the Hanford Reach, having been closed to the public for decades, preserves the only free-flowing stretch of the Columbia River and a number of endangered species.

The Tri-Cities' other claim to fame is Kennewick Man, a nearly complete human skeleton found in 1996 with a projectile point buried in his hip. Radiocarbon dating gave the remains an age of more than nine thousand years. Several local tribes promptly claimed Kennewick Man as an ancestor and filed for the right to rebury him immediately; anthropologists filed a countersuit for the right to study him. Currently, the remains repose at the Burke Museum in Seattle, where research will be allowed for a certain period of time. The remains are not on view, and the museum is very discreet regarding the research, which is still controversial in some circles (see *To See—Historic Sites*).

GUIDANCE Tri-Cities Visitor and Convention Bureau (509-735-8486 or 800-254-5824; www.visittri-cities.com), 1730 West Grandridge Boulevard, Kennewick 99336.

U.S. Department of Energy Hanford Site (www.hanford.gov), Richland. This isn't a place you can just walk up to, but two kinds of tours are available on certain dates: a tour of the B Reactor, pivotal to the Manhattan Project, and a general facility tour (including the B Reactor). For tour information, call Russ Fabre (509-373-2774) or Karen Sinclair (509-376-2151). Age and citizenship restrictions are enforced.

GETTING THERE Pasco, Kennewick, and Richland are at the junction of **I-82** and **US 395,** about 70 miles southeast of Yakima. **US 12** leads south from the Tri-Cities to Wallula Gap. West Richland and Benton City are on **WA 224; WA 240** leads northwest to Hanford.

Tri-Cities Airport (509-547-3378; www.portofpasco.com), 3601 North 20th Avenue, Pasco, is served by Delta, Horizon Air, United Express, and Allegiant.

AMTRAK (800-USA-RAIL; www.amtrak.com) runs a spur of the Empire Builder south from Spokane through Pasco, at 535 North First Avenue, to Portland, with bus links to Richland and West Richland.

Greyhound (509-547-3151 or 800-231-222; www.greyhound.com) stops in Pasco at 535 North First Avenue.

GETTING AROUND **Ben Franklin Transit** (509-547-5100; www.bft.org), 1000 Columbia Park Trail, Richland. Mon.–Sat. Bus service gets you around the Tri-Cities.

MEDICAL EMERGENCY **Kadlec Medical Center** (509-946-4611; www.kadlec .org), 888 Swift Boulevard, Richland.

Kennewick General Hospital (509-586-6111; www.kennewickgeneral.com), 900 South Auburn, Kennewick.

✴ To See

FARMERS' MARKETS **Market at the Parkway** (509-539-7229), at Richland Parkway, corner of Lee Boulevard and Jadwin Avenue, Richland. Open 9–1 Fri. June–Sept. Produce and crafts.

Pasco Farmers' Market (509-545-0738), at Fourth Avenue and West Columbia Street, Pasco. Open 8–12 Wed. and 8–1 Sat. May–Oct. The state's biggest open-air farmers' market.

Southridge Farmers' Market (509-528-4592), 3617 Plaza Way, Kennewick. Open 4–8 Thurs. June–Oct. Crafts, nuts, and baked goods as well as fruits and vegetables.

FOR FAMILIES *⌀* **Country Mercantile** (509-545-2192; www.countrymercantile .com), 232 Crestloch Road, Pasco; just off US 395. Open 7–7 daily. The mercantile is both farm stand and amusement center, selling fresh produce, jams, honeys, and all sorts of Northwest specialties. There's also a café and, in fall, a pumpkin patch, petting zoo, and corn maze.

⌀ ♿ **Playground of Dreams,** 6515 Columbia Drive Trail, Kennewick. Open dawn to dusk. With input from kids, two thousand volunteers built this 12,000-

square-foot playground in five days. Children can play on a pirate ship, castle, rope wall, and more. Handicapped-accessible.

HISTORIC SITES Columbia Park Trail, along Columbia Drive in Kennewick. This is the route of the earliest federal "highway" in the Northwest. In 1853 Congress voted for construction of military roads in the Oregon Territory. Secretary of War Jefferson Davis then ordered Captain George McClellan to build a road from old Fort Walla Walla (now underwater near Wallula Gap) to Puget Sound for the use of emigrants, who promptly started pouring in. One of the first groups was the Longmire party, which came over Naches Pass in the fall of 1853. Longmire eventually settled at the foot of Mount Rainier and built a health resort; the service complex near the park entrance is named for him (see the Mount Rainier National Park chapter in part 5, Line of Fire: The Cascades).

Kennewick Man. It happened near Columbia Park, near US 395 in Kennewick. The shore was lined with spectators watching the 1996 hydroplane races when a couple of young men noticed a human skull washing out of the riverbank. It turned out to be part of a human skeleton that at first was taken for that of a crime victim or perhaps an early settler. Soon, though, examiners found a projectile point in its hip, and the coroner ordered radiocarbon dating, which showed the remains to be more than nine thousand years old.

Local tribes claimed Kennewick Man as an ancestor and filed for the right to rebury him; anthropologists filed a countersuit for the right to study him. The matter was complicated by early reports that the skull had "Caucasoid" features—that is, it had some Caucasian-like features. This touched off a firestorm of protest in the tribal communities, who felt he was obviously one of theirs and should not be subjected to the indignities of research. Furthermore, they felt as though their heritage had been rifled enough. Years of litigation under the Native American Graves Protection and Repatriation Act, during which scientists were first forbidden, then allowed to study the bones, followed.

Currently the remains are at the Burke Museum in Seattle (see the Seattle chapter in part 3, Seattle Metropolitan Area), where research is allowed for a specified time, though this is still controversial. However, it's clear that Kennewick Man was a middle-aged male and that the projectile did not immediately kill him, for the bone was partly healed around the point. These are remarkable facts in themselves. Researchers take pains to point out that physically he was not recognizably "Caucasian" any more than he was recognizably "Indian." The find has galvanized American anthropology, redrawing theories of how the Americas were peopled and of human migration generally.

Lewis and Clark Interpretive Overlook, along Columbia Park Trail in Kennewick overlooking Bateman Island. This spot was as far as the explorers got up the Columbia; they arrived from down the Snake, camped at the confluence, and made a short sortie upstream before continuing their mission down to the sea. Four Corps of Discovery campsites have been identified in the Tri-Cities area, three used on their downstream trip and one on their return.

Sacajawea State Park (509-545-2361), 2503 Sacajawea Park Road, Pasco. On the nights of October 16–17, 1805, the Lewis and Clark party camped at this site at the confluence of the Snake and Columbia rivers. Here they hunted, fixed equipment, and met local inhabitants. This park commemorates their stay and particularly the Shoshone woman Sacajawea (or Sacagawea), wife of their interpreter, Toussaint Charbonneau (see *Wilder Places—Parks*). The **Sacajawea Interpretive Center** commemorates the journey of the only female member of the expedition; open 10–5 daily spring–Oct. An installation by Maya Lin, part of her **Confluence Project** series along the Columbia, tells the story of this place and its people in seven "Story Circles" at the park.

MUSEUMS ♂ **Columbia River Exhibition of History, Science and Technology Museum** (509-943-9000; www.crehst.org), 95 Lee Boulevard, Richland. Open 10–5 Mon.–Sat., 12–5 Sun. $4 adults, $3 seniors and children 7–16. At this particular location, history, science, and technology all have *nuclear* as a modifier. True, there's an exhibit on the scientific mission of Lewis and Clark and some presettlement history, but understandably the museum concentrates on nuclear technology and the story, scientific and social, of the Hanford nuclear site. Hands-on exhibits actually make the subject rather intelligible. Would you like to try a remote manipulator—a thing used to handle "hot" plutonium? You can (without the hot stuff). There's a 1963 nuclear reactor, waste tanks, and a Geiger counter comparing the radioactivity of things such as smoke detectors, fluorescent paint, various rocks, and other objects. Interesting, too, are exhibits on Hanford community life. Hanford quickly became a ready-made, albeit peculiar, city remote from any other, with government-issue housing allocated strictly according to social level. Plans and photos of these "alphabet houses" fill a hall downstairs, accompanied by comic-strip character Dupus Boomer, who provided an often wry, humorous commentary on Hanford life.

East Benton County Historical Society and Museum (509-582-7704), 205 Keewaydin Drive, Kennewick. Open 12–4 Tues.–Sat. $4 adults, $3 seniors, $1 children 5–17, active military free. The most impressive thing in this museum is the beautiful 1,100-square-foot petrified-wood floor, put together by a local man and donated to the museum. A small, discreet exhibit on the finding of Kennewick Man graces the entrance—he was found in this city, after all—but he currently resides at the Burke Museum in Seattle. Displays trace local history, from the petroglyphs out front to odd minerals to a 1920s dental office, and include donated memorabilia. It gives you pause when objects familiar to you in your youth turn up in a museum.

NATURAL WONDERS Wallula Gap, 12 miles south of Kennewick along US 12. As you drive south of the Tri-Cities, you'll notice a gap in the high benches along the Columbia, near the mouth of the Walla Walla River. This is Wallula Gap. At the end of the last Ice Age, when all the waters of prehistoric Lake Missoula came charging over the Columbia Plateau, this narrow gap was their only path off the plateau and seaward. In the resulting backup, water rose to a depth of 1,000 feet above the present site of the Tri-Cities, spreading up the river valleys far enough to flood Yakima and Walla Walla.

White Bluffs, about 20 miles along the Columbia River north of Richland. Rising several hundred feet above the river, the bluffs are a contrast to the dark basalt that generally covers the region. Formed of sediments deposited in prehistoric lakes 3 million to 5 million years ago, they contain many kinds of fossils: fish, plants, and prehistoric camels and horses. The bluffs are most easily seen from a boat ride up Hanford Reach.

SCENIC DRIVES Wallula Gap loop, about 70 miles via US 12, US 730, and US 395. This route follows the curve of the Columbia south to the Oregon border near Wallula Gap. If you look south from the gap, you'll see lines of windmills on the ridges along the Oregon-Washington border. This is the Stateline Energy Center, which opened in 2001 to harness the notorious Columbia Gorge winds and has become one of the world's biggest producers of wind-generated electricity. The route continues west into Oregon to Umatilla, crossing the Columbia at McNary Dam to follow US 295 back to the Tri-Cities.

UNIQUE ADVENTURES Hanford Site (Russ Fabre, 509-373-2774; Karen Sinclair, 509-376-2151; www.hanford.gov), off WA 240 north of Richland. Tours lasting four hours are offered several times a year. Free; preregistration, photo ID, and security check required; participants must be U.S. citizens age 18 or older. It's not every day you get to tour a top-secret military site. Well, it's not top-secret anymore, but it is still sensitive. Tours include fuel irradiation and processing sites and a walking tour of the B Reactor, as well as lots of austere desert countryside. You'll see the new waste treatment plant, too. Waste is a sensitive issue—not only the tailings that have to be dealt with somehow, but the million or so gallons of radioactive waste that have leaked into the soil and groundwater over the years. This is where most current Hanford efforts are centered.

✳ To Do

BICYCLING Several paved hiker-biker trails run along the Columbia River.

Columbia Park Trail, 6 miles from downtown Kennewick to the I-82 bridge.

Riverfront Trail, 7 miles from the I-82 bridge in Richland to Leslie Groves Park.

Sacajawea Heritage Trail, 23 miles of paved paths on both sides of the river joining both the Columbia Park and Riverfront trails.

Scott Cycle and Sports (509-374-8424), 704 South Ely Street, Kennewick. Check with them for bike rentals and trail information.

BOATING With three large rivers surrounding these three cities in the desert, boats abound, mostly of the motorized sort.

Columbia Park Marina (509-783-2196), 1776 Columbia Park Trail, Richland. Guest moorage and boat services.

CAMPING U.S. Corps of Engineers (509-547-2048) manages four camping parks in the area; reservations recommended.

Charbonneau, 642 Campground Road, Burbank; off WA 124 east of Pasco. Fifty-four paved hook-up sites. Closed in winter.

Fishhook, 4562 Fishhook Park Road, Prescott; off WA 124 northeast of Pasco. Fifty-three sites.

Hood, 592 Camp Circle, Burbank, 3 miles south of Pasco; take US 12 east, turn left on WA 124, and park on the left. Sixty-eight sites.

Windust, 5262 Burr Canyon Road, Pasco; on WA 263 northeast of Pasco. Twenty-eight sites, including four walk-in sites; no hook-ups. Closed in winter.

CANOEING AND KAYAKING Columbia Kayak Adventures (509-947-5901; www.columbiakayakadventures.com) offers custom tours of Hanford Reach and other waterways in this area. The informal Sunday Paddle Group meets at 9 AM for a short outing; some experience required.

GOLF Canyon Lakes Golf Course (509-582-3736), 3700 Canyon Lakes Drive, Kennewick. Eighteen holes.

Sun Willows Golf Course (509-545-3440), 2535 North 20th Avenue, Pasco. Eighteen holes.

West Richland Golf Course (509-967-2165), 4000 Fallon Drive, West Richland. Eighteen holes.

HIKING Within the Tri-Cities, walkers' options coincide with bikers' (see *Bicycling*). Here are a couple of locations farther afield.

Juniper Dunes Wilderness (Bureau of Land Management, 509-536-1200), off Pasco-Kahlotus Road, 15 miles northeast of Pasco; call for directions and access information. There are unmaintained trails here; bring your own water.

&. **McNary wildlife trail on the McNary National Wildlife Refuge** (509-546-8300), 1.9 miles; off US 12 southeast of Pasco. The first 700 feet of this trail leading to a bird-watching blind are wheelchair-accessible. See *Wilder Places—Wildlife Refuges*.

WINERY TOURS Red Mountain Appellation is located in the Tri-Cities area, with several wineries open at least seasonally. **Sunset Coach Tours** (800-941-2941) and **SUV Tours** (509-783-7060) offer tours, or devise your own visit with advice from **Washington Wine Tours** (www.washingtonwinetours.com). Here are three vintners.

Kiona Vineyards and Red Mountain Tasting Room (509-588-6716), 44612 North Sunset Road, Benton City. Open 12–5 daily.

Sandhill Winery (509-588-2699), 48313 North Sunset Road, Benton City. Open 11–5 Sat.–Sun.

Terra Blanca (509-588-6082), 34715 North Demoss Road, Benton City. Open 11–6 daily spring–fall; by appointment in winter.

✳ Wilder Places

PARKS Hanford Reach National Monument (509-546-8300; www.hanford reach.fws.gov), 51-mile stretch of the Columbia River. Open two hours before sunrise to two hours after sunset; call first about closures, washouts, and the like. Set aside to buffer the Hanford nuclear research facility, this is the last free-flowing stretch of the river above the tidal zone. *Remote* is the operative word. There are four restrooms (one year-round and three seasonal) on the 57,000 accessible acres and no other facilities. Access is mostly by boat, with two boat launches within the monument and another downstream in the Tri-Cities, and a few gravel roads. Despite this being the hottest and driest part of the Columbia Basin, the vast

Hanford Reach is rich in wildlife. Wintering waterfowl shelter on the river, an elk herd roams the riparian areas, and wily coyotes are plentiful. Certain areas may be closed at times for safety or to protect wildlife.

Sacajawea State Park (509-545-2361), 2503 Sacajawea Park Road, Pasco. Open 6:30 AM–dusk daily Mar. 15–Oct. This park commemorates the stay of Lewis and Clark in 1805 and is named for the Shoshone woman Sacajawea, wife of their interpreter, Toussaint Charbonneau. An interpretive center focusing on her role in the mission has just been renovated, with exhibits detailing the tribes that Lewis and Clark encountered on their journey from St. Louis to the Pacific.

WILDERNESS AREAS Juniper Dunes Wilderness (Bureau of Land Management, 509-536-1200), 7,140 acres; off Pasco-Kahlotus Road, 15 miles northeast of Pasco. This tract of desert features 130-foot-high sand dunes formed by the steady winds, as well as some of the last stands of western juniper in the state. If a desert escape from the Tri-Cities' sprawl sounds good, call for directions and access information. And bring water—there isn't any here.

WILDLIFE REFUGES McNary National Wildlife Refuge (509-547-4942), office at 64 Maple Street, Burbank; refuge off US 12 southeast of Pasco. This refuge's 15,000 acres of sloughs and backwaters harbor 100,000 waterfowl in the fall, and many other species generally. A trail leads to a bird-watching blind (see *To Do—Hiking*). As at most wildlife refuges, hunting is allowed in season.

✻ Lodging

The Tri-Cities see more visiting scientists and businesspeople than tourists (though that might change as the wineries in the region multiply). Most of the lodging, therefore, tends toward the institutional. The accommodations listed below are either exceptions or have redeeming local importance.

BED & BREAKFASTS

Kennewick
Cabin Suites Bed and Breakfast (509-374-3966; www.cabinsuites.com), 115 North Yelm. This regular ranch house in a residential neighborhood is just that—a home with three guest bedrooms, a dining room, two living rooms, and partial use of a kitchen. Bathrooms are shared. It's a friendly alternative to the mostly institutional accommodations in the area and is also convenient for groups. Whole house $205–265 (breakfast costs a few dollars extra); call for single-room rates.

GUESTHOUSES

Kennewick
✍ **Cherry Chalet** (509-783-6406; www.cherrychalet.com), 8101 West 10th Avenue. On the outskirts of the burbs, the Cherry Chalet sits on a 20-acre cherry farm (they also grow peaches, apples, and apricots). Leonard and Michele Sauer have run the house and farm for 12 years, creating a friendly, clean, and relaxed place with two bedrooms, one and a half baths, a living room, a kitchen, and a dining room. Stroll around the orchard or sit on the patio watching the koi. The new Sunrise Chalet has one bedroom, a bathroom, a dining area, and a deck. Cherry Chalet $160; Sunrise Chalet $140.

Richland
✍ **The Guest House at PNNL** (509-943-0400; www.pnl.gov/guesthouse), 620 Battelle Boulevard. If you have

business at Hanford or Pacific Northwest National Labs—even if you're a student intern—you can stay at this guesthouse. Rooms range from studios to small apartments to multiroom suites. It looks sort of like a college dorm, but it's comfortable enough, and it's hard to beat the rates. Children are welcome. Studios $93–95; apartments $97; multiroom suites $33–42 per bed; discounts for extended stays.

HOTELS
Kennewick
Clover Island Inn (866-586-0542; www.cloverislandinn.com), 435 Clover Island Drive. Technically on an island, the inn sits between the Blue Bridge and the landmark Cable Bridge. It has its own dock, and moorage is free for guests; other amenities include an outdoor pool, a spa, and a fitness room. Most of the 151 rooms have water views. Rates include continental breakfast. Queen or double-queen rooms $84–114; suites $199–349.

Richland
❦ **Red Lion Hotel** (509-946-7611 or 800-RED-LION; www.redlion.com), 802 George Washington Way. Right on the Columbia River, this 149-room Red Lion has the usual amenities from pool to fitness room to restaurant (see *Where to Eat*), plus it adjoins the 7-mile Riverfront Trail (see *To Do—Bicycling*). Pets welcome. From $130. There are also Red Lion hotels in Kennewick (509-783-0611), 1101 North Columbia Center Boulevard, and Pasco (509-547-0701), 2525 North 20th Avenue.

✳ Where to Eat
DINING OUT
Kennewick
The Cedars (509-582-2143), 355 Clover Island Drive. Open 5–9 daily.

Next to the Clover Island Inn (see *Lodging*), the Cedars enjoys the same river views. One of the more elegant venues in town, it's most appreciated for its steaks and prime rib but also serves pasta and seafood.

EATING OUT
Richland
Anthony's Homeport Columbia Point (509-946-3474), 550 Columbia Point Drive. Open 11–9:30 Mon.–Fri., 11–10:30 Fri.–Sat., 10–9:30 Sun. On the waterfront, like all Anthony's sites, it offers the same family menu and quality seafood. Complimentary daytime guest moorage is available, too.

Atomic Ale Brewpub (509-946-5465), 1015 Lee Boulevard. Open 11–10 Mon.–Thurs., 11–11 Fri.–Sat., 11–8 Sun. Across from Monterosso's (see below), with which it shares an owner, the brewpub offers its own handcrafted ales, such as Plutonium Porter and Half-Life Hefeweizen (businesses here get quite a lot of mileage out of the local nuclear industry). It's also known for its wood-fired pizzas, soups, and sandwiches served in a small-pub atmosphere. It's actually a remodeled A&W, but you wouldn't know it.

Monterosso's Italian Restaurant (509-946-4525), 1026 Lee Boulevard. Open for lunch 11–2 Tues.–Fri.; dinner 5–9 Mon.–Thurs., 5–10 Fri.–Sat. Monterosso's has been cooking in a 1947 Pullman car since 1995. The menu of pasta, homemade soups, veal, poultry, and seafood dishes provides pleasantly satisfying yet relaxed dining. Forties music plays in the background, and the car sways slightly if someone walks by.

Ripples Riverside Bar and Grill (509-946-7611), 802 George Washington Way (at the Red Lion Hotel—see *Lodging*). Open for breakfast, lunch, and dinner daily. Ripples serves steaks, soups, seafood, and general Northwest cuisine. It also has some of the better river views in town; since the Tri-Cities are a major port, much of the riverside has a rather industrial look.

✳ Entertainment

MUSIC **Battelle Performing Arts Center** (509-943-2787; www .performingabc.org), 1177 Jadwin Avenue, Richland. This is a clearing-house for various performing arts groups; shows range from musicals to classical music to classic films.

Mid-Columbia Symphony Orchestra (509-943-6602) performs at the Battelle Performing Arts Center (see above).

Richland Light Opera Company (509-967-5571; rloc.org), 5994 West Van Giesen, Richland, presents light opera in venues around Richland.

Three Rivers Folklife Society (509-528-2215; www.3rfs.org) sponsors the Tumbleweed Folk Music Festival each September, plus monthly concerts, song circles, and open-mike sessions.

✳ Special Events

September: **Pasco Fiery Foods Festival** (509-545-0738), Fourth Avenue and Lewis Street, Pasco. On the second weekend of September, two days of red-hot recipes culminate in a salsa contest.

December: **Christmas Light Boat Parade** (509-737-1166), Kennewick to Richland. Lighted, decorated boats parade from Clover Island to Howard Amon Park and back; viewing along the Columbia River.

WALLA WALLA AND THE PALOUSE

There are places where loess is definitely more. One of them is the Palouse, where glacial silt set down by Ice Age floods was blown about and eventually deposited in steep, rounded hills of deep soil covering 10,000 square miles of southeastern Washington and northern Idaho. This topsoil, called *loess,* has made the region a terrific producer of wheat and peas. The whole region turns bright green in spring as the new shoots come up (and then gold and then brown; it's dry even if it is fertile).

It wasn't for farming, though, that settlers came here. First a few missionaries arrived, including the ill-fated Whitmans, who wished to bring salvation to the Indians. Their presence encouraged early emigrants on the Oregon Trail, and their murder brought a greater military presence. Gold was then discovered in the nearby Idaho hills, and Walla Walla sprang up largely as a miners' supply center. It did quite well—well enough to draw immigrants from Germany, Italy, and Russia, who settled down to farming when the gold rush was over. Main Street is still lined with nicely preserved shops and banks from that eager era. And now, perhaps, the neighborhood is poised for a new burst of prosperity as vineyards spread up the Walla Walla Valley and, with them, the wine enthusiasts who come to visit.

GUIDANCE

Dayton Chamber of Commerce (509-382-4825 or 800-882-6299; www.historic dayton.com), 166 East Main Street, Dayton 99328.

Pullman Chamber of Commerce (509-334-3565 or 800-ENJOYIT; www.pullman chamber.com), 415 North Grand Avenue, Pullman 99163.

Tourism Walla Walla (877-WWVISIT; www.wallawalla.org), 8 South Second Avenue, Walla Walla 99362.

Umatilla National Forest Headquarters (541-278-3716; www.fs.fed.us/r6/uma), 2517 SW Hailey Avenue, Pendleton, OR 97801. District offices include **Pomeroy Ranger District** (509-843-1891), 71 West Main Street, Pomeroy 99347; **Walla Walla Ranger District** (509-522-6290), 1415 West Rose Street, Walla Walla 99362.

Walla Walla Chamber of Commerce (509-525-0850 or 877-WWVISIT; www .wwchamber.com), 29 East Sumach Street, Walla Walla 99362.

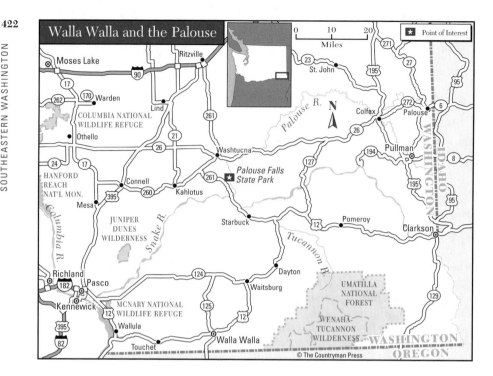

Walla Walla and the Palouse

GETTING THERE Walla Walla is accessible by **US 12** from the east and west and **WA 125** from the north and south. US 12 heads northeast through Waitsburg, Dayton, and Clarkston on the Idaho border. At Clarkston, **US 195** heads north to Pullman and Colfax. From Colfax, **WA 272** heads east to Palouse. From US 195 north of Colfax, **WA 23** heads through St. John to **I-90** at Sprague. Many other small highways connect little towns in the Palouse.

Pullman-Moscow Regional Airport (509-338-3223), 3200 Airport Complex North, Pullman.

Walla Walla Regional Airport (509-525-3100), 310 A Street, Walla Walla. Horizonair serves the area from this airport.

AMTRAK (800-USA-RAIL; www.amtrak.com) stops in Colfax at 610 South Main Street (Ace Hardware) and in Pullman at 1002 NW Nye Street.

Greyhound (800-231-2222; www.greyhound.com) stops in Colfax (509-397-4102), 610 South Main Street, and Pullman (509-334-1412), 1002 NW Nye Street.

GETTING AROUND **Valley Transit** (509-525-9140; www.valleytransit.com) serves Walla Walla and College Place with eight bus lines.

MEDICAL EMERGENCY **Pullman Regional Hospital** (509-332-2541), 1125 Washington Street, Pullman.

St. Mary Medical Center (509-525-3320; www.smmc.com), 401 West Poplar, Walla Walla.

Tri-State Memorial Hospital (509-758-5511), 1221 Highland Avenue, Clarkston.

Walla Walla General Hospital (509-525-0480; www.wwgh.com), 1025 South Second Avenue, Walla Walla.

✳ To See

CULTURAL SITES You'll see lots of **public art** in downtown Walla Walla. The city has been named one of the country's "100 Best Small Art Towns."

Walla Walla Community College (509-522-2500), 500 Tausick Way, Walla Walla; east of town. This institution is one of three colleges in this small agricultural town.

Walla Walla University (800-541-8900), College Place. This whole municipality west of town was set aside by Walla Walla's founders for higher education. Visitors are welcome to stroll the campus of this Seventh-Day Adventist institution.

Whitman College (509-527-5111; www.whitman.edu), 345 Boyer Avenue, Walla Walla. Whitman College was founded in 1859 in memory of Narcissa and Marcus Whitman, though it remains staunchly nonsectarian. With its old trees and neoclassical buildings, it is a sort of archetype of the rural university and one of the more highly regarded in the Northwest.

FARMERS' MARKETS ✍ **Walla Walla Farmers' Market** (509-520-3647), Crawford Park at Fourth Avenue and Main Street Open 9–1 Sat. late May–late Oct. Fresh produce and goodies are accompanied by live music. In summer look for Walla Walla onions, a sweet variety descended from seeds brought over by a Corsican immigrant.

FARMS AND GARDENS **Iris Test Garden** (509-751-9367; www.iristg.com), 16047A WA 12, Clarkston. Open daily mid-Apr.–mid-June. More than two thousand varieties of irises bloom on 12 acres. You're welcome to come and look, have a picnic at one of the tables, and maybe buy some rhizomes for your own garden.

FOR FAMILIES ✍ **Children's Museum of Walla Walla** (509-526-7529; www.cmww.org), 77 Wainwright Place, Walla Walla. Open 10–5 Thurs.–Sat., 12–5 Sun. $3.50. Intriguing kid-oriented exhibits and activities include participatory theater, a "doctor's office" where your child can actually play doctor under supervision, a building center, and exhibits on science, Indian life, and more.

HISTORIC HOMES **Perkins House** (509-397-3690), Colfax. Open 1–4 Thurs. and Sun. in summer. Free. This site includes the cabin built by James Perkins in 1870, which is the oldest building extant in Whitman County, and his restored 1886 Victorian house.

Walla Walla has nearly one hundred fine homes dating from 1865 to 1930. Prominent among them is the Kirkman House Museum (see *Museums*), but most are still privately owned. Most also are close to downtown, and a **self-guided walking tour** is available through the chamber of commerce (see *Guidance*). Other self-guided tours are available for Fort Walla Walla (see *Historic Sites*), downtown Walla Walla, and Pioneer Park (see *Wilder Places—Parks*).

HISTORIC SITES Downtown

Walla Walla has won awards for historical preservation and revitalization. A stroll down Main Street will take you past the following, as well as many other dignified veterans of Walla Walla's mercantile era:

Baker Boyer National Bank, the first skyscraper in town.

Liberty Theater (now Macy's), a whimsical 1917 building.

Die Brücke (1903), called this because it bridges Mill Creek.

Fort Walla Walla (509-527-4527), adjacent to Fort Walla Walla Museum (see *Museums*). Open 7 AM–11 PM daily. Free. This early trading and military post had three incarnations. The last, of which many buildings are still extant, was built in 1858 on the site of the current Veterans Administration Medical Center. A short walk (brochure available from the chamber of commerce; see *Guidance*) takes you through the parade grounds and past white wooden barracks and officers' quarters, as well as the chapel, stables, and granary. A military cemetery lies just below the museum.

HISTORIC DOWNTOWN WALLA WALLA

⚓ **Historic Dayton Depot** (509-382-2026; www.daytonhistoricdepot.org), 222 East Commercial Street, Dayton. Open 10–12 and 1–5 Wed.–Sat. May–Oct.; 11–4 Wed.–Sat. Nov.–Apr. $5 adults, children under 12 and those working on school projects free. This, the oldest train station in Washington, was in use from 1881 to 1971.

Whitman Mission National Historical Site (509-529-2761), on US 12, 7 miles west of Walla Walla. Grounds open dawn to dusk daily; visitors center open 8–6 daily in summer, 8–4:30 daily rest of the year. $3 adults, children under 17 free; free with National Parks Pass or America the Beautiful Pass; ticket good for seven days. In 1836, missionaries Marcus and Narcissa Whitman and John and Eliza Spalding trekked from New York to the Oregon Country to preach the Gospel. Narcissa and Eliza were the first non-Native women to make the transcontinental crossing. The Spaldings settled in what became eastern Idaho, while Marcus and Narcissa built their mission on this site near Fort Walla Walla. A visitors center details the sad history: Despite Narcissa's school and Marcus's medical practice, the latter's fiery sermons did not sit well with the Indians. When a measles epidemic killed half the Cayuse Indians in 1847, he was accused of poisoning them, and the Whitmans were massacred, along with their helpers and several children they had adopted. On the grounds, you can trace the outlines of the mission buildings. A trail leads to the hilltop obelisk commemorating the dead and another to the mass grave in a grove below.

MUSEUMS Asotin County Historical Museum (509-243-4659, Third and Fillmore streets, Asotin. Open 10–2 Tues.–Sat. Mar.–Oct. Donation accepted. Here you'll find an 1881 home, an 1882 organ, a schoolhouse, and an antique barge.

Bruce Memorial Museum (509-337-6157 or 509-337-6631), 318 Main Street, Waitsburg. Open 1–4 Fri.–Sat. June–Sept. Donation accepted. This restored 1883 mansion is just 21 miles northeast of Walla Walla.

Fort Walla Walla Museum (509-525-7703; www.fortwallawallamuseum.org), 755 Myra Road, Walla Walla. Open 10–5 daily Apr.–Oct.; living-history performances Sat.–Sun. afternoon June–Aug. $7 adults, $6 seniors and students, $3 children over six. Set in the green expanse of Fort Walla Walla Park (see *Wilder Places—Parks*), the museum's five modern gray rectangles arranged in a semicircle give an impression of the fort that once was here. The museum's mission is to portray and celebrate the region's pioneer heritage through varied and sometimes unusual exhibits: One entire building is occupied by a 33-mule-team combine, complete with life-sized sculpted mules. Themes run from Lewis and Clark, who passed nearby, to early commerce, transport, agriculture, military history, and daily life. Particularly affecting is the collection of 17 pioneer-era buildings that have been moved to the site. They include an 1867 schoolhouse, several cabins, an Italian immigrant homestead, and a frontier doctor's office, where an 1899 slip prescribes Bromo-Seltzer.

Kirkman House Museum (509-529-4373; www.kirkmanhousemuseum.org), 214 North Colville Street, Walla Walla. Open 10–4 Wed.–Sat., 1–4 Sun. $5 adults, $20 families. William Kirkman, an English immigrant who owned an unimaginably large ranch extending over much of southeastern Washington, built this massive Italianate brick house for his family. It remained their home from 1880, when the town underwent dramatic economic expansion, to 1919. In the 1970s, it was restored as a period house museum and contains some of the original furnishings. The **Walla Walla Textile Artists** demonstrate home textile production typical of the period in the adjacent **Weaver's Cottage** during museum hours.

Palus Museum (509-382-4820), 305 East Main Street, Dayton; 10 miles east of Waitsburg. Open 1–4 Fri.–Sat. Donation accepted. The museum houses a collection of Palouse Indian artifacts and a room on Lewis and Clark's passage through what is now the small town of Dayton on their way back east.

THE WHITMAN MISSION NATIONAL HISTORICAL SITE NEAR WALLA WALLA

Roy M. Chatters Newspaper and Printing Museum (509-878-1842 or 509-878-1742), Route 1, Box 6-A, Palouse 99161. Open by appointment only. Donation accepted. What a great name for a newspaper museum! Roy Chatters was a nuclear engineer with a passion for antique printing equipment. His museum displays old linotype machines, a flatbed press, and local archives back to the 1880s. It's now a branch of the Whitman County Historical Society.

Washington State University Museums

Several museums at WSU in Pullman bring art and science to the Palouse. Admission is free, but donations are accepted.

ᚷ **Museum of Art–WSU** (509-335-1910; www.wsu.edu/artmuse). Open 10–4 Mon.–Sat., 10–7 Thurs. in summer; 12–4 Tues.–Sat. fall–spring; closed July 3–Aug. 24. Presents changing exhibits in different media.

WSU Conner Museum (509-335-3553). Open 8–5 daily. This natural history museum features mounted and preserved specimens.

WSU Museum of Anthropology (509-335-3441). Open 9–4 Mon.–Fri. during academic year. Presents both physical and social anthropology, including prehistory of the Snake River area.

NATURAL WONDERS Champion trees. No sooner had Walla Walla become a bustling little town than its citizens nostalgically planted trees, remembering no doubt the glades of Missouri, New York, and even Italy. They brought in trees from Puget Sound, the nearby Blue Mountains, and the East Coast. The result is that the city has more than 50 state champion trees. They're concentrated mostly in Pioneer Park (see *Wilder Places—Parks*) and on the campus of Whitman College (see *Cultural Sites*) and include a 124-foot **black poplar;** a 99-foot **sycamore,** with a 16-foot circumference; and an 86-foot **northern catalpa,** which is also a national champion.

Snake River Canyon, along the Washington-Idaho border from Oregon to Clarkston. Also known as **Hell's Canyon,** this wild gorge extends from deep in Oregon north to Clarkston; with a drop from 9,000-foot peaks to 500 feet at the bottom, it's considered the deepest canyon in the United States. Outfitters in Asotin and Clarkston (see *To Do—Boating*) will be happy to take you down the rapids in a raft or jet boat, where you might be observed by bighorn sheep and mule deer. Fishing is also popular here, especially for sturgeon.

SCENIC DRIVES Palouse Scenic Byway, 208-mile paved loop with several spurs, starting in Pullman. Take WA 27 north through Palouse to Oakesdale (spur: continue north to Tekoa); WA 271 north to Rosalia; and US 195 south through Colfax (spurs: WA 26 west to Hooper, WA 272 east to Palouse) to Pullman (spurs: continue south to Clarkston, WA 194 west to Almota). Highways radiate like spokes from Pullman to the small towns of the rolling Palouse, the loess-covered breadbasket of Washington's far southeast. On or near the byway are Palouse Falls State Park, with its 200-foot cascade (see *Wilder Places—Parks*), historic homes and museums; and Washington State University in Pullman.

WINERY TOURS The Walla Walla Valley was the state's second federally recognized wine-growing area. Growth has been exponential; from one winery in 1977, the industry has mushroomed to 70, producing some quite distinguished wines. For a list of wineries and driving routes, contact **Walla Walla Valley Wine Alliance** (509-526-3117; wallawallawine.com), 13½ East Main Street, Walla Walla. Among the better-known wineries are these:

Canoe Ridge (509-527-0819; www.canoeridgevineyard.com), 1102 West Cherry Street, Walla Walla.

L'Ecole No. 41 (509-525-0940; www.lecole.com), 41 Lowden School Road, Lowden.

✷ To Do

BICYCLING Walla Walla's level terrain and low traffic volumes create a bike-friendly environment. A **map of bicycle routes** in and around town is available at the chamber of commerce (see *Guidance*).

Bicycle Barn (509-529-7860), 1503 East Isaacs, Walla Walla. Contact them for trail information.

BOATING Aardvark's Adventure Company (800-564-9737; www.aardvarks adventureco.com), 7357 Snake River Road, Asotin. Offers boat rentals.

Beamers Hells Canyon Tours (800-522-6966; www.hellscanyontours.com), 1451 Bridge Street, Clarkston. Full-day and half-day boat tours of Hells Canyon.

CAMPING Chief Timothy Park (509-751-0250 or 877-444-6777), on US 12 just west of Clarkston. An Army Corps of Engineers park. Sixteen tent sites, 33 RV sites, and 17 tent or RV sites.

&. **Fields Spring State Park** (509-256-3332), on WA 129 south of Clarkston. Twenty tent sites, 2 eight-person tepees, and 1 cabin sleeping four (Apr.–Oct.); ADA restroom. Call park office to reserve cabin or tepees; no reservations for tent sites.

Lewis and Clark Trail State Park (509-337-6457), on US 12 between Waitsburg and Dayton, 25 miles northeast of Walla Walla. Twenty-four standard sites Apr.–Sept.; 17 primitive sites open in winter.

Lyons Ferry Park (509-751-0240), on WA 261 just south of Palouse Falls. Two tent sites and 49 tent or RV sites without hook-ups. Closed in winter.

&. **Palouse Falls State Park** (509-646-9218), on WA 261, 36 miles northwest of Dayton. Ten tent sites, one ADA-compliant; toilet. No reservations.

Umatilla National Forest's Pomeroy District (see *Guidance*) has 10 first-come, first-served campgrounds, most without water. Among them are these:

Alder Thicket, on FR 40, 18 miles south of Pomeroy. Five sites; toilet.

Big Springs, on FR 4200-125, 26 miles south of US 12 at Pomeroy. Eight campsites; toilet. This is cool in the hot season.

Godman, on FR 46 south of Dayton. Eight tent sites; access to the Wenaha-Tucannon Wilderness (see *Wilder Places—Wilderness Areas*) and a spring (bring purifier).

Tucannon, on FR 4700-160, south of US 12 between Dayton and Pomeroy. Eighteen sites along the Tucannon River; popular with fishermen. Fee charged.

GOLF **Colfax Golf Course** (509-397-2122; www.colfaxgolf.com), 2402 North Cedar Street, Colfax. Nine holes.

Pheasant Creek Golf Course (866-430-4653), 1432 Touchet North Road, Touchet; on US 12 west of Walla Walla. Nine holes.

Touchet Valley Golf Course (509-382-4851), 209 North Pine Street, Dayton. Nine holes.

Veterans Memorial Golf Course (509-527-4507), 201 East Rees Avenue, Walla Walla. Eighteen holes.

HIKING **Bill Chipman Palouse Trail,** 7 miles from Pullman to Moscow, Idaho; trailhead on Bishop Boulevard behind the Quality Inn in Pullman. Open dawn to dusk daily. This level path is open to hikers, bikers, and skaters. Two restrooms, emergency phones, and interpretive signs are provided for your convenience.

Mill Creek trails, 20 miles; access is from Rooks Park, off Mill Creek Road, 6 miles east of Walla Walla. At 612 acres, Mill Creek, a water resource project of the U.S. Army Corps of Engineers (509-527-7160), is the largest tract of public land in Walla Walla County (see *Wilder Places—Parks*). The trails—some paved and some not—run mostly through grassland along the creek and canal and around Bennington Lake. It's shared by runners, cyclists, walkers, and skaters, so courtesy is called for.

Umatilla National Forest (see *Guidance*), sprawled over the Blue Mountains between Walla Walla and the Idaho border, and its **Wenaha-Tucannon Wilderness** (see *Wilder Places—Wilderness Areas*) offer miles of remote hiking, camping, and skiing. Access is from US 12 at Dayton or Pomeroy, or from WA 129 at Asotin. Some easier hikes include these:

Oregon Butte, 3 miles; from the Tepee trailhead on FR 4608, about 28 miles southeast of Dayton. A moderate ascent.

Squaw Spring, 3.5 miles; from the end of FR 4030. A gentle walk.

WINTER SPORTS **Ski Bluewood** (509-382-4725; www.bluewood.com), on FR 64, 21 miles southeast of Dayton. Bluewood, at an altitude of 5,600 feet, has two lifts, 24 runs at all difficulty levels, and a half-pipe for snowboarders.

Umatilla National Forest (see *Guidance*), which straddles the Oregon-Washington border, has plenty of opportunities for cross-country skiing on closed roads and designated trails.

✳ Wilder Places

PARKS **Camp William T. Wooten State Park** (509-843-1080), on FR 47 south of US 12 at Pomeroy. This "camp" centers on an Environmental Education Center run by Washington State Parks on 160 acres leased from the Washington Fish and Wildlife Service within a remote wildlife area. It offers hiking, canoeing, archery, and tennis, as well as group accommodations.

Chief Timothy Park (509-751-0250), on US 12 just west of Clarkston. Another Corps of Engineers park, this one near the confluence of the Snake and Clearwater rivers, has boat launches, a swimming area, a campground, and picnic sites. It is also slated to house one of a series of **Confluence Project** works by architect Maya Lin, who is creating monuments along the Snake and Columbia rivers commemorating contacts between Lewis and Clark and the Native peoples.

Fields Spring State Park (509-256-3332), on WA 129 south of Clarkston. This park's 792 forested acres are deep in the Blue Mountains. Open in summer for hiking, biking, wildlife and wildflower viewing, and camping, and in winter for snowshoeing and cross-country skiing. Paragliders use the park's 4,500-foot Puffer Butte.

⚲ **Fort Walla Walla Park** (509-527-4527), Dalles Military and Myra Road, Walla Walla. Surrounding Fort Walla Walla Museum (see *To See—Museums*), this 208-acre park includes the original military cemetery, a wildlife preserve, playgrounds, and a bicycle trail.

Lewis and Clark Trail State Park (509-337-6457), along US 12, 25 miles northeast of Walla Walla. This is a small 37-acre park along the Touchet River whose old-growth ponderosas and cottonwoods are a welcome relief from the treeless uplands. Situated on an Indian trading route that led from the Rockies to the Pacific Coast, this beautiful spot also witnessed the Corps of Discovery passing through in 1806 on their way home. Remains of some early homesteads are still visible. Summer interpretive programs include "living history" enactments of the Lewis and Clark journey. Swimming, walking trails, picnic sites, and camping are available.

Lyons Ferry Park (509-751-0240), on WA 261 just south of Palouse Falls. See *To Do—Camping*.

Mill Creek (509-527-7160), 3211 Reservoir Road, Walla Walla. Open 5 AM–10 PM; Rooks Park unit open 7 AM–sunset. This 612-acre tract of public land surrounding Mill Creek Dam and Bennington Lake is run by the U.S. Army Corps of Engineers. Looping around the lake and stream are 20 miles of paved hiking and biking trails (see *To Do—Hiking*). Egrets and other wild birds favor the spot.

&. *⚲* **Palouse Falls State Park,** off WA 261, 36 miles northwest of Dayton. Like Dry Falls south of Grand Coulee, Palouse Falls drops from a barren plateau down a gorge created by the Missoula Floods of twelve thousand or so years ago. But this falls is not dry; the cascade roars down its 200-foot drop, especially in spring and early summer, as it apparently has since the last Ice Age, oblivious to its desolate surroundings. A 0.25-mile ADA trail leads to an overlook. Camping and picnic tables are available, too.

Pioneer Park, bordered by Whitman, Alder, and Division streets near downtown Walla Walla. Venerable trees shade a 58-acre greensward encompassing a bandstand, an exotic bird aviary, a children's playground, and pleasant paths, all through the foresight of citizens who set aside this cow pasture in 1901 and planted trees both native and exotic. The park contains numerous state champions (see *To See— Natural Wonders*).

Steptoe Butte State Park, off US 195 north of Colfax. Day use only. A 3,612-foot-tall butte provides 200-mile views.

WILDERNESS AREAS Wenaha-Tucannon Wilderness, 177,465 acres; access via forest roads in Umatilla National Forest (see *Guidance*).

✳ Lodging

BED & BREAKFASTS

Clarkston Area

The Churchyard Inn (509-229-3200 or 800-227-2804; www.churchyardinn .com), 206 St. Boniface Street, Uniontown. First a parish house, then a convent, and now a B&B, the inn sits next to St. Boniface Church in quiet Uniontown, just north of Clarkston via US 195. The three-floor, cross-gabled house offers six guest rooms, most with private baths, gleaming woodwork, and antiques. Rates include a full breakfast; dinner available by arrangement. Consult about children and pets. $95–130.

Dayton

The Purple House Bed and Breakfast (509-382-3159 or 800-486-2574; www.purplehousebnb.com), 415 East Clay Street. It's actually more of a lilac color, with white trim; with its Queen Anne railings and fretwork, it looks like a candy house. Dr. Pietrzycki, literally on the frontiers of medicine, built it in 1882. Today its amenities include a library, a TV room, and an outdoor heated pool. One upstairs guest room has a shared bath; the downstairs master suite and carriage house have private baths. Rates include breakfast; other meals available by arrangement. $95–135.

Walla Walla

Green Gables Inn Bed and Breakfast (509-876-4373; www.greengables innnw.com), 922 Bonsella Street. The 6,000-square-foot Craftsman house has been through several permutations since its 1909 birth—as a private home, nurses' quarters for the nearby hospital, and, since a careful 1990 restoration, a capacious bed & breakfast. Five bedrooms and an apartment have all modern and antique comforts. Children under 12 welcome in the Carriage House apartment. No pets.

$139–225; minimum stay required some weekends.

Inn at Blackberry Creek (509-522-5233 or 877-522-5233; www.innat blackberrycreek.com), 1126 Pleasant Street. This white 1912 farmhouse now sits in a quiet residential neighborhood, screened from the street and neighbors by mature trees. A spring-fed creek fills a small pond in the backyard. Four guest rooms, each with a private bath, are quietly furnished with period antiques. Rates include a full breakfast; coffee, tea, and cookies are always on tap! Children over 12 welcome. $128–239; two-night minimum some weekends.

Wine Country Inn (509-386-3592), 915 Alvarado Terrace. A cozy 1930s house a couple of blocks from Whitman College, the inn has two pleasant two-bedroom suites. Rates include a full breakfast. $150–250.

CAMPGROUNDS

Walla Walla

Blue Valley RV Park (509-525-8282; www.bluevalleyrv.com), 50 West George Street. Sixty sites with full hook-ups and 21 tent sites, plus a laundry room, cable TV, Wi-Fi, and a common area with games, a book exchange, and a fireplace.

RV Resort Four Seasons (509-529-6072), 1440 Dalles Military Road. Eighty-nine sites with full hook-ups, plus a creek-side picnic area, cable TV, and wireless Internet access, but no tent camping.

HOTELS

Dayton

♿ **Weinhard Hotel** (509-382-4032), 235 East Main Street. Jacob Weinhard came to Dayton in 1880 to go into the brewing business, having learned it from his uncle Henry in Portland. He prospered to the point of opening a fine hotel in 1890, which stayed in use till 1963. When the hotel was renovated in 1994, as much as possible of the original woodwork was used, so that guests really feel they have gone back in time. The opulent lobby contains a grand piano and period furniture, while the 15 rooms have all the comforts of Victorian America plus some extras, such as private bathrooms, cable TV, and computer connections. $137.38 with tax in summer; discounted in winter.

Walla Walla

  ❧ **The Marcus Whitman Hotel** (509-525-2200 or 866-826-9422; www.marcuswhitmanhotel.com), 6 West Rose Street. You might wonder who stayed in this tall luxury hotel after it opened in 1928—after all, Walla Walla wasn't exactly the center of the universe. Led by the president of Baker Boyer National Bank (he of the downtown skyscraper; see *To See— Historic Sites*), the local business community was persuaded that a hotel and convention center was just the ticket to enhance prosperity. Remarkably, it succeeded; guests over the years included Presidents Eisenhower and Johnson, Louis Armstrong, and other celebrities. After a decline, Kyle Mussman bought it in 1999 and restored it to its opulent glory, with lots of gold leaf and deep carpets. The original tower contains two-room suites, while the new wing has smaller but still spacious, luxurious rooms, all with Italian furnishings (and all in shades of wine); several are ADA-compliant. There's also an on-site dining room (see *Where to Eat*). Rates include a "hot and healthy" breakfast. Pet-friendly rooms available. $119–230.

MOTELS

Walla Walla

Colonial Motel (509-529-1220; www .colonial-motel.com), 2279 East Isaacs Avenue. If you just need a clean, simple room, the 17-unit Colonial Motel is for you. Rooms do have cable TV, free Wi-Fi, refrigerators, air-conditioning, coffee machines, access to a barbecue area, and microwaves. Owners Dick and Carolyn Tuttle unobtrusively make sure you're safe and comfortable. $59–80.

RANCHES

Clarkston Area

❧ **Premier Alpacas of the Palouse** (509-229-3655; www.premieralpacas .com), Box 122, Uniontown 99179. This 100-year-old farm among rolling hills now raises and breeds alpacas. You can take part in farm activities or not, as you choose, but in any case you'll enjoy the peace and quiet of the rural Palouse. The original bunkhouse is now a guesthouse sleeping up to four, with a full bathroom and kitchenette. There's also an antiquesfurnished guest room in the main house with a designated bathroom across the hall. You have a choice of a continental or farm breakfast. Children welcome. No pets. Guesthouse $85–130; guest room $70–84.

✳ Where to Eat
DINING OUT

Dayton

Patit Creek Restaurant (509-382-2625), 725 East Dayton Street. Open for lunch and dinner Wed.–Fri., dinner only Sat. It may be in tiny Dayton, but it's got a first-class reputation for classic French cuisine and wild game. Reservations recommended.

Walla Walla

Backstage Bistro (509-526-0690; www.backstage-bistro.com), 230 East Main Street. Open for lunch and dinner Mon.–Sat., dinner only Sun. Downtown Walla Walla doesn't exactly hum on weekday nights, but there's a buzz inside the Backstage Bistro. The small, irregular space has a burgundy color scheme (there's a lot of that in wine country), an espresso bar, and cheerful, busy waitstaff. "Our goal is to provide so much joy and delight that people have no choice but to come back," they proclaim. After trying their fresh, crunchy spinach-mandarin salad and perfect chicken-rosemary ravioli, it might be hard not to. The menu's not big—several each of salads, pasta dishes, barbecue, and fine meats—but the ingredients are so fresh and prepared with such evident care that it's more than adequate. Live music several nights a month.

The Marc Restaurant (509-525-2200), at the Marcus Whitman Hotel (see *Lodging*). Open from 6 PM daily. Decorated in shades of burgundy, the Marc stocks about a hundred Walla Walla and regional wines. Chef Antonio Campolio puts together imaginative seasonal menus with products from local organic farms as well as wild seafood.

Whitehouse-Crawford (509-525-2222; www.whitehousecrawford.com), 55 West Cherry. Open 5–10 Wed.–Mon. Set in an old planing mill—another example of preservation by transformation—Whitehouse-Crawford emphasizes fresh, local produce with fine regional fish and meat. The menu lists as many desserts as main dishes. Reservations recommended.

EATING OUT

Pullman

Swilly's (509-334-3395; www.swillys.com), 200 NE Kamiaken. Open for lunch 11–3 Mon.–Fri.; dinner 5–9:30 Mon.–Sat. The name may be counterintuitive for a restaurant, but Swilly's is a fixture in downtown Pullman, well loved for its versatile menu, running from hearty soups and steak to mussels

and Brazilian stew. In good weather, you can dine outdoors.

Walla Walla

John's Wheatland Bakery (509-522-2253), 1828 East Isaacs. Open all day daily. If they don't have the baked goods you want at John's Wheatland, you probably don't need them. Rustic breads, breakfast pastries, fine desserts—all are improbably here on Walla Walla's commercial strip. Continental breakfast and "real food" lunches are also offered.

Merchants Ltd (509-525-0900; www.merchantsdeli.com), 21 East Main Street. Open 5 AM–2 PM Mon.–Sat. This old plank-floored store is the place for imported cheeses, oils, and other deli stuff you wouldn't expect to find in the far reaches of the Palouse. Besides which, it's buzzing at breakfast and busy at lunch, serving pastries, omelets, sandwiches, soups, salads, and a decent cup of tea.

South Fork Grill (509-522-4777), 1129 South Second Street. Open 11–9 Tues.–Sun. When the Creektown Café closed in 2010, it left a void that has now been filled at the same address. With burgers and sandwiches for lunch and crafted, seasonally changing menus for dinner, the South Fork has a little something for everyone. Chef Nimal, from Sri Lanka, also spices it up with a few well-placed curries. Eat in the snug wood dining room or, in summer, on the vine-bowered patio. Reservations recommended.

✳ Entertainment

MUSIC Walla Walla Symphony (509-529-8020; www.wwsymphony.com), 13½ East Main Street, Walla Walla. Founded in 1907, the oldest continuously operating symphony orchestra west of the Mississippi proudly offers a dozen or so concerts a year at Cordiner Hall on the campus of Whitman College (see *To See— Cultural Sites*).

✳ Selective Shopping

FOOD Ferdinand's (800-457-5442), 101 Food Quality Building, Washington State University, Pullman. Cougar Gold Cheese is one of the few university products to have won accolades from *Saveur* magazine; it also took a gold medal at the World Cheese Awards in London—Cheddar, England, you'll remember, is where cheddar began. You can buy it, and other WSU dairy products, at the aptly named campus outlet. Famous for its ice cream, too.

✳ Special Events

May: **Walla Walla Hot Air Balloon Stampede** (509-525-0850), County Fairgrounds, Walla Walla. The balloon festival dates from 1974, making it the second oldest in the nation after Albuquerque's. Upward of 50 balloons and thousands of visitors participate in this annual event, which is a sort of county fair of the hot-air world, with an antiques show, arts and crafts, races, children's activities, and a champagne reception.

June: **ArtWalla** (509-301-0185; www .artwalla.com), various locations in Walla Walla. This 10-day festival kicks off with a "meet the artists" night at the **Carnegie Art Center** (109 Palouse Street) and culminates in the Bronze Pour Gala at the **Walla Walla Foundry** (405 Woodland Avenue). In between are gallery walks, children's art activities, open studios, and more.

July: **Rockin' on the River** (509-758-7712; www.rockinontheriver.org), Gateway Golf Center, 725 Port Way, Clarkston. A family-friendly, daylong rock concert has music by regional bands.

Walla Walla Sweet Onion Festival (509-525-1031), County Fairgrounds, Walla Walla. Sweet onion dishes, music, games, and arts and crafts celebrate this famed local product.

August: **National Lentil Festival** (800-365-6948; www.lentilfest.com), Pullman. Lentils are a major Palouse crop, and the little bean is celebrated in various locations around Pullman with a cook-off, street fair, parade, crafts and sporting events, and more lentil dishes than you ever imagined.

Northeastern Washington

INTRODUCTION

The dominant natural feature of northeastern Washington has for eons been the Columbia River. Though its course has shifted with the vagaries of ice sheets and lava flows, it has generally tumbled down from its Canadian mountain source to sweep in great loops across the central Washington plains and thence through the Cascades, in their various incarnations, to the sea. Its salmon runs supported whole civilizations; it served as a trade route linking the coast to the interior; its waters permitted life to flourish on the arid Columbia Plateau.

The "river of the West" still defines much of the Northwest, particularly in this region. Whatever other impact the Columbia dam projects had—and it was considerable—they brought power to the people, and still do. The salmon runs are much reduced, of course. In this quadrant, the Grand Coulee Dam has backed the river up 151 miles into a great lake—Franklin Roosevelt Lake—cutting from the central desert to the northern forests. Its shores, except where they border Indian reservations, have been designated the Lake Roosevelt National Recreation Area. Other rivers come running to join it—the San Poil, Spokane, Kettle, Pend Oreille—all massing in unimaginable volume in the lunar landscape behind the dam.

This region comprises three starkly contrasting areas: Spokane, the only urban center; the great desert spreading southward and eastward from Grand Coulee, gouged and channeled and sparsely settled; and the north woods reaching from the Idaho border west to the fertile Okanogan Valley. It's a long way from Seattle—and anywhere else in the state.

GRAND COULEE AREA

The idea of damming the Columbia River at Grand Coulee was first broached in 1918 and, of course, roundly pooh-poohed. The fourth-biggest river basin in North America, draining 259,000 square miles, with an output of 160 million acre-feet per year and ferocious spring floods—you think you can dam *that?* Besides, there were already some private dams on the smaller tributaries that supplied irrigation and power for the then minute population of Washington's interior desert. In the unlikely event of population increase, the private utilities argued, the extra demand could easily be met by them.

Private power fought the dam. Even some farmers fought it, arguing that surplus crops were already driving prices down, so why produce more? However, the population did grow—little towns such as Coulee City, Wilbur, and Davenport—though not so much in the inner desert as downstream in Portland and in Seattle, where local power sources were soon exhausted. Then the Depression sent people on the road in search of work, and, presently, with war looming, military production facilities were needed near a source of cheap, abundant power. And so the Grand Coulee Dam was built, with the weight of Franklin D. Roosevelt behind it and an army of construction workers, service personnel, administrators, and engineers. At that time, few people gave much thought to the loss of salmon runs and the cultures that depended on them, except of course the Native Americans themselves. But they had to watch as the water rose, drowning falls where salmon and people had congregated for millennia, 150 miles back and into Canada, and see the same scene replay over the next two decades as dams went in up and down the Columbia and the Snake, till the whole river system was tamed.

It would be too much to say the desert bloomed. The sand and basalt scablands you see around Grand Coulee don't allow much to grow, though several towns sprouted around the project: Electric City, Grand Coulee, Coulee Dam. To the west and south, however, you'll find orchards and vineyards. The dams do allow Pacific shipping to Idaho, but mostly they produce copious electricity. Each drop that turns a turbine on the upper Columbia spins several more on its way downstream. This multiplier effect, and the public utilities, ensure power for everyone, just as FDR said. And whatever the admitted downsides of hydropower, northwesterners are likely to see to it that electricity of, by, and for the people shall not perish from face of the earth.

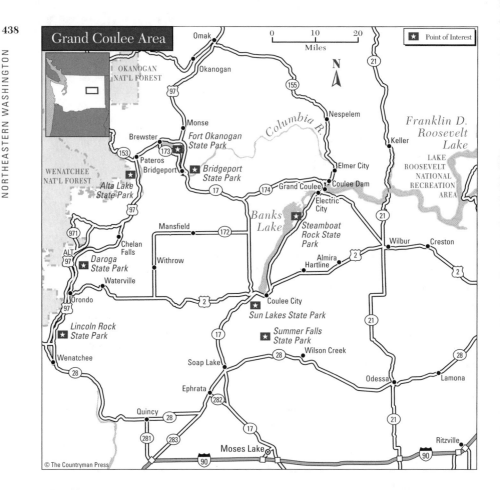

GUIDANCE Grand Coulee Area Chamber of Commerce (509-633-3074 or 800-268-5332; www.grandcouleedam.org), 306 Midway, WA 155, Box 760, Grand Coulee 99133.

GETTING THERE The major east-west highway through this region is **US 2,** from Orondo in the west to Davenport in the east. The dam and settlements of Grand Coulee, Coulee Dam, and Electric City are reached from the north at Omak or the south at Coulee City via **WA 155. WA 174** runs west to east through the area from Bridgeport to Wilbur (**WA 173** connects WA 174 to **US 97**). **WA 17** runs north from Ephrata to US 2 just west of Coulee City and on up to WA 174. **WA 21** runs north from WA 28 at Odessa through Wilbur to the Keller Ferry crossing. And **WA 25** runs north from US 2 at Davenport to cross the Spokane at its confluence with the Columbia.

The nearest airport is in Spokane (see the Spokane Area chapter).

The nearest **AMTRAK** (800-USA-RAIL; www.amtrak.com) stop is in Spokane (see the Spokane Area chapter).

Greyhound (800-231-2222; www.greyhound.com) stops in Okanogan (509-422-2801) at 310 South Second Street and Omak (509-826-5154) at 800 East Riverside Drive, but tickets are not sold at these locations.

MEDICAL EMERGENCY Coulee Community Hospital (509-633-1753), 411 Fortuyn Boulevard, Grand Coulee.

✳ To See

FARMERS' MARKETS Shaw's Fruit Stand (509-633-0133), 533 WA 155, Grand Coulee. Open 9–6 daily in season. Shaw's sells a cornucopia of fruits and vegetables from their own and other local orchards—10 kinds of cherries, 6 of plums, and 26 of apples. This is not to mention apricots, pumpkins, and just about anything else that grows on Washington's sunny side.

FOR FAMILIES ✐ **Northrup Canyon Horseback Riding** (509-641-1003); from WA 155 near milestone 19, 7 miles south of Grand Coulee Dam, turn up a gravel road. Hours vary; call to reserve. Take a gentle one-hour jaunt ($45) or a rugged half-day ride ($95) up Northrup Canyon. All ages are welcome; really small kids can take a ride in the corral.

HISTORIC SITES Davenport spring, in Davenport City Park near the museum at 600 Seventh Street. This was a welcome resting spot for traveling Indians, miners, and settlers, and it is probably why a town grew up here.

Fort Spokane (509-633-3830; www.nps.gov/laro), on WA 25, 23 miles north of Davenport. Open 9:30–5 daily Memorial Day–Labor Day; 9:30–5 Sat.–Sun. through Sept. Free. One of Washington's last frontier forts, Fort Spokane was put up at the confluence of the Spokane and Columbia rivers in 1880 to reinforce the U.S. military presence during the volatile late settlement period. In 1898, as the frontier closed, the fort became an Indian boarding school and tuberculosis sanatorium. Today the site is within the Lake Roosevelt National Recreation Area (see *Wilder Places—Recreation Areas*). A visitors center located in the old guardhouse, a 2-mile trail, and summer ranger programs interpret the history.

Grand Coulee Dam (509-633-9265; www.grandcouleedam.org); visitors center on WA 155 in Coulee Dam. Tours at 10, 12, 2, and 4 daily; visitors center open 9–5 daily. Grand Coulee Dam is billed as the eighth man-made wonder of the world. In the rough basalt wilderness of the Columbia Plateau, its rectilinear bulk barring the prodigious Columbia River looks as incongruous as a smooth monolith would in Olduvai Gorge. The largest concrete structure in North America and perhaps the most mammoth public works project of the 1930s, the dam opened in 1942 just in time to provide massive amounts of energy for the aluminum plants that grew up in the river basin, which in turn produced aluminum used to make airplanes for the war effort. Since the Columbia Basin was also conceived as a public utility district, it continues to have the cheapest electricity rates in the country and handy irrigation for an improbable number of orchards and wineries; today the federal Bureau of Reclamation runs the dam. (The salmon, naturally, didn't fare so well.)

On view in the visitors center are a few artifacts, including a hand-operated wooden pump that supplied underwater dam workers with air (it made me gasp just to look at it) and an uncomfortable-looking wheelchair that President Franklin D. Roosevelt used when he visited the site. You can also request one of four films, including two on the Ice Age floods (cautionary, perhaps) that carved out the coulees. Warning: Since September 11, 2001, bringing bags of any kind, including backpacks, purses, and camera bags, on the dam tour or into the dam visitors center is strictly forbidden. Queries about secure storage elicited the reply, "That's your responsibility."

MUSEUMS Douglas County Historical Museum (509-745-8435), 124 West Walnut Street, Waterville. Open 11–5 Tues.–Sat. Memorial Day–mid-Oct. Donation requested. This little museum conveys the flow of local history through pioneer artifacts, Indian items including possessions of Chief Moses, and even a local meteorite.

Lincoln County Historical Society and Museum (509-725-6711), 600 Seventh Street, Davenport. Open 9–5 Mon.–Sat. May–Sept. Donation accepted. In the rolling grain fields 35 miles west of Spokane, this little museum exhibits chunks of local history, such as farm machinery, Indian artifacts, and a blacksmith's shop.

NATURAL WONDERS The Channeled Scablands. From 17 million to 11 million years ago, lava flows emanated from fissures in the earth and covered the entire Columbia Plateau—what now comprises large parts of Washington and Oregon—with a layer of basalt that in places is 2 miles deep. Much, much later came floods as melting ice dams released waters that had been bound for thousands of years during the last Ice Age. One huge lake, prehistoric Lake Missoula, flooded catastrophically across Idaho and eastern Washington, not once but several times. The flow has been estimated at 10 times the volume of all today's rivers combined. The unimaginable force of the water and the debris it carried scoured the basalt plain, creating the channels, or coulees, that we see in the area today along US 2 from Davenport to Coulee City. This battered landscape covering most of central Washington is called the Channeled Scablands.

THE TOWN OF COULEE DAM WAS CREATED FOR THE BUILDERS OF GRAND COULEE DAM.

Dry Falls, off WA 17 just south of US 2. Visitors center open 10–6 daily mid-May–Sept. Donation requested. Dry Falls was formed in one of the coulees of the Channeled Scablands (see above). At the time, some 12,000–14,000 years ago, the falls wasn't dry but a raging torrent some 20 miles south of where it is now. The tremendous flow of the Lake Missoula floods eroded it backward to where it now stands, 400 feet high and 3 miles wide—nearly three times the size of Niagara Falls. The Dry Falls Interpretive Center, part of Sun Lakes State Park, details the falls' history and geology, as well as the story of J. Harlan Bretz, the geologist who figured it all out.

Lake Lenore Caves, off WA 17 between Soap Lake and Dry Falls. Here prehistoric lava flows engulfed a rhino, making a cast of its body in the cave rock.

Steamboat Rock, off WA 155 south of Grand Coulee. This massive basalt mesa juts 1,000 feet above Banks Lake. The huge basalt outcrop has been a landmark since people have been on the Columbia Plateau. From its mile-square tabletop, the distant Cascades appear like a tempting mirage above the thirsty plateau.

SCENIC DRIVES WA 155, 32 paved miles from Coulee City to Coulee Dam. This lonesome highway winds along the east shore of Banks Lake, with views of the lake on one side and the desolate Channeled Scablands on the other.

Crown Point overlook, 3 miles from Grand Coulee via WA 174. Open 6:30 AM–dusk. You can drive a few miles to the overlook at this state park for a grand view of Grand Coulee Dam.

WALKING TOURS Coulee Dam, on WA 155 near the dam. Wedged between forbidding cliffs and the Columbia River, this little town looks incongruously like Anytown, USA, circa 1930. "Engineers' Town," with its modest frame homes, dormitories, and planning center (now the city hall), was hurriedly built to house dam engineers and clerks on the river's west bank, while construction workers were relegated to temporary barracks to the east. A **self-guided walking tour** leads from the visitors center to City Hall, down neat, maple-shaded streets, and across the bridge. Flyers are available from the Grand Coulee Area Chamber of Commerce (see *Guidance*).

✳ To Do

BICYCLING Downriver Trail, 6.2-mile hiker-biker path in Coulee Dam. This flat trail goes along the river from the Coulee Dam Bridge to the boat launch.

Steamboat Rock State Park trails, off WA 155, 11 miles south of Electric City. Mountain bike trails in this rough terrain, with its heat and dust, are for hard-core cyclists.

Sun Lakes–Dry Falls State Park trails, off WA 17 just east of Coulee City. There are mountain bike trails here, too.

BOATING All kinds of boats dot Lake Roosevelt in summer, which means if you want a quiet sail or paddle, you should find a peaceful cove up lake (which is not too hard to do as the lake is 154 miles long); launch permits required. **Houseboat rentals** are one way to enjoy the lake in comfort.

COULEE DAM CITY HALL FORMERLY HELD THE OFFICES OF DAM ENGINEERS AND ADMINISTRATORS.

Roosevelt Recreational Enterprises (866-703-8232), on WA 17 at the Keller Ferry Marina.

CAMPING Daroga State Park (888-226-7688), on US 97, 6 miles north of Orondo (east side of Columbia River). Seventeen tent sites and 28 utility sites; showers, water, RV dump, toilets, trails, and boat launch.

Fort Spokane (509-725-2715 or 509-633-3830), 44150 District Office Lane, Davenport; about 59 miles northwest of Spokane in Lake Roosevelt National Recreation Area. Sixty-seven tent and trailer sites.

Steamboat Rock State Park (888-226-7688; www.parks.wa.gov), on WA 155, 13 miles south of Grand Coulee. Twenty-six tent sites, 100 RV sites, and 12 primitive boat-in sites on Banks Lake. In addition, 80 primitive sites are scattered about the lakeside 7 and 9 miles north of the main park area; these can't be reserved. For locations check the map on the website. Reservations for standard sites suggested in summer.

Sun Lakes–Dry Falls State Park (888-226-7688), on WA 17 south of Coulee City. One hundred fifty-two standard sites and 39 utility sites; very windy in summer.

GOLF Banks Lake Golf and Country Club (509-633-3588), 18949 Ludolph Road, Electric City. Eighteen holes.

Big Bend Golf and Country Club (509-647-5664), in Wilbur, 20 miles east of Grand Coulee at junction of US 2, WA 174, and WA 21. Nine holes.

HIKING Northrup Creek Trail, 3.5 miles, in Steamboat Rock State Park; on WA 155, 10 miles south of Grand Coulee. Northrup Canyon is a haven for bald

eagles in winter and rattlesnakes in summer. A trail leads gradually up Northrup
Creek, a strip oasis in these scablands, past an old homestead. The trail is closed in
winter to protect the eagles, but eagle viewing is possible from a viewpoint near
the trailhead.

the roof upon one of 12 supporting columns.

Daroga State Park (509-664-6380), on US 97, 6 miles north of Orondo. Camping, trails, and a boat launch are located on 1.5 miles of shoreline on the Columbia
River. Closed in winter.

Steamboat Rock State Park (509-633-1304), on WA 155 near Electric City, 13
miles south of Grand Coulee. Set on huge Banks Lake, a segment of the Columbia, the park around this massive basalt outcrop has been developed for water
sports, camping, and hiking; it contains both popular and remote areas. Wildflowers enliven the severe scablands in spring; eagles winter here.

Sun Lakes–Dry Falls State Park (509-632-5583), off WA 17 west of Coulee
City. With 4,000 acres, nine lakes, and miles of shoreline, there's camping, picnicking, boating, and fishing. See also *To See—Natural Wonders*.

**RECREATION AREAS Lake Roosevelt National Recreation Area Head-
quarters** (509-633-9441; www.nps.gov/laro), 1008 Crest Drive, Coulee Dam; open
8–4 Mon.–Fri. **District office** (509-633-3830) at Fort Spokane Visitor Center,
44150 District Office Lane North, Davenport; open 9:30–5 daily in summer. When
Grand Coulee Dam was completed, the Columbia River waters backed up, flooding waterfalls, drowning shoreline settlements, and creating a 154-mile-long lake
extending from the harsh scablands of coulee country north to the cool mountains
of the Canadian borderlands. Soon afterward, the new lake and its banks were designated a 100,390-acre national recreation area, named for the president who had
backed and practically created the dam. Boating, camping, fishing, and swimming
are the most popular activities; the southern reaches can become pretty crowded
as central Washingtonians seek respite from the surrounding parched desert.
Rangers lead activities from canoe trips to history and nature walks. Fishing and
hunting in season require permits either from the state or from the Colville Indian
Reservation (see the Okanogan Valley and Highlands chapter) and Spokane Indian
reservation (see the Kettle Falls and Selkirks chapter), which have jurisdiction
where they border the lake. The south shore is approached from US 2 at Wilbur
on WA 21 and at Davenport on WA 25. Supplies are available only from marina
concessions (see *To Do—Boating*) and very sparse lakeside settlements.

✳ Lodging

BED & BREAKFASTS

Grand Coulee

Gold House Inn Bed and Breakfast (509-633-1298 or 855-633-1298), 411 Partello Park. Eight simple rooms in this sprawling house all have private baths and air conditioning. Rates include breakfast. $55–98.

HOTELS

Waterville

Waterville Historic Hotel (509-745-8695 or 888-509-8180; www.waterville hotel.com), 102 East Park Street. This was an imposing hotel in 1903. Renovated and reopened in 1996, it retains many original furnishings. Twelve rooms each have the original steam heating, and some have private baths. Common areas include a cozy turn-of-the-20th-century lobby and porch. $49–189.

MOTELS

Coulee Dam

Columbia River Inn (509-633-2100 or 800-633-6421; info@columbiariver inn.com; www.columbiariverinn.com), 10 Lincoln Avenue. At this motel just across from the dam visitors center, each snug, pine-furnished room has a balcony view of the dam. Close the shutters to feel you're in a private Scandinavian lodge (the sauna adds to the effect, too). The staff couldn't be friendlier or more helpful. No pets. $105–210 in summer; $85–195 in winter.

Grand Coulee

Grand Coulee Center Lodge (aka Grand Coulee Center Motel) (509-633-2860 or 866-633-2860; www.grand couleemotel.com), 404 Spokane Way. There are thirty-two units, some with kitchenettes and some with two bedrooms. $49–145.

RESORTS

Electric City

Sunbanks Lake Resort (509-633-3786 or 888-822-7195; www.sunbanks resort.com), 57662 WA 155. On the shores of Banks Lake, which now fills most of the Grand Coulee, Sunbanks Lake Resort offers lodging ranging from rustic cabins to full-fledged villas; in peak season, the larger villas are rented only by the week. Tent and RV sites are available, too. Right on the water, it has access to 27 miles of lakefront and offers swimming, bike and boat rentals (including Jet Skis), and various amenities such as a **café** and miniature golf course—all things to nearly all people. Tent and RV sites $23–63; cabins and villas $45–525.

✳ Where to Eat

EATING OUT

Grand Coulee

La Presa Mexican Restaurant (509-633-3173), 515 East Grand Coulee Avenue. Open 10–10 daily. Since 1998, La Presa's family recipes have made it a local favorite.

Siam Palace (509-633-2921), 213 Main Street. Open for lunch Tues.–Fri. and dinner Tues.–Sat. Friendly service accompanies tasty Thai and Chinese dishes in this storefront eatery.

✳ Special Events

February: **Balde Eagle Festival** (www.eaglefestival.com), Grand Coulee. On the third weekend in February, this event (the extra "e" was acceptable in 1776) celebrates our national bird, three hundred of which winter in the Grand Coulee area. Events include eagle-watching tours, a raptor show, and (among other things) a duct-tape-pet art contest. Don't forget warm clothing; the plateau is cold in February.

OKANOGAN VALLEY AND HIGHLANDS

This region stretches from the edge of the Pasayten Wilderness east to the Kettle River and Lake Roosevelt. It's bordered on the south by the Columbia River and extends north to the Canadian border. The region includes two mountain passes on WA 20, the Colville Indian Reservation, and the gentle Okanogan Valley and foothills bumping up against the North Cascades. It's a vast area within the vaster northeastern quarter, full of wild rivers and silent forest.

Most towns in this region started out as small mining operations. When the Colville Reservation, now stretching from Coulee Dam nearly to Republic, was created, it reached all the way to the Canadian border. That changed fast when gold was discovered in the hills. The reservation was "opened," and towns including Oroville, Wauconda, and Republic sprang up. Most mines petered out after a couple of decades; today, much of the country is national forest and ranchland.

Fortunes changed. Digs in Republic now turn up troves of fossils finer than precious metals. Omak, along the Okanogan River, now has its stampede. The Colville Reservation, where high desert grades into forested hills, offers plenty of scope for remote and semiremote outdoor recreation. Oroville, properly speaking, is in the Okanogan Valley, a broad plain shaped like the Fertile Crescent and stretching into Canada. Sheltered on one side by the North Cascades and on the other by the Rocky Mountain foothills, its climate is significantly milder than that of either the mountains to the east or west or the desert to the south; fruit is grown here, and there are even attempts at vineyards. Which is not to say they don't get plenty of snow.

You won't find much nightlife in this region, or shopping, or even fine dining. You will find clean air and streams, enough stars to compensate for the lack of glitz, plenty of wildlife, and a spirit of self-sufficiency. As always, keep an eye on your gas gauge. If you travel in winter, keep tire chains and blankets in your car.

GUIDANCE **Colville Confederated Tribes** (509-634-2200 or 888-881-7684; www.colvilletribes.com).

Colville National Forest Headquarters (509-684-7000; www.fs.fed.us/r6 /colville), 765 South Main Street, Colville 99114. District offices include **Republic Ranger District** (509-775-7400), 650 East Delaware Avenue, Republic 99166.

Ferry County Chamber of Commerce and Visitor Information Center (509-779-4808; www.ferrycounty.com), Box 91, Malo 99150.

Okanogan County Tourism Council (888-431-3080; www.okanogancountry .com), Box 626, Omak 98441.

Omak Chamber of Commerce (509-826-1880; www.omakchamber.com), 401 Omak Avenue, Omak 98841.

Republic Chamber of Commerce (509-775-2704), 65 North Clark Avenue, Republic 99166.

Republic Regional Visitors' and Convention Bureau (509-775-3387; www .republicwa.com), 979 South Clark Avenue, Box 325, Republic 99166.

GETTING THERE US 97 from Brewster to Oroville is the main north-south highway to the west; it passes through Okanogan, Omak, and Tonasket. In the middle of the region, **WA 21** stretches from the Keller Ferry north through Republic and Curlew to the Canadian border. From Kettle Falls, **US 395** runs north to the border. **WA 20** is the main east-west route, from Tonasket through Wauconda and Republic to Kettle Falls. **WA 155** heads southeast from Omak through Nespelem and Elmer City to the Grand Coulee area.

GETTING AROUND You'll need a car in this vast, sparsely populated area.

MEDICAL EMERGENCY Ferry County Memorial Hospital (509-775-3333; Curlew branch 509-779-4049; www.fcphd.org), 36 Klondike Road, Republic.

Mid-Valley Hospital (509-826-1760), 810 Jasmine Street, Omak.

North Valley Hospital (509-486-2151; www.nvhospital.org), 126 South Whitcomb Avenue, Tonasket.

WA 155 CONNECTS THE GRAND COULEE AREA WITH THE OKANOGAN VALLEY.

Okanogan–Douglas District Hospital (509-689-2517), 507 Hospital Way, Brewster.

✴ To See

FARMERS' MARKETS Bridgeport Farmers' Market (509-686-3875), at 26th Street and Foster Creek Avenue, Bridgeport. Open 8:30–12:30 Fri. late June–mid-Oct.

Okanogan Valley Farmers' Market (509-826-0457). Two locations: American Legion Park, Okanogan, open 9–1 Sat. May–Oct.; at Central and Ash streets, Omak, open 3–7 Tues. May–Oct.

HISTORIC SITES Camp Growden, on Sherman Pass Scenic Byway (WA 20), about 15 miles west of Kettle Falls. This is the site where CCC youths worked the Colville National Forest in the 1930s.

Chief Joseph's Grave, in the cemetery just uphill from the Catholic church on C Street, Nespelem; from Coulee Dam take WA 155 north onto the Colville Reservation and drive about 12 miles. Chief Joseph would have preferred to have been buried in his native Wallowa Mountains, in Oregon, but the Nez Perce chief who led his people on a desperate 1877 flight from the U.S. Army was captured just short of the Canadian border, exiled to Oklahoma (where many members of his tribe perished), and finally sent to the Colville Reservation, where he died in 1904. His many requests for an allotment in the Wallowas, supported even by some army generals, were all refused. Offerings of feather bundles, sage bundles, pebbles, and plastic flowers cluster around the small obelisk marking his resting place in this windswept village cemetery.

Fort Okanogan, on WA 17, half a mile east of US 97. The state park in which the fort was situated has been closed due to maintenance and safety (and likely budget) considerations. This is unfortunate, because it was the first American settlement in what is now Washington. Founded by David Stuart of John Jacob Astor's Pacific Fur Company in 1811—the same year as Astoria, Oregon, was founded by Astor himself—it overlooked the confluence of the Okanogan and Columbia rivers and was a fur-trading post. Like Astoria, it ended up in the hands of the British a few years later. There's not much to see now, but a small sign at least informs passersby that is was there.

CAMP GROWDEN, A CIVILIAN CONSERVATION CORPS HERITAGE SITE, IS IN COLVILLE NATIONAL FOREST.

&. **Log Flume Heritage Site,** on Sherman Pass Scenic Byway (WA 20), a few miles west of Lake Roosevelt. This site shows how loggers transported timber before mechanization; the site includes a wheelchair-accessible trail.

Old Okanogan Mission, on US 97, about 8 miles north of Tonasket. The Jesuit father Etienne de Rouge arrived here in 1885 to build up the mission that his predecessor, Urban Grassi, had begun. De Rouge built a chapel, a church, and the first school in the county. All were destroyed by fire in 1910; the church was rebuilt, only to burn down again in 1971. The little monument by the road protects all that physically remains of the mission: the church bell that survived both fires.

Ranald MacDonald's Grave, in an Indian cemetery on Taroda Bridge Customs Road; from Republic, take WA 21 north to Curlew, turn left and follow the Kettle River about 10 miles, then turn right toward Ferry about 2 miles. Why does someone with the unlikely name of Ranald MacDonald lie in this lonely border country? Son of Hudson's Bay Company factor Archibald MacDonald and Chief Concomly's daughter Koale'zoa, the young Ranald was apparently intrigued by Japanese sailors shipwrecked near his mother's village. Instead of becoming a banker as his father wished, he ran off to sea and somehow convinced a ship's captain to help him stage his own shipwreck off the coast of Japan. Not surprisingly, the Japanese imprisoned him as an illegal alien and eventually deported him. But while under house arrest he had managed to teach English to some curious Japanese and above all had caught a glimpse of the society that so fascinated him. Not long afterward, some of those Japanese students acted as interpreters during the incursion of Commodore Perry and later negotiations opening Japan to foreign trade. Ranald spent much of his life roaming the world but remained an advocate for U.S.-Japanese relations. In later years, he rejoined relatives in northeastern Washington and ended his days on the Colville Reservation. Supposedly his last word was *sayonara*.

Ruby City town site, on Salmon Creek Road, about 12 miles northwest of Okanogan. There were silver strikes in Ruby City in the mid-1880s. In about 1888, a town was platted and built, only to be vacated in the early 1890s when the price of silver crashed. Now a marker shows where the town used to be; some foundations are still visible.

MUSEUMS Colville Tribal Museum (509-634-2589), 512 Mead Way, Coulee Dam. Open 10–6 Mon.–Sat. May–Dec.; 10–6 Tues.–Sat. Jan.–Apr. Free. This long-house-style building houses elaborate beadwork, basketwork, and costumes old and new by the 11 bands comprising the Colville Confederated Tribes, as well as historic artifacts, including one of the Lewis and Clark peace medals. Almost more affecting are the many black-and-white family photos.

Okanogan County Historical Museum (509-422-4272), 1410 Second Avenue North, Okanogan. Open 10–4 daily mid-May–mid-Sept. $2. This pioneer museum possesses an 1879 log cabin thought to be the oldest building in the county, as well as a replica Old West town and artifacts, dioramas, and photos detailing Okanogan's development.

Old Molson Ghost Town Museum (509-485-3292), 15 miles east of Oroville. Open 10–5 daily Memorial Day–Labor Day. Free. Molson was a gold rush town. It's called Old Molson now because, in 1909, the inhabitants were forced to move due to a land dispute with a rancher. But the old bank stands on its original foundation, and other period buildings, such as a jail and assay office, have been brought in from nearby. Farm equipment of the time completes the scene. Tours are self-guided; drive up and walk around.

Republic Historical Center, 15 North Kean Street, Republic; adjacent to the
Stonerose Interpretive Center (see *Natural Wonders*). Open 8–5 daily Memorial
Day–Labor Day; 8–5 Wed.–Sun. Labor Day–Oct. Donation requested. Republic's
mining past is recalled with assay and other mining equipment and historical
photos.

**NATURAL WONDERS Stonerose Interpretive Center and Eocene Fossil
Digging Site** (509-775-2295; www.stonerosefossil.org), 15-1 North Kean Street,
Republic. Interpretive center open 8–5 daily May–Labor Day; 8–5 Wed.–Sun.
Labor Day–Oct. Fossil digging site open 10–4 Tues.–Sat. May–Oct., plus 10–4
Sun. mid-June–mid-Sept. Fossil site admission sticker: $6 adults; $4 seniors, students, and children 6–18. Hammer and chisel rental: $4. When the dust of vol-
canic turmoil cleared about 50 million years ago, what is now Ferry County's
climate had changed from moist and tropical to warm and temperate. A lake lay
right where Republic is today, and over the years the remains of plants and small
animals sank to the lake bottom, where they were covered with mud. The mud
turned to shale, and presto!—a fossil bed. The interpretive center displays many
beautiful fossils from the site, including a remarkable five-petaled rose, snails, and
leaves of early pine and metasequoia. You can dig for plant and animal fossils yourself just a couple of blocks away. You are allowed to keep three of your finds but
must turn the rest over to the center.

SCENIC DRIVES Bangs Mountain Scenic Drive, 10 unpaved miles; from WA
20 about 10 miles west of junction with US 395. This route should be used only by
high-clearance, four-wheel-drive vehicles.

Sherman Pass Scenic Byway (WA 20), 35 paved miles from Republic to Kettle
Falls. This route winds through the tall firs of the Colville National Forest and
over Sherman Pass, at 5,575 feet the highest in the state.

WA 21, 53 paved miles from the Columbia to Republic. From the river's south
side, cross on the tiny, free **Keller's Ferry**—call the Colville Reservation for closures (see *Guidance*)—and continue north along the rushing San Poil River. Tra-
verse the reservation to Republic; you can go on to Canada if you like, another 32
miles.

WALKING TOURS Historic Republic Walking Tour. Leaflet available at the
Republic Historical Center (see *Museums*) for $5.95. The tiny town of Republic
dates from the mining boom of the late 1800s and early 1900s, and its town center
includes hotels and other businesses from that period.

✳ To Do

BOATING Roosevelt Recreational Enterprises (866-703-8232), at the Keller
Ferry Marina on WA 21, 14 miles north of Wilbur. Moorage facilities and boat
rentals, including houseboats.

CAMPING

Colville National Forest
Canyon Creek Campground, on WA 20 about 15 miles west of Kettle Falls.
Twelve tent and trailer sites; bathrooms but no water. No reservations.

Davis Lake, on CR 2695. Four tent sites; toilet but no water. No reservations.

Lake Ellen, on Inchelium Road. Fifteen tent and trailer sites; toilet but no water. No reservations.

Pierre Lake, on CR 4013. Sixteen tent and trailer sites; boat dock; bathrooms but no water. No reservations.

Trout Lake, on FR 020, 8.5 miles west of Kettle Falls. Five tent sites; toilet but no water. No reservations.

Colville Reservation
Colville Tribes (tribal tourism office, 888-881-7684) run numerous campgrounds on the reservation, often in beautiful, semi-remote settings. Fees apply for most campgrounds.

Keller Park, at the confluence of the San Poil and Columbia rivers, 2 miles south of Keller Ferry. Four acres with campsites, restrooms, picnic tables, and boat docks in a bucolic setting.

Thirteen Mile Creek Campground, off WA 21 near Republic. This base for backcountry horseback riding includes restrooms, a loading ramp, and fire rings.

National Park Service
Lake Roosevelt National Recreation Area (509-633-9441) runs 27 campgrounds along the length of the lake—large and small, accessible and remote. The Park Service charges $10 a night in summer for campsites reachable by car; those reachable only by boat or foot are free. NRA campgrounds in this region include Crystal Cove, Detillion, Halverson, Hawk Creek, Keller Ferry, Penix Canyon, Plum Point, Ponderosa, Porcupine Bay, and Spring Canyon. In addition, there are 7 campgrounds on the Colville Reservation section of the lake (see above); Colville sites are around $20.

Okanogan-Wenatchee National Forest
Beaver Lake, on FR 32 in Bodie. Eleven sites; water and toilet. No reservations.

Beth Lake, on CR 9480, about 3 miles from Beaver Lake. Fourteen sites; water and toilet. No reservations.

Bonaparte Lake, on Bonaparte Lake Road off WA 20 between Tonasket and Republic. Twenty-eight sites; water and toilets. No reservations.

Oriole, on FR 38-026 north of Conconully. Ten sites; water and toilet. No reservations.

State Parks
♿ **Bridgeport State Park** (888-266-7688), off WA 17 north of Bridgeport. Fourteen tent sites and 20 utility sites; ADA restrooms. No reservations.

♿ **Conconully State Park** (509-826-7408), on Conconully Road northwest of US 97 at Okanogan. Fifty-one tent sites and 15 utility sites; ADA restrooms. Several cabins will be added in 2012; $45–65. No reservations.

Curlew Lake State Park (509-775-3592), 62 State Park Road, Republic; off WA 21 about 8 miles north of Republic. Fifty-seven tent sites and 25 utility sites. No reservations.

♿ **Osoyoos Lake Veterans' Memorial Park** (509-476-2926), off US 97 just north of Oroville and just south of the Canadian border. Eighty-six standard sites (no utilities); ADA restroom.

Republic. Bills itself as the "toughest nine holes in the West."

HIKING **Colville National Forest** (see *Guidance*) offers unparalleled hiking and backpacking possibilities in its vast reaches. Most are higher-elevation (3,000–6,000 feet) backcountry trails, so take water, food, and warm clothes even in summer. Some options in the Republic–Kettle Falls area include these:

Columbia Mountain Loop, 7 miles; north of WA 20 at Sherman Pass, turn north on Kettle Trail Access Road, then walk 2 miles north to junction with Columbia Mountain Loop. Circumambulate the peak, viewing wildflowers and wildlife.

Hoodoo Canyon/Emerald Lake, 2.5 miles; from FR 9565 west of US 395 north of WA 20. This is a scenic streamside walk up Hoodoo Canyon.

Kettle Crest National Recreation Trail, 43 miles from White Mountain to Deer Creek Summit; crosses WA 20, 17 miles east of Republic, with access at Sherman Pass. This rugged backpackers' path runs north-south along the ridges of the Kettle Range. It can be done in segments or used to access other trails for day hikes.

Old Stage Trail, 5 miles to Kettle Crest Trail; off FR 2156 east of WA 21 near Curlew. Walk this early attempt to supply the nearby goldfields, up to the crest of the Kettle Range.

Sherman Peak Loop, 5.3 miles; south of WA 20 at Sherman Pass. Circumambulate this peak.

See also *Wilder Places—Recreation Areas*.

✴ Wilder Places

PARKS **Bridgeport State Park** (509-686-7231), off WA 17 north of Bridgeport. Just behind Chief Joseph Dam on the Columbia River, this park is a joint project of Washington State Parks and the U.S. Army Corps of Engineers. With beaches, boat ramps, campsites, and some shade, it's something of an oasis in summer.

Conconully State Park (509-826-7408), on Conconully Highway 22 miles northwest of US 97 at Okanogan. Open in winter for snow sports. Set between forested hills, with nearly a mile of shoreline on two lakes (Conconully Lake and Conconully Reservoir), this out-of-the-way park offers boating, fishing, swimming, and camping in summer.

Curlew Lake State Park (509-775-3592), 62 State Park Road, Republic; off WA 21, 8 miles north of Republic. Open 6:30 AM–dusk daily May 31–Oct. 30. Swimming, boating, camping, and picnicking amid 123 acres of flowered hills. Archaeological finds indicate the park was a summer campground area for local tribes.

Osoyoos Lake State Park (888-226-7688), off US 97 just north of Oroville. Open winter weekends for snow play. Osoyoos Lake, really a 14-mile-long wide spot in the Okanogan River, extends north into Canada. In summer it attracts campers with its sandy beaches and boating.

RECREATION AREAS **Lake Roosevelt National Recreation Area Headquarters** (509-633-9441; www.nps.gov/laro), 1008 Crest Drive, Coulee Dam. Open 8–4 Mon.–Fri. Building the Grand Coulee Dam backed up the waters of the

Columbia River 151 miles. Where the river once ran untrammeled down from the mountains and the salmon ran up it, there is now a deep, long, and placid lake reaching into Canada. The entire lakeshore has been designated a national recreation area, with campgrounds, boating, swimming, fishing, and hiking along its length—but bring supplies; settlements between Grand Coulee at the south end and Kettle Falls near the north are few and small. Rangers lead activities from canoe trips to history and nature walks. Fishing and hunting in season require permits either from the state or from the Colville Reservation, which has jurisdiction where it borders the lake. A drive or boat trip up the lake leads you from desert canyons to cool evergreen forests.

✷ Lodging

COTTAGES AND CABINS

Colville Reservation
Rainbow Beach (888-862-0978), 18 North Twin Lakes Road, Inchelium. This spot near Twin Lakes has rustic and modern cabins sleeping two to eight, as well as RV sites. Boat rentals are discounted for overnight guests. Fish and birds are abundant. RV sites $17; cabins $39–154.

Okanogan Area
✄ ♿ ♨ **Gibson's North Fork Lodge** (509-826-1475 or 800-555-1690; www.gibsonsnorthforklodge.com), 100 West Boone Avenue, Conconully. Four cabins sleeping four to six are simply but comfortably furnished and have their own kitchens and bathrooms. Handicapped-accessible, too. Close to Conconully Lake, the grounds include a games area and creek. Children and pets welcome. $80; two-night minimum on weekends.

HOTELS

Republic
♨ ♿ **The Prospector Inn Hotel** (509-775-3361 or 888-844-6480; www.theprospectorinn.com), 979 South Clark Avenue. The hotel's plank storefront puts you in mind of Republic's mining past, but inside are the amenities of a comfortable modern motel, including a handicapped-accessible room. If your muscles ache after a day of outdoor exertion, enjoy the sauna, then stroll Republic's broad, quiet main street. Rates include continental breakfast. Pets welcome with approval and fee. $51–150.

Tonasket
Hidden Hills Country Inn (509-486-1895 or 800-468-1890; www.hiddenhillsresort.com), 104 Hidden Hills Lane. This 1890s-style hotel (built in 1991) in the Okanogan Valley is part of a complex that includes a tiny theater for meetings and entertainment, a dining room, and a hopeful new winery. The 10 rooms all have private bathrooms. Rates include breakfast; dinner available with advance reservations. No children or pets. $120–130.

MOTELS

Omak
Omak Inn (509-826-3822), 912 Koala Drive. The Omak Inn features 49 comfortable motel-style rooms, an indoor pool and fitness center, and an on-site restaurant. $56–120.

Royal Motel (509-826-5715 or 866-504-7155), 514 Riverside Drive, Omak. An older, mom-and-pop motel with 10 units, the Royal is simple but clean and comfortable—and easy on the wallet. From $50.

Republic
Northern Inn (509-775-3371 or 888-801-1068; www.northern-inn.com), 852

South Clark Avenue. The rustic western storefront–style building hides two floors of clean, modern rooms and friendly service within walking distance of restaurants and other downtown attractions. $80.

RANCHES

Oroville

♂ & ❀ Eden Valley Guest Ranch

(509-485-4002; www.edenvalleyranch .net), 31 Eden Valley Lane. This 900-acre ranch 10 miles east of "town" raises hay, grain, and cattle. Ten cabins (one ADA-accessible) look rustic but have all amenities, including kitchens. Sided in reused materials from old (in some cases, prospectors') buildings, they blend into the hills. Ride horseback, hike, fish, raft the Okanogan River, watch wildlife or the stars, learn how a ranch works, or just loaf. You are in the far-from-everything West here. Slow down and enjoy it. Dogs and horses welcome ($5 for dogs; $10 for horses). Children welcome, too, of course. $110; $95 with minimum three-night stay.

Republic

♂ K Diamond K Ranch (888-345-

5355; www.kdiamondk.com), 15661 WA 21 South. A fork of the Sanpoil River runs through this 1,600-acre ranch in the foothills of the Kettle River Range. The Konz family will make sure you get a riding lesson upon arrival, and with their additional 30,000 leased acres of summer grazing, you've got room for serious riding, hiking, cattle driving, fishing, or loafing. Four cozy log rooms and two bathrooms make up the guest lodge; meals are shared around the family dining table. Rates include lodging, meals, riding, and use of ranch facilities. $95–179 per person depending on season; three-day minimum in summer.

Tonasket

♂ Canaan Ranch Bed and Barn

(509-486-1191 or 866-295-4217; www .canaanguestranch.com), 474 Cape LaBelle Road. Does 500 acres in a hidden mountain valley sound good? The Aeneas Valley east of Tonasket (you likely won't find it on a map) hides Canaan Ranch, home and breeding grounds for longhorn cattle, Polish Arabian horses, and border collies to cope with the livestock. Ride their horses (or bring your own), hike, fish, and watch wildlife or the northern lights. Two guest cabins in these wide-open spaces accommodate four to eight, and a bunkhouse apartment sleeps four. Bathrooms, showers, and a sauna are shared. There are also RV hook-ups. Children and horses welcome. RV sites $25; bunkhouse $100 (includes continental breakfast); cabins $135–150; discounts for extended stays.

✴ Where to Eat

EATING OUT

Omak

Breadline Café (509-826-5836; www .breadlinecafe.com), 102 South Ash. Open 11–9 Tues.–Fri., 9–9 Sat. The Breadline features locally raised beef, organic apples, and generally homemade, real food. The menu aims to please everyone from ranchers to foodies to vegans—quite an ambitious program in Omak, and apparently successful: The café has been open since 1980, serving soups, salads, and sandwiches for lunch and anything from crêpes to jambalaya for dinner.

The Corner Bistro (509-826-4188), 19 East Apple Avenue. Open 8 AM–9 PM Mon.–Sat., 8–8 Sun. Another farm-to-table restaurant, the Corner looks like any run-of-the-mill small-town eatery but offers well-prepared, fresh food with enough variety for vegetarians, carnivores, locavores, and the generally voracious.

Republic

Esther's Restaurant (509-775-2088), 90 North Clark Avenue. Open for lunch and dinner Mon.–Sat. Esther's is locally appreciated for its hearty and plentiful Mexican dishes.

Sportsmen's Roost (509-775-0404), 645 South Clark Avenue. Open 6 AM–10 PM Mon.–Fri., 7 AM–10 PM Sat.–Sun. Definitely a western country restaurant, Sportsmen's serves steaks, chicken, and other hearty fare.

✳ Special Events

August: **Omak Stampede** (509-826-1002; www.omakstampede.org), Omak. This rodeo, with its famous Suicide Race on horseback, has been going on for 70 years.

SPOKANE AREA

With a population of about 200,000, Spokane ties Tacoma for Washington's second-largest city. But it's more surprising to come on a city of this size at the far eastern end of the state. Whether you approach over the flatlands from the west and south or the dark mountains from the north and east, Spokane rises suddenly from the juncture of hill and plain—a blend of redbrick factories of a century ago, expansive parks, stately homes of railroad and lumber barons, and new suburbs.

Spokane pulled itself from near oblivion in the 1970s to host the 1974 world's fair. Even to make the bid was an act of audacity. Who had heard of Spokane, a run-down railway town 300 miles from a major city? But the town had known glory. It was one of the few in the state, and the only one in the interior, to have become a major railway hub in the late 1800s—many had aspired, but few had been chosen. Fortunes were made. Many homes and buildings remain from those heady days—the Finch home and the Davenport Hotel, to name a couple—mostly postdating the inevitable fire of 1889.

The Depression and other factors pulled the rug out, and the place fell into a long slumber. But this latest renaissance has kept going, bringing in some impressive restaurants, museums, an active performing-arts scene, wineries, and even (gasp) martini bars.

GUIDANCE Spokane Regional Convention and Visitors' Bureau (888-SPOKANE; www.visitspokane.com), 801 West Riverside Avenue, Suite 301, Spokane 99201.

Spokane Valley Chamber of Commerce (509-924-4994; www.spokanevalley chamber.org), 9507 East Sprague Avenue, Spokane Valley 99206.

West Plains Chamber of Commerce (509-747-8480; www.westplainschamber .org), 504 First Street, Cheney 99004.

GETTING THERE Highway access to Spokane is by **I-90** from the east (Coeur d'Alene, Idaho) or west (through Sprague and Four Lakes), **US 395** from the north (from Kettle Falls through Deer Park), and **US 195** from the south (from Colfax through Spangle). **US 2** reaches Spokane from the west via Davenport and Reardan, then heads north through Newport into Idaho. Smaller highways connect the outlying towns that circle the hub city of Spokane.

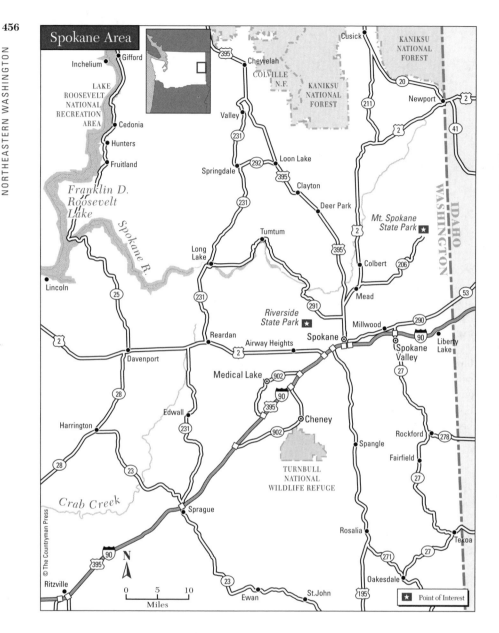

Spokane Area

Spokane International Airport (509-455-6455), just west of downtown via US 2 or I-90, is served by 16 carriers.

AMTRAK's (509-624-5144 or 800-USA-RAIL; www.amtrak.com) Empire Builder from Seattle to Chicago stops in Spokane at 221 First Avenue.

Greyhound (509-624-5251 or 800-231-2222; www.greyhound.com) stops in Spokane at 221 West First Street.

transit.com), at the Plaza, 701 West Riverside Avenue, Spokane, offers bus service
in and around Spokane.

MEDICAL EMERGENCY **Deaconess Medical Center** (509-458-5800), 800
West Fifth Avenue, Spokane.

Holy Family Hospital (509-482-0111), 5633 North Lidgerwood Street, Spokane.

Rockwood Clinic Urgent Care Centers (www.rockwoodclinic.com) has three
locations for urgent and outpatient care: **Downtown** (800-776-4048), 400 East
Fifth Avenue, Spokane; **Northside** (509-755-5340), 9001 North Country Homes
Boulevard, Spokane; and **Spokane Valley** (509-755-5595), 15412 East Sprague
Avenue, Spokane Valley.

Sacred Heart Medical Center (509-474-3131), 101 West Eighth Avenue,
Spokane.

Valley Hospital and Medical Center (509-924-6650), 12606 East Mission,
Spokane Valley.

✳ To See

FARMERS' MARKETS **Spokane Farmers' Market** (509-995-0182), corner of
Division Street and Second Avenue, Spokane. Open 8–1 Wed. and Sat. May–Oct.

FARMS AND FARM STANDS *ℐ* **Fleur de Provence** (509-466-4236), 7019
East Day–Mount Spokane Road, Mead. Pick your own lavender at this farm.

Green Bluff Growers (www.greenbluffgrowers.com) is an association of a few
dozen small farms in the hills northeast of Spokane. Pick your own fresh fruit or
buy it picked. Half a dozen festivals celebrate each seasons, so whether your weak-
ness is cherries, peaches, strawberries, or apples, you can indulge, often while
enjoying outdoor music, food, and crafts. Check the website for a list of members;
here are a couple.

Walter's Fruit Ranch (509-238-4709), 9807 East Day Road, Mead. Meet Rocky
the apple-picking dog here.

FOR FAMILIES *ℐ* **Cat Tales Zoological Park** (509-238-4126; www.cattales
.org), 17020 North Newport Highway (US 2), Mead. Open 10–6 Tues.–Sun. May–
Sept.; 10–4 Wed.–Sun. Oct.–Apr. $8 adults, $6 seniors and students, $5 children
under 13; infants who "cannot possibly escape from the stroller" free; seniors free
Sun. What would you do if you had more Bengal tigers than you could handle?
Well, aside from courting arrest for possession of an endangered species, you
would call Cat Tales. Cat Tales opened in 1991 as a private nonprofit zoo dedicated to rescuing unwanted, abused, or otherwise distressed felines. Today it's
home to 42 healthy tigers, cougars, Barbary lions, leopards, and other big cats with
a variety of personal histories (you would be surprised how many are taken in drug
raids).

ℐ **Looff Carrousel** in Riverfront Park (509-625-6601 or 800-366-PARK; www
.spokaneriverfrontpark.com), Spokane Falls Boulevard and Washington Street.
Operates from 11 AM Tues.–Sun. spring–fall; intermittently in winter; closed
Jan.–Feb. $2 adults, $1 seniors and children. This National Historic Landmark,

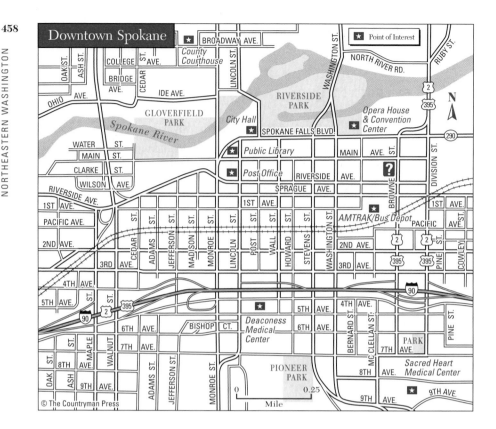

created in 1909 by the German carver Charles Looff, has 54 spirited horses, 2 dragon chairs, a tiger, and a giraffe, and it's a great ride. (I can vouch for it.) Children must be 42 inches tall unless accompanied by an adult.

✔ **Mobius** (509-624-5437; www.mobiusspokane.org), in the lower level of River Park Square, 808 West Main Avenue, Spokane. Open 10–5 Mon.–Sat., 11–5 Sun. $5.75 adults and children, $4.75 seniors and military, infants under one free. Kids can investigate the workings of water, weather, and land in "Geotopia"; learn about city safety; and operate kid-friendly construction equipment in this highly interactive children's museum. Exhibits highlight natural principles at work in the Spokane area as well as art and culture in faraway places. A related Mobius Science Center across the river is expected to open in 2012.

GARDENS Finch Arboretum (509-624-4832), 3404 West Woodland Boulevard, Spokane; off US 2 west of downtown. Open dawn to 10 PM fall–spring, 11 PM in summer. Free. Native and exotic trees in a landscaped 90-acre setting.

Manito Park (509-625-6200), 17th Avenue and Grand Boulevard, Spokane. Open 4 AM–11 PM in summer; 5 AM–10 PM in winter. Free. Opened in 1904, Manito's 90 acres on the South Hill are devoted almost entirely to a profusion of gardens—the Nishinomiya Japanese Garden, a formal rose garden, a French Renaissance garden, and a perennial garden, to name a few.

HISTORIC HOMES **Bing Crosby House** (509-323-5999 or 509-313-3847), 502 East Boone Avenue, Spokane. Call for hours. Free. Washington relishes its native sons—Bing's grandparents' house is preserved near Olympia (see the Olympia Area chapter in part 2, Southern Puget Sound), and his own boyhood home is here on the leafy campus of Gonzaga University. The family moved to Spokane from Tacoma in 1906, when he was an infant, and built this house in 1913. Bing actually attended Gonzaga, intending to become a lawyer. But he dropped out in his senior year to play music, probably disappointing his parents. (Years later, the university granted him an honorary degree.) The upper floor of the pleasant clapboard home now houses the offices of the Gonzaga University Alumni Association; downstairs is a collection of Bing Crosby memorabilia.

Brownes Addition

This neighborhood west of downtown Spokane, platted by the nouveaux riches of the late 1800s, contains many beautifully restored mansions. Several are on the National Register of Historic Places, as is the entire neighborhood. Among them are the following:

Amasa Campbell House, 2316 West First Avenue, Spokane. This massive half-timbered imitation Tudor home was designed by Kirtland Cutter in 1898 for mining magnate Amasa Campbell. It is now owned by the Northwest Museum of Arts and Culture (see *Museums*).

Bernhard Loewenberg home, 1923 West First Avenue, Spokane. This 1889 Queen Anne was the home of a dry-goods merchant.

Finch House, 2340 West First Avenue, Spokane. This 1898 neoclassical giant looks like a would-be White House, with tall Ionic columns. It was built by John Finch, Amasa Campbell's business partner (see above).

Patsy Clark Mansion, 2208 West Second Avenue, Spokane. Patrick Clark had architect Kirtland Cutter build him this 12,000-square-foot Italian-style villa complete with Italian sandstone, balustrades, balconies, and Tiffany glass in 1897. It has just been restored as an office building after several metamorphoses.

Cannon Hill District

Near Coeur d'Alene Park at Fourth Street and Chestnut Avenue, this Spokane neighborhood contains slightly later homes (1900–1907), including these:

Domer Home, 1603 West Ninth Street, Spokane. Particularly unusual is a huge half-round arch dominating the second floor.

Cliff House

Arbor Crest Wine Cellars (509-927-9463), 4705 Fruithill Road, Spokane. Open 12–5 daily. This cliff-top Florentine-style villa was built in 1924 by an eccentric with the improbable name of Royal Riblet. Royal was an inveterate tinkerer who came out from Iowa to design aerial tramways and ski lifts with his brother Byron; Royal then struck out on his own as an inventor. His patents include a mechanical parking garage, various automotive devices, and a square-wheeled tractor (preempted by the invention of caterpillar traction). The house of native rock and stucco was endlessly improved in accordance with Riblet's roving imagination: a gatehouse, a swimming pool, a life-sized checkerboard, a croquet court–cum–skating rink, an aerial tram to bring people and goods from the far bank of the Spokane River. (The tram was supplied with fishing poles so that visitors could, if they chose, pause midway and fish.) Indoor conveniences include an extraordinary number of electric outlets, an electric fireplace, two refrigerators, and a miniature tram to deliver mail, all of which attracted much attention in the intermountain West of the 1920s. Today the restored home is tastefully furnished for the occasional wedding or wine gathering. Arbor Crest's cellar is nearby on the premises, and a stroll among the gardens and vineyards leaves a pleasant aftertaste.

Green Bluff

Hutton Settlement (509-926-1027; www.huttonsettlement.org), at the foot of Green Bluff; off US 2 northeast of Spokane. Visits and tours by appointment. This collection of neat white cottages is an orphanage founded in 1919 by Levi Hutton, who was an orphan himself. Having struck it rich in the Idaho mines—not by mining but by investing—he decided to build a different kind of orphanage, where the children would live in small "family" groups presided over by a house mother. It continues in operation to this day, a testament to Hutton's foresight: He decreed, among other things, that the 319 acres he had donated could never be subdivided, and the foundation he set up to fund the home has lasted through wars and depressions.

Manito Park Area

Several stately homes ring this park on Spokane's South Hill:

Dan Morgan Home, 242 East Manito Place, Spokane. This 1908 Doric-columned house is a more restrained version of the Finch House (see *Brownes Addition*).

James Glover mansion, 323 West Eighth Avenue, Spokane. This 1888 Neo-Tudor mansion was the home of the man called the founder of Spokane.

Marycliff District

This area near Pioneer and Cliff parks on Spokane's South Hill has several Kirtland Cutter–designed homes, including these:

Corbin House, 815 West Seventh Street, Spokane. This is a neoclassical home.

Undercliff House, 703 West Seventh, Spokane. As this Tudoresque home attests, Cutter seems to have been most fascinated by the Tudor and Classical Greek styles.

HISTORIC SITES Cathedral of St. John the Evangelist (509-838-4277; www.stjohns-cathedral.org), 127 East 12th Avenue, Spokane. Tours 11–2 Wed., Fri., and Sat.; after services most Suns. Free. You have to blink a couple of times when you see the grand Gothic-style Episcopal cathedral looming over Spokane's South Hill—which is probably the effect its designers intended. Its soaring tower and stained glass would not look too out of place on Salisbury Plain.

Four Lakes Battle Monument, Four Lakes; just off I-90 about 10 miles southwest of Spokane. Following the Steptoe fiasco of 1858 (see below), Colonel George Wright of Walla Walla led a force of seven hundred soldiers in a punitive campaign against the Palouse, Yakama, Coeur d'Alene, and Spokane Indian tribes. With long-range rifles, sabers, and new minié bullets, they were better armed than Steptoe's crew. On September 1, 1858, the battle was joined and thousands of Indians (but no soldiers) were killed. A monument in the town of Four Lakes commemorates the event.

Gonzaga University (800-986-9585; www.gonzaga.edu), 502 West Boone Avenue, Spokane; just north of the Spokane River and east of downtown. Jesuits have been in northeastern Washington since the early 1840s. By 1887 they deemed the time right for a university and founded Gonzaga, which now occupies 108 leafy residential acres. Of interest are the Bing Crosby House (see *Historic Homes*) and ambitious St. Aloysius Parish Church, at 330 East Boone Street, completed in 1911 in an "adapted Romanesque" style.

Long Lake pictographs, on the north side of WA 291 about 20 miles northwest of Spokane. Shortly before this highway reaches the Long Lake Dam on the Spokane River, you can view a series of paintings depicting animals and humans on the granite cliff. Their meaning and origin is obscure. Use care negotiating the observation trail.

Spokane House Interpretive Center (509-465-5064; www.riversidestatepark .org), in Riverside State Park, 9711 West Charles Road, Nine Mile Falls. Open 10–4 Sat.–Sun. Memorial Day–Labor Day. Free. The original Spokane House has long since crumbled to dust. But it was the earliest trading post in what was to become Washington State, and it was inhabited from 1810 to 1826 by a motley community of British, French, Indian, and American fur trappers and traders. Eventually its location 60 miles from transportation on the Columbia River was found to be inconvenient, and the post was removed to Kettle Falls and renamed Fort Colvile (the British spelling). Digs in the 1950s and 1960s revealed its original location here. The interpretive center's displays of artifacts explain the history of the site.

Spokane Plains Battlefield, on US 2 about 10 miles east of Spokane. This State Heritage site commemorates a battle in 1858 between several Indian tribes and the U.S. Army in the wake of breaches of the 1855 treaty.

Steptoe Battlefield, off US 195 about 33 miles south of Spokane. This is another State Heritage site, commemorating a battle in 1858 between several Indian tribes and the U.S. Army. E. J. Steptoe was a colonel whose two military expeditions ended in routs, but nearby Steptoe Butte, now a state park about 20 miles south of the battlefield (see the Walla Walla and the Palouse chapter in part 6, Southeastern Washington) was named after him anyway.

MUSEUMS Carr's One of a Kind in the World Museum (509-489-8859), 5225 North Freya, Spokane. Open 1–4 Sat.–Sun. $8 adults, $7 seniors, children under nine free. This private museum features famous people's cars, including John F. Kennedy's 1962 Lincoln Continental, and other eclectic memorabilia.

North Spokane Farm Museum (509-466-2744), 6223 Ridgeway Road, Deer Park; on US 395 north of Spokane. Open 9–4 Apr.–Oct. 15; by appointment in winter. View farm implements of the area.

✐ **Northwest Museum of Arts and Culture** (509-456-3931; www.northwest museum.org), 2316 West First Avenue, Spokane. Open 10–5 Wed.–Sat., 5–9 first Fri. each month; closed holidays. $7 adults, $5 students and seniors, children under five free; by donation first Fri. each month. This Smithsonian-affiliated museum soars amid the stately homes of the Brownes Addition district (see *Historic Homes*). Its changing exhibits present a fascinating mesh of Northwest art, culture, and history—modern paintings inspired by Native basket-weave patterns, or early mapping of the Columbia Basin accompanied by watercolors by 19th-century artist Paul Kane. Most have something kids can get their hands on. Its collection of Columbia Plateau Indian artifacts is among the largest in the country. Admission includes the Campbell House next door (see *Historic Homes*).

Spokane Valley Heritage Museum (509-922-4570; www.valleyheritagecenter .org), 12114 East Sprague Avenue, Spokane Valley. Open 11–4 Wed.–Sat. $6 adults, $5 seniors, $4 students and children. The 1912 Township Hall was moved from the frontier town of Opportunity (now south of I-90 east of Spokane) to house the new Spokane Valley Heritage Museum, which opened August 2005 to showcase the history and development of the Spokane River valley.

NATURAL WONDERS Bowl and Pitcher, 4427 North Audrey L. White Parkway, Spokane. These basalt formations along the Spokane River frame boiling rapids in Riverside State Park. A swinging bridge across the river makes an exciting viewpoint.

Spokane Falls. View from the ground in Riverfront Park (see *Wilder Places—Parks*) or, for a bird's-eye view, take the park's **Skyride** over the falls ($7.25 adults; $6.25 seniors, military, and teens; $4 children 3–12). Once lost in a tangle of railway lines and yards, the jewel at the heart of Spokane came to light again when the city center was swept clean for the 1974 world's fair. Whitewater cascades down the upper and lower falls for a 90-foot drop down basalt cliffs.

SCENIC DRIVES Green Bluff orchard area, about 5 paved miles along Green Bluff Road, Dunn Road, Woolard Road, and Sands Road; from US 2 north of Spokane, turn right on Day–Mount Spokane Road, then left on Green Bluff Road. A tour of these country lanes, with explorations of nearby farms, makes a nice afternoon drive. On autumn afternoons, the roads can get crowded.

Mount Spokane Park Drive (WA 206), 15 paved miles from US 2 to Mount Spokane State Park. This winding route takes you up Deadman Creek into the folds of Mount Spokane and the foothills of the Rockies.

Turnbull National Wildlife Refuge Auto Tour Route, 5.5 miles. Drive through wetlands and woods south of Cheney, off WA 904 (see *Wilder Places—Wildlife Refuges*).

WA 291, about 33 miles from Riverside State Park to Long Lake Dam. This highway beside the Spokane River has views of the river and bluffs and a chance to see the Long Lake pictograph site about 5 miles east of the dam (see *Historic Sites*).

WALKING TOURS Cheney historical district (www.cityofcheney.org) comprises downtown buildings large and small, commercial and residential. Tour brochures can be downloaded or obtained from the West Plains Chamber of Commerce (see *Guidance*).

Spokane. A self-guided walking tour of **downtown,** with many buildings dating from the 1890s, is available from the Spokane Regional Convention and Visitors' Bureau (see *Guidance*). They can also provide you with historical or architectural itineraries. Of particular interest are the many **Kirtland Cutter homes** (www .spokaneoutdoors.com) built by this Washington architect who played a large part in rebuilding Spokane after the fire of 1889 and whose influence spread far beyond the Northwest. The **Historic Preservation office** (www.historicspokane .org) at City Hall is preparing walking-tour guides for Spokane's **16 designated historic districts;** available so far are guides for the Brownes Addition (see *Historic Homes*), Rockwood, and Hillyard neighborhoods, which have many fine old mansions.

WINERY TOURS Spokane Winery Association (509-926-0164; www.spokane wineries.net) has a list of regional wineries. Spokane might not be the first place you think of when you think of wine, and not many grapes are grown here, but the 19 local wineries are using grapes grown in the Yakima, Columbia, and Walla Walla valleys. Spokane's wineries stretch out from the downtown riverfront upstream and north into Green Bluff; most are family owned; and some maintain a very small, specialized production. Special wine events are the Spring Barrel Tasting on Mother's Day weekend and the Holiday Wine Festival the weekend before Thanksgiving, when all the wineries are open for tasting. Most of them are open on weekends at other times, and a lazy drive to a few cellars can make a pleasant afternoon.

✴ To Do

BICYCLING Back roads. Quiet highways wind through the countryside beyond Spokane's city limits. Cyclists enjoy the Palouse country to the south, along the Palouse Highway or Hangman Valley Road; the Medical Lake area to the southwest via WA 902; the meadows of Four Mound Prairie to the west, via Four Mound Road west of Riverside State Park; and the woods near Deer Park to the north, off US 395.

Centennial Trail (509-624-7188), 30 paved miles (37 miles planned) from Nine Mile Falls in Riverside State Park to the Idaho state line, plus another 40 miles to Lake Coeur d'Alene, Idaho. The Centennial Trail was dedicated in 1989 in honor of the centenary of Washington's statehood. Running alongside the Spokane River, the wide trail has plenty of room for all sorts of self-propelled travelers. Its route passes fossil beds and sites of archaeological and historical interest. The trail is intended for day use only, but access at many points along the way allows you to exit for the night. Maps are available at the Riverside State Park office (see *Wilder Places—Parks*).

Mount Spokane State Park (509-238-4258), 29500 Mount Spokane Drive, Mead; 25 miles northeast of Spokane off US 2 at end of WA 206. The park has 90 miles of mountain bike trails (see *Wilder Places—Parks*).

Riverside State Park (509-465-5064; www.riversidestatepark.org); off WA 291 northwest of downtown Spokane. This park has 50 miles of mountain bike trails (see *Wilder Places*).

Spokane Bicycle Club (509-747-5581), Box 62, Spokane 99210. Contact them for information on area cycling.

Turnbull National Wildlife Refuge Auto Tour Route, 5.5 miles; off WA 904 south of Cheney. This route through wetlands and woods is open to bicycles, too.

CAMPING Liberty Lake County Park (509-477-4730), south of I-90 east of Spokane. Open Apr. 15–Oct. 15. Twenty-two RV sites and 11 tent sites. No reservations.

Mount Spokane State Park (509-238-4258), 29500 Mount Spokane Drive, Mead; 25 miles northeast of Spokane off US 2 at the end of WA 206. Campsites open late May–mid-Sept. Eight tent and RV sites (no utilities; not ADA) on the mountain's spectacular flanks within the state park. No reservations.

& **Riverside State Park** (509-465-5064; reservations 888-226-7688; www.river sidestatepark.org), off WA 291 northwest of downtown Spokane. Sixteen tent sites and 16 RV sites, some wheelchair-friendly; access to fishing, boating, and hiking in the state park.

CANOEING, KAYAKING, AND RAFTING Little Spokane River, 7 miles within Little Spokane River Natural Area; put in at the painted rocks or St. George's School Road, both off Rutter Parkway. Boat this meandering stream and visit Indian pictographs along the way.

Riverside State Park (509-465-5064; www.riversidestatepark.org), off WA 291 northwest of downtown Spokane (see *Wilder Places—Parks*). Bring your own kayak or rent one within the park to boat the Spokane River here.

Spokane River. The lower Spokane has up to class III rapids. There's a put-in at Downriver Golf Course (see *Golf*), but it's wiser to go with an outfitter.

Wiley E. Waters (888-502-1900; www.riverrafting.com) offers guided kayak and raft trips on the Spokane River.

FOREST SERVICE CABIN RENTALS Quartz Mountain Fire Lookout, in Mount Spokane State Park (509-238-4258). Originally built in 1979 on top of Mount Spokane, the lookout was used until 1994. In 2004–2005 it was moved to this more remote location on Quartz Mountain and renovated (and its supporting tower incidentally lowered to 10 feet) and presto!—a backcountry cabin was born. Guests must be able to walk the 2.25 miles from the Selkirk Lodge shelter with their supplies. It sleeps up to four people on bunk beds. Water, a vault toilet, and other furnishings are provided. There's also an outdoor picnic table, a fire grate, and some fine views. $85 June 15–Sept. 15; $75 Sept. 16–Oct. 15.

GOLF City of Spokane (509-625-6200; www.spokaneparks.org, click on "golf") runs four 18-hole golf courses:

The Creek at Qualchan (509-448-9317), 301 East Meadow Lane.

Downriver Golf Course (509-327-5269), 3225 North Columbia Circle.

Esmeralda Golf Course (509-487-6291), 3933 East Kirtland.

Indian Canyon Golf Course (509-747-5353), 4304 West West Drive.

Spokane County (509-477-4730; www.spokanecounty.org) offers another three 18-hole golf courses:

Hangman Valley Golf Course (509-448-1212), 2210 East Hangman Valley Road, Spokane.

Liberty Lake Public Golf Course (509-225-6233), 24403 East Sprague Avenue, Liberty Lake.

Meadowwood Golf Course (509-255-9539), 24501 East Valleyway Avenue, Liberty Lake.

For more information check online (www.golfinspokane.com).

HIKING ♿ **Centennial Trail** (509-465-5064), 30 paved miles (37 miles planned) from Riverside State Park to the Idaho state line, plus 40 miles to Lake Coeur d'Alene, Idaho. This trail is open to hikers and skaters as well as cyclists (see *Bicycling*); most of it is also wheelchair-friendly.

♿ **Columbia Plateau Trail** (509-646-9218; www.parks.wa.gov/trails), 23 gravel miles from Cheney to Martin Road (7 miles east of Sprague); another 15 unimproved miles are open to hikers and bikers. This new trail follows an old Spokane–Portland railway line, complete with a crushed-rock surface. The 3.75 miles within Fish Lake County Park are paved and wheelchair-accessible. From there, the trail heads south through scenic Turnbull National Wildlife Refuge (see *Wilder Places—Wildlife Refuges*). When finished, it will run 130 miles through the harsh Channeled Scablands all the way to Pasco.

Deep Creek Canyon Loop, 4.6 miles, in Riverside State Park (509-465-5064; www.riversidestatepark.org), off WA 291 northwest of downtown Spokane (see *Wilder Places—Parks*). This trail offers fine reservoir views. The park has 55 miles of trails over varied terrain, including the Little Spokane River Trail (see below), though many are shared with mountain bikes.

Liberty Lake Regional Park loop trail, 7.5 miles. This has a 1,160-foot elevation gain but takes in a waterfall and views into Idaho (see *Wilder Places—Parks*).

Little Spokane River Trail, 5 miles in Riverside State Park (see Deep Creek Canyon Loop, above). Petroglyphs are visible on this trail.

Three Peaks Trail, 14 miles, in Mount Spokane State Park (509-238-4258), 29500 Mount Spokane Drive, Mead; 25 miles northeast of Spokane off US 2 at end of WA 206 (see *Wilder Places—Parks*). This long uphill hike is shorter but just as spectacular if you first drive to one of its higher trailheads. Mount Spokane State Park's 100 miles of trails, which are often shared with mountain bikes, also include trails used by Nordic skiers in winter.

WINTER SPORTS **Downriver Golf Course** (509-327-5269; www.spokaneparks .com), 3225 North Columbia Circle. Cross-country skiing is allowed here in winter.

Mount Spokane Ski and Snowboard Park (509-238-2220 or 509-443-1397), within Mount Spokane State Park, 29500 Mount Spokane Drive, Mead; 25 miles northeast of Spokane off US 2 at the end of WA 206 (see *Wilder Places—Parks*). Open 9–4 daily; night skiing Wed.–Sat. Jan.–mid-Mar. and part of Dec. Sno-Park permit required. This 5,883-foot peak can get 25 feet of snow in winter and has views into Idaho and Montana, five ski lifts for a 2,000-foot drop, and 15 miles of groomed cross-country trails. Snowmobilers also get their own groomed trails. Snowshoers and dogsleds have ample room to roam, too.

Riverside State Park (509-465-5064; www.riversidestatepark.org), off WA 291 northwest of downtown Spokane (see *Wilder Places—Parks*). Cross-country skiing is allowed on certain trails here in winter.

✳ Wilder Places

PARKS

Spokane City Parks
In 1907 the City of Spokane asked the Olmsted brothers, of New York–New England fame, to design a parks system. Today Spokane has more than 75 parks

ranging from small neighborhood green spaces to the grand Riverfront Park. Some highlights of the system are these:

Audubon Park, on Northwest Boulevard between Milton and Audubon streets. This is a stately green space.

Coeur d'Alene Park, at Fourth Avenue and Chestnut Street. Spokane's first park has 10 acres.

Downriver Park, Pettit Drive and Fort Wright Drive. This 95-acre wildlife corridor offers trails and natural springs.

Finch Arboretum, 3404 West Woodland Boulevard, off US 2 west of downtown. Native and exotic trees are planted on 90 landscaped acres (see *To See—Gardens*).

Manito Park, 17th Avenue and Grand Boulevard. Opened in 1904, Manito's 90 acres on the South Hill are devoted almost entirely to gardens (see *To See— Gardens*).

Riverfront Park (509-625-6600 or 800-366-PARK; www.spokaneriverfrontpark .com), Spokane Falls Boulevard and Washington Street. Besides 100 verdant acres for strolling, jogging, or sunbathing, the city's front yard offers such amusements as the 1909 Looff Carrousel (see *To See—For Families*) and the Skyride gondolas over Spokane Falls (see *To See—Natural Wonders*). Scattered through the park are reminders of Expo '74 (the 1974 world's fair): A venerable clock tower, emblem of Spokane, is all that remains of the Great Northern train station that was demolished to make way for the fair; a large tentlike web was once the U.S. pavilion. Whimsical attractions including the steel garbage-eating goat (environmentalism was the fair's theme), the giant *Red Wagon,* and the interactive fountain appeal to everyone's inner child.

Spokane County Parks

🦌 ♿ **Dishman Hills Natural Area,** 625 South Sargent Road, Spokane Valley. This 518-acre preserve has trails, a wheelchair-accessible path, and playground equipment.

Fish Lake County Park, just north of Cheney; from I-90 just west of Spokane, take US 195 south to Cheney-Spokane Road, turn right, go 7 miles to Myers Road, and follow the signs. $2 in summer. This 52-acre park has swimming, nonmotorized boating, paved trails, and a basketball court.

Liberty Lake Regional Park, 3707 South Zephyr Road; from I-90 east of Spokane, take the Liberty Lake exit, turn left on Valleyway to Lakeside, and turn right on Lakeside to Zephyr. This mountainside park with nearly 3,000 lakeside acres about 15 miles east of Spokane is popular for summer camping (see *To Do— Camping*) and swimming. Nearby is the Liberty Lake Public Golf Course (see *To Do—Golf*) and the 350-acre county park for off-road vehicles.

Little Spokane River Natural Area, adjoining Riverside State Park (see below). Jointly administered by Washington State Parks (through Riverside State Park) and Spokane County Parks, it's primarily for wildlife habitat but also for canoeing, kayaking, and wildlife watching.

State Parks

Mount Spokane State Park (509-238-4258), 29500 Mount Spokane Drive, Mead; 25 miles northeast of Spokane; take US 2 north from Spokane about 10 miles, then WA 206 east 15 miles. Open 6:30 AM–dusk in summer, 8 AM–10 PM in winter. From the top of 5,883-foot Mount Spokane, you can view the surrounding Selkirk Mountains, Idaho, and Canada, but you might be too busy checking the ski runs—the park draws downhill and Nordic skiers, snowmobilers, and general snow enthusiasts (see *To Do—Winter Sports*). Summer opens 100 miles of hiking trails (see *To Do—Hiking*), as many equestrian trails, and 90 miles of bike trails. There's camping, too (see *To Do—Camping*).

Riverside State Park (509-465-5064; www.riversidepark.org), on the northwestern edge of Spokane; from I-90 take exit 280, turn left onto Maxwell Street, which becomes Pettit Street, and park past the Downriver Golf Course (see *To Do—Golf*). Sprawling over 10,000 acres at the confluence of the Spokane and Little Spokane rivers, this state park is nearly all things to nearly all Spokanites: from pristine natural areas to dirt-bike zones, with hiking, skiing, river running, horseback riding, camping, and history (see *To See—Historic Sites*)—a recreational heaven just minutes from downtown.

WILDLIFE REFUGES & **Turnbull National Wildlife Refuge** (509-235-4723; www.turnbull.fws.gov), 26010 South Smith Road, Cheney; from I-90 west of Spokane take WA 904 to Cheney, then turn south on Cheney-Plaza Road and drive 4.5 miles to the entrance. Open dawn to dusk year-round. $3 per car Mar.–Oct. Where the Columbia Plateau bumps up against the foothills of the Rockies, Turnbull's combination of steppe, forest, and wetlands provides habitat for an unusual number of species. This is the eastern edge of the Channeled Scablands; as the Ice Age waned, the basalt plateau was scoured and channeled by unimaginable floods, yielding a severe landscape of dry canyons relieved by pines, wetlands, and views of the Bitterroots. Wildlife observation is the big draw: Watchable species include coyotes, deer, elk, and the occasional moose, not to mention 27 kinds of ducks. Unlike many refuges, Turnbull does not permit hunting or fishing, and public access is confined to 2,300 of its nearly 16,000 acres (move over, Daniel Boone). The Public Use Area includes a 5.5-mile tour loop open to cars, bicycles, and pedestrians, as well as shorter trails, including a 1-mile, wheelchair-accessible boardwalk.

✳ Lodging

BED & BREAKFASTS

Spokane

✦ **E. J. Roberts Mansion** (509-456-8839; www.ejrobertsmansion.com), 1923 West First Avenue. This 1889 mansion is popular for weddings and other events. The four antiques-furnished guest rooms each have a private bath. The grounds include a secret garden. Rates include breakfast. Children are welcome. No pets. $140–200.

Fotheringham House (509-993-8258; www.fotheringhamhouse.com), 2128 West Second Avenue. David Fotheringham was only 35 when he became Spokane's first mayor in 1891 and built his house in the city's upscale Brownes Addition (see *To See—Historic Homes*). Walnut antiques complement the original spiral staircase and intricate woodwork. Just steps from the Northwest Museum of Arts and Culture (see *To See—Museums*) and in the middle of a walking tour of historic homes (owners Valerie Blake and Kelley Dupuis can give you a self-guiding flyer), it's an ideal location for a quiet stay. Four guest rooms (only one with private bath) are furnished with antiques and period lamps but also offer free Wi-Fi. Rates include breakfast. $115–135.

Mariana Stolz House (509-483-4316 or 800-978-6587), 427 East Indiana Avenue. This Foursquare house has been around for more than a hundred years; some of the original fixtures are still in place. Four antiques-furnished rooms are available. $89–109.

☀ **On the Park Bed and Breakfast** (509-325-8396; www.ontheparkbb .com), 3527 North Audubon Street. Linda and Bob Mastronarde's 1920s home sits on Audubon Park (see *Wilder Places—Parks*) in a quiet west side neighborhood. The three guest rooms are named for honored relatives; each has its own bathroom, and two share a kitchenette; all have cozy pillow-top mattresses. Decorative touches alluding to the 1920s, 1930s, and 1940s include some fantastic antiques Linda has rescued from the Monroe Street antiques district (see *Selective Shopping*). Bob may have homemade cookies ready to welcome you and may surprise you with Danish *aebelskiver* as the centerpiece of a hearty breakfast (included in the rates). They'll also accommodate special dietary requirements. Ask about pets. $90–115.

GUESTHOUSES

Spokane
Odell House (509-879-4691; www .theodellhouse.com), 2325 West First Avenue. Just west of downtown, this house was built by the Odell family in 1899. A huge Queen Anne, it was converted to multiple units following World War II and now offers an alternative to expensive bed & breakfasts or cookie-cutter motels: rooms and apartments furnished in period style, some quite simple and others a bit grand, for long- or short-term rentals at reasonable rates. $50–145.

HOTELS

Spokane
☀ **The Davenport Hotel** (509-455-8888 or 800-899-1482; www.the davenporthotel.com), 10 South Post Street. The story goes that Louis Davenport's establishment started as a waffle stand in Spokane's boomtown days. Designed by Northwest architectural luminary Kirtland Cutter and now the grande dame of Spokane hotels, it opened in 1914 to, as Davenport put it, bring the world to Spokane. With ballroom decor alluding to Versailles and Venice, fine dining, and luxury Irish linens, it did. In fact, almost all the U.S. presidents of the 20th century stayed here. Even so, regional decline forced it to close in 1985. Bought and restored by local entrepreneurs Walt and Karen Worthy, it burst forth with renewed vigor in 2002, with much of the original decor sparklingly intact, fine dining in the Palm Court Grill (see *Where to Eat*), and the fountained foyer—called "Spokane's living room"—still welcoming guests. Even if you don't stay here, a tour is worthwhile just to hear the ghost stories, find coded messages in the ornate plaster friezes, and marvel at the architectural skills and opulence available on the frontier a hundred years ago. The 283 rooms feature gas fireplaces, bathrooms with capacious marble showers and jetted tubs, several phones, armchairs, desks, and Internet connection. Well-behaved pets welcome. Rooms $129–149; suites higher.

& **Hotel Lusso** (509-747-9750; hotel lusso.com), 808 West Sprague Avenue. Now owned by the Davenport. The Lusso's Italian theme runs throughout its interior design, from its Roman-style fountain to its elegant furnishings. Spokane's first "boutique" hotel, the Lusso opened in 1998 in an 1890 building as part of the city's rebirth, with 48 rooms comfortably appointed with easy chairs and ottomans. All rooms are nonsmoking. **Post Street Ale House** (509-789-6900), the on-site restaurant and pub, offers "comfortable food at comfortable prices." Rates include continental breakfast. No pets. Rooms $100–119; suites higher.

The Montvale Hotel (509-747-1919 or 866-668-8253; www.montvalehotel .com), 1005 West First Avenue. Built in 1899, the Montvale housed laborers in Spokane's boomtown days, then travelers, and then, like the town, it went into a long decline. Happily, it was restored and reopened as a 36-room hotel in 2005, with contemporary rooms and public areas that are a blend of art deco, modern, and historic styles. It shares the bustling downtown area with the Davenport and the Lusso (see above); there's room and action enough for all. $119–219.

LODGES

Mount Spokane Area
Bear Creek Lodge (509-238-9114; www.bearcreeklodgewa.com), 24817 North Mount Spokane Park Drive, Mead. Open year-round. At the foot of Mount Spokane, Bear Creek Lodge was originally a rustic ski lodge in the 1950s. Since then, it's been reconfigured; all 15 rooms have private baths, and the common room has two stone fireplaces. It's still simple: There are no phones, TVs, or cell service. **Bear Creek Lodge Restaurant and Lounge,** opened in 2003, specializes in steaks, ribs, and salmon—good intermountain grub; Wed. dinner specials. No pets. $59–225.

✳ Where to Eat
DINING OUT

Spokane
Luna (509-448-2383; www.luna spokane.com), 5620 South Perry Street. Open from 11 AM Mon.–Fri., from 9 AM Sat.–Sun. Located in what was formerly a post office in the south end, Luna has an eclectic menu that depends on local farmers and products. Choose from homemade pizzas, appetizers ranging from fresh clams to tuna tartare, and main dishes for everyone, including vegetarians. Reservations recommended.

Mizuna (509-747-2004; www.mizuna .com), 214 North Howard Street. Open 11–10 Mon.–Sat., 5–10 Sun. Located downtown, Mizuna has an ambitious, eclectic menu featuring choices such as mussels in white wine, sesame-miso ahi salad, and all-natural steak with pine nut butter, as well as vegetarian and vegan options.

& **Moxie** (509-456-3594; www.moxie moxie.com), 816 West Sprague Avenue. Open for dinner daily. Ian Wingate operated the first Moxie in Liberty Lake, till he was tapped to become executive chef at the Davenport Hotel. In 2004 he left the Davenport to open Moxie's second incarnation just across the street. It's become one of the chief Spokane venues for haute fusion cuisine, specializing in a Euro-Asian menu. Chef Wingate also painted the wave mural on the wall, with a nod to Hokusai. Reservations suggested.

The Palm Court Grill (509-789-6848; www.thedavenporthotel.com), in the Davenport Hotel, 10 South Post Street. Open for breakfast, lunch, and dinner daily. The restaurant at Spokane's classic hotel (see *Lodging*) has a classic menu, but that doesn't signify plain intermountain meat and potatoes—the beef tenderloin comes with béarnaise sauce, the baked chicken breast is stuffed with shiitake mushrooms and Gruyère, and the wild Northwest salmon melts in your mouth. The long wine list includes, naturally, Washington's finest. Also in the Davenport, the **Peacock Lounge**

offers—well, fine drinking, a ceiling entirely done in stained-glass peacock feathers, and light meals from the Palm Court's kitchen.

EATING OUT

Spokane

⚓ **Frank's Diner** (509-747-8798; www.franksdiners.com), 1516 West Second Avenue. Open 6 AM–8 PM Sun.–Thurs., 6 AM–9 PM Fri.–Sat. Frank's has been voted "best breakfast" in Spokane for 11 years running. Evidently people vote with their feet, because it's a hopping place at nine on a weekday morning. *Hearty* and *traditional* are the words: All possible permutations of eggs, hash browns, pancakes, and breakfast meats are on the menu, not to mention Frank's signature country gravy. Those who are watching their cholesterol can have Snoqualmie Oatmeal. Frank's is a railroad car restaurant—a 1906 Barney-Smith luxury car with glowing wood paneling, the personal carriage of the Northern Pacific's president till it was retired in 1931. Happily, it found a new life as a restaurant in Seattle, where it acquitted itself honorably for 60 years before being moved to Spokane. A Northside location (509-465-2464), 10929 North Newport Highway, occupies a 1913 Pullman car rescued from a forlorn railroad siding.

Mustard Seed Asian Café (509-483-1500), 4750 North Division Street. Open 11–9 Mon.–Thurs., 11–10 Fri.–Sat., 12–8 Sun. With a handful of locations in Montana, Idaho, and Washington, the Mustard Seed offers Asian–Pacific Rim cuisine at reasonable prices, from Japanese pot stickers to Bong Bong chicken and beyond. Most menu items are also available to go.

⚓ **The Onion** (509-747-3852; www.theonion.biz), 302 West Riverside. Open from 11 AM daily. The Onion is an informal, family-and-friends restaurant that serves only hormone-free burgers and has low-fat, low-carb options, as well as a children's menu. It's not fancy, but it's busy, hearty, and varied, with a menu running from their signature onion soup through steaks and burgers to salads, fish-and-chips, pasta dishes, and most basic American favorites. There's also a Northside location (509-482-6100), 7522 North Division Street.

& **Soulful Soups** (509-459-1190), 117 North Howard Street. Open 11 AM– 2 AM Mon.–Sat. Its first incarnation was as an 1890s saloon, and it still has the early pressed-tin ceiling. Home-made soups, salads, and sandwiches satisfy the inner person at this busy downtown lunch and snack spot.

⚓ **Steam Plant Grill** (509-777-3900; www.steamplantgrill.com), 159 South Lincoln Street. Open from 3 PM daily. From 1916 to 1986, the steam plant provided heat to most of downtown Spokane via a network of underground passages. After retirement, it took almost a decade to reawaken—as an office, retail, and restaurant complex. Renovators Ron and Julie Wells aimed to "enable diners to view and feel the unique atmosphere of an actual steam plant." Even if this is not your customary dining goal, the decor of catwalks and control panels is certainly unusual. The menu runs to a hearty Northwest mix of pasta, steaks, and seafood, and the beer is brewed on-site by Coeur d'Alene Brewing Company, whose motto is DRINK RESPONSIBLY. DRINK LOCALLY.

✳ Entertainment

MUSIC Spokane Opera (509-533-1150), the Metropolitan Performing Arts Center, 901 West Sprague Avenue, Spokane. Performances twice to four times a year.

Spokane Symphony (509-624-1200), Martin Woldson Theater, 1001 West Sprague Avenue, Spokane. Performs more than 60 diverse concerts a year.

THEATER ♪ **IMAX Theater at Riverfront Park** (509-625-6601), 507 North Howard, Spokane. Nature- and science-oriented IMAX features, as well as movies such as the Harry Potter series remastered for IMAX. Have adventures while getting off your feet. Handy to other park attractions if you're traveling with kids.

✳ Selective Shopping

River Park Square (509-363-0304; www.riverparksquare.com), 808 West Main Avenue, Spokane, is the new downtown mall featuring your usual Northwest stores and then some, plus the Mobius children's museum (see *To See—For Families*).

ANTIQUES Scattered north up Spokane's Monroe Street from the river to Dalton are a number of antiques shops where surprises sometimes await. Some of the dealers include the following:

Jewels Etc. (509-326-4099; www .jewelsetc.net), 618 North Monroe, Spokane.

Julie Button's Antiques and Collectibles (509-324-2018), 2907 North Monroe, Spokane.

United Hillyard Antique Mall (509-483-2647), 5016 North Market Street, Spokane. Two floors of exquisite finds in another up-and-coming antiques neighborhood.

✳ Special Events

May: ♿ **The Bloomsday Run** (509-838-1579; www.bloomsdayrun.org), 12 kilometers (7.5 miles) from Riverside Avenue to the Monroe Street Bridge, in Spokane. Timed to coincide with the Lilac Festival (see below), this run started in 1977 without apparent reference to James Joyce. On the crest of enthusiasm generated by Expo '74, Spokane's new, green downtown, and one visionary runner, a thousand participants ran the greenway. Today tens of thousands of runners, walkers, wheelchair users, and stroller pushers participate in the festive run.

Lilac Festival (509-535-4554; www .spokanelilacfestival.org), Spokane. Lilacs have proliferated in Spokane since the 1930s; there's even a "Lilac Hill" in Manito Park. The third weekend in May brings the Lilac Festival, with a parade, a lilac queen and princesses, and lilacs everywhere.

June: **Hoopfest** (509-634-2414; www .spokanehoopfest.net), Spokane. On the last weekend in June, Spokane's streets fill as thousands of players from 7 to 70 compete in an outdoor basketball tournament. The games take up 40 city blocks. Music, festivities, and food complement the games.

July: **Settlers' Days** (509-276-5900), at Mix Park, Perrins Field, and Swinyard Park, in Deer Park. This fair includes old-time contests, music, a parade, food booths, and crafts on the fourth weekend of July.

August: **Spokane Falls Northwest Indian Encampment and Powwow** (509-483-7535; www.spokaneriver frontpark.com), Spokane. Celebrate Native dancing, drumming, and crafts with Northwest tribes along the riverbanks the last weekend in August.

September: **Labor Day Dog Show and Herding Trials** (509-276-2444), Clayton Community Fairgrounds, about 12 miles northwest of Deer Park just off US 395. Observe the skills of sheepherding dogs and dogs in general.

KETTLE FALLS AND
THE SELKIRKS

The north woods of northeastern Washington are in the Selkirk Mountains, running at an angle from the confluence of the Spokane and Columbia rivers northeast to the border with Idaho and Canada (and beyond). These are western foothills of the Rockies, and flowing through them is the Pend Oreille River, which starts near Sandpoint, Idaho, and loops north into Canada before joining the Columbia at the border. The western edge of this region is along the edge of Lake Roosevelt down to Kettle Falls, then along US 395 south to Deer Park.

The few towns you find in this zone are small and weather-beaten—as well they might be, spending much of the winter under several feet of snow. Newport, northeast of Spokane, is right on the Idaho border on the Pend Oreille River. Also on the river are Cusick, Tiger, and Metaline. Just across the river is Metaline Falls, right up against Idaho and Canada; founded on minerals and hydropower, it is now an arts community. Kettle Falls has lake recreation rather than falls. Colville and Chewelah to the south are gateways to recreation. Here you will find clean air and streams, enough stars to compensate for the area's lack of glitz, plenty of wildlife, and a spirit of self-sufficiency. In this remote area, keep an eye on your gas gauge. If you travel in winter, keep tire chains and blankets in your car.

GUIDANCE Colville Chamber of Commerce (509-684-5973; www.colville .com), 121 East Astor, Colville 99114.

Colville National Forest Headquarters (509-684-7000; www.fs.fed.us/r6 /colville), 765 South Main Street, Colville 99114. District offices include **Kettle Falls office** (509-738-2300), 425 West Third Street, Kettle Falls 99141; **Newport Ranger District** (509-447-7300), 315 North Warren Avenue, Newport 99156; **Sullivan Lake Ranger District** (509-446-7500), 12641 Sullivan Lake Road, Metaline Falls 99153.

Greater Newport Area Chamber of Commerce (509-447-5812 or 877-818-1008; www.newportoldtownchamber.org), 325 West Fourth Street, Newport 99156.

Kaniksu/Idaho Panhandle National Forest (208-263-5111), 1500 US 2, Suite 110, Sandpoint, ID 83864.

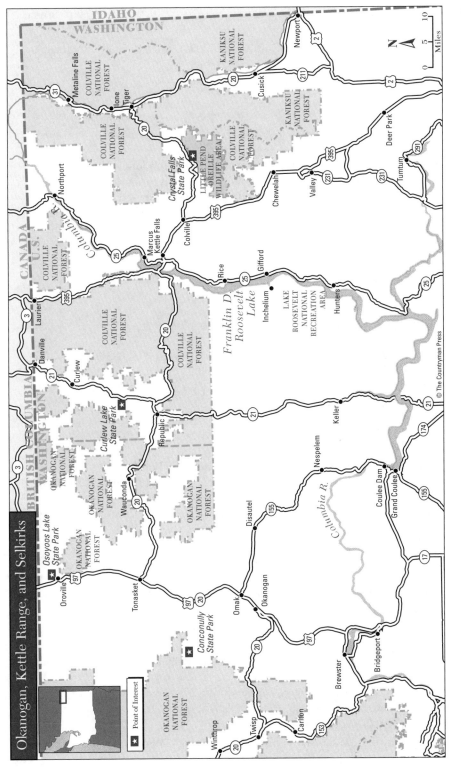

Okanogan, Kettle Range, and Selkirks

★ Point of Interest

© The Countryman Press

Kettle Falls Chamber of Commerce (509-738-2300), 265 West Third Street, Kettle Falls 99141.

The Metalines Chamber of Commerce (509-446-1721), Box 388, Metaline Falls 99153.

Pend Oreille River Tourism Alliance (509-447-5286; www.porta-us.com), Box 1182, Newport 99156.

Spokane Indian Reservation (509-458-6500; www.spokanetribe.com), 6105 Ford-Wellpinit Road, Wellpinit 99040; about 50 miles northwest of Spokane.

GETTING THERE In the west, the main north-south route is **US 395** from Spokane through Chewelah, Colville, and Kettle Falls to Canada; **WA 25** heads north from Davenport on **US 2** to Kettle Falls, then follows the Columbia northeast to Canada. In the east, US 2 heads north from Spokane to Newport, then heads east into Idaho. **WA 20** is the main east-west route, from Kettle Falls east through Colville and Tiger, where it turns south through Cusick and Newport. At Tiger, **WA 31** heads north to Metaline.

The closest air, train, and bus service is in Spokane (see the Spokane Area chapter).

GETTING AROUND You'll need a car in this remote area.

MEDICAL EMERGENCY Mount Carmel Hospital (509-685-5100; www.mt carmelhospital.org), 982 East Columbia, Colville.

Newport Hospital (509-447-2441), 714 West Pine Street, Newport.

St. Joseph's Hospital (509-935-8211), 500 East Webster Drive, Chewelah.

✳ To See

FARMERS' MARKETS Chewelah Farmers' Market (509-936-4353), Chewelah City Park, Park Street and Lincoln Avenue, Chewelah. Open 12–5 Fri. late May–mid-Oct.

Colville Farmers' Market (509-732-6619), corner of Third Avenue and Oak Street, Colville. Open 12–5 Wed. May–Oct.

HISTORIC SITES Lindsey House, at the County Fairgrounds, WA 20, Cusick. Open only during Pioneer Days in July and the Pend Oreille County Fair in late summer (see *Special Events*). This pioneer home is run by the Pend Oreille County Historical Society (see *Museums*).

Metaline Falls buildings. Of interest are the Cutter Theatre; the 1912 Larsen House, on Fifth Avenue between Grandview and the post office; and the Metaline Falls School, dating from 1912 to 1915. All are attributed to architect Kirtland Cutter (see the Spokane Area chapter).

Tiger Historical Center (509-447-5286), junction of WA 20 and WA 31, Tiger. Open June–Sept. Free. Nothing much is left at this lonely corner but the yellow clapboard Tiger Store, first built by George Tiger in 1906 (the present building dates from 1912). It served the little community of—Tiger!—in the years when

Washington's inhospitable far northeastern corner was being settled. Today it displays memorabilia of the era.

U.S. Fort Colville, 1 mile east of Colville on WA 294 and 2 miles north on Aladdin Road. Built in 1859, originally 3 miles east of Colville, this fort functioned till 1882, a bulwark in the turbulent years after the "settlement" of Indians on reservations. Today only a marker indicates the spot.

Washington Hotel (509-446-4415), 249 East Fifth Avenue, Metaline Falls. One of several historic buildings in Metaline Falls, the hotel was built in 1906 to house workers during the town's development and operated until just a few years ago. The gabled brick building is on the National Register of Historic Places.

MUSEUMS Kettle Falls Historical Center (509-738-6964), 1188 St. Paul's Mission Road, Kettle Falls; 3 miles west of town on US 395. Open 11–5 daily May 15–Sept. 15. Donation accepted. Like many falls on the Columbia River system, Kettle Falls was a bottleneck for migrating salmon and thus a major Indian fishing site and seasonal settlement. In 1826, British trappers established **Fort *Colvile*** nearby (not to be confused with the later U.S. Fort Colville, farther east near the town of Colville; see *Historic Sites*), enlisting some Indians in the fur trade, and Catholic missionaries soon followed. This small museum contains artifacts of the local Indians and fur traders and paintings depicting the history of the site. A short interpretive trail leads past hand-hewn **St. Paul's Mission** church, built by Father DeSmet and his Indian converts in 1847, to a view of what would be the falls but is now Lake Roosevelt. The site of Fort Colvile, too, lies beneath the waves.

Keller Heritage Center Museum and Park (509-684-5968), 700 North Wynne, Colville. Open 10–4 Mon.–Thurs. and 1–4 Fri.–Sun. May–Sept. $5 adults, $3 seniors, $2 children 5–18, $10 families. The Keller Heritage Center puts together pioneer buildings gleaned from around this remote corner of Washington—the town's first schoolhouse, cabins, a forge, and a 1930s fire tower—anchored by the fine 1910 Keller House, furnished as when built. The adjacent museum's artifacts display Colville's story in sequence, from geology and the fur trade to a print shop and pharmacy.

Pend Oreille County Historical Society Museum (509-447-5388), 402 South Washington Avenue, Newport. Open 10–4 daily May–mid-Oct. Donation requested. This 1908 train depot and adjoining grounds display tools and farm equipment from settlement days, three pioneer cabins, and a railroad exhibit featuring a Burlington Northern metal caboose. Next door is the Big Wheel, an engine that powered lumber mills on the site from 1909 to 1964.

ST. PAUL'S MISSION CHURCH IN KETTLE FALLS IS THE OLDEST CHURCH IN WASHINGTON.

NATURAL WONDERS Gardner Cave, in Crawford State Park (509-446-4065; see *Wilder Places—Parks*). Guided tours Thurs. and Mon. May–Sept.; call for hours. Free. This is the third-longest limestone gallery in Washington (1,055 feet), complete with stalactites, stalagmites, and other formations.

SCENIC DRIVES The Flowery Trail, 80 miles from Usk to Tiger—the long way. This back road takes you through stunning scenery over the Selkirk Mountains to Chewelah; then head north on US 395 to Colville and east on WA 20 to Tiger. (Continue south 31 miles on WA 20 to return to Usk.)

North Pend Oreille Scenic Byway (WA 31) (509-447-5286; www.porta-us.com), 27 paved miles from Tiger to the Canadian border. Winding along the silver Pend Oreille River between dark evergreen hills, the route from its junction with WA 20 presents ever-changing views and several small, half-forgotten mining towns. At the border, you could continue on the **International Selkirk Loop** (www.selkirk loop.org), a 280-mile drive joining several scenic highways through southern British Columbia, Idaho, and Washington, past snowcapped peaks, lakes, and waterfalls. If you want to do this, remember your passport.

Pend Oreille Valley Scenic Byway (WA 20), 50 paved miles from Tiger to Newport. Here, too, you have river and mountain views and small towns where you can still see log holding areas that supplied the Diamond Match Company.

WALKING TOURS Metaline Falls historic buildings. The tiny town of Metaline Falls, on WA 31 near the Idaho-Canada border, dates from the mining boom of the late 1800s and early 1900s. Its town center includes hotels and other businesses from that period. A self-guided walking tour is available from the Metalines Chamber of Commerce (see *Guidance*).

✳ To Do

BICYCLING Colville National Forest trails (509-684-7000; www.fs.fed.us/r6 /colville). Many hiking trails are also open to mountain bikes (see *Hiking*). Specific biking trails include these:

Chewelah Mountain Trail, 12 miles; off US 395 northeast of Chewelah. Maintained by 49 Degrees North Mountain Resort (see *Winter Sports*), this challenging trail is used for Nordic skiing in winter.

Geophysical Mountain Bike Trails, 7 miles; near Bead Lake about 20 miles north of Newport. This rolling forest terrain is in a winter wildlife range.

Wolf Donation Mountain Bike Trail System, 5 miles of varied terrain on the north edge of Newport.

BOATING Lake Roosevelt National Recreation Area (509-633-9441). All kinds of boats dot the lake in summer, which means if you want a quiet sail or paddle, you should find a peaceful cove up lake (not too hard, as the lake is 154 miles long); launch permits are required.

Lake Roosevelt Resort and Marina (800-635-7585), Box 340, Kettle Falls 99141. This vendor rents houseboats, one way to enjoy the lake in comfort.

Colville National Forest

Kettle Falls area: Pierre Lake, CR 4013. Sixteen tent and trailer sites; boat launch; restrooms but no water. No reservations.

Metalline area: East Sullivan and **West Sullivan,** on Sullivan Lake, CR 9345 about 5 miles east of Metaline Falls; 42 tent and trailer sites; water, toilets, beaches, and boat launch; reserve at 877-444-6777 or www.recreation.gov. **Millpond,** CR 9345 northeast of Ione, 2 miles from Sullivan Lake; 10 tent and trailer sites; water, toilet, and trail; no reservations. **Noisy Creek,** CR 9345 about 14 miles northeast of Ione; 19 tent and trailer sites; water, toilet, swimming, and boat launch; reserve at 877-444-6777 or www.recreation.gov.

Pend Oreille River area: Edgewater, CR 3669, 2 miles from Ione; 20 tent and trailer sites; water, toilet, and boat launch; reserve at 877-444-6777 or www .recreation.gov. **Panhandle,** CR 9325; 13 tent and trailer sites; water, toilet, and boat launch. **Pioneer Park Campground,** CR 9305; 17 tent and trailer sites; water, toilet, trail, and boat launch; reserve at 877-444-6777 or www.recreation.gov. **South Skookum Lake,** FR 3389 about 8 miles from Usk; 25 tent and trailer sites; water, toilet, and dock; no reservations. **Stagger Inn,** FR 302; from Nordman, Idaho, take ID 57 north 1.6 miles, then FR 302 for 10.7 miles; 4 primitive sites; toilet but no water; no reservations.

WA 20 area: Gillette Campground, on WA 20 about 13 miles from Ione; 30 tent and trailer sites; water, toilets, and trails; reserve at 877-444-6777 or www .recreation.gov. **Lake Leo,** on WA 20 about 7 miles from Gillette; 8 tent and trailer sites; water and boat launch; no reservations. **Lake Thomas,** on WA 20, 1 mile from Gillette; 16 tent sites; water and toilet; no reservations. **Little Twin Lakes,** on WA 20; 20 tent and trailer sites; fishing and boat launch; toilets but no water; no reservations.

Recreation Areas

Lake Roosevelt National Recreation Area (509-633-9441) runs 27 campgrounds—large and small, accessible and remote—along the length of the lake. The Park Service charges $10 in summer for campsites reachable by car; those reachable only by boat or foot are free. NRA campgrounds in this region include Bradbury Beach, Cloverleaf, Enterprise, Evans, Gifford, Hunters Park, Kettle Falls, Kettle River, Marcus Island, North Gorge, Snag Cove, and Summer Island. In addition, there are 11 campgrounds on the Spokane Reservation (see *Guidance*) section of the lake; Spokane sites are around $20.

GOLF Dominion Meadows (866-886-5508), 1861 East Hawthorne Avenue, Colville. Eighteen holes.

HIKING Pend Oreille–Sullivan Lake area has many hikes, which require access from a web of forest roads; contact **Colville National Forest Headquarters** (509-684-7000; www.fs.fed.us/r6/colville) for directions. Sullivan Lake, east of Metaline Falls, is surrounded by lovely paths:

Grassy Top Mountain, 3.75 miles; east of Sullivan Lake. A walk up this peak brings views of the Selkirks, with an elevation gain of only 900 feet.

Salmo-Priest Wilderness trails; contact **Sullivan Lake Ranger Station** (509-446-7500) for details. You can hike for days in this area northeast of the lake.

Trail No. 504, about 4 miles between Sullivan Lake and Noisy Creek campgrounds. This is a nice stroll along the eastern lakeshore.
See also *Wilder Places—Recreation Areas*.

WINTER SPORTS 49 Degrees North Mountain Resort (509-935-6649; www.ski49n.com), on Chewelah Peak; from US 395 at Chewelah, turn right on Flowery Trail Road for 10 miles. This little spot in the Colville National Forest offers 15 miles of cross-country trails, four chairlifts, and a surface lift for a vertical drop of 1,851 feet. Usually open Fri.–Tues. Thanksgiving–early Apr.

✳ Wilder Places

PARKS Crawford State Park (509-446-4065), 11 miles north of Metaline. Day use only; open 9–6 Thurs.–Mon. May–Aug. It's got 49 forested acres without any facilities, but the main attraction, Gardner Cave, is underground (see *To See— Natural Wonders*).

CRYSTAL FALLS ON THE LITTLE PEND OREILLE RIVER

Crystal Falls State Park, on WA 20, 14 miles east of Colville. View of falls on the Little Pend Oreille River.

RECREATION AREAS Lake Roosevelt National Recreation Area Headquarters (509-633-9441; www.nps.gov/laro), 1008 Crest Drive, Coulee Dam. Open 8–4 Mon.–Fri. **District Office** (509-738-2300), 1368 Kettle Park Road, Kettle Falls; generally open 9–5 daily in summer, Wed.–Sat. in winter. This 154-mile lake extends from the harsh scablands of coulee country north to the cool mountains of the Canadian borderlands; WA 25 runs along most of the eastern shore. The lake and its banks are designated a 100,390-acre national recreation area. Rangers lead activities from canoe trips to history and nature walks. Boating, camping, fishing, and swimming are the most popular activities. Obtain boat launch permits from headquarters or the district office (see above). Fishing and hunting in season require permits either from the state or from the Spokane Reservation (see *Guidance*), which has jurisdiction where it borders the lake. Supplies are available from only four marina concessions and very sparse lakeside settlements.

WILDERNESS AREAS **Salmo-Priest Wilderness,** 41,335 acres; in the far northeastern corner of Colville National Forest: From WA 31 at Metaline Falls, take Sullivan Lake Road east; turn left just before the Sullivan Lake Ranger Station (but stop there first for information). This is wilderness with a big "W." The tract is wet—western slopes catch the storms that make it over the Cascades—and wild. Bears, moose, cougars, and bobcats are to be expected; be prepared for the occasional wolf or grizzly bear, too. Virgin forests of western cedar, Douglas fir, and western hemlock are the biggest in eastern Washington.

WILDLIFE REFUGES **Little Pend Oreille National Wildlife Refuge** (509-684-8384), 1310 Bear Creek Road, Colville. Headquarters open 7:30–4 Mon.–Fri.; refuge open year-round but closed to vehicles Jan.–mid-Apr. This sprawling refuge covers more than 40,000 acres of mountains and wetlands on the western slopes of the Selkirks. Established mainly for migratory birds, it's also home to moose, lynx, cougars, and bears—one of the wilder wildlife refuges. A few dirt roads wander through the refuge, though most are closed in winter. Unusually, there are several primitive campgrounds in the refuge.

✳ Lodging

BED & BREAKFASTS

Newport
DannyAnn's Bed and Breakfast (509-447-3787; www.dannyanns.com), 131 North Spokane Avenue. This fine Craftsman house sits in a residential neighborhood and offers three unostentatious, comfy guest rooms and several common areas. Children over 14 welcome. No pets. $75–110.

COTTAGES AND CABINS

Colville
Whitetail Inn (509-684-8856), 1140 Marble Valley Basin Road; about 11 miles north of Colville. The "inn" is a two-room, hand-built log cabin in the woods, complete with bathroom and kitchenette. If you want perfect seclusion, you're likely to find it here. The owners offer guided horseback rides, too. No children. Consult about pets. $55–65.

Kettle Falls
🐾 **Blue Moose Rental Cabins** (509-738-6950 or 509-690-4937; www.blue moosecabins.com), 24387 US 395. Three cabins sit back in the woods off US 395 within a short walk of Lake

Roosevelt. This is a place for outdoor recreation—the woods, lake, and Kettle River offer fishing, boating, tubing, and more in summer, with plenty of snow in winter for cross-country skiing. The accommodations have full baths, kitchenettes, heat, and air-conditioning; they sleep three to seven. Linens are provided. $60; cash only.

INNS AND HOTELS

Newport
Inn at the Lake (509-447-5772 or 877-447-5772; www.innatthelake.com), 581 South Shore Diamond Lake Road. The Mediterranean-style villa with its terraced drop to the lakefront looks slightly displaced in the Rocky Mountain foothills, but inside, the cozy quilts and puffy comforters remind you where you are. Seven understatedly luxurious rooms each have their own bathroom; some have balconies. Consult about children and pets. $129–189.

LODGES

Colville
Lazy Bee B&B (509-732-8917), 3651 Deep Lake Boundary Road; 38 miles

north of Colville. This rustic house deep in the country has two guest rooms with shared bath, plus a living room, library, and no fewer than eight wood-burning fireplaces. There are no luxuries but time, space, and the great outdoors. Meals extra. Ask about children and pets. $60.

RANCHES

Kettle Falls

🐾 🏠 **Bull Hill Guest Ranch** (509-732-1171 or 877-285-5445; www.bull hill.com), 3738 Bull Hill Road; from US 395, drive north 20 miles or so along winding Lake Roosevelt, then take a steep dirt road another 2 miles past several NO TRESPASSING signs to the top of a hill. (Those who eschew surface travel can use the private airstrip.) *Remote* is the word—you'll see the Selkirk Mountains spread out before you. Moose, bears, and cougars roam the woods; 55 saddle horses and a fluctuating herd of cattle dot the meadows. Owners Don and Pete Guglielmino can arrange guided horseback rides—the nearby **China Bend winery** is a popular destination. You can also help them drive cattle, or just fish, hike the cedar forest, or take in the view from the hot tub. Their great-grandfather, Pietro Ansaldo, who somehow made his way here from northern Italy, filed the original 160-acre claim in 1903. It now extends to 10,000 owned and 40,000 leased acres on which you can ride happily into the sunset. Seven rustic, family-sized cabins are each equipped with a woodstove and full bathroom; an "executive" cabin has all the amenities plus mountain views. Meals are family-style in the combination kitchen, house, bar, and dining room (though families may wish the bar were elsewhere). Rates include all meals and ranch activities. $180–220 per person per day; discounts for children.

RESORTS

Cusick

🐾 **The Outpost Resort** (509-445-1531; www.theoutpostresort.net), 405351 WA 20. A rustic resort that offers four cabins, the Outpost is for outdoors-loving people and families. It has its own dock, swimming area, and

ONE OF THE RUSTIC CABINS AT BULL HILL GUEST RANCH

café on the lovely Pend Oreille River, plus a playground and boat rentals. $105–145 (two-night minimum); $360–540 per week.

✳ Where to Eat

EATING OUT

Metaline Falls

Cathy's Café (509-446-2447), 221 East Fifth Avenue. Open 6 AM–7:30 PM Mon.–Fri., 7 AM–7:30 PM Sat., 7–2 Sun. Homemade soups, salads, sandwiches, and pies are served in a comfortably straightforward setting. Breakfast is served all day.

Newport

Kelly's Restaurant and Lounge (509-447-3627), 324 West Fourth Street. Open 11–11 Mon.–Sat. Founded in 1894, Kelly's claims to be the second-oldest bar in Washington. Besides beer, you can get lunch and dinner daily.

Owen Grocery, Deli and Soda Fountain (509-447-3525), 337 South Washington Avenue. Open 7–6 Mon.–Fri., 8–6 Sat. Pick up groceries and sandwiches or have some ice cream, the latter served at the 1910 soda fountain counter.

✳ Special Events

July: ✐ **Chewelah Chataqua Festival of the Arts** (509-935-8991; www .chewelahchataqua.com), Chewelah. This little town hosts an arts-and-crafts festival—handcrafted items only— the second week in July. Food, music, and children's games accompany the festivities.

August: **Pend Oreille County Fair** (509-445-1367), County Fairgrounds, WA 20, Cusick. This agricultural fair has livestock, rodeo, food concessions, and more.

INDEX